To Barbara, my wife, my friend,
my companion, my life

Contents

Preface

This book is a translation, not from German to English, or Russian to Greek, but a translation from Pascal to Modula-2. The routines and procedures discussed here were originally written in MicroSoft Pascal and are described in the predecessor to this book, *Putting Pascal To Work* (TAB book No. 2691). The Pascal routines were used to create several hundred programs for a series of commercial applications. The programs are used every day by thousands of people and have proven useful.

The Pascal routines are collected into a library. The library is available in both the object code format that is typical of many library packages and in a source-code library that permits easy coding of library references. While the object and source library implementations are extensions to the Pascal language, Modula-2 has both of these features built into the language definition. For comparison, I wanted to see if the Modula-2 approach offered a better solution.

I am, after all, a working programmer. I support my family by designing and implementing data processing systems. I tend to judge all computer products by how well they help me perform my job. Naturally, in the course of writing this book, I compared Pascal and Modula-2 in this light. The question was quite simple: If I were to start over, knowing all that I know about both languages, which would I choose to use? The answer is Modula-2, but I must admit a slight hesitation in stating my choice.

Although the structure of the two languages is similar, Modula-2 has a definite edge in flexibility and expansibility. In the real world, however, the languages must be judged not only by their definition, but also by their implementation. In my opinion, the MicroSoft implementation of Pascal — the MS Pascal Compiler — comes very close to offsetting the benefits of the Modula-2 definition. Except for multitasking, MS Pascal has almost all of the features of the Modula-2 standard. Even the main feature of Modula-2, the ability to separately compile modules, can be handled in MS

Pascal. When coupled with some of the library features I discussed in *Putting Pascal to Work*, MS Pascal handles separate compilation of modules better than any of the currently available Modula-2 implementations.

Unfortunately, even though MS Pascal is the most powerful and complete implementation of Pascal for MS DOS computers, it is not the most popular. If popularity is measured in terms of number of units sold, Borland's Turbo Pascal has that distinction. Because of the significantly higher price for MS Pascal, the majority of programmers using Pascal with MS DOS use Turbo Pascal. It is extremely unfortunate that the two compilers are not more compatible.

Much of what makes MS Pascal suitable for large-scale commercial program development is not possible in Turbo Pascal. Turbo Pascal is certainly a useful tool, and because of its low price, a tool that is available to many programmers. But like Dr. Wirth himself, I caution the serious programmer not to use it for large and complex systems.

This, then, is why I would choose Modula-2. Both MS Pascal and Turbo Pascal begin with more or less the same standard definition of the Pascal language and extend it. MS Pascal extensions are intended to make the language more suitable for large, structured programs; Turbo Pascal extensions are aimed at fast compilations and broad general appeal. The different extensions make the two language implementations incompatible, and because the extensions are made to the Pascal compilers by changing the syntax of the language, it is almost impossible to make the two implementations compile the same source code.

Modula-2, on the other hand, is designed to be extended; the extensions are made *in* the language, not *to* the language. The extensions become just another set of library routines. If you don't like or don't need the extensions a given vendor has made to the language, then don't use them; write your own instead. This makes it possible to duplicate all of the functionality of the MS Pascal compiler in Modula-2 syntax. The MS Pascal extensions to the Pascal definition become available in many different Modula-2 implementations.

Introduction

There was, indeed, a Modula-1. It was simply called Modula when introduced by Dr. Nicklaus Wirth, head of the Institut fur Informatik at the Eidgenossische Technische Hochschule. In the introduction to his book *Programming in Modula-2*, Dr. Wirth explains that Modula evolved from experiments in multiprogramming conducted in the early 1970s. In 1977, when Dr. Wirth and his project team turned their attention to designing an integrated computing system, one that included both hardware and software, they created a new language that had its roots in both Modula and Dr. Wirth's earlier work with Pascal. Because the syntax of the new language was more similar to Modula, the new language became Modula-2.

The hardware side of the integration project is a totally unique computer called the Lilith. It was designed and built expressly for creating and executing Modula-2 programs. The Lilith computer even uses the Modula operating system, which was written, in part, using Modula-2. All of these tools were intended to work together.

The Lilith computer is powerful, fast, and compared to most personal computers, expensive. It is unlikely that many software developers will have access to a Lilith in the near future. Instead, if Modula-2 is to become a widely accepted language, it must be usable on hardware that is more readily available.

According to Jerry Pournelle (writing in the December 1985 issue of *BYTE Magazine*), Dr. Wirth has often expressed the following attitude about his Institute, ETH:

> ". . . [ETH] has a dual-purpose mission, to work at the frontiers of knowledge and to train students to understand the latest developments in technology. . . . ETH cannot become distracted by the requirement to make its technological achievements conform to industry's needs. It is enough that ETH develop generic technologies; industry must do the rest."

That, then, is the subject of this book: putting one of ETH's technological achievements, Modula-2, to work in today's computer industry. In the world of microcomputing, this means putting Modula-2 to work on IBM Personal Computers.

This book is not intended to teach Modula-2. (The Bibliography lists several excellent books that can be used to learn the language.) It assumes that the reader has a working knowledge of the language, a familiarity with compiled languages and the associated terminology, and a complete understanding of the MS DOS or PC DOS operating system. Instead, this book offers a general discussion of how the Modula-2 concept relates to the IBM PC standard and the rationale for using the language to develop commercial systems. There are also over one hundred practical routines, written in Modula-2, that serve as examples for the topics presented.

Chapter 1

Modula-2 in General

WHAT PROGRAMMING LANGUAGE IS BEST?

There are lots of opinions, based mostly on the "myths" of computer folklore. One of the most popular myths says that the choice of language depends on what you're doing. Are you writing operating systems? Use Assembler or C for speed. Do you need quick-and-dirty, one-shot number crunching? Use BASIC. To crunch a few more numbers, use Fortran. Or, if you really need to mash the numbers up good, use APL. All business programs should be written in COBOL—or RPG if you're using an IBM minicomputer. Pascal is a teaching language . . . Forth has never really caught on, it's too radically different . . . LISP is for processing lists. . . . Prolog is for artificial intelligence problems. Nobody uses PL/I . . . it's too slow. Ada is that big clumsy language that the U.S. Government sponsored . . . you've got to use it for the Department of Defense, but it will never fly in business. And then there's Modula-2, Dr. Niklaus Wirth's language for the Lilith project . . . you can't use it in the real world.

Most of these opinions are based on personal preference, reluctance to learn, or outright misconception. Most of them are wrong. The truth is, if you are willing (or forced) to work at it, you can use almost any language for almost any project. In the twenty odd years I've been working as a programmer, I've written statistical analysis programs in RPG; compilers and report generators in Fortran; operating systems and commercial applications in BASIC, and spreadsheet-like programs in COBOL. Not all of this was fun, and I certainly would not choose to do some of those things again, but they were all possible and the systems did work efficiently enough to be useful.

The "what you're doing" myth arose because the underlying design philosophy

1

of one language might allow a programmer to implement certain algorithms easier than other languages. Some languages minimize the number of words a programmer must write . . . some are easier for novices to learn . . . and some allow a veteran programmer to handle any problem that may arise. None of that determines which language is best.

To begin with, how do you define the term "best?" There are a lot of myths here, too. "Best" can mean fastest compilation or blazing execution. "Best" can mean "strongly typed," unless you're an advocate of BASIC, where "best" means no typing at all so you can define variables as you use them. "Best" can also mean procedure-oriented, data-oriented, line numbered, record-oriented, or whatever attribute you prefer. Ask a dozen programmers and you'll get a dozen answers.

Fortunately, there have been some scientific studies done on the subject. The results of these studies are gathered into the general principles called "structured programming." The bibliography of this book lists several books on the subject.

STRUCTURED PROGRAMMING

The studies that resulted in the concepts of structured programming defined "good" programs as programs that accomplish their assigned task, are easy to use, and cost least to maintain. The studies determined that most good programs have an easily identifiable and readily definable structure. They are built from a set of easily understood pieces that perform well-defined and predictable operations. The organization of these pieces into programs reflects the organization of the data on which the program operates. In a "good" program, the structure of the data determines the structure of the program.

The studies have shown that the principles of structured programming hold regardless of what kind of application is being programmed. "Good" programs, regardless of application, are structured programs. It follows, therefore, that the choice of "best" language should be heavily influenced by how well the language encourages structured programs.

When structured programming was first introduced, many people decided that it meant one thing: breaking a large system or program into smaller, more manageable pieces. Again, there were myths to determine how those pieces should be defined.

The myths said, "Every program has initialization to do, so a structured program obviously has an INITIALIZE routine. All file access begins with the FILEOPEN routine. There is always an ERROR handler. To avoid overhead, routines should only be nested a maximum of three deep. And, to make programs easier to follow, routines should be named to reflect their position in the hierarchy."

It happens that none of these so-called "rules" are valid. When applied, these rules produced structured programs that were split into pieces by a method called, for lack of a better term, "chunking."

In effect, "chunking" says: look at the system; split it into chunks so that the things that look like they go together are in the same chunk; program the chunks; link the chunks together and you've got a structured system. It was so simple that it had immediate appeal.

Data processing management quickly embraced structured programming because the theory clearly stated that large problems could be tackled as a pile of little problems. Once the large problem was "chunked," a hoard of programmers could be put to work programming the pieces. More programmers can do more work in less time, right? More pieces meant more programmers. The more people a manager needed, the bigger the programming department and the bigger the manager's clout within the company. The way DP management understood it, structured programming meant that one or two "senior analysts" could quickly design a system, chunk it, and turn it over to be programmed. The end result was "structured," so the system had to be good.

It didn't quite work out that way.

As it happens, a badly designed and implemented structured program is still a badly designed and implemented program; being structured doesn't make it any better.

The ramifications of "chunking" are explored by Edward Yourdon and Larry Constantine in their book, *Structured Design*. The authors recognize the tremendous benefits possible when applying the principles of structured programming to the implementation of computer systems, but also point out that those principles ". . . may be of little value if the basic *design* of the program or system is unsound." Therefore, the authors define a collection of "heuristics" for producing structured designs. (A heuristic is not a rule; it is a general principle that will usually produce good results. The results are not guaranteed, however, and the heuristic might have to be modified or even ignored in some circumstances.)

The pieces of a structured program are usually called *modules*. Yourdon and Constantine define a module as "a contiguous sequence of program statements, bounded by boundary elements, and having an aggregate identifier." The major goal of a structured design is to define how the system should be divided into modules in order to minimize "coupling" and maximize "cohesion." The term *coupling* refers to how individual modules are related to each other. The applicable heuristic says that the more independent modules are from each other, the better the design. *Cohesion* means whether or not the contents of an individual module really belong together. Yourdon and Constantine present several levels of cohesion, from probably very bad to probably very good, and define heuristics for determining the category into which a given module falls.

Modern computer programming languages such as Pascal, Modula-2, Ada, C, and Forth, are designed to minimize coupling between the pieces of a structured program. (Note: Yes, you can write structured programs in BASIC, or Assembler, or COBOL, or whatever, but the languages that were defined more recently are designed to make writing structured programs easier. Why make a job harder than it has to be?)

On the other hand, no computer language, including Modula-2, does anything to help a designer deal with maximizing the cohesion of the individual pieces in a system. To a certain extent, Modula-2 has made it necessary for a designer to be more aware of the potential problems.

MODULA-2 AND STRUCTURED DESIGNS

In most structured languages, the concept of a module applies most appropriately to a procedure, function, or subroutine. These are the elemental building blocks from which programs are constructed. As long as the system avoids the use of global variables, the coupling between these elements is entirely through the parameter lists defined for the routines. One element refers to another using the CALL mechanism.

By comparison, Modula-2 actually defines a specific language element called "MODULE." Large Modula-2 systems will always be designed as a collection of MODULES. Coupling between Modula-2 modules is through IMPORT and EXPORT lists, and those lists can, of course, include PROCEDURE names. In effect, a MODULE can be (and usually is) defined to have multiple entry points.

As Yourdon and Constantine point out, a module with multiple entry points is not necessarily bad, but the system designer must use extreme care to be certain that the PROCEDURES to which the entry points refer are not included in the module by coincidence. A module that exhibits "coincidental cohesion" is least desirable.

Modula-2 also requires additional considerations with regard to module coupling. Most other languages permit the elements of one module to refer to those in another at execution time only. These languages couple modules through the PUBLIC and EXTERNAL attributes and the CALL mechanism. Modula-2 permits module coupling at the source code level. A TYPE or CONSTANT defined in the DEFINITION of one module can be used at compile time in the source code of other MODULES.

MODULA-2 AND THE IBM PC

There are currently several Modula-2 compilers available for the IBM Personal Computer. I have worked with five of these. In keeping with the current trend in microcomputer language implementations, each of these packages actually includes more than just a compiler. Usually, the package includes an editor, a linker, and possibly, a debugger. The programs and modules that are described in this book have been implemented with two of these compilers; certain design considerations make use of the other compilers impractical. The packages are discussed in the following paragraphs.

The Modula Corporation

Dr. Richard Ohran was once a member of the faculty at the Eidgenossische Technische Hochschule where Dr. Niklaus Wirth invented Modula-2. Dr. Ohran is currently involved with the Modula Corporation, a company that is actively marketing both a Modula-2 compiler and the Lilith computer.

The early version of the Modula Corporation compiler generated *m-code*, rather than normal IBM PC object code. M-code requires an m-code run-time interpreter, which slows execution of the compiled programs. M-code is also based on a 64K address space, severely limiting the size of programs that can be developed. Modula Corporation eventually released a native code version of the compiler which produces more or less standard Intel object code and circumvents these problems.

Interface Technologies Corporation

ITC of Houston Texas offers a Modula-2 compiler that is bundled into a complete Modula-2 software development system, called M2SDS. This package includes not only the compiler but also a syntax-oriented editor, a library manager, a linker, and several utility libraries and programs. Some of the utility features are available at extra cost.

The editor, once you get use to its idiosyncrasies, makes source-code entry extremely fast. Because the editor does not permit syntax errors, the code will usually compile the first time. The editor does have the ability to read source files prepared by other means, but it insists that these files be error-free. That means that the M2SDS editor could not be used to translate the original Pascal source in which many of the routines in this book were written, which is unfortunate.

The compiler generates object code that is not compatible with any MicroSoft or IBM object files; you cannot, for example, link Assembler routines into an M2SDS program. (There are some very interesting ways around this. They are discussed later.) The M2SDS linker does produce standard MS DOS .EXE files. These .EXE files are often significantly smaller than those produced by the other compiler packages.

Logitech, Incorporated

Most of the routines discussed in this book were developed using the Modula-2 compiler offered by Logitech, Inc.

The compiler is fairly large, and, compared to M2SDS, fairly slow. While the package does include a very useful multi-window editor, the compiler will accept source prepared by any text editor. All of the files that the compiler uses and generates are standard DOS files.

The package has both a run-time debugger and a post-mortem debugger. Both of these are window-oriented, and if the appropriate options are specified when compiling, can be used to show source code. The debuggers are very useful.

Just to prove that there is no "free lunch," there are some problems with the Logitech package. The Logitech implementation uses a "run time" library to handle many of the functions of an executing program. I'll talk about that a bit in Chapter 2.

Farbware

David Farb, through his company named simply "Farbware," has produced a very useful Modula-2 compiler. Compared to some of the other Modula-2 packages, the Farbware system is small and compact, but it is still a complete implementation of the language. Unlike most of the others, the Farbware package produces standard MS DOS object files and uses the normal MS DOS linker to generate EXE files.

The Farbware package is constantly updated and improved, so some of the following statements might not be true of the currently available version, but as of this writing, there are several potential difficulties with the Farbware system.

First, the implementation does not include a standard BYTE data type. The BYTE data type is not included as part of Wirth's definition of Modula-2, but is mentioned in most of the literature as usually being available in Modula-2 implementations. Some of the routines in this book depend on the BYTE type. It should be a simple matter to define a new module that would export an acceptable definition.

Second, the Modula-2 standard states that all Modula-2 implementations should include an ALLOCATE and a DEALLOCATE procedure, usually found in a module named STORAGE. The Farbware implementation puts these routines in the SYSTEM module. Again, to use the Farbware system with the ETLING library in this book, you'll have to create a new module called STORAGE that exports the appropriate routines.

Like Pascal, Modula-2 defines the semicolon as a "statement separator" not a "statement terminator." But unlike Pascal, Modula-2 permits empty statements, which have a separator, but no body. In other words, in the following code fragment:

```
IF (dothis)
    THEN statement;
    END;
```

the semicolon after *"statement"* is legitimate in Modula-2. The Farbware implementation does not recognize this and reports multiple errors in most of the routines in the ETLING library.

Workman & Associates

Workman & Associates is a California-based company that distributes many quality software products for microcomputers. Some of their product line was written by other authors; some was developed by employees of the company. All of their products are first-rate, but are still constantly improved and modified.

One of the products Workman & Associates offer is an implementation of Modula-2—the FTL Modula-2 compiler. This compiler was originally implemented for CP/M operating systems by Dave Moore of Cerekof Computing in Brisbane, Australia. It has now been converted to MS DOS and is offered along with a very useful text editor and several additional utility programs.

FTL Modula-2 source code can be created by any ASCII text editor. (You don't need to use the FTL Editor, but it is a good choice if you don't have another.) The compiler produces non-MS DOS standard object files. These files must be linked together using the FTL linker. Also, unlike most of the other packages, this linker generates .COM rather that .EXE files. The .COM files do tend to be smaller and load quicker, but normal memory management restricts .COM files to a single 64K code segment and a single 64K data segment. All of the code in all of the modules your program requires must fit in the code segment. Static variables, constants, stack variables, and heap variables must all exist within the data segment. While you can still do useful work within these limits, FTL Modula-2 might not be suitable for all programs.

Because FTL Modula-2 has a single data segment, all POINTER and ADDRESS references can be made relative to the DS or ES registers. This means the FTL package implements these types as a single word, compatible with CARDINAL as the Wirth standard defines. This restricts the use of these types on an IBM PC to within the data segment, and causes some problems with the routines discussed in this book.

FTL Modula-2 also has a slightly different interpretation of the Modula-2 standard than some of the other packages. For example, the third, corrected edition of *Programing in Modula-2* does not clearly state whether or not an EXPORT list is required by a DEFINITION module. In several places, the book implies that the EXPORT list is not required because all identifiers in the DEFINITION are automatically exported. In other places, the EXPORT list is described and the difference between plain EXPORT and EXPORT QUALIFIED is discussed. Logitech and ITC choose to retain the EXPORT statement; FTL treats it as an erroneous entry, but only issues a warning if one is encountered.

In the FTL Modula-2 package, items IMPORTed by the DEFINITION of a module are also known within the IMPLEMENTATION. Many of the other packages require each part of a module to IMPORT individually.

WHICH ONE TO USE?

All of the packages discussed in this book have merit. They are certainly useful in their own environment. But the subject of this book is the translation of MS Pascal routines into Modula-2 and then using those routines to develop commercial systems on IBM Personal Computers. MS Pascal provides certain features that are not available in all of the Modula-2 packages. Some things, such as STRING and STRING data types, can be simulated in all of the packages, but certain features cannot. The MS Pascal routines require a BYTE data type; the routines use the total IBM PC address space, not just a single 64K code segment and a single 64K data segment; and, to implement the non-standard I/O routines discussed in this book, the routines require access to the IBM interrupt system.

Two packages fit these criteria better than the others. The Logitech and ITC packages provide all of the necessary features. Because the ITC syntax editor cannot be used in the translation process, the Logitech compiler was used in this book.

Chapter 2

Libraries

In programming terminology, a *library* is a collection of predefined language statements or machine instructions that are available for use in the implementation of a new program. Usually, the term *source library* is applied to language statements. Machine instructions that are compiled but not yet linked are found in an *object library,* and machine instructions that are compiled and loaded into memory during a program's execution may be part of a *run time* library.

Almost all modern computer languages use libraries in one or more of these forms, but unlike many others, Modula-2 places more emphasis on the subject. Other languages reserve the use of libraries for the compiler itself or treat libraries as an "added on" feature that functions outside the normal compilation process. Modula-2 demands that the programmer be aware of and actively involved with defining and implementing libraries.

When Wirth defined the syntax of the Modula-2, he specifically left out the definition of certain verbs. Wirth recognized that some things that a language must do are dependent on the machinery on which the compiler is implemented. Because of this, Modula-2 insists that the code dealing with machine-dependent operations be created in the form of library modules. This is why Modula-2 does not include any I/O statements; all I/O is machine dependent and must therefore be tailored to the specific hardware and operating system available.

In theory, each implementation of Modula-2 must supply the appropriate library modules. All packages discussed in this book do exactly that, and the source code for most of the library modules is included in the packages for the programmer. None of the packages discusses how to decide what to include in a library module. Neither Wirth nor any of the other authors deal with this directly.

PACKAGING

Most of the Modula-2 development systems have their own, nonstandard (at least non-MS DOS) linker that binds object (or object-like) files into an executable program. While each of these linkers is different, they all behave in a way that is similar to the MS DOS linker. *All* of the object code in each .OBJ file presented to the linker is included in the file that the linker produces. Even if a given program requires only one routine from an implementation containing 20 procedures, the code for the other 19 is included. To prevent .EXE files from growing too large, library modules should be defined to include only the code needed to do their job. Related but not necessarily required routines should be in separate modules.

With this in mind, it is tempting to simply put each routine in a separate module. Except for the M2SDS compiler, that's probably not a good idea. Here's why:

DOS allocates space for files one "cluster" at a time. A cluster is the term that DOS uses to refer to a unit of allocation; it contains one or more "sectors." When MS DOS formats a disk or diskette, it places magnetic markers on the surface that divides the surface into 512 byte areas; each area is a *sector*. The number of sectors in a cluster depends on the type of drive. Single-sided and high-capacity diskette drives have one sector per cluster; double-sided diskettes define two sectors per cluster. Hard disk drives have many variations, but, as an example, the 10-megabyte drive in an XT specifies eight sectors per cluster.

Since it's unlikely that the number of bytes in a file are evenly divisible by the number of bytes in a cluster, DOS almost always allocates too many bytes for a file. A little calculation will show that MS DOS will, on the average, waste half of the space in the last cluster allocated to each file.

Except for the M2SDS compiler, the Modula-2 packages put each module in a separate file. Lots and lots of little modules, containing one or two routines, will have lots and lots of wasted space. Because each module in a library can actually generate up to six separate files (such as the .DEF, .MOD, .SYM, .OBJ, .REF, and .LST files produced by the Logitech compiler), the amount of wasted space can pile up quickly.

The M2SDS package allows you to define "library" files; each library can contain many modules. The library file is allocated by DOS; M2SDS allocates space for modules within the file. As modules are added, changed, or deleted from an M2SDS library it does acquire some wasted space, but the package includes a "COMPRESS" utility that lets you rebuild the library to reclaim the wasted areas.

Although M2SDS does have a way around the DOS file allocation problem, the solution has drawbacks. The difficulty is that the library files can only be accessed through the M2SDS system. If you want to move modules, copy pieces of your library to diskettes, or edit a module, you have to use M2SDS. That is not always convenient. Furthermore, the M2SDS system does not include any "batch" facility. Any file manipulation must be done by hand, one file at a time. While the M2SDS approach is not that bad, I prefer to let DOS handle the module files directly. This gives me much more control over where the individual files are placed.

On the other hand, both M2SDS and Logitech use a "run-time" library approach for many of the standard operations that a Modula-2 program might require. A run-time library is, effectively, a large single module which contains many routines. When a Logitech compiled program is executed using this command:

M2 <program name>

the run time library is provided by the M2.EXE support file. But when a Logitech program is fully linked, the run time library is linked into the resulting program .EXE file. Like .OBJ files, all of the run-time library is linked into an .EXE file. Fortunately, almost all of the run-time library routines are useful.

There are no hard and fast rules with regard to packaging modules. Each circumstance should be judged on its own merits. There is a general discussion of the whole concept of packaging in *Structured Design* by Yourdon and Constantine. Note that the concepts of "module cohesion" apply both to the procedures in a Modula-2 module and to the module itself. Even procedures that are completely contained within modules and not exported to the outside world should be designed to exhibit a high degree of cohesion. Many Modula-2 modules are designed around the concept of "informational strength." Refer to Glenford Meyers book, *Reliable Software Through Composite Design,* for a discussion of this concept.

NAMES

All of the Modula-2 packages permit identifiers composed of any number of alphanumeric characters, as long as the first character is a letter. In keeping with the Wirth definition, all characters in an identifier are significant and the compilers are all case sensitive. (WRITE is not the same as Write.)

Having an unlimited number of characters from which to form identifiers is nice, but for programmers who must type their own source code, many characters in an identifier means many characters to type every time the identifier is used. On the other hand, short identifiers like "A" or "c2" do not contribute to the readability of the program. In my experience, identifiers composed of four to 10 characters are usually sufficient to provide a meaningful name and still save my typing finger. There are of course exceptions, but generally the names of things defined in the Etling Library have eight characters or less.

Because Modula-2 is case sensitive it can also be used to improve readability of source code. Several Modula-2 texts mentioned in the bibliography specify "standard programming conventions" that define when to use upper- and lowercase letters. Because Modula-2 keywords are by definition all capital letters, conventions state that all-uppercase words should be reserved for Modula-2. User-defined identifiers are all lowercase or some combination of upper- and lowercase.

Module Names

While I certainly agree that standard programming conventions do improve program readability, the restrictions specified in the other texts do cause some problems in the MS-DOS world. For example, module names should be chosen to correspond to the MS-DOS file in which the module is stored. MS-DOS names, whether you like it or not, wind up in all capital letters. That says that to avoid potential confusion, module names should be defined with all capital letters.

Again, each of the Modula-2 packages includes a predefined collection of library modules. In keeping with the general philosophy established on the original Modula-2 project, the library modules are called by names that are somewhat indicative of the things they contain. For example, the packages usually define a library module called "Storage," which contains the ALLOCATE and DEALLOCATE routines. When a library requires only eight, 10, or even 20 modules, meaningful names are easy to create. However, a library for a major application many contain 100 modules, especially when modules are created with .EXE file size in mind. Inventing that many names is not impossible, but it can be difficult. Eventually, names will be defined that are just a combination of letters and numbers. Giving modules meaningful names makes it easier to find a specific exported identifier. Trying to decide if GETTRAN is in module "TRAN1" or "TRAN2" causes names to lose their usefulness.

I believe that module names, like any "coding system," should either be completely meaningful or completely meaningless. A completely meaningful module name needs no further definition; the name completely describes the contents of the module. If you cannot define all names in the coding system to fit that criterion, then choose names that will force the user to look elsewhere for the definition; the names are completely meaningless. Meaningless names do not mislead.

The names chosen for the modules in the Etling Library in this book are completely meaningless, at least with regard to their exports. Instead, library module names are composed of six characters. To allow for other libraries using the same syntax, Etling Library module names begin with "EL," and the last four characters correspond to the number of the figure that describes the module in this book. Programs (i.e., modules that are executable), are identified by English or English-like words that do correspond to the function the program implements.

Other Identifiers

Type definitions in the Etling Library are also named with all capital letters. That does, of course, go against most current thinking in "readability." The general consensus seems to be that lowercase letters tend to make words easier to differentiate. Well, maybe . . . but I'm really more interested in using upper/lowercase combinations to differentiate usage. To me, it makes sense to be able to define a variable *account* of type ACCOUNT. Therefore, Type definitions in the Etling Library are named with all capitals; constants and variables are named with all lowercase letters. Procedures in the Etling Library are named with a combination of upper and lower letters, but always begin with a capital. (For clarity, when the text of this book mentions any PROCEDUREs, constants, or variables, the name is shown in italics.)

LISTINGS

This book includes a complete list of each and every module in the Etling Library. In the text, each type, constant, variable, or procedure from each module is presented in more or less the same order as they appear in the DEFINITION. This is not necessarily the same order in which these items appear in the module's IMPLEMENTATION. Often, one procedure in a module will require another. Some of the Modula-2 implementations insist upon strict adherence to the Modula-2 standard, which implies that an identifier must be declared before it can be used. Therefore, the IMPLEMENTATION of a module declares identifiers with this in mind.

A LIST OF IDENTIFIERS

Because the module names in the Etling Library are essentially meaningless, some mechanism must be provided to assist a programmer in locating things of interest. It should be a fairly simple exercise to write a program that would read a collection of .DEF files and print a sorted listing of exported items, but that is not quite enough. The listing should also include appropriate comments, and occasionally, things that are not exported from a module but nonetheless contribute to understanding the routines in the library.

The listings in Figs. 2-1, 2-2, and 2-3 define modules for building and printing such a list. (The programs include reference to many routines detailed later in the book.)

The Index

Keeping in mind what was said in the first chapter about myths regarding how to divide large programs into pieces, there is one general principle that I do tend to favor. If a specific file has a record-oriented data structure associated with it, I usually define a separate module that controls all access to that file. This "file access" module defines the record structure for the file and exportable procedures for accessing the data, but the calling sequences for these procedures refer to data fields, not records. Only the file access module knows the file's record structure.

A file access module "hides" record definitions. Information-hiding is an important principle of structured programming, and I think of the concept in terms of "the need to know." If a given routine can do its job without knowing certain information, I don't tell it. That way, if the information changes, it has no effect on that routine.

The only routines that need to know the specific record layout of a specific file are those routines that actually move data into or out of the record. By concentrating these routines within a single module, the record layout can change without affecting the rest of the system.

Figure 2-1 shows a module for controlling access to an index file associated with the Etling Source Library. The structure of this file will be discussed later, but think of it as keyed by an eight-character "member name" associated with an item in the Etling Library, and an additional eight characters specifying the name of the DEF module in which the item is defined. The data portion of the record is simply a LONGCARD variable, which points to the starting position of the item within the file.

Gathering the Members

Figure 2-2 shows INDEX, a main program. The program reads DEF source files and uses the *PutMemb* procedure from EL0201 to mark items of interest. INDEX depends on finding lines of source code that begin with the characters (*$. The first such line marks the start of an item; a second line beginning with (*$ marks the end.

As is often the case, much of INDEX is devoted to getting ready to do serious processing. Everything but the last 20 or 30 lines is initialization. The real work begins with the line that says:

```
IF (NOT FindParmLiteral('IN'),infile))
```

Beginning with this line, the program identifies the .DEF file, opens it, and then reads

Fig. 2-1. Library index file access.

```
DEFINITION MODULE EL0201;
   FROM EL0503 IMPORT   LONGCARD;
   EXPORT QUALIFIED   GetNMemb,PutMemb,ClsLib;

PROCEDURE GetNMemb(VAR member,filename:ARRAY OF CHAR;
                        VAR frstchar:LONGCARD):BOOLEAN;
(* This routine will return with the file and starting character, for the
   next member.  *)
PROCEDURE PutMemb(member,filename:ARRAY OF CHAR;frstchar:LONGCARD);
(* This routine will record the information for member in the NDX file.  *)
PROCEDURE ClsLib;
(* This routine closes the Library file.  *)
END EL0201.

:MPLEMENTATION MODULE EL0201;
   FROM SYSTEM IMPORT   ADR,TSIZE;
   FROM EL0303 IMPORT   equal;
   FROM EL0401 IMPORT   STRING,Literal,StrLen,ClearStr,MakeStr;
   FROM EL0503 IMPORT   LONGCARD,lczero;
   FROM EL0906 IMPORT   Cancel;
   FROM EL1002 IMPORT   FMODE,OPENKIND,DISP,LINECNTRL,LOCCNTRL,
                        OpnFile,ClsFile;
   FROM EL1003 IMPORT   GetLine;
   FROM EL1004 IMPORT   PutLine;
   FROM EL1007 IMPORT   RCRD,RFLDLIST,MakeRcrd,MakRFlds,MovFRcrd,MovTRcrd;
   FROM EL1012 IMPORT   SetFLoc;
   FROM EL1102 IMPORT   NODEPTR,NODE,NDXFCTRL,ChkNdxF;
   FROM EL1104 IMPORT   FindNdx,ReplNdx;
   FROM EL1105 IMPORT   MarkNdx;
   FROM EL1107 IMPORT   NextNdx;


CONST
   top      = TRUE;
   continue = TRUE;
   update   = TRUE;


TYPE
   MEMRDEF = RECORD
      member    :ARRAY [1..8] OF CHAR;
      filename  :ARRAY [1..8] OF CHAR;
      frstchar  :LONGCARD;
      END;
VAR
   ndxfctrl:NDXFCTRL;
   opnmode:FMODE;

PROCEDURE ChkOpen;
BEGIN
   WITH ndxfctrl DO
     IF (opnmode = makeold)
       THEN
         MakeStr(ddname,0,Literal('LIBNDX'));
         rcrdnmbr:=lczero;
         MakRFlds(3,rfldarea);
         WITH rfldarea^ DO
           loc[1]:=1;              len[1]:=8;
           loc[2]:=9;              len[2]:=8;
           loc[3]:=17;             len[3]:=TSIZE(LONGCARD);
           MakeRcrd(len[1]+len[2]+len[3],rcrd);
           END;
```

Fig. 2-1. continued

```
          hook.ptr:=NIL;
          hook.nmbr:=lczero;
      END;
    ChkNdxF(ddname,TSIZE(MEMRDEF),opnmode);
    END;
  END ChkOpen;

PROCEDURE GetNMemb(VAR member,filename:ARRAY OF CHAR;
                        VAR frstchar:LONGCARD):BOOLEAN;
VAR
  nmbr:LONGCARD;
BEGIN
  ChkOpen;
  WITH ndxfctrl DO
    MovTRcrd(rcrd,rfldarea,ADR(member),HIGH(member)+1,1);
    IF (NOT NextNdx(ddname,rcrd,nmbr,rfldarea^.loc[1],
                       rfldarea^.len[1],hook,top,continue))
      THEN RETURN FALSE
      ELSE
        MovFRcrd(rcrd,rfldarea,ADR(member),HIGH(member)+1,1);
        MovFRcrd(rcrd,rfldarea,ADR(filename),HIGH(filename)+1,2);
        MovFRcrd(rcrd,rfldarea,ADR(frstchar),TSIZE(LONGCARD),3);
        RETURN TRUE;
      END;
    END;
  END GetNMemb;


PROCEDURE PutMemb(member,filename:ARRAY OF CHAR;frstchar:LONGCARD);
VAR
  nmbr:LONGCARD;
BEGIN
  ChkOpen;
  WITH ndxfctrl DO
    MovTRcrd(rcrd,rfldarea,ADR(member),HIGH(member)+1,1);
    IF (FindNdx(ddname,rcrd,nmbr,rfldarea^.loc[1],
                          rfldarea^.len[1],hook,top))
      THEN
        MovTRcrd(rcrd,rfldarea,ADR(filename),HIGH(filename)+1,2);
        MovTRcrd(rcrd,rfldarea,ADR(frstchar),TSIZE(LONGCARD),3);
        ReplNdx(ddname,rcrd,nmbr,rfldarea^.loc[1],
                          rfldarea^.len[1],hook,top,NOT update);
      ELSE
        MovTRcrd(rcrd,rfldarea,ADR(filename),HIGH(filename)+1,2);
        MovTRcrd(rcrd,rfldarea,ADR(frstchar),TSIZE(LONGCARD),3);
        MarkNdx(ddname,rcrd,nmbr,rfldarea^.loc[1],
                          rfldarea^.len[1],hook,top,NOT update);
      END;
    END;
  END PutMemb;

PROCEDURE ClsLib;
BEGIN
  ClsFile(ndxfctrl.ddname,clsonly);
  END ClsLib;


BEGIN
  opnmode:=makeold;
END EL0201.
```

Fig. 2-2. Library index builder.

```
(*      INDEX, Source library member preprocessor
        Copyright (c) 1987 TAB BOOKS INC.
        Author: Don Etling

   This program expects a parameter list containing the following:

     IN=<device>:[<pathname>\]<filename>.<ext>
         LIBNDX=<device>:[<pathname>\]<filename>.<ext>

   For example:

     INDEX IN=A:BUILDLIB.DEF LIBNDX=D:BUILDLIB.LIB                      *)

MODULE INDEX;
  FROM SYSTEM IMPORT    BYTE;
  FROM EL0303 IMPORT    equal;
  FROM EL0304 IMPORT    cr,lf;
  FROM EL0401 IMPORT    STRING,MakeStr,StrLen,Literal,SetLen,nullstr,
                        MoveStr,SetChar,StrChar,SubStr;
  FROM EL0402 IMPORT    Concat;
  FROM EL0403 IMPORT    MatchStr,Positn;
  FROM EL0503 IMPORT    LONGCARD,lcone,LongCard,AddLCard;
  FROM EL0504 IMPORT    FRAMEPTR,MakFrame;
  FROM EL0801 IMPORT    GetParms,FindParm;
  FROM EL0803 IMPORT    AskParm;
  FROM EL0901 IMPORT    InitKB;
  FROM EL0902 IMPORT    crtads,nrmclr,ClrScrn,PstnCur,FindCRT;
  FROM EL0906 IMPORT    Cancel;
  FROM EL0908 IMPORT    TypeStr;
  FROM EL1002 IMPORT    FMODE,OPENKIND,DISP,LINECNTRL,OpnFile,ClsFile;
  FROM EL1003 IMPORT    GetLine;
  FROM EL0201 IMPORT    PutMemb;

CONST
  doall = TRUE;
  donthome = FALSE;
  home = TRUE;

VAR
  topframe,wrkframe,botframe,msgframe:FRAMEPTR;
  infile,line,crlf,h:STRING;
  inmode:FMODE;
  filename,member:ARRAY [1..8] OF CHAR;
  ioerr:BYTE;
  done,doit:BOOLEAN'
  frstchar,thisline
  i,j,k:CARDINAL;

BEGIN              (* Main *)
  MakeStr(infile,255,nullstr);
  MakeStr(line,255,nullstr);
  MakFrame(1,1,4,80,1,1,25,80,crtads,topframe);
  MakFrame(5,1,22,80,5,1,25,80,crtads,wrkframe);
  MakFrame(23,1,23,80,23,1,25,80,crtads,botframe);
  MakFrame(24,1,25,80,24,1,25,80,crtads,msgframe);
  ClrScrn(topframe^,nrmclr);
  ClrScrn(wrkframe^,nrmclr);
  ClrScrn(botframe^,nrmclr);
          MakeRcrd(len[1]+len[2]+len[3],rcrd);
          END;
        hook.ptr:=NIL;
```

Fig. 2-2. continued

```
        hook.nmbr:=lczero;
      END;
    ChkNdxF(ddname,TSIZE(MEMRDEF),opnmode);
    END;
  END ChkOpen;

PROCEDURE GetNMemb(VAR member,filename:ARRAY OF CHAR;
                            VAR frstchar:LONGCARD):BOOLEAN;
VAR
  nmbr:LONGCARD;
BEGIN
  ChkOpen;
  WITH ndxfctrl DO
    MovTRcrd(rcrd,rfldarea,ADR(member),HIGH(member)+1,1);
    IF (NOT NextNdx(ddname,rcrd,nmbr,rfldarea^.loc[1],
                      rfldarea^.len[1],hook,top,continue))
      THEN RETURN FALSE
      ELSE
        MovFRcrd(rcrd,rfldarea,ADR(member),HIGH(member)+1,1);
        MovFRcrd(rcrd,rfldarea,ADR(filename),HIGH(filename)+1,2);
        MovFRcrd(rcrd,rfldarea,ADR(frstchar),TSIZE(LONGCARD),3);
        RETURN TRUE;
      END;
    END;
  END GetNMemb;

PROCEDURE PutMemb(member,filename:ARRAY OF CHAR;frstchar:LONGCARD);
VAR
  nmbr:LONGCARD;
BEGIN
  ChkOpen;
  WITH ndxfctrl DO
    MovTRcrd(rcrd,rfldarea,ADR(member),HIGH(member)+1,1);
    IF (FindNdx(ddname,rcrd,nmbr,rfldarea^.loc[1],
                            rfldarea^.len[1],hook,top))
      THEN
        MovTRcrd(rcrd,rfldarea,ADR(filename),HIGH(filename)+1,2);
        MovTRcrd(rcrd,rfldarea,ADR(frstchar),TSIZE(LONGCARD),3);
        ReplNdx(ddname,rcrd,nmbr,rfldarea^.loc[1],
                          rfldarea^.len[1],hook,top,NOT update);
      ELSE
        MovTRcrd(rcrd,rfldarea,ADR(filename),HIGH(filename)+1,2);
        MovTRcrd(rcrd,rfldarea,ADR(frstchar),TSIZE(LONGCARD),3);
        MarkNdx(ddname,rcrd,nmbr,rfldarea^.loc[1],
                          rfldarea^.len[1],hook,top,NOT update);
      END;
    END;
  END PutMemb;

PROCEDURE ClsLib;
BEGIN
  ClsFile(ndxfctrl.ddname,clsonly);
  END ClsLib;

BEGIN
  opnmode:=makeold;
END EL0201.
```

Fig. 2-3. Library member lister.

```
(*  LISTER, Member lister
    Copyright (c) 1987 TAB BOOKS INC.
    Author: Don Etling

  This program expects a parameter list containing the following:

    DEF=<device>:[<pathname>\
    LIBNDX=<device>:[<pathname>]<NDXfile>

  For example:

    LISTER DEF=A: LIBNDX=B:MODULA.NDX                              *)

MODULE LISTER;
  FROM SYSTEM IMPORT      BYTE;
  FROM EL0303 IMPORT      equal;
  FROM EL0304 IMPORT      cr,lf;
  FROM EL0401 IMPORT      STRING,Literal,StrLen,MakeStr,SetLen,
                          SubStr,nullstr,CopyStr,StrSize,StrChar,SetChar;
  FROM EL0402 IMPORT      Concat,Insert,Delete;
  FROM EL0403 IMPORT      MatchStr,Positn;
  FROM EL0404 IMPORT      FixStr;
  FROM EL0503 IMPORT      LONGCARD,lcone,LongCard,AddLCard;
  FROM EL0504 IMPORT      FRAMEPTR,MakFrame;
  FROM EL0801 IMPORT      GetParms,FindParm;
  FROM EL0803 IMPORT      AskParm;
  FROM EL0902 IMPORT      crtads,nrmclr,ClrScrn,PstnCur;
  FROM EL0906 IMPORT      Cancel;
  FROM EL0908 IMPORT      TypeStr;
  FROM EL1002 IMPORT      FMODE,OPENKIND,DISP,LINECNTRL,
                          setpostn,OpnFile,ClsFile;
  FROM EL1003 IMPORT      GetLine;
  FROM EL1012 IMPORT      SetFLoc;
  FROM EL1201 IMPORT      pcp;
  FROM EL1202 IMPORT      LTBLPTR,SetRprt,PrtRprt,EndRprt,MakeLTbl,ClrLTbl;
  FROM EL0201 IMPORT      GetNMemb;

CONST
  doall = TRUE;
  donthome = FALSE;
  home = TRUE;
  ask  = TRUE;
  number = TRUE;
  date   = TRUE;
  time   = TRUE;

VAR
  topframe,wrkframe,botframe,msgframe:FRAMEPTR;
  inmode:FMODE;
  filename,member:ARRAY [0..7] OF CHAR;
  ioerr:BYTE;
  done,newpage:BOOLEAN;
  dsname,line,crlf,str,h1,h2,h3,h4,h5,h6:STRING;
  frstchar:LONGCARD;
  hdgs:LTBLPTR;
  i,j,pagenmbr,linenmbr:CARDINAL;

BEGIN
ClrScrn(msgframe^,nrmclr);
GetParms;
MakeStr(crlf,2,Literal('  '));
```

Fig. 2-3 continued

```
SetChar(crlf,1,cr);
SetChar(crlf,2,lf);
TypeStr(nrmclr,home,
        Literal('INDEX - Extract member definitions'),
         topframe^);
TypeStr(nrmclr,NOT home,crlf,topframe^);
TypeStr(nrmclr,NOT home,
        Literal('Copyright (c) 1986 TAB BOOKS INC '),
         topframe^);
TypeStr(nrmclr,NOT home,crlf,topframe^);
TypeStr(nrmclr,NOT home,
        Literal('Author: Don Etling'),
         topframe^);
TypeStr(nrmclr,NOT home,crlf,topframe^);
MakeStr(h,79,nullstr);
SetLen(h,79);
FOR i:=1 TO 79 DO
  SetChar(h,i,'-');
  END;
TypeStr(nrmclr,NOT home,h,topframe^);
TypeStr(nrmclr,home,h,botframe^);
IF (NOT FindParm(Literal('IN'),infile))
  THEN AskParm(Literal('IN'),Literal('IN'),infile,msgframe^);
  END;
inmode:=oldfile;
OpnFile(infile,inmode,ioerr,insist);
done:=FALSE;
doit:=FALSE;
frstchar:=lcone;
FOR i:=1 TO 8 DO
  filename[i]:=' ';
  END;
j:=Positn(Literal('.'),infile,1);
i:=j;
WHILE (StrChar(infile,i) <> ':')
                        AND (StrChar(infile,i) <> '\') DO
  DEC(i);
  END;
MoveStr(SubStr(i+1,j-i-1,infile),Literal(filename),1);
WHILE (GetLine(infile,line,rtrnend)) DO
  TypeStr(nrmclr,donthome,line,wrkframe^);
  IF (MatchStr(Literal('(*$'),line,1,1,3) = equal)
    THEN
      doit:=NOT doit;
      IF (doit)
        THEN
          i:=4;
          WHILE (i < StrLen(line))
                          AND (StrChar(line,i) = '-') DO
            INC(i);
            END;
          j:=StrLen(line)-4;
          WHILE (j > 1) AND (StrChar(line,j) = '-') DO
            DEC(j);
            END;
          MoveStr(SubStr(i,j-i+1,line),Literal(member),1);
          FOR k:=1 TO 8 DO
            IF (member[k] >= 'a') AND (member[k] <= 'z')
            THEN member[k]:=CHR(ORD('A') + ORD(member[k]) - ORD('a'));
            END;
          END;
```

Fig. 2-3 continued

```
              PutMemb(member,filename,frstchar);
          END;
      END;
    LongCard(StrLen(line),0,thisline);
    AddLCard(thisline,frstchar,frstchar);
      END;
ClsFile(Literal('*.*'),clsonly);
PstnCur(25,1,msgframe^);
END INDEX.
MakeStr(dsname,255,nullstr);
MakeStr(line,255,nullstr);
MakeStr(str,255,nullstr);
MakFrame(1,1,4,80,1,1,25,80,crtads,topframe);
MakFrame(5,1,22,80,5,1,25,80,crtads,wrkframe);
MakFrame(23,1,23,80,23,1,25,80,crtads,botframe);
MakFrame(24,1,25,80,24,1,25,80,crtads,msgframe);
ClrScrn(topframe^,nrmclr);
ClrScrn(wrkframe^,nrmclr);
ClrScrn(botframe^,nrmclr);
ClrScrn(msgframe^,nrmclr);
GetParms;
MakeStr(crlf,2,FixStr(Literal("cr*lf")));
MakeStr(h1,0,Literal('APPENDIX A. Library Member List'));
MakeStr(h2,0,Literal(' '));
MakeStr(h3,0,Literal(' '));
MakeStr(h4,79,nullstr);
SetLen(h4,79);
FOR i:=1 TO 79 DO
   SetChar(h4,i,'-');
   END;
MakeStr(h5,0,Literal(' '));
MakeStr(h6,0,Literal('Author: Don Etling'));
hdgs:=MakeLTbl(5,80);
CopyStr(h1,hdgs^.line[1]);
CopyStr(h2,hdgs^.line[2]);
CopyStr(h3,hdgs^.line[3]);
CopyStr(h4,hdgs^.line[4]);
CopyStr(h5,hdgs^.line[5]);
FOR i:=1 TO 5 DO
   WHILE (StrLen(hdgs^.line[i]) < StrSize(hdgs^.line[i])) DO
     Concat(Literal(' '),hdgs^.line[i]);
     END;
   END;
TypeStr(nrmclr,home,h1,topframe^);
TypeStr(nrmclr,NOT home,crlf,topframe^);
TypeStr(nrmclr,NOT home,h2,topframe^);
TypeStr(nrmclr,NOT home,crlf,topframe^);
TypeStr(nrmclr,NOT home,h6,topframe^);
TypeStr(nrmclr,NOT home,crlf,topframe^);
TypeStr(nrmclr,NOT home,h4,topframe^);
TypeStr(nrmclr,home,h4,botframe^);
SetRprt(pcp,62,ask,NOT number,NOT date,NOT time);
newpage:=TRUE;
FOR i:=1 TO HIGH(member)+1 DO
   filename[i]:=' ';
   member[i]:=' ';
   END;
WHILE (GetNMemb(member,filename,frstchar)) DO
   IF (NOT FindParm(Literal('DEF'),dsname))
     THEN AskParm(Literal('DEF'),Literal('DEF'),dsname,msgframe^);
     END;
```

Fig. 2-3 continued

```
    Concat(Literal(filename),dsname);
    WHILE (StrChar(dsname,StrLen(dsname)) = ' ') DO
      Delete(dsname,StrLen(dsname),1);
      END;
    Concat(Literal('.DEF'),dsname);
    inmode:=oldfile;
    OpnFile(dsname,inmode,ioerr,insist);
    IF (NOT SetFLoc(dsname,setpostn,1,frstchar))
      THEN Cancel(Literal('LISTER'),dsname,1,0);
      END;
    done:=TRUE;
    IF (linenmbr > 50)
      THEN linenmbr:=80;
      END;
    REPEAT
      IF (NOT GetLine(dsname,line,nortrnend))
        THEN done:=TRUE
        ELSE
          IF (MatchStr(Literal('(*$'),line,1,1,3) = equal)
            THEN
              done:=NOT done;
              IF (NOT done)
                THEN
                  CopyStr(Literal(filename),str);
                  WHILE (StrChar(str,StrLen(str)) = ' ') DO
                    Delete(str,StrLen(str),1);
                    END;
                  Concat(Literal('.'),str);
                  Delete(line,3,StrLen(str));
                  Insert(str,line,StrLen(line)-10);
                END;
            END;
          IF (NOT done)
            THEN
              TypeStr(nrmclr,donthome,line,wrkframe^);
              TypeStr(nrmclr,NOT home,crlf,wrkframe^);
              PrtRprt(line,newpage,0,hdgs,pagenmbr,linenmbr);
            END;
        END;
      UNTIL (done);
    ClsFile(dsname,clsonly);
    END;
  EndRprt;
  ClsFile(Literal('*.*'),clsonly);
  PstnCur(25,1,msgframe^);
  END LISTER.
```

the file line by line, looking for (*$. When a delimiting line is found, its contents are parsed to find the member name, and *PutMemb* is called to create the appropriate index entry. Because the index file is keyed on Member Name, PutMemb effectively produces a sorted list of items.

Producing a Listing

After INDEX gathers all of the library entries together, another program, LISTER, is used to list the items. LISTER uses *GetNMemb* to retrieve index records in alphabetical order by Member Name and then calls the report-generating routines from the Etling Library to produce a hard-copy list. Figure 2-3 shows LISTER and the Member listing it produces is shown in the Appendix.

Chapter 3

Low-Level Routines

Most Modula-2 programs are constructed from predefined and prepackaged procedures bundled together in multiple modules. The modules are bound together like bricks to build the program's structure. Like any well-made building, the structure must rest upon a sound foundation. The footing on which a Modula-2 program sits is the language itself, but the foundation is composed of the lowest level routines in the library of modules from which the program is built. In the Etling Library, there are eight modules that constitute the bottom level of the entire structure. They deal with the basic building blocks of the library.

BYTES

The IBM PC, and the IBM compatibles, are primarily "byte-oriented" machines. The actual central processor, or memory management unit, may be capable of addressing modes that group bytes together—two-byte words for the 8086 and 80286, four-byte words for the newer 80386—but the basic building block on these machines is an eight-bit byte. Therefore, most of the Modula-2 implementations for the IBM PC define a BYTE data type. Even the packages that do not have a BYTE type defined, permit references to byte addresses.

A Byte at a Time

Even though CARDINAL, INTEGER, and WORD types are composed of two bytes, none of the implementations define routines for dealing with just one of those bytes at a time. The first module in the Etling Library defines the necessary routines.

Fig. 3-1. Building words from bytes.

```
DEFINITION MODULE EL0301;
  FROM SYSTEM IMPORT    BYTE, WORD;
  EXPORT QUALIFIED      ByWord,LoByte,HiByte;

PROCEDURE ByWord(hibyte,lobyte:BYTE):WORD;
(* This routine will combine the two bytes to produce a single word.  *)
PROCEDURE LoByte(twobytes:WORD):BYTE;
(* This routine will return the least significant byte of twobytes.  *)
PROCEDURE HiByte(twobytes:WORD):BYTE;
(* This routine will return the most significant byte of twobytes.  *)
END EL0301.

IMPLEMENTATION MODULE EL0301;
  FROM SYSTEM IMPORT    BYTE, WORD;

TYPE
  BOTH = RECORD
    CASE KIND : BOOLEAN OF
        TRUE:     aword : WORD;
      ! FALSE: alobyte : BYTE;
                ahibyte : BYTE;
      END;
    END;

PROCEDURE ByWord(hibyte,lobyte:BYTE):WORD;
VAR
  both:BOTH;
BEGIN
  both.alobyte:=lobyte;
  both.ahibyte:=hibyte;
  RETURN both.aword;
  END ByWord;

PROCEDURE LoByte(twobytes:WORD):BYTE;
VAR
  both:BOTH;
BEGIN
  both.aword:=twobytes;
  RETURN both.alobyte;
  END LoByte;

PROCEDURE HiByte(twobytes:WORD):BYTE;
VAR
  both:BOTH;
BEGIN
  both.aword:=twobytes;
  RETURN both.ahibyte;
  END HiByte;

END EL0301.
```

Module EL0301 is shown in Figure 3-1. It contains three short procedures: *ByWord,* which builds a WORD from two BYTES; and *LoByte* and *HiByte,* which return the corresponding BYTE from the WORD parameter.

Byte Movements

All Modula-2 implementations define an "assignment" statement that is used to move data values from one storage location to another. But the assignment statement is only valid if the compiler is instructed to think of these locations as containing the same type of data. In other words, while this program fragment

```
VAR
    A:INTEGER;
    B:CARDINAL;
BEGIN
    A:=B;
END;
```

is not valid, this one is:

```
TYPE
    ANYRCRD = RECORD
        field1 : INTEGER;
        field2 : ARRAY [1..10] OF CHAR;
        END;
VAR
    s,t:ANYRCRD;

BEGIN
    s:=r;
END;
```

Unlike many other languages, Modula-2 permits RECORDs and even ARRAYs to be used in an assignment statement, as long as the variables involved are from "assignment compatible" types.

Unfortunately, there are times when data must be moved without regard to type. Modula-2 recognizes this, and provides both "Type Conversion" (change a value from one type to a corresponding value in another type) and "Type Transfer" (refer to the memory location of one variable as though it were of a different type), but both of these operations still impose some restrictions. The routines in module EL0302 (Fig. 3-2) treat data as nothing more than a sequence of bytes in memory. The routines in the module move sequences of bytes from one memory location to another; in effect, the value of any type can be moved to the memory location associated with any other type. If necessary, partial values can be used, for example:

```
VAR
    a:ARRAY [0..9] OF CHAR;
    c:CARDINAL;
BEGIN
    c:=100;
    MovByteL(c,a,0,7,TSIZE(CARDINAL));
    END;
```

This program fragment moves two bytes (the size of a CARDINAL type) from the

Fig. 3-2. Byte movement.

```
DEFINITION MODULE EL0302;
   FROM SYSTEM IMPORT    BYTE;
   EXPORT QUALIFIED      MovByteL,MovByteR,FillByte;

PROCEDURE MovByteL(VAR f,t:ARRAY OF BYTE;fi,ti,n:CARDINAL);
(* This routine will move n bytes from the byte address specified by f[fi]
   to the byte address specified by t[ti].  Transfer starts with the
   leftmost (i.e., lowest) memory location of both areas.  Note that there
   is no error checking done in conjunction with this routine.  *)
PROCEDURE MovByteR(VAR f,t:ARRAY OF BYTE;fi,ti,n:CARDINAL);
(* This routine will move n bytes from the byte address specified by f[fi]
   to the byte address specified by t[ti].  Transfer starts with the
   rightmost (i.e., highest) memory location of both areas.  Note that
   there is no error checking done in conjunction with this routine.  *)
PROCEDURE FillByte(value:BYTE;VAR t:ARRAY OF BYTE;ti,n:CARDINAL);
(* This routine will fill the memory area beginning with t[ti] with n
   bytes of value.  *)
END EL0302.


IMPLEMENTATION MODULE EL0302;
   FROM SYSTEM IMPORT    BYTE;

PROCEDURE MovByteL(VAR f,t:ARRAY OF BYTE;fi,ti,n:CARDINAL);
VAR
   i:INTEGER;
BEGIN
   FOR i:=0 TO n-1 DO
     t[ti]:=f[fi];
     INC(fi);
     INC(ti);
     END;
   END MovByteL;


PROCEDURE MovByteR(VAR f,t:ARRAY OF BYTE;fi,ti,n:CARDINAL);
VAR
   i:INTEGER;
BEGIN
   FOR i:=1 TO n DO
     t[ti]:=f[fi];
     DEC(fi);
     DEC(ti);
     END;
   END MovByteR;


PROCEDURE FillByte(value:BYTE;VAR t:ARRAY OF BYTE;ti,n:CARDINAL);
VAR
   i:INTEGER;
BEGIN
   FOR i:=ti TO ti + n-1 DO
     t[i] := value;
     END;
   END FillByte;

END EL0302.
```

memory location identified by the variable c to the eighth and ninth bytes of the array
a. Note that the location parameters are displacements from zero.

The routines in EL0302 can be used with any memory location, not just areas
addressed by variable names.

```
VAR
   f,t:ADDRESS;
BEGIN
   f:= the address of anything, even code . . .
   t:= . . . anything)
   MovByteL(f^,t^,0,0,1024);
END;
```

This fragment will move 1K bytes from one location to another without regard to the contents of the locations.

The routines in EL0302 are very powerful, but they are also very dangerous. Used carelessly, they can overwrite data, sections of program code, even areas of the operating system.

Byte Compares

Like most high-level languages, Modula-2 provides syntax to handle comparisons, but again, the syntax requires two operands of the same (or assignment compatible) type. Furthermore, the variables must be of an elementary type (i.e., one word or two words). Usually, comparison of structured types must be handled by programmer-written routines, but *CompArea*, the routine defined in module EL0303 (Fig. 3-3), will handle the comparisons of many structured types.

Because the parameters for *CompArea* are defined as ARRAY OF BYTE types, *CompArea* will compare any two memory locations. Although the routine does not insist on it, these memory locations are usually defined as character or byte arrays. Remember, on a "byte swapped" machine like an IBM PC, the WORD, CARDINAL, and INTEGER types are stored with the least significant byte first in memory. Using *CompArea* to compare two such types may not produce the expected results.

CHARACTERS

The Wirth definition of Module-2 specifically states that the value range of the type CHAR is based on the International Standards Organization's (ISO) standard of 128 (zero through 127) permissible values. Because the ISO standard leaves a few character positions undefined, with the understanding that these positions could be used according to national preferences, Wirth chose the American Standard Code for Information Interchange (ASCII) version as the standard character set for Modula-2.

The ASCII code was originally developed when the circuitry of electronic computers was organized in such a way that octal, or base 8, numbers were easiest to represent. Although the terminology isn't exactly right, the smallest unit of storage that an Octal machine can deal with, the octal "byte," has 128 possible values. It is logical for an octal machine to use ASCII coding.

Most modern computers, including the IBM PC, are built around the hexidecimal (base 16) numbering system. A hexidecimal byte has 256 possible values. Rather than waste the extra possibilities, hexidecimal machines usually define an additional 128 characters. The ASCII code used on octal machines, usually called "7-bit ASCII," was extended into "8-bit ASCII." On the IBM PC, the additional 128 characters

Fig. 3-3. Byte compares.

```
DEFINITION MODULE ELO303;
  FROM SYSTEM IMPORT    BYTE;
  EXPORT QUALIFIED      MATCHVAL,less,equal,greater,CompArea;

CONST
  less = -1;   equal = 0;   greater = 1;
TYPE
  MATCHVAL = [less..greater];
PROCEDURE CompArea(VAR area1:ARRAY OF BYTE; s1,11:CARDINAL;
                   VAR area2:ARRAY OF BYTE; s2,12:CARDINAL;
                       nbytes:CARDINAL):MATCHVAL;
(* This routine will compare the two arrays beginning at s1 and s2.  The
   compare is done according to the value of each corresponding byte in the
   areas.  The compare will continue for nbytes.

       If area1 < area2 then CompArea = less
       If area1 = area2 then CompArea = equal
       If area1 > area2 then CompArea = greater
*)
END ELO303.

IMPLEMENTATION MODULE ELO303;
  FROM SYSTEM IMPORT    BYTE;

PROCEDURE CompArea(VAR area1:ARRAY OF BYTE; s1,11:CARDINAL;
                   VAR area2:ARRAY OF BYTE; s2,12:CARDINAL;
                       nbytes:CARDINAL):MATCHVAL;
BEGIN
  IF (nbytes = 0)
    THEN IF (11 > 12)
      THEN nbytes:=11;
      ELSE nbytes:=12;
      END;
    END;
  WHILE (nbytes > 0) DO
    IF (area1[s1] <> area2[s2])
      THEN
        IF (area1[s1] < area2[s2])
          THEN RETURN less;
          ELSE RETURN greater;
          END;
      ELSE
        INC(s1);
        INC(s2);
        DEC(nbytes);
        IF (nbytes > 0)
          THEN IF (s1 > 11)
            THEN IF (s2 > 12)
              THEN RETURN equal
              ELSE RETURN less
              END;
            ELSE IF (s2 > 12)
              THEN RETURN greater
              END;
            END;
          END;
      END;
    END;
  RETURN equal;
  END CompArea;

END ELO303.
```

generated by this extra bit are used for foreign language and line drawing characters. But even that wasn't quite enough for the IBM designers. The IBM PC defines *extended ASCII*, a coding system that actually requires nine bits.

The use of extended ASCII on the IBM PC was made necessary by the IBM keyboard. The original IBM PC keyboard has 83 keys; by using some keys (like Shift, Ctrl, or Alt) in combination with others, the keyboard is capable of generating over 300 different characters. The IBM designers chose to use most of them; a feature that confuses the problems of dealing with keyboard input, which is discussed in Chapter 6.

Fortunately, the extended ASCII character set is arranged so that the extra characters are keyboard control characters. The "human language" characters (A through Z, 0 through 9, etc.) are part of the original ASCII definition. Because regular ASCII and extended ASCII characters will seldom appear in the same context, variables of type CHAR can still be defined to fit in a single byte, but be careful to recognize the potential problems.

Figure 3-4 shows EL0304, a module whose definition exports specific constants labeling specific values from the extended ASCII character set. (Note that for logical consistency, there is a EL0304 IMPLEMENTATION, but it has no code—perfectly legal in Modula-2.) These characters are all "control" characters, but not all of them are extended ASCII. The characters labeled *bksp, break, cr, deof, lf, tabr, tabl,* and *esc* are standard ASCII; this is a real nuisance when you must use them with extended ASCII. The keyboard handling routines discussed in Chapter 6 show a convenient way of dealing with the variations.

The Modula-2 character set has another major nuisance built into it. If you cannot represent a Modula-2 character constant as a quoted character (e.g., 'A') you must define it as an octal number. I haven't thought in octal in 15 years, and it took me quite a while to find a hexidecimal to octal conversion table. Coding EL0304 was harder than it should have been.

ADDRESS COMPARES

Most of the Modula-2 implementations provide compatibility between the AD-DRESS types and one or more of the standard numeric types. The compatibility is intended to permit a subset of arithmetic operations on ADDRESSES. The *CompAddr* routine in EL0305 (Fig. 3-5) provides ADDRESS compares.

EL0305 also includes *MemLoctn* and a corresponding type that can be used to determine where a specific address is located within the memory used by a program. The type, MEMLOCTN, is an enumerated type that specifies *inheap, instack,* or *incode. MemLoctn* will return the value appropriate for the ADDRESS specified as its parameter.

Correct operation of *MemLoctn* depends on the exact memory model in use by the Modula-2 implementation. M2SDS and LOGITECH use a model that is approximated by the diagram shown in Fig. 3-6. EL0305 defines a special ADDRESS, *strtheap,* that marks the beginning of the heap; any ADDRESS less than *strtheap* must be in the code of the executing program. Any ADDRESS greater than the ADDRESS at which the *MemLoctn* parameter is located is in the stack, and any ADDRESS in between is in the heap.

Fig. 3-4. Characters.

```
DEFINITION MODULE ELO304;
  EXPORT QUALIFIED
    fk1,   fk2,   fk3,   fk4,   fk5,   fk6,   fk7,   fk8,   fk9,   fk10,
    fk11, fk12, fk13, fk14, fk15, fk16, fk17, fk18, fk19, fk20,
    fk21, fk22, fk23, fk24, fk25, fk26, fk27, fk28, fk29, fk30,
    fk31, fk32, fk33, fk34, fk35, fk36, fk37, fk38, fk39, fk40,
    tabr, tabl, rtab, ltab, utab, dtab, home, end,  boxu, boxd,
    curl, curr, insr, del,  esc,
    altdec, allditto, dittokey, nextval, xmtcntrl,
    clearfld, seqval, help, bksp, break, cr, deof, lf, pgdn, pgup;

(* This module assigns meaningful names to the special control characters
   associated with the IBM PC keyboard.  Note that these characters include
   both the normal ASCII controls, and, the "Extended ASCII" characters
   defined by IBM.  *)
CONST
  bksp = 010C;    break = 003C;    cr    = 015C;    deof = 032C;
  lf   = 012C;    pgdn = 121C;    pgup  = 111C;    altdec = 072C;
(* STANDARD FUNCTION KEYS *)
  fk1  = 073C;    fk2 = 074C;    fk3 = 075C;    fk4 = 076C;    fk5 = 077C;
  fk6  = 100C;    fk7 = 101C;    fk8 = 102C;    fk9 = 103C;    fk10 = 104C;
(* SHIFT - FUNCTION KEYS *)
  fk11 = 124C;    fk12 = 125C;    fk13 = 126C;    fk14 = 127C;    fk15 = 130C;
  fk16 = 131C;    fk17 = 132C;    fk18 = 133C;    fk19 = 134C;    fk20 = 135C;
(* CNTRL - FUNCTION KEYS *)
  fk21 = 136C;    fk22 = 137C;    fk23 = 140C;    fk24 = 141C;    fk25 = 142C;
  fk26 = 143C;    fk27 = 144C;    fk28 = 145C;    fk29 = 146C;    fk30 = 147C;
(* ALT - FUNCTION KEYS *)
  fk31 = 150C;    fk32 = 151C;    fk33 = 152C;    fk34 = 153C;    fk35 = 154C;
  fk36 = 155C;    fk37 = 156C;    fk38 = 157C;    fk39 = 160C;    fk40 = 161C;
  (* FIELD TAB CHARS *)
  tabr = 011C; (*normal tab            *) tabl = 017C; (*shift tab            *)
  rtab = 115C; (*shift - NUM PAD 6 *) ltab = 113C; (*shift - NUM PAD 4 *)
  utab = 110C; (*shift - NUM PAD 8 *) dtab = 120C; (*shift - NUM PAD 2 *)
  home = 107C; (*shift - NUM PAD 7 *) end  = 117C; (*shift - NUM PAD 1 *)
  boxu = 111C; (*shift - NUM PAD 9 *) boxd = 121C; (*shift - NUM PAD 0 *)
  (* CURSOR MOVEMENT CONTROLS*)
  curl = 163C; (*ctrl NUM PAD 4    *) curr = 164C; (*ctrl NUM PAD 6    *)
  insr = 122C; (*shift - NUM PAD 0 *) del  = 123C; (*shift - NUM PAD . *)
  (* OVERALL CONTROL CHARACTERS *)
  esc      = 033C; (* Esc key        *) allditto = 023C; (*alt - R    *)
  nextval  = 027C; (*alt - I        *) dittokey = 040C; (*alt - D    *)
  xmtcntrl = 055C; (*alt - X (toggles tabbing into xmtonly fld) *)
  clearfld = 056C; (*alt - C        *) seqval   = 061C; (*alt - N    *)
  help     = 043C; (*alt - H        *)
END ELO304.

IMPLEMENTATION MODULE ELO304;

END ELO304.
```

TEMPORARY HEAP VARIABLES

One of the more important concepts in Modula-2 is the definition of *opaque* types, data types whose structure is hidden within an implementation module. Hiding the details of a type means that the details can change without requiring changes to any other module that uses the type. This is possible because, to the outside world, opaque types are actually pointers. Unlike normal pointer definitions

Fig. 3-5. Address comparisons.

```
DEFINITION MODULE EL0305;
   FROM SYSTEM IMPORT    ADDRESS;
   FROM EL0303 IMPORT    MATCHVAL;
   EXPORT QUALIFIED      strtheap,CompAddr,MEMLOCTN,MemLoctn;

TYPE
   MEMLOCTN = (inheap,instack,incode);
(* This TYPE is used to indicate where a given address falls within the
   currently executing program.  *)
VAR
   strtheap:ADDRESS;
(* This ADDRESS marks the first word of the heap area of the main process.
   Any variable between this ADDRESS and the current ADDRESS of the stack
   (i.e., SS:SP) must have been allocated by a call to NEW and is therefore
   a dynamic variable.  *)
PROCEDURE CompAddr(a1,a2:ADDRESS):MATCHVAL;
(* This routine will compare the two ADDRESS variables and return a
   corresponding value.

      If a1 < a2 then CompAddr = less
      If a1 = a2 then CompAddr = equal
      If a1 > a2 then CompAddr = greater
*)
PROCEDURE MemLoctn(a:ADDRESS):MEMLOCTN;
(* This routine will return a value specifing where the a ADDRESS is
   located.  *)
END EL0305.


   IMPLEMENTATION MODULE EL0305;
   FROM SYSTEM IMPORT    ADR,ADDRESS;
   FROM Storage IMPORT   ALLOCATE;
   FROM EL0303 IMPORT    MATCHVAL,equal,less,greater;

PROCEDURE CompAddr(a1,a2:ADDRESS):MATCHVAL;
BEGIN
   a1.SEGMENT := a1.SEGMENT + a1.OFFSET DIV 16;
   a1.OFFSET  := a1.OFFSET   MOD 16;
   a2.SEGMENT := a2.SEGMENT + a2.OFFSET DIV 16;
   a2.OFFSET  := a2.OFFSET MOD 16;
   IF (a1.SEGMENT < a2.SEGMENT)
     THEN RETURN less;
   ELSIF (a1.SEGMENT > a2.SEGMENT)
     THEN RETURN greater;
   ELSIF (a1.OFFSET < a2.OFFSET)
     THEN RETURN less;
   ELSIF (a1.OFFSET > a2.OFFSET)
     THEN RETURN greater;
     END;
   RETURN equal;
   END CompAddr;

PROCEDURE MemLoctn(a:ADDRESS):MEMLOCTN;
BEGIN
   IF (CompAddr(a,strtheap) = less)
     THEN RETURN incode;
   ELSIF (CompAddr(a,ADR(a)) = greater)
     THEN RETURN instack;
     ELSE RETURN inheap;
     END;
   END MemLoctn;
```

Fig. 3-5 continued
```
BEGIN
  NEW(strtheap);
END EL0305.
```

that are declared as a "POINTER TO something," the referent of an opaque type does not have to be defined in the DEFINITION of a module. The thing to which the opaque type refers is completely hidden within the IMPLEMENTATION.

That's the good news—but it's also the bad news. Things that are referenced by pointers must be allocated. The IMPLEMENTATION module that exports an opaque type must also export a PROCEDURE that allocates space for a variable of that type. And because that space is normally allocated on the heap, the module must also export a PROCEDURE to deallocate the variable when the caller is done with it. The

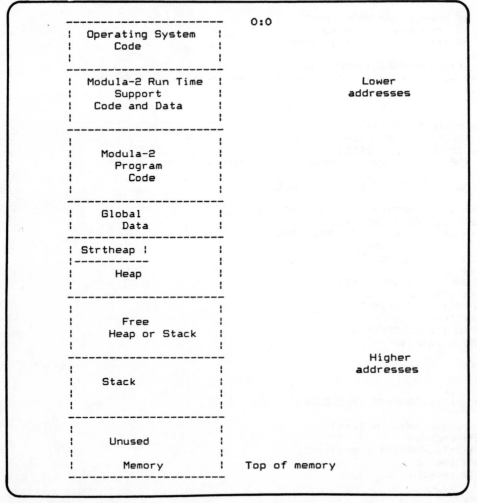

```
        --------------------    0:0
        !  Operating System  !
        !       Code         !
        !                    !
        --------------------
        !  Modula-2 Run Time !              Lower
        !      Support       !            addresses
        !  Code and Data     !
        !                    !
        --------------------
        !                    !
        !     Modula-2       !
        !      Program       !
        !       Code         !
        --------------------
        !     Global         !
        !      Data          !
        --------------------
        ! Strtheap !         !
        !----------          !
        !      Heap          !
        !                    !
        --------------------
        !                    !
        !      Free          !
        !  Heap or Stack     !
        !                    !
        --------------------              Higher
        !                    !          addresses
        !     Stack          !
        !                    !
        !                    !
        --------------------
        !                    !
        !     Unused         !
        !                    !
        !     Memory         !   Top of memory
        --------------------
```

Fig. 3-6. Memory models.

really bad news is that a programmer must *remember* to use the deallocate procedure *before* leaving the procedure in which the allocate was called.

To illustrate, consider the following:

```
PROCEDURE DoThis(VAR t:CHAR);
VAR
    ptr : POINTER TO ARRAY [1..100] OF CHAR;
    i    : CARDINAL;
BEGIN
    NEW(ptr);
    FOR c:=1 TO 100 DO
      ptr^ [i]:=t;
      END;
    END DoThis;
```

Notice that the space for *ptr* is allocated, but never deallocated. When *DoThis* returns to the caller, the space to which *ptr* points is marked by heap-management routines as being in use, but there is no way to get at it again. When *DoThis* is called a second time, a different 100 character area will be allocated. Do that often enough and you'll run out of heap. None of the Modula-2 packages catch this kind of error.

Opaque types and pointers are such powerful tools that I can't bring myself to criticize the concept. But neglecting to dispose of a pointer is a common mistake. I do it frequently—so frequently that I've devised a few "heuristics" for dealing with them.

First, in each section of code that must use a pointer, place the allocation for the pointer immediately after the BEGIN statement; the deallocation goes immediately before the associated END. Obviously, there are times when this isn't possible, but the general principle is sound. The idea is to reinforce the concept that allocations are done at the beginning and deallocations are done at the end. If you're careful to also obey a reasonable set of indentation rules, the corresponding procedure calls should be at the same level and fairly easy to spot (or, more importantly, to notice when the DEALLOCATE is missing).

Second, there is a way of defining "temporary heap" pointers. In the Etling Library, a temporary heap pointer is itself a dynamically allocated variable, allocated on the stack, that *by definition,* goes away when the procedure to which it is passed terminates. The space to which a temporary pointer refers is allocated in the heap, along with all other pointers, but the procedure that allocates a temporary pointer need not worry about deallocating it. The space will be automatically reused for the next temporary pointer.

The routines that control the temporary heap are defined in Module EL0307 (Fig. 3-7). This Module exports two procedures: *GetTHeap* and *ClrTHeap*, but the basis for its operation is the THEAP TYPE defined in the IMPLEMENTATION. The temporary heap is controlled by a chain of THEAP records that act as a "last in, first out" list.

As *GetTHeap* is called to allocate temporary heap pointers, it first calls *ClrTHeap*. I'll come back to that in a minute. The actual *GetTHeap* processing adds THEAP records to the end of the list. The chain is formed using the THEAP.*prev* field. THEAP.*adr* points to an area of THEAP.*nbytes* BYTES on the heap. The value of

Fig. 3-7. Temporary heap routines.

```
DEFINITION MODULE EL0307;
  FROM SYSTEM IMPORT    ADDRESS,ADR;
  EXPORT QUALIFIED      ClrTHeap,GetTHeap;

PROCEDURE ClrTHeap(adr:ADDRESS);
(* This routine will clear all variables allocated on the temporary heap
   that were referenced by a variable on the stack whose ADDRESS was after
   adr.  *)
PROCEDURE GetTHeap(VAR adr:ADDRESS;nbytes:CARDINAL);
(* This routine will allocate a variable on the temporary heap that is
   nbytes long and referenced by adr.  Note that any other temporary heap
   variables whose referenced ADDRESS is after adr will be cleared before
   the new area is allocated.  *)
END EL0307.

IMPLEMENTATION MODULE EL0307;
  FROM SYSTEM IMPORT    ADDRESS,ADR,TSIZE,BYTE;
  FROM Storage IMPORT   ALLOCATE,DEALLOCATE;
  FROM EL0303 IMPORT    less;
  FROM EL0305 IMPORT    CompAddr;

TYPE
  BYTEPTR  = POINTER TO ARRAY [1..65535] OF BYTE;
  THEAPPTR = POINTER TO THEAP;
  THEAP    = RECORD
    nbytes : CARDINAL;
    adr    : BYTEPTR;
    ref    : BYTEPTR;
    prev   : THEAPPTR;
    END;
VAR
  last : THEAPPTR;

PROCEDURE ClrTHeap(adr:ADDRESS);
VAR
  this:THEAPPTR;
BEGIN
  this:=last;
  WHILE (this <> NIL) DO
    IF (CompAddr(adr,this^.ref) = less)
      THEN this:=NIL;
      ELSE
        last:=this^.prev;
        DEALLOCATE(this^.adr,this^.nbytes);
        DEALLOCATE(this,TSIZE(THEAP));
        this:=last;
      END;
    END;
  END ClrTHeap;

PROCEDURE GetTHeap(VAR adr:ADDRESS;nbytes:CARDINAL);
VAR
  this : THEAPPTR;
BEGIN
  ClrTHeap(ADR(adr));
  ALLOCATE(this,TSIZE(THEAP));
  this^.ref:=ADR(adr);
  this^.nbytes:=nbytes;
  this^.prev:=last;
  last:=this;
  ALLOCATE(adr,nbytes);
```

```
    this^.adr:=adr;
    END GetTHeap;

)EGIN
    last   := NIL;
:ND EL0307.
```

THEAP.*adr* is returned to the caller as the value for *adr*. Each record also contains THEAP.*ref* that makes note of the address of *adr*. Because *adr* is always allocated on the program stack, THEAP.*ref* actually marks the values for the SS and SP registers when *adr* was defined. It is this value, the location of *adr* on the stack, that *GetTHeap* passes to *ClrTHeap*.

ClrTHeap removes records from the end of the THEAP chain, but only those records whose THEAP.*ref* field refers to a stack address that is equal to or greater than the *ClrTHeap adr* parameter. In other words, *ClrTHeap* reclaims heap area but only from calls that were made at or after the stack's current position. The only calls that could fit this criterion would be either at the same level within the current procedure *or* within procedures that the current procedure called. In either case, the THEAP entry is no longer needed.

Although not what it was intended for, *GetTHeap* can be used with variables. For example, consider the following:

```
TYPE
    LINE = ARRAY [1..100] OF CHAR;
    LINEPTR = POINTER TO LINE;
VAR
    a,b:LINEPTR;
BEGIN
    GetTHeap(a,100);
    GetTHeap(b,100);

    . . . . .
    END;
```

You must be careful when using *GetTHeap* this way. If *a* were defined on the stack after *b*, the second call to *GetTHeap* would clear the space allocated to *a*. The use for which *GetTHeap* is intended is discussed in detail in the next chapter.

Chapter 4

Strings

Early computer hardware, in the fifties and sixties, was expensive. It was significantly more expensive than the cost of programming and expensive enough to persuade the user that inconveniences were tolerable because "that's the way the computer does it." Users were willing to concede that to build an address list, you gave the machine data that said:

SMITH   JOHN

The order (i.e., last name, first name) was for the convenience of the computer; data entered this way is easier to sort. The extra blanks fill out the computers fixed length strings.

Today, hardware prices have plummeted to the point where the term "user friendly" controls commercial programming. Never mind the machinery, build the system so that users can continue to think in their terms . . . let the computer figure out what the users mean. Today, mailing lists are constructed from data entry that reads

JOHN SMITH

The program has to worry about *parsing* the string of characters into its component fields. The parsing operation implies taking a large string of varying length and splitting it into two or more smaller strings, again of varying length.

Modern languages, including Modula-2, allow string types to be treated almost

34

exactly like arrays. In *Programing in Modula-2*, Wirth describes the term "string" as a sequence of characters enclosed in quote marks as shown:

string = 'This is a string constant";

The Modula-2 standard states that string constants can be assigned to variables of type ARRAY [1..n] OF CHAR, as long as the length, n, is equal to or greater than the length of the string constant. And because Modula-2, unlike the original standard for Pascal, permits procedures to have parameters defined as "Open Arrays," it is possible to write Modula-2 routines that can handle strings of varying length. Modula-2 string constants can be *value parameters;* passed to PROCEDURES as an ARRAY OF CHAR and treated as any other array.

Even though Modula-2 provides a step in the right direction, it still has some problems with character strings. In many ways, Modula-2 is no better at handling strings than standard Pascal. First, some of the problems with Modula-2 character strings are discussed in the following paragraphs.

STANDARD MODULA-2 STRINGS

To handle strings of varying length, a program needs some way of determining the number of characters that a string contains. That is not the same as saying the size of the array that contains the string. If, for example, a variable is defined:

FirstName : ARRAY [1..10] OF CHAR;

it can hold, at most, 10 characters. Most given names are less than 10 characters long so there must be some way of deciding which of those ten characters are actually part of the name. There are two basic mechanisms for doing this: maintain a count of significant characters in another variable, or use some character to mark the end of significance within the string.

Standard Modula-2 uses the latter method. If you assign a string of length 5 to an ARRAY [1..10] OF CHAR, the last five characters of the array are set to CHR(0). When the time comes to reassemble a complete name from a FirstName and Last-Name array, a program need only look for CHR(0) to mark the end of each value.

This method presupposes that no legitimate string would ever have a CHR(0) as part of its value. Unfortunately, that isn't completely accurate.

One place where strings are used extensively in modern computing is in communications. The underlying premise in any type of transmission from one computer to another or from one computer to its peripheral devices (such as printers) is the transfer of messages composed of strings of characters. Some of these characters are used to control the communication process, and in some systems CHR(0) is used as one of these controls. Rather than including CHR(0) as a character in a constant string, Modula-2 forces you to define a special way of handling it — not impossible, but not convenient either.

Choosing any other value or character that fits in a single byte as the string terminator would cause similar problems. For commercial programming, the first method, keeping track of string length in a separate variable, avoids these potential problems.

Most of the Modula-2 packages actually do this for open arrays. When a procedure with an open array in its parameter list is called, the compiler generates code to place two values on the stack. One value specifies the starting address of the actual variable; the other value specifies the corresponding length (it is this value that the HIGH procedure accesses). Again, the length of the array is not the same as the number of characters in use.

The Modula-2 development packages referenced in this book deal with the problems of handling strings in several different fashions.

The Modula Corporation and the Farbware packages treat strings strictly as ARRAY OF CHAR variables with no further assistance. The Logitech library includes a module called "Strings" that offers several routines for copying one string to another or for inserting or deleting characters, but again, the string variables are simple ARRAY OF CHAR.

The Interface Technologies Corporation package defines a STRING type as an extension to the language; you can declare a variable of type STRING(n), where n is the maximum number of characters the variable can contain. The actual number of characters in use within the variable is maintained as the value in STRING[0]; therefore, a STRING type can be up to 255 character long. The ITC package also includes a library module named "Strings" that defines a half dozen or so routines that deal with the STRING type, all quite useful.

The string variables defined in all of the Modula packages have one thing in common: the variables to which they refer are defined on the stack. The allocation for these strings is done automatically by the compiler when the code for the corresponding VAR section is generated, and the memory space assigned to these strings becomes reusable immediately upon termination of the enclosing procedure. On the other hand, the useful length of any of these strings is limited, and except for the ITC package, none of the string implementations provides for varying the string length.

STRING REQUIREMENTS

Many of the books on Modula-2 referenced in the Bibliography offer alternatives to the standard Modula-2 string definitions. The routines that are discussed in the rest of this chapter are a composite of many of those alternatives, with an additional wrinkle or two that have I found useful.

I must admit that these string-related routines were very difficult to define, not because Modula-2 doesn't have the power or the flexibility to deal with strings, but because I wanted to duplicate, as much as possible, the string concepts available in MicroSoft Pascal. To me, the MS Pascal STRING and LSTRING types are perfect for dealing with strings in commercial programming. I wanted to duplicate these concepts, but I wanted the routines to be written in standard Modula-2, not in the extensions available in a single package.

Here are the criteria I used in developing these string-handling routines:

First, I wanted a string type that could be defined as a stack variable. Because string types are used so frequently in the rest of the library, I wanted a way to let the compiler handle allocation and deallocation. I wasn't quite able to arrive at this, but the GetTHeap routine discussed in Chapter 3 allows a very workable approximation.

Second, I wanted a string type that was completely compatible with ARRAY OF CHAR variables and (more importantly) string constants. I wanted to be able to use an ARRAY or a constant anywhere that a string was permitted, within the logical consistency of the operation. It isn't logical to use a constant as the target of an assignment operation (although, as it turns out, that is possible) but I did want to be able to use *either* a string or an ARRAY or a constant as the value to which an assigned string was set.

Third, I wanted a string type that would allow strings of varying length *and* various length. I wanted to be able to define, for each string, the maximum number of characters it could contain and the number of characters in use at any given moment.

Fourth, I wanted a convenient way of accessing each individual character in a string. Ideally, a character of *s*, where *s* is a STRING type, should be accessible as *s[i]*, just like the ARRAY type on which it is based. Again, this proved unattainable, but the required routines are not too unwieldly.

Fifth, I wanted the string-related operations to function as quickly and efficiently as possible without sacrificing the other four considerations.

The next section discusses how the Etling Library meets these goals.

STRING DEFINITIONS

In the Etling Library, the STRING type is defined in Module EL0401, shown in Fig. 4-1. Note that the STRING type is exported as opaque. The details of the STRING definition are hidden in the implementation. EL0401 also exports another type definition: CHRPTR = POINTER TO CHAR. This type doesn't need to be opaque; its definition is so specific there is no way it could change. The CHRPTR type is defined so that there may be a corresponding *ChrPtr* procedure; I'll discuss that in a moment.

The String Type. The definition for the STRING type that I finally settled on says that a STRING is actually a pointer to a record of type STRRCRD. A variable of type STRRCRD is *always* allocated on the heap, but the actual sequence of characters that constitute the associated ARRAY OF CHAR may not be. A STRRCRD contains five fields. STRRCRD.*max* defines the maximum number of characters the string contains. STRRCRD.*len* indicates the number of characters actually in use. STRRCRD.*dynamic* specifies whether or not the associated ARRAY OF CHAR is allocated dynamically (i.e., on the heap) or is simply an ARRAY OF CHAR allocated on the stack or as a string constant. If STRRCRD.*dynamic* = TRUE, then the field named STRRCRD.*char* is valid and it contains a dynamically allocated ARRAY OF CHAR on the heap. If STRRCRD.*dynamic* = FALSE, the field named STRRCRD.*cptr* is valid and it contains a pointer to an ARRAY OF CHAR that was not allocated specifically by the creation of the STRRCRD. Notice that STRRCRD.*cptr* is defined as a CHARSPTR, which is a POINTER to an ARRAY OF CHAR. In other words, for a dynamic string, this area of a STRRCRD contains the ARRAY that makes up the string and, for a nondynamic string, this area is a POINTER to the actual ARRAY.

EL0401 also exports several PROCEDUREs.

Literal. Literal is not actually a procedure; it's a procedure variable, of type LITERAL. The way in which Literal is defined and implemented illustrates some very powerful, and dangerous, features of Modula-2. The LITERAL type is defined as a PROCEDURE(ARRAY OF CHAR):STRING. Most textbooks on Modula-2 contain examples showing how any normal PROCEDURE, having the same calling sequence,

Fig. 4-1. Basic STRING definitions.

```
DEFINITION MODULE EL0401;
    FROM SYSTEM IMPORT      WORD,ADDRESS;
    FROM EL0303 IMPORT      MATCHVAL;
    EXPORT QUALIFIED        nullstr,STRING,CHRPTR,Literal,SubStr,MakeStr,
                            ClearStr,MoveStr,CopyStr,StrLen,StrSize,SetLen,
                            StrChar,SetChar,ChrPtr;


TYPE
    STRING;
(* A STRING variable is similar to an ARRAY OF CHARACTERS, except that the
    variable may be defined dynamically.  Each STRING variable has two
    additional associated values, accessible by StrLen and StrSize.  StrLen
    returns the number of characters in the STRING currently in use.
    StrSize returns the maximum number of characters the STRING may contain.
    The STRING routines include a Literal procedure that permits an array of
    char to be used anywhere a STRING is permitted.  *)
TYPE
    CHRPTR = POINTER TO CHAR;
(* A CHRPTR variable is a pointer to a CHARACTER.  The STRING routines
    include the ChrPtr procedure which will return a CHRPTR pointing to the
    appropriate character within a STRING.  *)
VAR
    nullstr : STRING;
(* The variable nullstr represents an empty string...zero length and no
    characters. *)
TYPE
    LITERAL = PROCEDURE(ARRAY OF CHAR):STRING;
VAR
    Literal : LITERAL;
(* The procedure variable, Literal, provides a way for a client module to
    use an array of chars as a STRING.  The parameter may be a string
    constant or a normal ARRAY OF CHAR.  Note that this routine creates a
    temporary STRING, referenced by an entry on the stack.  The Literal
    procedure should only be used to create a calling parameter...the
    temporary STRING may be overwritten by any other stack reference.  *)
PROCEDURE SubStr(n,l:CARDINAL;s:STRING):STRING;
(* This routine creates a new STRING, containing the l characters from s,
    beginning at StrChar(s,n).  Note that this routine creates a temporary
    STRING, similiar to the Literal routine.  *)
PROCEDURE MakeStr(VAR s:STRING;l:CARDINAL;init:STRING);
(* This routine will create a new STRING.  The CARDINAL, l, defines the
    total number of characters that the new STRING can contain...if it is
    zero, the length of the init parameter will determine the new STRING's
    maximum length.  The init parameter defines the new STRING's current
    length and initial contents.  Note that it is not logical to specify l =
    0 and init = nullstr.  On entry, the current value of s is assumed to be
    unknown.  *)
PROCEDURE ClearStr(VAR s:STRING);
(* This routine will deallocate the area defined by the STRING parameter.
    Note that this routine should only be used on STRING variables defined
    by MakeStr or SubStr.  If this routine is called with s pointing to a
    constant or stack STRING, the call will be ignored.  In either case, s
    will return NIL.  *)
PROCEDURE StrLen(s:STRING):CARDINAL;
(* This routine will return the current length of the STRING parameter. *)
PROCEDURE StrSize(s:STRING):CARDINAL;
(* This routine will return the maximum length of the STRING parameter. *)
PROCEDURE SetLen(s:STRING;l:CARDINAL);
(* This routine will set the current length of the STRING parameter to the
    value specified by l.  If l > StrSize(s), the routine will set l =
    StrSize(s).  *)
```

```
PROCEDURE StrChar(s:STRING;n:CARDINAL):CHAR;
(* This routine will return the character in s at the n'th position.  If n
   is greater than the StrLen(s), the routine will set n = StrLen(s).  If n
   = 0, the routine will set n = 1.  *)
PROCEDURE ChrPtr(s:STRING;n:CARDINAL):CHRPTR;
(* This routine will return a pointer to the character in s at the n'th
   position.  If n is greater than the StrLen(s), the routine will set n to
   StrLen(s).  If n = 0, the routine will set n = 1.  *)
PROCEDURE SetChar(s:STRING;n:CARDINAL;c:CHAR);
(* This routine will set the character in s at the n'th position to c.  If
   n is greater than the StrLen(s), the routine will set n to StrLen(s).
   If n = 0, the routine will set n = 1.  *)
PROCEDURE MoveStr(source,dest:STRING;d:CARDINAL);
(* This routine will move all characters from source into dest, begining
   at d.  If StrLen(dest) is not large enough to contain all of source, the
   move will be truncated.  If StrLen(source) < StrLen(dest) - d then dest
   will be filled with blanks.  Note that StrLen(dest) is not adjusted.  *)
PROCEDURE CopyStr(source,dest:STRING);
(* This routine will copy the contents of the first STRING to the second.
   If StrLen(source) is shorter than StrSize(dest), StrLen(dest) will be
   set to StrLen(source)..if StrLen(source) is larger than StrSize(dest),
   the move will be truncated.  *)
END ELO401.

IMPLEMENTATION MODULE ELO401;
   FROM Storage IMPORT   ALLOCATE,DEALLOCATE;
   FROM SYSTEM IMPORT    ADR,ADDRESS;
   FROM ELO302 IMPORT    MovByteL;
   FROM ELO307 IMPORT    GetTHeap;

CONST
   maxstr = 32767;
   dynamic = TRUE;
   fixedlen = 6;
TYPE
   CHARS     = ARRAY [1..maxstr] OF CHAR;
   CHARSPTR = POINTER TO CHARS;
   STRING   = POINTER TO STRRCRD;
   STRRCRD  = RECORD
     max      : CARDINAL;
     len      : CARDINAL;
     CASE dynamic:BOOLEAN OF
       TRUE  : char : CHARS;
     ! FALSE : cptr : CHARSPTR;
       END;
     END;

PROCEDURE StrLen(s:STRING):CARDINAL;
BEGIN
   RETURN s^.len;
   END StrLen;

PROCEDURE StrSize(s:STRING):CARDINAL;
BEGIN
   RETURN s^.max;
   END StrSize;

PROCEDURE SetLen(s:STRING;1:CARDINAL);
BEGIN
   IF (1 > StrSize(s))
     THEN s^.len:=StrSize(s);
     ELSE s^.len:=1;
```

Fig. 4-1 continued

```
    END;
  END SetLen;

PROCEDURE ChrPtr(s:STRING;n:CARDINAL):CHRPTR;
VAR
  a:ADDRESS;
BEGIN
  IF (n > StrLen(s))
    THEN n:=StrLen(s);
    END;
  IF (s^.dynamic)
    THEN a:=ADR(s^.char);
    ELSE a:=s^.cptr;
    END;
  IF (n > 1)
    THEN INC(a,n-1);
    END;
  RETURN a;
  END ChrPtr;

PROCEDURE StrChar(s:STRING;n:CARDINAL):CHAR;
VAR
  c:CHRPTR;
BEGIN
  c:=ChrPtr(s,n);
  RETURN c^;
  END StrChar;

PROCEDURE SetChar(s:STRING;n:CARDINAL;c:CHAR);
VAR
  as:CHRPTR;
BEGIN
  as:=ChrPtr(s,n);
  MovByteL(c,as^,0,0,1);
  END SetChar;

PROCEDURE MoveStr(source,dest:STRING;d:CARDINAL);
VAR
  sl,dl,s:CARDINAL;
  as,ad:CHRPTR;
  blank:CHAR;
BEGIN
  blank:=' ';
  dl:=StrLen(dest);
  sl:=StrLen(source);
  s:=1;
  WHILE (d <= dl) DO
    ad:=ChrPtr(dest,d);
    IF (s > sl)
      THEN MovByteL(blank,ad^,0,0,1);
      ELSE
        as:=ChrPtr(source,s);
        MovByteL(as^,ad^,0,0,1);
        INC(s);
      END;
    INC(d);
    END;
  END MoveStr;

PROCEDURE CopyStr(source,dest:STRING);
```

```
BEGIN
  IF (StrLen(source) > StrSize(dest))
    THEN SetLen(dest,StrSize(dest));
    ELSE SetLen(dest,StrLen(source));
    END;
  IF (StrLen(dest) > 0)
    THEN MoveStr(source,dest,1);
    END;
  END CopyStr;

PROCEDURE MakeStr(VAR s:STRING;n:CARDINAL;init:STRING);
BEGIN
  IF (n = 0)
    THEN n:=StrLen(init);
    END;
  ALLOCATE(s,fixedlen + n);
  s^.dynamic:=dynamic;
  s^.max:=n;
  s^.len:=StrLen(init);
  MoveStr(init,s,1);
  END MakeStr;

PROCEDURE ClearStr(VAR s:STRING);
BEGIN
  IF (s <> NIL) AND (s^.max > 0) AND (s^.dynamic)
    THEN DEALLOCATE(s,fixedlen + s^.max);
    END;
  s:=NIL;
  END ClearStr;

PROCEDURE MakeLit(l:CARDINAL;a:CHARSPTR):STRING;
VAR
  s:STRING;
BEGIN
  GetTHeap(s,fixedlen + 4);
  s^.max:=l+1;
  s^.len:=l+1;
  s^.dynamic:=FALSE;
  s^.cptr:=a;
  RETURN s;
  END MakeLit;

PROCEDURE SubStr(f,n:CARDINAL;s:STRING):STRING;
VAR
  sub:STRING;
BEGIN
  IF (f + n - 1 > StrLen(s))
    THEN n:=StrLen(s) - f + 1;
    END;
  GetTHeap(sub,fixedlen + 4);
  sub^.max:=n;
  sub^.len:=n;
  sub^.dynamic:=FALSE;
  sub^.cptr:=ChrPtr(s,f);
  RETURN sub;
  END SubStr;

BEGIN
  Literal    := LITERAL(MakeLit);
  MakeStr(nullstr,1,Literal(CHR(0)));
  SetLen(nullstr,0);
END EL0401.
```

can be used wherever a PROCEDURE type is referenced. What isn't clear is that because a PROCEDURE type is actually a POINTER to the entry point of a PROCEDURE, any ADDRESS is compatible. The means the referent of Literal could be any PROCEDURE or even an ARRAY containing the appropriate values. As long as the number of entries pushed on the stack by the caller corresponds to the number of items expected on the stack by the callee, everything works fine.

If you look in the initialization of the IMPLEMENTATION, you will see that Literal actually refers to the PROCEDURE named *MakeLit*. *MakeLit*'s calling sequence expects a CARDINAL and a CHARSPTR. Whenever Literal is called with a constant ARRAY OF CHAR, the compiler pushes the upper bound of the array and the address of the array on the stack. Because a CHARSPTR is a POINTER to an ARRAY OF CHAR (an ADDRESS, remember?), the *MakeLit* PROCEDURE expects the same sequence. (If appropriate, this concept makes a very convenient mechanism around Modula-2's inclination to copy constant array parameters onto the local stack of a procedure. While the copy philosophy may prevent the procedure from tampering with another procedure's data, it does slow down execution speed.)

Through *MakeLit,* Literal allows a calling program to treat any constant or variable ARRAY OF CHAR as though it were a STRING. To do this, *MakeLit* calls *GetTHeap* to allocate space for the appropriate STRRCRD on the temporary heap. The STRRCRD that *MakeLit* creates is only guaranteed to exist for as long as the corresponding temporary heap variable exists. Usually, Literal is used to supply a value in the calling sequence of another procedure, for example:

```
MoveStr(Literal('This is a constant'),string);
```

Because Literal is a function and does return a value, you might be tempted to use it to supply a value to a variable. As explained in the last chapter, this is permissible, but it should be done with care; the associated THEAP variable might get reused before you expect.

The STRING created by Literal can also be used on the receiving end of most of the STRING procedures. The following is legitimate:

```
MoveStr(string,Literal('---------'));
```

Because you won't be able to access the Literal again, this statement may not be logical, but it is valid. Normally, you would say this:

```
VAR
   aoc:ARRAY [1..10] OF CHAR;
BEGIN
   . . . .
   MoveStr(Literal('Some characters'),Literal(aoc));
   . . . .
   END;
```

One caution: A Modula-2 program is composed of statements; a statement is composed of one or more identifiers and symbols. A statement may be continued from one line to another, but each symbol or identifier must be entirely on one line. Because a string constant is a symbol, it, and its enclosing quotes, must fit all on one line. This limits the number of characters that can be fed to Literal to whatever limit the compiler imposes. Usually, this is around 100 characters.

There is a benefit to this technique that might not be obvious. When a program includes statements like

```
PROCEDURE DoSomething(s:ARRAY OF CHAR);
BEGIN
    . . . . .
    END;

VAR
    s : ARRAY [1..10] OF CHAR;
BEGIN
    s := '1234567890';
    DoSomething(s);
    . . . . .
```

then the compiler generates space for the '1234567890' in the constant area, space for the variable *s* on the stack of the main procedure, code to move the contents of the constant area to the variable area, and a complete copy of the contents of *s* on the stack for the *DoSomething* procedure. A simple move of 10 bytes can generate almost 100 bytes of code and data. As a general rule, programmers in modern structured languages should not worry about details like this, but a factor of 10 to 1 in wasted memory space requires at least a passing glance. Using Literal, you can decrease this factor considerably.

SubStr. A STRING operation often does not require the entire contents of an already existing STRING, but instead needs some sequence of characters from the middle. The SubStr function handles this. Like Literal, SubStr creates a STRRCRD in the temporary heap. Normally, it's used in the calling sequence of other procedures, as in the following:

```
CopyStr(SubStr(10,5,string1),string2);
```

MakeStr. Normal STRINGs (those that must be allocated and deallocated manually) are created by the MakeStr procedure. MakeStr can be used to allocate the area and give the resulting STRING an initial value. The contents of the *init* parameter are copied into the new STRING.

ClearStr. STRINGS created by MakeStr are destroyed by ClearStr. Before calling DEALLOCATE, the routine makes an effort to verify that the s parameter does indeed point to an allocated STRING. The main danger in ClearStr is that it may be called with a STRING parameter that has never been allocated. While it is unlikely that such a STRING would pass all three tests in ClearStr, it is still possible. Be aware that this might happen.

StrLen, StrSize, and SetLen. The EL0401 module includes three procedures that deal with the number of characters in a STRING. StrSize returns a CARDINAL value that corresponds to the maximum number of characters its STRING parameter can hold. StrLen indicates the number of characters currently in use. And, SetLen allows a calling routine to set the number of characters in use.

StrLen illustrates a common problem in many "general purpose" procedures; how do you go about reporting errors when the error might have been caused by the error reporting routines? For example, it is easy to make the mistake of calling StrLen with 1 set to a value greater then the maximum number of characters a particular STRING can contain. That's something *StrLen* should check for, and does, but aside from the fact that the error reporting routines won't be invented until Chapter 9, it might be the error reporting routines that have the problem. *StrLen* handles this situation by making a harmless but easily noticeable correction. If the value of the 1 parameter is greater than *StrSize(s)*, *SetLen* sets 1 to *StrSize(s)*. The program can continue to function without causing any damage.

MicroSoft Pascal, the original basis for the routines in this book, handles a similar problem by aborting the program. In MS Pascal, the COPYSTR procedure will copy one string variable to another. If the receiving string is shorter than the sender, the COPYSTR aborts. When the program in which this occurs includes the error-handling modules, the abort is accompanied by a short message, somewhat cryptic, but still useful. If the error reporting routines are excluded to conserve space in the EXE file, the program simply aborts with no message, nothing. It's difficult to find the problem when this occurs.

ChrPtr. The routine that returns a CHRPTR value for a STRING variable is called *ChrPtr*. It sole purpose is to return the address of the nth character in *s*. Most programs would never use this routine, but it is required by some of the other routines in the Library, and is therefore exported from the Module. Note that *ChrPtr* also corrects reference to characters outside the range of the STRING.

SetChar. To assign a value to a specific character in a STRING, use *SetChar*. Because *SetChar* calls *ChrPtr*, a caller can never access a character outside the limits of the STRING.

MoveStr and CopyStr. There are two STRING routines that permit the assignment of one STRING to another. *CopyStr* moves the entire contents, or at least as much as will fit, of the *source* STRING into the *dest* STRING. The transfer begins at the first character in each. The current length of *dest* is adjusted to reflect how many characters were actually transferred. *MoveStr*, on the other hand, allows the caller to specify which character in *dest* is to receive the first character of *source*. *MoveStr* does not adjust the current length of *dest*. For example, the following statements:

```
CopyStr(Literal('ABCDEF'),dest);
MoveStr(Literal(' - - '),dest,3);
```

will result in *dest* being set to 'AB--EF.'

MANIPULATING STRINGS

Module EL0402 contains three routines that manipulate the contents of a STRING variable. Because the STRRCRD to which a STRING points contains both a *max* and a *len* field, these routines can be used to change the number of characters in

Fig. 4-2. STRING manipulation routines.

```
DEFINITION MODULE ELO402;
   FROM ELO401 IMPORT    STRING;
   EXPORT QUALIFIED      Delete,Insert,Concat;

PROCEDURE Delete(dest:STRING;s,n:CARDINAL);
(* This routine will delete n characters from dest, beginning at s.  Any
   characters to the right will be moved left.  Note that the current
   length of dest is adjusted.  *)
PROCEDURE Insert(source,dest:STRING;d:CARDINAL);
(* This routine will insert source into dest, beginning at d.  Note that
   the current length of dest will be adjusted.  *)
PROCEDURE Concat(source,dest:STRING);
(* This routine will concatenate source onto the end of the characters
   currently defined in dest.  The length of dest will be adjusted
   accordingly.  *)
END ELO402.

IMPLEMENTATION MODULE ELO402;
   FROM SYSTEM IMPORT    ADR,ADDRESS;
   FROM ELO401 IMPORT    STRING,StrLen,SetLen,StrSize,SetChar,StrChar;

PROCEDURE Delete(dest:STRING;s,n:CARDINAL);
VAR
   l,i:CARDINAL;
BEGIN
   l:=StrLen(dest);
   IF (s + n > l + 1)
     THEN n:=l - s + 1;
     END;
   FOR i:=s TO l-n DO
     SetChar(dest,i,StrChar(dest,i+n));
     END;
   SetLen(dest,l-n);
   END Delete;

PROCEDURE Concat(source,dest:STRING);
VAR
   i,d,l:CARDINAL;
BEGIN
   IF (StrLen(dest) < StrSize(dest))
     THEN
       l:=StrLen(source);
       IF (StrLen(dest)+l > StrSize(dest))
         THEN l:=StrSize(dest) - StrLen(dest);
         END;
       d:=StrLen(dest)+1;
       SetLen(dest,l+StrLen(dest));
       FOR i:=1 TO l DO
         SetChar(dest,d,StrChar(source,i));
         INC(d);
         END;
     END;
   END Concat;

PROCEDURE Insert(source,dest:STRING; d:CARDINAL);
VAR
   n,i,j,l:CARDINAL;
BEGIN
   IF (d > StrLen(dest))
     THEN Concat(source,dest);
     ELSE
```

Fig. 4-2 continued

```
        l:=StrLen(source);
        IF (l + StrLen(dest) > StrSize(dest))
          THEN l:=StrSize(dest) - 1;
          END;
        IF (l > 0)
          THEN
            n:=StrLen(dest);
            j:=l+n;
            SetLen(dest,j);
            FOR i:=d TO n DO
              SetChar(dest,j,StrChar(dest,j-1));
              DEC(j);
              END;
            FOR i:=1 TO l DO
              SetChar(dest,d,StrChar(source,i));
              INC(d);
              END;
          END;
      END;
  END Insert;

END EL0402.
```

a STRING that are considered significant. *Delete* removes characters from a STRING, *Concat* adds characters onto the end of a STRING, and *Insert* adds characters into the middle of an existing STRING. Module EL0402 is shown in Fig. 4-2, and the comments in the DEFINITION document the operation of each of the routines.

LOOKING FOR PATTERNS

There are three general-purpose STRING pattern-matching routines in the Etling Library. These routines are contained in EL0403, shown in Fig. 4-3. *MatchStr* forms the basis for the other two. For simplicity, *MatchStr* is written in a straightforward fashion, using standard Modula-2 syntax. If speed is important, *MatchStr* could be rewritten in Machine code using CODE statements. Because both *Positn* and *Blank* use *MatchStr*, rewriting *MatchStr* would speed up all of these routines.

BUILDING BETTER STRING CONSTANTS

Standard Modula-2, and most of the Modula-2 compilers, don't quite make the grade when it comes to string constants. Modula-2 let's you say things like:

string = 'This is a string constant';

If you need to include any control characters, nonprintable characters, or extended ASCII characters in the string, however, you're in trouble. Your only recourse is to set up a variable ARRAY OF CHAR and assign the appropriate values to the individual elements—a time-consuming and error-prone process. There ought to be a way for the compiler to do the "grunt" work.

FixStr. Module EL0404 (see Fig. 4-4) exports a routine that makes string constants easier to handle. The routine *FixStr* requires a STRING parameter and it returns

Fig. 4-3. Patterns.

```
DEFINITION MODULE ELO403;
   FROM ELO303 IMPORT    MATCHVAL;
   FROM ELO401 IMPORT    STRING;
   EXPORT QUALIFIED      MatchStr,Positn,Blank;

PROCEDURE MatchStr(string1,string2:STRING;s1,s2,1:CARDINAL):MATCHVAL;
(* This routine will compare 1 characters in the STRINGs, beginning at s
   and s2.  The compare is done according to the arrangement of characters
   in the normal ASCII collating sequence.  The results of the compare are
   returned as follows:

      If string1 < string2 then MatchStr = less
      If string1 = string2 then MatchStr = equal
      If string1 > string2 then MatchStr = greater

   If, on entry, 1 = 0, the length of the longer STRING will control the
   length.  If one string is longer than the other (but contain equal
   characters) the routine will return indicating that the shorter string
   comes before the longer in the collating sequence.  *)
PROCEDURE Positn(pattern,source:STRING; s:CARDINAL):CARDINAL;
(* This routine will begin at s and search for an occurence of pattern in
   source.  If a match is found, the index of the first character will be
   returned as the function value.  If no match is found, or if s is
   greater than the length of source, the function will return 0.  *)
PROCEDURE Blank(source:STRING):BOOLEAN;
(* If all of the characters in source are equal to blank, this routine will
   return TRUE...at the first occurence of a non-blank, this routine will
   return FALSE.  *)
END ELO403.


IMPLEMENTATION MODULE ELO403;
   FROM ELO303 IMPORT    CompArea,MATCHVAL,equal,less,greater;
   FROM ELO401 IMPORT    STRING,CHRPTR,StrLen,SubStr,StrChar,ChrPtr;

PROCEDURE MatchStr(string1,string2:STRING;s1,s2,1:CARDINAL):MATCHVAL;
VAR
  c1,c2:CHRPTR;
BEGIN
  IF (StrLen(string1) = 0)
    THEN IF (StrLen(string2) = 0)
      THEN RETURN equal;
      ELSE RETURN less;
      END;
    ELSE IF (StrLen(string2) = 0)
      THEN RETURN greater;
      END;
    END;
  IF (1 = 0)
    THEN IF (StrLen(string1) > StrLen(string2))
      THEN 1:=StrLen(string1);
      ELSE 1:=StrLen(string2);
      END;
    END;
  c1:=ChrPtr(string1,s1);
  c2:=ChrPtr(string2,s2);
  RETURN CompArea(c1^,0,1,c2^,0,1,1);
  END MatchStr;

PROCEDURE Positn(pattern,source:STRING; s:CARDINAL):CARDINAL;
```

Fig. 4-3 continued
```
VAR
   match:MATCHVAL;
   ls,lp:CARDINAL;
BEGIN
   ls:=StrLen(source);
   lp:=StrLen(pattern);
   WHILE (s <= ls - lp + 1) DO
     match:=MatchStr(pattern,source,1,s,lp);
     IF (match = equal)
       THEN RETURN s;
       ELSE INC(s);
       END;
     END;
   RETURN 0;
   END Positn;

PROCEDURE Blank(source:STRING):BOOLEAN;
VAR
   i:CARDINAL;
BEGIN
   FOR i := 1 TO StrLen(source) DO
     IF (StrChar(source,i) <> ' ')
       THEN RETURN FALSE;
       END;
     END;
   RETURN TRUE;
   END Blank;

END ELO403.
```

Fig. 4-4. Fixing up STRING constants.
```
DEFINITION MODULE ELO404;
   FROM ELO401 IMPORT    STRING;
   EXPORT QUALIFIED      FixStr;

PROCEDURE FixStr(s:STRING):STRING;
(* This procedure rebuilds the contents of s, and returns, as its function
   value, the rebuilt STRING.  Normally, s contains special constructs and
   is the result of a call to Literal, as in:

       CopyStr(FixStr(Literal("'An example'*cr*lf")),string);

   Note that the constant is enclosed in double-quotes, with imbedded
   single quotes, and the * operator.  The * indicates that FixStr should
   concatentate the cr and lf characters onto the end of the 'An example'
   literal.  Any characters within single quotes are copied into the
   resulting string exactly as written.  Other characters may be specified
   by using their corresponding constant name (from ELO304);  by specifying
   CHR(x), where x defines the appropriate value;  or, as #hh, where the #
   indicates a hexi-decimal value defined by hh.  For example:

       CopyStr(FixStr(Literal("CHR(O)*CHR(16)*#20*#20")),string);
*)
END ELO404.

IMPLEMENTATION MODULE ELO404;
   FROM ELO302 IMPORT    MovByteL;
   FROM ELO303 IMPORT    CompArea,equal;
   FROM ELO401 IMPORT    STRING,StrLen,SetLen,StrChar,SetChar;
```

```
TYPE
  Memonic = RECORD
    m:ARRAY [1..4] OF CHAR;
    c:CHAR;
    END;
CONST
  quote     = 047C;
VAR
  t:ARRAY [1..70] OF Memonic;

PROCEDURE FixStr(s:STRING):STRING;
VAR
  l,f,i,n,j:CARDINAL;
  gotit,nope,done:BOOLEAN;
  m:ARRAY [1..4] OF CHAR;
  nbytes:CARDINAL;
BEGIN
  f:=1;
  l:=1;
  nbytes:=StrLen(s);
  WHILE (l <= nbytes) DO
    IF (StrChar(s,l) = quote)
      THEN
        INC(l);
        WHILE (StrChar(s,l) <> quote) DO
          SetChar(s,f,StrChar(s,l));
          INC(l);
          INC(f);
          END;
        INC(l,2);
      ELSE
        IF (StrChar(s,l) >= 'a') AND (StrChar(s,l) <= 'z')
          THEN
            j:=0;
            REPEAT
              m[j+1]:=StrChar(s,l+j);
              INC(j);
              UNTIL (l+j > nbytes) OR (StrChar(s,l+j) = '*');
            WHILE (j < 4) DO
              m[j+1]:=' ';
              INC(j);
              END;
            i:=1;
            gotit:=FALSE;
            REPEAT
              IF (CompArea(t[i].m,0,4,m,0,4,4) = equal)
                THEN gotit:=TRUE;
                ELSE INC(i);
                END;
              UNTIL (i > HIGH(t)+1) OR (gotit);
            IF (gotit)
              THEN
                SetChar(s,f,t[i].c);
                INC(f);
              END;
            WHILE (l <= StrLen(s)) AND (StrChar(s,l) <> '*') DO
              INC(l);
              END;
          ELSE
            n:=0;
            IF (StrChar(s,l) = 'C')
              THEN
```

Fig. 4-4 continued

```
                    INC(1,4);
                    WHILE (StrChar(s,1) >= '0')
                                   AND (StrChar(s,1) <= '9') DO
                      n:=10*n + ORD(StrChar(s,1)) - ORD('0');
                      INC(1);
                      END;
                  ELSE
                    INC(1);
                    done:=FALSE;
                    REPEAT
                      IF (StrChar(s,1) >= '0')
                                       AND (StrChar(s,1) <= '9')
                        THEN
                          n:=16*n + ORD(StrChar(s,1)) - ORD('0');
                          INC(1);
                        ELSE IF (StrChar(s,1) >='A')
                                     AND (StrChar(s,1) <= 'F')
                          THEN
                            n:=16*n + ORD(StrChar(s,1))-ORD('A') + 10;
                            INC(1);
                          ELSE done:=TRUE;
                          END;
                        END;
                      UNTIL (done);
                    END;
                  SetChar(s,f,CHR(n));
                  INC(f);
                  IF (StrChar(s,1) = ')')
                  THEN INC(1);
                  END;
              END;
            INC(1);
          END;
      END;
  FOR i:=f TO nbytes DO
    SetChar(s,i,CHR(0));
    END;
  DEC(f);
  SetLen(s,f);
  RETURN s;
  END FixStr;

PROCEDURE Init(m:ARRAY OF CHAR;c:CHAR;i:CARDINAL);
VAR
  j:CARDINAL;
BEGIN
  FOR j:=1 TO 4 DO
    t[i].m[j]:=m[j-1];
    END;
  t[i].c:=c;
  END Init;


BEGIN
  Init('bksp',010C,01);     Init('brea',003C,02);     Init('cr  ',015C,03);
  Init('deof',032C,04);     Init('lf  ',012C,05);     Init('pgdn',121C,06);
  Init('pgup',111C,07);     Init('altd',072C,08);     Init('fk1 ',073C,09);
  Init('fk2 ',074C,10);     Init('fk3 ',075C,11);     Init('fk4 ',076C,12);
  Init('fk5 ',077C,13);     Init('fk6 ',100C,14);     Init('fk7 ',101C,15);
  Init('fk8 ',102C,16);     Init('fk9 ',103C,17);     Init('fk10',104C,18);
  Init('fk11',124C,19);     Init('fk12',125C,20);     Init('fk13',126C,21);
  Init('fk14',127C,22);     Init('fk15',130C,23);     Init('fk16',131C,24);
```

```
      Init('fk17',132C,25);    Init('fk18',133C,26);    Init('fk19',134C,27);
      Init('fk20',135C,28);    Init('fk21',136C,29);    Init('fk22',137C,30);
      Init('fk23',140C,31);    Init('fk24',141C,32);    Init('fk25',142C,33);
      Init('fk26',143C,34);    Init('fk27',144C,35);    Init('fk28',145C,36);
      Init('fk29',146C,37);    Init('fk30',147C,38);    Init('fk31',150C,39);
      Init('fk32',151C,40);    Init('fk33',152C,41);    Init('fk34',153C,42);
      Init('fk35',154C,43);    Init('fk36',155C,44);    Init('fk37',156C,45);
      Init('fk38',157C,46);    Init('fk39',160C,47);    Init('fk40',161C,48);
      Init('tabr',011C,49);    Init('tabl',017C,50);    Init('rtab',115C,51);
      Init('ltab',113C,52);    Init('utab',110C,53);    Init('dtab',120C,54);
      Init('home',107C,55);    Init('end ',117C,56);    Init('boxu',111C,57);
      Init('boxd',121C,58);    Init('curl',163C,59);    Init('curr',164C,60);
      Init('insr',122C,61);    Init('del ',123C,62);    Init('esc ',033C,63);
      Init('alld',023C,64);    Init('next',027C,65);    Init('ditt',040C,66);
      Init('xmtc',055C,67);    Init('clea',056C,68);    Init('seqv',061C,69);
      Init('help',043C,70);
END ELO404.
```

the same STRING after reassembling it. The STRING parameter can be a regular STRING variable or it can be the result of a call to *Literal*. In the latter case, the contents of the ARRAY OF CHAR to which the STRING refers may be in the normal data space (i.e., declared in the VAR section of a PROCEDURE or MODULE), or, for a string constant, it may be in whatever area the compiler uses for constants. Logitech, for example, puts string constants in the appropriate code segment.

Modifying the contents of constants is not something that should be done casually, but, in the Modula-2 packages referenced in this book, it does appear to work with no detrimental side effects. The technique can probably be used with any structured data.

Fig. 4-5. Initializing STRING.

```
DEFINITION MODULE ELO405;
  FROM ELO401 IMPORT    STRING;
  EXPORT QUALIFIED      FillStr;

PROCEDURE FillStr(s:STRING;c:CHAR);
    (* This routine will fill s with the CHAR supplied.  *)
END ELO405.

IMPLEMENTATION MODULE ELO405;
  FROM ELO401 IMPORT    STRING,StrLen,SetLen,StrSize,SetChar;

PROCEDURE FillStr(s:STRING;c:CHAR);
VAR
  i:CARDINAL;
BEGIN
  SetLen(s,StrSize(s));
  FOR i:=1 TO StrLen(s) DO
    SetChar(s,i,c);
    END;
  END FillStr;

END ELO405.
```

INITIALIZING STRINGS

The last STRING-oriented module in the Etling Library is very small, but very necessary. Module EL0405 is shown in Fig. 4-5. This module exports a single routine, called *FillStr,* which fills it STRING parameter completely, from its first character to its *StrLen,* with the specified character. *FillStr* comes in very handy in commercial programming.

Chapter 5

Special Types

One heuristic inherent in the concept of structured programming states that you should be careful not to include items in the same module by coincidence.

Because that heuristic doesn't apply to chapters in a book, this chapter defines 5 modules that are here by coincidence. The only thing these modules really have in common is that they define special types used by other modules in the library.

CHARACTER SETS

Although standard Modula-2 defines all of the normal set operators, individual compilers can restrict the number of elements that a set can contain. The only standard set type that Modula-2 defines is the BITSET which is usually the size of one word, permitting at most 16 elements. However, commercial programming almost always requires operations on sets of characters. A complete character set for the IBM PC has 256 elements (actually, there are two 256 element character sets, considering the extended ASCII concept).

Wirth himself, in *Programing in Modula-2*, demonstrates how to build an ARRAY OF BITSET, providing a mechanism for defining and operating on sets of any size. Most of the Modula-2 texts listed in the bibliography expand upon these concepts. The routines in the Etling Library that deal with character sets are based on several of these definitions. The character set routines are exported by EL0501, shown in Fig. 5-1.

The Character Set Type. The character set type is called CHARSET and it is actually an array. The array has 16 elements. Each element is a BITSET, allowing for 16 values. Therefore, each CHARSET can handle up to 256 individual characters, exactly

Fig. 5-1. Character sets.

```
DEFINITION MODULE EL0501;
   FROM EL0401 IMPORT    STRING;
   EXPORT QUALIFIED      CHARSET,nullcset,numbers,capitals,lowcases,
                         IncCSet,ExcCSet,InCSet,EqCSet,MakeCSet;

CONST
   piecesize = 16; setsize = 256; pieces = 16; maxpiece = pieces - 1;
TYPE
   PIECERANGE = [0..maxpiece];
   CHARSET = ARRAY PIECERANGE OF BITSET;
VAR
   nullcset,numbers,capitals,lowcases : CHARSET;
(* Although these symbols are defined as variables, they should be treated
   as constants. *)
PROCEDURE IncCSet(ch:CHAR; VAR chset:CHARSET);
(* This routine will include the character ch in the Character Set defined
   by chset. *)
PROCEDURE ExcCSet(ch:CHAR; VAR chset:CHARSET);
(* This routine will remove the character ch from the Character Set
   defined by chset. *)
PROCEDURE InCSet(ch:CHAR; chset:CHARSET):BOOLEAN;
(* This routine will determine if the character ch is in the set defined
   by chset, returning TRUE if it does. *)
PROCEDURE EqCSet(chset1,chset2:CHARSET):BOOLEAN;
(* This routine will compare chset1 and chset2.  The function will return
   TRUE if the sets are equal. *)
PROCEDURE MakeCSet(chars:STRING;VAR chset:CHARSET);
(* This routine will create a CHARSET from the string defined by chars.
   Each character in chars will be included in chset. *)
END EL0501.


IMPLEMENTATION MODULE EL0501;
   FROM EL0401 IMPORT    STRING,StrLen,Literal,StrChar;

VAR
   piece:PIECERANGE;

PROCEDURE IncCSet(ch:CHAR; VAR chset:CHARSET);
BEGIN
   INCL( chset[ORD(ch) DIV piecesize], ORD(ch) MOD piecesize);
   END IncCSet;

PROCEDURE ExcCSet(ch:CHAR; VAR chset:CHARSET);
BEGIN
   EXCL( chset[ORD(ch) DIV piecesize], ORD(ch) MOD piecesize);
   END ExcCSet;

PROCEDURE InCSet(ch:CHAR; chset:CHARSET):BOOLEAN;
BEGIN
   RETURN ORD(ch) MOD piecesize IN chset[ ORD(ch) DIV piecesize ];
   END InCSet;

PROCEDURE EqCSet(chset1,chset2:CHARSET):BOOLEAN;
VAR
   i:CARDINAL;
BEGIN
   FOR i:=0 TO maxpiece DO
     IF (chset1[i] <> chset2[i])
       THEN RETURN FALSE;
       END;
     END;
```

```
   RETURN TRUE;
   END EqCSet;

PROCEDURE MakeCSet(chars:STRING;VAR chset:CHARSET);
VAR
   i:CARDINAL;
BEGIN
   chset:=nullcset;
   i:=1;
   REPEAT
     IncCSet(StrChar(chars,i),chset);
     INC(i);
     UNTIL (i > StrLen(chars));
   END MakeCSet;

BEGIN
   FOR piece:=0 TO maxpiece DO
     nullcset[piece]:={};
     END;
   MakeCSet(Literal('0123456789'),numbers);
   MakeCSet(Literal('ABCDEFGHIJKLMNOPQRSTUVWXYZ'),capitals);
   MakeCSet(Literal('abcdefghijklmnopqrstuvwxyz'),lowcases);
END EL0501.
```

what is needed for the IBM PC. Well, not exactly; remember the PC has the extended ASCII characters to complicate things. It would probably be acceptable to double the number of elements in the array, and handle all 512 possible values at one time, but both regular and extended ASCII characters are seldom used in the same context. When both groups are required, it's just as easy to use two CHARSET variables.

Charset Constants. For easy reference, the EL0501 module exports four CHAR-SET variables that contain standard groups of characters. (While these are exported as variables, any module that uses these items should treat them as constants.) The *nullcset* variable defines an empty CHARSET; *numbers* defines the set of all numeric characters, 0 through 9; *capitals* contains only capital letters; and, *lowcases* contains only lower case.

IncCSet and ExcCSet. The EL0501 module defines two routines that correspond to typical "set" operations. The *IncCSet* procedure will include a character in a set; the *ExcCSet* procedure removes a character. The IMPLEMENTATION shows how easy these routines are to create using standard Modula-2 BITSET operations. If you really find a need for "union" or "intersection" operations, they are easily defined. The other library routines do not need these operations, so EL0501 does not define them.

InCSet and EqCSet. The other library routines do need routines to determine if a given character is in a given CHARSET, or if one CHARSET is equal to another. That's what the *InCSet* and *EqCSet* routines do and again, the operations are very simple to implement using standard Modula-2.

MakeCSet. The last routine in EL0501 is *MakeCSet*, which is used to assign an initial value to a CHARSET. Even though it does not reference them directly, this routine was one of the main reasons for creating the *FixStr* and *Literal* procedures. In standard Modula-2, the accepted way of creating the capitals CHARSET would be as follows:

```
capitals:=nullcset;
InCSet('A',capitals);
InCSet('B',capitals);
InCSet('C',capitals);
InCSet('D',capitals);
InCSet('E',capitals);
```

Using *MakeCSet*, with *Fixstr* and *Literal,* this sequence becomes

MakeCSet(FixStr(Literal('ABCDEFGHIJKLMNOPQRSTUVWXYZ')),capitals);

This is not only much easier to write, it is much easier to read and understand.

DATES AND TIMES

EL0502 (Fig. 5-2) is a module that exports only two type definitions; one for DATE and one for TIME. Both types are 6-character arrays and are used to ensure that these commercially important concepts are standardized throughout the Etling Library. Note that the IMPLEMENTATION of EL0502 contains no code—perfectly acceptable in Modula-2.

Fig. 5-2. Dates and times.

```
DEFINITION MODULE EL0502;
  EXPORT QUALIFIED     DATE,TIME;

TYPE
  DATE = ARRAY [1..6] OF CHAR;
  TIME = ARRAY [1..6] OF CHAR;
(* These two types are used throughout the library to define a standard
   format for date and time variables.

      DATE is in yymmdd format.
      TIME is in hhmmss format.
*)
END EL0502.

IMPLEMENTATION MODULE EL0502;

END EL0502.
```

LONG CARDINALS

Later, when the I/O related routines are discussed in Chapter 10, the need arises for routines that can do arithmetic operations on 4-byte numeric quantities. A 4-byte number occupies two words on an IBM PC; twice the size of a normal Modula-2 INTEGER or CARDINAL.

Some of the Modula-2 compilers do offer a double-word data type, but the definitions and related operations are not consistent from one package to another. To avoid any confusion, the Etling Library introduces its own double-word arithmetic type, called LONGCARD, which is defined in EL0503 (shown in Fig. 5-3).

Fig. 5-3. Double-word cardinals.

```
DEFINITION MODULE EL0503;
   FROM EL0303 IMPORT    MATCHVAL;
   EXPORT QUALIFIED      LONGCARD,LongCard,AddLCard,SubLCard,MulLCard,
                         DivLCard,ComLCard,lczero,lcone;


TYPE
  LONGCARD = RECORD
    locard:CARDINAL;
    hicard:CARDINAL;
    END;
VAR
  lczero,lcone : LONGCARD;
PROCEDURE LongCard(loword,hiword:CARDINAL; VAR lcrd:LONGCARD);
(* This routine will create a double word CARDINAL on the heap, and return
   a pointer to it.  *)
PROCEDURE AddLCard(lcrd1,lcrd2:LONGCARD; VAR lcrdrslt:LONGCARD);
(* This routine will perform the equation :  lcrdrslt := lcrd1 + lcrd2   *)
PROCEDURE SubLCard(lcrd1,lcrd2:LONGCARD; VAR lcrdrslt:LONGCARD);
(*   This routine will perform the equation : lcrdrslt := lcrd1 - lcrd2  *)
PROCEDURE MulLCard(lcrd1,lcrd2:LONGCARD; VAR lcrdrslt:LONGCARD);
(*   This routine will perform the equation :
                   lcrdrslt := lcrd1.locard * lcrd2.locard         *)
PROCEDURE DivLCard(lcrd1,lcrd2:LONGCARD; VAR lcrdrslt,lcrdrem:LONGCARD);
(*   This routine will perform the equation :
                 lcrdrslt.loword := lcrd1 / lcrd2.loword
   The remainder is returned in lcrdrem.loword *)
PROCEDURE ComLCard(lcrd1,lcrd2:LONGCARD):MATCHVAL;
(*   This routine will compare the two LONGCARD parameters and return an
     integer indicating their relative value.

         If lcrd1 < lcrd2,    then ComLCard = less
         If lcrd1 = lcrd2,    then ComLCard = equal
         If lcrd1 > lcrd2,    then ComLCard = greater
*)
END EL0503.


IMPLEMENTATION MODULE EL0503;
   FROM EL0303 IMPORT    MATCHVAL,less,equal,greater;
   FROM SYSTEM IMPORT    SETREG,GETREG,CODE,AX,BX,CX,DX;


PROCEDURE LongCard(locard,hicard:CARDINAL;VAR lcrd:LONGCARD);
BEGIN
  lcrd.locard:=locard;
  lcrd.hicard:=hicard;
  END LongCard;

PROCEDURE AddLCard(lcrd1,lcrd2:LONGCARD;VAR lcrdrslt:LONGCARD);
VAR
  c1l,c1h,c2l,c2h,rl,rh:CARDINAL;
BEGIN
  c1l:=lcrd1.locard;
  c1h:=lcrd1.hicard;
  c2l:=lcrd2.locard;
  c2h:=lcrd2.hicard;
  SETREG(AX,c1l);
  SETREG(BX,c2l);
  SETREG(CX,c1h);
  SETREG(DX,c2h);
  CODE(  0F8H  );            (* CLC       *)
  CODE(11H,0D8H);            (* ADC AX,BX *)
  CODE(11H,0D1H);            (* ADC CX,DX *)
```

Fig. 5-3 continued

```
      GETREG(AX,rl);
      GETREG(CX,rh);
      lcrdrslt.locard:=rl;
      lcrdrslt.hicard:=rh;
    END AddLCard;

PROCEDURE SubLCard(lcrd1,lcrd2:LONGCARD;VAR lcrdrslt:LONGCARD);
VAR
  c1l,c1h,c2l,c2h,rl,rh:CARDINAL;
BEGIN
  c1l:=lcrd1.locard;
  c1h:=lcrd1.hicard;
  c2l:=lcrd2.locard;
  c2h:=lcrd2.hicard;
  SETREG(AX,c1l);
  SETREG(BX,c2l);
  SETREG(CX,c1h);
  SETREG(DX,c2h);
  CODE(  0F8H );              (* CLC         *)
  CODE(19H,0D8H);            (* SUB AX,BX *)
  CODE(19H,0D1H);            (* SUB CX,DX *)
  GETREG(AX,rl);
  GETREG(CX,rh);
  lcrdrslt.locard:=rl;
  lcrdrslt.hicard:=rh;
  END SubLCard;

PROCEDURE MulLCard(lcrd1,lcrd2:LONGCARD;VAR lcrdrslt:LONGCARD);
VAR
  c1l,c2l,c1h,c2h,rl,rh:CARDINAL;
  pp1l,pp1h,pp2l,pp2h,pp3l,pp3h:CARDINAL;
  t1,t2:LONGCARD;
BEGIN
  c1l:=lcrd1.locard;
  c1h:=lcrd1.hicard;
  c2l:=lcrd2.locard;
  c2h:=lcrd2.hicard;
  SETREG(AX,c1l);
  SETREG(BX,c2l);
  CODE(0F7H,0E3H);              (* MUL AX,BX *)
  GETREG(AX,pp1l);
  GETREG(DX,pp1h);
  SETREG(AX,c1l);
  SETREG(BX,c2h);
  CODE(0F7H,0E3H);              (* MUL AX,BX *)
  GETREG(AX,pp2l);
  GETREG(DX,pp2h);
  SETREG(AX,c1h);
  SETREG(BX,c2l);
  CODE(0F7H,0E3H);              (* MUL AX,BX *)
  GETREG(AX,pp3l);
  GETREG(DX,pp3h);
  t1.locard:=pp1l;
  t1.hicard:=pp1h;
  t2.locard:=0;
  t2.hicard:=pp2l;
  AddLCard(t1,t2,lcrdrslt);
  t1.locard:=0;
  t1.hicard:=pp3l;
  AddLCard(t1,lcrdrslt,lcrdrslt);
  END MulLCard;
```

```
PROCEDURE ComLCard(lcrd1,lcrd2:LONGCARD):MATCHVAL;
BEGIN
  IF (lcrd1.hicard < lcrd2.hicard)
    THEN RETURN less;
    ELSE IF (lcrd1.hicard > lcrd2.hicard)
      THEN RETURN greater;
      ELSE IF (lcrd1.locard < lcrd2.locard)
        THEN RETURN less;
        ELSE IF (lcrd1.locard > lcrd2.locard)
          THEN RETURN greater;
          ELSE RETURN equal;
          END;
        END;
      END;
    END;
  END ComLCard;

PROCEDURE DivLCard(lcrd1,lcrd2:LONGCARD;VAR lcrdrslt,lcrdrem:LONGCARD);
VAR
  m,n,t,ten:LONGCARD;
  match:MATCHVAL;
BEGIN
  match:=ComLCard(lcrd1,lcrd2);
  IF (match = less)
    THEN
      LongCard(0,0,lcrdrslt);
      lcrdrem := lcrd1;
    ELSE IF (match = equal)
      THEN
        LongCard(1,0,lcrdrslt);
        LongCard(0,0,lcrdrem);
      ELSE
        LongCard(0,0,lcrdrslt);
        LongCard(10,0,ten);
        REPEAT
          m := lcrd2;
          LongCard(1,0,n);
          REPEAT
            MulLCard(m,ten,t);
            match:=ComLCard(lcrd1,t);
            IF (match = greater)
              THEN
                m := t;
                MulLCard(n,ten,n);
              END;
          UNTIL (match <> greater);
          REPEAT
            SubLCard(lcrd1,m,lcrd1);
            AddLCard(n,lcrdrslt,lcrdrslt);
            match:=ComLCard(lcrd1,m);
            UNTIL (match < equal);
          match:=ComLCard(lcrd1,lcrd2);
          UNTIL (match < greater);
        IF (match = 0)
          THEN LongCard(0,0,lcrdrem);
          ELSE lcrdrem := lcrd1;
          END;
        END;
      END;
    RETURN;
    END DivLCard;
```

Fig. 5-3 continued

```
BEGIN
  LongCard(0,0,1czero);
  LongCard(1,0,1cone);
END EL0503.
```

The Longcard Type. A LONGCARD type is a record consisting of two CARDI-NAL elements. Each CARDINAL is accessible individually should the need arise.

LongCard. The routine that initializes LONGCARD variables is called *LongCard*. It assembles two CARDINAL parameters into the appropriate form.

AddLCard, SubLCard, MulLCard, and DivLCard. The LONGCARD arithmetic operations—add, subtract, multiply, and divide—are handled by the four LONG-CARD routines bearing the obvious names. The IMPLEMENTATION shows that the first three actually use direct machine code instructions to accomplish their tasks. The instructions shown in Fig. 5-3 use routines from the "SYSTEM" library module in the Logitech compiler; most of the other compilers have similar procedures available, but for those that don't there is another way to implement these procedures.

For example, if the EL0503 EXPORTed:

AddLCard = PROCEDURE (LONGCARD,LONGCARD,VAR LONGCARD);

then the IMPLEMENTATION OF EL0503 could contain the following:

```
FROM SYSTEM IMPORT
  ADR,BYTE;

TYPE
  LONGCARD = RECORD
    l : CARDINAL;
    h:  CARDINAL;
    END;
  ADDLCARD = PROCEDURE(LONGCARD,LONGCARD,VAR LONGCARD);
VAR
  AddLCard : ADDLCARD;

VAR
  add:ARRAY [1..36] OF BYTE;
BEGIN
  add[01]:=BYTE(055H);      (* push    bp              *)
  add[02]:=BYTE(089H);      (* mov     bp,sp           *)
  add[03]:=BYTE(0E5H);      (*                         *)
  add[04]:=BYTE(0B8H);      (* mov     ax,000e         *)
  add[05]:=BYTE(00EH);      (*                         *)
  add[06]:=BYTE(000H);      (*                         *)
  add[07]:=BYTE(0B9H);      (* mov     cx,0010         *)
  add[08]:=BYTE(010H);      (*                         *)
  add[09]:=BYTE(000H);      (*                         *)
  add[10]:=BYTE(0BBH);      (* mov     bx,000a         *)
  add[11]:=BYTE(00AH);      (*                         *)
  add[12]:=BYTE(000H);      (*                         *)
  add[13]:=BYTE(0BAH);      (* mov     dx,000c         *)
```

```
add[14]:=BYTE(00CH);     (*                          *)
add[15]:=BYTE(000H);     (*                          *)
add[16]:=BYTE(0F8H);     (* clc                      *)
add[17]:=BYTE(011H);     (* adc      ax,bx           *)
add[18]:=BYTE(0D8H);     (*                          *)
add[19]:=BYTE(011H);     (* adc      cx,dx           *)
add[20]:=BYTE(0D1H);     (*                          *)
add[21]:=BYTE(0C4H);     (* les      bx,[bp+0006]    *)
add[22]:=BYTE(05EH);     (*                          *)
add[23]:=BYTE(006H);     (*                          *)
add[24]:=BYTE(026H);     (* es:                      *)
add[25]:=BYTE(089H);     (* mov      [bx],ax         *)
add[26]:=BYTE(007H);     (*                          *)
add[27]:=BYTE(026H);     (* es:                      *)
add[28]:=BYTE(089H);     (* mov      [bx+0002],cx    *)
add[29]:=BYTE(04FH);     (*                          *)
add[30]:=BYTE(002H);     (*                          *)
add[31]:=BYTE(089H);     (* mov      sp,bp           *)
add[32]:=BYTE(0ECH);     (*                          *)
add[33]:=BYTE(05DH);     (* pop      bp              *)
add[34]:=BYTE(0CAH);     (* retf     000c            *)
add[35]:=BYTE(00CH);     (*                          *)
add[36]:=BYTE(000H);     (*                          *)

AddLCard:=ADDLCARD(ADR(add));
```

In case it isn't immediately obvious, this code fragment defines an ARRAY OF BYTE as a static variable. (For Modula-2 packages that do not define a BYTE type use an ARRAY OF CHAR.) The elements of the ARRAY are given values corresponding to the machine-code instructions required to access two 32-bit numbers on the stack, add them together, and store their sum in the memory location specified by an address stored on the stack, *exactly* what the *AddLCard* routine shown in Fig. 5-3 does. The last line of the code fragment assigns the address of this ARRAY to the PROCEDURE variable *AddLCard*. Effectively, this is a machine code subroutine, stored in an ARRAY in the data segment, that is callable just like any other Modula-2 procedure.

This is definitely great stuff, but it does have some drawbacks. First of all, it requires intimate knowledge of both the machine-language structure of the computer *and* detailed knowledge of the calling sequence used by the compiler. The statements shown are specifically for the Intel 8086, 80286, 80386 series of microprocessors and the stack structure used by the Logitech compiler. Even though the stack structure used by ITC compiler is very close to this, this exact sequence would not work with the M2SDS package; ITC pushes all VAR parameters on to the stack first, so the address referenced in add[21. .23] would be in a different location on the stack.

Another problem with this technique is the amount of code it takes to generate the ARRAY. The actual AddLCard routine in the add ARRAY requires only 36 bytes of memory. But in the Logitech package it requires a module containing over 200 bytes of code to generate it—not a very efficient use of memory.

Incidentally, note that the *DivLCard* routine is implemented using the other procedures. *DivLCard* first determines if *lcrd1* is less than or equal to *lcrd2*. If so, the answer, returned in *lcrdrslt* and *lcrdrem*, is obvious. If not, the routine finds the quotient by multiplying the divisor by ten and then performing successive subtractions. Each iteration generates another digit in the answer. When the divisor becomes greater than the dividend, the operation is complete. *DivLCard* is reasonably efficient (long division on a microcomputer is always slower than the other arithmetic operations) but use it with caution in repetitive situations.

ComLCard. Because the LONGCARD type is really a record, simple comparisons do not function properly. To compare two LONGCARD values, use the *ComLCard* routine.

SCREEN RELATED TYPES

The IBM PC supports two general types of CRT display: monochrome and color graphics. Originally the two were easy to differentiate, but as the hardware has matured, both IBM and a host of other manufactures have offered additional options. Luckily, they all require an adapter card in the machine and they all use a display buffer to contain the characters that appear on the screen. Therefore, they can all be dealt by the same routines.

The display buffer is an area in memory used by the electronics on the adapter card to determine what appears on the screen at each location. For a monochrome display, each location corresponds to a single character. Color graphic adapters can relate each location to a single character, or they can treat each "pixel" individually. In either case, a program can make characters appear on the screen by moving a character value to the appropriate location in the display buffer. The display adapter handles the formation of the character on the screen.

Chapter 9 discusses several routines for actually getting the characters into the display buffer, but EL0504 (see Fig. 5-4) defines several types, and associated routines, that describe the buffer. The types are presented here because they are required before the display operations.

CRTTYPES. Regardless of which kind of adapter is used, the display buffer can be envisioned as a two-dimensional ARRAY; each element of the ARRAY is a word, specifically, a DISPLAYWORD. From Modula-2 purposes, the DISPLAYWORD type is a RECORD of two bytes. The *chrbyte* field contains the actual character; the *colbyte* field contains the color attribute. As its name implies, the color attribute is used by the electronics in the adapter to control the color of the character on the screen. Even the monochrome adapter interprets this byte to cause underlining, high intensity, or reverse video. A DWPTR points to a DISPLAYWORD.

A SCREENMAP is an ARRAY OF DISPLAYWORD and an SMAPPTR points to it. Note that a SCREENMAP is limited to 16383 words; the maximum size array that most Modula-2 implementations can handle. The SCREENMAP type can be used to refer directly to the display adapter buffer or to arrays defined elsewhere in memory. EL0504 contains routines to move data between other arrays and the display buffer. To describe these areas, the routines use an artificial structure called a FRAME.

A FRAME type is a record that defines the size and shape of an array of DISPLAYWORD values, and the current location of an imaginary cursor within the area.

Fig. 5-4. Screen-related types.

```
DEFINITION MODULE EL0504;
   FROM SYSTEM IMPORT   BYTE,ADDRESS;
   EXPORT QUALIFIED     DISPLAYWORD,DWPTR,FRAME,FRAMEPTR,SCREENMAP,SMAPPTR,
                        MakeSMap,ClrSMap,MakFrame,ClrFrame,DsplyWrd,MovFrame;

TYPE
   DISPLAYWORD = RECORD
     chrbyte   : CHAR;
     colbyte   : BYTE;
     END;
   DWPTR = POINTER TO DISPLAYWORD;
   SCREENMAP = ARRAY [0..16383] OF DISPLAYWORD;
   SMAPPTR = POINTER TO SCREENMAP;
   FRAME = RECORD
     fl : CARDINAL;          (*  first line              *)
     fc : CARDINAL;          (*  first column            *)
     ll : CARDINAL;          (*  last line               *)
     lc : CARDINAL;          (*  last column             *)
     cl : CARDINAL;          (*  current line            *)
     cc : CARDINAL;          (*  current column          *)
     nl : CARDINAL;          (*  number of lines         *)
     nc : CARDINAL;          (*  number of columns       *)
     s  : SMAPPTR;           (*  address of SCREENMAP    *)
     dyn: BOOLEAN;           (*  kind of SCREENMAP       *)
     END;
   FRAMEPTR = POINTER TO FRAME;
PROCEDURE MakeSMap(nl,nc:CARDINAL;VAR s:SMAPPTR);
(* This routine will create a SCREENMAP on the heap, capable of containing
   the number of DISPLAYWORDs defined by the parameters.  Note that s is
   assumed to be undefined on entry.  *)
PROCEDURE ClrSMap(nl,nc:CARDINAL;VAR smap:SMAPPTR);
(* This routine will clear the SCREENMAP defined by smap from the heap.
   Note that the two cardinal parameters must correspond to the values used
   when the smap was created.  *)
PROCEDURE MakFrame(fl,fc,ll,lc,cl,cc,nl,nc:CARDINAL;
                        a:ADDRESS;VAR f:FRAMEPTR);
(* This routine will create a new Frame on the heap.  If a = NIL, the
   routine will also create an associated SCREENMAP, otherwise, f^.s will
   be set equal to a.  Note that f is assumed to be undefined on entry.  *)
PROCEDURE ClrFrame(VAR frame:FRAMEPTR);
(* This routine will clear the frame from the heap.  If frame.dyn = TRUE,
   the associated SCREENMAP will also be cleared.  *)
PROCEDURE DsplyWrd(l,c:CARDINAL;VAR frame:FRAME):DWPTR;
(* This routine will return the address of the DISPLAYWORD in the SCREENMAP
   associated with frame that is at line l, column c.  *)
PROCEDURE MovFrame(VAR f,t:FRAME);
(* This routine will move the contents of the screenmap refered to by f to
   the corresponsing area in t.  The move is done line by line, beginning
   at f.cl and t.cl and will extend for only as many lines and columns as
   will fit in t.  *)
END EL0504.


IMPLEMENTATION MODULE EL0504;
   FROM SYSTEM IMPORT   WORD,ADDRESS,BYTE;
   FROM Storage IMPORT  ALLOCATE,DEALLOCATE;
   FROM EL0302 IMPORT   MovByteL;

PROCEDURE MakeSMap(nl,nc:CARDINAL;VAR s:SMAPPTR);
BEGIN
   ALLOCATE(s,2*nl*nc);
   END MakeSMap;
```

Fig. 5-4 continued

```
PROCEDURE ClrSMap(nl,nc:CARDINAL;VAR s:SMAPPTR);
BEGIN
  DEALLOCATE(s,2*nl*nc);
  s:=NIL;
  END ClrSMap;

PROCEDURE MakFrame(fl,fc,ll,lc,cl,cc,nl,nc:CARDINAL;
                              a:ADDRESS;VAR f:FRAMEPTR);
BEGIN
  NEW(f);
  f^.fl:=fl;    f^.ll:=ll;    f^.fc:=fc;    f^.lc:=lc;
  f^.cl:=cl;    f^.cc:=cc;    f^.nl:=nl;    f^.nc:=nc;
  IF (a = NIL)
    THEN
      MakeSMap(nl,nc,f^.s);
      f^.dyn:=TRUE;
    ELSE
      f^.s:=a;
      f^.dyn:=FALSE;
    END;
  END MakFrame;

PROCEDURE ClrFrame(VAR f:FRAMEPTR);
BEGIN
  WITH f^ DO
    IF (f^.dyn)
      THEN ClrSMap(nl,nc,s);
      END;
    END;
  DISPOSE(f);
  END ClrFrame;

PROCEDURE DsplyWrd(l,c:CARDINAL;VAR f:FRAME):DWPTR;
VAR
  d:ADDRESS;
BEGIN
  d:=f.s;
  d.OFFSET:=d.OFFSET + 2*(f.nc*(l-1)+c-1);
  RETURN d;
  END DsplyWrd;

PROCEDURE MovFrame(VAR f,t:FRAME);
VAR
  l:CARDINAL;
  dt,df:DWPTR;
BEGIN
  FOR l:=0 TO t.ll-t.cl DO
    dt:=DsplyWrd(t.cl+1,t.fc,t);
    df:=DsplyWrd(f.cl+1,f.fc,f);
    MovByteL(df^,dt^,0,0,2*t.nc);
    END;
  END MovFrame;

END EL0504.
```

For example, the FRAME that describes the buffer for the monochrome adapter has the following values:

fl = 1; fc = 1; ll = 25; lc = 80;

nl = 25; nc = 80;

s.SEGMENT = b000H; s.OFFSET = 0000H;

The *cl* and *cc* values vary as required.

MakeSMap and ClrSMap. The *MakeSMap* and *ClrSMap* routines are available to create and destroy SCREENMAP variables on the heap. These routines are not normally used outside of the Library, but they are exported from EL0504 in case they might be needed.

MakFrame and ClrFrame. To create and destroy FRAME variables, use *MakFrame* and *ClrFrame*. *MakFrame* can be used with an existing SCREENMAP, as would be the case when the resulting FRAME refers to a display buffer; or, *MakFrame* can be instructed to also create a SCREENMAP variable on the heap.

DsplyWrd. To refer to an individual DISPLAYWORD within a SCREENMAP, use the *DsplyWrd* procedure. *DsplyWrd* returns a pointer (i.e., the ADDRESS) to the indicated word.

MovFrame. *MovFrame* moves the contents of the SCREENMAP associated with one FRAME into the corresponding SCREENMAP area of another. This permits quick movements into and out of a display buffer.

FIELD LISTS AND AREAS

There are two other general type definitions that are used by other routines in the Etling Library. Both are related to constructing arrays on the heap. The appropriate routines are in EL0305 which is shown in Fig. 5-5.

Fig. 5-5. Field lists.

```
DEFINITION MODULE EL0505;
   FROM SYSTEM IMPORT    WORD;
   EXPORT QUALIFIED      maxflds,maxarea,FLDLIST,FLPTR,AREA,AREAPTR,
                         MakeArea,ClrArea,MakFList,ClrFList;

CONST
   maxflds = 32766;
   maxarea = 32766;
TYPE
   FLDLIST = ARRAY [0..maxflds] OF CARDINAL;
   FLPTR = POINTER TO FLDLIST;
   AREA = ARRAY [0..maxarea] OF WORD;
   AREAPTR = POINTER TO AREA;
PROCEDURE MakeArea(l:CARDINAL;VAR a:AREAPTR);
(* This routine will create an area on the heap capable of holding l words.
   Note that the first word contains a count of the number of additional
   words allocated.  The routine assumes that the contents of a are of no
   consequence on entry.  *)
PROCEDURE ClrArea(VAR p:AREAPTR);
(* This routine clears the area to which p points.  *)
PROCEDURE MakFList(l:CARDINAL;VAR f:FLPTR);
(* This routine will create a list on the heap capable of holding l
   cardinal values.  Note that the first word contains a count of the
   number of additional cardinals allocated.  The routines assumes that the
   contents of f are of no consequence on entry.  *)
PROCEDURE ClrFList(VAR p:FLPTR);
(* This routine clears the list from the heap to which p points.  *)
END EL0505.
```

Fig. 5-5. continued

```
IMPLEMENTATION MODULE ELO505;
  FROM SYSTEM IMPORT    WORD;
  FROM Storage IMPORT   ALLOCATE,DEALLOCATE;

PROCEDURE MakeArea(l:CARDINAL;VAR a:AREAPTR);
BEGIN
  ALLOCATE(a,2*l+2);
  a^[0]:=WORD(l);
  END MakeArea;

PROCEDURE ClrArea(VAR a:AREAPTR);
BEGIN
  DEALLOCATE(a,CARDINAL(a^[0]));
  END ClrArea;

PROCEDURE MakFList(l:CARDINAL;VAR f:FLPTR);
BEGIN
  ALLOCATE(f,2*l+2);
  f^[0]:=l;
  END MakFList;

PROCEDURE ClrFList(VAR f:FLPTR);
BEGIN
  DEALLOCATE(f,f^[0]);
  END ClrFList;

END ELO505.
```

The FLDLIST and AREA Types. A FLDLIST type is an ARRAY OF CARDINAL allocated on the heap. The ARRAY bounds begins at zero, and the zero[th] element contains a count of the number of additional elements allocated. Similarly, an AREA is an ARRAY OF WORD. Again, the zero[th] element counts the number of additional words in the allocation.

MakeArea and ClrArea. The routines that deal with an AREA type are called *MakeArea* and *ClrArea*. Their operations are fairly trivial.

MakFLIst and ClrFLIst. Again, the routines for dealing with FLDLIST types are very simple.

Chapter 6

Conversions

Just about every computer language has a similar problem. The outside world, the user, understands characters; the inside world — the computer — deals in bits and bytes. Every computer language must have some way of converting from one form to another.

In many languages, the routines that do the converting are buried deep within the run-time library where the programmer never sees them. For example, in BASIC, when the program says "PRINT X," and X is an integer, something, somewhere, has to convert the value of "X" into a string of characters. In BASIC, the conversion routines, at least these particular routines, are not normally available to the programmer.

Modula-2, through the library modules furnished with the compiler packages, provides quite a few routines for converting numeric values between user representations and internal forms. These routines handle standard Modula-2 types; to handle the conversion required by the rest of the modules, the Etling Library implements a half-dozen routines of its own.

CONVERTING FROM STRINGS

Most of the modules in the Etling Library that require conversion, convert from a STRING to an internal representation. Even though the end result is different, all of these routines function in more or less the same way.

MakReal. The routine that converts a sequence of characters into a real number is called *MakReal*. It is the only routine in EL0601, shown in Fig. 6-1. The actual

Fig. 6-1. Converting from STRING to REAL.

```
DEFINITION MODULE EL0601;
  FROM EL0401 IMPORT    STRING;
  EXPORT QUALIFIED      MakReal;

PROCEDURE MakReal(source:STRING; s:CARDINAL; VAR stop:CARDINAL):REAL;
(* This routine will convert the sequence of numeric characters in source
   (beginning at s) into a REAL, which is returned as the function value.
   Conversion will stop when a non-numeric character is encountered, or the
   end of the STRING is reached.  On exit, stop will be set to the last
   character processed, or, will equal the length of source + 1.  *)
END EL0601.


IMPLEMENTATION MODULE EL0601;
  FROM EL0401 IMPORT    STRING,StrLen,StrChar;
  FROM EL0501 IMPORT    numbers,InCSet;

PROCEDURE MakReal(source:STRING; s:CARDINAL;VAR stop:CARDINAL):REAL;
VAR
  done,dp:BOOLEAN;
  sign,i:INTEGER;
  x,y:REAL;
BEGIN
  done:=FALSE;
  stop:=s;
  dp:=FALSE;
  x:=0.0;
  y:=1.0;
  IF (StrChar(source,s) = '-')
    THEN
       sign:=-1;
       stop:=s+1;
    ELSE
       sign:=+1;
       IF (StrChar(source,s) = '+')
         THEN stop:=s+1;
         ELSE stop:=s;
         END;
    END;
  REPEAT
    IF (stop > StrLen(source))
      THEN done:=TRUE;
      ELSE IF (StrChar(source,stop) = '.')
              OR (StrChar(source,stop) = ':')
         THEN dp:=TRUE;
         ELSE IF (InCSet(StrChar(source,stop),numbers))
           THEN
              i:=ORD(StrChar(source,stop)) - ORD('0');
              IF (dp)
                THEN
                   y:=y / 10.0;
                   x:=x + y * FLOAT(i);
                ELSE
                   x:=x*10.0 + FLOAT(i);
                END;
              INC(stop);
           ELSE done:=TRUE;
           END;
        END;
      END;
  UNTIL (done);
  IF (sign = 1)
```

```
      THEN RETURN x;
      ELSE RETURN -x;
      END;
    END MakReal;

  END EL0601.
```

operation of *MakReal* is trivial, but note that the routine does accept either a *"."* character or a *":"* as a decimal point. The *":"* character is explained in Chapter 13.

MakCard. EL0602, shown in Fig. 6-2, shows *MakCard* which converts a sequence of characters in a STRING into a CARDINAL. There are no surprises in this routine.

MakLCard. Converting the contents of a STRING into a LONGCARD is handled by *MakLCard* which is in EL0603 (see Fig. 6-3). Using the LONGCARD routines from EL0503 makes this routine even more trivial than the others.

Fig. 6-2. Converting from STRING to CARDINAL.

```
DEFINITION MODULE EL0602;
  FROM EL0401 IMPORT    STRING;
  EXPORT QUALIFIED      MakCard;

PROCEDURE MakCard(source:STRING; s:CARDINAL; VAR stop:CARDINAL):CARDINAL;
(* This routine will convert the sequence of numeric characters in source
   (beginning at s) into a CARDINAL, which is returned as the function
   value.  Conversion will stop when a non-numeric character is
   encountered, or the end of the STRING is reached.  On exit, stop will be
   set to the last character processed, or, to the length of source +1.  *)
END EL0602.

IMPLEMENTATION MODULE EL0602;
  FROM EL0401 IMPORT    STRING,StrLen,StrChar;
  FROM EL0501 IMPORT    numbers,InCSet;

PROCEDURE MakCard(source:STRING; s:CARDINAL;VAR stop:CARDINAL):CARDINAL;
VAR
  done:BOOLEAN;
  i:CARDINAL;
BEGIN
  stop:=s;
  i:=0;
  done:=FALSE;
  REPEAT
    IF (stop > StrLen(source))
      THEN done:=TRUE;
      ELSE IF (InCSet(StrChar(source,stop),numbers))
        THEN
          i:=10*i + ORD(StrChar(source,stop)) - ORD('0');
          INC(stop);
        ELSE done:=TRUE;
        END;
      END;
    UNTIL (done);
  RETURN i;
  END MakCard;

END EL0602.
```

Fig. 6-3. Converting from STRING to LONGCARD.

```
DEFINITION MODULE EL0603;
   FROM EL0401 IMPORT    STRING;
   FROM EL0503 IMPORT    LONGCARD;
   EXPORT QUALIFIED      MakLCard;

PROCEDURE MakLCard(source:STRING; s:CARDINAL;
                         VAR stop:CARDINAL;VAR l:LONGCARD);
(* This routine will convert the sequence of numeric characters in source
   (beginning at s) into a LONGCARD, which is returned in l.  Conversion
   will stop when a non-numeric character is encountered, or the end of the
   STRING is reached.  On exit, stop will be set to the last character
   processed, or, set to the length of source + 1.  *)
END EL0603.


IMPLEMENTATION MODULE EL0603;
   FROM EL0401 IMPORT    STRING,StrLen,StrChar;
   FROM EL0501 IMPORT    numbers,InCSet;
   FROM EL0503 IMPORT    LONGCARD,LongCard,lczero,MulLCard,AddLCard;

PROCEDURE MakLCard(source:STRING; s:CARDINAL;
                         VAR stop:CARDINAL;VAR l:LONGCARD);
VAR
   done:BOOLEAN;
   i:CARDINAL;
   m,ten:LONGCARD;
BEGIN
   stop:=s;
   done:=FALSE;
   l:=lczero;
   LongCard(10,0,ten);
   REPEAT
     IF (stop > StrLen(source))
       THEN done:=TRUE;
       ELSE IF (InCSet(StrChar(source,stop),numbers))
         THEN
           m.hicard:=0;
           m.locard:=ORD(StrChar(source,stop)) - ORD('0');
           MulLCard(l,ten,l);
           AddLCard(l,m,l);
           INC(stop);
         ELSE done:=TRUE;
         END;
       END;
     UNTIL (done);
   END MakLCard;

END EL0603.
```

MakInt. Integers are handled by *MakInt*, exported from EL0604 which is shown in Fig. 6-4.

CONVERTING TO STRINGS

As it happens, the routines in the Etling Library seldom require conversion from internal form to a STRING value. Consequently, the Library only contains two routines for dealing with these operations. These routines do, however, provide a valid prototype for creating any additional routines that might be required.

Fig. 6-4. Converting from STRING to INTEGER.

```
DEFINITION MODULE EL0604;
  FROM EL0401 IMPORT   STRING;
  EXPORT QUALIFIED     MakInt;

PROCEDURE MakInt(source:STRING; s:CARDINAL;
                      VAR stop:CARDINAL):INTEGER;
(* This routine will convert the sequence of numeric characters in source
   (beginning at s) into an INTEGER, which is returned as the function
   value.  Conversion will stop when a non-numeric character is
   encountered, or the end of the STRING is reached.  On exit, stop will be
   set to the last character processed, or, to the length of source + 1. *)
END EL0604.

IMPLEMENTATION MODULE EL0604;
  FROM EL0401 IMPORT   STRING,StrLen,StrChar;
  FROM EL0501 IMPORT   numbers,InCSet;

PROCEDURE MakInt(source:STRING; s:CARDINAL;VAR stop:CARDINAL):INTEGER;
VAR
  done:BOOLEAN;
  i:INTEGER;
  sign:INTEGER;
BEGIN
  done:=FALSE;
  stop:=s;
  i:=0;
  IF (StrChar(source,s) = '-')
    THEN
      sign:=-1;
      stop:=s+1;
    ELSE
      sign:=+1;
      IF (StrChar(source,s) = '+')
        THEN stop:=s+1;
        ELSE stop:=s;
        END;
    END;
  REPEAT
    IF (stop > StrLen(source))
      THEN done:=TRUE;
      ELSE IF (InCSet(StrChar(source,stop),numbers))
        THEN
          i:=10*i +
            INTEGER(ORD(StrChar(source,stop)) - ORD('0'));
          INC(stop);
        ELSE done:=TRUE;
        END;
      END;
  UNTIL (done);
  RETURN i*sign;
  END MakInt;

END EL0604.
```

CarToStr. Module EL0605 (Fig. 6-5) exports *CarToStr* which is used to convert a CARDINAL value into a STRING. The operation of this routine is simple and straightforward. Note that if the value of *nmbr* is greater than will fit in *width* characters, the routine fills the STRING with asterisks.

Fig. 6-5. Converting from CARDINAL to STRING.

```
DEFINITION MODULE EL0605;
  FROM EL0401 IMPORT    STRING;
  EXPORT QUALIFIED      CarToStr;

PROCEDURE CarToStr(nmbr,width:CARDINAL;dest:STRING);
(* This routine will convert nmbr into a sequence of width characters,
   with the value right justified in the STRING.  The routine assumes that
   dest is already defined and can hold at least width characters *)
END EL0605.

IMPLEMENTATION MODULE EL0605;
  FROM EL0401 IMPORT    Literal,STRING,SetLen,SetChar,StrLen,StrChar;

PROCEDURE CarToStr(nmbr,width:CARDINAL;dest:STRING);
VAR
  i:CARDINAL;
BEGIN
  SetLen(dest,width);
  WHILE (nmbr > 0) AND (width > 0) DO
    SetChar(dest,width,CHR(ORD('0')+(nmbr MOD 10)));
    DEC(width);
    nmbr:=nmbr DIV 10;
    END;
  IF (width = 0) AND (nmbr > 0)
    THEN FOR i:=1 TO StrLen(dest) DO
      SetChar(dest,i,'*');
      END;
    ELSE WHILE (width > 0) DO
      SetChar(dest,width,' ');
      DEC(width);
      END;
    END;
  IF (StrChar(dest,StrLen(dest)) = ' ')
    THEN SetChar(dest,StrLen(dest),'0');
    END;
  END CarToStr;

END EL0605.
```

Fig. 6-6. Converting from INTEGER to STRING.

```
DEFINITION MODULE EL0606;
  FROM EL0401 IMPORT    STRING;
  EXPORT QUALIFIED      IntToStr;

PROCEDURE IntToStr(nmbr:INTEGER;width:CARDINAL;dest:STRING);
(* This routine will convert nmbr into a sequence of width characters,
   with the value right justified in dest.  If the number is less than
   zero, a '-' will be included in dest.  *)
END EL0606.

IMPLEMENTATION MODULE EL0606;
  FROM EL0401 IMPORT    Literal,STRING,SetLen,SetChar,StrLen,StrChar;

PROCEDURE IntToStr(nmbr:INTEGER;width:CARDINAL;dest:STRING);
VAR
  i:CARDINAL;
  sign:CHAR;
BEGIN
```

```
IF (nmbr >= 0)
  THEN sign:=' ';
  ELSE
    sign:='-';
    nmbr:=ABS(nmbr);
    END;
SetLen(dest,width);
WHILE (nmbr > 0) AND (width > 0) DO
  SetChar(dest,width,CHR(ORD('0')+(nmbr MOD 10)));
  DEC(width);
  nmbr:=nmbr DIV 10;
  END;
IF (width = 0) AND (nmbr > 0)
  THEN FOR i:=1 TO StrLen(dest) DO
    SetChar(dest,i,'*');
    END;
  ELSE WHILE (width > 0) DO
    SetChar(dest,width,sign);
    sign:=' ';
    DEC(width);
    END;
  END;
IF (StrChar(dest,StrLen(dest)) = ' ')
  THEN SetChar(dest,StrLen(dest),'0');
  END;
END IntToStr;

END EL0606.
```

IntToStr. The routine that converts an INTEGER into a STRING is equally simple. It is called *IntToStr* and is exported from EL0606, which is shown in Fig. 6-6.

Chapter 7

Talking to DOS

The programs that control the operation of an IBM Personal Computer exist at four different levels.

The bottom level is built into the integrated electronic circuits in the machine's hardware. Many of these components have small programs "hardwired" into them. The programs might be physical connections among discrete elements or they might be encoded in Read Only Memory (ROM) circuits contained within their packages.

The second level is called BIOS, which is the acronym for Basic Input Output System. BIOS contains the primitive routines required to control the system hardware. BIOS operations are dictated by the hardware they control. The only reason the BIOS code would change is to reflect a change in hardware. Therefore, on the IBM PC, BIOS is recorded in ROM.

The third level of PC control is built into the two "hidden" files that are written on every disk or diskette formatted with the /S option. These files, called IBM-BIO.COM and IBMDOS.COM, contain routines to extend the functions in BIOS and to provide somewhat higher level access to the machine hardware. An excellent discussion of the concepts involved with these two files can be found in Peter Norton's book, *Inside the IBM PC*.

The highest level programs that control a PC can be divided into two broad categories: system programs and application programs. The best example of a system program is COMMAND.COM, the program that processes and implements DOS commands. COMMAND.COM uses routines in the two hidden files to accept character input from the keyboard, concatenate those characters into a command string, parse the command string, and based on its analysis, use hidden file routines to load and execute other system or application programs. Those programs in turn use some of the hidden file or BIOS routines to accomplish their tasks.

All of the Modula-2 packages available for the IBM PC have code contained within the object or run-time libraries supplied with the compilers to actually invoke DOS or BIOS routines. For example, when you say

WriteStr('Hi there')

in a Modula-2 program, the compiler translates your source code into a call to a routine that handles output to the CRT. The routine changes the

'Hi there'

into a suitable form and calls an IBMBIO.COM or IBMDOS.COM routine. This routine calls the routine in BIOS that generates the required sequence of instructions to the program stored in the CRT controller chip to cause the message to appear on your screen. This entire sequence of events is usually transparent to a programmer working in a high-level language, but there are instances when a specific application might need access to these low-level routines.

INTERRUPTS

Access to these routines is through a mechanism known as a *software-generated interrupt*. Unlike a *hardware interrupt*, which is an electrical signal to the central processor caused by a device that requires the processor's attention, a software interrupt is caused by an INT instruction within a program. Both kinds of interrupts tell the processor to stop what it is doing, push its flags onto the stack, load the address contained in a predefined memory location into the CS register, and begin performing the instructions at that location. The address loaded is an *interrupt vector*, which vectors control to an *interrupt service routine*. The memory location where the vector is stored is identified by an *interrupt number* and is within the first 1024 bytes of memory, which is sometimes called the *base page*. (To find the specific address of a vector in the base page, multiply the interrupt number by four.)

An INT instruction is similar to a CALL instruction, but there are two important differences. First, a CALL has to know the exact location of the instruction to which it will jump; an INT instruction only needs to know the interrupt number to tickle. Second, called routines reside within the program being executed; interrupt service routines can be any place in memory. The exact location of an interrupt service routine is unknown to the program that issues a software interrupt, and therefore, the size of the routine has no effect on the size of the program.

Any program at any location in memory can use an interrupt service routine, and either the program or the routine can be changed with no effect on the other. You can even replace an interrupt service routine with a routine of your own by simply changing the interrupt vector associated with the specific interrupt number.

All of the routines in BIOS, IBMBIO.COM, and IBMDOS.COM are available through software interrupts. DOS also uses some of the first 1024 bytes of memory to store values for control variables it needs. A complete listing of DOS interrupts and variables can be found in the Hardware Technical Reference Manual associated with your particular machine.

DOS Functions

One of the interrupt service routines (the one associated with INT 21H) provides access to what the DOS Technical Reference Manual refers to as "DOS Functions." These functions control memory management, I/O services, and even program loading. To use these functions, you load a *function number* in the high byte of the AX register, load data or control values into other registers, and issue a software interrupt using INT 21H.

All of the Modula-2 packages use these functions extensively. Most even provide a library routine that allows your program direct access to some of the available routines. The calling sequences for these routines vary widely between the packages, and some of them limit the specific function that you can access because certain DOS functions require more parameters than the package's routine provides.

Interrupt. A more useful routine, called *Interrupt,* is available in EL0701, shown in Fig. 7-1. *Interupt* provides complete access to all interrupts on a PC. The operation of *Interupt* requires use of the PC's registers. The syntax shown in Fig. 7-1 is for the Logitech compiler, but as the discussion of LONGCARD operations back in Chapter 5 mentioned, *Interupt* could be implemented as an ARRAY of BYTE.

Interupt also provides complete access to the CPU registers, including the flags register; *flags* can be used to pass the appropriate value to and from the routine. The constants defined in the library member named "flags" identify the various bits of the register. To set a flag before calling *Interupt,* use the following:

    INCL(BITSET(flags),zeroflg);

To test a bit on return from *Interupt,* use this:

    IF (zeroflg in BITSET(flags))

Vectors

As I discussed in the last section, both hardware and software interrupts are associated with a specific location in the first 1024 bytes of memory. This location contains the address of the routine to which control will be "vectored" when the interrupt is "tickled." By replacing this address with the address of another routine, a program can change how specific interrupts are treated.

MS DOS provides two functions that facilitate handling interrupt vectors. Access to these functions is provided by *GetVectr* and *SetVectr.* These two routines are exported from EL0702 as shown in Fig. 7-2. As you would expect, *GetVectr* retrieves the current address associated with a given interrupt. *SetVectr* will set a vector to a new address. An example of how these routines are used in EL1001 is discussed in Chapter 10.

PORTS: TALKING DIRECTLY TO THE HARDWARE

Interspersed with interrupt vectors and control variables in base page, an IBM Personal Computer has its Input/Output *ports.* In effect, an I/O port is a specific

Fig. 7-1. Interrupts.

```
DEFINITION MODULE EL0701;
   FROM SYSTEM IMPORT    BYTE,WORD;
   EXPORT QUALIFIED      Interupt,carryflg,parflg,auxcflg,zeroflg,signflg,
                         trapflg,intflg,dirflg,ovrflg;


CONST
   carryflg = 0;   parflg  = 2;   auxcflg = 4;   zeroflg = 6;
   signflg  = 7;   trapflg = 8;   intflg  = 9;   dirflg  = 10;   ovrflg = 11;
PROCEDURE Interupt(      number:BYTE;
                   VAR axreg,bxreg,cxreg,dxreg,dsreg,
                                    esreg,direg,sireg,flags:WORD);
(*   This routine will issue a software interupt to the interupt vector
     associated with number.  The remaining variables correspond to the
     machine registers.  Usuage of these variables depends on the interupt
     issued.  *)
END EL0701.


IMPLEMENTATION MODULE EL0701;
   FROM SYSTEM IMPORT   WORD,BYTE,CODE,AX,BX,CX,DX,DS,ES,DI,SI,SETREG,GETREG;


PROCEDURE Interupt(number:BYTE;VAR axreg,bxreg,cxreg,dxreg,dsreg,
                                    esreg,direg,sireg,flags:WORD);


VAR
   laxreg,lbxreg,lcxreg,ldxreg,ldsreg,lesreg,ldireg,lsireg,lflags:WORD;
   int:BYTE;


BEGIN
   laxreg := axreg;    lbxreg := bxreg;    lcxreg := cxreg;    ldxreg := dxreg;
   ldsreg := dsreg;    lesreg := esreg;    ldireg := direg;    lsireg := sireg;
   int    := number;
   SETREG(AX,int);
   CODE(2EH,0A2H,7FH,00H);           (*     MOV  CS:7Fh,AL   *)
   SETREG(AX,laxreg);
   SETREG(BX,lbxreg);
   SETREG(CX,lcxreg);
   SETREG(DX,ldxreg);
   SETREG(DS,ldsreg);
   SETREG(ES,lesreg);
   SETREG(DI,ldireg);
   SETREG(SI,lsireg);
   CODE(55H);             (* Save BP Register on Stack *)
   CODE(0CDH,16H);        (* Do the interupt - 16H replaced with INT *)
   CODE(5DH);             (* Retreive BP Register *)
   GETREG(AX,laxreg);
   GETREG(BX,lbxreg);
   GETREG(CX,lcxreg);
   GETREG(DX,ldxreg);
   GETREG(DS,ldsreg);
   GETREG(ES,lesreg);
   GETREG(DI,ldireg);
   GETREG(SI,lsireg);
   CODE(9CH);             (* Push FLAG Register onto Stack *)
   CODE(58H);             (* Pop FLAGS into AX *)
   GETREG(AX,lflags);
   flags := lflags;    axreg := laxreg;    bxreg := lbxreg;    cxreg := lcxreg;
   dxreg := ldxreg;    dsreg := ldsreg;    esreg := lesreg;    direg := ldireg;
   sireg := sireg;
   END Interupt;


END EL0701.
```

Fig. 7-2. Interrupt vectors.

```
DEFINITION MODULE ELO702;
  FROM SYSTEM IMPORT    WORD,ADDRESS;
  EXPORT QUALIFIED      GetVectr,SetVectr;

PROCEDURE GetVectr(number:WORD):ADDRESS;
(* This routine will return the ADDRESS to which the interupt vector
   associated with number points.  *)
PROCEDURE SetVectr(number:WORD;server:ADDRESS);
(* This routine will set the interupt vector associated with number to the
   address defined by server.  *)
END ELO702.

IMPLEMENTATION MODULE ELO702;
  FROM SYSTEM IMPORT    WORD,ADDRESS;
  FROM ELO301 IMPORT    ByWord,LoByte;
  FROM ELO701 IMPORT    Interupt;

PROCEDURE GetVectr(number:WORD):ADDRESS;
VAR
  ax,bx,cx,dx,ds,es,di,si:WORD;
  flags:BITSET;
  vector:ADDRESS;
BEGIN
  ax:=ByWord(35H,LoByte(number));
  Interupt(21H,ax,bx,cx,dx,ds,es,di,si,flags);
  vector.SEGMENT:=CARDINAL(es);
  vector.OFFSET:=CARDINAL(bx);
  RETURN vector;
  END GetVectr;

PROCEDURE SetVectr(number:WORD;server:ADDRESS);
VAR
  ax,bx,cx,dx,ds,es,di,si:WORD;
  flags:BITSET;
BEGIN
  ax:=ByWord(25H,LoByte(number));
  ds:=WORD(server.SEGMENT);
  dx:=WORD(server.OFFSET);
  Interupt(21H,ax,bx,cx,dx,ds,es,di,si,flags);
  END SetVectr;

END ELO702.
```

location in memory that is shared between the CPU and one of the adapter cards installed in the machine. The CPU and the adapter communicate by placing a byte or a word at the port address, and waiting for the other device to retrieve it. Basically, the occurrence of a device interrupt is a signal to the CPU that a byte or word is available at an associated I/O port. Each device usually has several consecutive base page addresses allocated for its port. One address might be for data and a second for control values. If the device is capable of both input and output, there might be a second set of addresses for the other mode.

I/O ports occupy space in memory, but to transfer data through the port, you must use machine instructions that are different from the normal memory access mnemonics. To send a value to an I/O port, you must use an OUT instruction; an IN instruction reads a value.

Byte or word I/O through a port represents the most primitive level of device communication on a personal computer, and is normally handled by the routines in BIOS or one of the hidden DOS files. There are times, however, when an application program needs to address an I/O port directly. The *PortIn* and *PortOut* procedures are shown in EL0703 (Fig. 7-3). (You will find an example of how to use these routines in Fig. 7-5, which defines the *Sound* procedure.)

DELAYS

There are circumstances when an executing program should pause and allow some time to pass before continuing its operation. One method for doing this is typified by the DOS PAUSE command. In a DOS batch file, PAUSE simply stops processing the file until you press a key. If you never press a key, execution never resumes—a PAUSE will wait forever. There are routines in the Library that operate in this fashion, but we also need a method for letting the program determine how long it will wait.

Figure 7-4 shows a routine for introducing delays into a program. This routine, called *Delay,* simply establishes an instruction loop lasting approximately one

Fig. 7-3. I/O ports.

```
DEFINITION MODULE EL0703;
   FROM SYSTEM IMPORT    WORD;
   EXPORT QUALIFIED      PortIn,PortOut;

PROCEDURE PortIn(number:WORD):WORD;
(* This routine inputs a single WORD (or BYTE, depending on the port
   accessed) from the I/O port specified by number.  Note that it is the
   responsibility of the caller to determine whether the entire word is
   meaningful.  *)
PROCEDURE PortOut(number,value:WORD);
(* This routine will send value to the I/O port idenitified by number.
   Note that it is the responsibility of the caller to determine whether
   both bytes of value have meaning.  *)
END EL0703.

IMPLEMENTATION MODULE EL0703;
   FROM SYSTEM IMPORT    WORD,SETREG,GETREG,AX,DX,CODE;

PROCEDURE PortIn(number:WORD):WORD;
VAR
   value:WORD;
BEGIN
   SETREG(DX,number);
   CODE(OECH);
   GETREG(AX,value);
   RETURN value;
   END PortIn;

PROCEDURE PortOut(number,value:WORD);
BEGIN
   SETREG(DX,number);
   SETREG(AX,value);
   CODE(OEEH);
   END PortOut;

END EL0703.
```

Fig. 7-4. Causing delays.

```
DEFINITION MODULE EL0704;
  EXPORT QUALIFIED      Delay;

PROCEDURE Delay(number:CARDINAL);
(* This routine will delay for the number of milliseconds specified.  Note
   that the delay is adjusted for XT or AT speeds, but is still
   approximate.  *)
END EL0704.

IMPLEMENTATION MODULE EL0704;
  FROM SYSTEM IMPORT    ADDRESS,WORD;

PROCEDURE Delay(number:CARDINAL);
VAR
  machtype:ADDRESS;
  count:CARDINAL;
  at:BOOLEAN;
BEGIN
  machtype.SEGMENT:=0F000H;
  machtype.OFFSET:=0FFFEH;
  IF (machtype^ = WORD(00FCH))
    THEN at:=TRUE;
    ELSE at:=FALSE;
    END;
  WHILE (number > 0) DO
    IF (at)
      THEN count:=50;
      ELSE count:=125;
      END;
    REPEAT
      DEC(count);
      UNTIL (count = 0);
    DEC(number);
    END;
  END Delay;

END EL0704.
```

millisecond (0.001 seconds), repeats the loop the number of times specified by *number,* and returns to the calling routine.

Note that *Delay* inspects the byte at memory location F000:FFFEH. That byte, which is in BIOS, indicates what type of IBM Personal Computer is executing the program. If the contents of the byte are equal to #FC, it indicates the machine is an IBM AT, and the timing constant is adjusted accordingly. The constants shown are really just an approximation. The actual elapsed time produced by running DELAY might vary by about 10% depending on how many times the loop gets interrupted. A couple of milliseconds one way or another doesn't really matter for short delays, but for delays on the order of an hour, 10% amounts to six minutes. The instruction loop approach doesn't work for longer delays. Later in this chapter, I'll talk about another way to introduce longer delays.

SOUNDS

Except for the sound you can make by writing a "control-G" character to the standard output device (the display), standard Modula-2 is mute.

Fig. 7-5. Making sounds.

```
DEFINITION MODULE ELO705;
   EXPORT QUALIFIED      ToneInit,ToneSet,ToneOn,ToneOff,Sound,
                         errfreq,errdur,qfreq,qdur;

CONST
   errfreq = 1046;   errdur  = 200;   qfreq   = 880;   qdur    = 100;

PROCEDURE ToneInit;
(* This routine will initialize the PC speaker system to produce a square
   wave using binary control values.  *)
PROCEDURE ToneSet(n:CARDINAL);
(* This routine selects the frequency of the square wave tone that will be
   output to the speaker system.  n determines the frequency f according to
   the formula:  f = 1,193,182 / n                          *)
PROCEDURE ToneOn;
(* This routine will turn on the timer and the speaker according to the
   criteria established by ToneSet.  *)
PROCEDURE ToneOff;
(* This routine turns of the speaker timer.  *)
PROCEDURE Sound(freq,duration:CARDINAL);
(* This routine uses the CPU timer to sound the PC's speaker.  freq is in
   cycles per second and duration is in milliseconds.  *)
END ELO705.

IMPLEMENTATION MODULE ELO705;
   FROM SYSTEM IMPORT    CODE,AX,CX,DX,SETREG,GETREG,WORD;
   FROM ELO503 IMPORT    LONGCARD,LongCard,DivLCard;
   FROM ELO703 IMPORT    PortIn,PortOut;
   FROM ELO704 IMPORT    Delay;

CONST
   timectrl = 0043H; timedata = 0042H; usetime2 = 00B6H; speaker  = 0061H;
   turnon   = 0003H;
VAR
   saveax:WORD;

PROCEDURE ToneInit;
BEGIN
   PortOut(timectrl,usetime2);
   END ToneInit;

PROCEDURE ToneSet(n:CARDINAL);
BEGIN
   PortOut(timedata,n);
   n:=n DIV 256;
   PortOut(timedata,n);
   END ToneSet;

PROCEDURE ToneOn;
VAR
   bits:CARDINAL;
BEGIN
   saveax:=PortIn(speaker);
   bits:=CARDINAL(saveax) DIV 4;
   bits:=4*bits + turnon;
   PortOut(speaker,bits);
   END ToneOn;

PROCEDURE ToneOff;
BEGIN
   PortOut(speaker,saveax);
```

Fig. 7-5 continued
```
  END ToneOff;

PROCEDURE Sound(freq,duration:CARDINAL);
VAR
  f,n:LONGCARD;
BEGIN
  LongCard(34DEH,0012H,f);
  LongCard(freq,0,n);
  DivLCard(f,n,n,f);
  ToneInit;
  ToneSet(n.locard);
  ToneOn;
  Delay(duration);
  ToneOff;
  END Sound;

END EL0705.
```

Figure 7-5 shows EL0705, which defines a collection of routines for making sounds, using the IBM PC speaker. The primary routine in this module is called *Sound,* but it uses several additional routines to help with this operation. There are actually several ways of producing sounds on a PC. *Sound* uses the method which accesses an I/O port assigned to a programmable counter/timer to establish the frequency, and a second I/O port that controls a switch (referred to as a "gate") to turn the speaker on and off. This is accomplished by calling the four helper routines in sequence.

ToneInit. The programmable counter/timer operates under control of the byte at 0043H. *ToneInit* uses *PortOut* to send the port a 00B6H. This instructs the port to use timer counter number 2, set the timer mode to receive the data one byte at a time (it might take several bytes to tell the timer all it needs to know), and to establish itself as a square-wave generator.

ToneSet. *ToneSet* establishes the frequency at which the timer operates by dividing a reference frequency (1,193,182 cycles per second) by the procedure's parameter, *n.* The resulting 16-bit integer is fed to the timer.

ToneOn. The speaker gate is controlled by the I/O port at 0061H. Because this address also controls other operations, *ToneOn* reads and saves the existing value, turns on the speaker and the timer by setting bits 0 and 1 on, and then outputs the new value back to the I/O port.

ToneOff. The sound is turned off by calling *ToneOff.* All it needs to do is reset the speaker port back to its original value.

Sound. The length of time that the sound is fed to the speaker is controlled by *duration,* and the frequency of the sound by *frequency.* To operate, *Sound* calls *ToneSet* and *ToneOn,* then passes *Duration* to *Delay,* which will not return for the specified number of milliseconds. When control does return, *Sound* calls *ToneOff.* Note that the sound continues while *Delay* operates; the sound must be both turned on *and* turned off. A program could conceivably call *ToneOn,* go do something else, and then come back much later to call *ToneOff,* although with only a single frequency being signaled, the effect of this might not be "user friendly."

Listing 7-5 contains a definition for another library member. "*Sounds*" is a standardized collection of values which can be fed to the *Sound* procedure. *Errfreg* and *errdur* are the values I use when I want to point out an error condition to the user. *qfreq* and *qdur* are for calling the user's attention to a question on the screen. By assigning standard names for these values, they are easier to remember and understand when they appear in a program listing. Also, using the same sound for the same condition throughout a system of programs helps the user become accustomed to how the system operates.

TIMERS

The timing device that *Sound* uses to control the PC's speaker is only one of three such devices included in an IBM Personal Computer. Timer 2 is used to control the speaker. Timer 1 is used to time and request refresh cycles for the DMA (direct memory access) channel, and Timer 0 is used to provide a constant time base for implementing a time-of-day clock.

Timer 0 runs in an interrupt enabled mode. It is attached to the device that handles all hardware interrupts for the PC, and it is given the highest priority. Timer 0 interrupts will be serviced before any other device. Timer 0 is programed by BIOS code during a "boot" to issue a hardware interrupt approximately 18.2 times per second. Every time an interrupt occurs, another BIOS routine adds 1 to a variable maintained in base page. The DOS TIME command establishes a starting value for this variable by converting values for hours, minutes, and seconds into an appropriate number. DATE, the DOS command that sets the system date, uses a similar base page variable to establish a starting date.

Other DOS commands and DOS functions reference these base-page variables whenever they need to create a "time stamp." For example, when a command (or an executing program) creates or changes a file, the DOS file access routines enter the current date and time values into the directory entry for the file.

For a time-of-day clock, a clock that counts 18.2 times per second is reasonably accurate, but it still translates to 0.055 seconds between tics. That isn't fast enough to create a millisecond delay (which is why *Delay* is necessary), but the DOS timing location is sufficient to implement long term delays.

SetTimer and ChkTimer. *SetTimer* and *ChkTimer* (see Module EL0706, Fig. 7-6), are Modula-2 routines that provide much longer delays. The module defines a global variable, *tics* that is initialized to point to the DOS timing location. The timing location is a double word, corresponding to a LONGCARD type. All of the arithmetic done in these routines uses LONGCARD data.

To use these routines, call *SetTimer* with the appropriate values to generate a value for *ticsleft*. Then you establish a loop that makes calls to *ChkTimer*, for example,

```
VAR
  ticsleft,timechkd:LONGCARD;
  hours,minutes,seconds:CARDINAL;

CONST
  relative = TRUE;
```

```
BEGIN
  hours    := 1;
  minutes  := 0;
  seconds  := 0;
  SetTimer(relative,hours,minutes,seconds,ticsleft,timechkd);
  WHILE (ChkTimer(hours,minutes,seconds,
                               ticsleft,timechkd) DO

    Write('Time remaining');
    WriteCard(hours:2);
    Write(':');
    WriteCard(minutes:2);
    Write(':');
    WriteCard(seconds:2);
    WriteLn;
    END;
```

Fig. 7-6. Timers.

```
DEFINITION MODULE EL0706;
  FROM EL0503 IMPORT    LONGCARD;
  EXPORT QUALIFIED      SetTimer,ChkTimer;

PROCEDURE SetTimer(relative:BOOLEAN;
                        hours,minutes,seconds:CARDINAL;
                        VAR ticsleft,timechkd:LONGCARD);
(* If relative = TRUE on entry, then hours, minutes and seconds define a
   time to be added to the current system time to define a target;
   otherwise, the values given are the target time.  In either case,
   ticsleft will return with the number of clock tics required to reach the
   target time, and, timechkd will indicate the value of the DOS BIOS timer
   location when ticsleft was defined.  Subsequent calls to ChkTimer will
   decrement the value of ticsleft.  *)
PROCEDURE ChkTimer(VAR hours,minutes,seconds:CARDINAL;
                        VAR ticsleft,timechkd:LONGCARD):BOOLEAN;
(* This function returns with the number of hours, minutes, and seconds
   remaining in ticsleft after being set by the appropriate call to
   SetTimer.  Note that all the parameters are changed by the call.  When
   ticsleft reaches zero, ChkTimer will return equal to FALSE.  *)
END EL0706.

IMPLEMENTATION MODULE EL0706;
  FROM SYSTEM IMPORT    ADDRESS;
  FROM EL0503 IMPORT    LongCard,LONGCARD,lczero,
                        AddLCard,SubLCard,MulLCard,DivLCard,ComLCard;

VAR
  cpday,cphr,cpmin,cpsec,ten,lch,lcm,lcs,tmp1,tmp2,tmp3,rem:LONGCARD;
  t:ADDRESS;
  tics:POINTER TO LONGCARD;

PROCEDURE SetTimer(relative:BOOLEAN;hours,minutes,seconds:CARDINAL;
                        VAR ticsleft,timechkd:LONGCARD);
BEGIN
  timechkd:=tics^;
  LongCard(hours,0,lch);
  LongCard(minutes,0,lcm);
  LongCard(seconds,0,lcs);
```

```
(* ticsleft = cphr*hours + cpmin*minutes + (cpsec*seconds) DIV 10 *)
  MulLCard(lch,cphr,tmp1);
  MulLCard(lcm,cpmin,tmp2);
  MulLCard(lcs,cpsec,tmp3);
  DivLCard(tmp3,ten,tmp3,rem);
  AddLCard(tmp1,tmp2,tmp1);
  AddLCard(tmp1,tmp3,ticsleft);
  IF (NOT relative)
    THEN
      IF (ComLCard(ticsleft,timechkd) = -1)
        THEN
          AddLCard(ticsleft,cpday,ticsleft);
          SubLCard(ticsleft,timechkd,ticsleft);
        ELSE
          SubLCard(ticsleft,timechkd,ticsleft);
        END;
    END;
  END SetTimer;

PROCEDURE ChkTimer(VAR hours,minutes,seconds:CARDINAL;
                   VAR ticsleft,timechkd:LONGCARD):BOOLEAN;
VAR
  now:LONGCARD;
  result:BOOLEAN;
BEGIN
  now:=tics^;
  IF (ComLCard(timechkd,now) = 1)
    THEN SubLCard(timechkd,cpday,timechkd);
    END;
  AddLCard(timechkd,ticsleft,ticsleft);
  timechkd:=now;
  IF (ComLCard(ticsleft,now) = 1)
    THEN SubLCard(ticsleft,now,ticsleft);
    ELSE LongCard(0,0,ticsleft);
    END;
  IF (ComLCard(ticsleft,lczero) = 0)
    THEN
      result:=TRUE;
      hours:=0;
      minutes:=0;
      seconds:=0;
    ELSE
      result:=FALSE;
      DivLCard(now,cphr,tmp1,rem);
      hours:=tmp1.locard;
      MulLCard(tmp1,cphr,tmp2);
      SubLCard(now,tmp2,now);
      DivLCard(now,cpmin,tmp1,rem);
      minutes:=tmp1.locard;
      MulLCard(tmp1,cpmin,tmp2);
      SubLCard(now,tmp2,now);
      DivLCard(now,cpsec,tmp1,rem);
      MulLCard(tmp1,ten,tmp1);
      seconds:=tmp1.locard;
    END;
  RETURN result;
  END ChkTimer;

BEGIN
  LongCard(00b0h,0018h,cpday);   (* cpday = 1573040 counts / day *)
  LongCard(0007h,0001h,cphr);    (* cphr  =   65543 counts / hr   *)
  LongCard(0444h,0000h,cpmin);   (* cpmin =    1092 counts / minute*)
```

Fig. 7-6. continued

```
  LongCard(00b6h,0000h,cpsec);   (* cpsec =   182 counts / second*)
  LongCard(10,0,ten);
  t.SEGMENT:=0040H;    t.OFFSET :=006CH;
  tics:=t;
END EL0706.
```

The example shows the loop displaying the remaining time, but it could be written to handle other more useful operations while the long delay is waiting to expire.

DATES AND TIMES

Commercial programs are often called upon to deal with a special kind of value: a date. In the business world, there are due dates, payroll dates, closing dates, and even report dates. Almost every program inputs, outputs, compares, or calculates dates. Chapter 14 defines routines for inputing and outputing dates for the user, but there are a couple other routines in the Etling Library that handle date strings.

In the commercial programs I write, date strings are always in one of two specific formats. When a date is presented to a user, the date is in the form "mm/dd/yy." This format always occupies eight characters, and both "mm" and "dd" are zero filled on the left. (January 1, 1980 would be shown as 01/01/80.) On the other hand, when a date is used internally by a program or is stored in a file, the date is six characters long, represented as "yymmdd." In this form, dates are easily compared and calculations are easier to handle.

The System Date

On an IBM Personal Computer, the most important (and often most overlooked) date is the date maintained by the operating system. This date is called the "system date," and it is set by the DOS DATE command. Many users have developed the habit of simply pressing the carriage return and allowing the date to default when DATE executes. Unfortunately, the system date is recorded in the directory every time a file is created or changed. When the system date and the time that goes along with it are allowed to default, all of the file date and time stamps are useless. In most commercial programs, this is intolerable.

There is, unfortunately, no way for a program to ensure that the system date and time are accurate. The best a program can do is show the current setting to the user and ask for verification that these values are indeed correct. If the user says the values are correct, the program has to accept the user's word. On the other hand, if the user says the values are wrong, the program should have some means of resetting them. The appropriate routines are in EL0707, shown in Fig. 7-7. Note that all of the routines in this module use the DATE and TIME types defined back in EL0502.

GetDate and SetDate. *GetDate* and *SetDate* use MS DOS interrupt 21H and functions 2AH and 2BH, respectively, to deal with the system date. There is nothing surprising here.

GetTime and SetTime. The routines that deal with the system time are *GetTime* and *SetTime*. They also use MS DOS functions to access the appropriate data.

GetWkDay. *GetWkDay* also uses the DOS function called 2AH to retrieve the system date variables, but unlike *GetDate*, this routine uses the value in AX which contains a number between zero and six, indicating the day of the week, to return an appropriate STRING.

Fig. 7-7. Standard dates and times.

```
DEFINITION MODULE ELO707;
  FROM ELO401 IMPORT    STRING;
  FROM ELO502 IMPORT    DATE,TIME;
  EXPORT QUALIFIED      GetDate,SetDate,GetTime,SetTime,GetWkDay;

PROCEDURE GetDate(VAR date:DATE);
(* This routine will return the current setting of the system date, in
   YYMMDD format.  *)
PROCEDURE SetDate(date:DATE):BOOLEAN;
(* This routine will set the system date to the corresponding value in
   date.  date is in YYMMDD format.  If the contents of date do not
   constitute a valid date, the routine will return FALSE.  *)
PROCEDURE GetTime(VAR time:TIME);
(* This routine will return the current setting of the system time, in
   HHMMDD format.  *)
PROCEDURE SetTime(time:TIME):BOOLEAN;
(* This routine will set the system time to the corresponding value in
   time.  time is in HHMMDD format.  If the contents of time do not
   constitue a valid time, the routine will return FALSE.  *)
PROCEDURE GetWkDay(wkday:STRING);
(* This routine will return a STRING containing the complete name of the
   day of week indicated by the current setting of the system clock.  *)
END ELO707.

IMPLEMENTATION MODULE ELO707;
  FROM SYSTEM IMPORT    WORD,BYTE;
  FROM ELO301 IMPORT    ByWord,LoByte,HiByte;
  FROM ELO401 IMPORT    Literal,STRING,SubStr,MakeStr,ClearStr,nullstr,
                        MoveStr,CopyStr;
  FROM ELO502 IMPORT    DATE,TIME;
  FROM ELO605 IMPORT    CarToStr;
  FROM ELO701 IMPORT    Interupt;

PROCEDURE GetDate(VAR date:DATE);
VAR
  ax,bx,cx,dx,ds,es,di,si,flags:WORD;
  str:STRING;
  i:CARDINAL;
BEGIN
  MakeStr(str,0,Literal('      '));
  ax:=ByWord(2AH,00H);
  Interupt(21H,ax,bx,cx,dx,ds,es,di,si,flags);
  CarToStr(CARDINAL(cx),6,str);
  MoveStr(SubStr(5,2,str),Literal(date),1);
  CarToStr(CARDINAL(ByWord(00H,HiByte(dx))),6,str);
  MoveStr(SubStr(5,2,str),Literal(date),3);
  CarToStr(CARDINAL(ByWord(00H,LoByte(dx))),6,str);
  MoveStr(SubStr(5,2,str),Literal(date),5);
  FOR i:=1 TO 6 DO
    IF (date[i] = ' ')
      THEN date[i]:='0';
      END;
    END;
  ClearStr(str);
  END GetDate;

PROCEDURE SetDate(date:DATE):BOOLEAN;
VAR
  ax,bx,cx,dx,ds,es,di,si,flags:WORD;
BEGIN
  ax:=ByWord(2BH,00H);
  cx:=WORD(10*(ORD(date[1])-ORD('0')) + ORD(date[2])-ORD('0'));
```

Fig. 7-7 continued

```
  dx:=WORD(
          100H*(10*(ORD(date[3])-ORD('0'))+ORD(date[4])-ORD('0'))
        +  (10*(ORD(date[5])-ORD('0'))+ORD(date[6])-ORD('0')));
  Interupt(21H,ax,bx,cx,dx,ds,es,di,si,flags);
  IF (LoByte(ax) <> BYTE(0))
    THEN RETURN FALSE;
    ELSE RETURN TRUE;
    END;
  END SetDate;

PROCEDURE GetTime(VAR time:TIME);
VAR
  ax,bx,cx,dx,ds,es,di,si,flags:WORD;
  str:STRING;
  i:CARDINAL;
BEGIN
  MakeStr(str,0,Literal('       '));
  ax:=ByWord(2CH,00H);
  Interupt(21H,ax,bx,cx,dx,ds,es,di,si,flags);
  CarToStr(CARDINAL(ByWord(00H,HiByte(cx))),6,str);
  MoveStr(SubStr(5,2,str),Literal(time),1);
  CarToStr(CARDINAL(ByWord(00H,LoByte(dx))),6,str);
  MoveStr(SubStr(5,2,str),Literal(time),3);
  CarToStr(CARDINAL(ByWord(00H,HiByte(dx))),6,str);
  MoveStr(SubStr(5,2,str),Literal(time),5);
  FOR i:=1 TO 6 DO
    IF (time[i] = ' ')
      THEN time[i]:='0';
      END;
    END;
  ClearStr(str);
  END GetTime;

PROCEDURE SetTime(time:TIME):BOOLEAN;
VAR
  ax,bx,cx,dx,ds,es,di,si,flags:WORD;
BEGIN
  ax:=ByWord(2DH,00H);
  cx:=WORD(10*(ORD(time[1])-ORD('0')) + ORD(time[2])-ORD('0'));
  dx:=WORD(
          100H*(10*(ORD(time[3])-ORD('0'))+ORD(time[4])-ORD('0'))
        +  (10*(ORD(time[5])-ORD('0'))+ORD(time[6])-ORD('0')));
  Interupt(21H,ax,bx,cx,dx,ds,es,di,si,flags);
  IF (LoByte(ax) <> BYTE(0))
    THEN RETURN FALSE;
    ELSE RETURN TRUE;
    END;
  END SetTime;

PROCEDURE GetWkDay(wkday:STRING);
VAR
  ax,bx,cx,dx,ds,es,di,si,flags:WORD;
  c:CARDINAL;
BEGIN
  ax:=ByWord(2AH,00H);
  Interupt(21H,ax,bx,cx,dx,ds,es,di,si,flags);
  c:=CARDINAL(ByWord(00H,LoByte(ax)));
  CASE c OF
    0:CopyStr(Literal('Sunday'),wkday);
  | 1:CopyStr(Literal('Monday'),wkday);
  | 2:CopyStr(Literal('Tuesday'),wkday);
```

```
: 3:CopyStr(Literal('Wednesday'),wkday);
: 4:CopyStr(Literal('Thursday'),wkday);
: 5:CopyStr(Literal('Friday'),wkday);
: 6:CopyStr(Literal('Saturday'),wkday);
    END;
  END GetWkDay;

END EL0707.
```

Fig. 7-8. Checking a date.

```
DEFINITION MODULE EL0708;
  FROM EL0502 IMPORT    DATE;
  EXPORT QUALIFIED      ChkDate;

PROCEDURE ChkDate(yymmdd:DATE;VAR yok,mok,dok:BOOLEAN):BOOLEAN;
(* This routine will check the contents of yymmdd to verify that it
   contains a valid date.  If any of the fields are in error, the routine
   will return false, and the appropriate BOOLEAN(s) will be set false.  *)
END EL0708.

IMPLEMENTATION MODULE EL0708;
  FROM EL0502 IMPORT    DATE;

PROCEDURE ChkDate(yymmdd:DATE;VAR yok,mok,dok:BOOLEAN):BOOLEAN;

  PROCEDURE Chop(yymmdd:DATE;s:CARDINAL;VAR f:CARDINAL):BOOLEAN;
  BEGIN
    IF (yymmdd[s] < '0') OR (yymmdd[s] > '9')
         OR (yymmdd[s+1] < '0') OR (yymmdd[s+1] > '9')
      THEN RETURN FALSE
      ELSE f:=10*(ORD(yymmdd[s]) - ORD('0'))
                        + ORD(yymmdd[s+1]) - ORD('0');
    END;
    RETURN TRUE;
    END Chop;

VAR
  iy,im,id:CARDINAL;
BEGIN
  yok:=Chop(yymmdd,0,iy);  mok:=Chop(yymmdd,2,im);  dok:=Chop(yymmdd,4,id);
  IF (mok)
    THEN IF (im < 1) OR (im > 12)
      THEN mok:=FALSE;
    END;
  END;
  IF (dok)
    THEN IF (id < 1)
      THEN dok:=FALSE;
      ELSE IF (id > 28)
        THEN IF (mok) AND (im IN {1,3,5,7,8,10,12})
          THEN IF (id <= 31)
            THEN dok:=TRUE;
            ELSE dok:=FALSE;
            END;
          ELSE IF (im <> 2)
            THEN IF (id <=30)
              THEN dok:=TRUE;
              ELSE dok:=FALSE;
              END;
```

Fig. 7-8 continued

```
          ELSE IF (yok) AND (iy MOD 4 = 0)
            THEN IF (id <= 29)
               THEN dok:=TRUE;
               ELSE dok:=FALSE;
               END;
            ELSE IF (id <= 28)
               THEN dok:=TRUE;
               ELSE dok:=FALSE;
               END;
            END;
          END;
        END;
      END;
    END;
  END;
 RETURN yok AND mok AND dok;
 END ChkDate;

END EL0708.
```

Checking Dates

SetDate uses code that is built into DOS to check the validity of the data it is passed. A routine that checks the validity of a date is quite useful in a commercial program. Unfortunately, if you were to use *SetDate* for that purpose, it would change the system date every time it was called. The routine shown in EL0708 *ChkDate*, (Fig. 7-8), will check a date without resetting the system date. The routine expects the date to be in the form "yymmdd." If the date is valid, the function will return true.

Chapter 8

Program Parameters

In electronics, a *black box* is any device that you can't see inside of; your only clues as to what goes on in there is what you see on the outside. On the outside, a black box might have switches or dials or plugs. If these things are properly labeled, and the box operates according to the instructions, you can use a black box for its stated purpose without understanding (or even knowing) how its insides operate. For me, most of the electronic devices I use (including computers) are black boxes. I know how to turn them on and I can generally operate them to accomplish what I want, but I don't really understand how they do what they do.

A properly designed black box has an interesting property. It knows how to operate, but it doesn't know what it is operating on. A radio, for example, knows how to translate an electromagnetic signal into an audio signal, but it doesn't know whether it has tuned in Bach, Boy George, or Waylon Jennings.

Ideally, a routine is a black box. By looking at the outside—at the procedure or function heading—you should be able to understand enough about the routine to use it. The switches, dials, and plugs that a routine uses are the parameters that you pass to it. The only thing you should have to know about a routine is what parameters it requires. The routine should have no effect on any data other than its parameters. Also, a well-designed routine does not know what it is operating on. The same routine that decides if

paycode = 'SALARY'

can also be used to determine that

mountain = 'EVEREST.'

The thing that makes a routine specific in its function but general in its usage, is the concept of parameters. A routine operates on its parameters, but in general it does not really care what they contain. (Obviously, there are some exceptions to this; some parameters are control parameters, and their contents dictate which of several operations a routine performs. But "good" routines generally have few control parameters.) Parameters are what allow you to write a routine such as:

PROCEDURE MoveIt(VAR this,that:STRING);

and then use the procedure to move *myname* to *payee* or *saturn* to *nextstop*.

Programs can also be written as black boxes. All of the DOS external commands are black box programs. You can use COPY.COM without understanding how it works, and the program will copy from one file to another without caring whether it is coping disk files, keystrokes, or printer files. To tell COPY.COM what to copy, you use parameters. The values you want COPY.COM to use for its parameters are included on the command line you use to invoke the program. For example, **COPY B:*.LST LPT1** passes B:*.LST2 and LPT1 as parameters. The operating system takes care of placing program parameters in a location where COPY.COM can find them.

When DOS executes any program, it builds an area in core into which the program is loaded. This area is called the *program segment*. At the beginning of this area, DOS builds a *program segment prefix* and copies all of the characters from the command line that invokes the program into a specific location in the PSP. The area set aside for these characters is only 127 bytes, which can be a problem. While this might be enough for most system programs, there are times when an application program must specify more characters than the area can handle, especially when it comes to defining files with pathnames.

The 127-byte limit is one reason why many DOS programs, and utility programs available from other sources, use cryptic abbreviations to supply values to program parameters. Do you remember what /B/4 means in the DOS FORMAT command? Often, to save space (and still be somewhat meaningful), parameters are positional. The values on the command line must be given in the same order each time. Some programs have optional parameters; if a given execution of a program doesn't require all parameters, you shouldn't be forced to supply a value. But with positional parameters, you must define a value for *each* parameter. Also, with positional parameters, you have no way of reminding yourself of the parameters for which you are supplying values; the only way of identifying which value goes with which parameter is by the position in which it appears.

I prefer program parameters based on keywords rather than positions. I would rather invoke a program like this:

PRINTER WIDTH=32 LENGTH=66 TITLE="CHAPTER 15"

To me this makes the reason for executing PRINTER easier to remember, and the reason for supplying the various values clearer. It is also convenient to be able to leave out parameters if they don't happen to be required for a given execution.

Suppose this program also requires a value for SPACING. If, as the example shows, you don't supply a value for that parameter, its up to the program (not the compiler or the operating system) to decide what to do about it. I discuss how to define such things in the following section.

THE BASIC PARAMETER ROUTINES

In the Etling Library, the routines in EL0801 (see Fig. 8-1) constitute the nucleus of the parameter-handling system. The routines require a record type, called PARM, and a pointer to that type, named PARMPTR. A PARM record contains three fields: *parmid* and *parmval* (both STRINGs), and *nextparm* (a PARMPTR). Using these types, the routines in the module construct a list of program parameters. The list is controlled by the two static variables, *firstparm* and *lastparm*. As their names imply, these variables point to the beginning and end of the parameter list.

The parameter list is a simple sequential linked list. No attempt is made to organize the list for rapid retrieval because the number of parameters defined for a typical program is usually small.

GetParms. A program that uses the program parameter routines from the Etling Library would begin with a call to *GetParms*. This routine collects the program parameters specified on the command line *and* gathers the system parameters from the DOS environment.

Both the routines in the Library and the DOS environment handler (refer to the DOS SET command for details) define parameters in more or less the same way. The general format is:

<parmid>=<parmval>

where <parmid> is replaced with any string of characters that identifies a parameter, and <parmval> is any string that defines the value the parameter is to assume. There are a couple of important differences between the Etling routines and DOS.

First, DOS will automatically change any lowercase characters in <parmid> to uppercase; the Etling routines will not. Lowercase characters are significant to the Etling routines and you must be careful to define parameters accordingly. Also, DOS permits embedded blanks in <parmval>. You can say this to DOS:

SET ALPHA=DDD AAA CCC

It will accept this as written. The Etling routines, on the other hand, use a blank character as a delimiter between several parameters on the same line. If you need to embed a blank in a <parmval>, enclose the entire <parmval> in double quotes. For example, consider the following:

PRINTER TITLE="CHAPTER ONE. MY LIFE BEGINS"

GetParms uses DOS function 62H to access the segment address of the program segment prefix assigned to the program. At an offset of 002CH bytes into this segment, DOS puts the address of the environment area in effect at the time of the

Fig. 8-1. Basic program parameter routines.

```
DEFINITION MODULE EL0801;
  FROM EL0401 IMPORT  STRING;
  EXPORT QUALIFIED    SetParm,BldParms,GetParms,GetNParm,FindParm,ClrParms;

PROCEDURE GetParms;
(* This routine will gather all of the program parameters passed from the
   operating system.  This includes both parameters on the command line and
   those in the DOS environment when the program is loaded.  *)
PROCEDURE BldParms(parmlist:STRING);
(* This routine will parse parmlist into individual parameters that will be
   added to the list of program parameters.  If the routine encounters a
   parameter in the form PARMFILE=<filename>, the routine will attempt to
   read additional parameters from that file.  Further, if it encounters a
   parameter stating ENVIRON=<seg>:<off>, the routine will use that address
   as a DOS environment area and build additional parameters from there. *)
PROCEDURE SetParm(parmid,parmval:STRING);
(* If a parameter already exists for parmid, and StrLen(parmval) = 0 this
   routine will delete the associated parameter from the list of parameters
   for the program.  If parmid does not exist, it will be added to the
   program list.  If parmid does exist and StrLen(parmval) <> 0, the
   parameter will be set to the new value.  *)
PROCEDURE FindParm(parmid,parmval:STRING):BOOLEAN;
(* If a program parameter matching parmid can be found, this routine will
   return TRUE and parmval will be set accordingly;  otherwise the routine
   will return FALSE and StrLLen(parmval) will equal zero.  *)
PROCEDURE GetNParm(parmid,parmval:STRING):BOOLEAN;
(* If, on entry, StrLLen(parmid) = 0, this routine will return the parmid
   and parmval for the first parameter in the program parameter
   list...otherwise, the routine will return the next parameter in the
   list.  If no more program parameters are defined, the routine will
   return false and the length of both parmid and parmval will equal 0.  *)
PROCEDURE ClrParms;
(* This routine will clear all existing program parameters.  *)
END EL0801.


IMPLEMENTATION MODULE EL0801;
  FROM SYSTEM IMPORT    SIZE,BYTE,WORD,ADDRESS;
  FROM Storage IMPORT   ALLOCATE,DEALLOCATE;
  FROM EL0301 IMPORT    LoByte,ByWord;
  FROM EL0302 IMPORT    MovByteL;
  FROM EL0303 IMPORT    equal;
  FROM EL0401 IMPORT    STRING,StrLen,SetLen,ClearStr,Literal,SubStr,
                        MakeStr,nullstr,CopyStr,StrChar,SetChar;
  FROM EL0402 IMPORT    Delete,Insert,Concat;
  FROM EL0403 IMPORT    MatchStr,Positn;
  FROM EL0701 IMPORT    Interupt;
  FROM EL0802 IMPORT    ReadParm;

TYPE
  PARMPTR = POINTER TO PARM;
  PARM = RECORD
    parmid  : STRING;
    parmval : STRING;
    nextparm: PARMPTR;
    END;
VAR
  frstparm,lastparm:PARMPTR;
PROCEDURE ChkParm(parmid:STRING;VAR thisparm:PARMPTR):BOOLEAN;
BEGIN
  thisparm:=frstparm;
  WHILE (thisparm <> NIL) DO
```

```
          IF (StrLen(parmid) = StrLen(thisparm^.parmid))
            THEN IF (MatchStr(parmid,thisparm^.parmid,
                                       1,1,StrLen(parmid)) = equal)
              THEN RETURN TRUE;
              END;
            END;
         thisparm:=thisparm^.nextparm;
         END;
      RETURN FALSE;
      END ChkParm;

PROCEDURE SetParm(parmid,parmval:STRING);
VAR
   thisparm,prevparm:PARMPTR;
BEGIN
   IF (StrLen(parmval) <> 0)
      THEN
         IF (ChkParm(parmid,thisparm))
            THEN
               ClearStr(thisparm^.parmval);
               MakeStr(thisparm^.parmval,0,parmval);
            ELSE
               NEW(thisparm);
               MakeStr(thisparm^.parmid,0,parmid);
               MakeStr(thisparm^.parmval,0,parmval);
               thisparm^.nextparm:=NIL;
               IF (frstparm = NIL)
                  THEN frstparm:=thisparm;
                  ELSE lastparm^.nextparm:=thisparm;
                  END;
               lastparm:=thisparm;
            END;
      ELSE
         IF (ChkParm(parmid,thisparm))
            THEN
               ClearStr(thisparm^.parmval);
               ClearStr(thisparm^.parmid);
               IF (frstparm = thisparm)
                  THEN
                     frstparm:=thisparm^.nextparm;
                     IF (lastparm = thisparm)
                        THEN lastparm:=frstparm;
                        END;
                  ELSE
                     prevparm:=frstparm;
                     WHILE (prevparm^.nextparm <> thisparm) DO
                        prevparm:=prevparm^.nextparm;
                        END;
                     prevparm^.nextparm:=thisparm^.nextparm;
                     IF (lastparm = thisparm)
                        THEN lastparm:=prevparm;
                        END;
                  END;
               DISPOSE(thisparm);
            END;
      END;
   END SetParm;

PROCEDURE BldParms(parmlist:STRING);
VAR
   fc,lc,i,pl:CARDINAL;
   skip:BOOLEAN;
   parmval,parmid:STRING;
```

Fig. 8-1 continued

```
BEGIN
  fc:=1;
  MakeStr(parmid,255,nullstr);
  MakeStr(parmval,255,nullstr);
  WHILE (fc < StrLen(parmlist)) DO
    skip:=TRUE;
    WHILE (skip) DO
      IF (fc > StrLen(parmlist))
        THEN skip:=FALSE;
        ELSE IF (StrChar(parmlist,fc) = ' ')
          THEN INC(fc);
          ELSE skip:=FALSE;
          END;
        END;
      END;
    IF (fc < StrLen(parmlist))
      THEN
        lc:=Positn(Literal('='),parmlist,fc);
        IF (lc = 0)
          THEN fc:=StrLen(parmlist)+1;
          ELSE
            CopyStr(SubStr(fc,lc-fc,parmlist),parmid);
            fc:=lc+1;
            IF (fc <= StrLen(parmlist))
              THEN
                IF (StrChar(parmlist,fc) <> '"')
                  THEN lc:=Positn(Literal(' '),parmlist,fc);
                  ELSE
                    fc:=fc+1;
                    lc:=Positn(Literal('"'),parmlist,fc);
                  END;
                IF (lc = 0)
                  THEN lc:=StrLen(parmlist)+1;
                  END;
                CopyStr(SubStr(fc,lc-fc,parmlist),parmval);
                fc:=lc+1;
              END;
          END;
      END;
    IF (StrLen(parmid) <> 0)
      THEN
        IF (MatchStr(Literal('PARMFILE'),parmid,1,1,0) = equal)
          THEN ReadParm(parmval);
          ELSE SetParm(parmid,parmval);
          END;
      END;
    END;
  ClearStr(parmid);
  ClearStr(parmval);
  END BldParms;

PROCEDURE ClrParms;
VAR
  thisparm,nextparm:PARMPTR;
BEGIN
  thisparm:=frstparm;
  WHILE (thisparm <> NIL) DO
    nextparm:=thisparm^.nextparm;
    ClearStr(thisparm^.parmid);
    ClearStr(thisparm^.parmval);
    DISPOSE(thisparm);
```

```
        thisparm:=nextparm;
      END;
    frstparm:=NIL;
    lastparm:=NIL;
    END ClrParms;


PROCEDURE FindParm(parmid,parmval:STRING):BOOLEAN;
VAR
    thisparm:PARMPTR;
BEGIN
  IF (ChkParm(parmid,thisparm))
    THEN
      CopyStr(thisparm^.parmval,parmval);
      RETURN TRUE;
    ELSE
      RETURN FALSE;
    END;
  END FindParm;


PROCEDURE GetNParm(parmid,parmval:STRING):BOOLEAN;
VAR
    thisparm:PARMPTR;
BEGIN
  IF (StrLen(parmid) = 0)
    THEN
      thisparm:=frstparm;
    ELSE
      IF (NOT ChkParm(parmid,thisparm))
        THEN RETURN FALSE;
        END;
      thisparm:=thisparm^.nextparm;
    END;
  IF (thisparm = NIL)
    THEN
      RETURN FALSE;
    ELSE
      CopyStr(thisparm^.parmid,parmid);
      CopyStr(thisparm^.parmval,parmval);
      RETURN TRUE;
    END;
  END GetNParm;


PROCEDURE GetParms;
VAR
    ax,bx,cx,dx,ds,es,di,si,flags:WORD;
    psp:ADDRESS;
    envptr:POINTER TO ARRAY [1..32768] OF CHAR;
    cmmdptr:POINTER TO ARRAY [0..127] OF CHAR;
    str:STRING;
    seg,i,j,l,m:CARDINAL;
BEGIN
    MakeStr(str,255,nullstr);
    ax:=ByWord(62H,00H);
    Interupt(21H,ax,bx,cx,dx,ds,es,di,si,flags);
    seg:=CARDINAL(bx);
    psp.SEGMENT:=seg;               psp.OFFSET:=2CH;
    psp.SEGMENT:=CARDINAL(psp^);    psp.OFFSET:=0;
    envptr:=psp;
    i:=1;
    WHILE (envptr^[i] <> CHR(0)) DO
      l:=i;
      CopyStr(nullstr,str);
```

Fig. 8-1 continued

```
    WHILE (envptr^[1] <> CHR(0)) DO
      SetLen(str,StrLen(str)+1);
      SetChar(str,StrLen(str),envptr^[1]);
      INC(1);
      END;
    BldParms(str);
    i:=1+1;
    END;
  psp.SEGMENT:=seg;    psp.OFFSET:=80H;
  cmmdptr:=psp;
  l:=ORD(cmmdptr^[0]);
  SetLen(str,1);
  FOR i:=1 TO 1 DO
    SetChar(str,i,cmmdptr^[i]);
    END;
  IF (1 > 0)
    THEN
      m:=Positn(Literal('='),str,1);
      IF (m > 0)
        THEN
          WHILE (m > 0) AND (StrChar(str,m) <> ' ') DO
            DEC(m);
            END;
          IF (m > 0)
            THEN Delete(str,1,m);
            END;
          BldParms(str);
        END;
    END;
  ClearStr(str);
  END GetParms;

BEGIN
  frstparm:=NIL;
  lastparm:=NIL
END EL0801.
```

load. DOS also places the remaining characters from the command line that invokes the program at an offset of 80H bytes into this segment. The byte at this location contains a count of the number of additional characters. To build the list of program parameters, *GetParms* simply references those areas and calls *BldParms* to construct the parameters.

The order in which *GetParms* builds parameters is significant. The parameters from the DOS environment are built first for a reason: the DOS environment constitutes a very useful "common" area for communicating parameters between programs. By issuing a DOS SET command, a DOS BATCH file can define a parameter that is accessible by all the multiple programs the BATCH file invokes. By collecting the DOS environment parameters first, these values become available for use as replacement values for command line or file parameters; I'll talk about this later in the chapter.

BldParms. *BldParms* handles the construction of program parameters. It separates a line of characters into individual parameters. The algorithm that *BldParms* uses is straightforward. It keeps track of the first character it is analyzing. It considers from there to the first equal sign to be <parmid>. If the character after the equal sign is a double quote, all characters from there up to the next double quote (excluding the quote marks) is the associated <parmval>. If the character is not a double quote, the <parmval> ends at the first blank. As with most of the Etling routines, *BldParms* contains only minimal error checking. If it cannot find an equal sign, it makes a guess, and continues; it assumes that you know what you are doing.

When *BldParms* has collected a valid <parmid> and <parmval> it calls *MatchStr* to see if <parmid> contains the value 'PARMFILE.' If it does, *GetParms* will call *ReadParm* (see the next section) to collect additional parameters from the file identified by <parmval>. A parameter whose <parmid> equals 'PARMFILE' can appear anywhere in the parameter list; even as an entry in a parameter file. Using this technique, a program has access to any number of parameters and is not limited to just the 127 characters permitted by DOS.

SetParm. The routine *BldParms* uses to create a new entry in the list of program parameters is called *SetParm*. *SetParm* can also be called from outside EL0801 to change the <parmval> for existing parameters or to delete a parameter entirely. *SetParm* decides what do to based on the value of *ChkParm*. *ChkParm* is a routine that is only used by the routines in the EL0801 Module and is not exported.

ChkParm. *ChkParm*'s job is to follow the list of program parameters to determine if the new parameter has already been defined. Note that if *ChkParm* indicates that the new parameter does not exist, it will be added on to the <u>end</u> of the list.

FindParm. Once *GetParms* has been called to build the list of program parameters, an executing program can retrieve the <parmval> for specific parameters by using *FindParm*. *FindParm* uses *ChkParm* to locate a given <parmid> in the program's list.

Together with *SetParm*, *FindParm* can be used to establish default values for a given *parameter*, For example:

```
IF (NOT FindParm(Literal('WIDTH'),width))
    THEN BEGIN
        CopyStr(Literal('132'),width);
        SetParm(Literal('WIDTH'),width);
        END;
```

FindParm can be called from anywhere within a program. Even the routines at the lowest level have complete access to program parameters without having to pass them down through the layers.

GetNParm. When an executing program is not quite sure which parameter it has to deal with, or if there is actually a list of possible values for a given situation, the program can call *GetNParm*. *GetNParm* allows a program to go through the parameter list sequentially. For example, if you could invoke a program called PRINTER by saying

```
PRINTER TITLE1="CHAPTER 1" TITLE2=MY LIFE AND TIMES"
```

you could include code within the program that looked like this:

```
CopyStr(nullstr,titleid);
```

```
WHILE (GetNParm(titleid,titleval)) DO
  IF (MatchStr(titleid,Literal('TITLE'),1,1,5) = equal)
    THEN . . . . .do whatever
```

These statements would look through the list of program parameters for any <parmid> beginning with the characters TITLE. When a match is found, the corresponding <parmval> can be used for whatever purpose is appropriate.

ClrParms. *ClrParms* will, as its name implies, clear the entire list of program parameters, and reset *firstparm* and *lastparm* to empty the list. Use this routine in a program that has access to several parameter files.

READING PARAMETERS FROM A FILE

The routine that *BldParms* uses to gather additional parameters from a PARMFILE is called *ReadParm* (Fig. 8-2, EL0802). *ReadParm* uses the I/O routines in the Etling Library to access the appropriate file. The I/O routines are discussed in Chapter 10. Note that as *ReadParm* reads each line from the file, it calls *BldParms* to construct a parameter. Because it might have been *BldParms* that called *ReadParm* in the first place, this is an example of indirect recursion. It's also an example of a way to get yourself in trouble using Modula-2.

A Modula-2 module can include a BEGIN and END pair that encompasses an initialization sequence for static variables within the module. When such a module is linked into a program, the compiler and linker generate code that causes this initialization code to be executed *before* the main code in the program. The initialization code is standard Modula-2; it can IMPORT and call any other procedure available in any other module. The Modula-2 standard states that modules requiring initialization are executed in the order in which they occur; usually, this is interpreted to mean the order in which they are IMPORTed. If the initialization code for one module requires another module and that other module also has initialization code, it must be executed <u>before</u> the first module's initialization. If the second module happens to reference something in the first, you've got a perfect situation for "gridlock."

The modules in the Etling Library are arranged in a sequence to avoid that: first compile the DEFINITION modules in numeric sequence, then the IMPLEMENTATION modules; finally always IMPORT modules in numeric sequence. If this sequence is followed, the gridlock problem will be circumvented. In the few instances —like EL0802—where an IMPLEMENTATION IMPORTs a routine from a later module, the module does not include initialization code.

ASK THE USER

AskParm. There are times when a program must ask the user to supply a parameter after the program starts executing. *AskParm*, shown in Fig. 8-3, is EXPORTed from EL0803 and can be used to prompt the user for optional or missing parameters. *AskParm* is normally used with *FindParm* to give the user a second chance to provide parameters. For example, look at the following segment:

```
IF (NOT FindParm(Literal('LENGTH'),length))
  THEN AskParm(Literal('Enter number of lines per page'),
               Literal('LENGTH'),length,frame);
```

Fig. 8-2. Reading parameters from a file.

```
DEFINITION MODULE EL0802;
   FROM EL0401 IMPORT    STRING;
   EXPORT QUALIFIED       ReadParm;

PROCEDURE ReadParm(ddname:STRING);
(* This routine will read program parameters from the file associated with
    ddname.  *)
END EL0802.

IMPLEMENTATION MODULE EL0802;
   FROM SYSTEM IMPORT     BYTE;
   FROM EL0401 IMPORT     STRING,MakeStr,ClearStr,nullstr;
   FROM EL0801 IMPORT     BldParms;
   FROM EL1002 IMPORT     OpnFile,FMODE,OPENKIND,LINECNTRL,DISP,ClsFile;
   FROM EL1003 IMPORT     GetLine;

PROCEDURE ReadParm(ddname:STRING);
VAR
  opnmode:FMODE;
  ioerr:BYTE;
  parmstr:STRING;
BEGIN
  MakeStr(parmstr,255,nullstr);
  opnmode:=oldfile;
  OpnFile(ddname,opnmode,ioerr,insist);
  WHILE (GetLine(ddname,parmstr,nortrnend)) DO
    BldParms(parmstr);
    END;
  ClsFile(ddname,clsonly);
  ClearStr(parmstr);
  END ReadParm;

END EL0802.
```

Fig. 8-3. Ask the user for a parameter.

```
DEFINITION MODULE EL0803;
   FROM EL0401 IMPORT    STRING;
   FROM EL0504 IMPORT    FRAME;
   EXPORT QUALIFIED       AskParm;

PROCEDURE AskParm(msg,parmid,parmval:STRING;VAR frame:FRAME);
(* This routine will use frame to ask the user to supply a value for the
    program parameter associated with parmid.  parmid and parmval will be
    added to the list of program parameters and parmval will be returned to
    the calling program.  *)
END EL0803.

IMPLEMENTATION MODULE EL0803;
   FROM EL0401 IMPORT     STRING,Literal,StrLen,CopyStr,SetLen,
                          MakeStr,ClearStr,SetChar;
   FROM EL0402 IMPORT     Insert,Concat;
   FROM EL0404 IMPORT     FixStr;
   FROM EL0501 IMPORT     CHARSET,nullcset,MakeCSet;
   FROM EL0504 IMPORT     FRAME;
   FROM EL0801 IMPORT     SetParm;
   FROM EL0902 IMPORT     nrmclr,ClrScrn;
   FROM EL0903 IMPORT     ReadKB;
   FROM EL0904 IMPORT     DsplyStr;
```

Fig. 8-3 continued

```
VAR
  normals,easciis:CHARSET;

PROCEDURE AskParm(msg,parmid,parmval:STRING;VAR frame:FRAME);
VAR
  eascii:BOOLEAN;
  kbchar:CHAR;
  str:STRING;
BEGIN
  ClrScrn(frame,nrmclr);
  MakeStr(str,255,Literal('Enter '));
  Concat(msg,str);
  SetLen(str,StrLen(str)+1);
  SetChar(str,StrLen(str),':');
  WITH frame DO
    DsplyStr(nrmclr,str,fl,fc,frame);
    REPEAT
      UNTIL (ReadKB(parmval,normals,easciis,
                     eascii,kbchar,frame,nrmclr));
    END;
  SetParm(parmid,parmval);
  ClearStr(str);
  END AskParm;

BEGIN
  MakeCSet(FixStr(Literal("cr")),normals);
  easciis:=nullcset;
END EL0803.
```

AskParm lets the calling program define the frame in which the user's prompt is to appear.

SAVING PARAMETERS TO A FILE

It's quite simple to write programs that, in effect, build a list of parameters for other programs to use. Use *SetParm* and *AskParm* to create the list and the *WrtParm* routine shown in Fig. 8-4 (from EL0804) to write the parameters to a file. Like *ReadParm*, *WrtParm* uses the I/O routines from Chapter 10 to open a file and copy the current parameter list into it.

REPLACEABLE PARAMETERS

DOS BATCH files are powerful and flexible. One of the concepts that contributes to this is *replaceable parameters*. Replaceable parameters allow you to define BATCH files containing variables (i.e., %0, %1, etc.) that are replaced with a value when the file is actually processed. The program parameter routines in the Etling Library have a similar facility, but with a friendlier twist.

FixParm. The routine that handles replaceable program parameters is called *FixParm* and is EXPORTed by EL0805, shown in Fig. 8-5. *FixParm* is normally used by the I/O routines in Chapter 10, but it is available for any program to call. The operation of *FixParm* is extremely simple, but the concept is also extremely powerful.

Fig. 8-4. Writing parameters to a file.

```
DEFINITION MODULE EL0804;
   FROM EL0401 IMPORT    STRING;
   EXPORT QUALIFIED      WrtParm;

PROCEDURE WrtParm(ddname:STRING);
(* This routine will write all currently defined program parameters to the
   file associated with ddname.  Note that if any parmval includes a space,
   that entire parmval will be enclosed in double quote characters.  The
   double-quote character cannot be included in a parmval.  *)
END EL0804.

IMPLEMENTATION MODULE EL0804;
   FROM SYSTEM IMPORT    BYTE;
   FROM EL0401 IMPORT    STRING,Literal,MakeStr,ClearStr,nullstr;
   FROM EL0403 IMPORT    Positn;
   FROM EL0801 IMPORT    GetNParm;
   FROM EL1002 IMPORT    OpnFile,FMODE,LINECNTRL,OPENKIND,ClsFile,DISP;
   FROM EL1004 IMPORT    PutLine;

PROCEDURE WrtParm(ddname:STRING);
VAR
   parmval,parmid:STRING;
   opnmode:FMODE;
   ioerr:BYTE;
BEGIN
   MakeStr(parmid,255,nullstr);
   MakeStr(parmval,255,nullstr);
   opnmode:=makenew;
   OpnFile(ddname,opnmode,ioerr,insist);
   WHILE (GetNParm(parmid,parmval)) DO
     PutLine(ddname,parmid,noendline);
     PutLine(ddname,Literal('='),noendline);
     IF (Positn(Literal(' '),parmval,1) > 0)
       THEN PutLine(ddname,parmval,endline);
       ELSE
         PutLine(ddname,Literal('"'),noendline);
         PutLine(ddname,parmval,noendline);
         PutLine(ddname,Literal('"'),endline);
       END;
     END;
   ClsFile(ddname,clsonly);
   ClearStr(parmid);
   ClearStr(parmval);
   END WrtParm;

END EL0804.
```

Fig. 8-5. Using replaceable program parameters.

```
DEFINITION MODULE EL0805;
   FROM EL0401 IMPORT    STRING;
   EXPORT QUALIFIED      FixParm;

PROCEDURE FixParm(parmval:STRING);
(* This routine will replace all occurences of [<id>] in parmval with the
   value associated with program parameter defined by <id>.  For example:

        DEVICE=C
        CLNTNMBR=1231
```

Fig. 8-5 continued

```
            SUBDIR=CLNT[CLNTNMBR]
            ACCOUNTS=[DEVICE]:\[SUBDIR]\ACCOUNTS.MST

   This sequence will be translated into:

            ACCOUNTS=C:\CLNT1231\ACCOUNTS.MST
*)
END EL0805.

IMPLEMENTATION MODULE EL0805;
   FROM EL0401 IMPORT    nullstr,STRING,Literal,StrLen,SetLen,CopyStr,
                         MakeStr,ClearStr,SubStr,StrSize;
   FROM EL0402 IMPORT    Delete,Insert,Concat;
   FROM EL0403 IMPORT    Positn;
   FROM EL0501 IMPORT    InCSet,numbers;
   FROM EL0801 IMPORT    FindParm;

PROCEDURE FixParm(parmval:STRING);
VAR
   i,j,k:CARDINAL;
   val,parmid:STRING;
BEGIN
   MakeStr(val,255,nullstr);
   MakeStr(parmid,255,nullstr);
   REPEAT
     i:=Positn(Literal('['),parmval,1);
     WHILE (i > 0) DO
       j:=Positn(Literal(']'),parmval,i);
       IF (j = 0)
         THEN i:=0;
         ELSE
           REPEAT
             k:=Positn(Literal('['),parmval,i+1);
             IF (k > 0) AND (k < j)
               THEN i:=k;
               ELSE k:=0;
               END;
             UNTIL (k = 0);
           CopyStr(SubStr(j+1,j-i+1,parmval),parmid);
           IF (NOT FindParm(parmid,val))
             THEN CopyStr(parmid,val);
             END;
           Delete(parmval,i,j-i);
           IF (StrLen(parmval) + StrLen(val) <= StrSize(parmval))
             THEN Insert(val,parmval,i);
             END;
           i:=Positn(Literal('['),parmval,1);
         END;
       END;
     UNTIL (i = 0);
   ClearStr(parmid);
   ClearStr(val);
   END FixParm;

END EL0805.
```

Any program parameter value can include replaceable values and any parameter ID can be used to supply the value. In Chapter 10, we'll see examples of how this can be put to use.

Chapter 9

Talking to the User

Programming is actually more art than science. The product of the art, however, is not an item to hang on the wall and admire, but a tool to handle and use. The product of the programming art—the program—is at its best when the user is no longer aware that it exists, but instead can concentrate on the problem he is using the program to solve. A good program simply does its job, and to the extent the user doesn't have to think about how to make it behave, a program does its job well. A good program is "user friendly."

To me, the term "user friendly" means that the program operates in a way that is intuitive for the user, or at least in a way that is easy for the user to learn. A good program doesn't dazzle or surprise, but presents a stable, standardized, and predictable face—a face with which the user can cope.

Obviously, the vast range of programs available for personal computers offers a huge crowd of faces to the user. A standard user interface has not yet been defined, but the IBM keyboard and display, and the recent trend toward "integrated" software are producing efforts in the right direction. Until an industry-wide standard is identified, the best a programmer can do is define and adhere to a standard user interface with the software he or she writes.

On an IBM Personal Computer, a program deals with the user over three separate channels: instructions and transient results are output to the display; the user's commands and data are input via the keyboard; and, permanent, user-readable data and results are printed on a printer. Controlling the printer is such a formidable topic that I've devoted an entire chapter to the subject later in this book. This chapter deals with the display and the keyboard.

Standard Modula-2 does suggest routines for dealing with the user devices, collected in a module called Terminal. The Terminal module is intended to handle character-by-character I/O to the user's console, in a manner similar to a teletype device, rather than as a CRT-based display system. These routines do not provide for cursor positioning, screen color, or any windowing operations.

Wirth's book, *Programing in Modula-2*, mentions several additional modules: Windows, TextWindows, and GraphicWindows, that are more suited to PC displays, but these modules are not part of the language. Whether or not they are implemented is entirely up to the compiler package. Most of the packages discussed in this book do not include these modules.

The packages that do include similar routines are limited by their intended environment. To be compatible with all MS DOS machines, these packages uses DOS function calls to implement user I/O. Because the DOS functions are written rather conservatively, these calls are not always suitable for commercial applications. So, to fill in the gaps and correct the limitations, the Etling Library contains routines to handle the keyboard and display operations.

THE KEYBOARD

As it happens, a large portion of the work done at the user interface on a personal computer involves collecting, dispersing, or interpreting characters. The collecting part begins with the keyboard.

The IBM PC keyboard actually has a microprocessor of its own built into its circuitry. This processor is responsible for detecting a keystroke (it signals both when the key is depressed and when it is released), for providing the "typematic" functions (so keys repeat if you hold it down longer than a second or so), and for communicating with the PC's central processor. The keyboard sends *scan codes*, indicating to the PC which key was pressed. The BIOS code translates these codes into characters and decides which keys generate extended ASCII characters. The BIOS routines are called by routines in IBMBIO.COM and IBMDOS.COM to provide character-by-character input to a system or application program.

The DOS routines that access keyboard BIOS are available through INT 21H. There are several different functions defined, and they vary as to whether or not the keyboard buffer is cleared, whether the routine waits for a keystroke or returns with a "not ready" status, and whether the character is echoed to the display. Function 06H is the best suited to commercial programs because it will return immediately if no character is pending, and it does not echo the character to the screen. In other words, function 06H does not force a program to stop while waiting for keyboard input. The program can continue to process, and the program can control whether and where a character appears on the display.

Additionally, function 06H does not check the character to determine if it is the Ctrl-Break character, the character that causes BASIC to interrupt execution of the program. Again, by using function 06H, the program has control over the consequences of the user pressing this key.

Module EL0901, shown if Fig. 9-1 has several routines for handling the keyboard. Normally, access to the keyboard begins with *InitKB*.

InitKB. The routine named *InitKB* references an address in base page. The byte

Fig. 9-1. Keyboard basics.

```
DEFINITION MODULE EL0901;
  EXPORT QUALIFIED       GetKBChr,FlushKB,InitKB;

PROCEDURE InitKB(caplock,numlock:BOOLEAN);
(* This routine will set the keyboard control states according to the
   values given.  *)
PROCEDURE FlushKB;
(* This routine will flush any pending characters from the keyboard
   buffer.  This can be used to prevent "type ahead" operations.  *)
PROCEDURE GetKBChr(VAR eascii:BOOLEAN;VAR kbchar:CHAR):BOOLEAN;
(* This routine will inspect the keyboard buffer and return FALSE if no
   character is pending.  If a character is available, the routine will
   return TRUE and kbchar will contain the character.  If the character is
   a standard ASCII character, eascii will return FALSE.  If the character
   is Extended ASCII (such as one of the function keys or cursor control
   keys), eascii will return true.  *)
END EL0901.

IMPLEMENTATION MODULE EL0901;
  FROM SYSTEM IMPORT    ADDRESS,WORD,BYTE;
  FROM EL0301 IMPORT    LoByte,ByWord;
  FROM EL0701 IMPORT    Interupt,zeroflg;

PROCEDURE InitKB(caplock,numlock:BOOLEAN);
CONST
  cap = ( 6 );   num = ( 5 );
VAR
  kbads:ADDRESS;
  kbflag:BITSET;
BEGIN
  kbads.SEGMENT:=0040H;    kbads.OFFSET :=0016H;
  kbflag:=BITSET(kbads^);
  IF (caplock)
    THEN kbflag:=kbflag + cap;
    ELSE kbflag:=kbflag - cap;
    END;
  IF (numlock)
    THEN kbflag:=kbflag + num;
    ELSE kbflag:=kbflag - num;
    END;
  kbads^:=WORD(kbflag);
  END InitKB;

PROCEDURE FlushKB;
VAR
  head,tail:ADDRESS;
BEGIN
  head.SEGMENT := 0040H;    head.OFFSET := 001AH;
  tail.SEGMENT := 0040H;    tail.OFFSET := 001CH;
  tail^ := head^;
  END FlushKB;

PROCEDURE GetKBChr(VAR eascii:BOOLEAN;VAR kbchar:CHAR):BOOLEAN;
VAR
  axreg,bxreg,cxreg,dxreg,dsreg,esreg,direg,sireg,flags:WORD;
BEGIN
  axreg:=ByWord(06H,00H);
  dxreg:=ByWord(00H,0FFH);
  Interupt(21H,axreg,bxreg,cxreg,dxreg,
                   dsreg,esreg,direg,sireg,flags);
  IF (zeroflg IN BITSET(flags))
```

Fig. 9-1 continued

```
        THEN RETURN FALSE;
        END;
    IF (LoByte(axreg) <> BYTE(OOH))
        THEN eascii:=FALSE;
        ELSE
            axreg:=ByWord(06H,OOH);
            dxreg:=ByWord(OOH,OFFH);
            Interupt(21H,axreg,bxreg,cxreg,dxreg,
                            dsreg,esreg,direg,sireg,flags);
            eascii:=TRUE;
        END;
    kbchar:=CHR(ORD(LoByte(axreg)));
    RETURN TRUE;
    END GetKBChr;

END ELO901.
```

at 0040:0017H is used by the keyboard routines in BIOS to indicate the state of the keyboard's shift keys. *InitKB* turns the appropriate bits on or off, depending on the value of the BOOLEAN parameters it is passed. (For further information on the usage of the bits in this byte, refer to the IBM Technical Reference Manual. Reference to these bits and other things in base page is dangerous. IBM specifically recommends *not* referring to addresses in BIOS. Subsequent releases of IBM equipment might change the meaning of certain locations.) *InitKB* is only intended to control the state of the Num Lock key and the Caps Lock key.

FlushKB. All of the DOS routines that deal with the keyboard operate on a short, 16 byte, keyboard buffer maintained by BIOS in base page. The buffer itself is located at 0040:001EH. The word at 0040:001AH, identified in the BIOS listing as BUFFER_HEAD, points to the first character stored in the buffer; 0040:001CH, BUFFER_TAIL, points to the last character. If the value stored at BUFFER_HEAD equals the value at BUFFER_TAIL, the buffer is empty.

Although it isn't exactly ideal, the routine named *FlushKB* references BUFF-ER_HEAD and BUFFER_TAIL, called *head* and *tail* in the routine. *FlushKB* references these addresses as a simple means of clearing the keyboard buffer. By setting the contents of BUFFER_HEAD to BUFFER_TAIL, *FlushKB* tells DOS the buffer is empty.

GetKBChr. The routine named *GetKBChr* uses DOS function 06H. If no character is pending, the call to *Interupt* returns with the zero flag in the FLAGS register set on, and *GetKBChr* will return immediately to its caller with a FALSE value. If a character is ready in the keyboard buffer, the *Interupt* call for function 06H will return with the zero flag clear, and *LoByte(ax)* will hold the character. If the user presses a key that translates to an extended ASCII character, *LoByte(ax)* will equal OOH, and *GetKBChr* must then make a second call to function 06H to read the actual character. If two calls are required, *eascii* will return TRUE; otherwise, it will be FALSE.

THE DISPLAY

The other side of the normal user interface on a personal computer, the output side, uses a CRT display. DOS has several function calls allocated for dealing with the display, and they operate by calling routines in BIOS to place characters at the proper location.

Unfortunately, the DOS routines impose some assumptions that are not always appropriate for commercial programs, and the BIOS routines are relatively slow. DOS assumes that when a character is written to the screen, the cursor should be positioned to the location immediately following. If the character is written to the last byte on a line, the cursor moves to the first byte on the next line and, if the next line happens to be off the end of the screen, the screen scrolls up. In other words, using the DOS function calls, you cannot write to the last byte on the last line without scrolling the screen. Because the Etling Library routines use the last line to display messages to the user, this is not satisfactory.

Also, because the routines in BIOS are designed to handle both the monochrome and the color monitors, they include code to synchronize the moving of characters into the display buffer with the timing control on the CRT. Ideally, characters should only be inserted into the buffer during the time when the electron gun in the CRT is turned off. (This is during the *horizontal retrace* interval, which is the time during which the electron beam is returning to its home position, before drawing the next line of pixels.) Otherwise, the display will show random patterns when the main processor uses the buffer. This phenomenon results in "snow" on the color monitor, but on the monochrome display and the enhanced color display, the snow is not apparent.

In applications that require moving a large block of characters to the screen rapidly, the only way to provide adequate speed is to move characters directly to the display buffers. Again, this does ignore IBM's recommendations, but it has been done by so many software packages that IBM has recognized the practice. Topview, IBM's multitasking operating system, allows such programs direct access to the screen buffer.

Colors

The memory that constitutes a display buffer contains one word for each screen location. The layout of words in the display buffer was discussed in Chapter 5, but Fig. 9-2 shows module EL0902, which exports routines to control access to the buffer. The module also exports several colors (*stdhilite, blink, nrmclr,* and *undrline*) that constitute standard color values used by the routines in this book. These colors were chosen for their effect on a monochrome display, which in my opinion is more suitable for text and data entry operations required by commercial applications than the color display. These attributes are legal for a color monitor but do not produce the effect their name implies. (For example, the *undrline* color becomes a very deep blue on the color display — making the characters even harder to read than is normally the case on these monitors. I'll talk more about this problem in Chapter 14.)

The Display Buffer

The CRT Address. All of the CRT-related routines in the Library determine the correct address by referencing a variable exported from EL0902. The variable is named *crtads,* and it contains the actual address in memory where the current display buffer is located.

Fig. 9-2. CRT basics.

```
DEFINITION MODULE ELO902;
  FROM SYSTEM IMPORT     BYTE;
  FROM ELO504 IMPORT     SMAPPTR,FRAME;
  EXPORT QUALIFIED       stdhilite,blink,nrmclr,undrline,crtads,wrkframe,
                         msgframe,FindCRT,PutCRT,ClrScrn,PstnCur,ScrollUp;

VAR
  stdhilite,blink,nrmclr,undrline:BYTE;
  crtads:SMAPPTR;
  wrkframe,msgframe:FRAME;
(* These variables define general screen related values for use in
   accessing the CRT.  crtads points to the display buffer for the current
   display.  wrkframe and msgframe divide the display buffer into two
   areas.  The larger area, wrkframe is used for most of the work done by a
   program...msgframe points to the last two lines on the CRT, which is the
   area normally used to display error and status messages to the user.  *)
PROCEDURE FindCRT;
(* This routine will determine which display adapter is currently in use,
   and set the appropriate address in the variable crtads.  Note that
   FindCRT should normally be called before any other routine that uses the
   CRT, but, crtads will default to the monochrome adapter. *)
PROCEDURE PutCRT(color:BYTE;character:CHAR;VAR frame:FRAME);
(* This routine will output character to the CRT, positioned within the
   frame specified.  If the character is a backspace and frame.cc is
   greater than frame.fc, the cursor is moved to [cl,cc-1]; regardless, a
   blank is moved to the new position.  If character is a line feed,
   frame.cl is set to frame.cl + 1.  If character is a carriage return,
   column is set to frame.cl.  Any other value for character is moved to
   the display buffer at [cl,cc], given the attribute specified by color,
   and column is set to column + 1.  *)
PROCEDURE ClrScrn(VAR frame:FRAME;color:BYTE);
(* This routine will fill the display adapter memory with color blanks
   with the frame specified.  *)
PROCEDURE PstnCur(line,column:CARDINAL;VAR frame:FRAME);
(* This routine will position the CRT cursor to the location specified, and
   frame.cl and frame.cc will be updated accordingly.  Note than no range
   checking is done, but, to avoid unpredictable results:

           1 <= line <= 25       1 <= column <= 80
*)
PROCEDURE ScrollUp(VAR frame:FRAME;color:BYTE);
(* This routine will scroll all of the lines on the display from frame.fl
   to frame.ll up one position, and the new line will be filled with color.
   On exit, frame.cl:=frame.ll.  *)
END ELO902.


IMPLEMENTATION MODULE ELO902;
  FROM SYSTEM IMPORT     BYTE,ADDRESS,WORD;
  FROM ELO301 IMPORT     ByWord,LoByte;
  FROM ELO302 IMPORT     MovByteL;
  FROM ELO304 IMPORT     bksp,cr,lf;
  FROM ELO504 IMPORT     FRAME,DWPTR,DsplyWrd;
  FROM ELO701 IMPORT     Interupt;

PROCEDURE FindCRT;
VAR
  equipment,bx,cx,dx,ds,es,di,si,flags:WORD;
BEGIN
  Interupt(11H,equipment,bx,cx,dx,ds,es,di,si,flags);
  IF ({4,5} <= BITSET(equipment))
    THEN crtadd.SEGMENT:=0B000H;
```

```
      ELSE crtadd.SEGMENT:=OB8OOH;
      END;
    crtads:=crtadd;
    wrkframe.s:=crtads;
    msgframe.s:=crtads;
    END FindCRT;

PROCEDURE PutCRT(color:BYTE;character:CHAR;VAR frame:FRAME);
VAR
    d:DWPTR;
BEGIN
    WITH frame DO
      IF (character = bksp)
        THEN
          IF (cc > fc)
            THEN cc:=cc-1;
            END;
          d:=DsplyWrd(cl,cc,frame);
          d^.chrbyte:=' ';
          d^.colbyte:=color;
      ELSIF (character = lf)
        THEN INC(cl);
      ELSIF (character = cr)
        THEN cc := fc;
        ELSE
          d:=DsplyWrd(cl,cc,frame);
          d^.chrbyte:=character;
          d^.colbyte:=color;
          INC(cc);
        END;
      END;
    END PutCRT;

PROCEDURE ClrScrn(VAR frame:FRAME;color:BYTE);
VAR
    nb,i:CARDINAL;
    d1,d2:DWPTR;
BEGIN
    WITH frame DO
      d1:=DsplyWrd(fl,fc,frame);
      d1^.chrbyte:=' ';
      d1^.colbyte:=color;
      nb:=2 * (lc - fc + 1);
      MovByteL(d1^,d1^,0,2,nb-2);
      FOR i:=fl+1 TO 11 DO
        d2:=DsplyWrd(i,fc,frame);
        MovByteL(d1^,d2^,0,0,nb);
        END;
      END;
    END ClrScrn;


PROCEDURE PstnCur(line,column:CARDINAL;VAR frame:FRAME);
VAR
    ax,bx,cx,dx,ds,es,di,si,flags:WORD;
BEGIN
    ax:=ByWord(02H,00H);
    bx:=ByWord(00H,00H);
    cx:=ByWord(00H,00H);
    dx:=ByWord(LoByte(line-1),LoByte(column-1));
    Interupt(10H,ax,bx,cx,dx,ds,es,di,si,flags);
    frame.cl:=line;
    frame.cc:=column;
    END PstnCur;
```

Fig. 9-2 continued

```
PROCEDURE ScrollUp(VAR frame:FRAME;color:BYTE);
VAR
  ax,bx,cx,dx,ds,es,di,si,flags:WORD;
BEGIN
  WITH frame DO
    ax:=ByWord(06H,01H);
    bx:=ByWord(color,00H);
    cx:=ByWord(LoByte(fl-1),LoByte(fc-1));
    dx:=ByWord(LoByte(ll-1),LoByte(lc-1));
    Interupt(10H,ax,bx,cx,dx,ds,es,di,si,flags);
    cl:=ll;
    END;
  END ScrollUp;

VAR
  crtadd:ADDRESS;
BEGIN
  stdhilite := BYTE(70H);     blink := BYTE(80H);
  nrmclr    := BYTE(07H); undrline := BYTE(01H);
  crtadd.SEGMENT   := 0B000H;   crtadd.OFFSET    := 0000H;
  FindCRT;
  crtads := crtadd;
  WITH wrkframe DO
    fl := 1;     ll := 23;    fc :=  1;    lc := 80;
    cl := 1;     cc :=  1;    nl := 25;    nc := 80;
    s  := crtads;
    END;
  WITH msgframe DO
    fl := 24;    ll := 25;    fc :=  1;    lc := 80;
    cl := 24;    cc :=  1;    nl := 25;    nc := 80;
    s  := crtads;
    END;
END EL0902.
```

EL0902 exports two other variables: *wrkframe* and *msgframe*. These two FRAME variables define universal areas on the user's display: the work area, and the message area. Both FRAMEs partition off areas in the display buffer. The *wrkframe* area is used for displaying data and retrieving user input. The *msgframe* area is reserved for displaying prompts to the user. Another module or a main program can modify its values and consequently change where error messages will appear on the screen if there is really a need to do so. I normally used lines 24 and 25 to display error messages, and *msgframe* is given default values accordingly.

FindCRT. The routine named *FindCRT* is included in the Library in case your software is intended to run on machines that might have either type of display. When *FindCRT* is called, it calls *Interupt* to access INT 11H. This interrupt vectors to a routine in BIOS that will return a word in the AX register that indicates all of the optional equipment installed in the machine on which the program is running. If bits 4 and 5 are set on, the machine is using a monochrome adapter. If these bits are not on, *FindCRT* will adjust the value of *crtads* to point to the correct location for the display buffer. (Again, for a complete description of the other bits returned by INT 11H, see the IBM Technical Reference Manual.)

PutCRT. *PutCRT* accesses the display buffer directly. If controls all character-by-character output to the display for all the routines in the Etling Library. Note that

PutCRT responds to carriage return and line feed characters but does not generate them. It assumes that the character it is asked to display will fit on the line it is told to use. Any "skip to a new line" logic must be in the calling routine. Refer to Figs. 9-5 and and 9-8 for examples of using *PutCRT*.

ClrScrn. Another routine that operates directly on the display buffer is called *ClrScrn*. As its name implies, *ClrScrn* will set all or part of the CRT screen to blanks in the color specified. The area to be cleared is defined by the coordinates specified in the FRAME. This, of course, implies that the area to be cleared need not cover the entire screen. *ClrScrn* can be used to clear a FRAME.

Display BIOS

There are three BIOS video I/O functions that do fit our purposes. The BIOS video I/O functions are available through INT 10H. Two of these functions are used by the routines in EL0902.

PstnCur. INT 10H, function 02H, positions the CRT cursor at the location specified by the DX register. (DH equals Line, DL equals Column.) *PstnCur* calls *Interupt* to access this function.

ScrollUp. The routine named *ScrollUp* calls INT 10H, function 06H, in the video I/O routines to cause the area within the FRAME to move up one line. Note that although the BIOS video routines include a function for scrolling the display down, I did not define a routine for doing this because I have never found a need for it. If you should find it useful, *ScrollUp* will provide a workable model.

PUTTING USER I/O TOGETHER

A conversation between the user and a program is actually a two-way affair. Usually, every time the user presses a key, a corresponding character should appear on the screen. (Sometimes this is not the case, and I'll deal with that later.)

Reading from the Keyboard

The *GetKBChr* routine shown back in Fig. 9-1 is the most primitive routine in the Etling Library for accessing the keyboard. *GetKBChr* operates a character at a time. Obviously, many programs deal with keyboard input in groups of several characters. THe Etling Library provides two different routines for doing this. One of these routines, *ReadKB*, gives the caller complete control over where the cursor will be positioned when user input begins. The other routine, named *InputKB*, functions more like an INPUT statement in BASIC; the cursor remains at its last used position. I'll talk about *InputKB* later in this chapter.

ReadKB. Figure 9-3 shows *ReadKB* exported from EL0903. The comments shown with the function heading are self-explanatory. The buffer in which the keystroke characters are passed back to the caller, *msg*, is defined as a STRING type so that up to 32K characters can be input at one time. However, *ReadKB* is intended to read fields from the keyboard, not lines. Fields generally are less than a full line wide. No assumptions are made in the program about the length of a line, but all of the characters in *msg* must fit within the FRAME defined.

Fig. 9-3. Read a keyboard message.

```
DEFINITION MODULE EL0903;
  FROM SYSTEM IMPORT     BYTE;
  FROM EL0401 IMPORT     STRING;
  FROM EL0501 IMPORT     CHARSET;
  FROM EL0504 IMPORT     FRAME;
  EXPORT QUALIFIED       ReadKB;

PROCEDURE ReadKB(msg:STRING; normals,easciis:CHARSET;VAR eascii:BOOLEAN;
                 VAR kbChar:CHAR;VAR frame:FRAME;color:BYTE):BOOLEAN;
(* This routine will attempt to read from the keyboard.  If no character is
   pending, control returns immediately to the caller, and the function
   will equal FALSE.  If at least one character is read, reading continues
   until one of the characters in either normals or easciis is read, and
   then, control returns with the function equal to TRUE.  msg is
   displayed, character by character as it is read, in the color specified.
   frame.cl and frame.cc are set accordingly.  If an attempt is made to
   enter more characters than msg can contain, Sound will be called to warn
   the user.  The character that ends the read is returned as kbchar with
   eascii set accordingly;  the terminating character is NOT displayed, and
   the terminating character is NOT included in msg.  The routine assumes
   that all of msg can fit within the frame defined.  *)
END EL0903.


IMPLEMENTATION MODULE EL0903;
  FROM SYSTEM IMPORT     BYTE;
  FROM EL0304 IMPORT     bksp;
  FROM EL0401 IMPORT     STRING,StrLen,nullstr,CopyStr,StrSize,SetLen,SetChar;
  FROM EL0402 IMPORT     Delete;
  FROM EL0501 IMPORT     CHARSET,InCSet;
  FROM EL0504 IMPORT     FRAME;
  FROM EL0705 IMPORT     Sound,errfreq,errdur;
  FROM EL0901 IMPORT     GetKBChr,FlushKB;
  FROM EL0902 IMPORT     PstnCur,PutCRT;


PROCEDURE ReadKB(msg:STRING; normals,easciis:CHARSET; VAR eascii:BOOLEAN;
                 VAR kbchar:CHAR;VAR frame:FRAME;color:BYTE):BOOLEAN;
VAR
  done:BOOLEAN;
BEGIN
  CopyStr(nullstr,msg);
  WITH frame DO
    PstnCur(cl,cc,frame);
    IF (NOT GetKBChr(eascii,kbchar))
      THEN RETURN FALSE;
      END;
    done:=FALSE;
    REPEAT
      IF (eascii)
        THEN done:=InCSet(kbchar,easciis);
        ELSE done:=InCSet(kbchar,normals);
        END;
      IF (NOT done)
        THEN
          IF (kbchar = bksp)
            THEN IF (cc = fc)
              THEN Sound(errfreq,errdur);
              ELSE
                Delete(msg,StrLen(msg),1);
                PutCRT(color,kbchar,frame);
                PstnCur(cl,cc,frame);
              END;
```

```
            ELSE IF (StrLen(msg) = StrSize(msg))
              THEN Sound(errfreq,errdur)
              ELSE
                SetLen(msg,StrLen(msg)+1);
                SetChar(msg,StrLen(msg),kbchar);
                PutCRT(color,kbchar,frame);
                IF (cc > lc)
                  THEN IF (cl > 11)
                    THEN Sound(errfreq,errdur);
                    ELSE cc:=fc;
                    END;
                  END;
                PstnCur(cl,cc,frame);
              END;
            END;
          REPEAT
            UNTIL (GetKBChr(eascii,kbchar));
        END;
      UNTIL (done);
    END;
  FlushKB;
  RETURN TRUE;
  END ReadKB;

END EL0903.
```

Displaying a Message for the User

There are also two display routines in the Etling Library. One of them, named *DsplyStr*, provides precise placement of the cursor before display begins. The other, *TypeMsg*, makes some assumptions about where the cursor should start, and like *InputKB*, is discussed later in this chapter.

DsplyStr. *DsplyStr*, shown in Fig. 9-4 (EL0904) will cause the contents of *msg* to appear on the screen. Unlike the WRITE or PUT statements in standard Modula-2, *DsplyStr* gives you complete control over where the message is shown, and in what color. Again, the routine is restricted to operate within the frame you define. Look at Fig. 9-5 for an example of using *DsplyStr*.

Fig. 9-4. Display a message on the CRT.

```
DEFINITION MODULE EL0904;
   FROM SYSTEM IMPORT    BYTE;
   FROM EL0401 IMPORT    STRING;
   FROM EL0504 IMPORT    FRAME;
   EXPORT QUALIFIED      DsplyStr;

PROCEDURE DsplyStr(color:BYTE;msg:STRING;sl,sc:CARDINAL;VAR frame:FRAME);
(* This routine will display the contents of msg on the CRT with the
   attribute of color.  The characters will be moved to the display buffer
   beginning at location [sl,sc] and, on return, the appropriate values in
   frame will be adjusted.  frame.cl and frame.cc will define the last
   position used.  frame.11 and frame.lc indicate the maximum values that
   can be accessed.  If, in the course of moving characters, frame.cc
   should exceed frame.lc, frame.cl will be set to frame.cl+1 and frame.cc
   will be set to frame.fc.  Should line exceed frame.11, the contents of
   the screen from [frame.fl,frame.fc] to [frame.11,frame.lc] will be
   scrolled up, and line will be unchanged.  *)
END EL0904.
```

Fig. 9-4. continued

```
IMPLEMENTATION MODULE EL0904;
  FROM SYSTEM IMPORT    SIZE,BYTE;
  FROM EL0401 IMPORT    STRING,StrLen,StrChar;
  FROM EL0504 IMPORT    FRAME;
  FROM EL0902 IMPORT    ScrollUp,PstnCur,PutCRT;

PROCEDURE DsplyStr(color:BYTE;msg:STRING;sl,sc:CARDINAL;VAR frame:FRAME);
VAR
  i:CARDINAL;
  done:BOOLEAN;
BEGIN
  WITH frame DO
    cl:=sl;      cc:=sc;
    IF (cl > 11)
      THEN ScrollUp(frame,color);
      END;
    PstnCur(cl,cc,frame);
    done:=FALSE;
    FOR i:=1 TO StrLen(msg) DO
      PutCRT(color,StrChar(msg,i),frame);
      IF (cc > lc)
        THEN
          cc:=fc;
          cl:=cl+1;
        END;
      IF (cl > 11)
        THEN ScrollUp(frame,color);
        END;
      PstnCur(cl,cc,frame);
      END;
    END;
  END DsplyStr;

END EL0904.
```

Displaying a Prompt

There are times when you want to display a message, and then wait for the user to reply with a single keystroke that indicates what action he wishes to take. The message you display under these circumstances is generally called a "prompt." One way to ensure that your systems and programs are easy for the user to learn is to always display prompts in the same location on the screen.

Message. The routine shown in Fig. 9-5 displays prompts. The routine is called *Message* and it is exported from EL0905. *Message* uses the area defined by *msgframe* to show its prompt on the display. It can be used to either wait for a response from the user or to return immediately so that some other routine can gather the user's reply. *Message* permits only a single character reply and is intended to be used as follows:

```
wait:=15;
MakeCSet(Literal('YN'),normals);
Message(Literal('Do you wish to continue?'),
        Literal('Y = Yes / N = no'),msgframe,wait,
              normals,nullcset,eascii,kbchar);
```

This statement will call *Message* and wait for the user to press either the Y key or the N key. No other keys will be accepted, and if the user does not press a key within 15 seconds (approximately) the *Sound* routine will be used to call for attention. The routine will retain control until a correct reply is made.

As I said before, *msgframe* is normally set to use lines 24 and 25 on the CRT to display prompts, but *Message* can be called with any two-line FRAME you require. Because, like many of the routines in the Etling Library, *Message* assumes you know what you want, it assumes that the *msg* you specify will fit in the area you define.

Fig. 9-5. A standard message handler.

```
DEFINITION MODULE EL0905;
   FROM EL0401 IMPORT    STRING;
   FROM EL0501 IMPORT    CHARSET;
   FROM EL0504 IMPORT    FRAME;
   EXPORT QUALIFIED      Message;

PROCEDURE Message(msg1,msg2:STRING; VAR msgframe:FRAME;
                     wait:CARDINAL; normals,easciis:CHARSET;
                     VAR eascii:BOOLEAN;VAR kbchar:CHAR);
(* This routine is a standardized error or instruction message handler. It
   uses two lines on the display to show a message to the user and then,
   either returns immediately (if both normals and easciis are equal to the
   null set) or waits for the user to enter one of the keys corresponding
   to a member of one of the sets.  The character that terminates the
   routine will return in kbchar.  eascii will indicate whether or not the
   character is an extended ASCII character.  If the user enters a
   character that is not in either set, .an appropriate error message is
   displayed and the standard error sound is made.  Both messages are
   displayed within msgframe.  If StrLen(msg1) > 0, it is displayed at
   msgframe[fl,fc].  msg2 is displayed on msgframe[ll,lc].  Existing
   contents of those lines are lost;  the screen is not scrolled.  If, on
   entry, wait > 0, the routine will use ChkTimer to allow the user
   approximately wait seconds to respond...if the user doesn't respond
   within that time, the routine will call Sound to attract attention.  *)
END EL0905.


IMPLEMENTATION MODULE EL0905;
   FROM SYSTEM IMPORT    SIZE,ADR;
   FROM EL0401 IMPORT    STRING,SetChar,StrLen,SetLen,Literal,
                         MakeStr,nullstr,MoveStr;
   FROM EL0501 IMPORT    CHARSET,InCSet,nullcset,EqCSet;
   FROM EL0503 IMPORT    LONGCARD;
   FROM EL0504 IMPORT    FRAME;
   FROM EL0705 IMPORT    Sound,qfreq,qdur,errfreq,errdur;
   FROM EL0706 IMPORT    SetTimer,ChkTimer;
   FROM EL0901 IMPORT    GetKBChr,FlushKB;
   FROM EL0902 IMPORT    PstnCur,nrmclr,ClrScrn;
   FROM EL0904 IMPORT    DsplyStr;

VAR
   msg:STRING;

PROCEDURE Message(msg1,msg2:STRING;VAR frame:FRAME;wait:CARDINAL;
                     normals,easciis:CHARSET;
                     VAR eascii:BOOLEAN;VAR kbchar:CHAR);
CONST
   relative = TRUE;
VAR
   l,c,i,hr,mi,se:CARDINAL;
```

Fig. 9-5 continued

```
      t,tc:LONGCARD;
      done,junk:BOOLEAN;
BEGIN
  ClrScrn(frame,nrmclr);
  WITH frame DO
    REPEAT
      IF (StrLen(msg1) > 0)
        THEN DsplyStr(nrmclr,msg1,fl,fc,frame);
        END;
      DsplyStr(nrmclr,msg2,11,fc,frame);
      PstnCur(fl,fc,frame);
      IF (EqCSet(normals,nullcset)) AND (EqCSet(easciis,nullcset))
        THEN RETURN
        END;
      IF (wait > 0)
        THEN SetTimer(relative,0,0,wait,t,tc);
        END;
      REPEAT
        done:=GetKBChr(eascii,kbchar);
        IF (wait > 0)
          THEN IF (ChkTimer(hr,mi,se,t,tc))
            THEN
              Sound(qfreq,qdur);
              SetTimer(relative,0,0,wait,t,tc);
            END;
          END;
        UNTIL (done);
      FlushKB;
      IF (eascii)
        THEN done:=InCSet(kbchar,easciis);
        ELSE done:=InCSet(kbchar,normals);
        END;
      IF (NOT done)
        THEN
          SetChar(msg,2,kbchar);
          DsplyStr(nrmclr,msg,11,fc,frame);
          Sound(errfreq,errdur);
        END;
      ClrScrn(frame,nrmclr);
    UNTIL (done);
  END;
END Message;

BEGIN
  MakeStr(msg,79,nullstr);
  SetLen(msg,79);
  MoveStr(Literal('< > is not a valid response'),msg,1);
END EL0905.
```

Displaying a Fatal Error

No matter how idiot-proof you try to make your programs, there is always some idiot hanging around out there that you didn't consider. Users are continually coming up with new ways to befuddle even the most user-friendly software, and occasionally, (but obviously not very frequently), you just plain miss a bug in an otherwise outstanding program. There will be times when your well-written and efficient code is presented with a circumstance that it just isn't prepared to handle. When that happens, you need a way to make a graceful exit. You need to tell the user, as politely as possible, "Hey . . . I just can't cope anymore. I'm gonna shut down, and here is as much as I know about why." The routine shown in Fig. 9-6 is intended to give you an out.

Cancel. *Cancel* is a standardized cancellation message generator. It uses *Message,* but it sets up its own FRAME, called *abortfrm* to display a "catastrophic" error message for the user. *Cancel* is exported from EL0906 (Fig. 9-6). The initialization section of the module sets *abortfrm* to *msgframe,* but *abortfrm* could be set to any two line FRAME you feel appropriate. An example of the format of *Cancel*'s message would be as follows:

Impossible error in GETLINE - No such record
(Status = 9)

The comments in Fig. 9-6 show the standard messages that *Cancel* will generate. As you read through the succeeding chapters, you will find many examples for using this routine.

SetPStat. When *Cancel* has displayed its message, it calls *SetPStat* to terminate the program's execution. The DOS function call 4CH will terminate the current process and transfer control to the invoking process. The function also sets the DOS ERRORLEVEL code, so that by using the DOS batch file IF statement, a terminating Modula-2 program can signal its success or failure to the operating system. Refer to the DOS manual for more information.

BrkHndlr. Occasionally, the user finds himself in a spot where he just can't continue. The user needs a way to say "Whoops! I didn't mean to do that!" That's why someone invented the Break key. Its a way for the user to interrupt the operation of a program. IBM recognized, however, that this isn't the kind of thing you would want to do by accident. So, the "break" operation on an IBM PC requires <u>two</u> keys be pressed simultaneously: the ctrl key and either the Break key or the "c" key. Even then there are times when you can hit these combinations accidentally.

When a user does press Ctrl-Break or Ctrl-C, the BIOS keyboard routine automatically vectors control to a specific interrupt vector. DOS calls the routine that sits on that interrupt, the Break Handler. EL0906 contains a routine to replace the standard DOS routine with something a little more consistent with the rest of the Library. Be aware that some of the Modula-2 packages, notably the one from Logitech, sometimes treat Ctrl-Break and Ctrl-C differently, and even treat Ctrl-Break itself differently depending on the circumstances. Because the documentation is not clear on these points, be certain you test your finished application to see what happens.

Keeping Track of Where You Are

All of the routines in the Etling Library that handle keyboard input and display output use FRAME variables. Two fields in a FRAME type keep track of the current location—the line and column—at which the cursor is placed within the frame. Therefore, routines that use FRAME types never have to ask DOS to locate the

Fig. 9-6. Cancel a program.
```
DEFINITION MODULE EL0906;
  FROM SYSTEM IMPORT    BYTE;
  FROM EL0401 IMPORT    STRING;
  FROM EL0504 IMPORT    FRAME;
  EXPORT QUALIFIED      Cancel,SetPStat,abortfrm,breakon;

VAR
  abortfrm:FRAME;
  breakon :BOOLEAN;
(* abortfrm is a variable, but it should be treated as a constant that
   defines the area of the crt in which cancel messages should be
   displayed.  breakon is used to signal the internal BrkHndlr routine as
   to whether or not it should permit the Ctrl-Break or Ctrl-C key
   combination to interrupt program execution.  *)
PROCEDURE Cancel(proc,msg:STRING;
                         msgnmbr:CARDINAL;status:BYTE);
(* This routine will terminate the current process and return to the
   invoker.  Usually, this means returning to the operating system.  This
   routine is intended to be used to indicate that a fatal error has
   occured, and the current process cannot continue to operate.  proc is
   used to identify the location where the cancel occurs...it is usually
   the name of the procedure where the call occurs, but, it can be any
   string of up to 20 characters.  msg can be used to show additional
   information about the error.  msgnmbr defines which standard error
   message should be displayed.  status will be used to set the error code
   that is passed to DOS...it can be accessed by the DOS IF and ERRORLEVEL
   commands.  The format of the error message that will be displayed is as
   follows:

        <message> (Status = <STATUS>)
        PROGRAM CANCELED

   The standard messages are:

      1 = Impossible error in <PROC> [<MSG>]
      2 = User requested abort in <PROC> [<MSG>]
      3 = Missing parm value for <MSG> in <PROC>
      4 = I/O error for <MSG> in <PROC>
      x = Undefined error code in <PROC> [<MSG>]
*)
PROCEDURE SetPStat(status:BYTE);
(* This routine will terminate the current process and set the process
   return code to status.  *)
END EL0906.

IMPLEMENTATION MODULE EL0906;
  FROM SYSTEM IMPORT    BYTE,SIZE,WORD,CODE,ADDRESS;
  FROM EL0301 IMPORT    ByWord,LoByte;
  FROM EL0304 IMPORT    fk10;
  FROM EL0401 IMPORT    STRING,Literal,MakeStr,ClearStr,
                        StrLen,CopyStr,nullstr;
  FROM EL0402 IMPORT    Concat;
  FROM EL0404 IMPORT    FixStr;
  FROM EL0501 IMPORT    CHARSET,nullcset,MakeCSet;
  FROM EL0504 IMPORT    FRAME;
  FROM EL0701 IMPORT    Interupt;
  FROM EL0702 IMPORT    SetVectr;
  FROM EL0902 IMPORT    msgframe,nrmclr;
  FROM EL0905 IMPORT    Message;

PROCEDURE SetPStat(status:BYTE);
```

```
VAR
  ax,bx,cx,dx,ds,es,di,si,flags:WORD;
BEGIN
  ax:=ByWord(04CH,status);
  Interupt(21H,ax,bx,cx,dx,ds,es,di,si,flags);
  END SetPStat;

PROCEDURE Cancel(proc,msg:STRING;msgnmbr:CARDINAL;status:BYTE);
VAR
  fn,ln:CHAR;
  str1,str2:STRING;
  eascii:BOOLEAN;
  kbchar:CHAR;

BEGIN
  MakeStr(str1,255,nullstr);
  MakeStr(str2,255,nullstr);
  WITH abortfrm DO
    CASE msgnmbr OF
      1:CopyStr(Literal('Impossible error in '),str1);
        Concat(proc,str1);
        IF (StrLen(msg) <> 0)
          THEN
            Concat(Literal(' '),str1);
            Concat(msg,str1);
          END;
    ! 2:CopyStr(Literal('User requested abort in '),str1);
        Concat(proc,str1);
        IF (StrLen(msg) <> 0)
          THEN
            Concat(Literal(' '),str1);
            Concat(msg,str1);
          END;
    ! 3:CopyStr(Literal('Missing parm value '),str1);
        IF (StrLen(msg) <> 0)
          THEN
            Concat(Literal('for '),str1);
            Concat(msg,str1);
          END;
        Concat(Literal('in '),str1);
        Concat(proc,str1);
    ! 4:CopyStr(Literal('I/O error '),str1);
        IF (StrLen(msg) <> 0)
          THEN Concat(msg,str1);
          END;
        Concat(Literal(' in '),str1);
        Concat(proc,str1);
      ELSE
        CopyStr(Literal('Undefined error code in '),str1);
        Concat(proc,str1);
        IF (StrLen(msg) <> 0)
          THEN
            Concat(Literal(' ('),str1);
            Concat(msg,str1);
            Concat(Literal(' )'),str1);
          END;
    END;
  fn:=CHR(ORD(status) DIV 16);
  ln:=CHR(ORD(status) - ORD(fn));
  IF (fn < CHR(10))
    THEN fn:=CHR(ORD('O') + ORD(fn))
    ELSE fn:=CHR(ORD('A') + ORD(fn) - 10);
```

Fig. 9-6 continued

```
      END;
    IF (ln < CHR(10))
      THEN ln:=CHR(ORD('O') + ORD(ln))
      ELSE ln:=CHR(ORD('A') + ORD(ln) - 10);
      END;
    CopyStr(Literal('(Status = '),str2);
    Concat(Literal(fn),str2);
    Concat(Literal(ln),str2);
    Concat(Literal(')'),str2);
    END;
  Message(str1,str2,abortfrm,0,nullcset,nullcset,eascii,kbchar);
  SetPStat(status);
  ClearStr(str1);
  ClearStr(str2);
  END Cancel;

PROCEDURE BrkHndlr;
(*  This routine is not known outside this module.  It sits on the
    Ctrl-Break exit address, and provides a way to inhibit program
    termination.
*)
VAR
  eascii:BOOLEAN;
  kbchar:CHAR;
BEGIN
  CODE(50H);              (* PUSH AX*)
  CODE(51H);              (* PUSH CX*)
  CODE(52H);              (* PUSH DX*)
  CODE(53H);              (* PUSH BX*)
  CODE(56H);              (* PUSH SI*)
  CODE(57H);              (* PUSH DI*)
  CODE(1EH);              (* PUSH DS*)
  CODE(06H);              (* PUSH ES*)
  IF (breakon)
    THEN
      Message(
          Literal('Verify...do you wish to terminate program?'),
          Literal('F1 = No, continue / F10 = Yes, stop'),
                  msgframe,15,
                  nullcset,easciis,eascii,kbchar);
      IF (kbchar = fk10)
        THEN Cancel(Literal('Ctrl-Break'),nullstr,2,0);
        END;
    END;
  CODE(07H);              (* PUSH ES*)
  CODE(1FH);              (* PUSH DS*)
  CODE(5FH);              (* PUSH DI*)
  CODE(5EH);              (* PUSH SI*)
  CODE(5BH);              (* PUSH BX*)
  CODE(5AH);              (* PUSH DX*)
  CODE(59H);              (* PUSH CX*)
  CODE(58H);              (* PUSH AX*)
  CODE(89H,0ECH);         (* MOV SP,BP*)
  CODE(5DH);              (* POP BP*)
  CODE(0CFH);             (* IRET *)
  END BrkHndlr;

VAR
  easciis : CHARSET;
BEGIN
  abortfrm:=msgframe;
```

```
   breakon:=TRUE;
   SetVectr(0023H,ADDRESS(BrkHndlr));
   MakeCSet(FixStr(Literal("fk1*fk10")),easciis);
END EL0906.
```

cursor. Well . . . almost never. Just in case, the Library includes a routine to ask DOS for help.

GetCursr. The routine shown in Fig. 9-7 uses INT 10H, Function 03H to determine the current location of the cursor. The routine is exported from EL0907 and is the only routine in the module. Because this routine is seldom required, it is in a separate module so that its code will not add to the size of a program unnecessarily. Admittedly, it is a small routine, but every little bit helps.

Teletype I/O

Most commercial applications lend themselves to a technique known as *full-screen data entry*, whereby the screen is divided into a series of fields that limits the areas where a user may enter data. Chapter 14 presents a full series of routines for doing this. Occasionally, a program doesn't need all that sophistication; sometimes a program's interaction with the user can be a simple series of questions and answers. This technique is usually called "Teletype I/O," because it was the only method available when Teletype and electric typewriters were the only interactive devices you could use to talk to computers. That's where *TypeStr* and *InputKB* come in. Both of these routines are exported from EL0908, The listing is shown in Fig. 9-8.

Fig. 9-7. Finding the cursor.

```
DEFINITION MODULE EL0907;
   EXPORT QUALIFIED      GetCursr;

PROCEDURE GetCursr(VAR line,column:CARDINAL);
(* This routine will return the current cursor position on the display
   currently in effect.  Note that line will be between 1 and 25...column
   will be between 1 and 80.  *)
END EL0907.

IMPLEMENTATION MODULE EL0907;
   FROM SYSTEM IMPORT    WORD;
   FROM EL0301 IMPORT    ByWord,LoByte,HiByte;
   FROM EL0701 IMPORT    Interupt;

PROCEDURE GetCursr(VAR line,column:CARDINAL);
VAR
   ax,bx,cx,dx,ds,es,di,si,flags:WORD;
BEGIN
   ax:=ByWord(03H,00H);
   bx:=ByWord(00H,00H);
   Interupt(10H,ax,bx,cx,dx,ds,es,di,si,flags);
   line:=ORD(HiByte(dx)) + 1;
   column:=ORD(LoByte(dx)) + 1;
   END GetCursr;

END EL0907.
```

Fig. 9-8. Simple teletype I/O.

```
DEFINITION MODULE ELO908;
   FROM SYSTEM IMPORT    BYTE;
   FROM ELO401 IMPORT    STRING;
   FROM ELO504 IMPORT    FRAME;
   EXPORT QUALIFIED      TypeStr,InputKB;

PROCEDURE TypeStr(color:BYTE;homecur:BOOLEAN;
                       msg:STRING; VAR frame:FRAME);
(* This routine will display the contents of msg on the current display in
   the color indicated.  If, on entry, homecur is TRUE, the cursor will be
   moved to the home position in the Frame, before the display.  Otherwise,
   the cursor will be left in its current position.  This routine works in
   conjunction with InputKB.  Both routines are restricted to the limits
   specified by frame.  *)
PROCEDURE InputKB(color:BYTE; msg,msgin:STRING;
                       VAR cl:CARDINAL;  VAR frame:FRAME);
(* This routine will display the contents of msg on the CRT and then read a
   string of characters from the keyboard up to but not including a
   carriage return.  When the carriage return is encountered, control
   returns to the calling routine, after a Line Feed is issued.  Normal
   backspace editing applies.  The characters entered by the user will be
   displayed in the color indicated.  All of the characters input must fit
   on the line at which input begins.  This routine is used in conjunction
   with TypeMsg.  Both routines restrict the cursor to within the limits
   defined by frame.  *)
END ELO908.


IMPLEMENTATION MODULE ELO908;
   FROM SYSTEM IMPORT    BYTE,SIZE;
   FROM ELO304 IMPORT    bksp,cr,lf;
   FROM ELO401 IMPORT    STRING,StrLen,StrChar,CopyStr,nullstr,
                         Literal,SetChar,SetLen;
   FROM ELO504 IMPORT    FRAME;
   FROM ELO705 IMPORT    Sound,errfreq,errdur;
   FROM ELO901 IMPORT    GetKBChr;
   FROM ELO902 IMPORT    PstnCur,ClrScrn,ScrollUp,PutCRT;
   FROM ELO907 IMPORT    GetCursr;


CONST
   donthome = FALSE;
VAR
   setcursr : BOOLEAN;

PROCEDURE TypeStr(color:BYTE;homecur:BOOLEAN;msg:STRING;VAR frame:FRAME);
VAR
   i:CARDINAL;
BEGIN
   WITH frame DO
     IF (homecur)
       THEN
         ClrScrn(frame,color);
         cl:=fl;
         cc:=fc;
         setcursr:=FALSE;
       ELSE
         IF (setcursr)
           THEN
             GetCursr(cl,cc);
             setcursr:=FALSE;
           END;
       END;
```

```
      PstnCur(cl,cc,frame);
    FOR i:=1 TO StrLen(msg) DO
      PutCRT(color,StrChar(msg,i),frame);
      IF (cc > lc)
        THEN
          cc:=fc;
          INC(cl);
        END;
      IF (cl > 11)
        THEN ScrollUp(frame,color);
        END;
      END;
    PstnCur(cl,cc,frame);
    END;
  END TypeStr;

PROCEDURE InputKB(color:BYTE;msg,msgin:STRING;
                            VAR cl:CARDINAL;VAR frame:FRAME);
CONST
  home = TRUE;
VAR
  eascii:BOOLEAN;
  kbchar:CHAR;
BEGIN
  CopyStr(nullstr,msgin);
  WITH frame DO
    IF (StrLen(msg) <> 0)
      THEN TypeStr(color,donthome,msg,frame);
      END;
    IF (setcursr)
      THEN
        GetCursr(cl,cc);
        setcursr:=FALSE;
      END;
    cl:=0;
    REPEAT
      REPEAT
        UNTIL (GetKBChr(eascii,kbchar));
      IF (kbchar <> cr)
        THEN
          IF (kbchar <> bksp)
            THEN
              IF (cc >= lc)
                THEN Sound(errfreq,errdur);
                ELSE
                  SetLen(msgin,StrLen(msgin)+1);
                  SetChar(msgin,1,kbchar);
                END;
            ELSE
              IF (cl > 1)
                THEN DEC(cl);
                END;
            END;
        END;
      PutCRT(color,kbchar,frame);
      PstnCur(cl,cc,frame);
      UNTIL (kbchar = cr);
    PutCRT(color,lf,frame);
    IF (cl > 11)
      THEN ScrollUp(frame,color);
      END;
    END;
```

Fig. 9-8 continued
```
  END InputKB;

BEGIN
  setcursr := TRUE;
END ELO9O8.
```

TypeStr. The *TypeStr* display routine is really intended to provide a continuous listing type of display within the confines of its FRAME parameter. *TypeStr* is used by the listing programs discussed back in Chapter 2.

InputKB. The other Teletype like routine is called *InputKB*. Note that *InputKB* can be used to prompt the user before input, and that unlike *ReadKB*, this routine will retain control until the user makes an entry.

Chapter 10

I/O

Even though the Modula-2 standard does not define any verbs or built-in routines for handling file input and output, in *Programing in Modula-2*, Wirth does offer suggested modules. Most of the Modula-2 implementations for the IBM PC took Wirth's suggestions and included similar modules in their packages.

I didn't.

Of course, I do have an advantage. I'm not trying to sell a package. I'm more interested in exploring the language to see what it can do. I can state, unequivocally, that my routines and the programs they produce will only operate with DOS 2.0 or later—preferably later. I don't have to worry about keeping my code compatible with earlier versions of DOS. I can also say that my routines use a completely nonstandard approach to Modula-2 I/O and might not be portable to environments other than the one for which they were intended. If your programs must operate on machines other than IBM PCs, or on operating systems other than DOS, the I/O routines presented in this chapter might have to be rewritten.

SOME NONSTANDARD I/O CONCEPTS

For some reason, I had problems with Pascal I/O operations right from the start. To this day, I cannot remember whether RESET opens a file for input operations alone, or if you can also write to it. The whole concept of PUTting a file variable never made sense to me, and the term "lazy evaluation" sounds like you don't get a raise this year.

When the routines in the Etling Library were originally written in Pascal, I decided to replace some of the more awkward (for me, at least) Pascal I/O concepts.

In the I/O routines that Wirth suggested for Modula-2, much of the Pascal awkwardness is gone, but there are still some things that the routines in the Etling Library offer that Wirth's do not. When I rewrote the Library in Modula-2, I decided to carry over the nonstandard techniques. Here they are.

File Names

In the Etling library, all files are identified by an identifier called a <ddname>. This identifier is a STRING, usually from 1 to 8 characters, but it can also contain up to 64 characters under certain circumstances. <ddname> stands for data definition name, and is the name by which a file is known *within* a program. The <ddname> is associated with another identifier called a <dsname>, for data set name. A <dsname> is a STRING containing up to 128 characters. The <dsname> defines the name by which the file is known *outside* the program.

The association between <ddname> and <dsname> is done via program parameters. For every <ddname> used within a program, there is usually a program parameter stating <dsname>=<ddname>, for example,

    OpnFile(Literal('PAYFILE'),opnmode,ioerr,insist);

This program fragment instructs the *OpnFile* routine (defined later in this chapter) to open the file identified by the constant, PAYFILE. *OpnFile* will call *FindParm* (defined in Chapter 8) to locate a program parameter whose <parmid> = 'PAYFILE'. If that parameter states

    PAYFILE=C:\PAYROLL\SALARY\WK0787.DAT

the file actually accessed by the program will be the WK0787.DAT file in the specified subdirectory. If the I/O routines do not find a parameter matching <ddname>, the value for <ddname> will be used as <dsname>. If you really need to, you can specify the name of the file to access without using a parameter. As the example shows, <dsname> can specify a full path name to the file. There is also another thing you can do with <dsname>. You can specify the volume on which it resides.

Volume Names

DOS 2.0 introduced the concept of disk and diskette volume names, but other than just making an entry in the directory, these volume names didn't accomplish much. The whole idea behind naming volumes is to provide a way of being certain that the correct diskette is mounted. On a mainframe, the operating system is responsible for detecting and verifying volume names. For microcomputers, the Etling routines will give this ability to a Modula-2 program.

Volume names for the Etling routines are included in the <dsname> associated with a file. The syntax for a <dsname> is defined like this:

    <dsname> = [<device>:]<filename>[.<ext>][,<volname>]
    <volname> = <filename>[.<ext>]

For example,

PAYFILE=A:HOURLY.TMP,071087.DAT

specifies that the file named HOURLY.TMP the program is to access is on the diskette whose <volname> is 071087.DAT. The directory entry for 071087.DAT can refer to any type of file (system, hidden, or normal), even the DOS volume name (if you're using DOS 3.0 or later). I'll talk more about volume names later in this chapter.

Directories

Some applications require that data files be separated into various classifications. For example, you might define a file that contains payroll data and arrange your system so that all of the data on salary payroll is in a directory named SALARY while all the hourly data is in HOURLY. The format of the data in each file would be the same and could be accessed by the same programs. To define which data to access during any given run of one of those programs, you could use the parameter system to say this:

PAYROLL=C:\PAYROLL\SALARY\071087.DAT

when you need to process salary payroll and this:

PAYROLL=C:\PAYROLL\HOURLY\071087.DAT

for the hourly calculations.

That works fine when you have only one or two files to deal with, but in a large application there could be five or six files that would have to be changed. The Etling Library routines provide an easier way. You can set up a batch file, named PAY.BAT (for example), that says this:

```
CD \PAYROLL
PAY PARMFILE=C:\PAYROLL\WKLY.PRM DIRNMBR=%1
CD \
```

and a parameter file that contains these statements:

```
PAYROLL=C:\PAYROLL\[DIRNMBR]\071087.DAT
TAXES=C:\PAYROLL\[DIRNMBR]\WITHOLD.DAT
FICA=C:\PAYROLL\[DIRNMBR]\FICA.DAT
INS=C:\PAYROLL\[DIRNMBR]\INS.DAT
```

When you need to execute the batch file to calculate salary payroll, you say **PAY SALARY** and the I/O routines will replace any occurrence of [DIRNMBR] with the current parameter setting for DIRNMBR. You can also use this facility for generic file names. If you define a parameter that says

GLRPTS=C:\GL\[DIRNMBR]-PL.001

you can set DIRNMBR to any five characters, and the I/O routines will access the appropriate file.

File Structure

In the I/O system defined by the Etling Library, files are identified within a program strictly by a <ddname>. There is no structure corresponding to the data type FILE as it is defined in standard Pascal. The concept of a buffer variable does not exist. Data can be read or written using any location in the data segment (or with some routines, using any location in memory).

The Etling Library I/O system treats all files as a sequence of bytes. The routines transfer data to or from files in groups of one or more bytes; the number of bytes transferred is controlled entirely by the program. Any byte in any file can have any value that a byte can contain, and under most circumstances no significance is attached to any byte value. (There are two routines, named *GetLine* and *PutLine,* that do recognize a carriage-return/line-feed sequence.)

The structure of the data within a file is controlled entirely by the program. There is nothing in the Etling basic I/O routines that implies some "inherent" data arrangement to the bytes in a file. There is no record length associated with a file; you can access the same file sequentially, randomly, with fixed or variable-length records. The location of the DOS file pointer is controlled entirely by the program.

Handles

Beginning with DOS 2.0 MicroSoft introduced the concept of a *file handle* to identify files to the DOS I/O function calls. A file handle is a 16-bit binary number that in effect points to the series of buffers and control variables that DOS maintains for the file. DOS predefines handles 0 through 4 and associates these numbers with the keyboard, display, error output device, auxiliary device, and printer. It is possible to refer to these five handles, but because the Etling routines provide I/O to these devices by other means, the first five handles are not used.

Now that I've talked about the concepts, let's look at the way they're implemented.

THE NUCLEUS OF THE ETLING I/O SYSTEM

The most primitive I/O routines in the Etling Library are contained in two modules, EL1001 and EL1002. Most of these routines are used by any program that does I/O to devices *other* than the keyboard or CRT.

Errors

The first module contains the error-reporting routines discussed in the following paragraphs.

RptIOErr. The *RptIOErr* procedure is the only routine exported from EL1001, shown in Fig. 10-1. It is this procedure that has the responsibility for reporting all errors that can be detected by the Library I/O system. It will generate over 70 different messages. Twelve of those messages (numbers 13H through 1FH) are relayed through the DOS critical error vector; I'll talk about that a little later. Most of the others come from the DOS function calls, but some are unique to the Etling Library. Depending on the value of *comeback, RptIOErr* will return control to the calling routine after reporting the message, or it will cancel the program.

As you will see from the routines in EL1002, most of the DOS functions return an indication of the success or failure of their operation using the carry bit in the flags register. if an error occurs, the DOS Function will set the carry bit, and the appropriate error code will be returned in the AX register. To test for this condition, routines use the following syntax:

IF ((carryflg IN BITSET[flags])

Most of the messages that *RptIOErr* generates are messages that the user of your program should probably never see. For example, the message "6 . . . invalid handle" indicates that one of the Library routines is trying to access a file that has not yet been opened; that is a program bug, not an execution error. The messages the user does see frequently, such as "176 . . . mount correct diskette" are mostly self-explanatory; if you encounter the other errors during the testing of your program, refer to the DOS Technical Reference for further information.

RptIOS. Even DOS doesn't detect all errors. Some errors are caught by BIOS or by the hardware. When these lower level routines find errors, they use interrupt 24H to vector to a routine known as the *critical error handler.* This is the routine responsible for issuing those cryptic DOS messages such as "Insert disk with batch file and strike any key when ready" or "Unrecoverable write error on target disk."

For most DOS programs, the DOS messages issued by the critical error handler are adequate, even if they are sometimes hard to decipher. But for applications programs that are intended to be used by people with no real training in computer jargon, DOS messages can be overwhelming. In an application program, the "Not ready reading drive A" message should be replaced with something more to the point, such as "Be certain the data diskette is in drive A and the diskette door is closed." The wording of the messages in *RptIOErr* are intended to be a little friendlier.

To be certain that DOS itself uses the messages in *RptIOErr* (as well as the BIOS and hardware routines), EL1001 replaces the default DOS critical error handler routine with *RptIOS,* the last routine in the EL1001 module. *RptIOS* sits on the interrupt vector; when it is invoked, it uses the contents of some of the registers to determine what caused the error. The error code itself is in the low-order byte of DI. To make this value correspond to the sequence of codes in *RptIOErr,* add 13H. Note that *RptIOS* will eventually return to the routine that caused the interrupt so that processing can continue.

When DOS does signal a disk error, the low-order byte of the AX register indicates which drive was involved. *RptIOS* uses this value as an index into the *vols* array; the message the user sees will include reference to the volume label the

Fig. 10-1. Dealing with DOS errors.

```
DEFINITION MODULE EL1001;
  FROM SYSTEM IMPORT    BYTE;
  FROM EL0401 IMPORT    STRING;
  EXPORT QUALIFIED      RptIOErr,vols;

VAR
  vols : ARRAY [0..25] OF STRING;
(* This array defines the volume lables the library routines think are
   associated with the corresponding device.  *)
PROCEDURE RptIOErr(ioerr:BYTE;dsname,procname:STRING; comeback:BOOLEAN);
(* This routine will translate ioerr to an appropriate message and will
   call Message to display it within msgframe.  If comeback is not TRUE,
   or, if the user responds with a Ctrl-Break, this routine will call
   Cancel, reporting procname as the source of the abort.  The format of
   the message is:

       Msg #<nn>...<error message>...(<DSNAME>)...
       F1 = Continue
*)
END EL1001.

IMPLEMENTATION MODULE EL1001;
  FROM SYSTEM IMPORT    SIZE,AX,DI,BP,SI,GETREG,CODE,ADR,BYTE,WORD,ADDRESS;
  FROM EL0301 IMPORT    ByWord,LoByte,HiByte;
  FROM EL0304 IMPORT    fk1,fk10,break;
  FROM EL0401 IMPORT    STRING,MakeStr,ClearStr,StrLen,
                        Literal,nullstr,SetChar;
  FROM EL0402 IMPORT    Insert,Concat;
  FROM EL0404 IMPORT    FixStr;
  FROM EL0501 IMPORT    MakeCSet,CHARSET,nullcset;
  FROM EL0504 IMPORT    FRAME;
  FROM EL0702 IMPORT    SetVectr;
  FROM EL0902 IMPORT    msgframe;
  FROM EL0905 IMPORT    Message;
  FROM EL0906 IMPORT    Cancel;

CONST
  wait = 15;
VAR
  easciis:CHARSET;

PROCEDURE RptIOErr(ioerr:BYTE;dsname,procname:STRING;comeback:BOOLEAN);
VAR
  msg:STRING;
  kbchar:CHAR;
  eascii:BOOLEAN;
BEGIN
  CASE ORD(ioerr) OF
    001H:MakeStr(msg,255,Literal('1...invalid DOS request'));
  ! 002H:MakeStr(msg,255,Literal('2...file not found'));
  ! 003H:MakeStr(msg,255,Literal('3...path not found'));
  ! 004H:MakeStr(msg,255,Literal('4...too many files open'));
  ! 005H:MakeStr(msg,255,Literal('5...access denied'));
  ! 006H:MakeStr(msg,255,Literal('6...invalid handle'));
  ! 007H:MakeStr(msg,255,Literal('7...memory control blocks destroyed'));
  ! 008H:MakeStr(msg,255,Literal('8...insufficient memory'));
  ! 009H:MakeStr(msg,255,Literal('9...invalid memory block address'));
  ! 00AH:MakeStr(msg,255,Literal('10...invalid environment'));
  ! 00BH:MakeStr(msg,255,Literal('11...invalid format'));
  ! 00CH:MakeStr(msg,255,Literal('12...invalid access code'));
  ! 00DH:MakeStr(msg,255,Literal('13...invalid data'));
```

```
! 00FH:MakeStr(msg,255,Literal('15...invalid drive'));
! 010H:MakeStr(msg,255,
        Literal('16...attempt to remove current directory'));
! 011H:MakeStr(msg,255,Literal('17...not same device'));
! 012H:MakeStr(msg,255,Literal('18...no more files'));
! 013H:MakeStr(msg,255,Literal('19...disk is write protected'));
! 014H:MakeStr(msg,255,Literal('20...unknown unit'));
! 015H:MakeStr(msg,255,Literal('21...device is not ready'));
! 016H:MakeStr(msg,255,Literal('22...unknown command'));
! 017H:MakeStr(msg,255,Literal('23...data error (CRC)'));
! 018H:MakeStr(msg,255,Literal('24...bad request structure length'));
! 019H:MakeStr(msg,255,Literal('25...invalid seek operation'));
! 01AH:MakeStr(msg,255,Literal('26...unknown media type'));
! 01BH:MakeStr(msg,255,Literal('27...sector not found'));
! 01CH:MakeStr(msg,255,Literal('28...printer not ready'));
! 01DH:MakeStr(msg,255,Literal('29...write fault'));
! 01EH:MakeStr(msg,255,Literal('30...read fault'));
! 01FH:MakeStr(msg,255,Literal('31...general failure'));
! 020H:MakeStr(msg,255,Literal('32...sharing violation'));
! 021H:MakeStr(msg,255,Literal('33...lock violation'));
! 022H:MakeStr(msg,255,Literal('34...disk change invalid'));
! 023H:MakeStr(msg,255,Literal('35...FCB unavailable'));
! 024H:MakeStr(msg,255,Literal('36...Sharing buffer overflow'));
! 032H:MakeStr(msg,255,Literal('50...network request not supported'));
! 033H:MakeStr(msg,255,Literal('51...remote computer not listening'));
! 034H:MakeStr(msg,255,Literal('52...duplicate name on network'));
! 035H:MakeStr(msg,255,Literal('53...network name not found'));
! 036H:MakeStr(msg,255,Literal('54...network busy'));
! 037H:MakeStr(msg,255,Literal('55...network device no longer exists'));
! 038H:MakeStr(msg,255,Literal('56...Net BIOS command limit exceeded'));
! 039H:MakeStr(msg,255,Literal('57...Network adapter hardware error'));
! 03AH:MakeStr(msg,255,Literal('58...incorrect response from network'));
! 03BH:MakeStr(msg,255,Literal('59...unexpected network error'));
! 03CH:MakeStr(msg,255,Literal('60...incompatible remote adapter'));
! 03DH:MakeStr(msg,255,Literal('61...print queue full'));
! 03EH:MakeStr(msg,255,Literal('62...not enough space for print file'));
! 03FH:MakeStr(msg,255,Literal('63...print file was deleted'));
! 040H:MakeStr(msg,255,Literal('64...network name was deleted'));
! 041H:MakeStr(msg,255,Literal('65...access denied'));
! 042H:MakeStr(msg,255,Literal('66...network device type incorrect'));
! 043H:MakeStr(msg,255,Literal('67...network name not found'));
! 044H:MakeStr(msg,255,Literal('68...network name limit exceeded'));
! 045H:MakeStr(msg,255,Literal('69...Net BIOS session limit exceeded'));
! 046H:MakeStr(msg,255,Literal('70...temporarily paused'));
! 047H:MakeStr(msg,255,Literal('71...network request not accepted'));
! 048H:MakeStr(msg,255,Literal('72...print/disk redirection paused'));
! 050H:MakeStr(msg,255,Literal('80...file already exists'));
! 052H:MakeStr(msg,255,Literal('82...cannot make directory'));
! 053H:MakeStr(msg,255,Literal('83...critical error handler failure'));
! 054H:MakeStr(msg,255,Literal('84...too many redirections'));
! 055H:MakeStr(msg,255,Literal('85...duplicate redirection'));
! 056H:MakeStr(msg,255,Literal('86...invalid password'));
! 057H:MakeStr(msg,255,Literal('87...invalid parameter'));
! 058H:MakeStr(msg,255,Literal('88...network device fault'));
  (* ---- NON-DOS error messages ---------------------- *)
! 0B0H:MakeStr(msg,255,Literal('176...mount correct diskette'));
! 0B1H:MakeStr(msg,255,
        Literal('177...no room on disk, record may be incomplete'));
! 0C0H:MakeStr(msg,255,
        Literal('192...modem not responding, check modem'));
! 0C1H:MakeStr(msg,255,
        Literal('193...communications adapter not installed'));
```

Fig. 10-1 continued

```
  ! OC2H:MakeStr(msg,255,Literal('194...communication data error'));
  ! OC3H:MakeStr(msg,255,Literal('195...communication buffer overflow'));
   ELSE MakeStr(msg,255,Literal('0...undefined error'));
   END;
 Insert(Literal('Msg '),msg,1);
 IF (StrLen(dsname) <> 0)
   THEN
      Concat(Literal('...('),msg);
      Concat(dsname,msg);
      Concat(Literal(')...'),msg);
   END;
 Message(msg,Literal('F1 = Continue'),
             msgframe,wait,nullcset,easciis,eascii,kbchar);
 IF (kbchar = break)
   THEN Cancel(procname,dsname,2,ioerr);
   ELSE IF (NOT comeback)
     THEN Cancel(procname,dsname,1,ioerr);
     END;
   END;
 ClearStr(msg);
 END RptIOErr;


PROCEDURE RptIOS;
(*  This routine is not known outside this module.  It sits on the DOS
    Critical Error Vector, and is called by DOS whenever an error is to be
    reported.
*)
TYPE
  HDRPTR  = POINTER TO DEVHEAD;
  DEVHEAD = RECORD
    next     : HDRPTR;
    attrib   : WORD;
    strat    : WORD;
    entry    : WORD;
    name     : ARRAY [1..8] OF CHAR;
    END;
CONST
  dortrn = TRUE;
  bit7 = 7;    bit15 = 15;
VAR
  i:CARDINAL;
  error:BYTE;
  direg,axreg,bpreg,sireg:WORD;
  hdrptr:HDRPTR;
  a:ADDRESS;
BEGIN
  CODE(50H);              (* PUSH AX *)
  CODE(51M);              (* PUSH BX *)
  CODE(52H);              (* PUSH CX *)
  CODE(53H);              (* PUSH DX *)
  CODE(56H);              (* PUSH SI *)
  CODE(57H);              (* PUSH DI *)
  CODE(1EH);              (* PUSH DS *)
  CODE(06H);              (* PUSH ES *)
  GETREG(DI,direg);
  GETREG(AX,axreg);
  GETREG(BP,bpreg);
  GETREG(SI,sireg);
  a.SEGMENT:=CARDINAL(bpreg);    a.OFFSET :=CARDINAL(sireg);
  hdrptr:=a;
```

```
i:=CARDINAL(direg) + 0013H;
error:=LoByte(i);
IF (bit7 IN BITSET(axreg)) AND (bit15 IN BITSET(hdrptr^.attrib))
  THEN
      RptIOErr(error,Literal(hdrptr^.name),
                              Literal('RptIOS'),dortrn);
  ELSE
    IF (error = BYTE(02H)) OR (error = BYTE(22H))
      THEN error:=BYTE(0B0H);
      END;
    RptIOErr(error,vols[ORD(LoByte(axreg))],
                              Literal('RptIOS'),dortrn);
  END;
CODE(07H);              (* POP ES    *)
CODE(1FH);              (* POP DS    *)
CODE(5FH);              (* POP DI    *)
CODE(5EH);              (* POP SI    *)
CODE(5BH);              (* POP DX    *)
CODE(5AH);              (* POP CX    *)
CODE(59H);              (* POP BX    *)
CODE(58H);              (* POP AX    *)
CODE(89H,0ECH);        (* MOV SP,BP *)
CODE(5DH);              (* POP BP    *)
CODE(0CFH);            (* IRET      *)
END RptIOS;

VAR
  i:CARDINAL;
BEGIN
  SetVectr(0024H,ADDRESS(RptIOS));
  MakeCSet(FixStr(Literal("fk1*brea")),easciis);
  FOR i:=0 TO HIGH(vols) DO
    MakeStr(vols[i],2,Literal(' :'));
    SetChar(vols[i],1,CHR(ORD('A')+i));
    END;
END EL1001.
```

Library thinks is in the device. The contents of this array is initialized in EL1001 to only include the device designator. Routines in EL1001 update these values when appropriate.

The process of defining error messages is one area where different versions of DOS are somewhat inconsistent. Back in DOS 1.0, there were only a dozen or so errors that DOS would detect and report. Some of the BIOS routines, particularly the disk handler, would signal a few more. As DOS grew, and its capabilities and complexities grew, the number of errors it would detect also expanded. Eventually, MicroSoft created a special DOS function call to help a program understand and deal with errors. Interrupt 21H, function 59H, is the "GET EXTENDED ERROR" routine. Because this function does not operate under DOS 2.0 and 2.1, it is not implemented in the Library.

If you were certain that your programs would only be used with DOS 3.0 or later, you might be tempted to rewrite *RptIOS* so that it used the DOS "GET EXTENDED ERROR" function to gather more complete information on the error. Don't. The DOS Technical Reference Manual specifically states that any routine used to replace the DOS critical error handler should avoid using any DOS functions beyond 0CH. As *RptIOS* is currently written, none of the routines it requires violates this restriction.

The I/O Primitives

To implement the I/O system, you need a half-dozen TYPE definitions and a collection of primitive routines. All of these items are exported by EL1002, shown in Fig. 10-2. EL1002 is quite a large module and is the primary reason that the error-handling routines were put in a separate module.

IOTYPES. The IOTYPES required by the I/O system are explained in detail by the comments in Fig. 8-2. The individual routines in the remainder of this chapter will give many examples for using these types, but the FMODE type might require some additional explanation.

In standard Pascal, there are two routines that are used to begin access to a file: RESET, and REWRITE. Essentially, RESET is used for an Input file; REWRITE is for an Output file. If a file does not exist, RESET doesn't care, it simply returns with an end-of-file indication immediately. REWRITE blithely assumes that regardless of whether the file exists, you want to write over whatever was there. The FileSystem module suggested by Wirth for Modula-2 expands on these operations, but FileSystem still requires the programmer to identify whether a file is opened for "reading," "writing," or "modifying." When I deal with files, I am usually more concerned with whether or not the file exists (or should exist) before my program starts messing with it.

There are times when I want to say, "If a file by this name exists, tell the user he has a problem, otherwise, go ahead and create the file." To accomplish this in standard Pascal, you would have first RESET the file in question, check to see if EOF is true immediately, and then either inform the user or REWRITE the file. There are times when you need to determine if a file already exists, so that if it doesn't, you can initialize some control variables. Again, in standard Pascal, it's a several-step process. The FileSystem module would have much the same problem.

The FMODE type is intended to allow a program to state explicitly whether or not a file should exist before it is accessed. Note that nothing in EL1002 says anything about whether a file is opened for reading or writing. The general philosophy of the Etling I/O system says *all* files are opened for input and output. While not all files fall in this category, the majority of files in an interactive commercial program are what would classically be called direct access files. A *direct-access file* uses a key or record number to allow a program to go directly to a specific location in the file without being forced to read from the beginning. In essence, DOS requires all direct-access files to be opened for both input and output. (This does cause some problems with Local Area Networks applications. Refer to the "DoOpen" routine for further information.)

Static I/O Variables and Constants. The routines in the EL1002 module require a single static variable for their operation. The data type, FID, and its associated FIDPTR are used to construct a chain of file definitions within the module. The static variable, *frstfid,* is used to anchor that chain. Because *frstfid* is used by other modules in the EL10 series, it is exported from EL1002.

EL1002 also defines and exports a collection of hexidecimal values used for setting or testing the attribute bytes associated with DOS files. Attribute bytes are also discussed in the DOS Technical Reference Manual.

Although most of the routines in EL1002 are exported, only two are normally used outside of the EL10 series of modules. To understand the operation of the

Fig. 10-2. Basic I/O routines.

```
DEFINITION MODULE EL1002;
    FROM SYSTEM IMPORT    WORD,BYTE,ADDRESS;
    FROM EL0401 IMPORT    STRING;
    FROM EL0503 IMPORT    LONGCARD;
    EXPORT QUALIFIED      FMODE,OPENKIND,DISP,LINECNTRL,LOCCNTRL,FIDPTR,FID,
                          DrvNmbr,FindHndl,DoClose,SetDTA,MountVol,FixName,
                          DoOpen,DoCreate,DoDel,DoSet,ClsFile,OpnFile,DoGet,
                          DoPut,FindDS,frstfid,nowrite,hidden,sysfile,volume,
                          subdir,archive;

TYPE
(* Non-Standard IO types. *)
    FMODE     = (newfile,oldfile,makenew,makeold,append);
    OPENKIND  = (insist,tryonce);
    DISP      = (clsonly,clsanddel);
    LINECNTRL = (endline,noendline,rtrnend,nortrnend);
    LOCCNTRL  = (setpostn,usepostn,seteof);
(* These type definitions are used by the IO control routines defined
   within the ETLING library.
```

FMODE refers to the status a file must have when it is first opened by
a program.

newfile ...   The file must not exist on the volume. A new file
               with the indicated name will be created.
oldfile ...   The file must exist on the volume.
makenew ...   If a file with the indicated name already exists on
               the volume, it will be deleted and a new file created.
makeold ...   If a file with the indicated name already exists on the
               volume, it will be used, otherwise a new file will be
               created.
append ...   Just like MAKEOLD, except that if the file exists, its file
               pointer will be set to the end of the file before any new
               data is written.

OPENKIND defines how error conditions should be treated when opening a
file.

insist ... Do not return to caller until file can be opened
            successfully.
tryonce ... Return to caller after one attempt to open file, regardless
            of error conditions.

DISP defines how a file should be handled after it is closed.

clsonly ... Simply close the file.
clsanddel . Close the file, then delete it from the directory.

LINCNTRL is used to control whether or not the Carriage Return / Line
Feed sequence is included in the read or write operation on a DOS text
file.

endline ... Write CR/LF after end of line.
noendline . Do not write the CR/LF after end of line.
rtrnend ... Include the CR/LF in the line read from a file.
nortrnend . Do not include the CR/LF in a read.

LOCCNTRL specifies how the file pointer is to be set before accessing a
file randomly.

setpostn .. Set the file pointer to the position indicated.

Fig. 10-2 continued

```
  usepostn .. Use the current file pointer position.
  seteof  ... Set the file pointer to the byte right after the end of file.  *)
  FIDPTR = POINTER TO FID;
  FID = RECORD
    nxtfid : FIDPTR;
    handle : WORD;
    ddname : STRING;
    END;
VAR
  frstfid  : FIDPTR;
  vols     : ARRAY [0..25] OF STRING;
CONST
(* These constants define bit patterns for testing the attribute bits
   associated with a file.  *)
  nowrite = 0001H;   hidden = 0002H;   sysfile = 0004H;   volume = 0008H;
  subdir  = 0010H;   archive = 0020H;
PROCEDURE DrvNmbr(dsname:STRING):CARDINAL;
(* This routine will convert the drive letter to a number.  If the dsname
   specified does not have a device, this routine will insert the current
   default drive in the name.  *)
PROCEDURE FindHndl(ddname:STRING; VAR lastfid,thisfid:FIDPTR):BOOLEAN;
(* This routine will search the list of file definitions to locate the
   file handle associated with the specified ddname.  If the file handle is
   not defined, the function will return FALSE.  *)
PROCEDURE DoClose(handle:WORD);
(* This routine will close the file associated with the indicated file
   handle.  If the close is un-successful, the routine will call Cancel. *)
PROCEDURE SetDTA(newdta:ADDRESS;VAR olddta:ADDRESS);
(* This routine will set the current DTA (disk transfer area) to the
   ADDRESS specified by newdta.  The DTA in effect when the routine is
   called will be returned in olddta.  *)
PROCEDURE MountVol(volname:STRING;askfirst:BOOLEAN);
(* This routine will ensure that the correct disk or diskette is mounted in
   the device associated with volname.  If, on entry, askfirst = TRUE, the
   user will be instructed to mount the correct volume...otherwise, the
   routine will check the device immediately.  Control will not return to
   the caller until the device is mounted.  *)
PROCEDURE FixName(dsname,volname:STRING);
(* This routine will fix up the dsname and separate out the volname, if one
   is specified.  If dsname includes the '!' character, each occurrence
   will be replaced with the value of the DIRNAME parameter defined for the
   main program.  The routine expects dsname to be in the form of an ASCIIZ
   string.  *)
PROCEDURE FindDS(ddname,dsname:STRING);
(* This routine will locate the dsname associated with ddname.  If the
   corresponding name entry cannot be found in the program parameters,
   dsname will equal ddname on return.  *)
PROCEDURE DoOpen(dsname:STRING; VAR handle:WORD;access:BYTE):BYTE;
(* This routine will attempt to open the file associated with dsname.  The
   results of the attempt will be returned as the function value.  The file
   will be opened using the DOS access specified by access, and, if the
   open is successful, the file handle will be returned in handle.  *)
PROCEDURE DoCreate(dsname:STRING;VAR handle:WORD):BYTE;
(* This routine will attempt to create a new entry in the directory
   associated with dsname.  If a similar file already exists, it will be
   truncated by this call.  If the call is successful, the file handle will
   be returned in handle.  The results of the call will be returned as the
   function value.  *)
PROCEDURE DoDel(dsname:STRING);
(* This routine will delete the file associated with dsname from the
   appropriate directory.  If the delete is unsuccessful, the routine will
```

```
       call Cancel.  *)
PROCEDURE DoSet(method:BYTE;handle,rlen:WORD; VAR rnmbr:LONGCARD);
(* This routine will set the file pointer for the specifed handle according
   to method:
        method = 0, The file will be set to the location specified by
                    rlen * (rnmbr - 1).
        method = 1, The file will be set to its current location
                    plus rlen * (rnmbr - 1).
        method = 2, The file will be set to the end of file plus
                    rlen * (rnmbr - 1).
   If an error occurs, this routine will call Cancel.  Otherwise, on
   return, rnmbr will point to the new record number.  *)
PROCEDURE ClsFile(ddname:STRING;how:DISP);
(* This routine will close the file associated with ddname and update its
   place in the directory accordingly.  If how = clsanddel, the file will
   be deleted from the directory, regardless of whether the file was ever
   opened.  Otherwise, a call to close a file that has not been opened is
   ignored.  If ddname = '*.*', ALL open files will be closed.  Note that
   it is good policy to close files after writing a series of records to
   ensure that the directory is properly updated.  If the file is left
   open, and the program is aborted or the user swaps diskettes, the
   directory could be corrupted.  *)
PROCEDURE OpnFile(ddname:STRING;VAR opnmode:FMODE;
                             VAR ioerr:BYTE;how:OPENKIND);
(* This routine will open the file associated with ddname.  If a program
   parameter whose parmid matches ddname exists, the corresponding parmval
   will be used as the file's dsname;  otherwise, ddname will be used for
   dsname.  opnmode indicates what status the file must have to be
   opened...it will return either newfile or oldfile to indicate if the
   file was created.  If the file is already open, the call is simply
   ignored.  If how = tryonce, only one attempt will be made to open the
   file and ioerr will return with a DOS error code indicating the success
   or failure of the attempt.  Otherwise, the routine will not return to
   the caller until the file can be opened.  Note that the general format
   for a file definition established via program parameters is:

        <ddname>=<dsname>[,<volumename>]


   If <volumename> is given, the device associated with <dsname> will be
   checked to verify that there is a file named <volumename> present on the
   device, BEFORE <dsname> is opened or closed.  *)
PROCEDURE DoGet(thisfid:FID;length:WORD;buf:ADDRESS):WORD;
(* This routine will attempt to transfer length bytes from the current
   position of the file associated with handle.  If an error occurs the
   routine will call Cancel and terminate.  Otherwise, the function value
   will return indicating the number of bytes actually transferred.  If on
   return, DoGet = 0, the end of file has been reached.  *)
PROCEDURE DoPut(thisfid:FID;length:WORD;buf:ADDRESS);
(* This routine will attempt to transfer length bytes to the file
   associated with handle at the current location of the file pointer.  If
   an error occurs, the routine will call Cancel and terminate the program.
   Note that if length bytes cannot be written, the routine assumes that
   the disk is full and cancels with the appropriate error.  *)
END EL1002.


IMPLEMENTATION MODULE EL1002;
   FROM SYSTEM IMPORT     ADR,BYTE,WORD,ADDRESS;
   FROM Storage IMPORT    ALLOCATE,DEALLOCATE;
   FROM EL0301 IMPORT     ByWord,LoByte,HiByte;
   FROM EL0303 IMPORT     equal,less,greater;
   FROM EL0304 IMPORT     fk1,fk10;
```

Fig. 10-2 continued

```
   FROM EL0401 IMPORT    STRING,CHRPTR,ChrPtr,nullstr,StrChar,SetChar,SetLen,
                         CopyStr,Literal,MakeStr,ClearStr,StrLen;
   FROM EL0402 IMPORT    Delete,Insert,Concat;
   FROM EL0403 IMPORT    MatchStr,Positn;
   FROM EL0404 IMPORT    FixStr;
   FROM EL0503 IMPORT    LONGCARD,LongCard,lczero,lcone,
                         SubLCard,MulLCard,AddLCard,DivLCard,ComLCard;
   FROM EL0701 IMPORT    carryflg,Interupt;
   FROM EL0801 IMPORT    FindParm;
   FROM EL0805 IMPORT    FixParm;
   FROM EL0906 IMPORT    Cancel,abortfrm;
   FROM EL1001 IMPORT    RptIOErr,vols;
CONST
  doscall = 21H;
PROCEDURE DrvNmbr(dsname:STRING):CARDINAL;
VAR
  device:CHAR;
  axreg,bxreg,cxreg,dxreg,dsreg,esreg,direg,sireg,flags:WORD;
BEGIN
  IF (StrChar(dsname,2) = ':')
    THEN
      device:=StrChar(dsname,1);
      IF (device < 'a')
        THEN RETURN CARDINAL(ORD(device) - ORD('A'));
        ELSE RETURN CARDINAL(ORD(device) - ORD('a'));
        END;
    ELSE
      axreg:=ByWord(19H,00H);
      Interupt(doscall,axreg,bxreg,cxreg,dxreg,
                                    dsreg,esreg,direg,sireg,flags);
      device:=CHR(ORD('A')+ORD(LoByte(axreg)));
      Insert(Literal(' :'),dsname,1);
      SetChar(dsname,1,device);
      RETURN CARDINAL(ORD(LoByte(axreg)));
    END;
  END DrvNmbr;
PROCEDURE FindHndl(ddname:STRING;VAR lastfid,thisfid:FIDPTR):BOOLEAN;
VAR
  done:BOOLEAN;
BEGIN
  done:=FALSE;
  thisfid:=frstfid;
  lastfid:=NIL;
  WHILE (thisfid <> NIL) AND (NOT done) DO
    IF (MatchStr(ddname,thisfid^.ddname,1,1,0) = equal)
      THEN done:=TRUE;
      ELSE
        lastfid:=thisfid;
        thisfid:=thisfid^.nxtfid;
      END;
    END;
  RETURN done;
  END FindHndl;
PROCEDURE DoClose(handle:WORD);
VAR
  axreg,bxreg,cxreg,dxreg,dsreg,esreg,direg,sireg,flags:WORD;
BEGIN
  axreg:=ByWord(3EH,00H);
  bxreg:=handle;
```

```
      Interupt(doscall,axreg,bxreg,cxreg,dxreg,
                            dsreg,esreg,direg,sireg,flags);
      IF (carryflg IN BITSET(flags))
        THEN Cancel(Literal('DoClose'),nullstr,4,LoByte(axreg));
        END;
      END DoClose;


PROCEDURE SetDTA(newdta:ADDRESS;VAR olddta:ADDRESS);
VAR
  axreg,bxreg,cxreg,dxreg,dsreg,esreg,direg,sireg,flags:WORD;
BEGIN
  axreg:=ByWord(2FH,OOH);
  Interupt(doscall,axreg,bxreg,cxreg,dxreg,
                              dsreg,esreg,direg,sireg,flags);
  olddta.SEGMENT:=CARDINAL(esreg);
  olddta.OFFSET:=CARDINAL(bxreg);
  axreg:=ByWord(1AH,OOH);
  dsreg:=WORD(newdta.SEGMENT);
  dxreg:=WORD(newdta.OFFSET);
  Interupt(doscall,axreg,bxreg,cxreg,dxreg,dsreg,esreg,direg,sireg,flags);
  END SetDTA;


PROCEDURE MountVol(volname:STRING;askfirst:BOOLEAN);
CONST
  dortrn = TRUE;
VAR
  dta:ARRAY [0..127] OF BYTE;
  newdta,olddta,nameadr:ADDRESS;
  iostat:BYTE;
  i:CARDINAL;
  axreg,bxreg,cxreg,dxreg,dsreg,esreg,direg,sireg,flags:WORD;
BEGIN
  IF (askfirst)
    THEN RptIOErr(0B0H,volname,Literal('MountVol'),dortrn);
    END;
  i:=DrvNmbr(volname);
  ClearStr(vols[i]);
  MakeStr(vols[i],0,volname);
  newdta:=ADR(dta[0]);
  SetDTA(newdta,olddta);
  nameadr:=ChrPtr(volname,1);
  REPEAT
    axreg:=ByWord(4EH,OOH);
    dsreg:=WORD(nameadr.SEGMENT);
    dxreg:=WORD(nameadr.OFFSET);
    cxreg:=WORD(volume);
    Interupt(doscall,axreg,bxreg,cxreg,dxreg,
                                dsreg,esreg,direg,sireg,flags);
    IF (carryflg IN BITSET(flags))
                    AND (axreg = WORD(0012H))
      THEN
        axreg:=ByWord(4EH,OOH);
        dsreg:=WORD(nameadr.SEGMENT);
        dxreg:=WORD(nameadr.OFFSET);
        cxreg:=WORD(hidden + sysfile + subdir);
        Interupt(doscall,axreg,bxreg,cxreg,dxreg,
                                dsreg,esreg,direg,sireg,flags);
      END;
    IF (NOT (carryflg IN BITSET(flags)))
      THEN iostat:=BYTE(OOH);
      ELSE
```

Fig. 10-2 continued

```
        IF (axreg = WORD(0002H)) OR (axreg = WORD(0015H))
                     OR (axreg = WORD(001FH))
          THEN iostat:=BYTE(OBOH);
          ELSE iostat:=LoByte(axreg);
          END;
        RptIOErr(iostat,volname,Literal('MountVol'),dortrn);
      END;
    UNTIL (iostat = BYTE(00H));
  SetDTA(olddta,olddta);
  END MountVol;

PROCEDURE FixName(dsname,volname:STRING);
VAR
  i,j,k:CARDINAL;
BEGIN
  SetLen(dsname,StrLen(dsname)+1);
  SetChar(dsname,StrLen(dsname),CHR(0));
  FixParm(dsname);
  i:=DrvNmbr(dsname);
  i:=Positn(Literal(','),dsname,1);
  IF (i = 0)
    THEN CopyStr(nullstr,volname);
    ELSE
      j:=Positn(Literal(':'),dsname,1);
      CopyStr(dsname,volname);
      Delete(volname,j+1,i-j);
      Delete(dsname,i,StrLen(dsname)-i);
                            (* leave Chr(0) attached *)
    END;
  END FixName;


PROCEDURE FindDS(ddname,dsname:STRING);
BEGIN
  IF (NOT FindParm(ddname,dsname))
    THEN CopyStr(ddname,dsname);
    END;
  END FindDS;

PROCEDURE DoOpen(dsname:STRING;VAR handle:WORD;access:BYTE):BYTE;
VAR
  nameadr:ADDRESS;
  axreg,bxreg,cxreg,dxreg,dsreg,esreg,direg,sireg,flags:WORD;
BEGIN
  nameadr:=ChrPtr(dsname,1);
  axreg:=ByWord(3DH,access);
  axreg:=WORD(BITSET(axreg) + {6});
  dxreg:=WORD(nameadr.OFFSET);
  dsreg:=WORD(nameadr.SEGMENT);
  Interupt(doscall,axreg,bxreg,cxreg,dxreg,dsreg,esreg,direg,sireg,flags);
  IF (carryflg IN BITSET(flags))
    THEN RETURN LoByte(axreg);
    ELSE
      handle:=axreg;
      RETURN 00H;
    END;
  END DoOpen;

PROCEDURE DoCreate(dsname:STRING;VAR handle:WORD):BYTE;
VAR
  nameadr:ADDRESS;
  axreg,bxreg,cxreg,dxreg,dsreg,esreg,direg,sireg,flags:WORD;
BEGIN
```

```
        nameadr:=ChrPtr(dsname,1);
        axreg:=ByWord(3CH,OOH);
        cxreg:=WORD(OOOOH);
        dxreg:=WORD(nameadr.OFFSET);
        dsreg:=WORD(nameadr.SEGMENT);
        Interupt(doscall,axreg,bxreg,cxreg,dxreg,dsreg,esreg,direg,sireg,flags);
        IF (carryflg IN BITSET(flags))
          THEN RETURN LoByte(axreg);
          ELSE
            handle:=axreg;
            RETURN OOH;
          END;
        END DoCreate;

PROCEDURE DoDel(dsname:STRING);
VAR
    nameadr:ADDRESS;
    axreg,bxreg,cxreg,dxreg,dsreg,esreg,direg,sireg,flags:WORD;
    i:CARDINAL;
BEGIN
    i:=Positn(Literal('NUL'),dsname,1);
    IF (i > O)
      THEN IF (i > 3) OR (i + 3 <> StrLen(dsname))
        THEN i:=O;
        END;
      END;
    IF (i = O)
      THEN
        nameadr:=ChrPtr(dsname,1);
        axreg:=ByWord(41H,OOH);
        dxreg:=WORD(nameadr.OFFSET);
        dsreg:=WORD(nameadr.SEGMENT);
        Interupt(doscall,axreg,bxreg,cxreg,dxreg,
                                      dsreg,esreg,direg,sireg,flags);
        IF (carryflg IN BITSET(flags))
          THEN IF (axreg <> WORD(OOO2H))
            THEN Cancel(Literal('DoDel'),dsname,4,LoByte(axreg));
            END;
          END;
      END;
    END DoDel;

PROCEDURE DoSet(method:BYTE;handle,rlen:WORD;VAR rnmbr:LONGCARD);
VAR
    axreg,bxreg,cxreg,dxreg,dsreg,esreg,direg,sireg,flags:WORD;
    junk:BOOLEAN;
    rem,rlc:LONGCARD;
BEGIN
    IF (ComLCard(rnmbr,lczero) <> equal)
      THEN
        SubLCard(rnmbr,lcone,rnmbr);
        rlc.locard:=CARDINAL(rlen);
        rlc.hicard:=O;
        MulLCard(rnmbr,rlc,rnmbr);
      END;
    axreg:=ByWord(42H,method);
    bxreg:=handle;
    cxreg:=WORD(rnmbr.hicard);
    dxreg:=WORD(rnmbr.locard);
    Interupt(doscall,axreg,bxreg,cxreg,dxreg,dsreg,esreg,direg,sireg,flags);
    IF (carryflg IN BITSET(flags))
      THEN Cancel(Literal('DOSET'),nullstr,2,LoByte(axreg));
```

Fig. 10-2 continued

```
      END;
    rnmbr.hicard:=CARDINAL(dxreg);
    rnmbr.locard:=CARDINAL(axreg);
    IF (ComLCard(rnmbr,lczero) <> equal)
      THEN DivLCard(rnmbr,rlc,rnmbr,rem);
      END;
    AddLCard(rnmbr,lcone,rnmbr);
    END DoSet;

PROCEDURE ClsFile(ddname:STRING;how:DISP);
CONST
    dontask  = FALSE;
VAR
    lastfid,thisfid,nextfid:FIDPTR;
    gothndl:BOOLEAN;
    dsname,volname:STRING;
BEGIN
    MakeStr(volname,255,nullstr);
    MakeStr(dsname,255,nullstr);
    IF (MatchStr(Literal('*.*'),ddname,1,1,0) = equal)
      THEN
        WHILE (frstfid <> NIL) DO
          ClsFile(frstfid^.ddname,how);
          END;
      ELSE
        gothndl:=FindHndl(ddname,lastfid,thisfid);
        IF (gothndl) OR (how = clsanddel)
          THEN
            FindDS(ddname,dsname);
            FixName(dsname,volname);
            IF (StrLen(volname) <> 0)
              THEN MountVol(volname,dontask);
              END;
            IF (gothndl)
              THEN
                DoClose(thisfid^.handle);
                IF (lastfid = NIL)
                  THEN frstfid:=thisfid^.nxtfid;
                  ELSE lastfid^.nxtfid:=thisfid^.nxtfid;
                  END;
                ClearStr(thisfid^.ddname);
                DISPOSE(thisfid);
              END;
            IF (how = clsanddel)
              THEN
                DoDel(dsname);
              END;
            END;
      END;
    ClearStr(volname);
    ClearStr(dsname);
    END ClsFile;

PROCEDURE OpnFile(ddname:STRING;VAR opnmode:FMODE;
                    VAR ioerr:BYTE;how:OPENKIND);
CONST
    dontask = FALSE;
    dortrn = TRUE;
VAR
    lastfid,thisfid:FIDPTR;
    dsname,volname:STRING;
```

```
      rnmbr:LONGCARD;
BEGIN
  MakeStr(volname,255,nullstr);
  MakeStr(dsname,255,nullstr);
  IF (FindHndl(ddname,lastfid,thisfid))
    THEN ioerr:=BYTE(OOH);
    ELSE
      NEW(thisfid);
      thisfid^.nxtfid:=frstfid;
      MakeStr(thisfid^.ddname,0,ddname);
      FindDS(ddname,dsname);
      FixName(dsname,volname);
      IF (StrLen(volname) <> 0)
        THEN MountVol(volname,dontask);
        END;
      REPEAT
        CASE opnmode OF
          newfile:
            ioerr:=DoOpen(dsname,thisfid^.handle,0);
            IF (ioerr = BYTE(02H))
              THEN ioerr:=DoCreate(dsname,thisfid^.handle);
              ELSE IF (ioerr = BYTE(OOH))
                THEN ioerr:=BYTE(50H);
                END;
              END;
        ! oldfile:ioerr:=DoOpen(dsname,thisfid^.handle,2);
        ! makenew:
            ioerr:=DoOpen(dsname,thisfid^.handle,0);
            IF (ioerr = BYTE(OOH)) OR (ioerr = BYTE(02H))
              THEN
                IF (ioerr = BYTE(OOH))
                  THEN
                    DoClose(thisfid^.handle);
                    DoDel(dsname);
                  END;
                ioerr:=DoCreate(dsname,thisfid^.handle);
                IF (ioerr = BYTE(OOH))
                  THEN opnmode:=newfile;
                  END;
              END;
        ! makeold:
            ioerr:=DoOpen(dsname,thisfid^.handle,2);
            IF (ioerr = BYTE(OOH))
              THEN
                opnmode:=oldfile;
              ELSE
                IF (ioerr = BYTE(02H))
                  THEN
                    ioerr:=DoCreate(dsname,thisfid^.handle);
                    IF (ioerr = BYTE(OOH))
                      THEN opnmode:=newfile;
                      END;
                  END;
              END;
        ! append:
            ioerr:=DoOpen(dsname,thisfid^.handle,2);
            IF (ioerr = BYTE(OOH))
              THEN
                opnmode:=oldfile;
                rnmbr.hicard:=0;
                rnmbr.locard:=0;
                DoSet(02H,thisfid^.handle,1,rnmbr);
```

Fig. 10-2 continued

```
                ELSE
                  IF (ioerr = BYTE(02)) OR (ioerr = BYTE(05))
                    THEN
                      ioerr:=DoCreate(dsname,thisfid^.handle);
                      IF (ioerr = BYTE(OOH))
                        THEN opnmode:=newfile;
                        END;
                    END;
                END;
            ELSE
              Cancel(Literal('OpnFile'),ddname,4,0);
            END;
        IF (how = insist) AND (ioerr <> BYTE(OOH))
          THEN RptIOErr(ioerr,dsname,Literal('OpnFile'),dortrn);
          END;
        UNTIL (ioerr = BYTE(OOH)) OR (how = tryonce);
      IF (ioerr <> BYTE(OOH))
        THEN
          ClearStr(thisfid^.ddname);
          DISPOSE(thisfid);
        ELSE
          frstfid:=thisfid;
        END;
    END;
  ClearStr(volname);
  ClearStr(dsname);
  END OpnFile;

PROCEDURE DoGet(thisfid:FID;length:WORD;buf:ADDRESS):WORD;
VAR
  axreg,bxreg,cxreg,dxreg,dsreg,esreg,direg,sireg,flags:WORD;
BEGIN
  axreg:=ByWord(3fh,OOh);
  bxreg:=thisfid.handle;
  cxreg:=length;
  dxreg:=WORD(buf.OFFSET);
  dsreg:=WORD(buf.SEGMENT);
  Interupt(doscall,axreg,bxreg,cxreg,dxreg,dsreg,esreg,direg,sireg,flags);
  IF (carryflg IN BITSET(flags))
    THEN Cancel(Literal('DoGet'),nullstr,4,LoByte(axreg));
    END;
  RETURN axreg;
  END DoGet;

PROCEDURE DoPut(thisfid:FID;length:WORD;buf:ADDRESS);
CONST
  notback = FALSE;
VAR
  axreg,bxreg,cxreg,dxreg,dsreg,esreg,direg,sireg,flags:WORD;
BEGIN
  axreg:=ByWord(40h,OOh);
  bxreg:=thisfid.handle;
  cxreg:=length;
  dxreg:=WORD(buf.OFFSET);
  dsreg:=WORD(buf.SEGMENT);
  Interupt(doscall,axreg,bxreg,cxreg,dxreg,dsreg,esreg,direg,sireg,flags);
  IF (carryflg IN BITSET(flags))
    THEN Cancel(Literal('DoPut'),nullstr,4,LoByte(axreg));
    END;
  IF (axreg <> length)
    THEN RptIOErr(OB1H,thisfid.ddname,Literal('DoPut'),notback);
```

```
      END;
   END DoPut;

BEGIN
   frstfid:=NIL;
END EL1002.
```

routines in EL1002, it is best to look at them in the sequence they would appear in a program. Before a file can be used within a program, it has to be opened. Wirth's FileSystem module defines several routines to open files, but in the Etling Library, all opens are done by a single routine: *OpnFile*.

OpnFile. *OpnFile* doesn't get upset if you call it to open a file that is already open. *OpnFile* also does not change the status of a file that is already open. *OpnFile* determines whether a file is open or not by calling *FindHndl* (discussed later in this chapter). If *OpnFile* is asked to open file for which the DOS handle has already been established, *OpnFile* sets *ioerr* to indicate "no error" and simply returns.

If a file is not open, *OpnFile* will build a new entry in the FID chain anchored by *frstfid*. It uses *FindDS* to locate a corresponding program parameter for *dsname*, or if one cannot be found, copy *ddname* into *dsname*. In either case, *OpnFile* calls *FixName* to parse and separate *dsname* into its component parts. When control returns from *FixName*, *OpnFile* will test to see if *FixName* extracted a value for *volname* from *dsname*. If so, *OpnFile* will call *MountVol* to be certain the correct volume is mounted.

The main body of *OpnFile* is a REPEAT loop with an embedded CASE statement that, depending on the value of *opnmode*, attempts to open the file in the proper fashion. All fives cases use *DoOpen* to actually open the file.

To successfully open a file with *opnmode = newfile*, *DoOpen* is told to open the file with "Read Access," which implies that the file must already exist. If the file does not exist, *DoOpen* will return with an error code of 02H, signaling "file not found." That is exactly what the *newfile* mode requires, so *DoCreate* is called to create the file. If *DoOpen* returns with no error (equal to zero), the file already exists, so *ioerr* is set to zero. Any other error is ignored for the moment.

For *oldfile* mode to be successful, the file is opened with "Read/Write Access." *DoOpen* will indicate the status of this operation.

A file defined as *makenew* is opened first as "Read Access." If an error of 02H (file not found) is indicated, *OpnFile* knows that it can safely call *DoCreate* to make a new file. However, if *DoOpen* finds no error, it means that the file has to be closed and deleted first. If *DoCreate* returns with no error, *opnmode* is set to *newfile* so that the calling routine knows that a new file was indeed created.

A *makeold* mode tries to open the file using "Read/Write Access." If the file already exists, this operation will return with no error, so *opnmode* will be set to *oldfile* to inform the caller. If the file does not exist, *DoOpen* will signal "file not found," and, *DoCreate* will be called to create it. If *DoCreate* returns no error, *opnmode* will be set to *newfile*.

The *append* file mode operates just like *makeold*, except that if the call to *DoOpen* returns no error, *OpnFile* knows that the file already exists and *DoSet* is called to position the file pointer to the end of the file.

Any other value for *opnmode* will cause the CASE statement to call *Cancel* and terminate the program.

If any of the file operations in the REPEAT loop detect an error for which they are not prepared to compensate, *OpnFile* looks at <u>how</u> to determine what to do. If *how* = *insist*, *OpnFile* will retain control in the REPEAT loop until the error is corrected. Otherwise, *OpnFile* returns to the caller with *ioerr* set to reflect the error it encountered, under the assumption that the caller will deal with the error condition.

OpnFile uses many of the other routines in module EL1002. The following paragraphs discuss these routines.

FindHndl. *FindHndl* is responsible for determining the DOS file handle associated with the file defined by *ddname*, assuming that the file has already been opened, and therefore, a corresponding entry has been made in the list of FID records. If the file has not yet been opened, *FindHndl* will return FALSE.

FixName. The first thing *FixName* does is concatenate a CHR(0) on the end of *dsname*. This makes *dsname* into an ASCIIZ string. ("ASCIIZ" is the name that the IBM Technical Reference Manual applies to a string of ASCII characters that is terminated by a byte containing a binary zero.) *FixName* then calls *FixParm* to fill in any replaceable program parameters that might be in *dsname*. Next, it calls *DrvNmbr* (see below), and when control returns, looks for a comma. If one occurs, the routine will extract *volname* from *dsname*. The <device> field from *dsname* is included in *volname*, but any associated <path> is not. The *volname* can be in a different directory.

DrvNmbr. The *DrvNmbr* function attempts to extract the letter corresponding to the <device> from *dsname*. If *dsname* does not specify <device>, *DrvNmbr* will call DOS function 19H to collect a number, returned in the lobyte of AX, corresponding to the current default disk device. The appropriate characters will be inserted into *dsname*. Regardless of the source of the <device>, *DrvNmbr* returns a value equal to the drive number. This value translates as 0=A:, 1=B:, etc.

MountVol. Before doing anything else, *MountVol* checks *askfirst* to determine if it should prompt the user with I/O message 176 before checking the specified drive. (Message 176 says "Mount correct diskette . . .") These are times when *MountVol* is used to tell the user to mount a particular diskette, and other times when it is used to make sure the correct diskette is still mounted. In the latter case, the prompt is not necessary, unless the correct diskette has been removed.

MountVol is responsible for maintaining the table of volume IDs contained in the *vols* array. Regardless of whether a new volume is mounted or not, *MountVol* clears the current value of *vols[i]*, where *i:=DrvNmbr(volname)*, and recreates this element using *volname* as the new volume identifier.

MountVol uses the *SetDTA* routine to change the data transfer area currently in effect for the program, and then establishes a REPEAT loop to check the volume. The REPEAT loop will not terminate until the correct file is found on the appropriate device. *MountVol* does not actually open the file named *volname*; it only looks at the directory and attempts to locate the first file whose name matches *volname*. To accomplish this, *MountVol* calls *Interupt* to invoke DOS function 4EH. This particular function uses the CX register to specify the "attribute" of the file. The attribute is stored in byte 11 of the directory entry. It is used by DOS to determine how the file may be treated by executing programs. Each bit in the attribute has a special meaning, and the appropriate values are shown in the Etling Library member named IOCONSTS.

For whatever reason, DOS permits function 4EH to do a generic search for any type of file but the DOS volume label. If you want the function to locate the label, you must search for the volume attribute by itself, and that is why *MountVol* actually does two calls to function 4EH. Unfortunately, under DOS 2.0 and 2.1 that doesn't work, and there does not appear to be any way to locate the label short of reading the entire directory and looking through it manually. MicroSoft apparently found, and fixed, this bug in DOS 3.0. Calls using the attribute work as advertised with that release of the operating system.

On the other hand, DOS 3.2 introduces another problem. The DOS SHARE command, introduced in DOS 3.1, was modified under 3.2 to use the volume label. If DOS 3.2 SHARE is loaded on a machine whose diskette drives are capable of detecting when the diskette drive door is opened (such as an IBM AT's high density drive), and a file is opened on that diskette, DOS will use the volume label to ensure that the user does not change the diskette until the file is closed. If the diskette does not have a volume label, SHARE doesn't interfere. If you use standard files as your "volume labels" (exactly what the Etling Library routines were intended for), SHARE won't cause any problems.

SetDTA. When DOS loads a program into memory and constructs the program segment prefix, it sets up a 128-byte area at location 80H that is called the DTA or data transfer area. The *data transfer area* is a small buffer area that DOS uses to contain data for file reads and writes when it performs I/O using FCBs (file control blocks). The FCB concept was built into early versions of DOS. Beginning with DOS 2.0, DOS introduced the file handle approach. If a program does not use any of the DOS functions that require an FCB, the DTA is only used as a buffer for the remaining characters from the command line that invokes the program (see the discussion for GetParms in Chapter 6).

Most of the routines in the Etling Library do use file handles, but there are a few instances where a routine might cause the DTA to be referenced. Because the default DTA contains the program parameters, any routine that does use the DTA must first call *SetDTA* to change the DTA address so that it points to another location. *SetDTA* first uses DOS function 2FH to retrieve the current DTA address (which it passes back to the caller in *olddta*) and then the routine uses function 1AH to set the new address.

DoOpen. The workhorse of the *OpnFile* sequence is the *DoOpen* routine, but its operation is really quite simple. It uses DOS function 3DH and the comments are self-explanatory. Beginning with DOS 3.0, the access byte passed to function 3DH is also used to specify the "file-sharing" mode to be used with the file. Although these modes are defined in terms of "read access" and "write access," they do not necessarily correspond to whether the file is read or written. Because almost all files referenced by the Library are opened as "read/write," *DoOpen* sets the file-sharing mode for all files for read/write. This could cause problems with some networks: files open in this mode are not buffered locally but are buffered by the file server. If a file has many short records (like a text file that is read one byte at a time), the application runs rather slowly.

DoCreate. The routine that will create a new file, *DoCreate*, uses DOS function 3CH and is also quite simple.

DoClose. *DoClose* is the routine that releases a file handle. Note that *DoClose* does not return an error. Instead, it calls *Cancel* to terminate the program if DOS function 3EH cannot close the file.

DoDel. Given a file's <ddname>, the *DoDel* routine will delete it from the directory using its <dsname>. When a file is deleted, DOS does not actually remove it from the directory, nor does it clear the space that the file occupied. The directory entry for a deleted file is marked with an E5H in the first byte of the area normally used by the file name. Assuming that you do not do something to reuse the file's space (such as opening a new file in its place or expanding an existing file), you can "undelete" a file by setting that first byte back to its original character.

DoSet. The *DoSet* routine is responsible for setting the position of a file's pointer. The *file pointer* is nothing more than a double word value indicating the next byte, in the file, that will be accessed by a read or write operation.

In case you are wondering, with a double-word file pointer the theoretical limit on the size of file that DOS can handle is somewhere around 4.2 <u>trillion</u> bytes. However, the practical limit is restricted to size of the DOS partition. The size of the DOS partition is limited by the size of the file allocation table (FAT) that the DOS FDISK program creates which is, in turn, related to the size of a disk cluster. The practical file limit is therefore about 32 million bytes. (That is also the maximum amount of disk space DOS can currently handle. A disk with more than 32 megabytes must be split into several "partitions." Each additional partition must be accessed by a DOS device driver.)

The DOS functions that use FCBs control the file pointer in terms of a record number and a record length. DOS 2.0 functions (the ones that the Etling routines use) dispense with the record concept entirely and permit the caller to ignore such things. This means that a calling routine can access the same file with several different record definitions, and the DOS functions will not interfere. For an example of this, refer to the way LISTER (in Chapter 2, Fig. 2-3) uses DEF files. For more information on the way *DoSet* works, refer to the discussion on *SetFLoc* later in this chapter.

Primitive Data Transfer

There are two routines in the EL1002 module that are not called from within the module but are included because they represent the most primitive form of file data transfer done by the Etling routines. There are two of these routines (one for input, one for output) and they both will call *Cancel* to terminate the program if they detect errors during their operations. They perform a cancel, rather than reporting the error to the user and asking for instruction, because by the time they are called, all user-correctable conditions have been detected and reported. If an error occurs when these routines are in control, the error must be something like a parity check or bad disk sector — something that the user can do nothing about. (Here is an example of "coincidental cohesion" that has merit; while these routines do not call and are not called by any other routines in EL1002, any other module that does I/O must include reference to these routines. Where else should they go?)

DoGet. The routine that handles all file input in the Etling Library is called *DoGet,* and it uses DOS function 3FH to read bytes from a file. Note that the bytes are read into an area identified as an ADDRESS. The actual byte, record, or buffer can be located anywhere in core.

DoPut. The output routine, *DoPut* uses DOS function 40H.

Terminating File Access

Whenever a Modula-2 program terminates, DOS automatically severs the connection between the program and any files it may have opened. If you need to terminate access to a file before the program shuts down, use *ClsFile*.

ClsFile. The last routine in the I/O Nucleus is *ClsFile*, which uses *DoClose*, the I/O primitive discussed earlier in this chapter used to break the connection between a file and a program. If the file has only been used for input, the DOS function that *DoClose* uses will dispose of the buffers associated with the file, and release the file handle. If the file has been used for output, the DOS function will write the contents of the file's buffers to the disk, dispose of the buffers, and update the file's directory entry before releasing the handle. Because of the file buffers, output files have special problems.

When an executing program writes to a file, the data that it writes is in reality only copied into a buffer maintained by DOS in memory. The contents of this buffer will not be written to the disk until the buffer is full. In other words, you cannot be absolutely certain that all of your data is indeed recorded on the disk until the file is closed. If your program is interrupted by the user (with Ctrl-Break or by a reboot) or a power failure occurs, the file might be left open. If that happens, some data might be left in memory. For this reason, it is good practice to close files periodically. The ideal circumstance would be to close a file after every record is written, but in most instances this severely degrades a program's performance.

Output files have another problem. If the file is on a removable medium, like a diskette, it is possible that the user would change diskettes before DOS got around to writing the files buffers. When this happens, you not only have a corrupted file, but DOS will occasionally rewrite the entire diskette directory. You can wind up with a completely unreadable diskette, because the directory recorded on it does not accurately reflect the files it contains. Again, to prevent that, call *ClsFile* at regular intervals. Like *OpnFile, ClsFile* will call *MountVol* before accessing the directory; this will ensure that the correct diskette is mounted before the directory is written.

Note that *ClsFile* can be called with **ddname = Literal('*.*')** which will close all open files in the program. To accomplish this, *ClsFile* goes through the chain of FIDs pointed to by *frstfid* and calls itself to close each *ddname* it finds.

DATA TRANSFER ROUTINES

The routines in the I/O nucleus are primarily concerned with attaching a file to a program. The actual transfer of data to or from a file is controlled by another series of routines. These routines are divided into two categories; routines that deal with text; and routines that deal with records. As a general rule, either kind of routine can be used on any file. As far as the Etling routines are concerned, there is nothing in a file that defines it as being text oriented or record oriented. The sole criterion that determines which set of routines you use is how do you want your program to deal with the file.

Etling routines do not handle any kind of data conversion. For example, you can use the following syntax in normal Pascal:

```
VAR
    I:INTEGER;
BEGIN
    I:=100;
    WRITELN(OUTPUT,I);
```

The Pascal compiler will generate instructions to convert the binary number stored in integer format in variable "I" into a sequence of ASCII characters for display on the OUTPUT file. The Etling routines do not provide this service. The Etling routines move bytes of data, unconverted, from memory to files (and vice versa). If you need to convert an integer to ASCII, you must provide the code to do that. The routines in Chapter 6 will help with whatever conversions you require. In most commercial applications, I have found that much data conversion can be avoided without sacrificing efficiency.

Text Routines

Usually, you use the text routines on files that contain lines. Each line contains human language words and is terminated by a carriage-return/line-feed sequence. The carriage return/line-feed sequence is a fairly universal end-of-line signal to text editors or word processing programs. It is, as its name implies, composed of a CHR(13) followed by a CHR(10). In hexidecimal, this is a 0D0AH.

GetLine. The routine that reads a line of text from a file is shown in Fig. 10-3. (EL1003.) This routine, *GetLine*, uses *DoGet* to read a character at a time from the file associated with *ddname*. The characters are returned to the calling program as a STRING named *line*. I normally use a STRING capable of containing 256 characters, but any length from 1 to *maxstr* will still operate correctly. The logic in *GetLine* looks for a carriage-return/lines-feed sequence, but it will treat any other occurrence of those two characters (e.g., CR*CR, LF*CR, etc.) as normal data. If the STRING is filled to capacity before the carriage-return/line-feed sequence is detected, the routine still returns normally. Note that you can use *getcrlf* to tell the routine whether or not the carriage-return/line-feed sequence should be included in *line* on return.

For an example of using *GetLine* without returning the carriage-return/Line feed, see *ReadParm* in Fig. 8-2. The LISTER program in Fig. 2-3 uses *GetLine* the other way.

PutLine. The routine used to output text to a file is called *PutLine,* exported from EL1004 as it appears in Fig. 10-4. The *line* variable can actually contain up to *maxstr* characters. *PutLine* will not issue the carriage-return/line-feed sequence until you tell it. This allows you to code multiple *PutLine* calls before ending a line. For example, you can use *PutLine* to print a line on a printer:

```
PutLine(Literal('LPT1'),
            Literal('GENERAL LEDGER - FOR THE MONTH OF '),
                        noendline);
PutLine(Literal('LPT1'),SubStr(3,2,date),noendline);
PutLine(Literal('LPT1'),Literal('/'),noendline);
PutLine(Literal('LPT1'),SubStr(1,2,date),endline);
```

Fig. 10-3. Reading a file line by line.

```
DEFINITION MODULE EL1003;
   FROM EL0401 IMPORT      STRING;
   FROM EL1002 IMPORT      LINECNTRL;
   EXPORT QUALIFIED        GetLine;

PROCEDURE GetLine(ddname,line:STRING; getcrlf:LINECNTRL):BOOLEAN;
(* This routine will begin reading a character at a time from the current
   position of the file associated with ddname.  Characters will be
   inserted in LINE until a carriage return/line feed sequence is
   encountered, or, until line is full.  If getcrlf = rtrnend, the cr/lf
   sequence will be included in line.  On return, StrLen(line) will be set
   accordingly.  If GetLine returns FALSE, the file is at EOF.  *)
END EL1003.


IMPLEMENTATION MODULE EL1003;
   FROM SYSTEM IMPORT      ADR,WORD;
   FROM EL0304 IMPORT      cr,lf,deof;
   FROM EL0401 IMPORT      STRING,Literal,StrLen,StrSize,CopyStr,
                           nullstr,StrChar,SetChar,SetLen;
   FROM EL0402 IMPORT      Delete;
   FROM EL0906 IMPORT      Cancel;
   FROM EL1002 IMPORT      DoGet,FindHndl,FIDPTR,LINECNTRL;

PROCEDURE GetLine(ddname,line:STRING;getcrlf:LINECNTRL):BOOLEAN;
VAR
   done,eof:BOOLEAN;
   thisfid,lastfid:FIDPTR;
   buffer:CHAR;
BEGIN
   IF (NOT FindHndl(ddname,lastfid,thisfid))
     THEN Cancel(Literal('GetLine'),ddname,4,0);
     END;
   done:=FALSE;
   eof:=FALSE;
   CopyStr(nullstr,line);
   WHILE (NOT done) DO
     IF (DoGet(thisfid^,1,ADR(buffer)) = WORD(0))
       THEN
         done:=TRUE;
         eof:=TRUE;
         IF (StrLen(line) <> 0)
               AND (StrChar(line,StrLen(line)) = deof)
           THEN Delete(line,StrLen(line),1);
           END;
     ELSIF (StrLen(line) = StrSize(line))
       THEN done:=TRUE;
       ELSE
         SetLen(line,StrLen(line)+1);
         SetChar(line,StrLen(line),buffer);
         IF (buffer = lf) AND (StrLen(line) > 1)
               AND (StrChar(line,StrLen(line)-1) = cr)
           THEN
             done:=TRUE;
             IF (getcrlf = nortrnend) AND (StrLen(line) > 2)
               THEN Delete(line,StrLen(line)-1,2);
               ELSE CopyStr(nullstr,line);
               END;
           END;
       END;
     END;
   RETURN NOT eof;
   END GetLine;

END EL1003.
```

Fig. 10-4. Writing lines.

```
DEFINITION MODULE EL1004;
   FROM EL0401 IMPORT    STRING;
   FROM EL1002 IMPORT    LINECNTRL;
   EXPORT QUALIFIED      PutLine;

PROCEDURE PutLine(ddname,line:STRING;putcrlf:LINECNTRL);
(* The contents of line will be written to the file associated with ddname.
   If putcrlf = endline, a carriage return / line feed sequence will be
   written after the end of the line.   *)
END EL1004.

IMPLEMENTATION MODULE EL1004;
   FROM SYSTEM IMPORT    ADR;
   FROM EL0304 IMPORT    cr,lf;
   FROM EL0401 IMPORT    STRING,StrLen,Literal,CHRPTR,ChrPtr;
   FROM EL0906 IMPORT    Cancel;
   FROM EL1002 IMPORT    DoPut,FindHndl,FIDPTR,LINECNTRL;

VAR
   crlf : ARRAY [1..2] OF CHAR;

PROCEDURE PutLine(ddname,line:STRING; putcrlf:LINECNTRL);
VAR
   thisfid,lastfid:FIDPTR;
BEGIN
   IF (NOT FindHndl(ddname,lastfid,thisfid))
     THEN Cancel(Literal('PutLine'),ddname,4,0);
     END;
   DoPut(thisfid^,StrLen(line),ChrPtr(line,1));
   IF (putcrlf = endline)
     THEN DoPut(thisfid^,2,ADR(crlf));
     END;
   END PutLine;

BEGIN
   crlf[1] := cr;
   crlf[2] := lf;
END EL1004.
```

Record Routines

Record routines are generally used on files that organize bytes into data fields. A repeating pattern of data fields defines a record.

Record-oriented routines permit a file to be accessed by record number, although in truth the routines translate this value into a byte offset from the beginning of the file and use the offset to actually position the file pointer. The offset is calculated by multiplying the length of record by the record number − 1. Using an offset value, the first record in a file starts at byte 0. Because the offset is calculated by each routine each time it is called, the record length you supply can vary from one access to another.

The record number associated with a record oriented file is defined as a four-byte number—a LONGCARD. This would imply that a file could contain 4096 K (64K times 64K) records, and each record could be 32K bytes long. That would produce a very big file. Again, the actual limit on the size of file is really 32 megabytes.

GetRcrd. The routine that reads data from a file in record-oriented format is called *GetRcrd* (Fig. 10-5). *GetRcrd* is the only routine in EL1005 and includes a call to *DoSet,* so it can be used to position the file pointer before reading a record. In other words, *GetRcrd* can be used to access a file randomly. The *locate* parameter determines how the file pointer will be positioned. If, on entry, *locate* = *usepostn,* the file will be accessed sequentially. If *locate* = *setpostn,* the record identified by *lastnmbr*

Fig. 10-5. Reading a record.

```
DEFINITION MODULE EL1005;
   FROM SYSTEM IMPORT    WORD,ADDRESS;
   FROM EL0401 IMPORT    STRING;
   FROM EL0503 IMPORT    LONGCARD;
   FROM EL1002 IMPORT    LOCCNTRL;
   EXPORT QUALIFIED      GetRcrd;

PROCEDURE GetRcrd(ddname:STRING;loccntrl:LOCCNTRL;
                  lastnmbr:LONGCARD;VAR nmbr:LONGCARD;
                  lentoget:WORD;VAR lengot:WORD; rcrd:ADDRESS):BOOLEAN;
(* This routine will attempt to read lentoget bytes from the file
   associated with ddname.  If, on entry, locate = setpostn, the file will
   be set to the byte indicated by:

        lentoget * (lastnmbr - 1)

   before the read is attempted.  Otherwise the file will be left at the
   position it was last set to.  If, in either case, the file is set to end
   of file, the function will return FALSE.  On return, lengot will
   indicate the number of bytes actually transferred.  *)
END EL1005.

IMPLEMENTATION MODULE EL1005;
   FROM SYSTEM IMPORT    ADR,ADDRESS,WORD;
   FROM EL0401 IMPORT    STRING,Literal;
   FROM EL0503 IMPORT    AddLCard,lcone,LONGCARD;
   FROM EL0906 IMPORT    Cancel;
   FROM EL1002 IMPORT    DoSet,DoGet,FindHndl,FIDPTR,LOCCNTRL;

PROCEDURE GetRcrd(ddname:STRING;locate:LOCCNTRL;
                  lastnmbr:LONGCARD;VAR nmbr:LONGCARD;
                  lentoget:WORD;VAR lengot:WORD;rcrd:ADDRESS):BOOLEAN;
VAR
  thisfid,lastfid:FIDPTR;
BEGIN
  IF (NOT FindHndl(ddname,lastfid,thisfid))
    THEN Cancel(Literal('GetLine'),ddname,4,0);
    END;
  IF (locate = setpostn)
    THEN DoSet(00H,thisfid^.handle,lentoget,lastnmbr);
    END;
  lengot:=DoGet(thisfid^,lentoget,rcrd);
  IF (lengot = WORD(0))
    THEN RETURN FALSE;
    ELSE
      AddLCard(lastnmbr,lcone,nmbr);
      RETURN TRUE;
      END;
  END GetRcrd;

END EL1005.
```

will be returned. For example, here is how *GetRcrd* can be used to read the retrieve the records from a file sequentially:

```
CONST
    lentoget = 100;
VAR
    nmbr:LONGCARD;
    lengot:WORD;
BEGIN
    nmbr:=0;
    WHILE (GetRcrd(ddname,usepostn,nmbr,nmbr,
                        lentoget,lengot,rcrd)) DO
        (*
                . . . . whatever
        *)
```

Because you would normally use the sequential access mode to read a file with the record length fixed at some value, *GetRcrd* should indicate that the end of file has been reached (by returning false) at the same time that *lengot* returns equal to zero. *GetRcrd* does not insist on this condition, however. Your program must decide what to do if this should happen.

When you use *GetRcrd* in the random access mode, be aware that the *DoSet* will call *Cancel* if you try to set the file to a record beyond what DOS thinks is the end of file.

You should also be aware that while *GetRcrd* will transfer a record from a file to any memory address, you should be careful when using that ability. For example, it would appear that you could use *GetRcrd* to read a screen image file directly into display memory. While this does indeed work most of the time, there are machines where the result will not be what you expected. If you try this on a PC with an expansion unit attached, and the display adapter happens to be in the expansion unit (rather than the system unit IBM recommends), the additional delay required to access memory outside the main box causes the first portion of the screen image to disappear. (One of my development machines is set up that way; it took me awhile to figure out what went wrong.)

PutRcrd. The record output routine is named *PutRcrd* and is exported from EL1006, shown in Fig. 10-6. Like *GetRcrd*, *PutRcrd* can be used to access a file either randomly or sequentially.

RECORD SUPPORT

While the Library routines do not insist on a record structure for a file, there are a few routines that make dealing with records easier. These routines are all collected in EL1007 and the module begins with a couple of special types.

RCRD and RFLDLIST. These two types define standard record support variables. A RCRD is a POINTER TO RCRDAREA. A RCRDAREA is intended to be allocated dynamically and contains a CARDINAL that defines the size of the area and an ARRAY OF BYTE. A RFLDLIST is a POINTER TO RFLDAREA. A RFLDAREA is also

Fig. 10-6. Writing a record.

```
DEFINITION MODULE EL1006;
    FROM SYSTEM IMPORT     WORD,ADDRESS;  .
    FROM EL0401 IMPORT     STRING;
    FROM EL0503 IMPORT     LONGCARD;
    FROM EL1002 IMPORT     LOCCNTRL;
    EXPORT QUALIFIED       PutRcrd;

PROCEDURE PutRcrd(ddname:STRING;locate:LOCCNTRL; lastnmbr:LONGCARD;
                       VAR nmbr:LONGCARD; len:WORD;rcrd:ADDRESS);
(* If, on entry, locate = setpostn, the file will be set to the byte
   indicated by:

           lentoget * (lastnmbr - 1)

   before the write is attempted.  Otherwise the file will be left at the
   position it was last set to.  len bytes from rcrd will be transferred to
   the file.  On return, nmbr will be updated accordingly.  *)
END EL1006.

IMPLEMENTATION MODULE EL1006;
    FROM SYSTEM IMPORT     ADR,ADDRESS,WORD;
    FROM EL0401 IMPORT     STRING,Literal;
    FROM EL0503 IMPORT     AddLCard,lcone,LONGCARD;
    FROM EL0906 IMPORT     Cancel;
    FROM EL1002 IMPORT     DoSet,DoPut,FindHndl,FIDPTR,LOCCNTRL;

PROCEDURE PutRcrd(ddname:STRING;locate:LOCCNTRL;lastnmbr:LONGCARD;
                        VAR nmbr:LONGCARD;len:WORD;rcrd:ADDRESS);
VAR
  thisfid,lastfid:FIDPTR;
BEGIN
  IF (NOT FindHndl(ddname,lastfid,thisfid))
    THEN Cancel(Literal(' PutRcrd'),ddname,4,0);
    END;
  IF (locate = setpostn)
    THEN DoSet(00H,thisfid^.handle,len,lastnmbr);
    END;
  DoPut(thisfid^,len,rcrd);
  AddLCard(lastnmbr,lcone,nmbr);
  END PutRcrd;

END EL1006.
```

Fig. 10-7. Standard record operations.

```
DEFINITION MODULE EL1007;
    FROM SYSTEM IMPORT     ADDRESS,BYTE;
    EXPORT QUALIFIED       maxrlen,maxrflds,RCRD,RFLDLIST,MakeRcrd,
                           ClrRcrd,MakRFlds,ClrRFlds,MovTRcrd,MovFRcrd;

CONST
  maxrlen = 32767;    maxrflds = 16383;
TYPE
  RCRDAREA = RECORD
    rcrdlen : CARDINAL;
    area    : ARRAY [1..maxrlen] OF BYTE;
    END;
  RCRD = POINTER TO RCRDAREA;
  RFLDAREA = RECORD
    nmbrflds : CARDINAL;
    loc      : ARRAY [1..maxrflds] OF CARDINAL;
    len      : ARRAY [1..maxrflds] OF CARDINAL;
    END;
  RFLDLIST = POINTER TO RFLDAREA;
```

Fig. 10-7 continued
```
PROCEDURE MakeRcrd(rcrdlen:CARDINAL;VAR rcrd:RCRD);
(* This procedure will create a record definition in memory capable of
   containing up to rcrdlen bytes.  *)
PROCEDURE ClrRcrd(VAR rcrd:RCRD);
(* This procedure will clear the record defintion specifed by rcrd.  *)
PROCEDURE MakRFlds(nmbrflds:CARDINAL;VAR rfldlist:RFLDLIST);
(* This routine will create field definition controls in memory capable of
   defining nmbrflds fields.  *)
PROCEDURE ClrRFlds(VAR rfldlist:RFLDLIST);
(* This routine clears the field definition controls specified by
   rfldlist.  *)
PROCEDURE MovFRcrd(VAR rcrd:RCRD;VAR rfldlist:RFLDLIST;
                        dest:ADDRESS;length,fldnmbr:CARDINAL);
(* This routine will move data from the rcrd^.area to the ADDRESS defined
   by dest.  The location of the data in the rcrd^.area is controlled by
   rfldlist^.loc[fldnmbr].  The number of bytes moved is length (If length
   = 0, length will be set to rfldlist^.len[fldnmbr]).  If length is less
   than rfldlist^.len[fldnmbr], excess bytes in the record will be ignored.
   If length is greater than rfldlist^.len[fldnmbr], the extra bytes in
   dest will be set to blank.  The variable associated with dest must be
   large enough to contain the data.  *)
PROCEDURE MovTRcrd(VAR rcrd:RCRD;VAR rfldlist:RFLDLIST;
                        source:ADDRESS;length,fldnmbr:CARDINAL);
(* This routine will move data from the ADDRESS defined by source into
   rcrd^.area[rfldlist^.loc^[fldnmbr]].  The number of bytes moved is
   controlled by rfldlist^.len[fldnmbr].  If length is less than
   rfldlist^.len[fldnmbr] then the remaining bytes in the rcrd^.area field
   will be set to blanks.  *)
END EL1007.


IMPLEMENTATION MODULE EL1007;
  FROM SYSTEM IMPORT    ADDRESS,BYTE,TSIZE;
  FROM Storage IMPORT   ALLOCATE,DEALLOCATE;
  FROM EL0302 IMPORT    MovByteL,FillByte;


PROCEDURE ClrRcrd(VAR rcrd:RCRD);
BEGIN
  DEALLOCATE(rcrd,TSIZE(CARDINAL)+rcrd^.rcrdlen);
  rcrd:=NIL;
  END ClrRcrd;


PROCEDURE MakeRcrd(rcrdlen:CARDINAL;VAR rcrd:RCRD);
BEGIN
  ALLOCATE(rcrd,TSIZE(CARDINAL)+rcrdlen);
  rcrd^.rcrdlen:=rcrdlen;
  END MakeRcrd;


PROCEDURE ClrRFlds(VAR rfldlist:RFLDLIST);
BEGIN
  DEALLOCATE(rfldlist,
            2*rfldlist^.nmbrflds*TSIZE(CARDINAL)+TSIZE(CARDINAL));
  rfldlist:=NIL
  END ClrRFlds;


PROCEDURE MakRFlds(nmbrflds:CARDINAL;VAR rfldlist:RFLDLIST);
BEGIN
  ALLOCATE(rfldlist,2*nmbrflds*TSIZE(CARDINAL)+TSIZE(CARDINAL));
  rfldlist^.nmbrflds:=nmbrflds;
  END MakRFlds;


PROCEDURE MovFRcrd(VAR rcrd:RCRD;VAR rfldlist:RFLDLIST;
                        dest:ADDRESS;length,fldnmbr:CARDINAL);
```

```
VAR
  w:CARDINAL;
BEGIN
  IF (length = 0) OR (length > rfldlist^.len[fldnmbr])
    THEN w:=rfldlist^.len[fldnmbr];
    ELSE w:=length;
    END;
  MovByteL(rcrd^.area[rfldlist^.loc[fldnmbr]],dest^,0,0,w);
  IF (w < length)
    THEN FillByte(BYTE(' '),dest^,w,length-w);
    END;
  END MovFRcrd;

PROCEDURE MovTRcrd(VAR rcrd:RCRD;VAR rfldlist:RFLDLIST;
                       source:ADDRESS;length,fldnmbr:CARDINAL);
VAR
  w:CARDINAL;
BEGIN
  IF (length = 0) OR (length > rfldlist^.len[fldnmbr])
    THEN w:=rfldlist^.len[fldnmbr];
    ELSE w:=length;
    END;
  MovByteL(source^,rcrd^.area[rfldlist^.loc[fldnmbr]],0,0,w);
  IF (w < rfldlist^.len[fldnmbr])
    THEN FillByte(BYTE(' '),rcrd^.area[rfldlist^.loc[fldnmbr]],
                            w,length-w);
    END;
  END MovTRcrd;

END EL1007.
```

intended to be a dynamic allocation, and it contains a counter and two ARRAY OF CARDINAL. Essentially, the RCRDAREA allocates the data area of a record and the RFLDAREA divides the area into individual fields. For each field, RFLDAREA.*loc[n]* defines the first byte of the field in the RCRDAREA, and RFLDAREA.*len[n]* specifies how many bytes are in the field.

These types provide a mechanism around a couple of "gotchas" in Modula-2. Standard Modula-2 allows the definition of a RECORD type, for example,

```
PERSON = RECORD
    firstname : ARRAY [1. .9] OF CHAR;
    initial   : CHAR;
    lastname : ARRAY [1. .20] OF CHAR;
    nmbrkids : CARDINAL;
    END;
```

How many bytes does this record contain? When you're using it in core, you probably don't care, but if you need to transfer it to or from a file, you have to figure it out. Depending on the Modula-2 package, you could come up with a different length. Some of the packages—the ones that do not support the BYTE type—insist that all variables and fields within a record begin on a WORD boundary. The PERSON record winds up 34 bytes long. On the other hand, some packages only insist that single BYTE fields be expanded to a full word. The "initial : CHAR " definition takes two bytes, but the *firstname* only requires nine, which leaves 33 bytes. Almost all the packages will insist that binary data—the CARDINAL field—be on a WORD boundary, which gives 32 bytes.

To avoid all this, use the types and routines in EL1007. A RCRDAREA can be an odd number of bytes. (The compiler might still round it off to a full word, but it doesn't matter.) Using the fields of the RFLDAREA, you can define fields that begin or end on a byte boundary with no trouble.

MakeRcrd and ClrRcrd. Use *MakeRcrd* and *ClrRcrd* to handle RCRDAREA definitions. Their operation is self-explanatory.

MakRFlds and ClrRflds. The routines that are used for RFLDAREA variables are called *MakRFld* and *ClrRFld*. The EL0201 module, defined back in Chapter 2, contains an example that uses these routines.

MovFRcrd and MovTRcrd. The routines that move data to or from a RCRDAREA are called *MovTRcrd* and *MovFRcrd,* respectively. Note that the source or destination of these movements is specified as an ADDRESS; any type variable at any location in memory can be used with these routines.

UTILITY I/O ROUTINES

The DOS functions have many I/O operations that standard Modula-2 does not implement. The Etling Library provides routines that access many of these functions, and the library adds a few things that even COMMAND.COM doesn't offer.

Avoiding Errors

The Etling Library offers two routines that are intended to prevent errors from occurring. In a commercial application, there are two conditions that spell disaster: using the wrong diskette, and running out of room on the right diskette. Here are the Etling routines that deal with these conditions.

ChkDisk. DOS function 36H provides a way of determining how much unoccupied space is available on a disk or diskette. The *ChkDisk* routine, shown in Fig. 10-8 (EL1008), gives an application program access to this function. *ChkDisk* will determine the amount of space remaining on the device associated with *ddname.* The number of free clusters on the device is returned in the variable, *remc.* To calculate the total number of bytes left, multiply *bytepers, secpers* and *remc.* The answer might require a LONGCARD variable.

Fig. 10-8. Check disk space.

```
DEFINITION MODULE EL1008;
    FROM SYSTEM IMPORT    WORD;
    FROM EL0401 IMPORT    STRING;
    EXPORT QUALIFIED      ChkDisk;

PROCEDURE ChkDisk(ddname:STRING; VAR secperc,remc,totc,bytepers:WORD);
(* This routine will return with values indicating the amount of free
   space remaining on the device associated with ddname.

        secperc  = Sectors per cluster.
        remc     = Remaining clusters.
        totc     = Total clusters on the device.
        bytepers = Byte per sector.
```

```
      If ddname does specify a valid device, the routine will call Cancel.   *)
END EL1008.

IMPLEMENTATION MODULE EL1008;
  FROM SYSTEM IMPORT    WORD;
  FROM EL0301 IMPORT    ByWord;
  FROM EL0401 IMPORT    STRING,Literal,nullstr,MakeStr,ClearStr;
  FROM EL0701 IMPORT    Interupt;
  FROM EL0906 IMPORT    Cancel;
  FROM EL1002 IMPORT    DrvNmbr,FindDS;

PROCEDURE ChkDisk(ddname:STRING;
                     VAR secperc,remc,totc,bytepers:WORD);
VAR
  dsname:STRING;
  ds,es,di,si,flags:WORD;
BEGIN
  MakeStr(dsname,255,nullstr);
  FindDS(ddname,dsname);
  secperc:=ByWord(36H,00H);          (*AX*)
  totc:=WORD(DrvNmbr(dsname)+1);     (*DX*)
  Interupt(21h,secperc,remc,bytepers,totc,ds,es,di,si,flags);
  IF (secperc = WORD(0FFFFH))
    THEN Cancel(Literal('ChkDisk'),dsname,4,0);
    END;
  ClearStr(dsname);
  END ChkDisk;

END EL1008.
```

ChkVol. The *ChkVol* routine, exported from EL1009 (Fig. 10-9), gives an application program access to the *MountVol* routine described earlier in this chapter. In an application that might read or write to diskettes, it is good practice to include a call to *ChkVol* before calling one of the file transfer routines, for example,

```
OpnFile(ddname,opnmode,ioerr,insist);
WHILE (not done) DO
    (*
          Whatever processing is required.
    *)
    ChkVol(ddname,ask);
    PutLine(ddname,line,endline);
    END;
```

Obviously, calls to *ChkVol* do take time. A program that includes this program fragment will run slower than a program that doesn't. However, if the amount of processing done in the program is such that the user could have time to remove a diskette and replace it with another, the *ChkVol* routine can avoid serious problems. The slight degradation in execution time is usually a minor inconvenience compared to the aggravation caused by scrambling a diskette.

The DOS Time Stamp

When DOS closes a file to which a program has written, it updates the date and time fields associated with the file in the directory. This happens every time a file that has been changed is closed. The date and time fields are very useful in tracking down

Fig. 10-9. Check volume ID.

```
DEFINITION MODULE EL1009;
  FROM EL0401 IMPORT    STRING;
  EXPORT QUALIFIED       ChkVol;

PROCEDURE ChkVol(ddname:STRING;askfirst:BOOLEAN);
(* This routine will make certain that the correct volume is mounted in the
   device associated with ddname.  If askfirst = TRUE, the user will be
   prompted to mount the volume before the first check is made.  Control
   does not return to the caller until the correct diskette is mounted.  *)
END EL1009.

IMPLEMENTATION MODULE EL1009;
  FROM EL0401 IMPORT    STRING,MakeStr,ClearStr,nullstr,StrLen;
  FROM EL1002 IMPORT    MountVol,FixName,FindDS;

PROCEDURE ChkVol(ddname:STRING;askfirst:BOOLEAN);
VAR
  dsname,volname:STRING;
  j:INTEGER;
BEGIN
  MakeStr(volname,255,nullstr);
  MakeStr(dsname,255,nullstr);
  FindDS(ddname,dsname);
  FixName(dsname,volname);
  IF (StrLen(volname) <> 0)
    THEN MountVol(volname,askfirst);
    END;
  ClearStr(volname);
  ClearStr(dsname);
  END ChkVol;

END EL1009.
```

bugs in a program, both while development is still under way and after the application has been released. You can use these fields to determine which version of your program is being used, or in what sequence data files were created. (Unfortunately, too many users, who do not have a clock card installed, simply skip over DOS's requests for DATE and TIME. Their system clock is seldom accurate, so the time stamp is not always as useful as it could be.)

The date and time fields in a DOS directory entry are allocated one word each. Obviously, to fit a value that says 13:30:37 on May 16, 1987 into two words, DOS must do some data manipulation. There are four routines in the Etling Library that will do this manipulation for a Modula-2 program. The routines are required by other library members to translate the DOS date and time fields, but they are also defined in the source library so that, if the need arises, an application program can also access them.

FDateToW and WToFDate. The routines that handle the file date are named *FDateToW* and *WToFDate*. *WToFDate* comes from EL1010 (Fig. 10-10), and *FDateToW* is exported from EL1011 (Fig. 10-11). The DOS date is compacted into a single word by using the bit pattern yyyyyyymmmmddddd. Bits 0 to 4 represent the day; bits 5 to 8 define the month; and bits 9 to 15 contain a number between 0 and 119. To translate bits 9 to 15 into a year value, add these bits to 1980. *FDateToW* will convert a string in

Fig. 10-10. Get a file time stamp.

```
DEFINITION MODULE EL1010;
  FROM EL0401 IMPORT    STRING;
  FROM EL0502 IMPORT    DATE,TIME;
  EXPORT QUALIFIED      WToFDate,WToFTime,GetFcdt;

PROCEDURE WToFDate(w:CARDINAL;VAR fdate:DATE);
(* This routine will convert the value of w, a word in the format used by
   DOS to store the date a file was last modified, into a string in the
   form yymmdd.  *)
PROCEDURE WToFTime(w:CARDINAL;VAR ftime:TIME);
(* This routine will convert the value of w, a word in the format used by
   DOS to store the time a file was last modified, into a string in the
   form hhmmss.  *)
PROCEDURE GetFcdt(ddname:STRING; VAR fdate:DATE;VAR ftime:TIME):BOOLEAN;
(* If the file associated with ddname does not exist, the function will
   return FALSE...otherwise the function will return TRUE and fdate and
   ftime will be set to the date and time that the file was last modified.
   fdate is in the form yymmdd.  ftime is in the form hhmmss.  *)
END EL1010.


IMPLEMENTATION MODULE EL1010;
  FROM SYSTEM IMPORT    WORD,BYTE;
  FROM EL0301 IMPORT    ByWord;
  FROM EL0401 IMPORT    STRING,nullstr,Literal,SubStr,
                        MakeStr,ClearStr,MoveStr;
  FROM EL0502 IMPORT    DATE,TIME;
  FROM EL0605 IMPORT    CarToStr;
  FROM EL0701 IMPORT    Interupt,carryflg;
  FROM EL0906 IMPORT    Cancel;
  FROM EL1002 IMPORT    FindHndl,OpnFile,FMODE,OPENKIND,DISP,ClsFile,FIDPTR;

PROCEDURE Land(w,p:WORD):CARDINAL;
BEGIN
  RETURN CARDINAL(BITSET(w) * BITSET(p));
  END Land;

PROCEDURE WToFDate(w:CARDINAL;VAR fdate:DATE);
VAR
  y,m,d:CARDINAL;
  str:STRING;
  i:CARDINAL;
BEGIN
  y:=w DIV 0200H;
  m:=Land(w,01E0H);
  m:=m DIV 0020H;
  d:=Land(w,001FH);
  y:=y+CARDINAL(1980);
  MakeStr(str,6,nullstr);
  ClearStr(str);
  CarToStr(y,6,str);
  MoveStr(SubStr(5,6,str),Literal(fdate),5);
  CarToStr(m,6,str);
  MoveStr(SubStr(5,6,str),Literal(fdate),3);
  CarToStr(d,6,str);
  MoveStr(SubStr(5,6,str),Literal(fdate),1);
  FOR i:=0 TO HIGH(fdate) DO
    IF (fdate[i] = ' ')
      THEN fdate[i]:='0';
      END;
    END;
  END WToFDate;
```

Fig. 10-10 continued

```
PROCEDURE WToFTime(w:CARDINAL;VAR ftime:TIME);
VAR
  h,m,s,i:CARDINAL;
  str:STRING;
BEGIN
  h:=w DIV 0800H;
  m:=Land(w,07E0H);
  m:=m DIV 0020H;
  s:=Land(w,001FH);
  MakeStr(str,6,nullstr);
  CarToStr(h,6,str);
  MoveStr(SubStr(5,6,str),Literal(ftime),1);
  CarToStr(m,6,str);
  MoveStr(SubStr(5,6,str),Literal(ftime),3);
  CarToStr(s,6,str);
  MoveStr(SubStr(5,6,str),Literal(ftime),5);
  FOR i:=0 TO HIGH(ftime) DO
    IF (ftime[i] = ' ')
      THEN ftime[i]:='0';
      END;
    END;
  ClearStr(str);
  END WToFTime;


PROCEDURE GetFcdt(ddname:STRING;VAR fdate:DATE;VAR ftime:TIME):BOOLEAN;
VAR
  ax,bx,cx,dx,ds,es,di,si,flags:WORD;
  lastfid,thisfid:FIDPTR;
  opnmode:FMODE;
  ioerr:BYTE;
BEGIN
  opnmode:=makeold;
  OpnFile(ddname,opnmode,ioerr,insist);
  IF (opnmode = newfile)
    THEN
      ClsFile(ddname,clsanddel);
      RETURN FALSE;
    ELSE
      IF (NOT FindHndl(ddname,lastfid,thisfid))
        THEN Cancel(Literal('GetFcdt'),ddname,4,0);
        END;
      ax:=ByWord(57H,00H);
      bx:=thisfid^.handle;
      cx:=WORD(0);
      dx:=WORD(0);
      Interupt(21h,ax,bx,cx,dx,ds,es,di,si,flags);
      IF (carryflg IN BITSET(flags))
        THEN Cancel(Literal('GetFcdt'),ddname,4,1);
        END;
      WToFDate(CARDINAL(dx),fdate);
      WToFTime(CARDINAL(cx),ftime);
      RETURN TRUE;
    END;
  END GetFcdt;


END EL1010.
```

Fig. 10-11. Set a file time stamp.

```
DEFINITION MODULE EL1011;
   FROM SYSTEM IMPORT    WORD;
   FROM EL0401 IMPORT    STRING;
   FROM EL0502 IMPORT    DATE,TIME;
   EXPORT QUALIFIED      FDateToW,FTimeToW,SetFcdt;

PROCEDURE FDateToW(VAR w:WORD;fdate:DATE);
(* This routine will convert the value of fdate, a string in the form
   yymmdd, into a single word in the format used by DOS to store the date a
   file was last modified.  *)
PROCEDURE FTimeToW(VAR w:WORD;ftime:TIME);
(* This routine will convert the value of ftime, a string in the form
   hhmmss, into a single word in the format used by DOS to store the time a
   file was last modified.  *)
PROCEDURE SetFcdt(ddname:STRING; fdate:DATE;ftime:TIME):BOOLEAN;
(* If the file associated with ddname does not exist, the function will
   return FALSE, otherwise the function will return TRUE, and the date and
   time stamp for the file will be set to the values indicated.  On entry,
   fdate has the form yymmdd;  ftime has the form hhmmdd.  *)
END EL1011.


IMPLEMENTATION MODULE EL1011;
   FROM SYSTEM IMPORT    WORD,BYTE;
   FROM EL0301 IMPORT    ByWord;
   FROM EL0401 IMPORT    STRING,Literal;
   FROM EL0502 IMPORT    DATE,TIME;
   FROM EL0701 IMPORT    Interupt,carryflg;
   FROM EL0906 IMPORT    Cancel;
   FROM EL1002 IMPORT    ClsFile,OpnFile,FMODE,OPENKIND,DISP,FIDPTR,FindHndl;

PROCEDURE FDateToW(VAR w:WORD; fdate:DATE);
VAR
   y,m,d:CARDINAL;
BEGIN
   y:=10*(ORD(fdate[1]) - ORD('0')) + ORD(fdate[2]) - ORD('0');
   IF (y < 80)
     THEN y:=y+2000;
     ELSE y:=y+1900;
     END;
   y:=y-1980;
   y:=y*CARDINAL(0400);
   m:=10*(ORD(fdate[3]) - ORD('0')) + ORD(fdate[4]) - ORD('0');
   m:=m*CARDINAL(0040);
   d:=10*(ORD(fdate[5]) - ORD('0')) + ORD(fdate[6]) - ORD('0');
   w:=WORD(BITSET(y) + BITSET(m));
   w:=WORD(BITSET(w) + BITSET(d));
   END FDateToW;

PROCEDURE FTimeToW(VAR w:WORD; ftime:TIME);
VAR
   h,m,s:CARDINAL;
BEGIN
   h:=10*(ORD(ftime[1]) - ORD('0')) + ORD(ftime[2]) - ORD('0');
   h:=h*CARDINAL(0800);
   m:=10*(ORD(ftime[3]) - ORD('0')) + ORD(ftime[4]) - ORD('0');
   m:=m*CARDINAL(0040);
   s:=10*(ORD(ftime[5]) - ORD('0')) + ORD(ftime[6]) - ORD('0');
   w:=WORD(BITSET(h) + BITSET(m));
```

Fig. 10-11 continued

```
   w:=WORD(BITSET(w) + BITSET(s));
   END FTimeToW;

PROCEDURE SetFcdt(ddname:STRING;fdate:DATE;ftime:TIME):BOOLEAN;
VAR
   ax,bx,cx,dx,ds,es,di,si,flags:WORD;
   lastfid,thisfid:FIDPTR;
   opnmode:FMODE;
   ioerr:BYTE;
BEGIN
   opnmode:=makeold;
   OpnFile(ddname,opnmode,ioerr,insist);
   IF (opnmode = newfile)
     THEN
       ClsFile(ddname,clsanddel);
       RETURN FALSE;
     ELSE
       IF (NOT FindHndl(ddname,lastfid,thisfid))
         THEN Cancel(Literal('SetFcdt'),ddname,4,0);
         END;
       ax:=ByWord(57H,01H);
       bx:=thisfid^.handle;
       FDateToW(dx,fdate);
       FTimeToW(cx,ftime);
       Interupt(21h,ax,bx,cx,dx,ds,es,di,si,flags);
       IF (carryflg IN BITSET(flags))
         THEN Cancel(Literal('SetFcdt'),ddname,4,1);
         END;
       RETURN TRUE;
     END;
   END SetFcdt;

END EL1011.
```

"YYMMDD" format into a single word in the DOS format. *WToFDate* will convert a word back into the "YYMMDD" format.

   FTimeToW and WToFTime. Figures 10-10 and Fig. 10-11 also show the routines that deal with the DOS file time field. These routines are called *FTimeToW* and *WToFTime*. *FTimeToW* converts a string containing a time in "hhmmss" format into the single word DOS requires. *WToFTime* will convert a word back the other way. The DOS time field assigns the bits of the time word using a hhhhhmmmmmmsssss pattern. Bits 0 to 4 contain the seconds; bits 5 to 10 the minutes; and bits 11 to 15 the hour at which the file was last changed. The number that represents seconds is actually in two second increments.

   SetFcdt and GetFcdt. To access the date and time fields for a file, use these routines. *SetFcdt* will change these fields for an existing file; *GetFcdt* will return the current values.

Locating the File Pointer

   SetFLoc. The *SetFLoc* routine shown in Fig. 10-12 (EL1012) has two uses. This routine can be used to set the file pointer for the file associated with *ddname* to the location specified. (For an example that uses *SetFLoc* this way, refer to the LISTER program defined in Chapter 2.) But if you call this routine with **method = seteof,** *rnmbr*

Fig. 10-12. Set a file pointer.

```
DEFINITION MODULE EL1012;
  FROM SYSTEM IMPORT    WORD;
  FROM EL0401 IMPORT    STRING;
  FROM EL0503 IMPORT    LONGCARD;
  FROM EL1002 IMPORT    LOCCNTRL;
  EXPORT QUALIFIED      SetFLoc;

PROCEDURE SetFLoc(ddname:STRING;method:LOCCNTRL;
                       rlen:WORD;VAR rnmbr:LONGCARD):BOOLEAN;
(* If the file associated with ddname does not exist, this function will
   return FALSE.  Otherwise, the function will return TRUE and the file
   pointer will be set according to the value in method.  If method =
   setpostn, the file pointer will be set to rlen * (rnmbr - 1).  If method
   = usepostn, the file pointer will be set to rlen * (rnmbr - 1) bytes
   past the current file position.  If method = seteof, the file pointer
   will be set to the end of file, and rnmbr will return with the number of
   rlen records the file contains.  *)
END EL1012.

IMPLEMENTATION MODULE EL1012;
  FROM SYSTEM IMPORT    WORD;
  FROM EL0401 IMPORT    STRING;
  FROM EL0503 IMPORT    LONGCARD,lczero;
  FROM EL1002 IMPORT    FindHndl,DoSet,FIDPTR,LOCCNTRL;

PROCEDURE SetFLoc(ddname:STRING;method:LOCCNTRL;
                       rlen:WORD;VAR rnmbr:LONGCARD):BOOLEAN;
VAR
  lastfid,thisfid:FIDPTR;
BEGIN
  IF (NOT FindHndl(ddname,lastfid,thisfid))
    THEN RETURN FALSE;
    ELSE
      CASE method OF
        setpostn:DoSet(00H,thisfid^.handle,rlen,rnmbr);
      ! usepostn:DoSet(01H,thisfid^.handle,rlen,rnmbr);
      ! seteof:
         rnmbr:=lczero;
         DoSet(02H,thisfid^.handle,rlen,rnmbr);
      ELSE
        RETURN FALSE;
      END;
      RETURN TRUE;
    END;
  END SetFLoc;

END EL1012.
```

returns equal to the number of records the file contains. To calculate the number of bytes in the file, multiply *rnmbr* by *rlen*. The answer might require a LONGCARD variable.

Directories

The ability of the Etling routines to access files using a complete DOS pathname makes the manipulation of directories, for the most part, unnecessary. There are times, however, when an application program might be forced to deal with directories directly. To facilitate this, the Etling Library contains four routines.

MkDir. The *MkDir* routine is exported from EL1013, shown in Fig. 10-13. It will create a directory as specified by *ddname*. Remember, you *can* create a directory with an extension; the command **MD TEST.TST** would create a directory named **TEST TST**.

Be careful with the *MkDir* routine; be certain that the *ddname* you specify does indeed name the directory you wish to create. If the routine detects an error, it will return that error as its function value under the assumption that the calling program should decide whether to report the error or ignore it.

Fig. 10-13. Make a directory.

```
DEFINITION MODULE EL1013;
   FROM SYSTEM IMPORT    WORD;
   FROM EL0401 IMPORT    STRING;
   EXPORT QUALIFIED      MkDir;

PROCEDURE MkDir(ddname:STRING):WORD;
(* This routine will attempt to create a directory according to the path
   defined in ddname.  If the operation is successful, the function will
   return = 0.  Otherwise, the routine will return equal to the error
   returned from DOS.  *)
END EL1013.


IMPLEMENTATION MODULE EL1013;
   FROM SYSTEM IMPORT    WORD,ADDRESS,ADR;
   FROM EL0301 IMPORT    ByWord;
   FROM EL0401 IMPORT    STRING,CHRPTR,StrLen,MakeStr,
                         ClearStr,nullstr,ChrPtr;
   FROM EL0701 IMPORT    Interupt,carryflg;
   FROM EL1002 IMPORT    FindDS,FindHndl,FixName,MountVol;

PROCEDURE MkDir(ddname:STRING):WORD;
CONST
   dontask = FALSE;
   dortrn  = TRUE;
VAR
   dsname,volname:STRING;
   ax,bx,cx,dx,ds,es,di,si,flags:WORD;
   adsname:ADDRESS;
BEGIN
   MakeStr(volname,255,nullstr);
   MakeStr(dsname,255,nullstr);
   FindDS(ddname,dsname);
   FixName(dsname,volname);
   IF (StrLen(volname) <> 0)
     THEN MountVol(volname,dontask);
     END;
   adsname:=ChrPtr(dsname,1);
   ax:=ByWord(39H,00H);
   dx:=WORD(adsname.OFFSET);
   ds:=WORD(adsname.SEGMENT);
   Interupt(21h,ax,bx,cx,dx,ds,es,di,si,flags);
   IF (carryflg IN BITSET(flags))
     THEN RETURN ax;
     ELSE RETURN WORD(0);
     END;
   ClearStr(volname);
   ClearStr(dsname);
   END MkDir;

END EL1013.
```

RmDir. Figure 10-14 shows *RmDir,* the routine for removing a directory from a disk or diskette. Of course, just like the DOS command, *RmDir* will return an error if you try to remove the current directory.

ChDir. Figure 10-15 shows EL1015 which exports *ChDir,* the Etling routine that will change the current directory on the device associated with *ddname*. Again, this routine will let the caller handle any errors. Note that *ddname* may refer to a *dsname,* which would be used to define the directory, or *ddname* may contain the directory itself.

Fig. 10-14. Remove a directory.

```
DEFINITION MODULE EL1014;
   FROM SYSTEM IMPORT    WORD;
   FROM EL0401 IMPORT    STRING;
   EXPORT QUALIFIED      RmDir;

PROCEDURE RmDir(ddname:STRING):WORD;
(* This routine will attempt to delete the directory according to the path
   defined in ddname.  If the operation is successful, the function will
   return = 0.  Otherwise, the routine will return equal to the error code
   returned from DOS.  *)
END EL1014.

IMPLEMENTATION MODULE EL1014;
   FROM SYSTEM IMPORT    WORD,ADDRESS,ADR;
   FROM EL0301 IMPORT    ByWord;
   FROM EL0401 IMPORT    STRING,CHRPTR,ChrPtr,MakeStr,ClearStr,nullstr,StrLen;
   FROM EL0701 IMPORT    Interupt,carryflg;
   FROM EL1002 IMPORT    FindDS,FindHndl,FixName,MountVol;

PROCEDURE RmDir(ddname:STRING):WORD;
CONST
   dontask = FALSE;
   dortrn  = TRUE;
VAR
   dsname,volname:STRING;
   ax,bx,cx,dx,ds,es,di,si,flags:WORD;
   adsname:ADDRESS;
BEGIN
   MakeStr(dsname,255,nullstr);
   MakeStr(volname,255,nullstr);
   FindDS(ddname,dsname);
   FixName(dsname,volname);
   IF (StrLen(volname) <> 0)
     THEN MountVol(volname,dontask);
     END;
   adsname:=ChrPtr(dsname,1);
   ax:=ByWord(3AH,00H);
   dx:=WORD(adsname.OFFSET);
   ds:=WORD(adsname.SEGMENT);
   Interupt(21h,ax,bx,cx,dx,ds,es,di,si,flags);
   IF (carryflg IN BITSET(flags))
     THEN RETURN ax;
     ELSE RETURN WORD(0);
     END;
   ClearStr(dsname);
   ClearStr(volname);
   END RmDir;

END EL1014.
```

Fig. 10-15. Change the current directory.

```
DEFINITION MODULE EL1015;
  FROM SYSTEM IMPORT    WORD;
  FROM EL0401 IMPORT    STRING;
  EXPORT QUALIFIED      ChDir;

PROCEDURE ChDir(ddname:STRING):WORD;
(* This routine will attempt to change the current directory according to
   the path defined in ddname.  If the operation is successful, the
   function will return = 0.  Otherwise, the routine will return equal to
   the error condition returned from DOS.  *)
END EL1015.


IMPLEMENTATION MODULE EL1015;
  FROM SYSTEM IMPORT    WORD,ADDRESS,ADR;
  FROM EL0301 IMPORT    ByWord;
  FROM EL0401 IMPORT    STRING,CHRPTR,ChrPtr,MakeStr,ClearStr,nullstr,StrLen;
  FROM EL0701 IMPORT    Interupt,carryflg;
  FROM EL1002 IMPORT    FindDS,FindHndl,FixName,MountVol;

PROCEDURE ChDir(ddname:STRING):WORD;
CONST
  dontask = FALSE;
  dortrn  = TRUE;
VAR
  dsname,volname:STRING;
  ax,bx,cx,dx,ds,es,di,si,flags:WORD;
  adsname:ADDRESS;
BEGIN
  MakeStr(dsname,255,nullstr);
  MakeStr(volname,255,nullstr);
  FindDS(ddname,dsname);
  FixName(dsname,volname);
  IF (StrLen(volname) <> 0)
    THEN MountVol(volname,dontask);
    END;
  adsname:=ChrPtr(dsname,1);
  ax:=ByWord(3BH,00H);
  dx:=WORD(adsname.OFFSET);
  ds:=WORD(adsname.SEGMENT);
  Interupt(21H,ax,bx,cx,dx,ds,es,di,si,flags);
  IF (carryflg IN BITSET(flags))
    THEN RETURN ax;
    ELSE RETURN WORD(0);
    END;
  ClearStr(dsname);
  ClearStr(volname);
  END ChDir;

END EL1015.
```

GetDir. The routine shown in Fig. 10-16 (EL1016), called *GetDir,* will return the full DOS pathname to the current directory in effect for the device associated with ddname. Note that the directory, returned in *dir,* contains a complete pathname, including the device and first backslash.

Accessing a File's Attribute

Along with the file's name and the date and time stamp, a DOS directory contains a single byte that is known as the file's attribute byte. This byte was

Fig. 10-16. Get the current directory.

```
DEFINITION MODULE EL1016;
  FROM SYSTEM IMPORT     WORD;
  FROM ELO401 IMPORT     STRING;
  EXPORT QUALIFIED       GetDir;

PROCEDURE GetDir(ddname,dir:STRING):WORD;
(* This routine will attempt to locate the current path defined for the
   device associated with ddname.  If no error occurs, dir will return the
   path.  The function value will indicate the success or failure of the
   operation.  *)
END EL1016.

IMPLEMENTATION MODULE EL1016;
  FROM SYSTEM IMPORT     WORD,ADDRESS,ADR;
  FROM ELO301 IMPORT     ByWord;
  FROM ELO401 IMPORT     STRING,SetLen,SetChar,Literal,StrLen;
  FROM ELO402 IMPORT     Delete,Concat;
  FROM ELO403 IMPORT     Positn;
  FROM ELO701 IMPORT     Interupt,carryflg;
  FROM EL1002 IMPORT     FindDS,FindHndl,DrvNmbr;

PROCEDURE GetDir(ddname,dir:STRING):WORD;
VAR
  ax,bx,cx,dx,ds,es,di,si,flags:WORD;
  i:CARDINAL;
  adsname:ADDRESS;
  str:ARRAY [1..64] OF CHAR;
BEGIN
  FindDS(ddname,dir);
  ax:=ByWord(47H,00H);
  dx:=WORD(DrvNmbr(dir));
  adsname:=ADR(str);
  ds:=WORD(adsname.SEGMENT);
  si:=WORD(adsname.OFFSET);
  Interupt(21H,ax,bx,cx,dx,ds,es,di,si,flags);
  IF (carryflg IN BITSET(flags))
    THEN RETURN ax;
    ELSE
      i:=Positn(Literal(':'),dir,1);
      IF (i > 0)
        THEN Delete(dir,i,StrLen(dir)-i);
        END;
      SetLen(dir,StrLen(dir)+1);
      SetChar(dir,StrLen(dir),'\');
      i:=1;
      WHILE (i < HIGH(str)+2) AND (str[i] <> CHR(0)) DO
        SetLen(dir,StrLen(dir)+1);
        SetChar(dir,StrLen(dir),str[i]);
        INC(i);
        END;
      RETURN WORD(0);
    END;
  END GetDir;

END EL1016.
```

discussed in conjunction with *MountVol* earlier in this chapter, but the attribute byte can be used to define file types other than the volume label. The list of attributes that a file can have is shown back in Fig. 10-1. There are several routines in the Etling Library that allow you to access and change this byte, all of them exported from EL1017, shown in Fig. 10-17.

FileAtt. The routine named *FileAtt* provides primitive access to a file's attribute. This routine is not normally called from outside the EL10 series of modules, but it is available should it be needed. *FileAtt* uses DOS function 43H to read or set the attribute byte for a file. Be aware that function 43H does not work quite the way it is supposed to under DOS 2.0 and 2.1. As I noted before, you cannot access a disk's volume label using this function, even though the DOS manual implies that you can.

FileAtt can also be used to change an existing file attribute, but there are two exceptions. You cannot change a volume label (even if you could get at it, which you can't), and you cannot change the attribute for a subdirectory. You can change the read-only, hidden, and system attributes.

ChkAttrb and SetAttrb. The two routines that access a file that are generally used by an application program are called *ChkAttrb* and *SetAttrb*. They operate as their names suggest.

Generic Filenames

FindFile. *FindFile,* the only routine in EL1018, shown in Fig. 10-18, allows you to specify a generic filename (one using the DOS wildcard characters, "*" and "?") and it will search the pathname on the volume for any file that matches. Use the file attributes defined in the *FileAtts* library member to establish a value for *kind,* but remember that DOS has a specific set of rules for combining these attributes. As the comments in the figure indicate, if *kind* equals zero, only normal files will be located. To locate any file (except the volume label) use *hidden* + *system* + *subdir*. To locate the volume label (under DOS 3.00 or later) use *volume* by itself.

Renaming Files

ReName. The module shown in Fig. 10-19 exports *ReName*. This routine allows you to invoke the DOS rename function. Unlike its DOS command counterpart, this routine can be used to rename a file to a different directory as well as specify the volume on which the file is located.

Using Volume Names

Before I leave the discussion of the Etling Library I/O routines, there is one final routine to present.

The Etling Library defines the concept of program-accessible volume names for diskettes. Volume names were originally created so that a program would have some way of making certain that the user had mounted the correct diskettes. These routines are more useful on a standard PC than on a machine with a fixed disk, but there might still be instances where any program may need to access a volume label. One place where this is particularly important is when one program needs to load and execute another, and the second program is on a diskette. Most of the Modula-2 packages have some "chain" or "overlay" facility that permits one program to load

Fig. 10-17. Dealing with file attributes.

```
DEFINITION MODULE EL1017;
  FROM SYSTEM IMPORT    BYTE,WORD;
  FROM EL0401 IMPORT    STRING;
  EXPORT QUALIFIED      FileAtt,ChkAttrb,SetAttrb;

PROCEDURE FileAtt(opcode:BYTE;dsname:STRING; VAR attrib:WORD):BYTE;
(* This routine will attempt to return the attribute for the file
   associated with dsname.  If an error occurs, the function will return
   set to the appropriate error code.  Otherwise the function will return =
   0, and if opcode = 0 attrib will be set to the attribute byte for the
   file, or if opcode = 1, the file attribute will be set to attrib.  *)
PROCEDURE ChkAttrb(ddname:STRING; VAR attrib:WORD):BOOLEAN;
(* This routine will return the attribute recorded for the file associated
   with ddname.  If function returns = FALSE, the file does not exist.
   Otherwise, attrib will contain the appropriate value.  *)
PROCEDURE SetAttrb(ddname:STRING; attrib:WORD):BOOLEAN;
(* This routine will set the attribute recorded for the file associated
   with ddname.  If function returns = FALSE, the file does not exist.
   Otherwise, attrib will become the new file attribute recorded for the
   file.  *)
END EL1017.


IMPLEMENTATION MODULE EL1017;
  FROM SYSTEM IMPORT    BYTE,WORD,ADDRESS,ADR;
  FROM EL0301 IMPORT    ByWord,LoByte;
  FROM EL0401 IMPORT    STRING,CHRPTR,ChrPtr,Literal,MakeStr,
                        ClearStr,nullstr,StrLen;
  FROM EL0701 IMPORT    Interupt,carryflg;
  FROM EL1001 IMPORT    RptIOErr;
  FROM EL1002 IMPORT    FindDS,FindHndl,MountVol,FixName;

CONST
  dortrn = TRUE;
  dontask = FALSE;

PROCEDURE FileAtt(opcode:BYTE;dsname:STRING;VAR attrib:WORD):BYTE;
VAR
  adsname:ADDRESS;
  ax,bx,cx,dx,ds,es,di,si,flags:WORD;
BEGIN
  ax:=ByWord(43H,opcode);
  adsname:=ChrPtr(dsname,1);
  ds:=WORD(adsname.SEGMENT);
  dx:=WORD(adsname.OFFSET);
  Interupt(21H,ax,bx,cx,dx,ds,es,di,si,flags);
  IF (carryflg IN BITSET(flags))
    THEN RETURN LoByte(ax);
    ELSE
      RETURN BYTE(0);
      attrib:=cx;
    END;
  END FileAtt;


PROCEDURE ChkAttrb(ddname:STRING; VAR attrib:WORD):BOOLEAN;
VAR
  dsname,volname:STRING;
  ioerr:BYTE;
BEGIN
  MakeStr(dsname,255,nullstr);
  MakeStr(volname,255,nullstr);
  FindDS(ddname,dsname);
```

Fig. 10-17 continued

```
  FixName(dsname,volname);
  IF (StrLen(volname) <> 0)
    THEN MountVol(volname,dontask);
    END;
  REPEAT
    ioerr:=FileAtt(00H,dsname,attrib);
    IF (ioerr <> BYTE(00H)) AND (ioerr <> BYTE(02H))
      THEN RptIOErr(ioerr,dsname,Literal('ChkAttrb'),dortrn);
      END;
    UNTIL (ioerr = BYTE(00H)) OR (ioerr = BYTE(02H));
  IF (ioerr = BYTE(00H))
    THEN RETURN TRUE;
    ELSE RETURN FALSE;
    END;
  ClearStr(dsname);
  ClearStr(volname);
  END ChkAttrb;

PROCEDURE SetAttrb(ddname:STRING;attrib:WORD):BOOLEAN;
VAR
  dsname,volname:STRING;
  ioerr:BYTE;
BEGIN
  MakeStr(dsname,255,nullstr);
  MakeStr(volname,255,nullstr);
  FindDS(ddname,dsname);
  FixName(dsname,volname);
  IF (StrLen(volname) <> 0)
    THEN MountVol(volname,dontask);
    END;
  REPEAT
    ioerr:=FileAtt(01H,dsname,attrib);
    IF (ioerr <> BYTE(00H)) AND (ioerr <> BYTE(02H))
      THEN RptIOErr(ioerr,dsname,Literal('SetAttrb'),dortrn);
      END;
    UNTIL (ioerr = BYTE(00H)) OR (ioerr = BYTE(02H));
  IF (ioerr = BYTE(00H))
    THEN RETURN TRUE;
    ELSE RETURN FALSE;
    END;
  ClearStr(dsname);
  ClearStr(volname);
  END SetAttrb;

END EL1017.
```

another, so I didn't write one. But if you do chain to programs on diskette, you will find *ReMount* useful.

ReMount. When a program terminates, it returns control to the process that invoked it. Normally, this means it returns control to DOS. If the program was begun by DOS under control of a batch file, DOS will attempt to read the next command from the file. If the batch file was on a diskette and the user has changed diskettes, DOS issues a message that says:

Insert disk with batch file
and press any key when ready

Fig. 10-18. Find a file.

```
DEFINITION MODULE EL1018;
   FROM SYSTEM IMPORT    WORD;
   FROM EL0401 IMPORT    STRING;
   FROM EL0502 IMPORT    TIME,DATE;
   FROM EL0503 IMPORT    LONGCARD;
   EXPORT QUALIFIED      FindFile;

PROCEDURE FindFile(ddname:STRING;kind:WORD; filename:STRING;
                   VAR attrib:WORD; VAR ftime:TIME;VAR fdate:DATE;
                       VAR filesize:LONGCARD):BOOLEAN;
(* This routine will search the path and volume associated with ddname for
   a file that matches the associated file name.  The file name may include
   global file search characters.  If StrLen(filename) = 0 on entry, the
   routine will assume that this is the first call;  otherwise, the routine
   will return the next matching file.  If, on entry, kine = 0, only normal
   files will be found.  Otherwise, all files whose attribute matches one
   of the attribute bits set will be returned.  When no more files can be
   found, the function will return FALSE.  *)
END EL1018.


IMPLEMENTATION MODULE EL1018;
   FROM SYSTEM IMPORT    BYTE,WORD,ADDRESS,ADR;
   FROM EL0301 IMPORT    ByWord,LoByte;
   FROM EL0302 IMPORT    MovByteL;
   FROM EL0401 IMPORT    STRING,CHRPTR,ChrPtr,Literal,MakeStr,ClearStr,
                         nullstr,CopyStr,StrLen,SetLen,SetChar;
   FROM EL0502 IMPORT    DATE,TIME;
   FROM EL0503 IMPORT    LONGCARD;
   FROM EL0701 IMPORT    Interupt,carryflg;
   FROM EL1002 IMPORT    FindDS,FixName,MountVol,SetDTA;
   FROM EL1010 IMPORT    WToFDate,WToFTime;

VAR
   dta:ARRAY [1..128] OF CHAR;


PROCEDURE FindFile(ddname:STRING;kind:WORD;filename:STRING;VAR attrib:WORD;
                   VAR ftime:TIME;VAR fdate:DATE;
                       VAR filesize:LONGCARD):BOOLEAN;
CONST
   dontask = FALSE;
VAR
   ax,bx,cx,dx,ds,es,di,si,flags:WORD;
   dsname,volname,str:STRING;
   adsname,olddta:ADDRESS;
   w:CARDINAL;
   i:INTEGER;
BEGIN
   MakeStr(dsname,255,nullstr);
   MakeStr(volname,255,nullstr);
   IF (StrLen(filename) <> 0)
     THEN
       ax:=ByWord(4FH,00H);
       CopyStr(Literal(dta),dsname);
     ELSE
       FindDS(ddname,dsname);
       FixName(dsname,volname);
       IF (StrLen(volname) <> 0)
         THEN MountVol(volname,dontask);
         END;
       ax:=ByWord(4EH,00H);
     END;
```

Fig. 10-18 continued
```
  SetDTA(ADR(dta),olddta);
  adsname:=ChrPtr(dsname,1);
  ds:=WORD(adsname.SEGMENT);
  dx:=WORD(adsname.OFFSET);
  cx:=kind;
  Interupt(21h,ax,bx,cx,dx,ds,es,di,si,flags);
  IF (carryflg IN BITSET(flags))
    THEN RETURN FALSE;
    ELSE
      MovByteL(dta,attrib,21,0,1);
      MovByteL(dta,w,22,0,2);
      WToFDate(w,fdate);
      MovByteL(dta,w,24,0,2);
      WToFTime(w,ftime);
      MovByteL(dta,filesize,26,0,4);
      i:=31;
      CopyStr(nullstr,filename);
      WHILE (dta[i] <> CHR(0)) DO
        SetLen(filename,StrLen(filename)+1);
        SetChar(filename,StrLen(filename),dta[i]);
        INC(i);
        END;
      RETURN TRUE;
    END;
  SetDTA(olddta,olddta);
  ClearStr(dsname);
  ClearStr(volname);
  END FindFile;

END EL1018.
```

Fig. 10-19. Rename a file.
```
DEFINITION MODULE EL1019;
  FROM EL0401 IMPORT    STRING;
  EXPORT QUALIFIED      Rename;

PROCEDURE Rename(ddname,newname:STRING):BOOLEAN;
(* This routine will rename the file associated with ddname to the new name
   specified.  The files need not be in the same directory, but must be on
   the same volume.  Only the file associated with ddname may state the
   volumne name.  If the file does not exist, the function will return
   FALSE.  *)
END EL1019.


IMPLEMENTATION MODULE EL1019;
  FROM SYSTEM IMPORT    WORD,ADDRESS;
  FROM EL0301 IMPORT    ByWord;
  FROM EL0401 IMPORT    STRING,CHRPTR,ChrPtr,MakeStr,ClearStr,nullstr,StrLen;
  FROM EL0701 IMPORT    Interupt,carryflg;
  FROM EL1002 IMPORT    FindDS,FixName,MountVol;

PROCEDURE Rename(ddname,newname:STRING):BOOLEAN;
CONST
  dontask = FALSE;
VAR
  ax,bx,cx,dx,ds,es,di,si,flags:WORD;
  dsname,volname:STRING;
  adsname:ADDRESS;
```

```
BEGIN
  MakeStr(dsname,255,nullstr);
  MakeStr(volname,255,nullstr);
  FindDS(ddname,dsname);
  FixName(dsname,volname);
  IF (StrLen(volname) <> 0)
    THEN MountVol(volname,dontask);
    END;
  ax:=ByWord(56H,00H);
  adsname:=ChrPtr(dsname,1);
  ds:=WORD(adsname.SEGMENT);
  dx:=WORD(adsname.OFFSET);
  adsname:=ChrPtr(newname,1);
  es:=WORD(adsname.SEGMENT);
  di:=WORD(adsname.OFFSET);
  Interupt(21H,ax,bx,cx,dx,ds,es,di,si,flags);
  IF (carryflg IN BITSET(flags))
    THEN RETURN FALSE;
    ELSE RETURN TRUE;
    END;
  ClearStr(dsname);
  ClearStr(volname);
  END Rename;

END EL1019.
```

Fig. 10-20. Remount volumes.

```
DEFINITION MODULE EL1020;
  EXPORT QUALIFIED Remount;

PROCEDURE Remount;
(* This procedure is usually called at the end of a main program.  It will
   search for a program parameter with <parmid> = REMOUNT.  If the
   parameter is found, this routine will use its <parmval> to determine
   which diskettes should be mounted when the program ends.  The format for
   <parmval> is:

        REMOUNT=<device>:,<volname> <device>:,<volname>[...]

   Note that, if neccessary, Remount can specify a volume for each of
   several devices.  Each entry is delimited with a semicolon.   *)
END EL1020.

IMPLEMENTATION MODULE EL1020;
  FROM EL0401 IMPORT    STRING,Literal,StrLen,MakeStr,
                        ClearStr,nullstr,CopyStr;
  FROM EL0402 IMPORT    Delete;
  FROM EL0403 IMPORT    Positn;
  FROM EL0801 IMPORT    FindParm;
  FROM EL1002 IMPORT    ClsFile,clsonly,FixName;
  FROM EL1009 IMPORT    ChkVol;

PROCEDURE Remount;
CONST
  dontask = FALSE;
VAR
  str,vol:STRING;
  i:CARDINAL;
BEGIN
  MakeStr(str,255,nullstr);
```

Fig. 10-20 continued

```
   MakeStr(vol,255,nullstr);
   ClsFile(Literal('*.*'),clsonly);
   IF (FindParm(Literal('REMOUNT'),str))
      THEN
         WHILE (StrLen(str) <> 0) DO
            i:=Positn(Literal(' '),str,0);
            IF (i = 0)
               THEN CopyStr(nullstr,str);
               ELSE
                  FixName(str,vol);
                  ChkVol(vol,dontask);
                  Delete(str,1,i);
               END;
            END;
         END;
   ClearStr(str);
   ClearStr(vol);
   END Remount;

END EL1020.
```

To a user who is not necessarily aware that he is executing a batch file in the first place, the message is not very friendly. The Etling Library includes a routine for displaying a message that the user might find more informative.

The routine is called *ReMount,* and it is shown in EL1020, Fig. 10-20. If you write a program that could be executed from a batch file on a diskette, the last thing it should do before it terminates is call *ReMount.* In addition to using *ChkVol* to tell the user to mount the correct diskettes in each diskette drive, *ReMount* will issue a global close to *ClsFile.* The following call:

    ClsFile(Literal('*.*'),clsonly)

will ensure that all open files are closed before the program terminates.

THE CONFIG.SYS FILE

Everyone who uses DOS 2.0 (or greater) is probably familiar with the special DOS system file named CONFIG.SYS. (If you've never heard of this file, read the appropriate chapter in your DOS manual. You'll find some very interesting things in there.)

Both standard Modula-2 I/O and the nonstandard I/O routines in the Etling Library show a remarkable improvement in the time to access disk or diskette files if you include the following commands in your CONFIG.SYS file:

    FILES=20
    BUFFERS=20

The file access methods defined in the next chapter also benefit from these options.

Chapter 11

File Access Methods

The I/O routines defined in the last chapter simply transfer bytes to and from files; the routines do not know anything about how these bytes are arranged, and except for the carriage return/line-feed sequence, the routines do not attach any particular significance to the bytes themselves. It is up to the application program to define how the bytes are grouped together and to decide how these groups are stored in the file.

Although, in theory, many different arrangements of data into files are possible, there are some arrangements that are more useful to commercial applications than others. In recognition of this fact, main-frame operating systems define mechanisms called *access methods*. An *access method* is a predefined method for grouping data into records and for storing or retrieving these records in files. Some of the more popular main-frame methods are called VSAM (for Virtual Storage Access Method), ISAM (Indexed Sequential Access Method), or BDAM (Basic Direct Access Method).

The Etling Library defines four different methods for accessing files. The TEXT file method that uses the carriage-return/line-feed sequence is implemented by the *GetLine* and *PutLine* routines discussed in Chapter 10. The *GetRcrd* and *PutRcrd* routines handle the direct access method; a program can read or write data records by specifying a record number—the program has "direct access" to each record. The two remaining access methods are the subject of this chapter.

INDEXED FILES

The Etling Library contains a series of routines that provide random access to files indexed by a balanced binary tree. An excellent treatment of the entire theory of binary tree structures can be found in Niklaus Wirth's book, *Algorithms + Data*

Structures = Programs. (In fact, many of the library routines were based on Wirth's algorithms and therefore share many of the same procedure, function, or variable names. The Wirth routines were heavily modified to include file access.)

Binary trees

The term "binary tree" refers to the fact that elements of the structure are arranged in such a way that any element can be located based on a series of binary decisions. Access to the structure begins at the top—sometimes called the "root," —although the Etling Library routines refer to it as the "hook" or "hanger." Figure 11-1 illustrates a binary tree structure.

In the figure, the 26 letters of the alphabet are arranged in a balanced binary tree structure. "P" is the hanger element. To locate any other element in the structure, simply compare its key to the key of the current element. If the key you wish to find is less than the current key, follow the path to the left; all greater keys are to the right. Beginning with "P," a program can locate any other key with only four comparisons. Using this technique on a file means that a program can locate any record in a file containing 64K times 64K records (the number of records accessible by a LONG-CARD) with only 32 compares. In practice, most files on a personal computer would have less than 10,000 records. A binary tree structure would provide very rapid access to such files. Even when files contain hundreds of thousands of records, access is still fast enough for most purposes.

To reduce the number of compares required to find an element in a binary tree, the tree structure should be kept "in balance." According to the Wirth book, a tree is considered to be balanced if, and only if, the height of the two subtrees hanging from every record differ by, at most, one. Using this definition, the tree in Fig. 11-1 is balanced even though "X" has a subtree containing seven records to the left and a subtree containing only two records to the right.

NDX Files

In the Etling Library, binary tree files are referred to as NDX files. As a general rule, I tend to use NDX as the extension for any file using the tree structure.

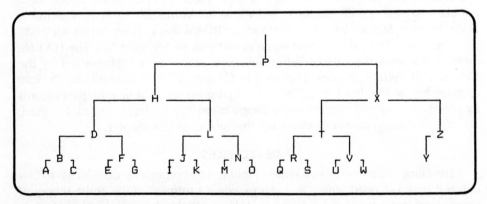

Fig. 11-1. A balanced binary tree structure.

An NDX file is a file of fixed length records, and there must be at least one record in the file. Each record consists of 10 bytes of control information followed by at least four bytes of data. The control information implements the binary tree structure. Imbedded in the data portion of the record is an NDX KEY; a contiguous string of characters that is unique among all records in the file. The library routines allow a program to access records based on the contents of this key. An NDX record could be defined as follows:

```
NDXRCRD = RECORD
   left     : LONGCARD;
   right    : LONGCARD;
   balance  : LONGCARD
   data     : RECORD
      xxx      : ARRAY [. . .] OF BYTE;
      key      : ARRAY [. . .] OF BYTE;
      yyy      : ARRAY [. . .] OF BYTE;
      END;
   END;
```

The field named NDXRCRD.*left* contains the address of the record at the top of the subtree containing all records whose keys are less than this record. NDXRCRD.*right* has the address of the top of the subtree of keys greater than this. In both cases, a zero value indicates that there are no more records lower in the structure.

NDXRCRD.*balance* uses the values from *matchval* in the Library to indicate whether or not the subtree hanging from the record is in balance. If balance = less, there is one more level to the left than to the right; balance = equal means that the tree from this record down has an equal number of records in both directions: balance = greater means more levels to the right.

Access to an NDX file begins at record number 1 in the file. Record 1 is a header record containing information that helps to locate the other records in the file. The format of the header record could be defined like this:

```
HDRRCRD = RECORD
   frstfree : LONGCARD;
   lastrcrd : LONGCARD;
   unused   : CARDINAL;
   hanger   : LONGCARD;
   unused   : ARRAY [. . .] OF BYTE;
   END;
```

The HDRRCRD.*lastrcrd* field contains the address of the last record physically written to the file; in effect, it marks the end of the file. (DOS will allow a program to write a record after the end of a file, but it will return an error if a program attempts to read past the end.) As each new record is added to the file, this value might or might not be incremented. The amount of space physically allocated to an NDX file can increase, but it cannot decrease. When records are deleted from an NDX file, the space they occupied is still part of the file; Any new records added will reuse the same space. Usually, an NDX file grows until it reaches some limit related to the application, and then as records are deleted in normal processing, the size stays more or less constant.

As records are deleted from an NDX file, their physical space is added to a chain of "free" records in the file. HDRRCRD.*frstfree* contains the address of the first free chain record in the file. Records are added into this chain sorted by record number.

HDRRCRD.*hanger* has the address of the record that represents the top of the tree in the file. Note that this variable actually occupies part of the area used for data in other records. (Because of this, the data are a must be at least four bytes long.) It is possible that a given NDX file might not include a HDRRCRD.*hanger* value. There are circumstances where a file might contain multiple trees; the *hanger* for each tree would be recorded as part of the data in another file, for example:

```
TEAM = RECORD
    teamname  : ARRAY [1. .10] OF CHAR;
    address   : ARRAY [1. .30] OF CHAR;
    city      : ARRAY [1. .20] OF CHAR;
    state     : ARRAY [1. .2] OF CHAR;
    zip       : ARRAY [1. .9] OF CHAR;
    firstchild : LONGCARD;
    END;


CHILD = RECORD
    lastname  : ARRAY [1. .20] OF CHAR;
    firstname : ARRAY [1. .20] OF CHAR;
    team      : ARRAY [1. .10] OF CHAR;
    END;
```

The TEAM record type defines the data portion of one NDX file; the CHILD record defines the data portion of another. TEAM records contain *firstchild*; a LONGCARD that identifies the *hanger* of the tree of CHILD records in the other file that is associated with the specified team. All of the appropriate NDX routines define a parameter, called *top*, that allows the calling program to indicate if the file contains its own "top of tree," or if the actual *hanger* is contained in another file. As the CHILD record shows, it is also possible to have the key for one record (a TEAM record in the example) defined as part of the data area in a record in another file. Using these techniques it is possible to define fairly complex data relationships, but remember that unlike a so-called "database handler," a program using these techniques is responsible for maintaining the necessary cross references.

Both TEAM and CHILD are defined using explicit field definitions for the fields they contain. These fields are shown just as an example; normally, I would use the RCRDAREA and RFLDAREA technique described by EL1007.

Furthermore, note that the definition of the records within the called *does not* include reference to *left, right,* and *balance.* The caller only need concern itself with the data area of an NDX record; the NDX routines handle the rest.

The Basic NDX Routines

The basic NDX routines are actually split into 2 modules. The NDX type definitions and six routines required by all NDX access are in EL1101, shown in Fig. 11-1. EL1102 (Fig. 11-2) contains helper routines for maintaining tree balance. The routines in EL1102 are only required by the modules that add or delete records.

NDX Types. The NDX routines require a couple of type definitions. These types define the data structures required to handle the binary tree structure in core. NODE, the record definition for an element of the tree, looks a lot like the physical record stored in an NDX file, but it is important to note that in core, *left* and *right* are pointers, not record addresses. As physical NDX records are read or built in memory, the record addresses are kept as a field in the NODEPTR record.

For convenience, the EL1101 module also exports a NDXFCTRL type. This is a record structure that can be used to store all of the control variables required by an NDX file. It isn't mandatory that you have an NDXFCTRL variable associated with an NDX file; the type is only defined as a reminder of the data you would normally define.

ChkNdxF and ClrNdx. Because of the special considerations associated with the tree structure, there are several routines that must be used to begin and end access to an NDX file. Normally, a program that uses an NDX file would begin access with a call to *ChkNdxF* and terminate access with calls to *ClrNdx*.

ChkNdxF is a special routine that will create, if necessary, the header for a new file. Because *ChkNdxF* uses *OpnFile* to actually open the file, the logic associated with *opnmode* is the same as discussed in Chapter 10.

If *OpnFile* does cause a new file to be created, *opnmode* will return equal to *newfile*. In this case, *ChkNdxF* will create a header record for the file using the following initial values:

```
HDRRCRD.frstfree := 0;
HDRRCRD.lastrcrd := 1;
HDRRCRD.hanger   := 0;
```

As new records are added to the file, the NDX routines will adjust these values accordingly. Even if a new file is created, *ChkNdxF* will always return with **opnmode = oldfile**. This is to prevent repeated *ChkNdxF* calls from re-initializing the header record. Note that the length of the header record is controlled by *rcrdlen*. The length of each record in the NDX file must be constant.

Note that as the comments in Fig. 11-2 warn, if the NDX file is on diskette, *ChkNdxF* should be called periodically to make certain that the proper diskette is still mounted. Many of the NDX routines use a parameter named *updtdir* that allows the caller to specify whether or not the directory entry for a file should be updated when a new record is added to the file. If a given program uses **updtdir = TRUE**, the file will will be closed after a write. *ChkNdxF* must be called before the file can be accessed again.

The NDX routines are designed to keep a certain amount of the tree structure in core as a file is being accessed. This decreases the number of actual disk accesses that must be made to find a specific record and therefore provides faster access.

Fig. 11-2. NDX file basics.

```
DEFINITION MODULE EL1102;
  FROM EL0401 IMPORT    STRING;
  FROM EL0503 IMPORT    LONGCARD;
  FROM EL1002 IMPORT    FMODE;
  FROM EL1007 IMPORT    RCRD,RFLDLIST;
  EXPORT QUALIFIED      NODEPTR,NODE,NDXFCTRL,ndxclen,ChkNdxF,ClrNdx,
                        GetNdx,PutNdx,MakeNode,ChkLoad;

TYPE
  NODEPTR = RECORD
    ptr       : POINTER TO NODE;
    nmbr      : LONGCARD;
    END;
  NODE = RECORD
    left      : NODEPTR;
    right     : NODEPTR;
    balance   : INTEGER;
    rcrd      : RCRD;
    END;
  NDXFCTRL = RECORD
    ddname    : STRING;
    rcrdnmbr  : LONGCARD;
    rcrd      : RCRD;
    rfldarea  : RFLDLIST;
    hook      : NODEPTR;
    END;
CONST
  ndxclen = 10;
PROCEDURE ChkNdxF(ddname:STRING;rcrdlen:CARDINAL; VAR opnmode:FMODE);
(* This procedure ensures that the NDX file associated with ddname is
   opened and ready for access.  Note that if the operation results in a
   new file being created, its header record will be properly initialized.
   On entry opnmode should be set to the value required for the desired
   operation...it will always return = oldfile.  This routine should be the
   first NDX routine called for a specific file and, if the file is on
   diskette, the routine should be recalled periodically to ensure that the
   proper diskette is still mounted.  *)
PROCEDURE ClrNdx(VAR hook:NODEPTR);
(* This routine will dispose of the chain of nodes specified by hook and
   thereby clear the heap for reuse.  *)
PROCEDURE GetNdx(ddname:STRING;nmbr:LONGCARD; VAR left,right:LONGCARD;
                      VAR bal:INTEGER;VAR thisrcrd:RCRD);
(* This routine will read the NDX record identified by nmbr from the file
   associated with ddname.  *)
PROCEDURE PutNdx(ddname:STRING; nmbr,left,right:LONGCARD;bal:INTEGER;
                      thisrcrd:RCRD);
(* This procedure will write the NDX record identified by nmbr to the file
   associated with ddname.  *)
PROCEDURE MakeNode(VAR thisnode:NODEPTR;length:CARDINAL);
(* This routine will create a new NODEPTR record.  *)
PROCEDURE ChkLoad(ddname:STRING;VAR p:NODEPTR;rcrdlen:CARDINAL);
(* This routine will determine if the record associated with p has been
   loaded into memory...if not, the routine will load it.  *)
END EL1102.

IMPLEMENTATION MODULE EL1102;
  FROM SYSTEM IMPORT    ADR,BYTE;
  FROM Storage IMPORT   DEALLOCATE,ALLOCATE;
  FROM EL0302 IMPORT    FillByte,MovByteL;
  FROM EL0303 IMPORT    equal;
  FROM EL0401 IMPORT    STRING,Literal;
```

```
      FROM EL0503 IMPORT    LONGCARD,lczero,lcone,ComLCard;
      FROM EL0906 IMPORT    Cancel;
      FROM EL1002 IMPORT    FMODE,OpnFile,ClsFile,OPENKIND,LOCCNTRL;
      FROM EL1005 IMPORT    GetRcrd;
      FROM EL1006 IMPORT    PutRcrd;
      FROM EL1007 IMPORT    RCRD,MakeRcrd,ClrRcrd;

  CONST
    t1 = 'The Etling Library';
    t2 = 'All programs and modules, Copyright (c) 1987 TAB BOOKS INC.';
    t3 = 'Author: Don Etling';

  PROCEDURE GetNdx(ddname:STRING;nmbr:LONGCARD;VAR left,right:LONGCARD;
                     VAR bal:INTEGER;VAR thisrcrd:RCRD);
  VAR
    ndxptr:RCRD;
    l:CARDINAL;
  BEGIN
    MakeRcrd(thisrcrd^.rcrdlen+ndxclen,ndxptr);
    IF (NOT GetRcrd(ddname,setpostn,nmbr,nmbr,
                       ndxptr^.rcrdlen,l,ADR(ndxptr^.area)))
      THEN Cancel(Literal(' GetNdx'),ddname,1,0);
      END;
    MovByteL(ndxptr^.area,left,0,0,4);
    MovByteL(ndxptr^.area,right,4,0,4);
    MovByteL(ndxptr^.area,bal,8,0,2);
    MovByteL(ndxptr^.area,thisrcrd^.area,10,0,thisrcrd^.rcrdlen);
    ClrRcrd(ndxptr);
    END GetNdx;

  PROCEDURE PutNdx(ddname:STRING;nmbr,left,right:LONGCARD;bal:INTEGER;
                     thisrcrd:RCRD);
  VAR
    ndxptr:RCRD;
  BEGIN
    MakeRcrd(thisrcrd^.rcrdlen+ndxclen,ndxptr);
    MovByteL(left,ndxptr^.area,0,0,4);
    MovByteL(right,ndxptr^.area,0,4,4);
    MovByteL(bal,ndxptr^.area,0,8,2);
    MovByteL(thisrcrd^.area,ndxptr^.area,0,10,thisrcrd^.rcrdlen);
    PutRcrd(ddname,setpostn,nmbr,nmbr,
                       ndxptr^.rcrdlen,ADR(ndxptr^.area));
    ClrRcrd(ndxptr);
    END PutNdx;

  PROCEDURE MakeNode(VAR thisnode:NODEPTR;length:CARDINAL);
  BEGIN
    NEW(thisnode.ptr);
    thisnode.ptr^.left.ptr:=NIL;
    thisnode.ptr^.right.ptr:=NIL;
    thisnode.ptr^.left.nmbr:=lczero;
    thisnode.ptr^.right.nmbr:=lczero;
    thisnode.ptr^.balance:=equal;
    MakeRcrd(length,thisnode.ptr^.rcrd);
    FillByte(BYTE(0),thisnode.ptr^.rcrd^.area,0,length);
    END MakeNode;

  PROCEDURE ChkLoad(ddname:STRING;VAR p:NODEPTR;rcrdlen:CARDINAL);
  BEGIN
    IF (p.ptr = NIL) AND (ComLCard(p.nmbr,lczero) <> equal)
      THEN
        MakeNode(p,rcrdlen);
```

Fig. 11-2 continued

```
      WITH p.ptr^ DO
        GetNdx(ddname,p.nmbr,left.nmbr,right.nmbr,balance,rcrd);
        END;
      END;
  END ChkLoad;

PROCEDURE ChkNdxF(ddname:STRING;rcrdlen:CARDINAL;VAR opnmode:FMODE);
VAR
  dummy:RCRD;
  status:BYTE;
BEGIN
  OpnFile(ddname,opnmode,status,insist);
  IF (opnmode = newfile)
    THEN
      MakeRcrd(rcrdlen,dummy);
      FillByte(BYTE(0),dummy^.area,0,rcrdlen);
      PutNdx(ddname,lcone,lczero,lcone,0,dummy);
      ClrRcrd(dummy);
    END;
  opnmode:=oldfile;
  END ChkNdxF;

PROCEDURE ClrNdx(VAR hook:NODEPTR);
BEGIN
  IF (hook.ptr <> NIL)
    THEN
      ClrNdx(hook.ptr^.left);
      ClrNdx(hook.ptr^.right);
      ClrRcrd(hook.ptr^.rcrd);
      DISPOSE(hook.ptr);
      hook.ptr:=NIL;
    END;
  END ClrNdx;

END EL1102.
```

Closing an NDX file (with *ClsFile*) does not automatically release the heap space used by the tree structure. The calling routine is responsible for deciding when that should be done, and it should call *ClrNdx* to handle the necessary DISPOSEs. Note that *ClrNdx* will call itself recursively to clear the entire tree structure from *hook* on down.

GetNdx and PutNdx. The two routines that read or write physical records to and from an NDX file are *GetNdx* and *PutNdx*. Both routines operate by creating a new record on the heap that is 10 bytes longer than *thisrcrd* (the RCRD passed from the calling program). Both routines use *MovByteL* to move the control information into the record. Note that neither routine is normally called from outside the NDX routines.

MakeNode and ChkLoad. The two routines that are responsible for loading NDX records into the tree structure maintained in memory are called *MakeNode* and *ChkLoad. ChkLoad* makes certain that a record referenced by the NODEPTR *p* is indeed loaded; if not, it calls *MakeNode* to create the necessary variables on the heap and loads the record into them. Neither routine is normally called from outside the NDX routines.

Fig. 11-3. NDX file balance helpers.

```
DEFINITION MODULE EL1103;
   FROM ELO401 IMPORT    STRING;
   FROM EL1102 IMPORT    NODEPTR;
   EXPORT QUALIFIED      Sb1,Sb2,R1rr,R1ll,R2rl,R2lr,FlushNdx;

PROCEDURE Sb1(VAR bal:INTEGER;VAR x,y:NODEPTR;VAR lower:BOOLEAN);
(*  This routine will set the appropriate balance for x and y. *)
PROCEDURE Sb2(VAR p2,p1,p:NODEPTR);
(*  This routine will set the appropriate balance for p1 and p.  *)
PROCEDURE R1rr(VAR p,p1:NODEPTR);
(*  Rotate tree once right to right. *)
PROCEDURE R1ll(VAR p,p1:NODEPTR);
(*  Rotate tree once left to left. *)
PROCEDURE R2rl(VAR p,p1,p2:NODEPTR);
(*  Rotate tree twice right to left. *)
PROCEDURE R2lr(VAR p,p1,p2:NODEPTR);
(*  Rotate tree twice left to right *)
PROCEDURE FlushNdx(ddname:STRING;VAR p:NODEPTR);
(* This routine will ensure that the entire tree from a given node downward
   is written to the NDX file.  *)
END EL1103.

IMPLEMENTATION MODULE EL1103;
   FROM ELO303 IMPORT    equal,greater,less;
   FROM ELO401 IMPORT    STRING;
   FROM EL1102 IMPORT    NODEPTR,PutNdx;

PROCEDURE Sb1(VAR bal:INTEGER;VAR x,y:NODEPTR;VAR lower:BOOLEAN);
BEGIN
   IF (bal = equal)
     THEN
       x.ptr^.balance:=greater;
       y.ptr^.balance:=less;
       lower:=FALSE;
     ELSE
       x.ptr^.balance:=equal;
       y.ptr^.balance:=equal;
     END;
   END Sb1;

PROCEDURE Sb2(VAR p2,p1,p:NODEPTR);
BEGIN
   IF (p2.ptr^.balance = less)
     THEN p.ptr^.balance:=greater;
     ELSE p.ptr^.balance:=equal;
     END;
   IF (p2.ptr^.balance = greater)
     THEN p1.ptr^.balance:=less;
     ELSE p1.ptr^.balance:=equal;
     END;
   END Sb2;

PROCEDURE R1rr(VAR p,p1:NODEPTR);
BEGIN
   p.ptr^.right:=p1.ptr^.left;
   p1.ptr^.left:=p;
   END R1rr;

PROCEDURE R1ll(VAR p,p1:NODEPTR);
BEGIN
   p.ptr^.left:=p1.ptr^.right;
```

Fig. 11-3 continued

```
    p1.ptr^.right:=p;
    END R111;

PROCEDURE R2r1(VAR p,p1,p2:NODEPTR);
BEGIN
    p2:=p1.ptr^.left;
    p1.ptr^.left:=p2.ptr^.right;
    p2.ptr^.right:=p1;
    p.ptr^.right:=p2.ptr^.left;
    p2.ptr^.left:=p;
    Sb2(p2,p,p1);
    p:=p2;
    END R2r1;

PROCEDURE R21r(VAR p,p1,p2:NODEPTR);
BEGIN
    p2:=p1.ptr^.right;
    p1.ptr^.right:=p2.ptr^.left;
    p2.ptr^.left:=p1;
    p.ptr^.left:=p2.ptr^.right;
    p2.ptr^.right:=p;
    Sb2(p2,p1,p);
    p:=p2;
    END R21r;

PROCEDURE FlushNdx(ddname:STRING;VAR p:NODEPTR);
BEGIN
    IF (p.ptr <> NIL)
      THEN
        FlushNdx(ddname,p.ptr^.left);
        FlushNdx(ddname,p.ptr^.right);
        WITH p.ptr^ DO
          PutNdx(ddname,p.nmbr,left.nmbr,right.nmbr,balance,rcrd);
          END;
      END;
    END FlushNdx;

END EL1103.
```

Helper routines

Module EL1103 (Fig. 11-3) contains six routines that help routines in the other modules maintain the balance of a tree structure, and a single routine that is used to "flush" the contents of a list of NODES to disk.

Sb1 and Sb2. Two of the routines that assist in rebalancing the tree structure after a record is deleted are called *Sb1* and *Sb2*. Refer to Wirth's book, *Algorithms + Data Structures = Programs,* for an explanation of these routines.

R1rr, R1ll, R2rl, and R2lr. There are four routines in the Etling Library that rebalance an NDX file after a new record is inserted. Again, refer to the Wirth book for details of their operation.

FlushNdx. The *FlushNdx* routine is responsible for flushing a tree structure from memory to the file. *FlushNdx* will call itself recursively to write all records in the tree structure from the starting point downward. Again, remember that even though *FlushNdx* calls *PutNdx* to write records to the file, there is no guarantee that the DOS buffers that contain the records are written to the file. Only a *ClsFile* will guarantee that the buffers are flushed.

Finding and/or Replacing Existing Records

EL1104, shown in Fig. 11-4, contains the routines for locating an existing record in an NDX file. Because the logic involved with replacing a record requires first finding it, the routine that replaces an existing record is also in this module.

FindNdx. *FindNdx* will retrieve existing records in an NDX file. To do this, *FindNdx* uses the internal routine, *ChkNode* (described in the next section) to follow the tree structure until it comes to a record whose key matches the key portion of *rcrd*. The tree that *FindNdx* searches is defined by the parameter, *hook*. If *hook.ptr* is equal to NIL on entry, it indicates that the tree has not yet been accessed; if *top* is equal to TRUE, *FindNdx* will load the header record to begin access at the top of the file tree. (If *top* equals FALSE and *hook.ptr* equal, NIL, *FindNdx* will simply return FALSE to indicate that no record was found.)

If, after following the tree, *ChkNode* is unable to locate a record whose key matches *rcrd*, *FindNdx* will return FALSE to indicate that the record does not exist in the file. If the record can be found, *FindNdx* will be true, and *rcrd* will contain the data portion of the appropriate NDX record.

ChkNode. The logic that searches the NDX file for a matching key is defined as a separate routine so that it may call itself recursively. That routine is named *ChkNode*. The routine uses *ChkLoad* to be certain that the appropriate elements are in core, *CompArea* to decide which branch to follow, and *ClrNdx* to tidy up the tree as it follows down the structure. If *CompArea* indicates that a requested record lies along the left branch, *ChkLoad* uses *ClrNdx* to clear the records from core that constitute the right branch; if the record is in the right branch, the left branch is cleared.

ChkNode is also used by *ReplNdx*. Therefore, it includes a parameter named *dorewrt* that controls whether or not the located record is rewritten to the file. If, on entry, *dorewrt* = TRUE, the contents of *rcrd* will be used to replace the contents of the record on file.

ReplNdx. There are times when a program only needs to replace the data portion of an existing NDX record. *ReplNdx* handles this operation. *ReplNdx* uses *ChkNode*, just like *FindNdx*, to locate the appropriate record and tells *ChkNode* to rewrite it.

Adding Records to an NDX File

MarkNdx. New records are added to an NDX file using *MarkNdx*. The record to be added is contained in *rcrd*. The key of the record is located at *rcrd*[*keyloc*] to *rcrd*[*keyloc* + *keylen* − 1]. *MarkNdx* assumes that the key portion of *rcrd* is unique within the file. If a record with a matching key does exist, *MarkNdx* might produce unpredictable results. Because a program that adds record to an NDX file would normally call *FindNdx* to determine whether or not the record exists *before* accepting input data, *MarkNdx* assumes that if it is called, the key does not yet exist.

The routine that actually adds a new record is called *InsrtKey* and is discussed a little later in this chapter, but first note the logic in *MarkNdx*. If *InsrtKey* returns with *written* = FALSE, it indicates that the tree structure has been changed but that the

Fig. 11-4. Locate an NDX record.

```
DEFINITION MODULE EL1104;
  FROM EL0401 IMPORT    STRING;
  FROM EL0503 IMPORT    LONGCARD;
  FROM EL1007 IMPORT    RCRD;
  FROM EL1102 IMPORT    NODEPTR;
  EXPORT QUALIFIED      FindNdx,ReplNdx;

PROCEDURE FindNdx(ddname:STRING;VAR rcrd:RCRD; VAR nmbr:LONGCARD;
                      keyloc,keylen:CARDINAL;
                  VAR hook:NODEPTR;top:BOOLEAN):BOOLEAN;
(* This routine will attempt to locate a record in the file associated with
   ddname whose key matches the key portion of rcrd.  If a matching record
   exists, its contents will be returned in rcrd, nmbr will be set to the
   appropriate record number, and the function will return true.  If a
   record cannot be found, nmbr will return = 0 and the function will be
   false.  *)
PROCEDURE ReplNdx(ddname:STRING;VAR rcrd:RCRD;
                  VAR nmbr:LONGCARD;keyloc,keylen:CARDINAL;
                  VAR hook:NODEPTR;top:BOOLEAN; updtdir:BOOLEAN);
(* If a record with a matching key can be found in the NDX file associated
   with ddname, it will be replaced by rcrd, and its record number will be
   returned in nmbr.  If no match can be found, nmbr will return = 0, and
   no change will be made to the file.  If the record is replaced, and
   updtdir = TRUE, the file will be closed so that the directory will be
   properly updated.  *)
END EL1104.


IMPLEMENTATION MODULE EL1104;
  FROM EL0302 IMPORT    MovByteL;
  FROM EL0401 IMPORT    STRING;
  FROM EL0303 IMPORT    CompArea,less,greater,equal;
  FROM EL0503 IMPORT    LONGCARD,ComLCard,lczero,lcone;
  FROM EL1002 IMPORT    ClsFile,DISP;
  FROM EL1007 IMPORT    RCRD,MakeRcrd,ClrRcrd;
  FROM EL1102 IMPORT    NODEPTR,ChkLoad,PutNdx,GetNdx,ClrNdx;


PROCEDURE ChkNode(ddname:STRING;VAR p:NODEPTR;VAR nmbr:LONGCARD;
                  VAR rcrd:RCRD;keyloc,keylen:CARDINAL;dorewrt:BOOLEAN);
BEGIN
  ChkLoad(ddname,p,rcrd^.rcrdlen);
  CASE CompArea(rcrd^.area,keyloc-1,keylen,
                    p.ptr^.rcrd^.area,keyloc-1,keylen,keylen) OF

    equal:
      nmbr:=p.nmbr;
      IF (NOT dorewrt)
        THEN MovByteL(p.ptr^.rcrd^.area,
                          rcrd^.area,0,0,rcrd^.rcrdlen);

        ELSE
          MovByteL(rcrd^.area,p.ptr^.rcrd^.area,0,0,rcrd^.rcrdlen);
          WITH p.ptr^ DO
            PutNdx(ddname,nmbr,left.nmbr,right.nmbr,balance,rcrd);
            END;
        END;
    | less:
      IF (p.ptr^.right.ptr <> NIL)
        THEN ClrNdx(p.ptr^.right);
        END;
      IF (ComLCard(p.ptr^.left.nmbr,lczero) <> equal)
        THEN ChkNode(ddname,p.ptr^.left,nmbr,rcrd,keyloc,keylen,dorewrt)
        ELSE nmbr:=lczero;
        END;
```

```
    ELSE
      IF (p.ptr^.left.ptr <> NIL)
        THEN ClrNdx(p.ptr^.left);
        END;
      IF (ComLCard(p.ptr^.right.nmbr,lczero) <> equal)
        THEN ChkNode(ddname,p.ptr^.right,nmbr,rcrd,keyloc,keylen,dorewrt)
        ELSE nmbr:=lczero;
        END;
      END;
  END ChkNode;

PROCEDURE FindNdx(ddname:STRING;VAR rcrd:RCRD;
                      VAR nmbr:LONGCARD;keyloc,keylen:CARDINAL;
                        VAR hook:NODEPTR;top:BOOLEAN):BOOLEAN;

VAR
  d1,d2:LONGCARD;
  bal:INTEGER;
  dummy:RCRD;
BEGIN
  nmbr:=lczero;
  IF (hook.ptr = NIL) AND (top)
    THEN
      MakeRcrd(rcrd^.rcrdlen,dummy);
      GetNdx(ddname,lcone,d1,d2,bal,dummy);
      MovByteL(dummy^.area,hook.nmbr,0,0,4);
      ClrRcrd(dummy);
    END;
  IF (ComLCard(hook.nmbr,lczero) <> equal)
    THEN ChkNode(ddname,hook,nmbr,rcrd,keyloc,keylen,FALSE);
    END;
  IF (ComLCard(nmbr,lczero) = equal)
    THEN RETURN FALSE;
    ELSE RETURN TRUE;
    END;
  END FindNdx;

PROCEDURE ReplNdx(ddname:STRING;VAR rcrd:RCRD;
                      VAR nmbr:LONGCARD;keyloc,keylen:CARDINAL;
                        VAR hook:NODEPTR;top:BOOLEAN;updtdir:BOOLEAN);
VAR
  d1,d2:LONGCARD;
  bal:INTEGER;
  dummy:RCRD;
BEGIN
  nmbr:=lczero;
  IF (hook.ptr = NIL) AND (top)
    THEN
      MakeRcrd(rcrd^.rcrdlen,dummy);
      GetNdx(ddname,lcone,d1,d2,bal,dummy);
      MovByteL(dummy^.area,hook.nmbr,0,0,4);
      ClrRcrd(dummy);
    END;
  IF (ComLCard(hook.nmbr,lczero) <> equal)
    THEN ChkNode(ddname,hook,nmbr,rcrd,keyloc,keylen,TRUE);
    END;
  IF (updtdir)
    THEN ClsFile(ddname,clsonly);
    END;
  END ReplNdx;

END EL1104.
```

modified records have not yet been written to the file; *MarkNdx* will call *FlushNdx* to handle this. If on entry to *MarkNdx, top* equals TRUE, it indicates that the NDX file has only one tree and that the header record contains the address to the top of tree record. If, in the course of adding the record to the file, *InsrtKey* causes the file hanger to change, *MarkNdx* contains code to update the header record. Finally, if the calling program indicates that the file directory entry should be updated (i.e., *updtdir* equals TRUE) *MarkNdx* will call *ClsFile*.

InsrtKey. The routine that inserts a new record into a binary tree is called *InsrtKey* (see EL1105, Fig. 11-5). *InsrtKey* is defined as a separate procedure, rather than as code within *MarkNdx*, because it needs to be able to call itself recursively. *InsrtKey* should never be called from outside the NDX routines.

InsrtKey is a fairly complicated routine. The theory behind its logic is discussed in Wirth's book (refer to the discussion of "search" on page 220). The parameters used by *InsrtKey* do need some explanation. The *ddname* is of course the <ddname> of the file in which the record will be inserted. The *nmbr* will eventually return to *MarkNdx* with the number of the record in the file at which *rcrd* is written. The *keyloc* and *keylen* define the location and size of the key within *rcrd*. The *p* is used to follow the tree structure in memory; as each call to *InsrtKey* is made, *p* reflects the element begin considered. The *higher* returns to the caller equal to TRUE if, in the course of inserting the record, the tree structure associated with *p* grew higher (e.g., another level was added to the structure hanging from the element *p*). The *written* returns to the caller equal to FALSE if the tree structure hanging from *p* must be rewritten to the file to reflect the changes in the structure.

When *InsrtKey* finally arrives at the point in the tree where the new record should be inserted, *p.nmbr,* the record number associated with last element accessed, will equal zero. When this occurs, *InsrtKey* calls *MakeNode* and *GetFNdx* to create the new record, changes *higher* and *written* to reflect that the structure has changed, and returns back through the chain of recursive calls to *MarkNdx*.

If *p.nmbr* is not equal to zero when *InsrtKey* is called, the routine will use *ChkLoad* to make certain that the appropriate portion of the tree structure is in memory, and then use *CompArea* to determine in which branch of the tree the new record belongs. If the new key is lower in the collating sequence than the key associated with *p, InsrtKey* will call itself using the left branch; a higher key belongs in the right branch (note that there is no logic to deal with an equal key). Regardless of which branch is taken, on return from the recursive call. *InsrtKey* behaves more or less the same. First, it checks *higher* to see if the number of levels in the branch has changed. If *higher* is true, *InsrtKey* uses a CASE statement to determine which way the tree has been tilted and calls the appropriate balancing routine (*R1ll, R2lr, R1rr*, or *R2rl*) to rotate the elements to bring the tree back into balance. When *InsrtKey* returns far enough back through its recursive calls so that *higher* is not longer true, it uses *written* to decide if the subtree associated with the current element needs rewriting.

GetFNdx. When *InsrtKey* finds the place where a new record belongs, it calls *GetFNdx* to retrieve a physical record from the file in which to store it. *GetFNdx* refers to *hdrrcrd.frstfree*. If records have been deleted from the file and free records are imbedded within the existing file space, *hdrrcrd.frstfree* will be greater than zero and *GetFNdx* can use the first record in the free record chain to contain the new entry. If

Fig. 11-5. Add a new NDX record.

```
DEFINITION MODULE EL1105;
   FROM EL0401 IMPORT    STRING;
   FROM EL0503 IMPORT    LONGCARD;
   FROM EL1007 IMPORT    RCRD;
   FROM EL1102 IMPORT    NODEPTR;
   EXPORT QUALIFIED      MarkNdx;

PROCEDURE MarkNdx(ddname:STRING;VAR rcrd:RCRD;
                    VAR nmbr:LONGCARD;keyloc,keylen:CARDINAL;
                      VAR hook:NODEPTR;top,updtdir:BOOLEAN);
(* This routine will add a record to the NDX file associated with ddname.
   If a matching record already exists, the results of this routine are
   undefined...be sure to call FindNdx first to see if a record exists.  If
   a new record is created, nmbr will return with the appropriate record
   number.  If, on entry, updtdir = TRUE, the file will be closed so that
   the directory will be properly updated.  *)
END EL1105.


IMPLEMENTATION MODULE EL1105;
   FROM SYSTEM IMPORT    BYTE;
   FROM EL0302 IMPORT    MovByteL,FillByte;
   FROM EL0303 IMPORT    CompArea,less,equal,greater;
   FROM EL0401 IMPORT    STRING;
   FROM EL0503 IMPORT    LONGCARD,lcone,lczero,AddLCard,ComLCard;
   FROM EL1002 IMPORT    ClsFile,DISP;
   FROM EL1007 IMPORT    RCRD,MakeRcrd,ClrRcrd;
   FROM EL1102 IMPORT    MakeNode,GetNdx,PutNdx,ChkLoad,NODEPTR;
   FROM EL1103 IMPORT    FlushNdx,R1rr,R2rl,R1ll,R2lr;

PROCEDURE GetFNdx(ddname:STRING;VAR nmbr:LONGCARD;rcrdlen:CARDINAL);
VAR
   rcrd:RCRD;
   frstfree,lastrcrd,frstndx,d1,d2:LONGCARD;
   bal:INTEGER;
BEGIN
   MakeRcrd(rcrdlen,rcrd);
   FillByte(BYTE(0),rcrd^.area,0,rcrd^.rcrdlen);
   GetNdx(ddname,lcone,frstfree,lastrcrd,bal,rcrd);
   MovByteL(rcrd^.area,frstndx,0,0,4);
   IF (ComLCard(frstfree,lczero) = equal)
     THEN
       AddLCard(lastrcrd,lcone,lastrcrd);
       nmbr:=lastrcrd;
       PutNdx(ddname,nmbr,lczero,lczero,0,rcrd);
     ELSE
       nmbr:=frstfree;
       GetNdx(ddname,nmbr,frstfree,d1,bal,rcrd);
     END;
   MovByteL(frstndx,rcrd^.area,0,0,4);
   PutNdx(ddname,lcone,frstfree,lastrcrd,0,rcrd);
   ClrRcrd(rcrd);
   END GetFNdx;


PROCEDURE InsrtKey(ddname:STRING;VAR nmbr:LONGCARD;
                    VAR rcrd:RCRD;keyloc,keylen:CARDINAL;
                        VAR p:NODEPTR;VAR higher,written:BOOLEAN);
VAR
   where:INTEGER;
   p1,p2:NODEPTR;
BEGIN
   IF (ComLCard(p.nmbr,lczero) = equal)
```

Fig. 11-5 continued

```
THEN
  MakeNode(p,rcrd^.rcrdlen);
  GetFNdx(ddname,p.nmbr,rcrd^.rcrdlen);
  higher:=TRUE;
  written:=FALSE;
  p.ptr^.balance:=equal;
  MovByteL(rcrd^.area,p.ptr^.rcrd^.area,0,0,rcrd^.rcrdlen);
  nmbr:=p.nmbr;
ELSE
  ChkLoad(ddname,p,rcrd^.rcrdlen);
  where:=CompArea(rcrd^.area,keyloc-1,keylen,
                  p.ptr^.rcrd^.area,keyloc-1,keylen,keylen);
  IF (where = less)
    THEN
      InsrtKey(ddname,nmbr,rcrd,keyloc,keylen,
               p.ptr^.left,higher,written);
      IF (higher)
        THEN
          CASE p.ptr^.balance OF
            greater:
              p.ptr^.balance:=equal;
              higher:=FALSE;
          ! equal:p.ptr^.balance:=less;
          ! less:
              p1:=p.ptr^.left;
              IF (p1.ptr^.balance = less)
                THEN
                  R1ll(p,p1);
                  p.ptr^.balance:=equal;
                  p:=p1;
                ELSE R2lr(p,p1,p2);
                END;
              p.ptr^.balance:=equal;
              higher:=FALSE;
            ELSE
            END;
        ELSE
          IF (NOT written)
            THEN
              written:=TRUE;
              FlushNdx(ddname,p);
            END;
        END;
    ELSE
      InsrtKey(ddname,nmbr,rcrd,keyloc,keylen,
               p.ptr^.right,higher,written);
      IF (higher)
        THEN
          CASE p.ptr^.balance OF
            less:
              p.ptr^.balance:=equal;
              higher:=FALSE;
          ! equal:p.ptr^.balance:=greater;
          ! greater:
              p1:=p.ptr^.right;
              IF (p1.ptr^.balance = greater)
                THEN
                  R1rr(p,p1);
                  p.ptr^.balance:=equal;
                  p:=p1;
                ELSE R2rl(p,p1,p2);
```

```
                    END;
                p.ptr^.balance:=equal;
                higher:=FALSE;
              ELSE
              END;
          ELSE IF (NOT written)
            THEN
                written:=TRUE;
                FlushNdx(ddname,p);
              END;
            END;
        END;
    END;
  END InsrtKey;

PROCEDURE MarkNdx(ddname:STRING;VAR rcrd:RCRD;
                  VAR nmbr:LONGCARD;keyloc,keylen:CARDINAL;
                    VAR hook:NODEPTR;top,updtdir:BOOLEAN);

VAR
  d1,d2,frstndx:LONGCARD;
  bal:INTEGER;
  dummy:RCRD;
  higher,written:BOOLEAN;
BEGIN
  higher:=FALSE;
  written:=TRUE;
  frstndx:=hook.nmbr;
  InsrtKey(ddname,nmbr,rcrd,keyloc,keylen,hook,higher,written);
  IF (NOT written)
    THEN FlushNdx(ddname,hook);
    END;
  IF (top) AND (ComLCard(frstndx,hook.nmbr) <> equal)
    THEN
      MakeRcrd(rcrd^.rcrdlen,dummy);
      GetNdx(ddname,lcone,d1,d2,bal,dummy);
      MovByteL(hook.nmbr,dummy^.area,0,0,4);
      PutNdx(ddname,lcone,d1,d2,bal,dummy);
      ClrRcrd(dummy);
    END;
  IF (updtdir)
    THEN ClsFile(ddname,clsonly);
    END;
  END MarkNdx;

END EL1105.
```

hdrrcrd.frstfree is equal to zero, *GetFNdx* will call *PutNdx* to create a new record past the end of the current file at *hdrrcrd.lastrcrd* + 1. In either case, *GetFNdx* will rewrite the header record to update the entries accordingly.

Deleting Records

The routines that delete records from an NDX file are contained in EL1106, shown in Fig. 11-6.

FreeNdx. The routine that removes records from the tree structure in an NDX file is named *FreeNdx*. Again, *FreeNdx* relies on *DelKey*, an internal routine that can be called recursively, to do most of the work. When control returns to *FreeNdx*, it may

Fig. 11-6. Delete an NDX record.

```
DEFINITION MODULE EL1106;
  FROM EL0401 IMPORT    STRING;
  FROM EL1007 IMPORT    RCRD;
  FROM EL1102 IMPORT    NODEPTR;
  EXPORT QUALIFIED      FreeNdx;

PROCEDURE FreeNdx(ddname:STRING;VAR rcrd:RCRD; keyloc,keylen:CARDINAL;
                    VAR hook:NODEPTR; top,updtdir:BOOLEAN);
(* This routine will attempt to delete the NDX record whose key matches the
   key portion of rcrd from the file associated with ddname.  If a record
   with a matching key exists, the record will be removed from the normal
   tree within the file, the record's contents will be set to binary
   zeroes, and the record's number will be added to the chain of free
   records in the file.  If a record with a matching key does not exist,
   the results of this routine are undefined.  If a record is removed, and
   updtdir = TRUE on entry, the file will be closed before returning so
   that the directory will be properly updated.  *)
END EL1106.


IMPLEMENTATION MODULE EL1106;
  FROM Storage IMPORT   DEALLOCATE;
  FROM SYSTEM IMPORT     BYTE;
  FROM EL0302 IMPORT     MovByteL;
  FROM EL0303 IMPORT     CompArea,less,equal,greater;
  FROM EL0401 IMPORT     STRING;
  FROM EL0503 IMPORT     LONGCARD,lcone,lczero,ComLCard;
  FROM EL1002 IMPORT     ClsFile,DISP;
  FROM EL1007 IMPORT     RCRD,MakeRcrd,ClrRcrd;
  FROM EL1102 IMPORT     MakeNode,GetNdx,PutNdx,ChkLoad,NODEPTR;
  FROM EL1103 IMPORT     FlushNdx,Sb1,Sb2,R1rr,R2rl,R1ll,R2lr;

PROCEDURE PutFNdx(ddname:STRING;nmbr:LONGCARD;rcrdlen:CARDINAL);
VAR
  last,next,d1,d2:LONGCARD;
  rcrd:RCRD;
  bal:INTEGER;
BEGIN
  MakeRcrd(rcrdlen,rcrd);
  next:=lcone;
  REPEAT
    last:=next;
    GetNdx(ddname,last,next,d1,bal,rcrd);
    UNTIL (ComLCard(next,lczero) = equal)
                    OR (ComLCard(next,nmbr) = greater);
  PutNdx(ddname,last,nmbr,d1,bal,rcrd);
  PutNdx(ddname,nmbr,next,lczero,0,rcrd);
  ClrRcrd(rcrd);
  END PutFNdx;


PROCEDURE DelKey(ddname:STRING;VAR rcrd:RCRD;keyloc,keylen:CARDINAL;
                    VAR p:NODEPTR;VAR lower,written:BOOLEAN);
VAR
  q:NODEPTR;

  PROCEDURE Balance1(VAR p:NODEPTR;VAR lower:BOOLEAN);
  VAR
    p1,p2:NODEPTR;
  BEGIN
  CASE p.ptr^.balance OF
    less:p.ptr^.balance:=equal;
  ! equal:
```

```
            p.ptr^.balance:=greater;
            lower:=FALSE;
      ! greater:
            p1:=p.ptr^.right;
            ChkLoad(ddname,p1,rcrd^.rcrdlen);
            IF (p1.ptr^.balance <> less)
              THEN
                R1rr(p,p1);
                Sb1(p1.ptr^.balance,p,p1,lower);
                p:=p1;
              ELSE
                ChkLoad(ddname,p1.ptr^.left,rcrd^.rcrdlen);
                R2rl(p,p1,p2);
                p2.ptr^.balance:=equal;
              END;
        ELSE END;
      END Balance1;


PROCEDURE Balance2(VAR p:NODEPTR;VAR lower:BOOLEAN);
VAR
  p1,p2:NODEPTR;
BEGIN
    CASE p.ptr^.balance OF
      greater:p.ptr^.balance:=equal;
      ! equal:
            p.ptr^.balance:=less;
            lower:=FALSE;
      ! less:
            p1:=p.ptr^.left;
            ChkLoad(ddname,p1,rcrd^.rcrdlen);
            IF (p1.ptr^.balance <> greater)
              THEN
                R1ll(p,p1);
                Sb1(p1.ptr^.balance,p1,p,lower);
                p:=p1;
              ELSE
                ChkLoad(ddname,p1.ptr^.right,rcrd^.rcrdlen);
                R2lr(p,p1,p2);
                p2.ptr^.balance:=equal;
              END;
        ELSE END;
      END Balance2;


PROCEDURE Del(VAR r:NODEPTR;VAR lower:BOOLEAN);
BEGIN
    ChkLoad(ddname,r,rcrd^.rcrdlen);
    IF (ComLCard(r.ptr^.right.nmbr,lczero) <> equal)
      THEN
        Del(r.ptr^.right,lower);
        IF (lower)
          THEN Balance2(r,lower);
          END;
      ELSE
        MovByteL(r.ptr^.rcrd^.area,p.ptr^.rcrd^.area,0,0,
                          p.ptr^.rcrd^.rcrdlen);
        p.nmbr:=r.nmbr;
        q.ptr:=r.ptr;
        r:=r.ptr^.left;
          lower:=TRUE;
        END;
      END Del;
```

Fig. 11-6 continued

```
BEGIN
  ChkLoad(ddname,p,rcrd^.rcrdlen);
  CASE CompArea(rcrd^.area,keyloc-1,keylen,
                    p.ptr^.rcrd^.area,keyloc-1,keylen,keylen) OF
    less:
      DelKey(ddname,rcrd,keyloc,keylen,p.ptr^.left,lower,written);
      IF (lower)
        THEN Balance1(p,lower)
        ELSE IF (NOT written)
          THEN
            written:=TRUE;
            FlushNdx(ddname,p);
          END;
        END;
  ! greater:
      DelKey(ddname,rcrd,keyloc,keylen,p.ptr^.right,lower,written);
      IF (lower)
        THEN Balance2(p,lower)
        ELSE IF (NOT written)
          THEN
            written:=TRUE;
            FlushNdx(ddname,p);
          END;
        END;
    ELSE
      q:=p;
      IF (ComLCard(q.ptr^.right.nmbr,lczero) = equal)
        THEN
          p:=q.ptr^.left;
          lower:=TRUE;
        ELSE IF (ComLCard(q.ptr^.left.nmbr,lczero) = equal)
          THEN
            p:=q.ptr^.right;
            lower:=TRUE;
          ELSE
            Del(q.ptr^.left,lower);
            IF (lower)
              THEN Balance1(p,lower);
              END;
          END;
        END;
      PutFNdx(ddname,q.nmbr,rcrd^.rcrdlen);
      ClrRcrd(q.ptr^.rcrd);
      DISPOSE(q.ptr);
      q.ptr:=NIL;
      written:=FALSE;
    END;
  END DelKey;

PROCEDURE FreeNdx(ddname:STRING;VAR rcrd:RCRD;keyloc,keylen:CARDINAL;
                    VAR hook:NODEPTR;top,updtdir:BOOLEAN);
VAR
  dummy:RCRD;
  d1,d2,frstndx:LONGCARD;
  lower,written:BOOLEAN;
  balance:INTEGER;
BEGIN
  lower:=FALSE;
  written:=TRUE;
  frstndx:=hook.nmbr;
  DelKey(ddname,rcrd,keyloc,keylen,hook,lower,written);
```

```
IF (NOT written)
  THEN FlushNdx(ddname,hook);
  END;
IF (top) AND (ComLCard(frstndx,hook.nmbr) <> equal)
  THEN
    MakeRcrd(rcrd^.rcrdlen,dummy);
    GetNdx(ddname,lcone,d1,d2,balance,dummy);
    MovByteL(hook.nmbr,dummy^.area,0,0,4);
    PutNdx(ddname,lcone,d1,d2,balance,dummy);
    ClrRcrd(dummy);
  END;
IF (updtdir)
  THEN ClsFile(ddname,clsonly);
  END;
END FreeNdx;

END EL1106.
```

call *FlushNdx* to write changed records. If the tree being followed is the only tree in the file, *FreeNdx* might modify the control fields in the header record for the file. And, if *updtdir* equals TRUE on entry, *FreeNdx* will call *ClsFile* to ensure that the directory entry for the file is updated correctly.

DelKey. *DelKey* handles the removal of records from the tree structure. Like *InsrtKey*, its logic is fairly complex and it has several internal routines to help with its operations. Basically, *DelKey* is *InsrtKey* in reverse. The routine calls itself recursively until it finds the record to be deleted, and then calls *PutFNdx* to add the record into the chain of free records in the file. When the record is removed from the structure, *DelKey* uses *balance1, Balance2, Sb1, Sb2, R1rr, R1ll, R2rl,* and *R2lr* to bring the tree back into balance. As it happens, rebalancing the tree after a deletion is more complicated than after an insertion. Again, refer to Wirth's book for details.

PutFNdx. *PutFNdx* adds records to the chain of free records in an NDX file. Note that *PutFNdx* uses a REPEAT loop to locate the next free record whose address is greater than *nmbr*. The new free record is added at that point. Because the next new NDX record to be added to a file uses the first record in the free chain, keeping the chain in order by record number tends to bunch all "live" records near the beginning of the file. This tends to improve retrieval speed, but does have a severe detrimental effect on the speed with which records are deleted. If your application involves deleting large numbers of records at one time (as would happen in an end of month "purge" operation), you might want to simply add free chain records on the end.

Reading from Beginning to End

A program often must read records from an NDX file sequentially. Unlike a text file where records are retrieved strictly in the sequence in which they were written, the records in an NDX file are retrieved in key sequence. Sometimes the program doesn't want to read all of the records in a file but instead wishes to start at some specific key. The routines that make these operations possible are in EL1107, shown in Fig. 11-7.

NextNdx. When a program needs to read the next record in a tree structure it uses *NextNdx*. If, on entry, *continue* equal FALSE, *NextNdx* will begin accessing the file at the record whose key is equal to or greater than the key in *rcrd*. If *continue*

Fig. 11-7. Get the next NDX record.

```
DEFINITION MODULE EL1107;
   FROM EL0401 IMPORT    STRING;
   FROM EL0503 IMPORT    LONGCARD;
   FROM EL1007 IMPORT    RCRD;
   FROM EL1102 IMPORT    NODEPTR;
   EXPORT QUALIFIED      NextNdx;

PROCEDURE NextNdx(ddname:STRING;VAR rcrd:RCRD;
                   VAR nmbr:LONGCARD;keyloc,keylen:CARDINAL;
                   VAR hook:NODEPTR; top,continue:BOOLEAN):BOOLEAN;
(* This routine will locate a record in the NDX file associated with ddname
   whose key is equal to or greater than the key in rcrd.  If continue =
   TRUE on entry, only a record with a greater key will be returned.  If a
   record exists, the function will return true and nmbr will contain the
   number of the record.  If no more records exist, the function will
   return false and nmbr = 0.  *)
END EL1107.


IMPLEMENTATION MODULE EL1107;
   FROM EL0302 IMPORT    MovByteL,FillByte;
   FROM EL0303 IMPORT    CompArea,less,equal,greater;
   FROM EL0401 IMPORT    STRING;
   FROM EL0503 IMPORT    LONGCARD,lcone,lczero,ComLCard;
   FROM EL1007 IMPORT    RCRD,MakeRcrd,ClrRcrd;
   FROM EL1102 IMPORT    GetNdx,ChkLoad,NODEPTR,ClrNdx;


PROCEDURE TraceR(ddname:STRING;VAR p:NODEPTR;VAR nmbr:LONGCARD;
                   VAR rcrd:RCRD;keyloc,keylen:CARDINAL;continue:BOOLEAN);
VAR
   where:INTEGER;
BEGIN
   ChkLoad(ddname,p,rcrd^.rcrdlen);
   where:=CompArea(rcrd^.area,keyloc-1,keylen,
                    p.ptr^.rcrd^.area,keyloc-1,keylen,keylen);
   IF (where = less)
     THEN IF (ComLCard(p.ptr^.left.nmbr,lczero) = equal)
       THEN
         where:=equal;
         continue:=FALSE;
       ELSE
         IF (p.ptr^.right.ptr <> NIL)
           THEN ClrNdx(p.ptr^.right);
           END;
         TraceR(ddname,p.ptr^.left,
                          nmbr,rcrd,keyloc,keylen,continue);
         IF (ComLCard(nmbr,lczero) = equal)
           THEN
             ChkLoad(ddname,p,rcrd^.rcrdlen);
             where:=equal;
             continue:=FALSE;
           END;
       END;
     END;
   IF (where = equal)
     THEN IF (continue)
       THEN
         nmbr:=lczero;
         where:=greater;
       ELSE
         nmbr:=p.nmbr;
         IF (ComLCard(nmbr,lczero) <> equal)
```

```
              THEN MovByteL(p.ptr^.rcrd^.area,rcrd^.area,
                                       0,0,rcrd^.rcrdlen);
            END;
        END;
      END;
    IF (where = greater)
      THEN
        IF (p.ptr^.left.ptr <> NIL)
          THEN ClrNdx(p.ptr^.left);
          END;
        IF (ComLCard(p.ptr^.right.nmbr,lczero) <> equal)
          THEN TraceR(ddname,p.ptr^.right,nmbr,rcrd,
                                       keyloc,keylen,continue);
          ELSE nmbr:=lczero;
          END;
      END;
    END TraceR;
PROCEDURE NextNdx(ddname:STRING;VAR rcrd:RCRD;
                  VAR nmbr:LONGCARD;keyloc,keylen:CARDINAL;
                  VAR hook:NODEPTR;top,continue:BOOLEAN):BOOLEAN;
VAR
  dummy:RCRD;
  d1,d2:LONGCARD;
  balance:INTEGER;
BEGIN
  IF (hook.ptr = NIL) AND (top)
    THEN
      MakeRcrd(rcrd^.rcrdlen,dummy);
      GetNdx(ddname,lcone,d1,d2,balance,dummy);
      MovByteL(dummy^.area,hook.nmbr,0,0,4);
      ClrRcrd(dummy);
    END;
  IF (ComLCard(hook.nmbr,lczero) <> equal)
    THEN TraceR(ddname,hook,nmbr,rcrd,keyloc,keylen,continue)
    ELSE nmbr:=lczero;
    END;
  IF (ComLCard(nmbr,lczero) = equal)
    THEN RETURN FALSE
    ELSE RETURN TRUE;
    END;
  END NextNdx;
END EL1107.
```

equals TRUE, *NextNdx* will only look for a record with a greater key. In either case, *NextNdx* returns with the next record in the structure, or false if no more records exist. A program can use this routine to read a complete file from beginning to end or to start reading somewhere within the file and continue until some condition is met. Note that to read from the beginning of the file, set the key portion of *rcrd* to all CHR(0)'s on the first access.

TraceR. Once again, the logic for following a tree from left to right is contained in a separate routine, *TraceR,* so that it can call itself. Its logic is quite similar to most of the other routines already discussed.

Reading Backwards

In the same way that the records in an NDX file can be retrieved in key sequence, they can also be read in reverse key sequence. The routines that read an NDX file backward are shown in Fig. 11-8 (EL1108).

Fig. 11-8. Get the previous NDX record.

```
DEFINITION MODULE EL1108;
  FROM EL0401 IMPORT    STRING;
  FROM EL0503 IMPORT    LONGCARD;
  FROM EL1007 IMPORT    RCRD;
  FROM EL1102 IMPORT    NODEPTR;
  EXPORT QUALIFIED      LastNdx;

PROCEDURE LastNdx(ddname:STRING;VAR rcrd:RCRD;
                    VAR nmbr:LONGCARD;keyloc,keylen:CARDINAL;
                        VAR hook:NODEPTR;top,continue:BOOLEAN):BOOLEAN;
(* This routine will locate a record in the NDX file associated with ddname
   whose key is equal to or less than the key in rcrd.  If continue = TRUE
   on entry, only a record with a lesser key will be returned.  If a record
   exists, the function will return true and nmbr will contain the number
   of the record.  If no more records exist, the function will return false
   and nmbr = 0.  *)
END EL1108.


IMPLEMENTATION MODULE EL1108;
  FROM EL0302 IMPORT    MovByteL,FillByte;
  FROM EL0303 IMPORT    CompArea,less,equal,greater;
  FROM EL0401 IMPORT    STRING;
  FROM EL0503 IMPORT    LONGCARD,lcone,lczero,ComLCard;
  FROM EL1007 IMPORT    RCRD,MakeRcrd,ClrRcrd;
  FROM EL1102 IMPORT    GetNdx,ChkLoad,NODEPTR,ClrNdx;

PROCEDURE TraceL(ddname:STRING;VAR p:NODEPTR;VAR nmbr:LONGCARD;
                    VAR rcrd:RCRD;keyloc,keylen:CARDINAL;continue:BOOLEAN);
VAR
  where:INTEGER;
BEGIN
  ChkLoad(ddname,p,rcrd^.rcrdlen);
  where:=CompArea(rcrd^.area,keyloc-1,keylen,
                    p.ptr^.rcrd^.area,keyloc-1,keylen,keylen);
  IF (where = greater)
    THEN IF (ComLCard(p.ptr^.right.nmbr,lczero) = equal)
      THEN
        where:=equal;
        continue:=FALSE;
      ELSE
        IF (p.ptr^.left.ptr <> NIL)
          THEN ClrNdx(p.ptr^.left);
          END;
        TraceL(ddname,p.ptr^.right,nmbr,rcrd,keyloc,keylen,continue);
        IF (ComLCard(nmbr,lczero) = equal)
          THEN
            ChkLoad(ddname,p,rcrd^.rcrdlen);
            where:=equal;
            continue:=FALSE;
          END;
      END;
    END;
  IF (where = equal)
    THEN IF (continue)
      THEN
        nmbr:=lczero;
        where:=less;
      ELSE
        nmbr:=p.nmbr;
        IF (ComLCard(nmbr,lczero) <> equal)
          THEN MovByteL(p.ptr^.rcrd^.area,
```

```
                                  rcrd^.area,0,0,rcrd^.rcrdlen);
            END;
          END;
        END;
    IF (where = less)
      THEN
        IF (p.ptr^.right.ptr <> NIL)
          THEN ClrNdx(p.ptr^.right);
          END;
        IF (ComLCard(p.ptr^.left.nmbr,lczero) <> equal)
          THEN TraceL(ddname,p.ptr^.left,nmbr,rcrd,
                                    keyloc,keylen,continue)
          ELSE nmbr:=lczero;
          END;
      END;
    END TraceL;

PROCEDURE LastNdx(ddname:STRING;VAR rcrd:RCRD;
                  VAR nmbr:LONGCARD;keyloc,keylen:CARDINAL;
                  VAR hook:NODEPTR;top,continue:BOOLEAN):BOOLEAN;
VAR
  dummy:RCRD;
  d1,d2:LONGCARD;
  balance:INTEGER;
BEGIN
  IF (hook.ptr = NIL) AND (top)
    THEN
      MakeRcrd(rcrd^.rcrdlen,dummy);
      GetNdx(ddname,lcone,d1,d2,balance,dummy);
      MovByteL(dummy^.area,hook.nmbr,0,0,4);
      ClrRcrd(dummy);
    END;
  IF (ComLCard(hook.nmbr,lczero) <> equal)
    THEN TraceL(ddname,hook,nmbr,rcrd,keyloc,keylen,continue)
    ELSE nmbr:=lczero;
    END;
  IF (ComLCard(nmbr,lczero) = equal)
    THEN RETURN FALSE;
    ELSE RETURN TRUE;
    END;
  END LastNdx;

END EL1108.
```

LastNdx. If a program should need to read an NDX file from the end to the beginning, the routine named *LastNdx* will handle it. Like *NextNdx,* fit can be used to start at the end of the file (set *rcrd*'s key to CHR(225)) or at some place in the middle and read backwards from there.

TraceL. The recursive routine that follows a tree structure from right to left is called *TraceL.* It operates in reverse from *TraceR.*

LINKED FILES

The last access method defined in the Etling LIbrary handles files that consist of individual records, linked together to form chains. Again, the theory of linked records is discussed in Niklaus Wirth's book.

Figure 11-9 illustrates the concept of a linked list structure. Each element of the list contains, in addition to the data that makes up the record, a control variable that

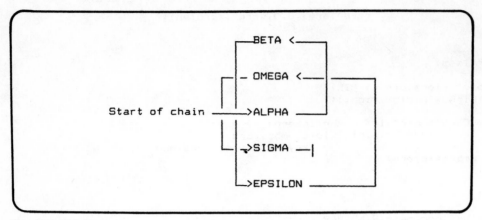

Fig. 11-9. Link files.

points to the next record in the list. The physical placement of the records in the file does not in any way indicate the order in which they will be retrieved. It is the order in which the links are arranged that determines the retrieval sequence. Therefore, although the records in the figure are stored in the order "BETA, OMEGA, ALPHA, SIGMA, EPSILON," the link structure permits them to be retrieved as though they were stored alphabetically.

The major advantage to the linked list concept, over a standard sequential file, is that it is possible to "insert" a new record into the middle of the list without being forced to rewrite the entire list. You can add the record to the end of the file and rearrange the link pointers so the new record can retrieved in the proper sequence.

LNK Files

In the Etling Library, linked list records are stored in files with a LNK extension. Each record must be at least four bytes long. The records are all stored as an ARRAY OF BYTE, and the control variables are maintained by the LNK routines, so there is no need for special data types.

Each record in an LNK file has the same format:

```
LNKRCRD = RECORD
   nextlink : LONGCARD;
   data    : ARRAY OF BYTE;
   END;
```

Only the data area is accessible to a calling routine; the control variable, *nextlink,* is used internally by the LNK routines.

Like NDX files, LNK files begin with a special header record. The format of the header record could be defined as follows:

```
HDRRCRD = RECORD
   frstfree : LONGCARD;
```

```
lastrcrd : LONGCARD;
unused : ARRAY OF BYTE;
END;
```

The *hdrrcrd.frstfree* field points to the chain of free records in the file. As with NDX files, free records are records that were used to contain records but have since been deleted from the normal access.

The Nucleus of the Link File Routines

The routines that form the basis for the link file routines, along with a LNKFCTRL type, are contained in EL1110, shown in Fig. 11-10. Again, use of the LNKFCTRL type is not mandatory.

ChkLnkF. All access to a LNK file should begin with a call to *ChkLnkF*. If the call to *OpnFile* causes a new file to be created, *opnmode* will return equal to *newfile*. This will cause *ChkLnkF* to initialize the header record in the LNK file. The fields of the header record are initialized as follows:

```
hdrrcrd.frstfree := 0;
hdrrcrd.lastrcrd := 1;
```

As with an NDX file, a program that uses a LNK file should call *ChkLnkF* periodically to ensure that the file is open. Unlike an NDX file, the LNK routines do not provide a way to close a file and update the directory automatically. If a given application requires, the program should close the LNK file periodically to ensure that the records are properly flushed to diskette.

Note that *ChkLnkF* calls *PutLink* to write the header record to the file.

PutLink. *PutLink* is the routine that handles all transfers of LNK records to the file. *PutLink* builds a record that is four bytes longer than the data area defined by *rcrd*. That four bytes is used to hold the link pointer to the next record in the chain. Note that while *PutLink* is callable from outside the LNK routines, it does not modify the link pointers. As the comments in Fig. 11-10 warn, *PutLink* should only be called to replace the contents of an existing record, but in most situations, *ReplLink* is a better choice.

GetLink. The routine that transfers data from a LNK file to memory is named *GetLink*. Like *PutLink,* this routine builds a record area four bytes longer than the data area in *rcrd*. In addition to being used by several of the internal LNK routines, *GetLink* is available to other routines. It can be used to follow a chain of LNK records, for example:

```
thislink:= { start of chain }
REPEAT
   GetLink(ddname,rcrd,thislink,nextlink);
        { . . .whatever processing. . . }
   thislink := nextlink;
   UNTIL (ComLCard(thislink,lczero) = equal);
```

Fig. 11-10. LNK file basics.

```
DEFINITION MODULE EL1110;
  FROM EL0401 IMPORT      STRING;
  FROM EL0503 IMPORT      LONGCARD;
  FROM EL1002 IMPORT      FMODE;
  FROM EL1007 IMPORT      RCRD,RFLDLIST;
  EXPORT QUALIFIED        LNKFCTRL,GetLink,PutLink,ChkLnkF;

TYPE
  LNKFCTRL = RECORD
    ddname    : STRING;
    rcrdnmbr  : LONGCARD;
    rcrd      : RCRD;
    rfldarea  : RFLDLIST;
    END;
PROCEDURE ChkLnkF(ddname:STRING;rcrdlen:CARDINAL;VAR opnmode:FMODE);
(* This routine will ensure the LNK file associated with ddname is opened
   and ready for access.  If the operation results in a new file being
   created, this routine will initialize its header record correctly.   On
   entry, opnmode should be set to the value indicating the proper
   operation...on return, it will always equal oldfile.  This routine
   should be the first LNK routine called for a given file, and, it should
   be recalled periodically to ensure that the file is still open.  *)
PROCEDURE PutLink(ddname:STRING;thisnmbr,nextline:LONGCARD;rcrd:RCRD);
(* This routine will write a record to the LNK file associated with ddname.
   Note that this routine does not link records together and it should only
   be called by an application routine to replace the data portion of an
   existing LNK record.  *)
PROCEDURE GetLink(ddname:STRING;VAR rcrd:RCRD;
                            thislink:LONGCARD;VAR nextlink:LONGCARD);
(* This routine will attempt to read the record pointed to by thislink from
   the LNK file associated with ddname.  On return, nextlink will point to
   the next record in the same chain, or will be set to zero if thislink is
   the chain end.  *)
END EL1110.

IMPLEMENTATION MODULE EL1110;
  FROM SYSTEM IMPORT      ADR,BYTE,WORD;
  FROM EL0302 IMPORT      MovByteL,FillByte;
  FROM EL0401 IMPORT      STRING,Literal;
  FROM EL0503 IMPORT      LONGCARD,lcone,lczero;
  FROM EL0906 IMPORT      Cancel;
  FROM EL1002 IMPORT      OpnFile,FMODE,LOCCNTRL,OPENKIND;
  FROM EL1005 IMPORT      GetRcrd;
  FROM EL1006 IMPORT      PutRcrd;
  FROM EL1007 IMPORT      RCRD,MakeRcrd,ClrRcrd;

CONST
  t1 = 'The Etling Library';
  t2 = 'All programs and modules, Copyright (c) 1986 TAB BOOKS INC.';
  t3 = 'Author: Don Etling';

PROCEDURE PutLink(ddname:STRING;thislink,nextlink:LONGCARD;rcrd:RCRD);
VAR
  dummy:RCRD;
BEGIN
  MakeRcrd(rcrd^.rcrdlen+4,dummy);
  MovByteL(nextlink,dummy^.area,0,0,4);
  MovByteL(rcrd^.area,dummy^.area,0,4,rcrd^.rcrdlen);
  PutRcrd(ddname,setpostn,thislink,thislink,
                    dummy^.rcrdlen,ADR(dummy^.area));
  ClrRcrd(dummy);
```

```
  END PutLink;
PROCEDURE GetLink(ddname:STRING;VAR rcrd:RCRD;
                   thislink:LONGCARD;VAR nextlink:LONGCARD);
VAR
  dummy:RCRD;
  len:WORD;
BEGIN
  MakeRcrd(rcrd^.rcrdlen+4,dummy);
  IF (NOT GetRcrd(ddname,setpostn,thislink,nextlink,
               dummy^.rcrdlen,len,ADR(dummy^.area)))
    THEN Cancel(Literal('GetLink'),ddname,1,0);
    END;
  MovByteL(dummy^.area,nextlink,0,0,4);
  MovByteL(dummy^.area,rcrd^.area,4,0,rcrd^.rcrdlen);
  ClrRcrd(dummy);
  END GetLink;

PROCEDURE ChkLnkF(ddname:STRING;rcrdlen:CARDINAL;VAR opnmode:FMODE);
VAR
  dummy:RCRD;
  ioerr:BYTE;
  lastrcrd:LONGCARD;
BEGIN
  OpnFile(ddname,opnmode,ioerr,insist);
  IF (opnmode = newfile)
    THEN
      MakeRcrd(rcrdlen+4,dummy);
      FillByte(CHR(0),dummy^.area,0,rcrdlen+4);
      lastrcrd:=lcone;
      MovByteL(lastrcrd,dummy^.area,0,0,4);
      PutLink(ddname,lcone,lczero,dummy);
      ClrRcrd(dummy);
    END;
  opnmode:=oldfile;
  END ChkLnkF;

END EL1110.
```

Adding New Records to a LNK File

The routine that adds records to an LNK file is exported from EL1111. (Refer to Fig. 11-11.)

MakeLinK. The *MakeLink* routine uses the value in *oldlink* to determine whether the record being added constitutes the start of a new chain or if the record is being added into an existing chain. The routine assumes that the "start of chain" value is stored somewhere else. When the position of the record in the chain is determined, *MakeLink* uses the header record to find the first free record in the file. If no records have been deleted from the file, *hdrrcrd.frstfree* will be zero and the new record will be added to the end of the file. If records have been deleted, the free chain space will be reused.

Deleting a LNK Record

DelLink. Figure 11-12 shows EL1112, which exports the routine that is used to delete a record from an LNK file. It is called *DelLink,* and it will remove a record from a chain and insert its record number into the chain of free-space records.

Fig. 11-11. Add a new LNK record.

```
DEFINITION MODULE EL1111;
   FROM EL0401 IMPORT    STRING;
   FROM EL0503 IMPORT    LONGCARD;
   FROM EL1007 IMPORT    RCRD;
   EXPORT QUALIFIED      MakeLink;

PROCEDURE MakeLink(ddname:STRING;oldlink:LONGCARD;
                   rcrd:RCRD;VAR newlink:LONGCARD);
(* This routine will add a new record to the LNK file associated with
   ddname.  On entry, if oldline = 0, a new chain will be started,
   otherwise, rcrd will be chained from the record specified by oldlink.
   newlink will return with the record number of the new record.  Note that
   rcrd does not include space for the LNK pointers.  The LNK routines
   maintain the chain in an area that is separate from the rcrd area.  *)
END EL1111.


IMPLEMENTATION MODULE EL1111;
   FROM SYSTEM IMPORT    ADR,BYTE,WORD;
   FROM EL0302 IMPORT    MovByteL,FillByte;
   FROM EL0303 IMPORT    equal;
   FROM EL0401 IMPORT    STRING;
   FROM EL0503 IMPORT    LONGCARD,lcone,lczero,AddLCard,ComLCard;
   FROM EL1007 IMPORT    RCRD,MakeRcrd,ClrRcrd;
   FROM EL1110 IMPORT    GetLink,PutLink;


PROCEDURE MakeLink(ddname:STRING;oldlink:LONGCARD;
                   rcrd:RCRD;VAR newlink:LONGCARD);
VAR
  next,lastrcrd,nextfree:LONGCARD;
  dummy:RCRD;
BEGIN
  MakeRcrd(rcrd^.rcrdlen,dummy);
  FillByte(CHR(0),dummy^.area,0,rcrd^.rcrdlen);
  GetLink(ddname,dummy,lcone,nextfree);
  MovByteL(dummy^.area,lastrcrd,0,0,4);
  IF (ComLCard(nextfree,lczero) = equal)
    THEN
      AddLCard(lastrcrd,lcone,lastrcrd);
      newlink:=lastrcrd;
      PutLink(ddname,newlink,lczero,dummy);
    ELSE
      newlink:=nextfree;
      GetLink(ddname,dummy,newlink,nextfree);
    END;
  MovByteL(lastrcrd,dummy^.area,0,0,4);
  PutLink(ddname,lcone,nextfree,dummy);
  IF (ComLCard(oldlink,lczero) = equal)
    THEN next:=lczero
    ELSE
      GetLink(ddname,dummy,oldlink,next);
      PutLink(ddname,oldlink,newlink,dummy);
    END;
  PutLink(ddname,newlink,next,rcrd);
  ClrRcrd(dummy);
  END MakeLink;

END EL1111.
```

Fig. 11-12. Delete an LNK record.

```
DEFINITION MODULE EL1112;
   FROM EL0401 IMPORT    STRING;
   FROM EL0503 IMPORT    LONGCARD;
   FROM EL1007 IMPORT    RCRD;
   EXPORT QUALIFIED      DelLink;

PROCEDURE DelLink(ddname:STRING;rcrdlen:INTEGER;
                  lastlink:LONGCARD;VAR thislink:LONGCARD);
(* This routine will remove a record from the current chain in the LNK file
   associated with ddname.  If lastlink is not equal to zero on entry, the
   corresponding record will be accessed and the next link to which it
   points will be removed from the chain.  If lastlink is equal to zero on
   entry, the record identified by thislink will be removed.  In either
   case, thislink will return pointing to the next record in the chain, or
   will return equal to zero if the end of chain has been reached.  *)
END EL1112.

IMPLEMENTATION MODULE EL1112;
   FROM EL0303 IMPORT    equal,greater;
   FROM EL0401 IMPORT    STRING;
   FROM EL0503 IMPORT    LONGCARD,lcone,lczero,ComLCard;
   FROM EL1007 IMPORT    RCRD,MakeRcrd,ClrRcrd;
   FROM EL1110 IMPORT    GetLink,PutLink;

PROCEDURE DelLink(ddname:STRING;rcrdlen:INTEGER;
                  lastlink:LONGCARD;VAR thislink:LONGCARD);
VAR
   last,next,nextlink:LONGCARD;
   dummy:RCRD;
BEGIN
   MakeRcrd(rcrdlen,dummy);
   IF (ComLCard(lastlink,lczero) = equal)
     THEN GetLink(ddname,dummy,thislink,nextlink)
     ELSE
       GetLink(ddname,dummy,lastlink,thislink);
       GetLink(ddname,dummy,thislink,nextlink);
       PutLink(ddname,lastlink,nextlink,dummy);
     END;
   next:=lcone;
   REPEAT
     last:=next;
     GetLink(ddname,dummy,last,next);
     UNTIL (ComLCard(next,lczero) = equal)
                OR (ComLCard(next,thislink) = greater);
   PutLink(ddname,last,thislink,dummy);
   PutLink(ddname,thislink,next,dummy);
   thislink:=nextlink;
   ClrRcrd(dummy);
   END DelLink;

END EL1112.
```

Replacing an Existing Record
ReplLink. The routine shown in Fig. 11-13 is called *ReplLink,* and it can be used to replace the data portion of an existing .LNK record. This routine is safer to use than *PutLink* because it does not reference *NextLink. ReplLink* is exported from EL1113.

Fig. 11-13. Replace a LNK record.

```
DEFINITION MODULE EL1113;
   FROM EL0401 IMPORT    STRING;
   FROM EL0503 IMPORT    LONGCARD;
   FROM EL1007 IMPORT    RCRD;
   EXPORT QUALIFIED      ReplLink;
PROCEDURE ReplLink(ddname:STRING;rcrd:RCRD;thisline:LONGCARD);
(* This routine will replace the data in the LNK file record associated
   with ddname and identified by thislink.   No change is made to the
   associated chain.   *)
END EL1113.
IMPLEMENTATION MODULE EL1113;
   FROM EL0401 IMPORT    STRING;
   FROM EL0503 IMPORT    LONGCARD;
   FROM EL1007 IMPORT    RCRD,MakeRcrd,ClrRcrd;
   FROM EL1110 IMPORT    GetLink,PutLink;
PROCEDURE ReplLink(ddname:STRING;rcrd:RCRD;thislink:LONGCARD);
VAR
   dummy:RCRD;
   next:LONGCARD;
BEGIN
   MakeRcrd(rcrd^.rcrdlen,dummy);
   GetLink(ddname,dummy,thislink,next);
   PutLink(ddname,thislink,next,rcrd);
   ClrRcrd(dummy);
   END ReplLink;

END EL1113.
```

AN EXAMPLE

The four access methods available in the Etling Library can be used to define very simple or very complex file structures. In theory, it is possible to build true "hierarchical" or "relational" databases using these access methods, and in fact, most of the "database management" packages available for personal computers implement their file handling using similar techniques.

The EL0201 module declared back in Chapter 2 uses an NDX file to index a standard text file. An example of a direct access file can be found in Chapter 13 in the discussion of the INX files used by the on-screen "help" facility.

The record definitions shown earlier in this chapter, in conjunction with the top of tree variable in an NDX file, illustrates how several. NDX files can be used to create a hierarchical structure.

Figure 11-14 shows the source code for a complete module that uses an .NDX file together with a .LNK file. The module named EL1114 contains all of the file descriptions, record layouts, and calls to the I/O routines for two files. One file contains the name and address data for families; the other the first name, birth date, and Player Pass number for each of the family's children that participates in organized soccer. In other words, the two files define the membership list for an Amateur Soccer Club. This module is part of a larger program that allows the user to add, change, delete, or print records in that list. (The modules that implement the rest of the program are discussed in later chapters.)

EL1114 does include type definitions for a NAMERCRD and a KIDRCRD. Neither is actually used. The definitions are there only for documentation; the position and

Fig. 11-14. File access routines.

```
DEFINITION MODULE EL1114;
   FROM EL0401 IMPORT    STRING;
   FROM EL0503 IMPORT    LONGCARD;
   EXPORT QUALIFIED      BegName,WrtName,ClsName,DelName,GetNName,
                         ReadName,PutKid,GetKid;


PROCEDURE BegName;
(* This routine will begin access to the files associated with the ddnames
   FAMILY and KIDS.  It should be the first routine called.  *)
PROCEDURE WrtName(name,address,city,state,zip,phone:STRING;
                          frstdtl:LONGCARD):BOOLEAN;
(* This routine will attempt to write a new record to the FAMILY file. If
   a record with the corresponding NAME and ADDRESS already exists, the
   function will return false, otherwise the data will be added to the
   file. *)
PROCEDURE DelName(name,address,city,state,zip,phone:STRING):BOOLEAN;
(* This routine will attempt to delete the FAMILY record identified by the
   consts.  If the record exists, it will be deleted and the function will
   return true.  *)
PROCEDURE ClsName;
(* This routine will close the FAMILY and KIDS files and clear all
   associated indexes from the heap.  *)
PROCEDURE GetNName(name,address,city,state,zip,phone:STRING;
                        VAR frstdtl:LONGCARD):BOOLEAN;
(* This routine will return the next FAMILY record from the file.  If no
   more records exists, the function will return false.  To begin access,
   call this routine with NAME = all CHR(0);  *)
PROCEDURE ReadName(name,address,city,state,zip,phone:STRING;
                        VAR frstdtl:LONGCARD):BOOLEAN;
(* This routine will attempt to read the record from the FAMILY file
   identified by the constants.  If such a record exists, the function will
   return true, and frstdtl will contain the address of the first kid
   record in the KIDS file.  *)
PROCEDURE PutKid(firstname,birthdate,pass,note:STRING;
                          VAR lastdtl:LONGCARD);
(* This routine will write a kid record to the KIDS file.  Note that on
   entry, lastdtl should contain the address of the last kid record written
   for the current FAMILY.  If lastdtl = 0, a new chain of kid records will
   be started.  on exit, lastdtl will contain the address of the new
   record.  *)
PROCEDURE GetKid(firstname,birthdate,pass,note:STRING;
                        VAR nextdtl:LONGCARD);
(* This routine will return with the next kid record from the KIDS file in
   the chain associated with nextdtl.  when nextdtl returns equal to zero,
   there are no more links in the chain after the current.  *)
END EL1114.


IMPLEMENTATION MODULE EL1114;
   FROM SYSTEM IMPORT    ADR,TSIZE,SIZE;
   FROM EL0303 IMPORT    equal;
   FROM EL0401 IMPORT    STRING,Literal,StrLen,ClearStr,MakeStr,ChrPtr;
   FROM EL0503 IMPORT    LONGCARD,lczero,ComLCard;
   FROM EL1002 IMPORT    FMODE,OPENKIND,DISP,OpnFile,ClsFile;
   FROM EL1007 IMPORT    RCRD,RFLDLIST,MakeRcrd,MakRFlds,MovFRcrd,MovTRcrd,
                         ClrRFlds,ClrRcrd;
   FROM EL1102 IMPORT    NODEPTR,NODE,NDXFCTRL,ChkNdxF,ClrNdx;
   FROM EL1104 IMPORT    FindNdx;
   FROM EL1105 IMPORT    MarkNdx;
   FROM EL1106 IMPORT    FreeNdx;
   FROM EL1107 IMPORT    NextNdx;
   FROM EL1110 IMPORT    ChkLnkF,LNKFCTRL,GetLink,PutLink;
```

Fig. 11-14 continued

```
   FROM EL1111 IMPORT    MakeLink;
   FROM EL1112 IMPORT    DelLink;

CONST
   top      = TRUE;
   continue = TRUE;
   update   = TRUE;
TYPE
   NAMERCRD = RECORD
     name      : ARRAY [1..35] OF CHAR;
     address   : ARRAY [1..35] OF CHAR;
     city      : ARRAY [1..20] OF CHAR;
     state     : ARRAY [1..3] OF CHAR;
     zip       : ARRAY [1..9] OF CHAR;
     phone     : ARRAY [1..10] OF CHAR;
     frstdtl   : LONGCARD;
     END;
   KIDRCRD = RECORD
     firstname : ARRAY [1..30] OF CHAR;
     birthdate : ARRAY [1..6] OF CHAR;
     pass      : ARRAY [1..15] OF CHAR;
     note      : ARRAY [1..20] OF CHAR;
     END;
VAR
   famfctrl:NDXFCTRL;
   kidfctrl:LNKFCTRL;
   fammode,kidmode:FMODE;

PROCEDURE BegName;
BEGIN
   WITH famfctrl DO
     IF (fammode = makeold)
       THEN
         MakeStr(ddname,0,Literal('FAMILY'));
         rcrdnmbr:=lczero;
         MakRFlds(8,rfldarea);
         WITH rfldarea^ DO
           loc[1]:=1;              len[1]:=112;
           loc[2]:=1;              len[2]:=35;
           loc[3]:=36;             len[3]:=35;
           loc[4]:=71;             len[4]:=20;
           loc[5]:=91;             len[5]:=3;
           loc[6]:=94;             len[6]:=9;
           loc[7]:=103;        •   len[7]:=10;
           loc[8]:=113;            len[8]:=TSIZE(LONGCARD);
           MakeRcrd(len[1]+len[8],rcrd);
           END;
         hook.ptr:=NIL;
         hook.nmbr:=lczero;
       END;
     ChkNdxF(ddname,rcrd^.rcrdlen,fammode);
     END;
   WITH kidfctrl DO
     IF (kidmode = makeold)
       THEN
         MakeStr(ddname,0,Literal('KIDS'));
         rcrdnmbr:=lczero;
         MakRFlds(4,rfldarea);
         WITH rfldarea^ DO
           loc[1]:=1;              len[1]:=30;
           loc[2]:=31;             len[2]:=6;
```

```
                loc[3]:=37;                 len[3]:=15;
                loc[4]:=52;                 len[4]:=20;
                MakeRcrd(len[1]+len[2]+len[3]+len[4],rcrd);
                END;
            END;
        ChkLnkF(ddname,rcrd^.rcrdlen,kidmode);
        END;
    END BegName;

PROCEDURE ToFile(name,address,city,state,zip,phone:STRING;frstdtl:LONGCARD);
BEGIN
    WITH famfctrl DO
        MovTRcrd(rcrd,rfldarea,ChrPtr(name,1),    StrLen(name)    ,2);
        MovTRcrd(rcrd,rfldarea,ChrPtr(address,1),StrLen(address),3);
        MovTRcrd(rcrd,rfldarea,ChrPtr(city,1),   `StrLen(city)    ,4);
        MovTRcrd(rcrd,rfldarea,ChrPtr(state,1),   StrLen(state)   ,5);
        MovTRcrd(rcrd,rfldarea,ChrPtr(zip,1),     StrLen(zip)     ,6);
        MovTRcrd(rcrd,rfldarea,ChrPtr(phone,1),   StrLen(phone)   ,7);
        MovTRcrd(rcrd,rfldarea,ADR(frstdtl),      SIZE(frstdtl)   ,8);
        END;
    END ToFile;

PROCEDURE FromFile(name,address,city,state,zip,phone:STRING;
                            VAR frstdtl:LONGCARD);
BEGIN
    WITH famfctrl DO
        MovFRcrd(rcrd,rfldarea,ChrPtr(name,1),    StrLen(name)    ,2);
        MovFRcrd(rcrd,rfldarea,ChrPtr(address,1),StrLen(address),3);
        MovFRcrd(rcrd,rfldarea,ChrPtr(city,1),    StrLen(city)    ,4);
        MovFRcrd(rcrd,rfldarea,ChrPtr(state,1),   StrLen(state)   ,5);
        MovFRcrd(rcrd,rfldarea,ChrPtr(zip,1),     StrLen(zip)     ,6);
        MovFRcrd(rcrd,rfldarea,ChrPtr(phone,1),   StrLen(phone)   ,7);
        MovFRcrd(rcrd,rfldarea,ADR(frstdtl),      SIZE(frstdtl)   ,8);
        END;
    END FromFile;

PROCEDURE WrtName(name,address,city,state,zip,phone:STRING;
                        frstdtl:LONGCARD):BOOLEAN;
BEGIN
    BegName;
    ToFile(name,address,city,state,zip,phone,frstdtl);
    WITH famfctrl DO
        IF (FindNdx(ddname,rcrd,rcrdnmbr,rfldarea^.loc[1],
                                rfldarea^.len[1],hook,top))
        THEN RETURN FALSE;
        ELSE
            MarkNdx(ddname,rcrd,rcrdnmbr,rfldarea^.loc[1],
                            rfldarea^.len[1],hook,top,update);
            RETURN TRUE;
            END;
        END;
    END WrtName;

PROCEDURE DelName(name,address,city,state,zip,phone:STRING):BOOLEAN;
VAR
    lastdtl:LONGCARD;
BEGIN
    BegName;
    ToFile(name,address,city,state,zip,phone,lastdtl);
    WITH famfctrl DO
        IF (NOT FindNdx(ddname,rcrd,rcrdnmbr,rfldarea^.loc[1],
                                rfldarea^.len[1],hook,top))
```

Fig. 11-14 continued

```
          THEN RETURN FALSE;
          ELSE MovFRcrd(rcrd,rfldarea,ADR(lastdtl), SIZE(lastdtl),8);
          END;
      END;
    WITH kidfctrl DO
      WHILE (ComLCard(lastdtl,lczero) <> equal) DO
        DelLink(ddname,rcrd^.rcrdlen,lczero,lastdtl);
        END;
      END;
    WITH famfctrl DO
      FreeNdx(ddname,rcrd,rfldarea^.loc[1],rfldarea^.len[1],
                          hook,top,update);

      END;
    RETURN TRUE;
    END DelName;

PROCEDURE ClsName;
BEGIN
  IF (fammode <> makeold)
    THEN
      WITH famfctrl DO
        ClrNdx(hook);
        ClrRcrd(rcrd);
        ClrRFlds(rfldarea);
        ClearStr(ddname);
        ClsFile(ddname,clsonly);
        END;
      WITH kidfctrl DO
        ClrRcrd(rcrd);
        ClrRFlds(rfldarea);
        ClearStr(ddname);
        ClsFile(ddname,clsonly);
        END;
      kidmode:=makeold;
      fammode:=makeold;
    END;
  END ClsName;

PROCEDURE GetNName(name,address,city,state,zip,phone:STRING;
                   VAR frstdtl:LONGCARD):BOOLEAN;
BEGIN
  BegName;
  ToFile(name,address,city,state,zip,phone,frstdtl);
  WITH famfctrl DO
    IF (NOT NextNdx(ddname,rcrd,rcrdnmbr,rfldarea^.loc[1],
                         rfldarea^.len[1],hook,top,continue))
      THEN RETURN FALSE;
      ELSE
        FromFile(name,address,city,state,zip,phone,frstdtl);
        RETURN TRUE;
      END;
    END;
  END GetNName;

PROCEDURE ReadName(name,address,city,state,zip,phone:STRING;
                   VAR frstdtl:LONGCARD):BOOLEAN;
BEGIN
BegName;
ToFile(name,address,city,state,zip,phone,frstdtl);
WITH famfctrl DO
  IF (NOT FindNdx(ddname,rcrd,rcrdnmbr,rfldarea^.loc[1],
```

```
                                 rfldarea^.len[1],hook,top))
         THEN RETURN FALSE;
         ELSE
            MovFRcrd(rcrd,rfldarea,ADR(frstdtl), SIZE(frstdtl),8);
            RETURN TRUE;
         END;
      END;
   END ReadName;

PROCEDURE PutKid(firstname,birthdate,pass,note:STRING;
                              VAR lastdtl:LONGCARD);
BEGIN
   WITH kidfctrl DO
      MovTRcrd(rcrd,rfldarea,ChrPtr(firstname,1),StrLen(firstname) ,1);
      MovTRcrd(rcrd,rfldarea,ChrPtr(birthdate,1),StrLen(birthdate) ,2);
      MovTRcrd(rcrd,rfldarea,ChrPtr(pass,1),     StrLen(pass)       ,3);
      MovTRcrd(rcrd,rfldarea,ChrPtr(note,1),     StrLen(note)       ,4);
      MakeLink(ddname,lastdtl,rcrd,lastdtl);
      END;
   END PutKid;

PROCEDURE GetKid(firstname,birthdate,pass,note:STRING;
                              VAR nextdtl:LONGCARD);
BEGIN
   WITH kidfctrl DO
      GetLink(ddname,rcrd,nextdtl,nextdtl);
      MovFRcrd(rcrd,rfldarea,ChrPtr(firstname,1),StrLen(firstname) ,1);
      MovFRcrd(rcrd,rfldarea,ChrPtr(birthdate,1),StrLen(birthdate) ,2);
      MovFRcrd(rcrd,rfldarea,ChrPtr(pass,1),     StrLen(pass)       ,3);
      MovFRcrd(rcrd,rfldarea,ChrPtr(note,1),     StrLen(note)       ,4);
      END;
   END GetKid;

BEGIN
   fammode      := makeold;
   kidmode      := makeold;
END EL1114.
```

length of each of the fields in the records is controlled by the RFLDAREA contained within the corresponding control record. (Remember, depending on which Modula-2 package you are using, the type definitions may not accurately reflect the position of the fields within the record.)

The FAMILY file is an .NDX file that uses the definition for NAMERCRD to divide the data area of its records into individual fields. All but the last four bytes of the record define the key. This means that the file can handle many families with the same last name; the names may be the same, but the address will be different.

The FAMILY record includes a field named *frstdtl*. This field contains the record address for the first *kidrcrd* associated with the family. The *kidrcrd* is stored in the KIDS file, a .LNK file. Using this technique, a given FAMILY can have one child in the club, or many children, without allocating more space than is absolutely required.

All access to the membership files must go though the routines in the EL1114 module. None of the other modules in the program knows where or how the data is stored. By restricting knowledge about record layouts and file access methods to this single module, you can localize the effect of a change in the file definition. Other routines in the program might need to use the data the file contains, but their access to the data is through the parameter lists of the procedures this module defines.

Chapter 12

Dealing with the Printer

I firmly believe that there is justice in this world. I believe that sooner or later, every little wrong gets righted . . . every little insult gets returned . . . every little hurt gets repaid. Because of that, I believe that someone, somewhere, is keeping track of the number of times a microcomputer salesperson utters the phrase, "It's IBM compatible." Someday, they'll get paid back for that.

In addition, I believe that every time one of those people says, "Hey! Here's the printer you want to buy! It's better/faster/cheaper/bigger/wider (pick one or two) than the IBM printer, and it's 100% IBM Compatible!" they get five marks beside their name. The truth of the matter is, there really isn't such a thing as an IBM compatible printer.

When the IBM Personal Computer was first introduced, they came out with "The IBM Personal Computer Printer." Shortly thereafter, there was "The IBM Personal Computer Graphics Printer." Nothing else is exactly like either one of those, and they are not even exactly like each other.

The differences in printers range from monumental to subtle. The difference between a "letter quality" printer, like a Diablo 630, and the little IBM Graphics, is quickly obvious, but the others keep their differences well hidden. The Okidata MicroLine 92 is the most IBM-compatible of the compatibles I have worked with, but even with its "Plug'n Play" option there is still at least one difference. The IBM Graphics printer prints compressed characters at 16.5 characters per inch; the Okidata does 17.1 character per inch. This is not a big difference, but it's significant if you're trying to print between the lines on preprinted forms.

Not only do printers vary in physical size, shape, paper handling path, and

216

method of transferring data from the PC (i.e., serial or parallel), they also vary in what they are capable of doing. Some printers print graphics, some print letter quality, some use daisy wheels, some use thermal paper. Some printers can use colors, others use lasers. The list is almost endless.

CONTROLLING THE PRINTER

Regardless of what a printer is capable of doing, something, somewhere, has to command it to do its tricks. There are two basic ways of doing that.

First, most printers have physical switches that a user can push to select printer functions. Almost all printers have 3 or 4 switches on their front panel (in addition to the "on/off" switch) that control the more frequently accessed functions, and buried somewhere on the printer main circuit board there are usually eight or 16 DIP switches that handle the more exotic operations. Hardware switches work fine for options that you set once and forget (like "skip over perforation"), but when you need to change options under program control, your only choice is the second method for controlling printers.

The second method is to issue a *printer control code*. A printer control code is a sequence of one or more characters that the printer will recognize as a command to invoke one of its special functions. The problem with printer control codes is this: To use them to control the printer, something has to insert them in the string of characters to be printed. There are two ways of doing this: let the program that wants to print the characters in the first place generate the control codes, or put something in between the program and the printer that generates the codes.

The problem with letting the program generate the codes is that each printer has its own ideas about what character sequence should do what function. Hard coding printer control sequences in the program would either restrict the program to operation with a single printer, or waste space by allowing for printers that weren't used on a particular system.

Putting something between a program and a printer usually involves revectoring the software interrupt associated with printer operation to point at a routine called a *device driver*. A device driver intercepts all characters before they are transmitted to the printer. If any of these characters are control characters, the driver will translate a standard sequence known to the operating system into a specific sequence required to invoke the same function on the nonstandard printer.

There are two problems (again) with a device driver approach. First, every printer requires its own driver. While the user is only forced to deal with the driver for his particular printer, someone has to write drivers for all the rest. Second, the choice of what constitutes a "standard sequence known to the operating system" is not clear-cut. It seems that every program that uses device drivers picked one printer (and no two programs picked the same one) and used its control codes as standard. All of the other device drivers the program defined were built around that one printer.

The Printer Routines

The Etling Library tackles the problem of controlling the printer from a slightly different angle.

The Library defines a series of routines that provide access to the printer. When a program needs to output characters to the printer, it calls one of the Library routines. To generate a sequence of printer control characters, the program imbeds an arbitrary "printer mnemonic" in the string to be printed. To the Etling Library routines, a *printer mnemonic* is any sequence of characters enclosed in two occurrences of the escape character (CHR(27)). For example, Fig. 12-1 defines a list of constants that can be used for identifying some of the more common printer mnemonics. The mnemonics are not printer control characters; they only identify controls. The actual control sequences must be supplied elsewhere. Here is how it works:

All of the routines that handle printer access in the Etling Library are in the same module, EL1202. This module uses several types, constants, and variables. The complete listing of EL1201 is shown in Fig. 12-1.

Opening the Printer

OpnPrint. To DOS the printer is a device, just like a disk or diskette drive. While the printer does not have files that can be selected individually, it still must be "opened" so that the necessary buffers and control variables can be allocated in the DOS work areas. The routine named *OpnPrint,* exported from EL1202, eventually gets around to calling *OpnFile* to open the printer, but first *OpnPrint* does a couple of other things.

First, *OpnPrint* attempts to find a program parameter for a <parmid> of PPORT. If the parameter exists, it indicates that the procedure that defines printer controls, *LPrintCF,* has already been called and the device to which the printer is attached (the <parmval> for PPORT) has already been defined. If PPORT does not exist, *LPrintCF* is called to establish these parameters.

Rather than always directing output directly to the printer, the print routines can be instructed to reroute the output to a disk file. The file the routines produce under these circumstances is a standard text file; it can be edited with a text editor, read into another program, or copied to the printer using COPY at some more convenient time. (On a mainframe, this technique of directing printed output to a disk file is called *spooling*. On the other hand, the term "print spooler" on a micro generally means a large buffer either in memory or in some external device that allows the program to write into one end while the printer pulls characters out the other.)

As the comments in Fig. 12-1 indicate, *OpnPrint* uses its parameter *asktoset* to decide if it should ask the user about spooling or instruct the user to set the paper to top of form. Note that before asking about either of these options, the routine looks for a program parameter for WARNPRINT; if the parameter is found and its <parmval> is NO, both questions will be skipped. This allows you to print automatically. If WARNPRINT is not found, the routine looks for a program parameter for PRTSPOOL. If the parameter is not found, the routine assumes that spooling is not to be enabled for this particular program.

Once the printer controls are loaded and the question of spooling is settled, *OpnPrint* calls *OpnFile* to physically open the <dsname> associated with PPORT. Note that PPORT might refer to one of the actual DOS printer devices (e.g., LPT1, LPT2, etc.) or it might reference the file used for spooling. For an example of this, refer to LISTER in Chapter 2.

After the printer is open, *OpnPrint* calls the routine that transfers characters to

Fig. 12-1. Basic printer routines.

```
DEFINITION MODULE EL1201;
   FROM EL0401 IMPORT    STRING;
   EXPORT QUALIFIED      Print,ClsPrint,OpnPrint,
                         pbl,pcb,pce,pcl,pcp,pcr,pff,pfl,pdb,pde,peb,pee,
                         pel,plf,pub,pue,pwb,pwe;

VAR
(*
   Constants for defining printer mnemonics
*)
   pbl, (* ESC+'BL'+ESC      Ring Bell                 *)
   pcb, (* ESC+'CB'+ESC      Begin compressed          *)
   pce, (* ESC+'CE'+ESC      End compressed            *)
   pcl, (* ESC+'CL'+ESC      Clear Printer Buffer      *)
   pcp, (* ESC+'CP'+ESC      Clear printer to default  *)
   pcr, (* ESC+'CR'+ESC      Carriage Return           *)
   pff, (* ESC+'FF'+ESC      Form Feed                 *)
   pdb, (* ESC+'DB'+ESC      Begin Double Strike       *)
   pde, (* ESC+'DE'+ESC      End Double Strike         *)
   peb, (* ESC+'EB'+ESC      Begin Emphasized          *)
   pee, (* ESC+'EE'+ESC      End Emphasized            *)
   pel, (* ESC+'EL'+ESC      End Line (usually CR*LF)  *)
   plf, (* ESC+'LF'+ESC      Line feed                 *)
   pub, (* ESC+'UB'+ESC      Begin Underline           *)
   pue, (* ESC+'UE'+ESC      End Underline             *)
   pwb, (* ESC+'WB'+ESC      Begin Double width        *)
   pwe, (* ESC+'WE'+ESC      End Double width          *)
   pfl: (* ESC+'FL66'+ESC Set form length   (66 may be replaced with
                              any two digits specifing the number of
                              lines per page  *)
        STRING;
PROCEDURE OpnPrint(asktoset,eject:BOOLEAN);
(* This procedure will open the file associated with the ddname PRINTER,
   and read that file to define the controls for the printer.  If a program
   parameter for that ddname is not given, printed output will be directed
   to LPT1 with a default set of controls.  If asktoset = true, this
   procedure will look for a parm named PRTSPOOL...if it exists, the user
   will be given the option of directing printed output there.  Otherwise
   the user will be asked to align the paper before returning.  If eject =
   TRUE, a form feed will be sent to the file.  *)
PROCEDURE ClsPrint(eject:BOOLEAN);
(* This procedure will close the device associated with PPORT.  If eject is
   true on entry, a form feed will be written before the file is closed. *)
PROCEDURE Print(msg:STRING);
(* This routine will output the contents of msg to the device associated
   with PPORT.  The actual assignment for that device is normally found in
   the file associated with the ddname PRINTER, and that file also contains
   the appropriate values for the printer control mnemonics.  Any and all
   printer control to be done in the course of printing this message should
   be imbedded in the string in the form of mnemonics enclosed within two
   occurences of the ESC character...CHR(27).  These mnemonics will be
   translated into an appropriate character string based on the translation
   table.  For example, if msg includes:
                      ESC+'FF'+ESC
   and the printer involved is an IBM PC Graphics Printer, a CHR(12) will
   be written to the printer.  The mnemonics are defined in PRTCONSTS.  *)
END EL1201.

IMPLEMENTATION MODULE EL1201;
   FROM SYSTEM IMPORT    BYTE,SIZE;
   FROM Storage IMPORT   ALLOCATE,DEALLOCATE;
```

Fig. 12-1 continued

```
  FROM EL0303 IMPORT      equal;
  FROM EL0304 IMPORT      esc,break,fk1,fk2;
  FROM EL0401 IMPORT      SubStr,STRING,Literal,nullstr,SetLen,MakeStr,
                          ClearStr,StrLen,MoveStr,CopyStr,StrChar,SetChar;
  FROM EL0402 IMPORT      Delete,Insert;
  FROM EL0403 IMPORT      MatchStr,Positn;
  FROM EL0404 IMPORT      FixStr;
  FROM EL0501 IMPORT      CHARSET,MakeCSet,IncCSet,nullcset;
  FROM EL0902 IMPORT      msgframe;
  FROM EL0905 IMPORT      Message;
  FROM EL0906 IMPORT      Cancel;
  FROM EL0801 IMPORT      FindParm,SetParm;
  FROM EL1002 IMPORT      FMODE,OpnFile,ClsFile,OPENKIND,DISP,LINECNTRL;
  FROM EL1003 IMPORT      GetLine;
  FROM EL1004 IMPORT      PutLine;

TYPE
  PCPTR = POINTER TO PCONTROL;
  PCONTROL = RECORD
    mem     :STRING;
    escseq:STRING;
    next    :PCPTR;
    END;
CONST
  t1 = 'The Etling Library';
  t2 = 'All programs and modules, Copyright (c) 1986 TAB BOOKS INC.';
  t3 = 'Author: Don Etling';
  wait = 15;
VAR
  first:PCPTR;
  dospool:BOOLEAN;
  printer,pport,lpt1,spooling,prtspool:STRING;
  fk1fk2,fk1break:CHARSET;

PROCEDURE MakeMem(mem:ARRAY OF CHAR):STRING;
VAR
  s:STRING;
BEGIN
  MakeStr(s,4,Literal('    '));
  SetChar(s,1,esc); SetChar(s,2,mem[0]);
  SetChar(s,3,mem[1]); SetChar(s,4,esc);
  RETURN s;
  END MakeMem;

PROCEDURE Default(mem:ARRAY OF CHAR;escseq:STRING);
VAR
  this:PCPTR;
BEGIN
  NEW(this);
  this^.next:=first;
  first:=this;
  this^.mem:=MakeMem(mem);
  MakeStr(this^.escseq,0,escseq);
  END Default;

PROCEDURE LPrintCF;
VAR
  str,escseq:STRING;
  i,j,n,m:CARDINAL;
  opnmode:FMODE;
  ioerr:BYTE;
```

```
     this,last:PCPTR;
BEGIN
  MakeStr(str,255,nullstr);
  MakeStr(escseq,255,nullstr);
  WHILE (first <> NIL) DO
    last:=first;
    first:=first^.next;
    ClearStr(last^.escseq);
    ClearStr(last^.mem);
    DISPOSE(last);
    END;
  first:=NIL;
  IF (NOT FindParm(printer,str))
    THEN
      SetParm(pport,lpt1);
      Default('LF',FixStr(Literal("'C'*lf")));
      Default('CR',FixStr(Literal("'C'*cr")));
      Default('FF',FixStr(Literal("'C'*ff*'C'*cr")));
      Default('EL',FixStr(Literal("'C'*cr*'C'*lf")));
      Default('CP',FixStr(Literal("'C'*CHR(27)*'C'*CHR(6)")));
    ELSE
      opnmode:=oldfile;
      OpnFile(printer,opnmode,ioerr,insist);
      IF (GetLine(printer,str,nortrnend))
        THEN SetParm(pport,str);
        END;
      WHILE (GetLine(printer,str,nortrnend)) DO
        IF (StrLen(str) < 4)
          THEN Cancel(Literal('LPrintCF'),str,1,0);
          ELSE
            NEW(this);
            this^.next:=first;
            first:=this;
            MakeStr(this^.mem,4,Literal('    '));
            SetChar(this^.mem,1,esc);
            SetChar(this^.mem,2,StrChar(str,1));
            SetChar(this^.mem,3,StrChar(str,2));
            SetChar(this^.mem,4,esc);
            Delete(str,1,3);
            CopyStr(nullstr,escseq);
            WHILE (StrLen(str) > 0) DO
              IF (StrChar(str,1) = 'A') OR (StrChar(str,1) = 'H')
                THEN
                  SetLen(escseq,StrLen(escseq)+2);
                  SetChar(escseq,StrLen(escseq)-1,StrChar(str,1));
                  SetChar(escseq,StrLen(escseq),CHR(0));
                  Delete(str,1,1);
                ELSE IF (StrLen(str) < 3)
                  THEN Cancel(Literal('LPrintCF'),str,1,2);
                  ELSE
                    m:=0;
                    FOR j:=1 TO 3 DO
                      m:=m*10+ORD(StrChar(str,j)) - ORD('0');
                      END;
                    SetLen(escseq,StrLen(escseq)+2);
                    SetChar(escseq,StrLen(escseq)-1,'C');
                    SetChar(escseq,StrLen(escseq),CHR(m));
                    Delete(str,1,3);
                  END;
                END;
              END;
            MakeStr(this^.escseq,0,escseq);
```

Fig. 12-1 continued

```
              END;
          END;
      ClsFile(printer,clsonly);
    END;
  ClearStr(str);
  ClearStr(escseq);
  END LPrintCF;

PROCEDURE Print(msg:STRING);
VAR
  i,j,k,m:CARDINAL;
  this:PCPTR;
  done:BOOLEAN;
  str:STRING;
BEGIN
  MakeStr(str,255,msg);
  i:=0;
  REPEAT
    j:=Positn(Literal(esc),str,i+1);
    i:=Positn(Literal(esc),str,j+1);
    IF (j > 0) AND (i > 0)
      THEN
        this:=first;
        done:=FALSE;
        WHILE (this <> NIL) AND (NOT done) DO
          IF (MatchStr(this^.mem,str,1,j,3) = equal)
            THEN done:=TRUE;
            ELSE this:=this^.next;
            END;
          END;
        IF (done)
          THEN
            k:=1;
            Delete(str,j,3);
            WHILE (k < StrLen(this^.escseq)) DO
              IF (StrChar(this^.escseq,k) = 'C')
                THEN
                  INC(k);
                  Insert(Literal(' '),str,j);
                  SetChar(str,j,StrChar(this^.escseq,k));
                  INC(j);
                ELSE
                  m:=0;
                  WHILE (StrChar(str,j) <> esc) DO
                    IF (StrChar(this^.escseq,k) = 'A')
                      THEN INC(j);
                      ELSE
                        m:=m*10 + ORD(StrChar(str,j))-ORD('0');
                        Delete(str,j,1);
                      END;
                    END;
                  END;
                IF (StrChar(this^.escseq,k) = 'H')
                  THEN
                    Insert(Literal(' '),str,j);
                    SetChar(str,j,CHR(m));
                    INC(j);
                  END;
                INC(k);
                END;
            Delete(str,j,1);
```

```
          END;
      END;
    UNTIL (j = 0) OR (i = 0);
  PutLine(pport,str,noendline);
  ClearStr(str);
  END Print;

PROCEDURE ClsPrint(eject:BOOLEAN);
BEGIN
  IF (eject)
    THEN Print(pff);
    END;
  ClsFile(pport,clsonly);
  END ClsPrint;

PROCEDURE OpnPrint(asktoset,eject:BOOLEAN);
VAR
  opnmode:FMODE;
  ioerr:BYTE;
  str:STRING;
  eascii:BOOLEAN;
  kbchar:CHAR;
BEGIN
  MakeStr(str,255,nullstr);
  IF (NOT FindParm(pport,str))
    THEN LPrintCF;
    END;
  IF (asktoset)
    THEN
      IF (FindParm(Literal('WARNPRINT'),str))
        THEN IF (MatchStr(Literal('NO'),str,1,1,0) = equal)
          THEN asktoset:=FALSE;
          END;
        END;
      IF (NOT FindParm(prtspool,str))
        THEN dospool:=FALSE;
        ELSE
          dospool:=TRUE;
          IF (asktoset)
            THEN
              Message(
          Literal('Where do you wish to direct printed output'),
                    Literal('F1 = Printer / F2 = Spool File'),
                    msgframe,wait,nullcset,fk1fk2,eascii,kbchar);
              IF (kbchar = fk1)
                THEN dospool:=FALSE
                END;
              END;
          IF (dospool)
            THEN SetParm(pport,str);
            END;
        END;
      IF (dospool)
        THEN SetParm(spooling,Literal('YES'));
        ELSE
          IF (asktoset)
            THEN Message(Literal(
            'Make certain that printer paper is aligned and power is on'),
                  Literal('F1 = continue'),
                    msgframe,wait,nullcset,fk1break,eascii,kbchar);
          ELSE kbchar:=fk1;
          END;
```

Fig. 12-1 continued

```
              IF (kbchar = break)
                THEN Cancel(Literal('OpnPrint'),spooling,2,0)
                ELSE SetParm(spooling,Literal('NO'));
                END;
          END;
      END;
    IF (dospool)
      THEN opnmode:=append
      ELSE opnmode:=oldfile;
      END;
    OpnFile(pport,opnmode,ioerr,insist);
    Print(pcp);
    IF (eject)
      THEN Print(pff);
      END;
    ClearStr(str);
    END OpnPrint;

BEGIN
    pbl := MakeMem('BL');    pcb := MakeMem('CB');    pce := MakeMem('CE');
    pcl := MakeMem('CL');    pcp := MakeMem('CP');    pcr := MakeMem('CR');
    pff := MakeMem('FF');    pfl := MakeMem('FL');    pdb := MakeMem('DB');
    pde := MakeMem('DE');    peb := MakeMem('EB');    pee := MakeMem('EE');
    pel := MakeMem('EL');    plf := MakeMem('LF');    pub := MakeMem('UB');
    pue := MakeMem('UE');    pwb := MakeMem('WB');    pwe := MakeMem('WE');
    first    := NIL;
    dospool  := FALSE;
    MakeStr(spooling ,0,Literal('SPOOLING'));
    MakeStr(printer  ,0,Literal('PRINTER'));
    MakeStr(pport    ,0,Literal('PPORT'));
    MakeStr(lpt1     ,0,Literal('LPT1'));
    MakeStr(prtspool ,0,Literal('PRTSPOOL'));
    MakeCSet(FixStr(Literal("fk1*fk2")),fk1fk2);
    MakeCSet(FixStr(Literal("fk1*brea")),fk1break);
END EL1201.
```

the printer (its name is *Print*) to send it the mnemonic identified by the constant *pcp*. This mnemonic means "clear the printer and reset." If the *OpnPrint* parameter *eject* is equal to true, the routine will also send *pff* for "issue form feed."

LPrintCF. The routine that is responsible for building the table that translates printer mnemonics into printer control sequences is *LPrintCF*. This routine is not exported from EL1202. It uses the TYPE definitions contained in the module to build a list of CONTROL records. A CONTROL record translates a mnemonic into a control sequence (and it contains a pointer to the next record in the list).

LPrintCF builds the list of CONTROL records by either reading the file associated with the program parameter PRINTER, or by using the *Default* procedure to create a list of the five default mnemonics. If the PRINTER file is defined, it should include the following records.

The first record in the file associated with the <ddname> PRINTER should indicate the device to which the printer is attached. This record should contain a single word, such as LPT1, LPT2, or even COM1 or COM2. When *OpnPrint* opens the device and spooling is not in effect, that is the name of the DOS device that will be opened.

The remaining lines in the PRINTER file define the translation of printer mnemonics known within the program into printer-control sequences that the particular printer attached to the PPORT device will recognize. Each of the remaining lines has this form:

<mnemonic>=<control sequence>

The value for <mnemonic> is any two characters. The list in Fig. 12-1 is only a starting point; you can define additional <mnemonic> codes if your application warrants it. The routine that intercepts <mnemonic>s in the print string only looks for a match in the CONTROL record list; it does not attach any special significance to the code.

The <control sequence> portion of each line in the PRINTER file defines the sequence of characters that should be sent to the printer whenever the particular mnemonic is encountered. To allow for characters that cannot be entered directly into the file using a text editor, the character sequence is specified using three decimal digits to represent each character. For example, for an IBM Graphics Printer, the sequence ESC*"−1" causes the printer to begin underlining characters. A PRINTER file defined for a program that used an IBM Graphics Printer would include a line that said this:

UB=027045049

Usually, the printer-control sequence is just a string of ASCII characters, but occasionally, a control sequence has to include a numeric indication of some kind. The sequence that sets the number of lines per page is an example of this on most printers. The sequence for an IBM Graphics is ESC*"C"*CHR(n), where n is the number of lines.

Note that the printer is sent a character, but the character is controlled by n. To set a Graphics printer to a page length of 55 lines, you would send it ESC*"C"*CHR(55). Some printers want n specified as a string of ASCII digits. For example, the Okidata 92 would use ESC*"F55" to accomplish the same thing.

When a control sequence does require a number, use an A or a H to indicate how it is to be sent to the printer. For an IBM Graphics Printer, the PRINTER file should include a line that states:

FL=027067H

A PRINTER file for the Okidata would say:

FL=027070AA

Note that the latter example shows two A characters; there should be one A for each digit to be sent. In both cases, a program would embed the string ESC*"FF55'*ESC in the print line.

LPrintCF includes the helper procedure, *Default*. If *LPrintCF* cannot find PRINTER, it will build a default list of CONTROL records. The default list includes only the simplest of printer controls, but if a given application will be using the report-genera-tion routines defined later in this chapter, this list contains the mnemonics that are mandatory for providing minimum printer control. One of those mnemonics, *pel*, is used to signal "end of line." On most printers, the *pel* control sequence is carriage-return/line-feed, but if a particular printer has a switch setting that provides a line feed automatically whenever a carriage return (the IBM printers *do* have this option), you can redefine *pel* to function accordingly.

The number of mnemonics defined in the printer-control files is determined entirely by the application and the printer models that it might support. The list of mnemonics defined in Fig. 12-1 reflects the operations that most microcomputer printers are capable of performing, but the list is by no means complete. If you are writing an application that will only be used on printers capable of doing something not in the list, all you need do is define a mnemonic for use in your programs and create a control file that translates the mnemonic into a control sequence.

Printing

Print. The routine that transfers character strings from a program to the printer or spool files is exported from EL1202, and is known as *Print*. *Print* is responsible for trapping imbedded printer mnemonics and converting them into actual printer con-trol sequences using the list built by *LPrintCF*. If *Print* is given a *msg* to print that has an unmatched ESC character, or if *msg* contains a mnemonic that is not in the *LPrintCF* list, the characters are sent along to the printer without modification.

ClsPrint. Like any other file or device, PPORT should be closed when the program has completed its use. The routine that closes the print device is named *ClsPrint*, also exported from El1202. *ClsPrint* can be used to issue a final form feed before closing. This ensures that the last page of one report is not cluttered up with the first page of the next.

REPORTS

It isn't enough to control the printer, a commercial program needs to have something to say to it. Fortunately, commercial applications never lack for something to put down on paper. The process of printing reports, regardless of what the report contains, requires some fairly consistent operations. The report should be broken up into distinct pages, each page should be numbered and should begin with heading lines that describe the report in such a way that it can be identified from all other reports the system might produce. All of these things can be done with a collection of standard routines from the Etling Library.

The report-generation routines are all contained in the EL1202 module. This module uses several variables (shown in Fig. 12-2). The routines are designed to oversee the production of one report at a time, and these variables keep track of the controls associated with that one report.

SetRprt. The first thing a program must do, if it uses the report generation routines, is define values for the report control variables. This is accomplished with a call to *SetRprt*. The comments in Fig. 12-2 are self-explanatory. Note that *SetRprt* does not output anything to the printer; it only defines the control values that will be used by the other routines.

   PrtRprt. The routine that outputs a report line to the printer is called *PrtRprt*. The routine requires several special type definitions that are also exported from the module. The types define LINETBL, an array of STRINGs, and LTBLPTR, a pointer to a LINETBL. These types are used to allocate a table of strings on the heap. The strings

Fig. 12-2. Report-generation routines.

```
DEFINITION MODULE EL1202;
   FROM EL0401 IMPORT    STRING;
   EXPORT QUALIFIED      LINETBL,LTBLPTR,PrtRprt,EndRprt,SetRprt,maxlines,
                         MakeLTbl,ClrLTbl;
CONST
  maxlines = 256;
TYPE
  LTBLPTR = POINTER TO LINETBL;
  LINETBL = RECORD
    nmbr : CARDINAL;
    line : ARRAY [1..maxlines] OF STRING;
    END;
PROCEDURE SetRprt(pcs:STRING;pagelength:CARDINAL;
                  asktoset,npage,dpage,tpage:BOOLEAN);
(* This procedure will define the control variables for a new report.  The
   character size used will be controlled by pcs...it should be set to the
   appropriate memnonic from PRTCONST.  The total number of lines that will
   be printed on a page (including headings) is controlled by pagelength.
   If asktoset = true, the user will be asked to position the paper to the
   top of a new page before printing begins.  If npage, dpage, and/or tpage
   are true, the first three lines of the headings printed on each page
   will include the page number, date, and time.  *)
PROCEDURE EndRprt;
(* This procedure will end the production of the report begun by SetRprt.
   It will close the printer, thereby causing whatever is the buffer to
   print, and reset the appropriate controls.  *)
PROCEDURE PrtRprt(prtline:STRING;VAR newpage:BOOLEAN; skiplines:CARDINAL;
                  hdgs:LTBLPTR;VAR pagenmbr,linenmbr:CARDINAL);
(* This procedure will print prtline on a report that has been previously
   defined by a call to SetRprt.  If newpage = true, a form feed will be
   issued and the lines pointed to by hdgs will be printed, before prtline.
   pagenmbr and linenmbr always reflect the current position of the print
   head after printing takes place.  SetRprt will set pagenmbr to
   zero...the first call to PrtRprt after that will cause the actual start
   of the first page.  skiplines indicates the number of lines to skip
   before printing prtline.  If, on entry, skiplines = 0, prtline will be
   printed on the current line of the current page.  The routine always
   issues a pel (the end-of-line printer mnemonic) after prtline...that
   control need not be imbedded in prtline.  Note that newpage will always
   return false.  *)
PROCEDURE MakeLTbl(nlines,length:CARDINAL):LTBLPTR;
(* This procedure will build a Line Table, for use with the report handling
   routines in this module.  The table will have nlines lines, each of
   length characters.  *)
PROCEDURE ClrLTbl(VAR h:LTBLPTR);
(* This routine will clear a line table. *)
END EL1202.

IMPLEMENTATION MODULE EL1202;
   FROM SYSTEM IMPORT    TSIZE;
   FROM Storage IMPORT   ALLOCATE,DEALLOCATE;
   FROM EL0401 IMPORT    STRING,nullstr,Literal,MakeStr,ClearStr,StrLen,
                         CopyStr,StrChar,SetChar;
```

Fig. 12-2 continued

```
FROM EL0402 IMPORT    Concat,Delete;
FROM EL0502 IMPORT    DATE,TIME;
FROM EL0605 IMPORT    CarToStr;
FROM EL0707 IMPORT    GetDate,GetTime;
FROM EL1201 IMPORT    Print,OpnPrint,ClsPrint,pel,pff;

CONST
  eject = TRUE;
PROCEDURE PrtHdgs(hdgs:LTBLPTR;VAR pagenmbr,linenmbr:CARDINAL);
VAR
  str1,str2:STRING;

  PROCEDURE PrtIt(line:STRING);
  BEGIN
    Print(line);
    Print(pel);
    END PrtIt;

BEGIN
  MakeStr(str1,8,nullstr);
  MakeStr(str2,255,nullstr);
  IF (pagenmbr > 0)
    THEN Print(pff);
    ELSE Print(pcs);
    END;
  pagenmbr:=pagenmbr+1;
  linenmbr:=1;
  IF (linenmbr <= hdgs^.nmbr)
    THEN
      CopyStr(hdgs^.line[linenmbr],str2);
      IF (donmbr)
        THEN
          CarToStr(pagenmbr,3,str1);
          Delete(str2,StrLen(hdgs^.line[linenmbr])-7,8);
          Concat(Literal('Page '),str2);
          Concat(str1,str2);
        END;
      PrtIt(str2);
      linenmbr:=2;
      IF (linenmbr <= hdgs^.nmbr)
        THEN
          CopyStr(hdgs^.line[linenmbr],str2);
          IF (dodate)
            THEN
              Delete(str2,StrLen(hdgs^.line[linenmbr])-7,8);
              Concat(frmddate,str2);
            END;
          PrtIt(str2);
          linenmbr:=3;
          IF (linenmbr <= hdgs^.nmbr)
            THEN
              CopyStr(hdgs^.line[linenmbr],str2);
              IF (dotime)
                THEN
                  Delete(str2,StrLen(hdgs^.line[linenmbr])-7,8);
                  Concat(frmdtime,str2);
                END;
              PrtIt(str2);
              linenmbr:=4;
            END;
        END;
```

```
      END;
  WHILE (linenmbr <= hdgs^.nmbr) DO
    PrtIt(hdgs^.line[linenmbr]);
    linenmbr:=linenmbr+1;
    END;
  ClearStr(str1);
  ClearStr(str2);
  END PrtHdgs;

PROCEDURE PrtRprt(prtline:STRING;VAR newpage:BOOLEAN;skiplines:CARDINAL;
                       hdgs:LTBLPTR;VAR pagenmbr,linenmbr:CARDINAL);
VAR
  i:CARDINAL;
  sub:STRING;
BEGIN
  IF (prtopen = FALSE)
    THEN
      OpnPrint(doask,NOT eject);
      doask:=FALSE;
      IF (dodate)
        THEN
          GetDate(date);
          SetChar(frmddate,1,date[3]);
          SetChar(frmddate,2,date[4]);
          SetChar(frmddate,3,'/');
          SetChar(frmddate,4,date[5]);
          SetChar(frmddate,5,date[6]);
          SetChar(frmddate,6,'/');
          SetChar(frmddate,7,date[1]);
          SetChar(frmddate,8,date[2]);
        END;
      IF (dotime)
        THEN
          GetTime(time);
          SetChar(frmdtime,1,time[1]);
          SetChar(frmdtime,2,time[2]);
          SetChar(frmdtime,3,':');
          SetChar(frmdtime,4,time[3]);
          SetChar(frmdtime,5,time[4]);
          SetChar(frmdtime,6,':');
          SetChar(frmdtime,7,time[5]);
          SetChar(frmdtime,8,time[6]);
        END;
      pagenmbr:=0;
      linenmbr:=maxlines;
      prtopen:=TRUE;
      END;
  IF (linenmbr+skiplines >= length) OR (newpage)
    THEN PrtHdgs(hdgs,pagenmbr,linenmbr);
    END;
  FOR i:=1 TO skiplines DO
    Print(pel);
    linenmbr:=linenmbr+1;
    END;
  Print(prtline);
  Print(pel);
  linenmbr:=linenmbr+1;
  newpage:=FALSE;
  END PrtRprt;

PROCEDURE SetRprt(PCS:STRING;pagelength:CARDINAL;
                    asktoset,npage,dpage,tpage:BOOLEAN);
BEGIN
```

Fig. 12-2 continued

```
  MakeStr(pcs,0,PCS);
  donmbr:=npage;    dodate:=dpage;    dotime:=tpage;
  doask:=asktoset;
  length:=pagelength;
  END SetRprt;

PROCEDURE EndRprt;
BEGIN
   IF (prtopen)
     THEN ClsPrint(eject);
     END;
  prtopen:=FALSE;
  END EndRprt;

PROCEDURE MakeLTbl(nlines,length:CARDINAL):LTBLPTR;
VAR
   h:LTBLPTR;
   i:CARDINAL;
BEGIN
   ALLOCATE(h,nlines*TSIZE(STRING)+2);
   FOR i:=1 TO nlines DO
     MakeStr(h^.line[i],length,nullstr);
     END;
   h^.nmbr:=nlines;
   RETURN h;
   END MakeLTbl;

PROCEDURE ClrLTbl(VAR h:LTBLPTR);
VAR
   i:CARDINAL;
BEGIN
   FOR i:=1 TO h^.nmbr DO
     ClearStr(h^.line[i]);
     END;
   DEALLOCATE(h,h^.nmbr*TSIZE(STRING)+2);
   END ClrLTbl;

VAR
   length:CARDINAL;
   pcs,frmddate,frmdtime:STRING;
   donmbr,dodate,dotime,doask,prtopen:BOOLEAN;
   date:DATE;
   time:TIME;
BEGIN
   prtopen:=FALSE;
   MakeStr(frmddate,8,Literal('          '));
   MakeStr(frmdtime,8,Literal('          '));
END EL1202.
```

define the literals that are to appear in the headings. The module also exports *MakeLTbl* and *ClrLTbl,* two routines for creating and destroying LINETBL variables.

PrtRprt uses the parameter named *hdgs* to define the heading lines that will appear at the top of each page. If, when *SetRprt* was called, *npage, dpage,* and/or *tpage* were equal to TRUE, a page number, report date, and report time are inserted at the end of the first three lines in *hdgs*. (The routine assumes that the lines have reserved room for these literals.)

Note that *PrtRprt* contains all of the logic required to ensure that the printer is open, that there is sufficient room on the page to print *prtline* (after skipping the number of lines specified by *skiplines*), and to skip to the top of a new page if necessary. This relieves the calling program of all responsibility for the mechanics of printing the report; the caller can concentrate on the format of the report and let *PrtRprt* worry about how it gets to the printed page.

Fig. 12-3. Mailing-list file reporting.

```
DEFINITION MODULE EL1203;
   FROM EL0401 IMPORT    STRING;
   FROM EL0503 IMPORT    LONGCARD;
   EXPORT QUALIFIED      PrtList,PrtLbls;

PROCEDURE PrtList(name,address,city,state,zip,phone:STRING;
                 VAR frstdtl:LONGCARD;
                     firstname,birthdate,pass,note:STRING):CHAR;
(* This routine handles printing of the membership list.  On entry, name
   should contain the family name at which printing is to begin.  *)
PROCEDURE PrtLbls(name,address,city,state,zip,phone:STRING;
                 VAR frstdtl:LONGCARD;
                     firstname,birthdate,pass,note:STRING):CHAR;
(* This routine handles printing of the mailing labels.  On entry, name
   should contain the family name at which printing is to begin.  *)
END EL1203.

(* Copyright (c) 1987 TAB BOOKS INC.
   Author: Don Etling
*)
IMPLEMENTATION MODULE EL1203;
   FROM EL0303 IMPORT    equal;
   FROM EL0304 IMPORT    fk1,fk6,fk7,fk9;
   FROM EL0401 IMPORT    STRING,Literal,StrChar,StrLen,SetLen,SubStr,
                         SetChar,nullstr,ClearStr,MakeStr,MoveStr,CopyStr;
   FROM EL0402 IMPORT    Delete,Insert,Concat;
   FROM EL0404 IMPORT    FixStr;
   FROM EL0405 IMPORT    FillStr;
   FROM EL0501 IMPORT    CHARSET,MakeCSet,nullcset;
   FROM EL0503 IMPORT    LONGCARD,lczero,ComLCard;
   FROM EL0801 IMPORT    FindParm;
   FROM EL0902 IMPORT    msgframe;
   FROM EL0905 IMPORT    Message;
   FROM EL0906 IMPORT    Cancel;
   FROM EL1201 IMPORT    pel,pcp,pcb,Print,OpnPrint,ClsPrint;
   FROM EL1202 IMPORT    PrtRprt,SetRprt,EndRprt,LTBLPTR,MakeLTbl;
   FROM EL1114 IMPORT    GetNName,GetKid;

CONST
   asktoset = TRUE;
   npage = TRUE;    dpage = TRUE;    tpage = TRUE;    eject = TRUE;
VAR
   fk1fk6,fk7fk9,fk6fk9:CHARSET;
   pcppcb,pcppce:STRING;

PROCEDURE MoveDtl(VAR dtlnmbr:LONGCARD;
                     firstname,birthdate,pass,note,prtline:STRING);
BEGIN
   GetKid(firstname,birthdate,pass,note,dtlnmbr);
   MoveStr(firstname,prtline,37);
   MoveStr(SubStr(3,2,birthdate),prtline,70);
```

Fig. 12-3 continued

```
    SetChar(prtline,72,'/');
    MoveStr(SubStr(5,2,birthdate),prtline,73);
    SetChar(prtline,75,'/');
    MoveStr(SubStr(1,2,birthdate),prtline,76);
    MoveStr(pass,prtline,79);
    MoveStr(note,prtline,95);
  END MoveDt1;

PROCEDURE PrtList(name,address,city,state,zip,phone:STRING;
                  VAR frstdt1:LONGCARD;
                      firstname,birthdate,pass,note:STRING):CHAR;
CONST
  length = 62;
VAR
  hdgs:LTBLPTR;
  dt1,str:STRING;
  kbchar:CHAR;
  eascii,newpage:BOOLEAN;
  i,pagenmbr,linenmbr:CARDINAL;
BEGIN
  MakeStr(dt1,132,nullstr);
  MakeStr(str,255,nullstr);
  Message(
      Literal('Verify...print all Families from here on printer'),
            Literal('F7 = Yes / F9 = No'),
            msgframe,15,nullcset,fk7fk9,eascii,kbchar);
  IF (kbchar = fk7)
    THEN Message(
        Literal('Be certain standard paper is loaded in printer'),
            Literal('F7 = Ready / F9 = Stop'),
            msgframe,15,nullcset,fk7fk9,eascii,kbchar);
    END;
  IF (kbchar = fk7)
    THEN
      IF (NOT FindParm(Literal('FAMILY'),str))
        THEN Cancel(Literal('FAMILY'),Literal(' '),4,0);
        END;
      Insert(Literal('LISTING OF FILENAME = '),str,1);
      hdgs:=MakeLTbl(4,132);
      FillStr(hdgs^.line[1],' ');
      MoveStr(str,hdgs^.line[1],1);
      FillStr(hdgs^.line[2],' ');
      FillStr(hdgs^.line[3],' ');
      MoveStr(Literal('          NAME AND ADDRESS           '),
                                        hdgs^.line[3],1);
      MoveStr(Literal('          FIRST NAME          '),
                                        hdgs^.line[3],37);
      MoveStr(Literal('  BIRTH    PASS NUMBER          NOTES'),
                                        hdgs^.line[3],69);
      FillStr(hdgs^.line[4],' ');
      MoveStr(Literal('--------------------------------'),
                                        hdgs^.line[4],1);
      MoveStr(Literal('-------------------------------'),
                                        hdgs^.line[4],37);
      MoveStr(Literal('--------'),hdgs^.line[4],69);
      MoveStr(Literal('----------------'),hdgs^.line[4],78);
      MoveStr(Literal('--------------------'),hdgs^.line[4],94);
      SetRprt(pcppcb,length,asktoset,npage,dpage,tpage);
      WHILE (GetNName(name,address,city,state,zip,phone,frstdt1)) DO
        IF (linenmbr + 9 > length)
            THEN newpage:=TRUE;
```

```
                END;
            FillStr(dtl,' ');
            MoveStr(name,dtl,1);
            IF (ComLCard(frstdtl,lczero) <> equal)
              THEN MoveDtl(frstdtl,firstname,birthdate,pass,note,dtl);
                END;
            PrtRprt(dtl,newpage,0,hdgs,pagenmbr,linenmbr);
            FillStr(dtl,' ');
            MoveStr(address,dtl,1);
            IF (ComLCard(frstdtl,lczero) <> equal)
              THEN MoveDtl(frstdtl,firstname,birthdate,pass,note,dtl);
                END;
            PrtRprt(dtl,newpage,0,hdgs,pagenmbr,linenmbr);
            FillStr(dtl,' ');
            MoveStr(city,dtl,1);
            MoveStr(state,dtl.22);
            MoveStr(zip,dtl,27);
            IF (ComLCard(frstdtl,lczero) <> equal)
              THEN MoveDtl(frstdtl,firstname,birthdate,pass,note,dtl);
                END;
            PrtRprt(dtl,newpage,0,hdgs,pagenmbr,linenmbr);
            FillStr(dtl,' ');
            MoveStr(Literal('        PHONE: '),dtl,1);
            MoveStr(SubStr(1,3,phone),dtl,14);
            MoveStr(SubStr(4,3,phone),dtl,19);
            MoveStr(SubStr(7,4,phone),dtl,23);
            IF (ComLCard(frstdtl,lczero) <> equal)
              THEN MoveDtl(frstdtl,firstname,birthdate,pass,note,dtl);
                END;
            PrtRprt(dtl,newpage,0,hdgs,pagenmbr,linenmbr);
            FillStr(dtl,' ');
            WHILE (ComLCard(frstdtl,lczero) <> equal) DO
              MoveDtl(frstdtl,firstname,birthdate,pass,note,dtl);
              PrtRprt(dtl,newpage,0,hdgs,pagenmbr,linenmbr);
              END;
            PrtRprt(hdgs^.line[4],newpage,0,hdgs,pagenmbr,linenmbr);
            END;
          CopyStr(Literal('*************** END OF LIST ************'),dtl);
          PrtRprt(dtl,newpage,0,hdgs,pagenmbr,linenmbr);
          EndRprt;
          END;
      ClearStr(dtl);
      ClearStr(str);
      RETURN fk9;
      END PrtList;

PROCEDURE PrtLbls(name,address,city,state,zip,phone:STRING;
                  VAR frstdtl:LONGCARD;
                      firstname,birthdate,pass,note:STRING):CHAR;
VAR
    spaces,str:STRING;
    kbchar:CHAR;
    eascii:BOOLEAN;
BEGIN
    MakeStr(spaces,255,nullstr);
    MakeStr(str,80,nullstr);
    Message(
        Literal('Verify...print all labels from here on printer'),
        Literal('F6 = Yes / F9 = No'),
            msgframe,15,nullcset,fk6fk9,eascii,kbchar);
    IF (kbchar = fk6)
      THEN Message(
```

Fig. 12-3 continued

```
                   Literal('Be certain labels are loaded in printer'),
                     Literal('F6 = Ready / F9 = Stop'),
                        msgframe,15,nullcset,fk6fk9,eascii,kbchar);
         END;
       IF (kbchar = fk6)
         THEN
       IF (NOT FindParm(Literal('SPACES'),spaces))
         THEN CopyStr(Literal('            '),spaces);
         END;
       OpnPrint(asktoset,NOT eject);
     Print(pcppce);
     REPEAT
       Message(Literal('Check label pattern'),
               Literal('F1 = Again / F6 = Print Labels'),
               msgframe,15,nullcset,fk1fk6,eascii,kbchar);
       IF (kbchar = fk1)
         THEN
           Print(pcp);
           Print(spaces);
           Print(Literal('XXXXXXXXXXXXXXXXXXXXXXXXXXXXXXXXXXX'));
           Print(pel);
           Print(spaces);
           Print(Literal('XXXXXXXXXXXXXXXXXXXXXXXXXXXXXXXXXXX'));
           Print(pel);
           Print(spaces);
           Print(Literal('XXXXXXXXXXXXXXXXXXXXXXXXXXXXXXXXXXX'));
           Print(pel);
           Print(pel);
           Print(pel);
         END;
       UNTIL (kbchar = fk6);
     WHILE (GetNName(name,address,city,state,zip,phone,frstdtl)) DO
       Print(pel);
       Print(pel);
       Print(spaces);
       Print(name);
       Print(pel);
       Print(spaces);
       Print(address);
       Print(pel);
       Print(spaces);
       CopyStr(city,str);
       WHILE (StrChar(str,StrLen(str)) = ' ') DO
         Delete(str,StrLen(str),1);
         END;
       Print(str);
       Print(Literal(' '));
       Print(state);
       Print(Literal(' '));
       Print(zip);
       Print(pel);
       Print(pel);
       END;
     END;
   ClsPrint(NOT eject);
   ClearStr(spaces);
   ClearStr(str);
   RETURN fk9;
   END PrtLbls;


BEGIN
```

```
   MakeCSet(FixStr(Literal('fk1*fk6')),fk1fk6);
   MakeCSet(FixStr(Literal('fk6*fk9')),fk6fk9);
   MakeCSet(FixStr(Literal('fk7*fk9')),fk7fk9);
   MakeStr(pcppcb,0,FixStr(Literal('pcp*pcb')));
   MakeStr(pcppce,0,FixStr(Literal('pcp*pce')));
 END EL1203.
```

EndRprt. The *EndRprt* routine should be the last routine called in a program that uses the report-generation routines. If the *prtopen* variable in the module indicates that a report has been started, *EndRprt* will call *ClsPrint* and instruct it to issue a page eject.

AN EXAMPLE

LISTER (discussed back in Chapter 2) uses the report-generation routines in the Etling Library to produces its library listings. Figure 12-3 shows another example. It lists the source code for another module in the Membership List program begun in the last chapter, module EL1203.

The EL1204 module contains routines to produce both a complete membership listing and mailing labels. The membership list is handled by *PrtList;* the mailing labels by *PrtLbls.* The first routine uses the report-generation routines; the second routine calls the print routines directly.

Chapter 13

Windows . . . Sort of

The magic word is "windows." That's the word that all software developers use to show that their stuff is more "state of the art" than anyone else can offer. Everyone —MicroSoft, IBM, Digital Research, even Apple—uses the word as undeniable proof that their systems are easier to learn and user friendlier because their systems "do windows." They will will tell you that "all your troubles are over because once you buy our system all the other developers will start developing software to take advantage of all the great things that our windows can do." Well, not to be left out, let me state, positively, there are routines in the Etling Library that do windows.

Right. So what's a window?

Fortunately for software developers, no one has gotten around to defining the term, exactly. It can mean whatever seems appropriate for the package the developer is trying to sell, and until someone establishes the "de facto standard," the term "windows" is going to mean a lot of different things. Whichever definition is finally accepted, there are a few basic principles that will be included.

The concept of "windows" begins with the realization that the main output device to the user, the display, is *not* a typewriter or teleprinter. The display is not limited to having one line at a time appear at the bottom of a page as a roll of paper moves upward. When used with memory mapping electronics, the display can show, almost instantly, a whole page . . . a complete picture . . . a total thought.

The display *is* a window, and because of the speed with which the contents of memory can be changed, the display is a *moving* window. Unlike the print head on paper, the display window moves up and down, right and left. And when memory is

236

completely rewritten, the display can make a quantum leap, bypassing the two-dimensional scroll to display an entirely different view in an instant.

If one view is good, are not several views better? That's another attribute of most windowing systems; the ability to show several "windows" on the screen at once. In fact, some windowing systems, like IBM's TOPVIEW, are really operating systems.

TOPVIEW windows have two functions. First, the system itself uses one or more windows on the screen to show menus, optional parameters, or portions of directory listings. Second, TOPVIEW can load several programs into memory at one time and allocate a window through which the user can moniter the program's operation. Depending on the resources each program requires, TOPVIEW can keep some running while others are in a state of suspension. Depending on the mixture of programs and how each program must interface with the screen, the display might show several windows, or the entire screen might be dedicated to one program.

Some systems that use windows, like Borland's SIDEKICK, will open a window at the touch of a key. What appears in the window is part of SIDEKICK, not another program.

For the record, the routines in the Etling Library are more like SIDEKICK than TOPVIEW. The display can show multiple windows, but all of the windows are part of the same program's operations. The Etling Library routines do not provide a "multi-tasking" operating system; the routines only permit one program to divide the display into several areas for interfacing with the user.

The Etling Library provides two related yet distinctly different types of window. There are "reference" windows and "data entry" windows. A *reference window* is a window that displays reference information for the user; the user may be able to move around in the window, but he cannot change the information it displays. A data entry window can both display information and allow the user to change it or enter new values. Data entry windows are discussed in the next chapter, but this chapter presents the simplest kind of reference window.

SIMPLE REFERENCE WINDOWS

The basic principle behind simple reference windows is the FRAME data type, described back in Chapter 5. If you recall from that discussion, a FRAME is a record structure that can be used to delineate an area within a SCREENMAP, which is an ARRAY of DISPLAYWORD. In other words, a FRAME refers to an area of display (or display-like) memory.

The area in which a reference window appears on the screen can be defined as a FRAME. If the information to which the user will refer is also defined as a FRAME and allocated somewhere else in memory, displaying that information on the screen becomes relatively easy.

ShwFrame. Figure 13-1 shows EL1301 which exports a single routine named *ShwFrame*. *Shwframe* handles the appearance of a reference FRAME on the display. The parameter list for *ShwFrame* requires two FRAME variables; the *f* FRAME defines the information, and the *t* FRAME defines the area in which the information should appear on the screen. *SheFrame* allows *f* to be larger and of different dimensions than *t*. The user can use the cursor control keys to move the contents of *f* around, within the confines of *t*.

Fig. 13-1. Dealing with frames.

```
DEFINITION MODULE EL1301;
  FROM EL0501 IMPORT    CHARSET;
  FROM EL0504 IMPORT    FRAME;
  EXPORT QUALIFIED       ShwFrame;

PROCEDURE ShwFrame(VAR f,t:FRAME;VAR normals,easciis:CHARSET;
                   VAR eascii:BOOLEAN;VAR kbchar:CHAR);
(* This routine will display the contents of f on the crt within the area
   specified by t.  If the f contains more lines or columns than t, this
   routine will permit the user to scroll using the cursor control keys.
   When the user presses one of the keys specified, control will return to
   the calling program.  *)
END EL1301.


IMPLEMENTATION MODULE EL1301;
  FROM SYSTEM IMPORT    ADDRESS,ADR;
  FROM EL0302 IMPORT    MovByteL;
  FROM EL0304 IMPORT    home,end,tabl,tabr,utab,dtab,curr,curl;
  FROM EL0501 IMPORT    InCSet,CHARSET;
  FROM EL0504 IMPORT    FRAME,MovFrame;
  FROM EL0705 IMPORT    Sound,errfreq,errdur;
  FROM EL0901 IMPORT    InitKB,GetKBChr;
  FROM EL0902 IMPORT    ClrScrn,nrmclr;


PROCEDURE ShwFrame(VAR f,t:FRAME;VAR normals,easciis:CHARSET;
                   VAR eascii:BOOLEAN;VAR kbchar:CHAR);
CONST
  lockcap    = TRUE;    locknum    = TRUE;
VAR
  done:BOOLEAN;
BEGIN
  InitKB(lockcap,NOT locknum);
  done:=FALSE;
  f.cl:=f.fl;    f.cc:=f.fc;    t.cl:=t.fl;    t.cc:=t.fc;
  REPEAT
    MovFrame(f,t);
    REPEAT
      UNTIL (GetKBChr(eascii,kbchar));
    IF ((eascii) AND (InCSet(kbchar,easciis)))
       OR ((NOT eascii) AND (InCSet(kbchar,normals)))
      THEN done:=TRUE;
      ELSE
        CASE kbchar OF
          home : f.cl:=f.fl; f.cc:=f.fc;
          ! end  : f.cl:=f.ll-f.fl; f.cc:=f.lc-f.fc;
          ! utab :IF (f.cl > f.fl)
                    THEN DEC(f.cl);
                    ELSE Sound(errfreq,errdur);
                    END;
          ! dtab :IF (f.cl < f.ll-f.fl)
                    THEN INC(f.cl);
                    ELSE Sound(errfreq,errdur);
                    END;
          ! curr,tabr :IF (f.cc < f.lc-f.fc)
                    THEN INC(f.cc);
                    ELSE Sound(errfreq,errdur);
                    END;
          ! curl,tabl :IF (f.cc > f.fc)
                    THEN DEC(f.cc);
                    ELSE Sound(errfreq,errdur);
                    END;
```

```
        ELSE
           Sound(errfreq,errdur);
           END;
        END;
     UNTIL (done);
   ClrScrn(f,nrmclr);
   InitKB(lockcap,locknum);
   END ShwFrame;

END EL1301.
```

Fig. 13-2. Help.

```
DEFINITION MODULE EL1302;
   FROM EL0401 IMPORT    STRING;
   FROM EL0504 IMPORT    FRAME;
   EXPORT QUALIFIED      Help;

PROCEDURE Help(helpname,inxname:STRING;msgno:CARDINAL;VAR hlpframe:FRAME);
(* This routine will provide an on-screen help message corresponding to the
   contents of msgno.  The file identified by helpname contains the actual
   messages...the file associated with inxname is used as an index to those
   messages.  These files must be prepared by the NDXHELP program.  The
   messages appear on the screen in the area in hlpframe.  If the message
   requires more than that number of lines, this routine will permit the
   user to scroll them up and down, using the cursor control keys.  When
   the user presses the help key, this routine will clear that area and
   return to the calling procedure.  *)
END EL1302.

IMPLEMENTATION MODULE EL1302;
   FROM SYSTEM IMPORT    WORD,BYTE,ADR,ADDRESS;
   FROM Storage IMPORT   ALLOCATE,DEALLOCATE;
   FROM EL0302 IMPORT    MovByteL;
   FROM EL0304 IMPORT    help;
   FROM EL0401 IMPORT    STRING,Literal,StrLen,MakeStr,ClearStr,
                         nullstr,StrChar;
   FROM EL0501 IMPORT    CHARSET,MakeCSet,nullcset;
   FROM EL0503 IMPORT    LongCard,LONGCARD;
   FROM EL0504 IMPORT    DsplyWrd,DWPTR,FRAMEPTR,FRAME,MakFrame,
                         ClrFrame,MovFrame;
   FROM EL0902 IMPORT    nrmclr,ClrScrn;
   FROM EL0906 IMPORT    Cancel;
   FROM EL1001 IMPORT    RptIOErr;
   FROM EL1002 IMPORT    OpnFile,ClsFile,LOCCNTRL,LINECNTRL,
                         OPENKIND,FMODE,DISP;
   FROM EL1003 IMPORT    GetLine;
   FROM EL1005 IMPORT    GetRcrd;
   FROM EL1012 IMPORT    SetFLoc;
   FROM EL1301 IMPORT    ShwFrame;

PROCEDURE Help(helpname,inxname:STRING;msgno:CARDINAL;VAR hlpframe:FRAME);
VAR
   h,t:FRAMEPTR;
   i,j,nlines:CARDINAL;
   rcrd:RECORD
     frst:LONGCARD;
     nlines:CARDINAL;
     END;
   nmbr:LONGCARD;
   d,d1,d2:DWPTR;
```

Fig. 13-2 continued

```
    lengot:WORD;
    ioerr:BYTE;
    line:STRING;
    hmode,imode:FMODE;
    ishelp,eascii:BOOLEAN;
    kbchar:CHAR;

BEGIN
  MakeStr(line,255,nullstr);
  IF (StrLen(helpname) = 0)
  THEN ishelp:=FALSE;
  ELSE
    hmode:=oldfile;
    REPEAT
      OpnFile(helpname,hmode,ioerr,tryonce);
      IF (ioerr = BYTE(0))
        THEN ishelp:=TRUE;
        ELSE
          ishelp:=FALSE;
          IF (ioerr = BYTE(2))
            THEN ioerr:=BYTE(0);
            ELSE RptIOErr(ioerr,helpname,Literal('Help'),TRUE);
          END;
        END;
      UNTIL (ioerr = BYTE(0));
  END;
IF (ishelp)
  THEN
    imode:=oldfile;
    OpnFile(inxname,imode,ioerr,insist);
    LongCard(msgno,0,nmbr);
    IF (NOT GetRcrd(inxname,setpostn,
                            nmbr,nmbr,6,lengot,ADR(rcrd)))
      THEN ishelp:=FALSE;
      ELSE IF (rcrd.nlines < hlpframe.nl)
        THEN nlines:=hlpframe.nl;
        ELSE nlines:=rcrd.nlines;
        END;
      END;
  END;
IF (NOT ishelp)
  THEN nlines:=hlpframe.nl;
  END;
MakFrame(1,1,nlines,hlpframe.nc,1,1,nlines,hlpframe.nc,NIL,t);
ClrScrn(t^,nrmclr);
IF (ishelp)
  THEN
    IF (rcrd.nlines = 0)
      THEN ishelp:=FALSE;
      ELSE
        IF (NOT SetFLoc(helpname,setpostn,1,rcrd.frst))
          THEN Cancel(Literal('Help'),helpname,1,0);
          END;
        FOR i:=1 TO rcrd.nlines DO
          IF (NOT GetLine(helpname,line,nortrnend))
            THEN Cancel(Literal('Help'),helpname,1,1);
            END;
          FOR j:=1 TO StrLen(line) DO
            d:=DsplyWrd(i,j+2,t^);
            d^.chrbyte:=StrChar(line,j);
            END;
```

```
              END;
            END;
          ClsFile(helpname,clsonly);
          ClsFile(inxname,clsonly);
        END;
   IF (NOT ishelp)
      THEN FOR i:=1 TO StrLen(msg) DO
          d:=DsplyWrd(1,i,t^);
          d^.chrbyte:=StrChar(msg,j);
          END;
        END;
   FOR i:=1 TO nlines DO
      d1:=DsplyWrd(i,1,t^);
      d2:=DsplyWrd(i,t^.nc,t^);
      IF (i = 1) OR (i = nlines)
        THEN
          d1^.chrbyte:='*';
          d2^.chrbyte:='*';
        ELSE
          d1^.chrbyte:=CHR(18);
          d2^.chrbyte:=CHR(18);
        END;
      END;
   WITH hlpframe DO
      MakFrame(fl,fc,ll,lc,fl,fc,nl,nc,NIL,h);
      END;
   MovFrame(hlpframe,h^);
   ShwFrame(t^,hlpframe,nullcset,helpcset,eascii,kbchar);
   MovFrame(h^,hlpframe);
   ClrFrame(t);
   ClrFrame(h);
   ClearStr(line);
   END Help;

VAR
   msg:STRING;
   helpcset:CHARSET;
BEGIN
   MakeCSet(Literal(help),helpcset);
   MakeStr(msg,0,Literal('No help available for this item.'));
END EL1302.
```

PROVIDING HELP

The other "buzz word" phrase used in connection with "windows" is "context sensitive help." All this really means is that the program or system has a method of determining what the user is supposed to be doing and what context the action is in, and can provide a reference window that somehow helps him do it. *ShwFrame* handles the window, and the following routine provides the help. (Determining what the user is doing is discussed in the next chapter.)

Help. Module EL1302, shown in Fig. 13-2, exports *Help,* the routine that implements the additional help facility. *Help* uses its *hlpframe* parameter to display messages on the screen for the user. The messages are taken from the file associated with *helpname.* The *helpname* file has an associated *inxname* file, which provides a direct index into the help messages. Each help message is numbered and the *inxname* file is used to indicate the location at which the message identified by *msgno* begins in the *helpname* file.

Fig. 13-3. Help file builder.

```
(*  NDXHELP, Help file indexer
    Copyright (c) 1987 TAB BOOKS INC.
    Author: Don Etling

    This program will read a text file and create an NDX file to it.
    Entries in the index are controlled by encountering a line in the
    following form:

            ($HELPMSG:<fr>[-<lr>][,USE:<pr>)

    The program expects a parameter list containing:

            HLPFILE=<helpfilename> INXFILE=<inxfilename>                    *)

MODULE NDXHELP;
  FROM SYSTEM IMPORT      BYTE,ADR,WORD;
  FROM EL0303 IMPORT      equal;
  FROM EL0304 IMPORT      cr,lf;
  FROM EL0401 IMPORT      STRING,MakeStr,StrLen,Literal,SetLen,
                          nullstr,MoveStr,SetChar,StrChar,SubStr;
  FROM EL0402 IMPORT      Concat;
  FROM EL0403 IMPORT      MatchStr,Positn;
  FROM EL0503 IMPORT      LONGCARD,lcone,LongCard,AddLCard;
  FROM EL0504 IMPORT      FRAMEPTR,MakFrame;
  FROM EL0602 IMPORT      MakCard;
  FROM EL0801 IMPORT      GetParms,FindParm;
  FROM EL0803 IMPORT      AskParm;
  FROM EL0901 IMPORT      InitKB;
  FROM EL0902 IMPORT      crtads,nrmclr,ClrScrn,PstnCur,FindCRT;
  FROM EL0906 IMPORT      Cancel;
  FROM EL0908 IMPORT      TypeStr;
  FROM EL1002 IMPORT      FMODE,OPENKIND,DISP,LINECNTRL,setpostn,
                          OpnFile,ClsFile;
  FROM EL1003 IMPORT      GetLine;
  FROM EL1005 IMPORT      GetRcrd;
  FROM EL1006 IMPORT      PutRcrd;

CONST
  hlpfile    = 'HLPFILE';
  inxfile    = 'INXFILE';
  home       = TRUE;
VAR
  hlpmode,inxmode:FMODE;
  rcrd:RECORD
    frst:LONGCARD;
    nlines:CARDINAL;
    END;
  r,fr,lr,i,j:CARDINAL;
  nmbr,frst,length:LONGCARD;
  doing:BOOLEAN;
  lengot:WORD;
  topframe,wrkframe,botframe,msgframe:FRAMEPTR;
  line,crlf,h:STRING;
  ioerr:BYTE;

BEGIN              (* Main *)
  MakeStr(line,255,nullstr);
  MakFrame(1,1,4,80,1,1,25,80,crtads,topframe);
  MakFrame(5,1,22,80,5,1,25,80,crtads,wrkframe);
  MakFrame(23,1,23,80,23,1,25,80,crtads,botframe);
  MakFrame(24,1,25,80,24,1,25,80,crtads,msgframe);
```

```
ClrScrn(topframe^,nrmclr);
ClrScrn(wrkframe^,nrmclr);
ClrScrn(botframe^,nrmclr);
ClrScrn(msgframe^,nrmclr);
GetParms;
MakeStr(crlf,2,Literal('  '));
SetChar(crlf,1,cr);
SetChar(crlf,2,lf);
TypeStr(nrmclr,home,
        Literal('NDXHELP - Help file NDX Builder'),
        topframe^);
TypeStr(nrmclr,NOT home,crlf,topframe^);
TypeStr(nrmclr,NOT home,
        Literal('Copyright (c) 1987 TAB BOOKS INC '),
        topframe^);
TypeStr(nrmclr,NOT home,crlf,topframe^);
TypeStr(nrmclr,NOT home,
        Literal('Author: Don Etling'),
        topframe^);
TypeStr(nrmclr,NOT home,crlf,topframe^);
MakeStr(h,79,nullstr);
SetLen(h,79);
FOR i:=1 TO 79 DO
   SetChar(h,i,'-');
   END;
TypeStr(nrmclr,NOT home,h,topframe^);
TypeStr(nrmclr,home,h,botframe^);
hlpmode:=oldfile;
inxmode:=makenew;
doing:=FALSE;
frst:=lcone;
OpnFile(Literal(hlpfile),hlpmode,ioerr,insist);
OpnFile(Literal(inxfile),inxmode,ioerr,insist);
WHILE (GetLine(Literal(hlpfile),line,rtrnend)) DO
   TypeStr(nrmclr,NOT home,line,wrkframe^);
   LongCard(StrLen(line),0,length);
   AddLCard(frst,length,frst);
   IF (MatchStr(Literal('($HELPMSG:'),line,1,1,10) <> equal)
     THEN rcrd.nlines:=rcrd.nlines+1;
     ELSE
       IF (doing)
         THEN FOR r:=fr TO lr DO
           LongCard(r,0,nmbr);
           PutRcrd(Literal(inxfile),setpostn,nmbr,nmbr,6,ADR(rcrd));
           END;
         END;
       rcrd.frst:=frst;
       fr:=MakCard(line,11,i);
       IF (StrChar(line,i) <> '-')
         THEN lr:=fr;
         ELSE lr:=MakCard(line,i+1,i);
         END;
       IF (StrChar(line,i) <> ',')
         THEN doing:=TRUE;
         ELSE
           j:=MakCard(line,i+5,i);
           LongCard(j,0,nmbr);
           IF (NOT GetRcrd(Literal(inxfile),setpostn,
                       nmbr,nmbr,6,lengot,ADR(rcrd)))
             THEN Cancel(Literal('buildhlp'),Literal(inxfile),1,0);
             END;
           FOR r:=fr TO lr DO
```

Fig. 13-3 continued

```
                LongCard(r,0,nmbr);
                PutRcrd(Literal(inxfile),setpostn,nmbr,nmbr,6,ADR(rcrd));
                END;
              doing:=FALSE;
          END;
        rcrd.nlines:=0;
      END;
    END;
  IF (doing)
    THEN FOR r:=fr TO lr DO
      LongCard(r,0,nmbr);
      PutRcrd(Literal(inxfile),setpostn,nmbr,nmbr,6,ADR(rcrd));
      END;
    END;
  ClsFile(Literal(hlpfile),clsonly);
  ClsFile(Literal(inxfile),clsonly);
  PstnCur(25,1,msgframe^);
END NDXHELP.
```

Help displays its messages by its creating its own FRAME, assembling the message within it, and then using *ShwFrame* to display the message for the user. Note that if there is no message for a particular *msgno* (or, for that matter, if the *helpname* file does not exist), the message says "No help available for this item."

NDXHELP. Figure 13-3 shows NDXHELP, a program that will build help message files. NDXHELP builds an inxfile that indexes the messages in the hlpfile. An inxfile is a direct access file; each record in the file contains a fixed number of bytes and is directly accessible by record number. Each record in the inxfile points to a message in the hlpfile; the record number corresponds to the message number in the hlpfile. The inxfile record also contains an indication of the number of lines in the message.

As the comments in Fig. 13-3 indicate, each help message in the hlpfile is defined by a command in the following format:

{$HELPMSG:<fr>[−<lr>][,USE:<pr>]}

The three variables, <fr>, <lr>, and <pr>, are integer values that indicate the message number (or numbers) to be associated with the message. The value for <fr> is required; the other values are optional. If −<lr> is given, the help message will apply to all message numbers from <fr> to <lr>. If ,USE:<pr> is given, NDXHELP will copy the assignment for <pr>. In other words, it reuses a previous message.

Chapter 14

Data Entry

The data entry windowing system defined in the Etling Library is implemented by the deScreen routines. These "**d**ata **e**ntry **Screen**" routines are patterned after several screen-handling systems used on various mainframe computers. Hewlett-Packard calls their system "VIEW/3000;" IBM implements the same techniques in CICS (Customer Information Control System).

The basic assumption behind all of these systems, deScreen included, is that most computer users are accustomed to dealing with *forms*. Forms are printed documents with blank spaces in which the user writes information. An employment application is a form; each year the IRS redesigns the Income Tax forms. One way to develop user friendly systems is to take advantage of the user's familiarity with forms when defining the way in which data is entered into a program.

With this in mind, the deScreen routines provide a way to construct, display, and control the user's interaction with forms on the PC display.

There is one problem with implementing a "form on the screen" system for personal computers. Many forms will not fit in a space that is only 25 lines by 80 columns. For example, Fig. 14-1 shows a registration form that might be used by an amateur soccer league to register the individual teams that make up the league. The form is intended to be filled in by hand, so the exact number of characters each field can contain varies. It is difficult, therefore, to say exactly how much space the form would require on the screen, but it is approximately 132 characters wide by 40 lines long.

Some screen-oriented data entry systems would require you to redesign the

```
============================REGISTRATION FORM============================
TEAM NAME:_____    DIVISION: ____  SEASON:_____  YEAR 19__

SOCCER CLUB NAME:_____    COACHES NAME:_____
        ADDRESS:_____        ADDRESS:_____
           CITY:_____           CITY:_____
          STATE:___ ZIP:_____            STATE:___ ZIP:_____ PHONE (___)___-___
```

	PLAYER'S NAME	B.DATE	PASS #	PHONE	ADDRESS	CITY	ST.	ZIP
1		_-_		_-_				
2		_-_		_-_				
3		_-_		_-_				
4		_-_		_-_				
5		_-_		_-_				
6		_-_		_-_				
7		_-_		_-_				
8		_-_		_-_				
9		_-_		_-_				
10		_-_		_-_				
11		_-_		_-_				
12		_-_		_-_				
13		_-_		_-_				
14		_-_		_-_				
15		_-_		_-_				
16		_-_		_-_				
17		_-_		_-_				
18		_-_		_-_				
19		_-_		_-_				
20		_-_		_-_				
21		_-_		_-_				
22		_-_		_-_				
23		_-_		_-_				
24		_-_		_-_				
25		_-_		_-_				

```
REGISTRAR _____  DATE __-__-__
```

Fig. 14-1. Soccer team registration form.

form so that it required less space. Other systems force you to collect the data the form represents in several steps. The deScreen routines have a different approach.

SCREEN MAPS

The deScreen routines use a SCREENMAP, defined somewhere in main memory (other than display memory) to contain the form definition. That SCREENMAP can be smaller than the display memory, or it can be much larger than the display can show at one time. To interface with the user, the deScreen routines provide a way to show a smaller SCREENMAP anywhere on the display, or to use the display as a "window" into the larger SCREENMAP.

With a SCREENMAP that is larger than the display can show, the window can move around in the form, but rather than allowing the user to position the window at random (as *ShwFrame,* described in the last chapter, would do) the deScreen routines permit the program to define a logical flow from one place to another, depending on the data to be collected. To assist with defining this flow, the deScreen routines group data into discrete fields.

Fields

Certain areas of a deScreen SCREENMAP are designated as data fields. Just like a record field, a deScreen field is a contiguous area that represents some elemental unit of information. In a deScreen SCREENMAP, all fields are strings of ASCII characters. There are, however, two different types of deScreen fields. A numeric field can contain only numeric characters; an alpha field can contain any ASCII character.

Boxes

The deScreen SCREENMAP is divided into one or more *boxes*. A box is similar to a FRAME, defined back in Chapter 5, but while a FRAME refers to an area on the display, a box relates to an area in a deScreen map *and* to a FRAME on the CRT. In effect, a box projects an area of a deScreen into display memory.

Colors

When you define a field in a deScreen, you also specify the color in which it is to appear on the display. The deScreen routines, like the rest of the display access routines in the Etling Library, will work equally well with the Monochrome, Color Graphics, or Enhanced Color Graphics adapters available for the IBM PC product line. But because the deScreen routines access display memory directly without going through BIOS, there is a significant amount of "snow" generated on the Color Graphics adapter by some of the deScreen operations. The deScreen technique loses a lot of its appeal when it is used with the standard color adapter. The Monochrome adapter and the Enhanced Color adapter work fine, and because of their higher resolution, produce character images that are acceptable for data entry.

The choice of what color attribute to use for the display generated by a deScreen is entirely up to the screen designer. (The *IBM Technical Reference Manual* for each model of IBM PC has an appendix that lists all of the legal color attributes versus the color they generate on both the color and monochrome display.) There are, however, certain concepts to keep in mind.

First, avoid color attributes that generate black characters on a white background for the monochrome display. This is particularly true for areas of the SCREENMAP that will tend to stay on the screen for long periods of time. As is the case for all CRT display tubes, the monochrome display relies on a layer of phosphor on the inside of the glass tube to help "retain" the image drawn by the electron gun at the back of the tube. When an electron hits this phosphor, the phosphor glows for a short period of time after the guns moves on. The glow retains the image long enough to fool your eye and brain into thinking that the glow is continuous.

The problem is that when an inverse video image is shown on the screen, a fairly large area of the phosphor must glow. Eventually, the image will begin to etch itself into the phosphor coating. Then, the image will become visible even when the CRT is turned off. This will, of course, happen for any character displayed for long periods of time, but, it affects larger areas of the screen with inverse video.

The second point to keep in mind when defining colors is that the deScreen routines that control a user's access also highlight the entire field in which the user is working. This draws the user's attention to the field quicker than a single blinking cursor (which is still present in the field to mark the current character). The deScreen routines allow the program to specify what color is to be used for this highlight. I normally use *stdhilite* (hexidecimal 70) from the COLORS entry in the Etling Library, but you can choose any color you find acceptable. Note that *stdhilite* does produce inverse video on a monochrome display, but because the user seldom stays in any one field for a long time, the effect of this on the display's phosphor is minimized.

The last point with regard to color on a deScreen is this; combining color with the line-drawing graphics characters will emphasize the form on the screen concept. Use the line drawing characters, shown in Fig. 14-2 to outline boxes and columns, and, then use one of the color attributes that produces underlined characters to define each data entry field. Unfortunately, a color attribute value of 1, (which is what *undrline* in the COLORS library entry uses) will produce a very deep blue character on a black background on either of the color displays. A value of 49 (which also underlines characters on the monochrome) produces an acceptable combination on

```
   ┌    ┬    ┐                 ╔    ╦    ╗
  218  194  191               201  203  187

   ├    ┼    ┤                 ╠    ╬    ╣
  195  197  180               204  206  185

   └    ┴    ┘                 ╚    ╩    ╝
  192  193  217               200  202  188


        ─         │         ║         ═
       196       179       186       205


   ╒    ╤    ╕                 ╓    ╥    ╖
  213  209  184               214  210  183

   ╞    ╪    ╡                 ╟    ╫    ╢
  198  216  181               199  215  182

   ╘    ╧    ╛                 ╙    ╨    ╜
  212  207  190               211  208  189
```

```
To enter one of the characters into a text file using an editor,
press the ALT key, and enter the 3 digits under the character
using the numeric key pad.
```

Fig. 14-2. Line-drawing graphic character set.

a color display; the characters are shown as deep blue characters on a cyan background.

THE SCREEN COMPILER

Definition of a SCREENMAP is entirely under your control. Figure 14-3 shows MAKESCRN, which is essentially a screen compiler. It will translate a series of commands contained in a text file (with a SCD extension) into a file containing a SCREEN-MAP. The file it generates is an IMG file. In addition to the SCREENMAP, an IMG file defines several control areas used by the deScreen routines to interpret box and field definitions. The SCREENMAP and the control areas are built by MAKESCRN under control of the commands in the SCD file.

To execute MAKESCRN, you need to provide two parameters. The batch file, DOSCRN.BAT, handles its execution. DOSCRN.BAT contains the following:

```
MAKESCRN SCD=%1.SCD IMG=%1.IMG
TESTSCRN IMG=%1.IMG SCROLLTAB=¦ ¦
```

TESTSCRN is a program that tests a completed deScreen image file and is discussed later in this chapter. If you wish MAKESCRN to produce a printed copy of the DEF file, include parameters for PRINTER and PRTSPOOL.

MAKESCRN Commands

All MAKESCRN commands share the same general format. Each command is a single line in the SCD file. There is no "continuation" character, so each command

Fig. 14-3. Makescrn commands.

```
*<comment>

C,<max fields>,<max line>,<max columns>,<max boxes>;

B,<box number>,
    <1st map line>,<1st map column>,
      <number map lines>,<number map columns>,
        <1st display line>,<1st display column>,
          <max display lines>,<number display columns>;

T,<line>,<column>,<length>,<color>,<text string>;

A,<fld number>,<line>,<column>,<length>,<color>,
        <fld type>,<default string>;

N,<fld number>,<line>,<column>,<length>,<color>,
        <fld type>,<default string>;

Z,<fld number>,<line>,<column>,<length>,<color>,
        <fld type>,<default string>;

R,<number repeats>;

Q;

E;
```

must fit on one line. Because MAKESCRN is built from routines in the Etling Library, it uses *GETLINE* to read the SCD file. In *GetLine*, lines may contain up to 32K characters, but because most text editors are incapable of producing a line that long, MAKESCRN's line is restricted to 255 characters in length).

Figure 14-3 summarizes the MAKESCRN commands. Each MAKESCRN command begins with a single character that identifies its function. Each command ends with an optional semicolon. The first noncomment command in a SCD file must be a control command.

Many MAKESCRN commands require a list of parameters. Some parameters are numbers (which can be separated from one another by any non-numeric character) but some parameters require strings of alpha characters. It is best if you standardize on one character to use as delimiter; I use a comma.

Figure 14-4 shows a complete SCD file. This file creates a deScreen image file for the soccer team registration form shown in Fig. 14-1. As is often the case, the deScreen makes some minor modifications to the form; this time, some of the field lengths are truncated to a more displayable (but still serviceable) length. In the following discussion, refer to Fig. 14-4 for an example of each command.

Comments. The SCD file may contain comments to help you remember what form the file defines or to assist with the definition. Any line that begins with an asterisk is a comment line. Comment lines are ignored by MAKESCRN. I generally include "ruler lines" in each SCD file. A ruler line is a comment line that contains nothing but the numbers 1 through whatever, and helps to determine the position of other fields. For example,

```
*          1         2         3         4
* 12345678901234567890123456789012345678901234. .
```

Fig. 14-4. DEF file for the registration form.

```
*
*
*
C,317,38,160,4;
B,1,1,2,9,79,1,2,9,79
B,2,10,1,3,160,10,1,3,80;
B,3,13,1,25,160,13,1,10,80;
B,4,38,1,1,160,23,1,1,80;
*          12345678901234567890123456789012345678901234567890123456789012345678901234567890
*                   1         2         3         4         5         6         7         8
T,01,01,80,2,
T,02,01,80,2,   TEAM NAME: 12345678901234567890     DIVISION: 1234  SEASON: 12345678, 1985
T,03,01,80,2,
T,04,01,80,2,      CLUB: 12345678901234567890123456     COACH: 12345678901234567890123456
T,05,01,80,2,   ADDRESS: 12345678901234567890123456   ADDRESS: 12345678901234567890123456
T,06,01,80,2,      CITY: 12345678901234567890123456      CITY: 12345678901234567890123456
T,07,01,80,2,     STATE: 123    ZIP: 123456789          STATE: 123  ZIP: 123456789
T,08,01,80,2,                                           PHONE: (123) 123-1234
T,09,01,80,2,
A,1,2,15,20,49, ,
A,2,2,51,4,49, ,
A,3,2,65,8,49, ,
Z,4,2,77,2,49, ,85;
A,5,4,15,25,49, ,
A,6,5,15,25,49, ,
```

```
A,7,6,15,25,49, ,
A,8,7,15,3,49, ,
A,9,7,26,9,49, ,
A,10,4,53,25,49, ,
A,11,5,53,25,49, ,
A,12,6,53,25,49, ,
A,13,7,53,3,49, ,
A,14,7,62,9,49, ,
N,15,8,54,3,49, ,
A,16,8,59,3,49, ,
N,17,8,63,4,49, ,
T,10,01,80,2,
T,11,01,80,2,
T,12,01,80,2,
T,38,01,80,2,
T,10,81,80,2,
T,11,81,80,2,
T,12,81,80,2,
T,38,81,80,2,
```

```
R,25;
T,13,01,80,2,
T,13,81,80,2,
```

```
L,13,2,2,2,01;
A,18,13,5,20,49, ,
Z,43,13,26,2,49, ,
Z,68,13,29,2,49, ,
Z,93,13,32,2,49, ,
A,118,13,35,15,49, ,
A,143,13,51,3,49, ,
A,168,13,55,3,49, ,
A,193,13,59,4,49, ,
A,218,13,106,20,49, ,
A,243,13,127,15,49, ,
A,268,13,143,3,49, ,
A,293,13,147,9,49, ,
Q;
E;
```

Control Command. The first non-comment command in a SCD file must be a control command. There must be one, and only one, control command in a SCD file. A control command contains four parameters, in the following format:

C,<max fields>,<max lines>,<max columns>,<max boxes>

The <max fields> parameter specifies the maximum number of fields the deScreen contains. There must be at least one field defined. The upper limit for <max fields> is around 6000, but a deScreen containing this many fields would probably exceed some of the other limits. I have built deScreens with as many as 2000 fields with no problem.

The <max lines> and <max columns> parameters define the limits of the SCREENMAP. Both of these numbers must be between one and 255, but <max lines> multiplied by <max columns> must be less than 16K. Again, the SCREENMAP these parameters specify must be less than the 32K upper limit placed on all structure definitions.

The last parameter, <max boxes>, specifies how many boxes are defined within the map. There must be at least one box defined, and the upper limit is around 2000. Again, a deScreen with this many boxes would probably run out of space elsewhere.

Box Command. For each box defined in the Control command, there must be a corresponding Box command. The Box command's format is as follows:

```
B,<box number>,
      <1st map line>,<1st map column>,
      <number of map lines>,<number of map columns>,
      <1st display line>,<1st display column>,
      <number of display lines>,<number of display columns>;
```

Obviously, <box number> must be between one and the limit set by the <max boxes> parameter defined in the control command. The <1st map line> and <1st map column> parameters define the upper left corner of the box, and <number map lines> and <number map columns> define the extent of the box in the deScreen SCREENMAP. The other four parameters do the same thing for the box on the display. (Note that unlike a FRAME, the lower right corner of a box is defined as <1st line> plus <number of lines> minus 1.) For example, consider the following:

```
B,1,1,1,10,80,5,40,5,40;
```

This box command defines box number 1. The box begins at line 1, column 1 in the SCREENMAP and contains 10 lines and 80 columns. When box number 1 is shown on the display, it will appear at line 5, column 40, and will only show 5 lines and 40 columns.

The deScreen routines give a program complete control over which boxes appear on the display at any given time, but all the boxes that are on the screen are treated as a unit when it comes to scrolling. All boxes that begin on the same SCREENMAP line will be scrolled vertically if they are on the display at the same time. All boxes that begin with the same column will be scrolled horizontally.

Text Command. Much of what appears on a deScreen is descriptive information such as column headings, user instructions, or graphic characters to outline specific fields. These kinds of things are defined in a deScreen using the Text command. A Text command has the following format:

```
T,<line>,<column>,<length>,<color>,<text string>;
```

The <line> and <column> parameters define the starting point for the <text string> in the SCREENMAP (*not* on the display). <length> is the number of characters that <text string> contains, and <color> is the color attribute that is to be used for every character in the <text string>. I generally use a color attribute of 2 for text areas. This produces normal green on black characters not only on the monochrome display but also on both color monitors. An example of the Text command would be as follows:

```
T,2,1,17,2     TEAM NAME:    ;
```

This command would cause the literal "   TEAM NAME: " (note the surrounding blanks) to be defined on line 2, column 1 of the SCREENMAP.

Text lines are entered into the SCREENMAP in the order in which they appear in the SCD file. It is legal to have several commands refer to the same area; the <text string> associated with the last command encountered determines the end result.

Text commands also provide another service; they define the limits of horizontal scrolling. Because the deScreen routines are field oriented, the routines arrange to keep all of the field in which the cursor is positioned, on the display at one time. From the user's standpoint, however, it looks better if the surrounding line drawing characters are also on the screen. To do this the routines must have some way of identifying the amount of the SCREENMAP to show. Therefore, each deScreen image that requires more than 80 columns to display any given line should divide the line into individual areas and mark the boundaries of each area with a SCROLLTAB character. The choice of character is entirely up to you; I generally use the double vertical line character (CHR(186)) from the line-drawing set.

To use the SCROLLTAB character, define the deScreen text lines to use the character as a "tab stop." For example, if the SCROLLTAB were equal to ¦, a text line that said

T,10,1,30,2, ¦ xxxxxxx ¦ xxxxxxxx ¦ xx ¦

would define four tab positions. If the box in which this line was contained required more than 80 columns to display, the user could tab across line 10, and each successive field would scroll onto the display.

In some instances, a deScreen might require that a portion of each line remain on the display as another portion scrolls horizontally. The soccer team registration form shown in Fig. 14-1 is an example. The layout of this form is obviously too large to fit in a 25 by 80 display. It would be possible to break each horizontal line using a SCROLLTAB, but that would permit the line number and player's name columns to scroll off the screen to the left when the city, state, zip, or phone fields were being accessed. Because any deScreen defined for this form would probably also be used for data inquiry, it would be more convenient for the user if the line number and player's name could stay on the screen while the fields from B.DATE over did the scrolling.

The deScreen routines provide a mechanism for doing this, or at least for giving that appearance. Figure 14-4 lists a SCD file for the registration form. Note that boxes 2, 3, and 4 require 160 columns. The Text commands that define the literals associated with lines 11 through 38 in the SCREENMAP use a special control character (CHR(1)) to indicate the areas of each line that are *not* to be overlaid when a horizontal scroll occurs. In other words, columns 81 through 103 of each line are not used, and, although the box in which they are contained might be mapped onto the display, the contents of these columns are not shown. Note that character 81 on each line from 13 to 37 is set to CHR(186), the scrolltab.

Alpha Command. An alpha field is defined in a deScreen SCREENMAP using an Alpha command. An alpha field can, by definition, contain any character from the character set defined as follows:

CHARSET[' '. .'~']

Note, however, that the deScreen routines might intercept some characters; see the discussion on *ReadScrn* and *ReadFlds*. The format of an Alpha command is:

A,<fld number>,<line>,<column>,<length>,<color>,<fld type>,<default string>;

Every field in a deScreen is assigned a unique field number. The actual value for <fld number> must be between one and <max fields>, given on the control command. The field number is used by the calling program to communicate with the deScreen routines. The field numbers need not be defined consecutively; in fact, you can skip numbers altogether, but because space will still be allocated in the control tables for the skipped fields, this is inefficient.

The values for <line> and <column> indicate the starting position for the field in the SCREENMAP. The field extends for <column> + <length> − 1 positions. Therefore, each field must fit on one line. When the field is initially created in the SCREENMAP, it will be given the color attribute specified by <color>. I normally use a value of 49. The contents of <default string> will be moved into the field area. It will override any characters placed there previously. As Fig. 14-4 shows, I often use a sequence of numbers in a Text command to illustrate the length of each field; then later, when I define the value for <default string>, I use the correct initial value. The number sequence aids in locating fields and defining lengths.

The other parameter, <fld type>, has three possible values. If <fld type> is blank, the field is defined as a normal field. The user will be permitted to position the cursor in the field and enter alpha numerical characters. If <fld type> is a "C," the field is a constant field; the user will not be allowed in the field. Instead, the field will be used by the calling program to display data that only changes under program control. If the <fld type> is an "X," the field is known as a *transmit only* field. A transmit only field is normally the same as a constant field; it is given an initial constant value by the calling program and is unavailable to the user. However, if the user first enters an Alt-X, the deScreen routines will permit access to the transmit only fields in the current box. In other words, transmit only fields contain data that the user would seldom change.

An example of an Alpha command would be:

A,15,4,87,10,49, , Standard ;

This command defines field number 15, an alpha field, and places it on line 4, column 87. It is 10 characters long, and its initial value is " Standard " in color 49.

Note that space for each field is defined in the deScreen SCREENMAP. The characters that the user enters into each field are stored in the SCREENMAP, where they remain unchanged until the deScreen is cleared or until the user changes them. There is generally no reason to allocate additional space for all field values in the calling program. For example, even though the deScreen defined in Fig. 14-5 has space for 25 lines of player information, the program that uses this deScreen would never need to access more than one player at a time. The program only needs to allocate space for one line of data.

Numeric Command. The format for a Numeric command is

N,<fld number>,<line>,<column>,<length>,<fld type>,<default string>;

All of the parameters are the same as for an alpha field, with the exception of <default string>. The default string for a numeric field is also used to indicate where the decimal point occurs in the number. The deScreen routines recognize the colon (":") as a decimal point. (Many accounting forms use this technique; it helps to distinguish the decimal point from an extraneous mark on the paper). For example, consider the following:

N,33,20,10,6,49,C, 0:00;

This numeric command defines field number 33, which begins on line 20, column 10. The field is six characters long (the decimal point must be counted as a character) and it will be displayed in color 49. The field is a program constant, and it will have an initial value of: 0:00.

When the cursor is positioned in a numeric field, the user is prohibited from entering anything other than a numeric character. In deScreen, numeric characters are defined as the set ['0'. .'9','−','+', '.','.',':']. The deScreen routines are built around the way an adding machine handles numbers. If the decimal is not entered, it is assumed to be present at the proper number of decimal places. To enter the number −100.00 into a field, the user can enter 10000−, 100.−, −100., −10000, or even −100.00.

Fig. 14-5. The deScreen IMG builder.

```
(*   MAKESCRN, deScreen image builder
     Copyright (c) 1987 TAB BOOKS INC.
     Author: Don Etling

This program expects a parameter list containing the following entries:

    SCD=<scrnfile> IMG=<imagefile>
    [PRINTER=<prtcontrolfilename>.<extension>]
    [PRTSPOOL=<prtspoolfilename>.<extension>]

All four parameters may specify a complete DOS path to their respective
files.  Only SCD is mandatory;  if it cannot be found, the program will
CANCEL.  Normally, <scrnfile> will have an SCD extension...<imagefile>
will have an IMG extension.

The program will use SCD to locate a deScreen defintion file named
<scrnfile>.  That file is a standard ASCII text file containing
deScreen commands that this program can use to create the file
associated with IMG.  The IMG file is used by the deScreen routines in
the ETLING library.  Note that if IMG is not given, the program will
create the image file in a file named IMG.

If the PRINTER parameter is given, a listing of the contents of
<scrnfile> will be produced.  If PRTSPOOL is given, the listing will be
written to the associated disk file...otherwise the listing will be
directed to the printer.
```

Fig. 14-5 continued

```
    The <scrnfile> file is composed of lines.  Each line begins with a
    character that identifies the command that it contains.  Refer to the
    documentation for details.                                          *)

MODULE MAKESCRN;
  FROM SYSTEM IMPORT      ADR,ADDRESS,BYTE,WORD;
  FROM Storage IMPORT     ALLOCATE;
  FROM ELO301 IMPORT      LoByte;
  FROM ELO302 IMPORT      MovByteL;
  FROM ELO303 IMPORT      equal;
  FROM ELO304 IMPORT      cr,lf;
  FROM ELO401 IMPORT      STRING,Literal,StrLen,MakeStr,SetLen,ClearStr,
                          nullstr,CopyStr,StrSize,StrChar,SetChar;
  FROM ELO402 IMPORT      Concat,Insert,Delete;
  FROM ELO403 IMPORT      MatchStr,Positn;
  FROM ELO404 IMPORT      FixStr;
  FROM ELO503 IMPORT      LONGCARD,lcone,lczero,LongCard,AddLCard;
  FROM ELO504 IMPORT      FRAMEPTR,MakFrame;
  FROM ELO505 IMPORT      AREAPTR,MakeArea,maxarea,FLPTR;
  FROM ELO602 IMPORT      MakCard;
  FROM ELO605 IMPORT      CarToStr;
  FROM ELO801 IMPORT      GetParms,FindParm;
  FROM ELO803 IMPORT      AskParm;
  FROM ELO902 IMPORT      crtads,nrmclr,ClrScrn,PstnCur;
  FROM ELO904 IMPORT      DsplyStr;
  FROM ELO906 IMPORT      Cancel;
  FROM ELO908 IMPORT      TypeStr;
  FROM EL1002 IMPORT      FMODE,OPENKIND,DISP,LINECNTRL,
                          setpostn,OpnFile,ClsFile;
  FROM EL1003 IMPORT      GetLine;
  FROM EL1006 IMPORT      PutRcrd;
  FROM EL1012 IMPORT      SetFLoc;
  FROM EL1201 IMPORT      pcp;
  FROM EL1202 IMPORT      LTBLPTR,SetRprt,PrtRprt,EndRprt,MakeLTbl,ClrLTbl;
  FROM EL1406 IMPORT      SDPTR,FLDTYPE,FLDTYPES,
                          numtype,alptype,xmttype,contype,zerofill;

CONST
  controls  = 'C'; endofcoms  = 'E'; textcom    = 'T'; boxcom      = 'B';
  alphacom  = 'A'; numbercom  = 'N'; fillzero   = 'Z'; linenumcom  = 'L';
  repeatcom = 'R'; quitrepeats = 'Q'; xmitonlyfld = 'X'; constantfld = 'C';
  comment   = '*';
  donthome  = FALSE; dohome     = TRUE; ask        = TRUE;
  f1 = 5;  11 = 25;  fd = 1;  lc = 80;
  asktoset = TRUE;  npage = TRUE;  dpage = TRUE;  tpage = TRUE;
  pagwid   = 132;   paglen  = 61;
  maxcard  = 65535;

VAR
  comtype,fflag: CHAR;
  i,j,1,c:CARDINAL;
  fnumber,flength,fline,fcolumn,fcolor,totalwords,nrpts,nerrs:CARDINAL;
  imgmode,defmode:FMODE;
  ioerr:BYTE;
  p:SDPTR;
  a:ADDRESS;
  printing,newpage:BOOLEAN;
  hdgs:LTBLPTR;
  pagenmbr,linenmbr:CARDINAL;
  topframe,wrkframe,botframe,msgframe:FRAMEPTR;
  comline,str,h1,h2,h3,h4,h5,h6,crlf:STRING;
```

```
PROCEDURE ListIt(line:STRING;printing:BOOLEAN);
BEGIN
   IF (printing)
     THEN
       PrtRprt(line,newpage,0,hdgs,pagenmbr,linenmbr);
       END;
   TypeStr(nrmclr,donthome,line,wrkframe^);
   TypeStr(nrmclr,donthome,crlf,wrkframe^);
   END ListIt;

PROCEDURE ListErr(msgno,limit:CARDINAL;flag:CHAR);
VAR
   str,nstr:STRING;
BEGIN
   MakeStr(nstr,5,nullstr);
   MakeStr(str,255,nullstr);
   nerrs:=nerrs+1;
   IF (limit > maxcard)
     THEN
       CarToStr(limit,5,nstr);
       WHILE (StrChar(nstr,1) = ' ') DO
         Delete(nstr,1,1);
         END;
     END;
   CASE msgno OF
     1:MakeStr(str,80,Literal('...line number must be between 1 and '));
   : 2:MakeStr(str,80,Literal('...column number must be between 1 '));
   : 3:MakeStr(str,80,Literal(
         '...for this field, field length must be between 1 and '));
   : 4:MakeStr(str,80,Literal('...field color must be between 0 and 255'));
   : 5:MakeStr(str,80,Literal('...field number must be between 1 and '));
   .: .6:MakeStr(str,80,Literal(
         '...there is already an entry for field number'));
   : 7:MakeStr(str,80,Literal('...flag field =  '));
       SetChar(str,StrLen(str),fflag);
       Concat(Literal(' is invalid'),str);
   : 8:MakeStr(str,80,Literal('...box number must be between 1 and '));
   : 9:MakeStr(str,80,Literal(
         '...first map line in box must be between 1 and '));
   : 10:MakeStr(str,80,Literal(
         '...first map column in box must be between 1 and '));
   : 11:MakeStr(str,80,Literal(
         '...number of map lines in box must be between 1 and '));
   : 12:MakeStr(str,80,Literal(
         '...number of map columns in box must be between 1 and '));
   : 13:MakeStr(str,80,Literal(
         '...first screen line in box must be between 1 and 25'));
   : 14:MakeStr(str,80,Literal(
         '...first screen column in box must be between 1 and 80'));
   : 15:MakeStr(str,80,Literal(
         '...number of screen lines in box must be between 1 and '));
   : 16:MakeStr(str,80,Literal(
         '...number of screen columns in box must be between 1 and '));
   : 17:MakeStr(str,80,Literal('...line outside screen for line number '));
   : 18:MakeStr(str,80,Literal('...invalid field number'));
   : 20:MakeStr(str,80,Literal(
         '...number of repeats must be between 1 and '));
   : 21:MakeStr(str,80,Literal(
         '...command unknown or invalid in repeat sequence'));
   : 22:MakeStr(str,80,Literal('...unknown command'));
   : 23:MakeStr(str,80,Literal('***no limits given - abort'));
   : 24:MakeStr(str,80,Literal(
         '...number of fields must be between 0 and 32k'));
```

Fig. 14-5 continued

```
: 25:MakeStr(str,80,Literal(
        '...number of lines must be between 1 and 255'));
: 26:MakeStr(str,80,Literal(
        '...number of columns must be between 1 and 255'));
: 27:MakeStr(str,80,Literal(
        '...number boxes must be between 1 and lines * columns'));
: 28:MakeStr(str,80,Literal('...number lines * number column > 32k'));
    ELSE
      END;
  ListIt(str,printing);
  ClearStr(str);
  ClearStr(nstr);
  END ListErr;

PROCEDURE ReadNext(def:STRING;VAR comtype:CHAR;comline:STRING);
BEGIN
  REPEAT
    IF (NOT GetLine(def,comline,nortrnend))
      THEN comtype:=endofcoms;
      ELSE
        comtype:=StrChar(comline,1);
        ListIt(comline,printing);
        END;
    UNTIL (comtype <> comment);
  END ReadNext;

PROCEDURE GetCoord(VAR i:CARDINAL):BOOLEAN;
BEGIN
  fline:=MakCard(comline,i,i);
  IF (fline < 1) OR (fline > p^.smml)
    THEN
      ListErr(1,p^.smml,' ');
      RETURN FALSE;
    END;
  fcolumn:=MakCard(comline,i+1,i);
  IF (fcolumn < 1) OR (fcolumn > p^.smmc)
    THEN
      ListErr(2,p^.smmc,' ');
      RETURN FALSE;
    END;
  flength:=MakCard(comline,i+1,i);
  IF (flength < 1) OR (flength > p^.smmc-fcolumn+1)
    THEN
      ListErr(3,p^.smmc-fcolumn+1,' ');
      RETURN FALSE;
    END;
  fcolor:=MakCard(comline,i+1,i);
  IF (fcolor < 0) OR (fcolor > 255)
    THEN
      ListErr(4,maxcard,' ');
      RETURN FALSE;
    END;
  RETURN TRUE;
  END GetCoord;

PROCEDURE MoveImg(VAR j:CARDINAL);
VAR
  i:CARDINAL;
BEGIN
  FOR i:=0 TO flength-1 DO
    p^.sm^[p^.smmc*(fline-1)+fcolumn+i].colbyte:=LoByte(fcolor);
```

```
      IF (j <= StrLen(comline))
        THEN
          p^.sm^[p^.smmc*(fline-1)+fcolumn+i].chrbyte:=StrChar(comline,j);
          j:=j+1;
        ELSE p^.sm^[p^.smmc*(fline-1)+fcolumn+i].chrbyte:=' ';
        END;
      END;
    END MoveImg;

PROCEDURE DoText;
VAR
  i:CARDINAL;
BEGIN
  i:=3;
  IF (GetCoord(i))
    THEN
      i:=i+1;
      MoveImg(i);
    END;
  END DoText;

PROCEDURE MveCntrl;
VAR
  i:CARDINAL;
  done:BOOLEAN;
BEGIN
  WITH p^.ct^[fnumber] DO
    CASE comtype OF
      alphacom: fldtype:=FLDTYPE{alptype};
    | numbercom,fillzero:
        done:=FALSE;
        i:=0;
        REPEAT
          IF (p^.sm^[p^.smmc*(fline-1)+fcolumn+i].chrbyte = ':')
            THEN done:=TRUE
            ELSE i:=i+1;
            END;
          UNTIL (done) OR (i >= flength);
        IF (done)
          THEN fldprec:=flength-i-1
          ELSE fldprec:=0;
          END;
        IF (comtype = fillzero)
          THEN fldtype:=FLDTYPE{zerofill};
          END;
        fldtype:=fldtype + FLDTYPE{numtype};
      ELSE
        END;
    CASE fflag OF
      xmitonlyfld: fldtype:=fldtype + FLDTYPE{xmttype};
    | constantfld: fldtype:=fldtype + FLDTYPE{contype};
      ELSE
        END;
    fldline:=fline;
    fldclmn:=fcolumn;
    fldlen:=flength;
    END;
  END MveCntrl;

PROCEDURE CheckNum(j:CARDINAL):BOOLEAN;
BEGIN
  IF (j < 1) OR (j > p^.maxfield)
```

Fig. 14-5 continued

```
      THEN
        ListErr(5,p^.maxfield,' ');
        RETURN FALSE;
      ELSE IF (p^.ct^[j].fldlen = 0)
        THEN RETURN TRUE;
        ELSE
          ListErr(6,j,' ');
          RETURN FALSE;
        END;
      END;
  END CheckNum;

PROCEDURE DoAlpha;
VAR
  i:CARDINAL;
  ok:BOOLEAN;
BEGIN
  fnumber:=MakCard(comline,3,i);
  ok:=CheckNum(fnumber);
  IF (ok)
    THEN i:=i+1;ok:=GetCoord(i);
    END;
  IF (ok)
    THEN
      i:=i+1;fflag:=StrChar(comline,i);
      IF (fflag = ' ') OR (fflag = xmitonlyfld) OR (fflag = constantfld)
        THEN ok:=TRUE;
        ELSE
          ok:=FALSE;
          ListErr(7,maxcard,fflag);
        END;
    END;
  IF (ok)
    THEN
      i:=i+2;
      MoveImg(i);
      MveCntrl;
    END;
  END DoAlpha;

PROCEDURE DoNmbr;
VAR
  i:CARDINAL;
  ok:BOOLEAN;
BEGIN
  fnumber:=MakCard(comline,3,i);
  ok:=CheckNum(fnumber);
  IF (ok)
    THEN
      i:=i+1;
      ok:=GetCoord(i);
    END;
  IF (ok)
    THEN
      i:=i+1;fflag:=StrChar(comline,i);
      IF (fflag = ' ') OR (fflag = xmitonlyfld) OR (fflag = constantfld)
        THEN ok:=TRUE
        ELSE
          ok:=FALSE;
          ListErr(7,maxcard,fflag);
        END;
```

```
        END;
    IF (ok)
      THEN
        i:=i+2;
        MoveImg(i);
        MveCntrl;
        END;
    END DoNmbr;

PROCEDURE DoBox;
VAR
  i:CARDINAL;
  boxnumber:CARDINAL;
BEGIN
  boxnumber:=MakCard(comline,3,i);
  IF (boxnumber < 1) OR (boxnumber > p^.maxbox)
    THEN ListErr(8,p^.maxbox,' ');
    ELSE WITH p^.bx^[boxnumber] DO
      fmlib:=MakCard(comline,i+1,i);
      fmcib:=MakCard(comline,i+1,i);
      nmlib:=MakCard(comline,i+1,i);
      nmcib:=MakCard(comline,i+1,i);
      fslib:=MakCard(comline,i+1,i);
      fscib:=MakCard(comline,i+1,i);
      nslib:=MakCard(comline,i+1,i);
      nscib:=MakCard(comline,i+1,i);
      cfmlibos:=0;
      cfmcibos:=0;
      IF (fmlib < 1) OR (fmlib > p^.smml)
        THEN ListErr(9,p^.smml,' ');
        END;
      IF (fmcib < 1) OR (fmcib > p^.smmc)
        THEN ListErr(10,p^.smmc,' ');
        END;
      IF (fmlib < 1) OR (nmlib > p^.smml-fmlib+1)
        THEN ListErr(11,p^.smml-fmlib+1,' ');
        END;
      IF (nscib < 1) OR (nmcib > p^.smmc-fmcib+1)
        THEN ListErr(12,p^.smmc-fmcib+1,' ');
        END;
      IF (fslib < 1) OR (fslib > 25)
        THEN ListErr(13,maxcard,' ');
        END;
      IF (fscib < 1) OR (fscib > 80)
        THEN ListErr(14,maxcard,' ');
        END;
      IF (nslib < 1) OR (nslib > 25-fslib+1)
        THEN ListErr(15,25-fslib+1,' ');
        END;
      IF (nscib < 1) OR (nscib > 80-fscib+1)
        THEN ListErr(16,80-fscib+1,' ');
        END;
      END;
    END;
  END DoBox;

PROCEDURE CopyScrn;
VAR
  i,j:CARDINAL;
BEGIN
  i:=fline+1;
  FOR j:=2 TO nrpts DO
```

Fig. 14-5 continued

```
      IF (i > p^.smm1)
        THEN ListErr(17,j,' ')
        ELSE MovByteL(p^.sm^[p^.smmc*(fline-1)+fcolumn],
                      p^.sm^[p^.smmc*(i-1)+fcolumn],0,0,2*flength);
      END;
    i:=i+1;
    END;
  END CopyScrn;

PROCEDURE CopyFlds;
VAR
  i,j:CARDINAL;
BEGIN
  i:=fnumber+1;
  FOR j:=2 TO nrpts DO
    IF (NOT CheckNum(i))
      THEN ListErr(18,i,' ');
      ELSE
        p^.ct^[i].fldline:=p^.ct^[fnumber].fldline+j-1;
        p^.ct^[i].fldclmn:=p^.ct^[fnumber].fldclmn;
        p^.ct^[i].fldlen:=p^.ct^[fnumber].fldlen;
        p^.ct^[i].fldprec:=p^.ct^[fnumber].fldprec;
        p^.ct^[i].fldtype:=p^.ct^[fnumber].fldtype;
      END;
    i:=i+1;
    END;
  END CopyFlds;

PROCEDURE DoLn;
VAR
  ln:STRING;
  i,j,k,num:CARDINAL;
BEGIN
  MakeStr(ln,255,nullstr);
  i:=3;
  IF (GetCoord(i))
    THEN
      num:=MakCard(comline,i+1,i);
      k:=fline;
      IF (i < 1) OR (i > p^.smm1)
        THEN ListErr(1,p^.smm1,' ');
        ELSE FOR i:=1 TO nrpts DO
          CarToStr(num,flength,ln);
          FOR j:=1 TO flength DO
            p^.sm^[p^.smmc*(k-1)+fcolumn+j-1].colbyte:=LoByte(fcolor);
            IF (StrChar(ln,j) = ' ')
              THEN p^.sm^[p^.smmc*(k-1)+fcolumn+j-1].chrbyte:='0'
              ELSE p^.sm^[p^.smmc*(k-1)+fcolumn+j-1].chrbyte:=StrChar(ln,j);
              END;
            END;
          k:=k+1;
          num:=num+1;
          END;
        END;
    END;
  ClearStr(ln);
  END DoLn;

PROCEDURE DoRpts;
VAR
  i:CARDINAL;
```

```
BEGIN
  nrpts:=MakCard(comline,3,i);
  IF (nrpts < 1) OR (nrpts > p^.smml)
    THEN ListErr(20,p^.smml,' ')
    ELSE REPEAT
      ReadNext(Literal('SCD'),comtype,comline);
      IF (comtype <> quitrepeats)
        THEN CASE comtype OF
          textcom:
            DoText;
            CopyScrn;
        : alphacom:
            DoAlpha;
            CopyFlds;
            CopyScrn;
        : numbercom,fillzero:
            DoNmbr;
            CopyFlds;
            CopyScrn;
        : linenumcom:DoLn;
          ELSE
            ListErr(21,maxcard,' ');
          END;
        END;
      UNTIL (comtype = quitrepeats);
    END;
  END DoRpts;

PROCEDURE SwapCard(VAR i1,i2:CARDINAL):CARDINAL;
VAR
  i3:CARDINAL;
BEGIN
  i3:=i1;
  i1:=i2;
  i2:=i3;
  RETURN 1;
  END SwapCard;


PROCEDURE BldBoxes;
VAR
  a:ADDRESS;
  nt: CARDINAL;
  i,j:CARDINAL;
  str:STRING;
  boxnumber:CARDINAL;
BEGIN
  MakeStr(str,255,nullstr);
  p^.sdlen:=22+2*p^.smml*p^.smmc+10*p^.maxfield+26*p^.maxbox;
  a:=p^.bx;
  a.OFFSET:=a.OFFSET+26*p^.maxbox;
  WITH p^ DO
    FOR boxnumber:=1 TO p^.maxbox DO
      bx^[boxnumber].tabs.ptr:=a;
      nt:=0;
      WITH bx^[boxnumber] DO
        FOR i:=1 TO p^.maxfield DO
          IF (NOT (contype IN ct^[i].fldtype))
            THEN WITH ct^[i] DO
              IF (fldline >= fmlib)
                 AND (fldline < (fmlib+nmlib))
                 AND (fldclmn >= fmcib)
                 AND (fldclmn < (fmcib+nmcib))
```

Fig. 14-5 continued

```
                    THEN
                       nt:=nt+1;
                       bx^[boxnumber].tabs.ptr^[nt]:=i;
                    END;
                 END;
              END;
           END;
        END;
     bx^[boxnumber].tabs.maxtabs:=nt;
     IF (nt > 0)
        THEN
           REPEAT
              j:=0;
              FOR i:=1 TO nt-1 DO
                 IF (ct^[bx^[boxnumber].tabs.ptr^[i]].fldline
                       > ct^[bx^[boxnumber].tabs.ptr^[i+1]].fldline)
                    THEN j:=SwapCard(bx^[boxnumber].tabs.ptr^[i],
                                         bx^[boxnumber].tabs.ptr^[i+1]);
                    ELSE IF (ct^[bx^[boxnumber].tabs.ptr^[i]].fldline
                             = ct^[bx^[boxnumber].tabs.ptr^[i+1]].fldline)
                       THEN IF (ct^[bx^[boxnumber].tabs.ptr^[i]].fldclmn
                                > ct^[bx^[boxnumber].tabs.ptr^[i+1]].fldclmn)
                          THEN j:=SwapCard(bx^[boxnumber].tabs.ptr^[i],
                                         bx^[boxnumber].tabs.ptr^[i+1]);
                       END;
                    END;
                 END;
              END;
           UNTIL (j = 0);
        END;
     a.OFFSET:=a.OFFSET+2*nt;
     p^.sdlen:=p^.sdlen+2*nt;
     CarToStr(boxnumber,5,str);
     Insert(Literal('boxnumber = '),str,1);
     ListIt(str,printing);
     CarToStr(nt,5,str);
     Insert(Literal('tabs = '),str,1);
     ListIt(str,printing);
     END;
  END;
  ClearStr(str);
  END BldBoxes;

PROCEDURE WrtImg;
VAR
  nmbr:LONGCARD;
BEGIN
  imgmode:=makenew;
  OpnFile(Literal('IMG'),imgmode,ioerr,insist);
  PutRcrd(Literal('IMG'),setpostn,lczero,nmbr,
                                 WORD(p^.sdlen),ADR(p^.sdlen));
  ClsFile(Literal('IMG'),clsonly);
  END WrtImg;

PROCEDURE GetComs;
VAR
  i,j:CARDINAL;
  a:ADDRESS;
BEGIN
  WITH p^ DO
     a:=p;
     a.OFFSET:=a.OFFSET+26;
```

```
    sm:=a;
    a.OFFSET:=a.OFFSET+2*smml*smmc;
    ct:=a;
    a.OFFSET:=a.OFFSET+2*5*maxfield;
    bx:=a;
    FOR i:=1 TO smml*smmc DO
      sm^[i].colbyte:=BYTE(03H);
      sm^[i].chrbyte:=' ';
      END;
    FOR i:=1 TO maxfield DO
      ct^[i].fldlen:=0;
      ct^[i].fldtype:=FLDTYPE();
      ct^[i].fldprec:=0;
      ct^[i].fldline:=0;
      ct^[i].fldclmn:=0;
      END;
    END;
  REPEAT
    ReadNext(Literal('SCD'),comtype,comline);
    CASE comtype OF
      boxcom            :DoBox;
    : textcom           :DoText;
    : alphacom          :DoAlpha;
    : numbercom,fillzero:DoNmbr;
    : repeatcom         :DoRpts;
    : endofcoms         :
        BldBoxes;
        WrtImg;
      ELSE
        ListErr(22,maxcard,' ');
        END;
    UNTIL (comtype = endofcoms);
  END GetComs;
BEGIN
  MakFrame(1,1,4,80,1,1,25,80,crtads,topframe);
  MakFrame(5,1,22,80,5,1,25,80,crtads,wrkframe);
  MakFrame(23,1,23,80,23,1,25,80,crtads,botframe);
  MakFrame(24,1,25,80,24,1,25,80,crtads,msgframe);
  ClrScrn(topframe^,nrmclr);
  ClrScrn(wrkframe^,nrmclr);
  ClrScrn(botframe^,nrmclr);
  ClrScrn(msgframe^,nrmclr);
  GetParms;
  MakeStr(crlf,2,FixStr(Literal("cr*lf")));
  MakeStr(h1,0,Literal('MAKESCRN - deScreen IMG File Builder'));
  MakeStr(h2,0,Literal('Copyright (c) 1986 TAB BOOKS INC '));
  MakeStr(h3,0,Literal(' '));
  MakeStr(h4,79,nullstr);
  SetLen(h4,79);
  FOR i:=1 TO 79 DO
    SetChar(h4,i,'-');
    END;
  MakeStr(h5,0,Literal(' '));
  MakeStr(h6,0,Literal('Author: Don Etling'));
  TypeStr(nrmclr,dohome,h1,topframe^);
  TypeStr(nrmclr,NOT dohome,crlf,topframe^);
  TypeStr(nrmclr,NOT dohome,h2,topframe^);
  TypeStr(nrmclr,NOT dohome,crlf,topframe^);
  TypeStr(nrmclr,NOT dohome,h6,topframe^);
  TypeStr(nrmclr,NOT dohome,crlf,topframe^);
  TypeStr(nrmclr,NOT dohome,h4,topframe^);
  TypeStr(nrmclr,dohome,h4,botframe^);
  SetRprt(pcp,62,ask,npage,dpage,tpage);
```

Fig. 14-5 continued

```
newpage:=TRUE;
GetParms;
MakeStr(comline,255,nullstr);
MakeStr(str,255,nullstr);
printing:=FindParm(Literal('PRINTER'),str);
IF (printing)
  THEN
    newpage  := TRUE;
    pagenmbr := 0;
    linenmbr := 0;
    hdgs:=MakeLTbl(5,80);
    CopyStr(h1,hdgs^.line[1]);
    CopyStr(h2,hdgs^.line[2]);
    CopyStr(h3,hdgs^.line[3]);
    CopyStr(h4,hdgs^.line[4]);
    CopyStr(h5,hdgs^.line[5]);
    IF (NOT FindParm(Literal('SCD'),str))
      THEN Cancel(Literal('makescrn'),Literal('SCD'),7,0);
      END;
    Concat(Literal(' - '),hdgs^.line[1]);
    Concat(str,hdgs^.line[1]);
    FOR i:=1 TO 5 DO
      WHILE (StrLen(hdgs^.line[i]) < StrSize(hdgs^.line[i])) DO
        Concat(Literal(' '),hdgs^.line[i]);
        END;
      END;
    SetRprt(pcp,paglen,asktoset,npage,dpage,tpage);
  END;
nerrs:=0;
ALLOCATE(a,65520);
p:=a;
defmode:=oldfile;
OpnFile(Literal('SCD'),defmode,ioerr,insist);
ReadNext(Literal('SCD'),comtype,comline);
IF (comtype <> controls)
  THEN ListErr(23,maxcard,' ');
  ELSE
    p^.sdlen:=0;
    p^.maxfield:=MakCard(comline,3,i);
    IF (p^.maxfield < 0) OR (p^.maxfield > maxcard)
      THEN ListErr(24,maxcard,' ');
      END;
    p^.smml:=MakCard(comline,i+1,i);
    IF (p^.smml < 1) OR (p^.smml > 255)
      THEN ListErr(25,maxcard,' ');
      END;
    p^.smmc:=MakCard(comline,i+1,i);
    IF (p^.smmc < 1) OR (p^.smmc > 255)
      THEN ListErr(26,maxcard,' ');
      END;
    p^.maxbox:=MakCard(comline,i+1,i);
    IF (p^.maxbox < 1) OR (p^.maxbox > p^.smml*p^.smmc)
      THEN ListErr(27,maxcard,' ');
      END;
    IF (p^.smml * p^.smmc > maxcard)
      THEN ListErr(28,maxcard,' ');
      END;
    IF (nerrs = 0)
      THEN GetComs;
      END;
  END;
ClsFile(Literal('SCD'),clsonly);
END MAKESCRN.
```

Zero Numeric Command. The deScreen routines do provide a way to zero-fill a numeric field: simply specify the field using a Z command. The syntax of the Z command is identical to the Numeric command. Note that the fields associated with B.DATE in Fig. 14-4 are declared as zero-filled numerics. In the deScreen routines, zero-filling always occurs on the left.

REPEAT COMMAND. The Repeat command provides a shorthand method for defining the body of many forms. The format for the R commands is:

```
R,<number repeats>;
```

The Repeat command instructs the MAKESCRN program to repeat the series of commands that follow. All commands between the R and the next Q command will be repeated the number of times specified. Repeat commands *may not* be nested.

The area of the Soccer Registration Form where Player data is recorded is actually 25 lines containing data in the same format. Fig. 14-4 uses a Repeat command to define these lines without entering each line definition individually. Note that the definition for each field is repeated as it is encountered. The command that says:

```
A, 18,13,5,20,49, ,
```

creates fields 18, 19, 20, etc. The repeat logic assumes that, in addition to incrementing the field number, it should also increment the line number. Therefore, field 18 is on line 13, field 19 is on field 14, and so on.

When several fields are on the same line within a repeat loop, each field command must allow for the number of fields a repeated field definition would require. In other words, the repeat loop says:

```
R,25;
A,18,13,5,20,49, ,
Z,43,13,26,2,49, ,
```

The first zero-filled numeric begins 25 fields after the alpha field.

LINE COMMAND. Sometimes each line in the body of a form should be numbered. One way to do this is to define a constant field on each line and let the calling program assign a value for each. An easier way is to use the L command. An L command can only appear within a repeat loop. The format for an L command is:

```
L,<line>,<column>,<length>,<color>,<initial value>;
```

The <line> and <column> parameters specify the starting location for the value. It is, by definition, a numeric string of <length> digits. It will appear in <color> and the first line on which it appears will show <initial value>; each succeeding line will be incremented by one.

Quit Command. The Quit command terminates a repeat loop. Its format is simply:

```
Q;
```

End Command. The last command in a SCD must be an E command. Its format is equally simple:

E;

MAKESCRN Operations

Like all Modula-2 programs, you must begin reading the source code for MAKESCRN at the end of the listing. After gathering the program parameters (*Get-Parms*), MAKESCRN sets up the appropriate FRAME variables and shows its title on the screen. If you have instructed MAKESCRN to also produce a listing as it compiles the deScreen (by including a PRINTER or PRTSPOOL parameter for the program), MAKESCRN also sets up suitable report headings.

Once the preliminaries are out of the way, MAKESCRN calls ALLOCATE to establish a work area. The work area defined is as large as most Modula-2 packages will permit—almost 64K bytes. The area is referenced by *a*, which is an ADDRESS variable. The value of *a* is immediately assigned to *p*, a variable of type SDPTR. The SDPTR type is defined in Fig. 14-6.

An SDPTR is a pointer to a SCRNDEF. The SCRNDEF type is a record, but, its an unusual kind of record. The first 26 bytes of a SCRNDEF contain fixed fields, just like any other record, but the remaining bytes in the SCRNDEF are divided among four control tables. The actual size of each table, and therefore the position of each table in the SCRNDEF, varies according to the deScreen being defined. The four tables are, in order of their appearance: the SCREENMAP, containing exact images of the deScreen text areas; the FDTBL (for field definition table) which contains position and size information for every field; the BDTBL (box definition table) which defines the control variables for every box; and, last, the BOXTABMAPS, which are integer arrays for each box indicating the order in which the fields in the box are to be accessed.

The fixed portion of a SCRNDEF begins with a STRING. When the SCRNDEF is written to a file, this field is not actually used, but when the record is in core, the *dd* field contains the filename used to access the .IMG file. The next five fields in a SCRNDEF are CARDINALS that keep track of the various table sizes. The *sdlen* field contains the total number of bytes in the SCRNDEF. Even though MAKESCRN allocates almost 64K bytes, the actual number of bytes used for the SCRNDEF will be somewhat smaller than that; *sdlen* will contain the actual number. The next four fields in a SCRNDEF (*smml*, *smmc*, *maxfield*, and *maxbox*) contain the maximum number of lines, columns, fields, and boxes defined. These values are taken from the control command specified in the DEF file.

The next three fields (*sm*, *ct*, and *bx*) are all pointers. They contain the addresses of the portion of the SCRNDEF record that is used for the SCREENMAP, FDTBL, and BDTBL arrays. The definitions for each of these types is also shown in Fig. 14-6. Again, the unusual thing about their usage in the SCRNDEF is the fact that they are defined as though they pointed to the maximum possible size of each array. The actual sizes are adjusted in MAKESCRN.

The code in MAKESCRN is fairly straightforward. I leave its investigation to you. Note that when the SCRNDEF is completed, it is written to the IMG file. The number of bytes written is the actual length of the SCRNDEF, minus the 4 bytes used for the filename pointer.

Fig. 14-6. deScreen types.

```
DEFINITION MODULE EL1406;
   FROM SYSTEM IMPORT      WORD,BYTE,ADDRESS;
   FROM EL0401 IMPORT      STRING;
   FROM EL0501 IMPORT      CHARSET;
   FROM EL0504 IMPORT      DISPLAYWORD,FRAME;
   FROM EL0505 IMPORT      maxarea;
   EXPORT QUALIFIED        hlpframe,ecntrl,ncntrl,alptype,xmttype,contype,
                           zerofill,numtype,changed,FLDTYPES,FLDTYPE,FLDDEF,
                           FDTBL,FDTPTR,BOXDEF,BDTBL,BDTPTR,SDPTR,SMAP,
                           SMPTR,SCRNDEF;

CONST
   maxtabs = 8192;    maxboxes = 255;    numtype = 7;    alptype = 6;
   xmttype = 5;        contype = 4;      zerofill = 3;   changed = 2;

TYPE
(* These are the internal types required for the operation of the deScreen
   routines.  They are only used by the MakeScrn program and the DESCREEN
   modules...not by the calling programs.  *)
   FLDTYPES =[0..15];
   FLDTYPE = SET OF FLDTYPES;
   FLDDEF = RECORD
     fldtype :FLDTYPE;
     fldlen   :CARDINAL;
     fldprec :CARDINAL;   (*Number of digits right
                                        of decimal for num.*)
     fldline :CARDINAL;   (*Map line on which field appears *)
     fldclmn :CARDINAL;   (*Map column *)
     END;
   FDTBL = ARRAY [1..6500] OF FLDDEF;      (*  MAX POSSIBLE FIELDS *)
   FDTPTR = POINTER TO FDTBL;
   BOXDEF = RECORD
     fmlib     : CARDINAL;    (* FIRST MAP LINE IN BOX           *)
     fmcib     : CARDINAL;    (* FIRST MAP COLUMN IN BOX         *)
     nmlib     : CARDINAL;    (* NUMBER OF MAP LINES IN BOX      *)
     nmcib     : CARDINAL;    (* NUMBER OF MAP COLUMNS IN BOX    *)
     fslib     : CARDINAL;    (* FIRST SCREEN LINE IN BOX        *)
     fscib     : CARDINAL;    (* FIRST SCREEN COLUMN IN BOX      *)
     nslib     : CARDINAL;    (* NUMBER OF SCREEN LINES IN BOX   *)
     nscib     : CARDINAL;    (* NUMBER OF SCREEN COLUMNS IN BOX *)
     cfmlibos  : CARDINAL;    (* CURRENT FIRST MAP LINE
                                            IN BOX ON SCREEN *)
     cfmcibos  : CARDINAL;    (* CURRENT FIRST MAP COLUMN
                                            IN BOX ON SCREEN *)
        (*NOTE:  CURRENT MAP LINE = fmlibox - fmlib
                                 + CURRENT SCREEN LINE      *)
     tabs: RECORD
       ptr      : POINTER TO ARRAY [1..8192] OF CARDINAL;
       maxtabs : CARDINAL;
       END;
     END;
   BDTBL = ARRAY [1..maxboxes] OF BOXDEF;      (*MAX POSSIBLE BOXES*)
   BDTPTR = POINTER TO BDTBL;
   SDPTR =   POINTER TO SCRNDEF;
   SMAP =   ARRAY [1..maxarea] OF DISPLAYWORD;(*MAX POSSIBLE SIZE *)
   SMPTR = POINTER TO SMAP;
   SCRNDEF = RECORD
     dd                 : STRING;        (* filename *)
     sdlen              : CARDINAL;
     smml               : CARDINAL;
     smmc               : CARDINAL;
```

Fig. 14-6 continued

```
      maxfield              : CARDINAL;
      maxbox                : CARDINAL;
      sm                    : SMPTR;
      ct                    : FDTPTR;
      bx                    : BDTPTR;
    (*  SCREENMAP;
      FDTBL;
      BDTBL;
      BOXTABMAPS;*)
      END;
VAR
  hlpframe          : FRAME;
  ecntrl,ncntrl : CHARSET;
END EL1406.

IMPLEMENTATION MODULE EL1406;
  FROM EL0302 IMPORT    MovByteL;
  FROM EL0304 IMPORT    help,curl,curr,tabr,rtab,tabl,ltab,utab,dtab,home,
                        end,boxu,boxd,cr,insr,bksp,del,allditto,dittokey,
                        nextval,xmtcntrl,clearfld,seqval,altdec,esc;
  FROM EL0401 IMPORT    STRING,Literal;
  FROM EL0501 IMPORT    CHARSET,InCSet,numbers,MakeCSet;
  FROM EL0504 IMPORT    FRAME;
  FROM EL0902 IMPORT    crtads;

CONST
  T1 = 'The Etling Library';
  T2 = 'All programs and modules, Copyright (c) 1987 TAB BOOKS INC.';
  T3 = 'Author: Don Etling';
VAR
  wrkframe:FRAME;
  e:ARRAY [1..20] OF CHAR;
  n:ARRAY [1..4] OF CHAR;
  i:CARDINAL;
BEGIN
  i:=19;
  MovByteL(i,n,0,0,2);
  e[1] :=tabl;       e[2] :=rtab;       e[3] :=ltab;      e[4] :=utab;
  e[5] :=dtab;       e[6] :=home;       e[7] :=end;       e[8] :=boxu;
  e[9] :=boxd;       e[10]:=curl;       e[11]:=curr;      e[12]:=insr;
  e[13]:=del;        e[14]:=allditto; e[15]:=nextval; e[16]:=dittokey;
  e[17]:=xmtcntrl; e[18]:=clearfld; e[19]:=seqval;   e[20]:=help;
  MakeCSet(Literal(e),ecntrl);
  n[1]:=tabr;   n[2]:=cr;   n[3]:=bksp;   n[4]:=esc;
  MakeCSet(Literal(n),ncntrl);
  wrkframe.fl:=1;    wrkframe.fc:=1;    wrkframe.ll:=23;    wrkframe.lc:=80;
  wrkframe.cl:=1;    wrkframe.cc:=1;    wrkframe.nl:=23;    wrkframe.nc:=80;
  wrkframe.s :=crtads;
  hlpframe.fl:=24;   hlpframe.fc:=1;    hlpframe.ll:=25;    hlpframe.lc:=80;
  hlpframe.cl:=24;   hlpframe.cc:=1;    hlpframe.nl:=2;     hlpframe.nc:=80;
  hlpframe.s :=crtads;

END EL1406.
```

TESTSCRN

Figure 14-7 shows TESTSCRN, a program that allows you to test completed deScreen IMG files without writing a program to control it.

To execute TESTSCRN, provide it with two parameters, for example:

TESTSCRN IMG=REGFORM.IMG SCROLLTAB= ¦ ¦

This command will execute TESTSCRN using the image file containing the Soccer Registration form. Note that the second parameter is SCROLLTAB and it is assigned a value corresponding to the character to be used as the tab marker when the image is accessed.

When TESTSCRN executes, it will display a prompt that says:

Q = Quit, S = Show, C = Clear? . .

If you respond with a Q (followed by a carriage return), the program will terminate. If you respond with an S or a C, the program will prompt:

NUMBER OF BOXES TO SHOW, BOX NUMBERS? . .

or

NUMBER OF BOXES TO CLEAR, BOX NUMBERS? . .

In either case, enter the number of boxes you wish to have take part in the operation, followed by the individual box numbers. For example, to show the boxes in REG-FORM.IMG, you would enter this:

4,1,2,3,4 *(followed by a carriage return)*

If you were clearing boxes, TESTSCRN would return to the original prompt at this point. If you are showing boxes, TESTSCRN will display the next prompt:

NUMBER OF BOXES TO READ, BOX NUMBERS? . . .

Here you respond with the number of boxes for which you wish to access the data fields. With REGFORM.IMG, you would enter the following:

2,1,3 *(followed by a carriage return)*

This would allow you to move the cursor around in the fields contained in boxes 1 and 3, which are the only boxes in REGFORM.IMG that have fields into which you can enter data.

TESTSCRN assumes you know what you want to do. It has very little error-checking logic built into it. It assumes that the boxes you attempt to show or clear do indeed exist in the IMG. It also assumes that the boxes you wish to read exist, and that they are shown on the screen and contain readable fields. If you respond to one of the prompts incorrectly, TESTSCRN's behavior is unpredictable. You might be forced to reboot.

Fig. 14-7. The deScreen image tester.

```
(*  TESTSCRN - deScreen IMG tester
    Copyright (c) 1987 TAB BOOKS INC.
    Author: Don Etling

    This program expects a parameter list containing the following entries:
    IMG=<scrnfile>
      [SCROLLTAB=<char>]

    <scrnfile> may specify a complete DOS path to the file, and it is
    mandatory;  if it cannot be found, the program will CANCEL.  SCROLLTAB
    is optional, but if it is specified, it defines the character that the
    deScreen routines will use to mark the limits of a scroll to the left
    or right.                                                           *)

MODULE TESTSCRN;
  FROM EL0304 IMPORT   cr,lf,fk1;
  FROM EL0401 IMPORT   STRING,Literal,StrLen,MakeStr,SetLen,nullstr,StrChar;
  FROM EL0501 IMPORT   CHARSET,nullcset,IncCSet;
  FROM EL0504 IMPORT   FRAMEPTR,MakFrame;
  FROM EL0505 IMPORT   AREAPTR,FLPTR,MakFList,ClrFList;
  FROM EL0602 IMPORT   MakCard;
  FROM EL0705 IMPORT   Sound,errfreq,errdur;
  FROM EL0801 IMPORT   GetParms,FindParm;
  FROM EL0902 IMPORT   crtads,nrmclr,ClrScrn,PstnCur,stdhilite;
  FROM EL0903 IMPORT   ReadKB;
  FROM EL0904 IMPORT   DsplyStr;
  FROM EL1406 IMPORT   SDPTR;
  FROM EL1409 IMPORT   LoadScrn;
  FROM EL1411 IMPORT   ShowBox,ClearBox;
  FROM EL1412 IMPORT   ReadScrn;

CONST
  TITLE1   = 'TESTSCRN - deScreen image tester';
  TITLE2   = 'Copyright (c) 1986 TAB BOOKS INC.';
  TITLE3   = 'Author: Don Etling';
VAR
  str,kbmsg:STRING;
  rlptr,slptr:FLPTR;
  kbchar,horscrltab:CHAR;
  c,i,j,lastbox,lastfld,n,line,column:CARDINAL;
  chgd,done,eascii:BOOLEAN;
  thisscrn:SDPTR;
  wrkframe,msgframe:FRAMEPTR;
  crcharset,fk1charset:CHARSET;
BEGIN
  MakFrame(1,1,25,80,1,1,25,80,crtads,wrkframe);
  MakFrame(24,1,25,80,24,1,25,80,crtads,msgframe);
  ClrScrn(wrkframe^,nrmclr);
  crcharset:=nullcset;
  IncCSet(cr,crcharset);
  fk1charset:=nullcset;
  IncCSet(fk1,fk1charset);
  GetParms;
  MakeStr(str,255,nullstr);
  MakeStr(kbmsg,255,nullstr);
  done:=FALSE;
  IF (FindParm(Literal('SCROLLTAB'),str))
  THEN horscrltab:=StrChar(str,1);
  ELSE horscrltab:=CHR(186);
  END;
  LoadScrn(Literal('IMG'),thisscrn);
  REPEAT
    ClrScrn(msgframe^,nrmclr);
```

```
        DsplyStr(nrmclr,Literal('Q = QUIT, S = SHOW, C = CLEAR?..'),
                        msgframe^.fl,msgframe^.fc,msgframe^);
      SetLen(kbmsg,0);
      REPEAT
        UNTIL (ReadKB(kbmsg,crcharset,nullcset,
                        eascii,kbchar,msgframe^,nrmclr));
      kbchar:=StrChar(kbmsg,1);
      CASE kbchar OF
        'Q':done:=TRUE;
      ! 'S':
          ClrScrn(msgframe^,nrmclr);
          DsplyStr(nrmclr,Literal('NUMBER OF BOXES TO SHOW,BOX NUMBERS?..'),
                    msgframe^.fl,msgframe^.fc,msgframe^);
          SetLen(kbmsg,0);
          REPEAT
            UNTIL (ReadKB(kbmsg,crcharset,nullcset,
                            eascii,kbchar,msgframe^,nrmclr));
          n:=MakCard(kbmsg,1,i);
          MakFList(n,slptr);
          FOR j:=1 TO n DO
            slptr^[j]:=MakCard(kbmsg,i+1,i);
            END;
          ClrScrn(msgframe^,nrmclr);
          DsplyStr(nrmclr,Literal('NUMBER OF BOXES TO READ,BOX NUMBERS?..'),
                    msgframe^.fl,msgframe^.fc,msgframe^);
          SetLen(kbmsg,0);
          REPEAT
            UNTIL (ReadKB(kbmsg,crcharset,nullcset,
                            eascii,kbchar,msgframe^,nrmclr));
          n:=MakCard(kbmsg,1,i);
          MakFList(n,rlptr);
          FOR j:=1 TO n DO
            rlptr^[j]:=MakCard(kbmsg,i+1,i);
            END;
          ShowBox(thisscrn,slptr);
          ReadScrn(thisscrn,slptr,rlptr,0,lastbox,
                      0,lastfld,TRUE,chgd,
                      nullcset,fk1charset,stdhilite,horscrltab,
                      eascii,kbchar);
          ClrFList(slptr);
          ClrFList(rlptr);
      ! 'C':
          ClrScrn(msgframe^,nrmclr);
          DsplyStr(nrmclr,Literal('NUMBER OF BOXES TO CLEAR,BOX NUMBERS?..'),
                    msgframe^.fl,msgframe^.fc,msgframe^);
          SetLen(kbmsg,0);
          REPEAT
          UNTIL (ReadKB(kbmsg,crcharset,nullcset,
                            eascii,kbchar,msgframe^,nrmclr));
        n:=MakCard(kbmsg,1,i);
        MakFList(n,slptr);
        FOR j:=1 TO n DO
          slptr^[j]:=MakCard(kbmsg,i+1,i);
          END;
        ClrScrn(msgframe^,nrmclr);
          ClearBox(thisscrn,slptr);
          ClrFList(slptr);
        ELSE
          Sound(errfreq,errdur);
          END;
      UNTIL (done);
END TESTSCRN.
```

When you are testing a deScreen, you have access to all of the keyboard controls built into the deScreen routines. Fig. 14-8 summarizes those controls. In TESTSCRN, one key has a special purpose; F1 returns to the main program from the deScreen routines. TESTSCRN will then repeat its original prompt.

THE deScreen ROUTINES

Once the deScreen IMG file is created, you can use TESTSCRN to show it on the display, and use the deScreen keyboard characters to move around in the SCREEN-MAP. However, the characters you type into the fields go away when you leave TESTSCRN. To hold on to the characters and to save the data, you need a program. The Etling Library contains a whole series of routines to help you do this.

A word of caution. The deScreen routines do check to be certain that the box or field numbers to which they are asked to refer do indeed fall within the limits associated with the SCRNDEF defined by the SDPTR; however, the routines contain very little else in terms of error checking. The deScreen routines assume that the calling program knows what it wants to do.

In (and Out) of Memory

The deScreen routines in the Etling Library all operate around the IMG file and the SCRNDEF it contains. To use the SCRNDEF, you must first load it into memory, and when you're done, you have to clear it out. The routines that do these operations are contained in EL1409, shown in Fig. 14-9.

LoadScrn. The routine that loads a deScreen IMG file into memory is called *LoadScrn.* The comments in Fig. 14-9 explain how to use *LoadScrn* and point out once again that the SCRNDEF is attached to the ADDRESS variable that is passed to the routine. This variable is the only direct reference in the calling program to the entire deScreen work area.

Note that *LoadScrn* opens the file associated with the <ddname> defined by *scrnfile,* and after copying the value of *scrnfile* into the *p.dd* variable, the routine reads only the first 2 bytes from the file. The first 2 bytes contain *sdlen,* and that value is used to ALLOCATE an area in exactly the right size for the SCRNDEF. The SCRNDEF is loaded into this area in another read. *LoadScrn* then adjusts the addresses for *sm, ct, bx* and the *tab* lists.

FreeScrn. When a program has completed the processing associated with a specific deScreen, it should call *FreeScrn* to return the allocated space back to the segmented heap manager.

Dealing with Fields

Loading a deScreen into memory does not in any way affect what is shown on the user's display. To the calling program, the deScreen SCREENMAP is essentially a huge keyboard and display buffer. The characters that are entered by the user might appear on the display, but they are not automatically transferred into variables that are accessible to the calling program. To access the characters in a field, the calling

Fig. 14-8. deScreen control keys.

```
        KEY                     FUNCTION
------------------     ----------------------------------------------
      TAB              Move cursor one field to right.
   Right Arrow

   Shift TAB           Move cursor one field to left.
   Left Arrow

   Backspace           Delete character to left, and move cursor. If the
                         cursor is at the left end of a field, move cursor
                         to right of left field.

Carriage Return        Move cursor to first field on next line.

      HOME             Move cursor to first field in current box.

      END              Move cursor to last field in current box.

   PAGE UP             Move cursor to first field in previous box.

   PAGE DOWN           Move cursor to first field in next box.

    Up Arrow           Move cursor to field directly above current field.

  Down Arrow           Move cursor to field directly below current field.

    Delete             Delete character to right of cursor, move all other
                         characters left one postion.

    Insert             Move all characters to right of cursor one position
                         to the right, and insert a new character at the
                         current position.

Ctrl Right Arrow       Move cursor one character to the right. Do not
                         overwrite the current character.

Ctrl Left Arrow        Move cursor one character to the left. Do not
                         overwrite the current character.

    Alt X              Toggle Transmit only field. If the user has been
                         denied access, pressing Alt X will permit access.
                         If the user has been permitted access, pressing
                         Alt X will deny access.

    Alt R              All-Ditto. This control will duplicate the contents
                         of the current field in all fields in the same box
                         directly below the current field.

    Alt D              Ditto. This key copies the contents of the field
                         directly above the current field into the current
                         field.

    Alt I              Increment. This key copies the contetns of the field
                         directly above the current field and increments
                         its contents by 1 before copying it into the cureent
                         field.

    Alt N              Sequence. This key will copy the contents of the
                         current field into all fields directly below the
                         current field, and, increment each field by one.
```

Fig. 14-8 continued

    Alt C   Clear. This key will clear all characters (except
                     the decimal point) from the current field.

    Alt X   Help. This key invokes the deScreen "help" feature.
                     Refer to the discussion for the HELPSCRN routine.

Fig. 14-9. Loading deScreens.

```
DEFINITION MODULE EL1409;
   FROM SYSTEM IMPORT    ADDRESS;
   FROM EL0401 IMPORT    STRING;
   EXPORT QUALIFIED      FreeScrn,LoadScrn;

PROCEDURE FreeScrn(VAR thisscrn:ADDRESS);
(* This routine will clear the deScreen definition associated with thisscrn
   and release the space it occupies.  *)
PROCEDURE LoadScrn(scrnfile:STRING; VAR thisscrn:ADDRESS);
(* This is the first routine in the deScreen series.  It is used to load a
   deScreen ".img" file and establish the required control variables in
   core.  If the <dsname> associated with scrnfile can be opened and read
   successfully thisscrn will return pointing to the defined control area.
   (If the file cannot be loaded successfully, the routine will call
   Cancel).  The variable thisscrn should be allocated by the caller in
   such a way that it is un-molested during screen access.  The first call
   to any deScreen routine should be to LoadScrn which will allocate and
   initialize core for this area...subsequent calls use this variable to
   inform the screen handling routines which definition is being used.
   Therefore, a single program may use multiple screens with a different
   thisscrn for each.  *)
END EL1409.


IMPLEMENTATION MODULE EL1409;
   FROM SYSTEM IMPORT    ADR,ADDRESS,WORD,BYTE;
   FROM Storage IMPORT   ALLOCATE,DEALLOCATE;
   FROM EL0401 IMPORT    STRING,Literal,ClearStr,MakeStr;
   FROM EL0503 IMPORT    lczero,LONGCARD;
   FROM EL0906 IMPORT    Cancel;
   FROM EL1002 IMPORT    FMODE,OpnFile,LOCCNTRL,OPENKIND,DISP,ClsFile;
   FROM EL1005 IMPORT    GetRcrd;
   FROM EL1406 IMPORT    SDPTR;

PROCEDURE FreeScrn(VAR thisscrn:ADDRESS);
VAR
  p:SDPTR;
BEGIN
  p:=thisscrn;
  ClearStr(p^.dd);
  DEALLOCATE(thisscrn,p^.sdlen+4);
  END FreeScrn;

PROCEDURE LoadScrn(scrnfile:STRING;VAR thisscrn:ADDRESS);
VAR
  opnmode:FMODE;
  ioerr:BYTE;
  nmbr:LONGCARD;
  length,lengot:WORD;
  p:SDPTR;
  h:ADDRESS;
  i:CARDINAL;
```

```
BEGIN
  opnmode:=oldfile;
  OpnFile(scrnfile,opnmode,ioerr,insist);
  IF (NOT GetRcrd(scrnfile,setpostn,lczero,nmbr,
                              WORD(2),lengot,ADR(length)))
    THEN Cancel(Literal(' LoadScrn'),scrnfile,1,0);
    END;
  ALLOCATE(thisscrn,CARDINAL(length)+4);
  p:=thisscrn;
  h:=thisscrn;
  lengot:=WORD(0);
  IF (NOT GetRcrd(scrnfile,setpostn,lczero,nmbr,
                              length,lengot,ADR(p^.sdlen)))
    THEN Cancel(Literal(' LoadScrn'),scrnfile,1,1);
    END;
  ClsFile(scrnfile,clsonly);
  WITH p^ DO
    MakeStr(dd,0,scrnfile);
    h.OFFSET:=h.OFFSET+26;
    sm:=h;
    h.OFFSET:=h.OFFSET+2*(smml*smmc);
    ct:=h;
    h.OFFSET:=h.OFFSET+10*maxfield;
    bx:=h;
    h.OFFSET:=h.OFFSET+26*maxbox;
    FOR i:=1 TO maxbox DO
      IF (bx^[i].tabs.maxtabs > 0)
        THEN
          bx^[i].tabs.ptr:=h;
          h.OFFSET:=h.OFFSET+2*bx^[i].tabs.maxtabs;
        END;
      END;
    END;
  END LoadScrn;

END EL1409.
```

program must use one of the deScreen routines that transfer data to or from the SCREENMAP. These routines are contained in EL1410, shown in Fig. 14-10.

GetFld and PutFld. To retrieve the contents of a field, use *GetFld.* You specify the field to retrieve by identifying *fldnmbr* and defining *thisscrn*. The contents of the field are returned in *fldvalue*. The number of characters returned is controlled by the length of *fldvalue*. If the field definition in the SCRNDEF contains fewer characters than *fldvalue* could contain, *fldvalue* will be filled with spaces.

To transfer data to the SCREENMAP, use *PutFld. PutFld* also identifies the field by *fldnmbr,* and the number of characters transferred is controlled by the length of *fldvalue*. If *fldvalue* has fewer characters than the field definition in the SCRNDEF requires, the field will be filled with spaces.

BlankFld. A program frequently needs to clear the contents of one or more fields in a SCREENMAP. The routine named *BlankFld,* will clear any field, regardless of which type it is. If the field is numeric, the decimal point is left unchanged.

ChgColor. *ChgColor* is the routine that changes the color of a deScreen field. *ChgColor* operates on the SCREENMAP, not on the display.

Fig. 14-10. Moving field values.

```
DEFINITION MODULE EL1410;
  FROM SYSTEM IMPORT    BYTE,ADDRESS;
  FROM EL0401 IMPORT    STRING;
  EXPORT QUALIFIED      BlankFld,ChgColor,GetFld,PutFld;

PROCEDURE BlankFld(fldnmbr:CARDINAL;VAR thisscrn:ADDRESS);
(* This routine will fill the deScreen field associated with fldnmbr in
   thisscrn with blanks (except that the ":" in a numeric field will be
   left in its proper position).  Note that the change is made in the
   control area, not on the display.  *)
PROCEDURE ChgColor(VAR thisscrn:ADDRESS;fldnmbr:CARDINAL;
                          color:BYTE;switch:BOOLEAN);
(* thisscrn refers to a deScreen loaded by LoadScrn.  The color attribute
   of the indicated field will be changed.  If, on entry, switch is true
   color will be OR'd with existing attribute.  If false, color will be
   XOR'd to #FF and then AND'd to the exisiting attibute.  (i.e., switch =
   true turns color on, = false turns it off).  Note that the change is
   made in the control area, not on the crt.  *)
PROCEDURE GetFld(fldnmbr:CARDINAL;fldvalue:STRING;VAR thisscrn:ADDRESS);
(* A deScreen procedure that returns the current value of the specified
   field from the identified screen definition.  *)
PROCEDURE PutFld(fldnmbr:CARDINAL;fldvalue:STRING;VAR thisscrn:ADDRESS);
(* A deScreen procedure that moves fldvalue into the identified screen
   definition.  *)
END EL1410.


IMPLEMENTATION MODULE EL1410;
  FROM SYSTEM IMPORT    WORD,BYTE,ADDRESS;
  FROM EL0301 IMPORT    LoByte,ByWord;
  FROM EL0401 IMPORT    STRING,StrLen,Literal,SetChar,StrChar;
  FROM EL0906 IMPORT    Cancel;
  FROM EL1406 IMPORT    SDPTR,FLDTYPE,FLDTYPES,numtype,changed;

PROCEDURE BlankFld(fldnmbr:CARDINAL;VAR thisscrn:ADDRESS);
VAR
  p:SDPTR;
  i:CARDINAL;
BEGIN
  p:=thisscrn;
  WITH p^ DO
    IF (fldnmbr < 1) OR (fldnmbr > maxfield)
      THEN Cancel(Literal(' BlankFld'),p^.dd,1,BYTE(0));
      ELSE WITH ct^[fldnmbr] DO
        FOR i:=fldclmn TO fldclmn+fldlen-1 DO
          IF (sm^[smmc*(fldline-1)+i].chrbyte <> ':')
            THEN sm^[smmc*(fldline-1)+i].chrbyte:=' ';
            ELSE IF (NOT (numtype IN fldtype))
              THEN sm^[smmc*(fldline-1)+i].chrbyte:=' ';
              END;
            END;
          END;
        END;
        INCL(fldtype,changed);
      END;
    END;
  END;
END BlankFld;

PROCEDURE ChgColor(VAR thisscrn:ADDRESS;fldnmbr:CARDINAL;
                          color:BYTE;switch:BOOLEAN);
VAR
  p:SDPTR;
```

```
    i:CARDINAL;
   newcolor:WORD;
BEGIN
  p:=thisscrn;
  WITH p^ DO
    IF (fldnmbr < 1) OR (fldnmbr > maxfield)
      THEN Cancel(Literal('ChgColor'),p^.dd,1,BYTE(0));
      ELSE WITH ct^[fldnmbr] DO
        newcolor:=ByWord(00h,
                          sm^[smmc*(fldline-1)+fldclmn].colbyte);
        IF (switch)
          THEN newcolor:=WORD(BITSET(newcolor) +
                                    BITSET(ByWord(00h,color)));
          ELSE newcolor:=WORD(BITSET(newcolor) -
                                    BITSET(ByWord(00h,color)));
          END;
        FOR i:=fldclmn TO fldclmn+fldlen-1 DO
          sm^[smmc*(fldline-1)+i].colbyte:=LoByte(newcolor);
          END;
        END;
      END;
    END;
  END ChgColor;

PROCEDURE GetFld(fldnmbr:CARDINAL;fldvalue:STRING;VAR thisscrn:ADDRESS);
VAR
  p:SDPTR;
  i:CARDINAL;
BEGIN
  p:=thisscrn;
  WITH p^ DO
    IF (fldnmbr < 1) OR (fldnmbr > maxfield)
      THEN Cancel(Literal('GetFld'),p^.dd,1,BYTE(0));
      ELSE WITH ct^[fldnmbr] DO
        FOR i:=1 TO StrLen(fldvalue) DO
          IF (i > fldlen)
            THEN SetChar(fldvalue,i,' ');
            ELSE SetChar(fldvalue,i,
                      sm^[smmc*(fldline-1)+fldclmn+i-1].chrbyte);
            END;
          END;
        END;
      END;
    END;
  END GetFld;

PROCEDURE PutFld(fldnmbr:CARDINAL;fldvalue:STRING;VAR thisscrn:ADDRESS);
VAR
  p:SDPTR;
  i:CARDINAL;
BEGIN
  p:=thisscrn;
  WITH p^ DO
    IF (fldnmbr < 1) OR (fldnmbr > maxfield)
      THEN Cancel(Literal(' PutFld'),p^.dd,1,BYTE(0));
      ELSE WITH ct^[fldnmbr] DO
        FOR i:=1 TO fldlen DO
          IF (i > StrLen(fldvalue))
            THEN sm^[smmc*(fldline-1)+fldclmn+i-1].chrbyte:=' '
            ELSE sm^[smmc*(fldline-1)+fldclmn+i-1].chrbyte:=
                                          StrChar(fldvalue,i);
            END;
```

Fig. 14-10 continued

```
            END;
          INCL(fldtype,changed);
          END;
      END;
    END;
  END PutFld;

END EL1410.
```

Moving from the SCRNDEF to the Display

A program can actually load several different IMG files into the segmented heap at one time; to make one of these deScreen appear on the display, you need to use some other routines. These routines are all exported from EL1411, shown in Fig. 14-11.

ShowBox. *ShowBox* is the routine that moves all or part of one or more boxes from the SCRNDEF to the display. The boxes to be displayed are defined in *showblst*. *showblst* is a FLDLIST, an ARRAY OF CARDINAL. The values identify the box numbers to show. Note that *ShowBox* calls *ShowScrn,* to do the work. For each box, *ShowBox* sets *cfmlibos* and *cfmcibos* to their initial values. These variables stand for "current first map line in box on screen" and "current first map column in box on screen." They are set to *fmlib* and *fmcib* ("first map line in box and first map column in box"), respectively. In other words, *cfmlibos* and *cfmcibos* keep track of where the upper left corner of the display window associated with the box is located within the box in the SCREENMAP. That is not necessarily the same as the upper left corner of the box.

ShowScrn. The *ShowScrn* routine contains the code that actually moves the contents of a SCREENMAP to the crt. Note that *ShowScrn* checks each character in the first line of the SCREENMAP, to see if it is CHR(1), the special control character that prevents the display from being overlaid. If a control character is encountered, that portion of the display is not involved in the move.

ClearBox. Sometimes a program needs to clear a particular box from the display. The routine named *ClearBox* will do this job. Note that *cfmlibos* and *cfmcibos* are set back to zero. *ClearBox* uses *ClrScrn* to actually clear the display; no change is made to the SCREENMAP.

The Nucleus of the deScreen Routines

The EL1412 module contains the nucleus of the deScreen routines. Any program that accesses a deScreen must use the routines in this module. The module is quite large, and it exports quite a few routines. To understand its operation, begin with the *ReadScrn* routine (refer to Fig. 14-12).

ReadScrn. The major portion of the EL1412 module is within ReadScrn. Any program that uses a deScreen to either gather or display data, will usually call *ReadScrn* (either directly or indirectly through *ReadFlds*). *ReadScrn* has several jobs, but its main purpose is to read one character at a time from the keyboard and either display it on the crt or perform the control function that the character indicates.

ReadScrn has a large parameter list; the comments in the .DEF file explain the

Fig. 14-11. Moving boxes.

```
DEFINITION MODULE EL1411;
   FROM SYSTEM IMPORT    ADDRESS;
   FROM EL0505 IMPORT    FLPTR;
   FROM EL1406 IMPORT    SMAP;
   EXPORT QUALIFIED      ShowBox,ClearBox,ShowScrn;

PROCEDURE ShowScrn (VAR image:SMAP;
          ml,            (*MAX LINES IN DEF                *)
          mc,            (*MAX COLUMNS IN DEF              *)
          fdl,           (*FIRST DEF LINE TO MOVE          *)
          fdc,           (*FIRST DEF COLUMN TO MOVE        *)
          fcl,           (*FIRST CRT LINE TO FILL          *)
          fcc,           (*FIRST CRT COLUMN TO FILL        *)
          ncltf,         (*NUMBER OF CRT LINES TO FILL   *)
          tnc:CARDINAL);   (*NUMBER OF CRT COLLUMN TO FILL*)
(* This routine is used to transfer a screen image from the definition to
   the crt screen.  It is used only internally by the deScreen routines and
   is not directly available to other procedures.  *)
PROCEDURE ShowBox(VAR thisscrn:ADDRESS;showblst:FLPTR);
(* This routine will move the appropriate contents of the deScreen boxes
   identified by showblst onto the display.  thisscrn refers to a descreen
   control area loaded by LoadScrn.  *)
PROCEDURE ClearBox(VAR thisscrn:ADDRESS;showblst:FLPTR);
(* This routine will clear the area of the display occupied by the deScreen
   boxes associated with showblst.  thisscrn refers to a deScreen control
   area loaded by LoadScrn.  *)
END EL1411.


IMPLEMENTATION MODULE EL1411;
   FROM SYSTEM IMPORT    ADDRESS;
   FROM EL0302 IMPORT    MovByteL;
   FROM EL0401 IMPORT    STRING,Literal;
   FROM EL0504 IMPORT    FRAMEPTR,MakFrame,ClrFrame;
   FROM EL0505 IMPORT    FLPTR;
   FROM EL0902 IMPORT    ClrScrn,nrmclr,crtads;
   FROM EL0906 IMPORT    Cancel;
   FROM EL1406 IMPORT    SDPTR,SMAP;


PROCEDURE ShowScrn (VAR image:SMAP;
                        ml,mc,fdl,fdc,fcl,fcc,ncltf,tnc:CARDINAL);
VAR
   i,j,nc:CARDINAL;
   ok:BOOLEAN;
BEGIN
  REPEAT
    nc:=0;ok:=TRUE;
    WHILE (ok) DO
      IF (image[mc*(fdl-1)+fdc+nc].chrbyte <> CHR(1))
        THEN ok:=FALSE
        ELSE IF (nc = tnc)
          THEN ok:=FALSE
          ELSE INC(nc);
          END;
        END;
      END;
    IF (nc > 0)
      THEN
        FOR i:=0 TO ncltf-1 DO
          MovByteL(image,crtads^,2*(mc*(i+fdl-1) + fdc-81),
                               2*(80*(i+fcl-1) + fcc-1),2*nc);
          END;
```

Fig. 14-11 continued

```
        tnc:=tnc-nc;fdc:=fdc+nc;fcc:=fcc+nc;
        nc:=0;
      END;
    IF (tnc > 0)
      THEN
        nc:=0;ok:=TRUE;
        WHILE (ok) DO
          IF (image[mc*(fdl-1)+fdc+nc].chrbyte = CHR(1))
            THEN ok:=FALSE
            ELSE IF (nc = tnc)
              THEN ok:=FALSE
              ELSE INC(nc);
              END;
            END;
          END;
        FOR i:=0 TO ncltf-1 DO
          MovByteL(image,crtads^,2*(mc*(i+fdl-1) + fdc-1),
                                2*(80*(i+fcl-1) + fcc-1),2*nc);
          END;
        tnc:=tnc-nc;fdc:=fdc+nc;fcc:=fcc+nc;
      END;
    UNTIL (tnc <= 0);
  END ShowScrn;

PROCEDURE ShowBox(VAR thisscrn:ADDRESS;showblst:FLPTR);
VAR
  i:CARDINAL;
  p:SDPTR;
BEGIN
  p:=thisscrn;
  i:=1;
  WHILE (i <= showblst^[0]) DO
    IF (showblst^[i] < 1) OR (showblst^[i] > p^.maxbox)
      THEN Cancel(Literal('ShowBox'),p^.dd,1,0);
      ELSE WITH p^.bx^[showblst^[i]] DO
        ShowScrn(p^.sm^,p^.smml,p^.smmc,fmlib,
                              fmcib,fslib,fscib,nslib,nscib);
        cfmlibos:=fmlib;
        cfmcibos:=fmcib;
        i:=i+1;
        END;
      END;
    END;
  END ShowBox;

PROCEDURE ClearBox(VAR thisscrn:ADDRESS;showblst:FLPTR);
VAR
  i:CARDINAL;
  p:SDPTR;
  f:FRAMEPTR;
  a:ADDRESS;
BEGIN
  p:=thisscrn;
  i:=1;
  WHILE (i <= showblst^[0]) DO
    IF (showblst^[i] < 1) OR (showblst^[i] > p^.maxbox)
      THEN Cancel(Literal('ClearBox'),p^.dd,1,0);
      ELSE WITH p^.bx^[showblst^[i]] DO
        cfmlibos:=0;
        cfmcibos:=0;
        MakFrame(fslib,fscib,fslib+nslib-1,fscib+nscib-1,
```

```
                              fslib,fscib,25,80,crtads,f);
        ClrScrn(f^,nrmclr);
        ClrFrame(f);
        i:=i+1;
        END;
      END;
    END;
  END ClearBox;

END EL1411.
```

parameters in detail. The routine is also large; so large that it is broken up into some twenty odd smaller routines.

ReadScrn begins by locating the program parameters that identify the files containing the "Help" messages for the deScreen. (The help files are discussed at the end of this section.) Next, *ReadScrn* will determine the box and the field within the box in which it should begin operation. When the starting location is determined, *ReadScrn* establishes a repeat loop. Within the loop, *ReadScrn* will set up a smaller loop that waits for the user to enter a character on the keyboard. If the character is in either the *easciis* set or *normals* set sent by the calling program, *ReadScrn* will close up shop and return to the caller. If the character is in one of the *ReadScrn* control CHARSETs, *ReadScrn* will call *Control* to handle whatever operation is associated with the character. Otherwise, *ReadScrn* will call *CanPChr* to make certain that the character fits the type of field in which the cursor is positioned and that the field has room for another character; if so, *ReadScrn* will call *PutChar;* if not, *ReadScrn* will signal an error.

Both *Control* and *PutChar* might result in moving the cursor out of the field in which it was originally located. (A *PutChar* might fill a field, and the cursor must be moved to the first character of the next field. Many of the *Control* operations change the field location directly.) Neither routine will actually do the field change, but will instead signal *ReadScrn* (using *chgfld*) that a change is necessary. *ReadScrn* uses *LeaveFld* and *EnterFld* to do the actual manipulation.

Control is internal to *ReadScrn,* but except for *CanPChr* and *PutChar,* the other routines are easier to understand in terms of how they relate to *Control. Control* is discussed in the next paragraph; *CanPChr* and *PutChar* are the last routines discussed in this section.

Implementing Keyboard Controls

The EL1412 Module defines two CHARSET variables: one containing extended ASCII characters, and the other containing normal ASCII. These are the characters that *ReadScrn* and *Control* recognize as keyboard controls. If the user should enter one of these characters, and the appropriate code is not specified as a member of *easciis* or *normals* (the CHARSET parameters that the calling program would use to signal *ReadScrn* to return), *ReadScrn* will call *Control* to perform the associated operation.

Control. First, *Control* checks *kbchar* to determine if *insrtchr,* a BOOLEAN that signals whether or not the user is inserting characters in the middle of a field, should be toggled off. If *kbchar* is NOT one of the characters shown, insertion can continue;

Fig. 14-12. Basic deScreen routines.

```
DEFINITION MODULE EL1412;
  FROM SYSTEM IMPORT      WORD,BYTE,ADDRESS;
  FROM EL0401 IMPORT      STRING;
  FROM EL0501 IMPORT      CHARSET;
  FROM EL0505 IMPORT      FLPTR;
  FROM EL1406 IMPORT      FLDDEF,FDTBL,BOXDEF,BDTBL,SMAP;
  EXPORT QUALIFIED        MoveCur,CanDTab,CanLTab,CanRTab,CanUTab,CanECur,
                          CanHCur,AlignNum,IncFld,IsBlank,ShftLFld,ShftRFld,
                          ShowFld,CanDBox,CanUBox,CanPChr,ClrFld,DoDelete,
                          PutChar,ScrlScrn,ChgCAtt,SetCur,EnterFld,LeaveFld,
                          ChgBox,ReadScrn;

PROCEDURE MoveCur(VAR box:BOXDEF;VAR curline,curclmn:CARDINAL;
                            increment:INTEGER);
(* This routine moves the cursor to the new location. *)
PROCEDURE CanDTab (xmttabok:BOOLEAN;VAR box:BOXDEF;VAR flds:FDTBL;
                VAR curtab:CARDINAL;curclmn:CARDINAL):BOOLEAN;
(* This routine will check to be sure that the screen includes a field to
    which the cursor can tab down.  *)
PROCEDURE CanLTab(xmttabok:BOOLEAN;VAR box:BOXDEF;VAR flds:FDTBL;
                VAR curtab:CARDINAL):BOOLEAN;
(* This routine will check to be sure that the screen includes a field to
    which the cursor can tab left.  *)
PROCEDURE CanRTab(xmttabok:BOOLEAN;VAR box:BOXDEF;VAR flds:FDTBL;
                VAR curtab:CARDINAL):BOOLEAN;
(* This routine will check to be sure that the screen includes a field to
    which the cursor can tab right.  *)
PROCEDURE CanUTab (xmttabok:BOOLEAN;VAR box:BOXDEF;VAR flds:FDTBL;
                VAR curtab:CARDINAL;curclmn:CARDINAL):BOOLEAN;
(* This routine will check to be sure that the screen includes a field to
    which the cursor can tab up.  *)
PROCEDURE CanECur (xmttabok:BOOLEAN;VAR box:BOXDEF;VAR flds:FDTBL;
                VAR curtab:CARDINAL):BOOLEAN;
(* This routine will check to be certain that the cursor can be moved to
    the first field in the current box.  *)
PROCEDURE CanHCur (xmttabok:BOOLEAN;VAR box:BOXDEF;VAR flds:FDTBL;
                VAR curtab:CARDINAL):BOOLEAN;
(* This routine will check to be certain that the cursor can be moved to
    the last field in the current box.  *)
PROCEDURE AlignNum(mc,ml:CARDINAL;VAR image:SMAP;VAR fld:FLDDEF);
(* This routine will align the characters in a numeric field so that the
    decimal point is properly positioned.  *)
PROCEDURE IncFld(fld:STRING);
(* This routine will add '1' to the contents of the numeric field defined
    by fld.  *)
PROCEDURE IsBlank(mc,ml:CARDINAL;VAR image:SMAP;VAR fld:FLDDEF):BOOLEAN;
(* This routine will check the contents of the field specified by fld and
    return TRUE if it is all blank.  *)
PROCEDURE ShftLFld(mc,ml:CARDINAL;VAR image:SMAP;
                        fldline,frstcol,lastcol:CARDINAL);
(* This routine will shift the contents of a field to the left. *)
PROCEDURE ShftRFld(mc,ml:CARDINAL;VAR image:SMAP;
                        fldline,frstcol,lastcol:CARDINAL);
(* This routine will shift the contents of a field to the right. *)
PROCEDURE ShowFld(mc,ml:CARDINAL;VAR image:SMAP;
                    VAR box:BOXDEF;VAR fld:FLDDEF);
(* This routine moves a field from the image to the screen. *)
PROCEDURE CanDBox(VAR boxes:BDTBL;VAR readblst:FLPTR;
                VAR currb,newbox:CARDINAL;
                    xmttabok:BOOLEAN;VAR flds:FDTBL):BOOLEAN;
(* This routine checks to see if another box is below the current one. *)
```

```
PROCEDURE CanUBox(VAR boxes:BDTBL;VAR readblst:FLPTR;
                  VAR currb,newbox:CARDINAL;
                     xmttabok:BOOLEAN;VAR flds:FDTBL):BOOLEAN;
(* This routine checks to see if another box is above the current one. *)
PROCEDURE CanPChr(mc,ml:CARDINAL;VAR image:SMAP;VAR fld:FLDDEF;
                  VAR curline,curclmn:CARDINAL;pchar:CHAR):BOOLEAN;
(* This routine will make sure that a character can be put to the current
   position. *)
PROCEDURE ClrFld(mc,ml:CARDINAL;VAR image:SMAP;
                 VAR box:BOXDEF;VAR fld:FLDDEF);
(* This routine will clear all the field identified by fld. *)
PROCEDURE DoDelete(mc,ml:CARDINAL;VAR image:SMAP;VAR box:BOXDEF;
                   VAR fld:FLDDEF; VAR curclmn:CARDINAL);
(*  This routine will delete a character at the current cursor position. *)
PROCEDURE PutChar(mc,ml:CARDINAL;VAR image:SMAP;
                  VAR boxes:BDTBL;VAR flds:FDTBL;
                   VAR curbox,curfld,curline,curclmn:CARDINAL;
                    pchar:CHAR;VAR insrtchr:BOOLEAN):BOOLEAN;
(* This routine will move pchar to the current cursor position and adjust
   the field accordingly.  *)
PROCEDURE ScrlScrn (mc,ml:CARDINAL;VAR image:SMAP;
                    VAR showblst:FLPTR;VAR boxes:BDTBL;
                     VAR curbox,curfld:CARDINAL;VAR flds:FDTBL;
                      hortab:CHAR):BOOLEAN;
(* This routine scrolls the display. *)
PROCEDURE ChgCAtt (VAR box:BOXDEF;VAR fld:FLDDEF;setcolor:BYTE);
(* This routine will change the color of the field associated with fld. *)
PROCEDURE SetCur(mc,ml:CARDINAL;VAR image:SMAP;VAR fld:FLDDEF;
                          fromleft:BOOLEAN):CARDINAL;
(* This routine determines the cursor position. *)
PROCEDURE EnterFld(mc,ml:CARDINAL;VAR image:SMAP;
                   VAR showblst:FLPTR; VAR boxes:BDTBL;VAR flds:FDTBL;
                    VAR curbox,curtab,curfld,curline,curclmn:CARDINAL;
                     hlclr:BYTE;hortab:CHAR;fromleft:BOOLEAN);
(* This routine handles the operations for moving into a field. *)
PROCEDURE LeaveFld(mc,ml:CARDINAL;VAR image:SMAP;VAR boxes:BDTBL;
                   VAR flds:FDTBL;curbox,curfld:CARDINAL);
(* This routine handles the operations required to leave a field. *)
PROCEDURE ChgBox(mc,ml:CARDINAL;VAR image:SMAP;VAR showblst:FLPTR;
                 VAR boxes:BDTBL;VAR flds:FDTBL;VAR newbox,curtab:CARDINAL;
                  oldbox,lastfld:CARDINAL;hortab:CHAR):BOOLEAN;
(* This routine handles the change from one box to another. *)
PROCEDURE ReadScrn(VAR thisscrn:ADDRESS;VAR showblst,readblst:FLPTR;
                   frstbox:CARDINAL;VAR lastbox:CARDINAL;
                   frstfld:CARDINAL;VAR lastfld:CARDINAL;
                   oktochg:BOOLEAN;VAR chgd:BOOLEAN;
                 VAR normals,easciis:CHARSET;hlclr:BYTE;hortab:CHAR;
                 VAR eascii:BOOLEAN;VAR kbchar:CHAR);
(* This routine gives the calling program access to a deScreen for
   controlling data entry.  The appropriate screen must have been loaded
   (using LoadScrn) and is referred to by ThisScrn.  ShowBLst defines the
   list of box numbers that are to appear on the screen during this
   access...these boxes will all scroll as appropriate.  readblst defines
   the list of boxes into which data may be entered.  Note the the two
   lists do not have to be the same, but every element in readblst should
   also be in showblst.  frstbox defines the readblst box where reading is
   to be begin...(note:  readblst[?] = frstbox).  If frstbox = 0 on entry,
   reading will begin at readblst[1].  On exit, lastbox will be set to the
   box being accessed when the user decided that input was complete.
   frstfld defines the field number where reading is to begin.  If frstfld
   = 0 on entry, reading will begin at the first field in frstbox.  If
   frstfld <> 0 on entry, then frstbox must also not be zero, and reading
```

Fig. 14-12 continued

```
       will begin at the field specified.  (If frstfld is not in frstbox, the
       procedure will cancel).  Calling this routine with frstbox and/or
       frstfld not equal to zero allows a calling program to continue reading
       where it left off, as opposed to starting over at the beginning of a
       list.   If oktochg is false on entry, this routine will not permit the
       user to enter data into the screen...instead, the cursor control
       characters can be used to view data.  If oktochg is true on entry, and
       any data is entered or changed, chgd will return true.  hlclr defines
       the color that is to be used to highlight the field currently being
       read...this is usually stdhilite.  hortab defines the character that is
       to be used to mark a horizontal tab position of sideways scrolling...its
       use depends on the screen being accessed.  normals and easciis define
       sets of characters that the routine is to use as a termination signal.
       When a character from one of those sets is encountered, the routine will
       return to the caller with kbchar equal to the character that terminated
       the read, and, eascii set accordingly.  *)
END EL1412.

IMPLEMENTATION MODULE EL1412;
   FROM SYSTEM IMPORT     ADR,ADDRESS,WORD,BYTE;
   FROM EL0302 IMPORT     MovByteL;
   FROM EL0304 IMPORT     help,curl,curr,tabr,rtab,tabl,ltab,utab,dtab,home,
                          end,boxu,boxd,cr,insr,bksp,del,allditto,dittokey,
                          nextval,xmtcntrl,clearfld,seqval,altdec,esc;
   FROM EL0401 IMPORT     STRING,Literal,StrLen,MakeStr,ClearStr,CopyStr,
                          nullstr,SetLen,SetChar,StrChar;
   FROM EL0402 IMPORT     Concat,Delete,Insert;
   FROM EL0403 IMPORT     Positn;
   FROM EL0501 IMPORT     CHARSET,InCSet,numbers,MakeCSet;
   FROM EL0504 IMPORT     DISPLAYWORD,FRAME,DsplyWrd,DWPTR;
   FROM EL0505 IMPORT     FLPTR,FLDLIST;
   FROM EL0705 IMPORT     Sound,errfreq,errdur;
   FROM EL0801 IMPORT     FindParm;
   FROM EL0901 IMPORT     FlushKB,GetKBChr;
   FROM EL0902 IMPORT     PstnCur,crtads;
   FROM EL0906 IMPORT     Cancel;
   FROM EL1406 IMPORT     hlpframe,ecntrl,ncntrl,alptype,xmttype,contype,
                          zerofill,numtype,changed,FLDTYPES,FLDTYPE,FLDDEF,
                          FDTBL,FDTPTR,BOXDEF,BDTBL,BDTPTR,SDPTR,
                          SMAP,SMPTR,SCRNDEF;
   FROM EL1410 IMPORT     GetFld,PutFld;
   FROM EL1411 IMPORT     ShowBox,ShowScrn;
   FROM EL1302 IMPORT     Help;

PROCEDURE MoveCur(VAR box:BOXDEF;VAR curline,curclmn:CARDINAL;inc:INTEGER);
BEGIN
   IF (inc < 0)
     THEN DEC(curclmn,ABS(inc));
     ELSE INC(curclmn,inc);
     END;
   WITH box DO
     PstnCur(curline+fslib-cfmlibos,curclmn+fscib-cfmcibos,wrkframe);
     END;
   END MoveCur;

PROCEDURE CanDTab (xmttabok:BOOLEAN;VAR box:BOXDEF;VAR flds:FDTBL;
              VAR curtab:CARDINAL;curclmn:CARDINAL):BOOLEAN;
VAR
   i:CARDINAL;
   tabfound: BOOLEAN;
BEGIN
```

```
      i:=curtab;
      tabfound:=FALSE;
      WITH box DO
         WHILE (i < tabs.maxtabs) AND (NOT tabfound) DO
            INC(i);
            IF (flds[tabs.ptr^[i]].fldline > flds[tabs.ptr^[curtab]].fldline)
               THEN
                  WITH flds[tabs.ptr^[i]] DO
                     IF (curclmn >= fldclmn) AND (curclmn < fldclmn+fldlen)
                        THEN IF (xmttabok)
                           THEN tabfound:=TRUE
                           ELSE IF (NOT (xmttype IN fldtype))
                              THEN tabfound:=TRUE;
                              END;
                           END;
                        END;
                     END;
               END;
            END;
         END;
      IF (tabfound)
         THEN curtab:=i;
         END;
      RETURN tabfound;
      END CanDTab;

PROCEDURE CanLTab(xmttabok:BOOLEAN;VAR box:BOXDEF;VAR flds:FDTBL;
                  VAR curtab:CARDINAL):BOOLEAN;
VAR
   i:CARDINAL;
   tabfound:BOOLEAN;
BEGIN
   tabfound:=FALSE;
   i:=curtab;
   WHILE (i > 1) AND (NOT tabfound) DO
      DEC(i);
      IF (xmttabok)
         THEN tabfound:=TRUE
         ELSE IF (NOT (xmttype IN flds[box.tabs.ptr^[i]].fldtype))
            THEN tabfound:=TRUE;
            END;
         END;
      END;
   IF (tabfound)
      THEN curtab:=i;
      END;
   RETURN tabfound;
   END CanLTab;


PROCEDURE CanRTab(xmttabok:BOOLEAN;VAR box:BOXDEF;VAR flds:FDTBL;
                  VAR curtab:CARDINAL):BOOLEAN;
VAR
   i:CARDINAL;
   tabfound:BOOLEAN;
BEGIN
   i:=curtab;
   tabfound:=FALSE;
   WHILE (i < box.tabs.maxtabs) AND (NOT tabfound) DO
      INC(i);
      IF (xmttabok)
         THEN tabfound:=TRUE
         ELSE IF (NOT (xmttype IN flds[box.tabs.ptr^[i]].fldtype))
            THEN tabfound:=TRUE;
```

Fig. 14-12 continued

```
        END;
      END;
    END;
  IF (tabfound)
    THEN curtab:=i;
    END;
  RETURN tabfound;
  END CanRTab;


PROCEDURE CanUTab (xmttabok:BOOLEAN;VAR box:BOXDEF;VAR flds:FDTBL;
              VAR curtab:CARDINAL;curclmn:CARDINAL):BOOLEAN;
VAR
  i:CARDINAL;
  tabfound: BOOLEAN;
BEGIN
  i:=curtab;
  tabfound:=FALSE;
  WITH box DO
    WHILE (i > 1) AND (NOT tabfound) DO
      DEC(i);
      IF (flds[tabs.ptr^[i]].fldline < flds[tabs.ptr^[curtab]].fldline)
        THEN
          WITH flds[tabs.ptr^[i]] DO
            IF (curclmn >= fldclmn) AND (curclmn < fldclmn+fldlen)
              THEN IF (xmttabok)
                THEN tabfound:=TRUE
                ELSE IF (NOT (xmttype IN fldtype))
                  THEN tabfound:=TRUE;
                  END;
                END;
              END;
            END;
        END;
      END;
    END;
  IF (tabfound)
    THEN curtab:=i;
    END;
  RETURN tabfound;
  END CanUTab;


PROCEDURE CanECur (xmttabok:BOOLEAN;VAR box:BOXDEF;VAR flds:FDTBL;
              VAR curtab:CARDINAL):BOOLEAN;
VAR
  new:CARDINAL;
BEGIN
  new:=box.tabs.maxtabs+1;
  IF (CanLTab(xmttabok,box,flds,new))
    THEN
      IF (new <> curtab)
        THEN
          curtab:=new;
          RETURN TRUE;
        ELSE RETURN FALSE;
        END;
    ELSE RETURN FALSE;
    END;
  END CanECur;


PROCEDURE CanHCur (xmttabok:BOOLEAN;VAR box:BOXDEF;VAR flds:FDTBL;
              VAR curtab:CARDINAL):BOOLEAN;
```

```
VAR
  new:CARDINAL;
BEGIN
  new:=0;
  IF (CanRTab(xmttabok,box,flds,new))
    THEN
      IF (new <> curtab)
        THEN
          curtab:=new;
          RETURN TRUE;
        ELSE RETURN FALSE
        END;
    ELSE RETURN FALSE;
    END;
  END CanHCur;

PROCEDURE AlignNum(mc,ml:CARDINAL;VAR image:SMAP;VAR fld:FLDDEF);
VAR
  i,j:CARDINAL;
  str:STRING;
  sign,c:CHAR;
  done,nonzero:BOOLEAN;
BEGIN
  nonzero:=FALSE;
  sign:=' ';
  MakeStr(str,255,nullstr);
  WITH fld DO
    FOR i:=fldclmn TO fldclmn+fldlen-1 DO
      c:=image[mc*(fldline-1)+i].chrbyte;
      IF (c = '-') OR (c = '+')
        THEN sign:=c
        ELSE IF (InCSet(c,numbers)) OR (c = '.')
          THEN
            SetLen(str,StrLen(str)+1);
            SetChar(str,StrLen(str),c);
            IF (c <> '0') AND (c <> '.')
              THEN nonzero:=TRUE;
              END;
          END;
        END;
      END;
    IF (StrLen(str) = 0)
      THEN
        FOR i:=1 TO fldlen DO
          SetLen(str,StrLen(str)+1);
          SetChar(str,StrLen(str),' ');
          END;
        IF (fldprec > 0)
          THEN SetChar(str,fldlen-fldprec,':');
          END;
      ELSE
        i:=Positn(Literal('.'),str,1);
        IF (i = 0)
          THEN IF (fldprec > 0)
            THEN
            WHILE (fldprec > StrLen(str)) DO
              Insert(Literal('0'),str,1);
              END;
            i:=StrLen(str) - fldprec + 1;
            Insert(Literal('.'),str,i);
          END;
        END;
```

Fig. 14-12 continued

```
    IF (i <> 0)
      THEN
        IF (StrLen(str) > i+fldprec)
          THEN Delete(str,i+fldprec+1,
                                StrLen(str)-i-fldprec)
          ELSE WHILE (StrLen(str) < i+fldprec) DO
            SetLen(str,StrLen(str)+1);
            SetChar(str,StrLen(str),'0');
            END;
          END;
        IF (i <= fldlen - fldprec - 1)
          THEN SetChar(str,i,altdec);
          ELSE
            Delete(str,i,1);
            Insert(Literal(altdec),str,fldlen-fldprec);
          END;
      END;
    IF (zerofill IN fldtype)
      THEN
        WHILE (StrLen(str) < fldlen) DO
          Insert(Literal('0'),str,1);
          END;
        IF (sign = '-') AND (nonzero)
          THEN
            Insert(Literal('0'),str,1);
            SetChar(str,1,sign);
          END;
      ELSE
        done:=FALSE;
        REPEAT
          IF (StrLen(str) <= 1)
            THEN done:=TRUE
            ELSE IF (StrChar(str,1) = '0')
              THEN Delete(str,1,1)
              ELSE done:=TRUE;
              END;
            END;
          UNTIL (done);
        IF (sign = '-') AND (nonzero)
          THEN
            Insert(Literal('0'),str,1);
            SetChar(str,1,sign);
          END;
        WHILE (StrLen(str) < fldlen) DO
          Insert(Literal(' '),str,1);
          END;
        IF (NOT nonzero) AND (fldprec > 0)
                              AND (fldlen > fldprec +1)
          THEN SetChar(str,fldlen-fldprec-1,'0');
          END;
      END;
    END;
FOR i:=1 TO fldlen DO
  image[mc*(fldline-1)+fldclmn+i-1].chrbyte:=StrChar(str,i);
      END;
    END;
  ClearStr(str);
  END AlignNum;

PROCEDURE IncFld(fld:STRING);
VAR
```

```
      c,j,n:CARDINAL;
BEGIN
  c:=1;j:=StrLen(fld);
  WHILE (j > 0) AND (c = 1) DO
    IF (InCSet(StrChar(fld,j),numbers))
      THEN
        n:=ORD(StrChar(fld,j))-ORD('0')+c;
        IF (n < 10)
          THEN c:=0
          ELSE n:=n-10;
          END;
        SetChar(fld,j,CHR(ORD('0')+n));
      ELSE IF (StrChar(fld,j) = ' ')
        THEN
          SetChar(fld,j,'1');
          c:=0;
        END;
      END;
    DEC(j);
    END;
  END IncFld;

PROCEDURE IsBlank(mc,ml:CARDINAL;VAR image:SMAP;VAR fld:FLDDEF):BOOLEAN;
VAR
  i:CARDINAL;
  blnksofar:BOOLEAN;
BEGIN
  blnksofar:=TRUE;
  i:=fld.fldclmn;
  WHILE (i < fld.fldclmn+fld.fldlen) AND (blnksofar) DO
    IF (image[mc*(fld.fldline-1)+i].chrbyte = ' ')
        OR (image[mc*(fld.fldline-1)+i].chrbyte = altdec)
      THEN DEC(i);
      ELSE blnksofar:=FALSE;
      END;
    END;
  RETURN blnksofar;
  END IsBlank;

PROCEDURE ShftLFld(mc,ml:CARDINAL;VAR image:SMAP;
                          fldline,frstcol,lastcol:CARDINAL);
VAR
  i:CARDINAL;
BEGIN
  FOR i:=frstcol TO lastcol-1 DO
    image[mc*(fldline-1)+i].chrbyte:=image[mc*(fldline-1)+i+1].chrbyte;
    END;
  image[mc*(fldline-1)+lastcol].chrbyte:=' ';
  END ShftLFld;

PROCEDURE ShftRFld(mc,ml:CARDINAL;VAR image:SMAP;
                          fldline,frstcol,lastcol:CARDINAL);
VAR
  i:CARDINAL;
BEGIN
  FOR i:=lastcol TO frstcol+1 BY -1 DO
    image[mc*(fldline-1)+i].chrbyte:=image[mc*(fldline-1)+i-1].chrbyte;
    END;
  image[mc*(fldline-1)+frstcol].chrbyte:=' ';
  END ShftRFld;

PROCEDURE ShowFld(mc,ml:CARDINAL;VAR image:SMAP;
                     VAR box:BOXDEF;VAR fld:FLDDEF);
```

Fig. 14-12 continued

```
VAR
  i,cl,cc:CARDINAL;
  d:DWPTR;
BEGIN
  WITH fld DO
    WITH box DO
      cl:=fldline+fslib-cfmlibos;
      cc:=fldclmn+fscib-cfmcibos;
      FOR i:=0 TO fldlen-1 DO
        d:=DsplyWrd(cl,cc+i,wrkframe);
        d^.chrbyte:=image[mc*(fldline-1)+fldclmn+i].chrbyte;
        END;
      END;
    END;
  END ShowFld;

PROCEDURE CanDBox(VAR boxes:BDTBL;VAR readblst:FLPTR;
                     VAR currb,newbox:CARDINAL;
                         xmttabok:BOOLEAN;VAR flds:FDTBL):BOOLEAN;
VAR
  tab1,rb:CARDINAL;
  boxfound:BOOLEAN;
BEGIN
  boxfound:=FALSE;
  rb:=currb+1;
  WHILE (rb <= readblst^[0]) AND (NOT boxfound) DO
    IF (boxes[readblst^[rb]].tabs.maxtabs = 0)
      THEN rb:=rb+1
      ELSE
        tab1:=0;
        IF (CanRTab(xmttabok,boxes[readblst^[rb]],flds,tab1))
          THEN boxfound:=TRUE
          ELSE rb:=rb+1;
          END;
      END;
    END;
  IF (boxfound)
    THEN
      currb:=rb;
      newbox:=readblst^[rb];
    END;
  RETURN boxfound;
  END CanDBox;

PROCEDURE CanUBox(VAR boxes:BDTBL;VAR readblst:FLPTR;
                     VAR currb,newbox:CARDINAL;
                         xmttabok:BOOLEAN;VAR flds:FDTBL):BOOLEAN;
VAR
  tab1,rb:CARDINAL;
  boxfound:BOOLEAN;
BEGIN
  boxfound:=FALSE;
  rb:=currb-1;
  WHILE (rb > 0) AND (NOT boxfound) DO
    IF (boxes[readblst^[rb]].tabs.maxtabs = 0)
      THEN rb:=rb-1
      ELSE
        tab1:=0;
        IF (CanRTab(xmttabok,boxes[readblst^[rb]],flds,tab1))
          THEN boxfound:=TRUE
          ELSE rb:=rb-1;
```

```
            END;
          END;
        END;
    IF (boxfound)
      THEN
        currb:=rb;
        newbox:=readblst^[rb];
      END;
    RETURN boxfound;
    END CanUBox;

PROCEDURE CanPChr(mc,ml:CARDINAL;VAR image:SMAP;VAR fld:FLDDEF;
                    VAR curline,curclmn:CARDINAL;pchar:CHAR):BOOLEAN;
VAR
  i:CARDINAL;
  ok:BOOLEAN;
BEGIN
  WITH fld DO
    IF (alptype IN fldtype)
      THEN IF (pchar >= ' ') AND (pchar <= '~')
        THEN ok:=TRUE;
        ELSE ok:=FALSE;
        END;
      ELSE IF (InCSet(pchar,numbers))
            OR (pchar = ' ') OR (pchar = '+') OR (pchar = '-')
            OR (pchar = ':') OR (pchar = '.')
        THEN
          ok:=TRUE;
          IF (pchar = '.')
            THEN IF (fldprec = 0)
              THEN ok:=FALSE;
              END;
            END;
          IF (ok)
            THEN IF (curclmn > fldclmn+1)
              THEN IF (image[mc*(fldline-1)+curclmn-1].chrbyte = '+')
                      OR (image[mc*(fldline-1)+curclmn-1].chrbyte = '-')
                THEN IF (image[mc*(fldline-1)+curclmn-2].chrbyte <> ' ')
                  THEN ok:=FALSE;
                  END;
                END;
              END;
            END;
          IF (ok) AND ((pchar = '-') OR (pchar = '+')
                                    OR (pchar = '.') OR (pchar =':'))
            THEN
              i:=fldclmn;
              WHILE (i < fldclmn+fldlen) AND (ok) DO
                IF (image[mc*(fldline-1)+i].chrbyte = pchar)
                  THEN ok:=FALSE
                  ELSE INC(i);
                  END;
                END;
            END;
        ELSE ok:=FALSE
        END;
      END;
    END;
  END;
  RETURN ok;
  END CanPChr;

PROCEDURE ClrFld(mc,ml:CARDINAL;VAR image:SMAP;
                    VAR box:BOXDEF;VAR fld:FLDDEF);
```

Fig. 14-12 continued

```
VAR
  i:CARDINAL;
BEGIN
  WITH fld DO
    IF (alptype IN fldtype)
      THEN FOR i:=fldclmn TO fldclmn+fldlen-1 DO
        image[mc*(fldline-1)+i].chrbyte:=' '
        END;
      ELSE FOR i:=fldclmn TO fldclmn+fldlen-1 DO
        IF (i <> fldlen-fldprec)
          THEN image[mc*(fldline-1)+i].chrbyte:=' ';
          END;
        END;
      END;
    END;
  ShowFld(mc,ml,image,box,fld);
  END ClrFld;


PROCEDURE DoDelete(mc,ml:CARDINAL;VAR image:SMAP;
                   VAR box:BOXDEF;VAR fld:FLDDEF;VAR curclmn:CARDINAL);
BEGIN
  WITH fld DO
    IF (alptype IN fldtype)
      THEN ShftLFld(mc,ml,image,fldline,curclmn,fldclmn+fldlen-1)
      ELSE IF (curclmn < fldclmn+fldlen-fldprec-1)
        THEN ShftRFld(mc,ml,image,fldline,fldclmn,curclmn)
        ELSE ShftLFld(mc,ml,image,fldline,curclmn,fldclmn+fldlen-1);
        END;
      END;
    END;
  ShowFld(mc,ml,image,box,fld);
  END DoDelete;


PROCEDURE PutChar(mc,ml:CARDINAL;VAR image:SMAP;
                  VAR boxes:BDTBL;VAR flds:FDTBL;
                  VAR curbox,curfld,curline,curclmn:CARDINAL;
                  pchar:CHAR;VAR insrtchr:BOOLEAN):BOOLEAN;
VAR
  bumpcursor:INTEGER;
  d:DWPTR;
BEGIN
  WITH flds[curfld] DO
    IF (insrtchr)
      THEN ShftRFld(mc,ml,image,fldline,curclmn,fldclmn+fldlen-1);
      END;
    IF (curclmn+1 = fldclmn+fldlen)
      THEN bumpcursor:=-1
      ELSE bumpcursor:=1;
      END;
    image[mc*(fldline-1)+curclmn].chrbyte:=pchar;
    END;
  IF (insrtchr)
    THEN ShowFld(mc,ml,image,boxes[curbox],flds[curfld])
    ELSE WITH flds[curfld] DO
      WITH boxes[curbox] DO
      d:=DsplyWrd(fldline+fslib-cfmlibos,curclmn+fscib-cfmcibos,wrkframe);
      d^.chrbyte:=image[mc*(flds[curfld].fldline-1)+curclmn].chrbyte;
      END;
      END;
    END;
  IF (bumpcursor = -1)
```

```
        THEN
          insrtchr:=FALSE;
        IF (numtype IN flds[curfld].fldtype)
          THEN
            AlignNum(mc,ml,image,flds[curfld]);
            ShowFld(mc,ml,image,boxes[curbox],flds[curfld]);
          END;
        RETURN TRUE;
      ELSE
        IF (bumpcursor > 0)
          THEN
            curclmn:=curclmn+CARDINAL(bumpcursor);
            WITH boxes[curbox] DO
             PstnCur(curline+fslib-cfmlibos,curclmn+fscib-cfmcibos,wrkframe);
            END;
        END;
      RETURN FALSE;
    END;
  END PutChar;

PROCEDURE ScrlScrn (mc,ml:CARDINAL;VAR image:SMAP;
                      VAR showblst:FLPTR;VAR boxes:BDTBL;
                       VAR curbox,curfld:CARDINAL;VAR flds:FDTBL;
                        hortab:CHAR):BOOLEAN;
TYPE
  DIRECTION = (up,down,left,right);

  PROCEDURE OnScrn(VAR box:BOXDEF;VAR fld:FLDDEF;
                        VAR scrldir:DIRECTION):BOOLEAN;
  BEGIN
    WITH box DO
      WITH fld DO
        IF (fldline >= cfmlibos)
          THEN IF (fldline < cfmlibos + nslib)
            THEN IF (fldclmn >= cfmcibos)
              THEN IF (fldclmn+fldlen <= cfmcibos+nscib)
                THEN RETURN TRUE;
                ELSE scrldir:=right;
                END;
              ELSE scrldir:=left;
              END;
            ELSE scrldir:=down;
            END;
          ELSE scrldir:=up;
          END;
        END;
      END;
    RETURN FALSE;
    END OnScrn;
VAR
  cursb,i:CARDINAL;
  scrldir:DIRECTION;
  gotcha,horchg,verchg,done:BOOLEAN;
BEGIN
  horchg:=FALSE;
  verchg:=FALSE;
  cursb:=1;done:=FALSE;
  WHILE (cursb <= showblst^[0]) AND (NOT done) DO
    IF (curbox = showblst^[cursb])
      THEN done:=TRUE
      ELSE INC(cursb);
      END;
```

Fig. 14-12 continued

```
      END;
  IF (NOT done)
    THEN Cancel(Literal(' ScrlScrn'),nullstr,1,0);
    END;
  WHILE (NOT OnScrn(boxes[showblst^[cursb]],flds[curfld],scrldir)) DO
    WITH boxes[showblst^[cursb]] DO
      CASE scrldir OF
        up:
           DEC(cfmlibos);
           verchg:=TRUE;
      ! down:
           INC(cfmlibos);
           verchg:=TRUE;
      ! left:
           horchg:=TRUE;
           cfmcibos:=flds[curfld].fldclmn;
           WHILE(cfmcibos > fmcib)
               AND
               (image[mc*(flds[curfld].fldline-1)+cfmcibos].chrbyte
                             <> hortab) DO
             DEC(cfmcibos);
             END;
      ! right:
           horchg:=TRUE;
           cfmcibos:=cfmcibos+flds[curfld].fldlen;
           WHILE (cfmcibos < fmcib+nmcib-1)
                 AND
               (image[mc*(flds[curfld].fldline-1)+cfmcibos].chrbyte
                           <> hortab) DO
             INC(cfmcibos);
             END;
        END;
      END;
    END;
  IF (verchg) OR (horchg)
    THEN FOR i:=1 TO showblst^[0] DO
      gotcha:=FALSE;
      IF (verchg) AND (boxes[showblst^[i]].cfmlibos > 0)
          AND (boxes[showblst^[i]].fmlib = boxes[showblst^[cursb]].fmlib)
        THEN
          gotcha:=TRUE;
          boxes[showblst^[i]].cfmlibos:=boxes[showblst^[cursb]].cfmlibos;
        END;
      IF (horchg) AND (boxes[showblst^[i]].cfmcibos > 0)
          AND (boxes[showblst^[i]].fmcib = boxes[showblst^[cursb]].fmcib)
        THEN
          gotcha:=TRUE;
          boxes[showblst^[i]].cfmcibos:=boxes[showblst^[cursb]].cfmcibos;
        END;
      IF (gotcha)
        THEN WITH boxes[showblst^[i]] DO
          ShowScrn(image,ml,mc,cfmlibos,cfmcibos,fslib,fscib,nslib,nscib);
          END;
        END;
      END;
    END;
  IF (horchg) OR (verchg)
    THEN RETURN TRUE;
    ELSE RETURN FALSE;
    END;
  END ScrlScrn;
```

```
PROCEDURE ChgCAtt (VAR box:BOXDEF;VAR fld:FLDDEF;setcolor:BYTE);
VAR
   i,cl,cc:CARDINAL;
   d:DWPTR;
BEGIN
   cl:=fld.fldline+box.fslib-box.cfmlibos;
   cc:=fld.fldclmn+box.fscib-box.cfmcibos;
   FOR i:=0 TO fld.fldlen-1 DO
     d:=DsplyWrd(cl,cc+i,wrkframe);
     d^.colbyte:=setcolor;
     END;
   END ChgCAtt;


PROCEDURE SetCur(mc,ml:CARDINAL;VAR image:SMAP;VAR fld:FLDDEF;
                              fromleft:BOOLEAN):CARDINAL;
VAR
   i:CARDINAL;
   lastblank:BOOLEAN;
BEGIN
   WITH fld DO
     IF (fromleft)
       THEN RETURN fldclmn;
       ELSE
         lastblank:=FALSE;
         i:=fldlen-1;
         WHILE (i > 0) AND (NOT lastblank) DO
           IF (image[mc*(fldline-1)+fldclmn+i-1].chrbyte = ' ')
             THEN DEC(i);
             ELSE IF (numtype IN fldtype)
               THEN IF (image[mc*(fldline-1)+fldclmn+i-1].chrbyte = altdec)
                 THEN DEC(i);
                 ELSE lastblank:=TRUE;
                 END;
               ELSE lastblank:=TRUE;
               END;
             END;
           END;
         RETURN fldclmn+i;
       END;
     END;
   END SetCur;


PROCEDURE EnterFld(mc,ml:CARDINAL;VAR image:SMAP;VAR showblst:FLPTR;
                     VAR boxes:BDTBL;VAR flds:FDTBL;
                       VAR curbox,curtab,curfld,curline,curclmn:CARDINAL;
                         hlclr:BYTE;hortab:CHAR;fromleft:BOOLEAN);
VAR
BEGIN
   curfld:=boxes[curbox].tabs.ptr^[curtab];
   junk:=ScrlScrn(mc,ml,image,showblst,boxes,curbox,curfld,flds,hortab);
   WITH flds[curfld] DO
     ChgCAtt(boxes[curbox],flds[curfld],hlclr);
     curline:=fldline;
     END;
   curclmn:=SetCur(mc,ml,image,flds[curfld],fromleft);
   WITH boxes[curbox] DO
     PstnCur(curline+fslib-cfmlibos,curclmn+fscib-cfmcibos,wrkframe);
     END;
   END EnterFld;


PROCEDURE LeaveFld(mc,ml:CARDINAL;VAR image:SMAP;VAR boxes:BDTBL;
                     VAR flds:FDTBL;curbox,curfld:CARDINAL);
```

Fig. 14-12 continued

```
VAR
   i,cl,cc:CARDINAL;
BEGIN
   ChgCAtt(boxes[curbox],flds[curfld],
           image[mc*(flds[curfld].fldline-1)+flds[curfld].fldclmn].colbyte);
   IF (numtype IN flds[curfld].fldtype)
      THEN
         AlignNum(mc,ml,image,flds[curfld]);
         ShowFld(mc,ml,image,boxes[curbox],flds[curfld])
      END;
   END LeaveFld;


PROCEDURE ChgBox(mc,ml:CARDINAL;VAR image:SMAP;VAR showblst:FLPTR;
                    VAR boxes:BDTBL;VAR flds:FDTBL;VAR newbox,curtab:CARDINAL;
                       oldbox,lastfld:CARDINAL;hortab:CHAR):BOOLEAN;
VAR
   junk:BOOLEAN;
   oldfld:CARDINAL;
BEGIN
   IF (oldbox > 0)
      THEN
         oldfld:=boxes[oldbox].tabs.ptr^[1];
         LeaveFld(mc,ml,image,boxes,flds,oldbox,lastfld);
         junk:=ScrlScrn(mc,ml,image,showblst,boxes,oldbox,oldfld,flds,hortab);
      END;
   IF (newbox = 0)
      THEN RETURN FALSE
      ELSE
         curtab:=0;
         RETURN CanRTab(FALSE,boxes[newbox],flds,curtab);
      END;
   END ChgBox;


PROCEDURE ReadScrn(VAR thisscrn:ADDRESS;VAR showblst,readblst:FLPTR;
                          frstbox:CARDINAL;VAR lastbox:CARDINAL;
                          frstfld:CARDINAL;VAR lastfld:CARDINAL;
                          oktochg:BOOLEAN;VAR chgd:BOOLEAN;
                    VAR normals,easciis:CHARSET;hlclr:BYTE;hortab:CHAR;
                    VAR eascii:BOOLEAN;VAR kbchar:CHAR);
VAR
   s:SDPTR;
   xmttabok,eor,insrtchr,done,blkfld,chgfld,fromleft:BOOLEAN;
   ok,showall,foundfld:BOOLEAN;
   currb,curline,curclmn,curtab,holdtab,i:CARDINAL;
   tempfld,helpname,inxname:STRING;

PROCEDURE Control(showblst,readblst:FLPTR;VAR thisscrn:ADDRESS;
               mc,ml:CARDINAL;VAR image:SMAP;VAR boxes:BDTBL;VAR flds:FDTBL;
               frstbos:CARDINAL;VAR lastbox:CARDINAL;
               frstfld:CARDINAL;VAR lastfld:CARDINAL;
               oktochg:BOOLEAN;VAR chgd:BOOLEAN;
            VAR xmttabok,insrtchr,chgfld,fromleft:BOOLEAN;
               helpname,inxname:STRING;
            hlclr:BYTE;kbchar,hortab:CHAR):BOOLEAN;
VAR
   didit:BOOLEAN;
BEGIN
   didit:=TRUE;chgfld:=FALSE;fromleft:=TRUE;
   IF (kbchar <> insr) AND (kbchar <> bksp)
      AND (kbchar <> curl) AND (kbchar <> curr) AND (kbchar <> help)
      THEN insrtchr:=FALSE;
```

```
     END;
CASE kbchar OF
  help:Help(helpname,inxname,lastfld,hlpframe);
! xmtcntrl:xmttabok:=(NOT xmttabok);
! curl:IF (curclmn > flds[lastfld].fldclmn)
    THEN MoveCur(boxes[lastbox],curline,curclmn,-1)
    ELSE IF (CanLTab(xmttabok,boxes[lastbox],flds,curtab))
      THEN
        insrtchr:=FALSE;
        chgfld:=TRUE;
      ELSE didit:=FALSE;
      END;
    END;
! curr:IF (curclmn < flds[lastfld].fldclmn + flds[lastfld].fldlen-1)
    THEN MoveCur(boxes[lastbox],curline,curclmn,1)
    ELSE IF (CanRTab(xmttabok,boxes[lastbox],flds,curtab))
      THEN
        insrtchr:=FALSE;
        chgfld:=TRUE;
      ELSE didit:=FALSE;
      END;
    END;
! tabr,rtab: IF (CanRTab(xmttabok,boxes[lastbox],flds,curtab))
    THEN chgfld:=TRUE
    ELSE didit:=FALSE;
    END;
! tabl,ltab:IF (CanLTab(xmttabok,boxes[lastbox],flds,curtab))
    THEN chgfld:=TRUE
    ELSE didit:=FALSE;
    END;
! utab:IF (CanUTab(xmttabok,boxes[lastbox],flds,curtab,curclmn))
    THEN chgfld:=TRUE
    ELSE didit:=FALSE;
    END;
! dtab:IF (CanDTab(xmttabok,boxes[lastbox],flds,curtab,curclmn))
    THEN chgfld:=TRUE
    ELSE didit:=FALSE;
    END;
! home:IF (CanHCur(xmttabok,boxes[lastbox],flds,curtab))
    THEN chgfld:=TRUE
    ELSE didit:=FALSE;
    END;
! end:IF (CanECur(xmttabok,boxes[lastbox],flds,curtab))
    THEN chgfld:=TRUE
    ELSE didit:=FALSE;
    END;
! boxu:
    frstbox:=lastbox;
    IF (NOT CanUBox(boxes,readblst,currb,lastbox,xmttabok,flds))
      THEN didit:=FALSE
      ELSE IF (NOT ChgBox(mc,ml,image,showblst,boxes,
                          flds,lastbox,curtab,frstbox,lastfld,hortab))
        THEN didit:=FALSE
        ELSE
          lastfld:=0;
          chgfld:=TRUE;
          didit:=TRUE;
        END;
      END;
! boxd:
    frstbox:=lastbox;
    IF (NOT CanDBox(boxes,readblst,currb,lastbox,xmttabok,flds))
```

Fig. 14-12 continued

```
          THEN didit:=FALSE
          ELSE IF (NOT ChgBox(mc,ml,image,showblst,boxes,
                              flds,lastbox,curtab,frstbox,lastfld,hortab))
            THEN didit:=FALSE
            ELSE
               lastfld:=0;
               chgfld:=TRUE;
               didit:=TRUE;
            END;
          END;
  ! cr:
      foundfld:=FALSE;
      i:=curtab;done:=FALSE;
      WHILE (NOT done) AND (NOT foundfld) DO
        IF (CanRTab(xmttabok,boxes[lastbox],flds,i))
          THEN IF (flds[boxes[lastbox].tabs.ptr^[i]].fldline > curline)
            THEN foundfld:=TRUE
            ELSE done:=FALSE
            END;
          ELSE done:=TRUE;
          END;
        END;
      IF (NOT foundfld)
        THEN didit:=FALSE
        ELSE
          curtab:=i;
          chgfld:=TRUE;
        END;
  ! insr:IF (NOT oktochg)
      THEN didit:=FALSE
      ELSE insrtchr:=(NOT insrtchr);
      END;
    ELSE IF (NOT oktochg)
      THEN didit:=FALSE
      ELSE
        chgd:=TRUE;
        INCL(flds[lastfld].fldtype,changed);
        CASE kbchar OF
          bksp:IF (insrtchr)
            THEN
              didit:=FALSE;
              DoDelete(mc,ml,image,boxes[lastbox],flds[lastfld],curclmn)
            ELSE
              IF (curclmn+1 = flds[lastfld].fldclmn+flds[lastfld].fldlen)
                AND (image[mc*(flds[lastfld].fldline-1) +
                               curclmn].chrbyte <> ' ')
          THEN done:=TRUE
          ELSE done:=FALSE;
          END;
        IF (NOT done)
          THEN IF (curclmn > flds[lastfld].fldclmn)
            THEN
              MoveCur(boxes[lastbox],curline,curclmn,-1);
              done:=TRUE;
            ELSE IF (CanLTab(xmttabok,boxes[lastbox],flds,curtab))
              THEN
                chgfld:=TRUE;
                fromleft:=FALSE;
                done:=TRUE;
              END;
            END;
```

```
              END;
         IF (NOT done)
            THEN didit:=FALSE
            ELSE
               image[mc*(flds[lastfld].fldline-1)+curclmn].chrbyte
                                       :=' ';
               ShowFld(mc,ml,image,boxes[lastbox],flds[lastfld]);
            END;
      END;
!
  del:
    didit:=TRUE;
    DoDelete(mc,ml,image,
                    boxes[lastbox],flds[lastfld],curclmn);
!
  clearfld:
    ClrFld(mc,ml,image,boxes[lastbox],flds[lastfld]);
    chgfld:=TRUE
  ELSE
    holdtab:=curtab;
    showall:=FALSE;
    CASE kbchar OF
      dittokey:IF (CanUTab(xmttabok,boxes[lastbox],
                                    flds,curtab,curclmn))
        THEN
          MakeStr(tempfld,flds[boxes[lastbox].tabs.
                         ptr^[holdtab]].fldlen,nullstr);
          GetFld(boxes[lastbox].tabs.ptr^[curtab],
                         tempfld,thisscrn);
          PutFld(boxes[lastbox].tabs.ptr^[holdtab],
                         tempfld,thisscrn);
          ClearStr(tempfld);
          showall:=TRUE;
        END;
     ! allditto:
          MakeStr(tempfld,flds[lastfld].fldlen,nullstr);
          GetFld(lastfld,tempfld,thisscrn);
          blkfld:=IsBlank(mc,ml,image,flds[lastfld]);
          done:=FALSE;
          WHILE (NOT done) DO
            IF (CanDTab(xmttabok,boxes[lastbox],
                                 flds,curtab,curclmn))
               THEN IF (IsBlank(mc,ml,image,
                          flds[boxes[lastbox].tabs.ptr^[curtab]])
                          = blkfld)
            THEN done:=TRUE
            ELSE PutFld(boxes[lastbox].tabs.
                          ptr^[curtab],tempfld,thisscrn)
            END;
          ELSE done:=TRUE;
          END;
        END;
      showall:=TRUE;
    ClearStr(tempfld);
! nextval:IF (NOT (numtype IN flds[boxes[lastbox].tabs.
                                 ptr^[holdtab]].fldtype))
    THEN didit:=FALSE
    ELSE IF (NOT CanUTab(xmttabok,
                 boxes[lastbox],flds,curtab,curclmn))
      THEN didit:=FALSE
      ELSE IF (NOT (numtype IN flds[boxes[lastbox].tabs.
                                 ptr^[holdtab]].fldtype))
```

Fig. 14-12 continued

```
            THEN didit:=FALSE
            ELSE IF (flds[boxes[lastbox].tabs.
                                  ptr^[curtab]].fldlen
                 <>  flds[boxes[lastbox].tabs.
                                  ptr^[holdtab]].fldlen)
              THEN didit:=FALSE
              ELSE
                MakeStr(tempfld,flds[boxes[lastbox].
                              tabs.ptr^[curtab]].fldlen,nullstr);
                GetFld(boxes[lastbox].tabs.ptr^[curtab],
                              tempfld,thisscrn);
                IncFld(tempfld);
                PutFld(boxes[lastbox].tabs.ptr^[holdtab],
                              tempfld,thisscrn);
                showall:=TRUE;
                ClearStr(tempfld);
              END;
            END;
          END;
        END;
  | seqval:IF (NOT (numtype IN flds[boxes[lastbox].tabs.
                                  ptr^[holdtab]].fldtype))
        THEN didit:=FALSE
        ELSE
          MakeStr(tempfld,flds[lastfld].fldlen,nullstr);
          GetFld(lastfld,tempfld,thisscrn);
          done:=FALSE;
          WHILE (NOT done) DO
            IF (NOT CanDTab(xmttabok,boxes[lastbox],
                              flds,curtab,curclmn))
              THEN done:=TRUE
              ELSE IF (NOT IsBlank(mc,ml,image,
                            flds[boxes[lastbox].tabs.
                                  ptr^[curtab]]))
                THEN done:=TRUE
                ELSE
                  IncFld(tempfld);
                  PutFld(boxes[lastbox].tabs.
                              ptr^[curtab],tempfld,thisscrn);
                END;
              END;
            END;
          showall:=TRUE;
                  ClearStr(tempfld);
                END;
              ELSE
                didit:=FALSE;
              END;
            IF (showall)
              THEN
                chgfld:=TRUE;
                ShowBox(thisscrn,showblst);
              END;
            curtab:=holdtab;
          END;
      END;
    END;
  RETURN didit;
  END Control;

BEGIN     (* - R E A D S C R N - *)
```

```
eor:=FALSE;
xmttabok:=FALSE;
insrtchr:=FALSE;
chgd:=FALSE;
s:=thisscrn;
MakeStr(helpname,255,nullstr);
MakeStr(inxname,255,nullstr);
IF (FindParm(s^.dd,helpname))
   THEN
     i:=Positn(Literal('.'),helpname,1);
     IF (i > 0)
       THEN Delete(helpname,i,StrLen(helpname)-i+1);
       END;
     CopyStr(helpname,inxname);
     Concat(Literal('.HLP'),helpname);
     Concat(Literal('.INX'),inxname);
   END;
WITH s^ DO
   IF (frstbox = 0)
     THEN
       currb:=1;
       lastbox:=readblst^[1];
     ELSE
       currb:=1;done:=FALSE;
       lastbox:=frstbox;
       WHILE (currb <= readblst^[0]) AND (NOT done) DO
         IF (frstbox = readblst^[currb])
           THEN done:=TRUE
           ELSE currb:=currb+1;
           END;
         END;
       IF (NOT done)
         THEN Cancel(Literal('ReadScrn'),nullstr,1,1);
         END;
     END;
   IF (NOT ChgBox(smmc,smml,sm^,showblst,bx^,ct^,lastbox,curtab,
                               frstbox,0,hortab))
     THEN Cancel(Literal('ReadScrn'),nullstr,1,3);
     END;
   IF (frstfld = 0)
     THEN
       curtab:=0;
       IF (NOT CanRTab(FALSE,bx^[readblst^[currb]],ct^,curtab))
       THEN IF (NOT CanRTab(TRUE,bx^[readblst^[currb]],ct^,curtab))
         THEN Cancel(Literal('ReadScrn'),nullstr,1,0);
         END;
       END;
     frstfld:=bx^[readblst^[currb]].tabs.ptr^[curtab];
   ELSE
     curtab:=1;done:=FALSE;
     WHILE (curtab <= bx^[lastbox].tabs.maxtabs) AND (NOT done) DO
       IF (frstfld = bx^[lastbox].tabs.ptr^[curtab])
         THEN done:=TRUE
         ELSE curtab:=curtab+1;
         END;
       END;
     IF (NOT done)
       THEN Cancel(Literal('ReadScrn'),nullstr,1,2);
       END;
   END;
EnterFld(smmc,smml,sm^,showblst,bx^,ct^,lastbox,curtab,lastfld,
             curline,curclmn,hlclr,hortab,TRUE);
```

Fig. 14-12 continued

```
REPEAT
  chgfld:=FALSE;
  REPEAT
    UNTIL (GetKBChr(eascii,kbchar));
  IF (InCSet(kbchar,normals) AND (NOT eascii))
            OR            (InCSet(kbchar,easciis) AND (eascii))
    THEN
      eor:=TRUE;
      ok:=TRUE;
      chgfld:=TRUE;
    ELSE IF (InCSet(kbchar,ncntrl) AND (NOT eascii))
            OR                (InCSet(kbchar,ecntrl) AND (eascii))
      THEN ok:=Control(showblst,readblst,thisscrn,
                  smmc,smml,sm^,bx^,ct^,
                  frstbox,lastbox,frstfld,lastfld,
                  oktochg,chgd,xmttabok,insrtchr,
                  chgfld,fromleft,helpname,inxname,
                  hlclr,kbchar,hortab)
      ELSE IF (NOT oktochg)
        THEN ok:=FALSE
        ELSE IF (eascii)
          THEN ok:=FALSE
          ELSE
            ok:=CanPChr(smmc,smml,sm^,ct^[lastfld],
                                      curline,curclmn,kbchar);
            IF (ok)
              THEN
                chgd:=TRUE;
                INCL(ct^[lastfld].fldtype,changed);
                IF (PutChar(smmc,smml,sm^,bx^,ct^,lastbox,lastfld,
                                  curline,curclmn,kbchar,insrtchr))
                  THEN
                    chgfld:=CanRTab(xmttabok,bx^[lastbox],ct^,curtab);
                  END;
              END;
          END;
        END;
      END;
    END;
  IF (NOT ok)
    THEN
      Sound(errfreq,errdur);
      FlushKB;
    ELSE IF (chgfld)
      THEN
        IF (lastfld > O)
          THEN LeaveFld(smmc,smml,sm^,bx^,ct^,lastbox,lastfld);
          END;
        IF (NOT eor)
          THEN EnterFld(smmc,smml,sm^,showblst,bx^,ct^,
                        lastbox,curtab,lastfld,curline,curclmn,
                        hlclr,hortab,fromleft);
          END;
      END;
    END;
  UNTIL (eor);
  END;
ClearStr(helpname);
ClearStr(inxname);
END ReadScrn;
```

```
CONST
  T1 = 'The Etling Library';
  T2 = 'All programs and modules, Copyright (c) 1986 TAB BOOKS INC.';
  T3 = 'Author: Don Etling';
VAR
  wrkframe:FRAME;
  e:ARRAY [1..20] OF CHAR;
  n:ARRAY [1..4] OF CHAR;
  i:CARDINAL;
BEGIN
  i:=19;
  MovByteL(i,n,0,0,2);
  e[1]:=tab1;        e[2]:=rtab;       e[3]:=ltab;      e[4]:=utab;
  e[5]:=dtab;        e[6]:=home;       e[7]:=end;       e[8]:=boxu;
  e[9]:=boxd;        e[10]:=curl;      e[11]:=curr;     e[12]:=insr;
  e[13]:=del;        e[14]:=allditto;  e[15]:=nextval;  e[16]:=dittokey;
  e[17]:=xmtcntrl;   e[18]:=clearfld;  e[19]:=seqval;   e[20]:=help;
  MakeCSet(Literal(e),ecntrl);
  n[1]:=tabr;   n[2]:=cr;   n[3]:=bksp;   n[4]:=esc;
  MakeCSet(Literal(n),ncntrl);
  wrkframe.fl:=1;    wrkframe.fc:=1;    wrkframe.ll:=23;   wrkframe.lc:=80;
  wrkframe.cl:=1;    wrkframe.cc:=1;    wrkframe.nl:=23;   wrkframe.nc:=80;
  wrkframe.s :=crtads;
  hlpframe.fl:=24;   hlpframe.fc:=1;    hlpframe.ll:=25;   hlpframe.lc:=80;
  hlpframe.cl:=24;   hlpframe.cc:=1;    hlpframe.nl:=2;    hlpframe.nc:=80;
  hlpframe.s :=crtads;

END EL1412.
```

otherwise, it must be turned off. The rest of the routine looks complicated, but is in reality three large nested CASE statements. If the character is one of the values that do not change the contents of a field (i.e., *help, xmtcntrl,* etc.), the first part of the CASE statement determines what to do. Otherwise, if the character indicates some change to a single field and the user is permitted to change the contents of a field (*oktochg* is equal to TRUE), the second CASE statement gets control. If the changes involves multiple fields, the third CASE statement handles that. If the operation is successful, *Control* will return equal to TRUE.

Moving the Cursor

The characters that control cursor movement within a deScreen fall into three different categories: keys that move between boxes, keys that move between fields, and keys that move within fields. Because the routines in each category use routines in the other, we'll look at the last category first.

MoveCur. *Control* recognizes two control characters that cause the cursor to move one position *without* destroying the contents of the current field (as backspace or forward space would do). These characters are the *curl* and *curr* characters. If the user presses one of these keys, *Control* will determine if the resulting movement would cause the cursor to leave the current field. If so, *Control* will call *CanRTab* or *CanLTab* to make certain the move is legitimate. If the movement does not require the cursor to leave the field. *Control* will call *MoveCur* to set the cursor to its new position, both on the display and in the SCREENMAP.

Changing Fields

There are several routines involved with moving the deScreen cursor from one field to another. Such movement, whether caused by the user entering a control key or invoked automatically when the current field is full, is divided into two distinct steps. First, *Control* verifies that there is indeed another field in the current box to which the cursor can be moved (if not, *Sound* is called to alert the user). Second, if there is a field in the proper direction, *Control* sets *chgfld* to cause *ReadScrn* to make the switch.

CanDTab, CanLTab, CanRTab, and CanUTab. There are four directions that the cursor could move, so there are four routines that make certain a move is possible. All four routines operate similarly. Each of these routines can be invoked in response to the user entering the corresponding key. *CanDTab* is related to the *dtab* key (Shift–Number Pad 2); *CanLTab* is the *tabl* (Shift Tab) or *ltab* (Shift–number pad 4); *CanRTab* is *tabr* (normal tab) or *rtab* (Shift–number pad 6); and *CanUTab* is *utab* (Shift–number pad 8).

In all cases, if the cursor is already at the appropriate boundary of the list of fields that the SCRNDEF array named *box.tabs* contains, the routines will return FALSE immediately. Otherwise, the routines will increment or decrement an index into the array until the boundary is reached or another field is found. Note that *CanDTab* and *CanUTab* look for a field on another line that would contain the column indicated by the current cursor position; on the other hand, *CanRTab* and *CanLTab* will simply move through the list of fields. *CanRTab* (or *CanLTab*) might wind up in the first (or last) field of the next (or previous) line. Note that these routines will only permit access to a transmit only field if *xmttabok* = TRUE.

CanECur and CanHCur. If the user enters an *endt* (Shift–number pad 1) or *home* (Shift–number pad 7) character, *Control* will call one of these routines. *CanECur* will attempt to set the value of *curtab* to the last field in the current box; *CanHCur* will use the first field in the current box. These routines call *CanLTab* or *CanRTab* to determine if an appropriate field exists.

EnterFld and LeaveFld. There are two routines that handle moving into or out of a deScreen field. *LeaveFld* handles the exit; *EnterFld* the entrance.

EnterFld uses *curtab* to locate the value for *curfld* in the list of tabs defined for the current box. *EnterFld* then calls *ScrlScrn* to map the location of the field onto the display. Next, *EnterFld* will call *ChgCAtt* to change the color attribute to *hlclr* for all characters in the field on the display, adjust the value for *curclmn*, and position the display cursor's to the proper location.

When the deScreen routines leave a field, they call *LeaveFld*. *LEAVEFLD* uses *ChgCAtt* to change the color attribute for all characters in the field on the display back to the color of the field in the SCRNDEF's SCREENMAP. Also, if the field being left is a numeric field, *LeaveFld* will call *AlignNum* to align the field with its decimal point, and *ShowFld* to show the results of the alignment.

ScrlScrn. There is a single routine in the Etling Library that is responsible for all of the horizontal or vertical scrolling that a deScreen is capable of doing. That routine is called *ScrlScrn*. When *ScrlScrn* is called, the value of *curfld* indicates the number of the field into which the cursor is about to be positioned. *ScrlScrn* has an internal routine, *OnScrn*, that it uses to determine which direction the current box must be moved in order to show that field on the display. *OnScrn* will signal a move in only one direction at a time, so several calls might be required before the correct position is determined. Once the move is established, *ScrlScrn* goes through the list of boxes on the screen (contained in *showblst*) and adjusts the values for *cfmlibos* and *cfmcibos* accordingly. The appropriate portion of each box is then shown on the display using *ShowScrn*.

Note that *ScrlScrn* uses the upper left corner of each box to determine whether or not a given box should participate in the scroll. Boxes that start on the same line (in the SCRNDEF's SCREENMAP) will all scroll vertically at the same time; boxes that begin in the same column will scroll horizontally at the same time. In the Soccer Team Registration form .DEF file, shown back in Fig. 14-4, box number 1 is intentionally begun in SCREENMAP column 2 so that it will not scroll horizontally with the other boxes.

ChgCAtt. The deScreen routine that changes the color attribute for a field is named *ChgCAtt*. Note that it changes the color on the display, not in the SCRNDEF's SCREENMAP.

SetCur. When the cursor moves into a new field, it might or might not be positioned to the first character in the field, depending on which direction it is coming from, and the type of field into which it is moving. If the cursor is coming from the left, the cursor is positioned at the leftmost character in the new field. If the cursor is coming from the right (as would be the case if the user backspaced into the field), the cursor is set to the last non-blank character in the field. *SetCur* handles this logic. The value of *SetCur* returns equal to the new cursor column position in the SCRNDEF's SCREENMAP, not on the display.

AlignNum. When the cursor leaves a numeric field, the contents of the field must be adjusted to align the numeric value with the decimal point in the field. *AlignNum* handles this task. To simplify its operation, *AlignNum* copies the contents of the field into a STRING character by character, inserts whatever characters are required to fill the field with zeros (on either side of the decimal point) and then copies the field back to the SCREENMAP.

ShowFld. If one of the *Control* operations results in the contents of a field begin changed, the operation only changes the contents of the field in the SCRNDEF's SCREENMAP. To change the contents of the field on the display, the routine will call *ShowFld*. It moves the characters (not the colors) from the SCREENMAP to the display, one character at a time.

Changing boxes

The TESTSCRN program, described earlier in this chapter, allows you to move between boxes, but in general I recommend that you avoid designing deScreens that use this option. It seems to confuse most users. If you do implement a system that gives the user access to multiple boxes at the same time, the *boxu* (Shift – number pad 9) and *boxd* (Shift – number pad 3) keys signal a box change. As with a field change, a box change is a two-step process.

CanDBox and CanUBox. The routines that ensure a box change is possible are named *CanDBox* and *CanUBox*. They increment or decrement an index into *readblst*, determining if another box is on the display in the appropriate direction. If there is another box, they will call *CanRTab* to enter the new box at the first field. (Note that *both* routines start at the first field in the new box.)

ChgBox. After Control uses *CanUBox* or *CanDBox* to determine if another box is included in *readblst,* it calls the routine named *ChgBox* to actually move the cursor into the new box. This routine is also used directly by *ReadScrn* to define the first box to access.

If *ChgBox* is called with *oldbox* greater than zero, the routine calls *LeaveFld* to move the cursor out of the field it was in, and then calls *ScrlScrn* to reposition the old box on the display. If *newbox* is greater than zero, *ChgBox* will call *CanRTab* to locate the first field in the new box.

Moving Down a Line

When filling out a form, a user might not always have all of the data for every field on each line. For example, in completing the Soccer Registration Form in Fig. 14-1, the user might not have addresses for each player. One way to skip over fields using the deScreen routines is to simple press the *tabr* character once for each field. Because the fields to be skipped are at the end of a line, a simpler way to skip them all is to press the *enter* key. When *Control* recognizes the *cr* character, it automatically invokes *CanRTab* until it encounters a field that is on the next line. The cursor is relocated to the left-most field on the line following the original.

Changing the Contents of a Field

The routines discussed so far in connection with the *Control* routine do not affect the contents of a field in a deScreen; they only move from one location to another. If, on entry to *ReadScrn* and subsequently on entry to *Control,* the parameter named *oktochg* is FALSE, that is all the user is permitted to do; move the cursor around on the screen. If, on entry, *oktochg* equals TRUE, the user may also change the contents of fields. The routines that enter characters are discussed in the Entering Characters Section later in this chapter, but there are some other operations in *Control* that can affect a field's contents.

One key is actually more of a "toggle" (similar to the *xmtcntrl* key). When the user presses the *insr* key (Shift–Number Pad 0) on the keyboard, *Control* says insrtchr = NOT insrtchr If *insrtchr* ends up TRUE, then as long as the cursor stays within the same field, any new characters will be inserted in the middle of the field at the current cursor position. Characters to the right of the cursor will be shifted right to make room for the new character.

Deleting Characters

There are three ways in which the user can delete characters from an existing field. If, while typing data, the user makes an obvious mistake and presses the wrong key, he or she can immediately erase the incorrect character by pressing the backspace key. The backspace key deletes the character to the left of the cursor and moves the cursor over one position. The other control characters invoke routines that implement their operation.

DoDelete. If the user presses the *del* key (Shift–Number Pad period), *Control* calls *DoDelete* to delete the character at the current cursor position. *DoDelete* doesn't exactly delete the character; it simply moves the rest of the characters over one position, thereby covering over the offending character. To handle the move, *DoDelete* calls either *ShftRFld* or *ShftLFld* depending on the circumstances. The contents of an alpha field are always shifted to the left (using *ShftLFld*), but the direction a numeric field is shifted depends on which side of the decimal point the cursor is on. If the cursor is to the left of the decimal, the field is shifted right; if the cursor is to the right of the decimal, the field is shifted left. Because the user might or might not have entered a decimal, and the field might or might not be aligned, using the *del* key on a numeric field does not always produce the results the user might have wanted.

ShftLFld and ShftRFLd. The routines that move the contents of a field left and right are named *ShftLFld* and *ShftRFld*, respectively. They operate only on the SCREENMAP, not on the display. Both change the original character in the last position referenced to *blank*.

ClrFld. When the user presses the *clearfld* (Alt–C) key, *Control* calls *ClrFld*. That routine sets every character in the field (in the SCREENMAP) to *blank*, except of course the decimal point in a numeric field. *ClrFld* then calls *ShowFld* to display the cleared field for the user.

Duplicating Fields

Because deScreen is built around a "form on the screen" concept, it is possible to design screens that organize fields into columns of data. (The Soccer Team Registration form contains a column of Player Pass numbers.) Sometimes the user might need to do the same operation on all of the data in a particular column. *Control* provides some of the more common data column operations using a single keystroke.

When the user presses the *dittokey* (Alt–D), *Control* will copy the contents of the field above the current field. To do this, *Control* first locates the field above by using *CanUTab*, then it calls *GetFld* and *PutFld*.

Occasionally, a user might want to replicate the contents of the current field all the way down the data column. The *allditto* key (Alt–R) will instruct *Control* to use *GetFld* to retrieve the contents of the current field; then, using *CanDTab* to locate fields on subsequent lines, it calls *PutFld* to duplicate these contents in the other fields. Note that the *allditto* key works selectively; if the current field is blank, *Control* will only duplicate the field down to the next field that is blank; if the current field is not blank, *Control* will stop duplicating when it encounters a non-blank field. This permits the user to set limits.

IsBlank. The routine that determines if a specific field contains nothing but blanks (or the decimal point, if the field is numeric) is called *IsBlank*. It returns a BOOLEAN value to indicate the contents of the field.

Numbering Lines

Almost all forms that contain columns of data use one of these columns to number the lines on the form. In the Soccer Team Registration form, the line numbers are preprinted, both on the paper form and on the deScreen using a line number command. There are times when one of the columns contains numbers that might not number the line, but still are sequential from one line to the next. If, for example, the registration form was used not only to list players on a team but also to assign Player Pass Numbers, the data entered in this field would fit into this category.

The deScreen routines provide several convenient ways to enter data into such a field. The *nextval* (Alt–I) key causes *Control* to use *GetFld* to retrieve the value of the field on the line above the current field, increment its value by one, and use *PutFld* to set the value of the current field. The *seqval* (Alt–N) key tells *Control* to copy the contents of the current field all the way down the form, incrementing the value by one as it goes. Obviously, both keys are only permitted to operate on a numeric field.

IncFld. When the contents of a numeric field need to be incremented, *Control* calls *IncFld*. *IncFld* adds 1 to the ASCII contents of the field and handles all of the required carry operations.

Entering Characters

If the user presses a key that *ReadScrn* does not recognize as a control character that would invoke *Control*, *ReadScrn* assumes that the character is to be entered as data into the current cursor position of the current field. Note: *ReadScrn* first checks *oktochg*. If that parameter is FALSE, the user is not permitted to enter characters.

CanPChr. If the user is permitted to enter characters, *ReadScrn* calls *CanPChr* to make sure the character legitimately belongs in the current field. If the field is an alpha field, *CanPChr* will accept any character between ' ' and '~'. If the field is a numeric, *CanPChr* verifys that the character is indeed a numeric character and that it makes sense in light of the current contents of the field. (Only one decimal point is permitted, only one sign, etc.)

PutChar. If *CanPChr* determines that the character the user has entered does constitute a legitimate character for the current field, *ReadScrn* uses *PutChar* to move the character into the SCREENMAP and display it on the CRT. If the user has toggled *insrtchr* on, the contents of the field will be shifted right one position before the new characters is inserted. If adding the new character fills the field, *PutChar* will return to *ReadScrn* equal to TRUE. This indicates that *ReadScrn* should invoke the logic to change fields.

Providing Help

No matter how carefully you design your screen, you will never make the data required for every field obvious to every user. Sometimes you must provide a little more information. The deScreen routines have a mechanism for doing this. The user is given access to the additional help through *ReadScrn*. The first thing *ReadScrn* does is define the names of the files in which the help messages are contained. Then, whenever the user presses the *helpkey*, *Control* invokes the *Help* routine defined in the last chapter.

Reading a Partial Box

The *ReadScrn* routine provides access to all of the non-constant fields in one or more boxes. Often a program needs to restrict the user to a subset of the fields in a single box. The deScreen routine that offers this facility is named *ReadFlds*. *ReadFlds* is exported from EL1413, shown in Fig. 14-13.

Fig. 14-13. Read a list of fields.

```
DEFINITION MODULE EL1413;
   FROM SYSTEM IMPORT     BYTE,ADDRESS;
   FROM EL0501 IMPORT     CHARSET;
   FROM EL0505 IMPORT     FLPTR;
   EXPORT QUALIFIED       ReadFlds;

PROCEDURE ReadFlds(VAR thisscrn:ADDRESS;showblst:FLPTR;
                       boxnumber:CARDINAL;flds:FLPTR;
                       frstfld:CARDINAL;VAR lastfld:CARDINAL;
                       oktochg:BOOLEAN;VAR chgd:BOOLEAN;
                   VAR normals,easciis:CHARSET;hlclr:BYTE;hortab:CHAR;
                       VAR eascii:BOOLEAN;VAR kbchar:CHAR);
(* This routine gives the calling program access to a subset of the fields
   defined for a single box in the deScreen defined by thisscrn.  The
   routine operates by creating a new box with the definition defined for
   boxnumber, but with the list of fields defined by flds, and then calling
   the readscrn function.  Refer to the explanation of ReadScrn for further
   details.  *)
END EL1413.


IMPLEMENTATION MODULE EL1413;
   FROM SYSTEM IMPORT     ADDRESS,BYTE;
   FROM EL1406 IMPORT     SDPTR;
   FROM EL1412 IMPORT     ReadScrn;
   FROM EL0501 IMPORT     CHARSET;
   FROM EL0505 IMPORT     FLPTR,MakFList,ClrFList;

PROCEDURE ReadFlds(VAR thisscrn:ADDRESS;showblst:FLPTR;
                       boxnumber:CARDINAL;flds:FLPTR;
                       frstfld:CARDINAL;VAR lastfld:CARDINAL;
                       oktochg:BOOLEAN;VAR chgd:BOOLEAN;
                   VAR normals,easciis:CHARSET;hlclr:BYTE;hortab:CHAR;
                       VAR eascii:BOOLEAN;VAR kbchar:CHAR);
VAR
  p:SDPTR;
  holdtab:ADDRESS;
  holdmax,lastbox,i:CARDINAL;
  readblst:FLPTR;
BEGIN
  p:=thisscrn;
  MakFList(1,readblst);
  readblst^[1]:=boxnumber;
  holdtab:=p^.bx^[boxnumber].tabs.ptr;
  holdmax:=p^.bx^[boxnumber].tabs.maxtabs;
  FOR i:=1 TO flds^[0] DO
    p^.bx^[boxnumber].tabs.ptr^[i]:=flds^[i];
    END;
  p^.bx^[boxnumber].tabs.maxtabs:=flds^[0];
  ReadScrn(thisscrn,showblst,readblst,0,lastbox,frstfld,lastfld,
               oktochg,chgd,normals,easciis,hlclr,hortab,eascii,kbchar);
  p^.bx^[boxnumber].tabs.ptr:=holdtab;
  p^.bx^[boxnumber].tabs.maxtabs:=holdmax;
  ClrFList(readblst);
  END ReadFlds;

END EL1413.
```

ReadFlds. The *ReadFlds* routine will only operate on one box at a time, and it requires the calling program to provide it with a list of the fields within the box that it is to access. To operate, *ReadFlds* modifies the list of tabs for the box and then calls *ReadScrn* as though the box only contained the subset of fields.

Accessing Field Attributes

Because the calling program does not have access to the deScreen SCRNDEF directly, the deScreen routines include several that provide information about the SCREENMAP.

MaxFlds. *MaxFlds,* exported from EL1414, shown in Fig. 14-14, will return to the calling program with the total number of fields defined in the SCRNDEF.

FldLngth. The routine shown in Fig. 14-15 (exported from EL1415) is named *FldLngth,* and it will tell the calling program the defined length of the identified field.

FldChgd. If the user changes the contents of a field during a call to *ReadScrn* or *ReadFlds,* the routine will set a flag in the *fldtype* variable maintained for the field in the SCRNDEF. The routine exported from EL1416 and shown in Fig. 14-16, *FldChgd,* will interrogate that flag and return to the calling program with the appropriate value. Note that *FldChgd* also turns off the flag.

Reporting Errors

A standardized method for entering data should have a standardized way of telling the user when he has entered data that is in error. The deScreen routines include some standardized error-reporting routines.

First you should realize that the deScreen philosophy is built around a "head down" date-entry technique. This technique implies that the user is not necessarily

Fig. 14-14. Determine the number of fields in a deScreen.

```
DEFINITION MODULE EL1414;
   FROM SYSTEM IMPORT    ADDRESS;
   EXPORT QUALIFIED      MaxFlds;

PROCEDURE MaxFlds(VAR scrn:ADDRESS):CARDINAL;
(* This function will return the total number of fields defined for the
   deScreen definiton specified.  Note that the count includes constant
   fields as well as variable fields.  *)
END EL1414.

IMPLEMENTATION MODULE EL1414;
   FROM SYSTEM IMPORT    ADDRESS;
   FROM EL1406 IMPORT    SDPTR;

PROCEDURE MaxFlds(VAR thisscrn:ADDRESS):CARDINAL;
VAR
   p:SDPTR;
BEGIN
   p:=thisscrn;
   RETURN p^.maxfield;
   END MaxFlds;

END EL1414.
```

Fig. 14-15. Get a field's length.

```
DEFINITION MODULE EL1415;
   FROM SYSTEM IMPORT    ADDRESS;
   EXPORT QUALIFIED      FldLngth;

PROCEDURE FldLngth(fld:CARDINAL;VAR scrn:ADDRESS):CARDINAL;
(* This function will return the number of bytes in the deScreen field
   specified.  *)
END EL1415.


IMPLEMENTATION MODULE EL1415;
   FROM SYSTEM IMPORT    ADDRESS;
   FROM EL0401 IMPORT    STRING,Literal;
   FROM EL0906 IMPORT    Cancel;
   FROM EL1406 IMPORT    SDPTR;

PROCEDURE FldLngth(fld:CARDINAL;VAR thisscrn:ADDRESS):CARDINAL;
VAR
   p:SDPTR;
BEGIN
   p:=thisscrn;
   WITH p^ DO
     IF (fld < 1) OR (fld > maxfield)
       THEN Cancel(Literal(' FldLngth'),p^.dd,1,0);
       END;
     RETURN ct^[fld].fldlen;
     END;
   END FldLngth;

END EL1415.
```

looking at the display, but instead has his or her head down, copying from some document. Because of this, the types of errors that a user might make during data entry are divided into two classifications: errors that should be reported immediately, and errors that should be reported later. For errors in the first classification, the deScreen routines call *Sound* to get the user's attention. Immediate errors are errors that indicate the user has lost track of what was being entered. Trying to enter an alpha character in a numeric field, or trying to tab past the end of the box are both examples of this kind of error.

The other kind of error is an error of content: the user enters a value that, although it has the right kind of characters in the right sequence, does not constitute a valid value for the field. An example of this kind of error is when the user enters a data of 13/43/12 (the numbers are right; they just don't add up to a valid date). The deScreen routines do not detect these kinds of errors; it's up to the calling program to make sense out of the values the user enters. The deScreen routines do, however, have a standardized way of reporting these kinds of errors, and they assume that the calling program will report content errors all at the same time. The routines further assume that all of the content errors are in the same box. All of these routine are exported from EL1417, which is shown in Fig. 14-17.

FlgAsErr. After calling *ReadScrn* or *ReadFlds,* a program that uses the deScreen error-reporting routines should go through the fields in the SCREENMAP one at a time and check for content errors. Because content errors in one field might affect or be caused by the contents in another, this is often the only way of detecting certain

Fig. 14-16. Determine if a field has changed.

```
DEFINITION MODULE EL1416;
  FROM SYSTEM IMPORT    ADDRESS;
  EXPORT QUALIFIED      FldChgd;

PROCEDURE FldChgd(fldnmbr:CARDINAL;VAR thisscrn:ADDRESS):BOOLEAN;
(* This routine will return true if the flag maintained for the field in
   the specified scrn indicates that a change has been made to contents of
   the field since the last time that the flag was reset.  If no change has
   been made, the function will return false.  In either case, the field
   flag will be reset before control returns.  Note that when a screen is
   loaded, all flags are set to "No change".  *)
END EL1416.


IMPLEMENTATION MODULE EL1416;
  FROM SYSTEM IMPORT    ADDRESS;
  FROM EL0401 IMPORT    STRING,Literal;
  FROM EL0906 IMPORT    Cancel;
  FROM EL1406 IMPORT    FLDTYPES,SDPTR,changed;

PROCEDURE FldChgd(fldnmbr:CARDINAL;VAR thisscrn:ADDRESS):BOOLEAN;
VAR
  p:SDPTR;
  chgd:BOOLEAN;
BEGIN
  p:=thisscrn;
  WITH p^ DO
    IF (fldnmbr < 1) OR (fldnmbr > maxfield)
      THEN Cancel(Literal(' FldChgd'),p^.dd,1,0);
      ELSE WITH ct^[fldnmbr] DO
        IF (changed IN fldtype)
          THEN chgd:=TRUE;
          ELSE chgd:=FALSE;
          END;
        EXCL(fldtype,changed);
        RETURN chgd;
        END;
      END;
    END;
  END FldChgd;

END EL1416.
```

mistakes.) As each such error is detected, the calling program should call *FlgAsErr*. *FlgAsErr* builds a list of errors using the data types defined in Fig. 14-17. The comments in the figure explain this process.

ReDoErrs. After all of the content errors are flagged, the calling program should use *ReDoErrs* to allow the user to see and correct them. *ReDoErrs* gives the user the option of either correcting one error at a time, or dealing with the entire box at once. In the first option, *ReDoErrs* will display a message indicating the error.

ShowErrs. To draw the user's attention to the fields that are in error, *ReDoErrs* calls *ShowErrs*. *ShowErrs* does nothing more than step through the list of errors, calling *ChgColor* to change the color of each error field. Normally, *ShowErrs* uses the color attribute for *blink,* thereby making the field blink on the screen.

ClrErrs. The last routine that *ReDoErrs* calls is *ClrErrs*. *ClrErrs* will dispose of any

Fig. 14-17. Dealing with errors.

```
DEFINITION MODULE EL1417;
   FROM SYSTEM IMPORT    BYTE,ADDRESS;
   FROM EL0401 IMPORT    STRING;
   FROM EL0505 IMPORT    FLPTR;
   EXPORT QUALIFIED      ERRPTR,ERRRCRD,ERRCNTRL,STDEMSG,
                         FlgAsErr,RedoErrs,ShowErrs,ClrErrs;


TYPE
(* These definitions must be copied into any routine that uses the deScreen
   error routines.  Note that a variable of type ERRCNTRL should be
   allocated by the calling routine in such a way that it remains
   unmolested while error checking is occuring.  The field frsterr in that
   variable should be initialized to nil by the calling before the first
   call to FlgAsErr.  *)
   ERRPTR  = POINTER TO ERRRCRD;
   ERRRCRD = RECORD
      nexterr       :ERRPTR;
      fldnmbr       :CARDINAL;
      errnmbr       :CARDINAL;
      majerr        :BOOLEAN;
      END;
   ERRCNTRL = RECORD
      nmbrmaj:CARDINAL;
      nmbrmin:CARDINAL;
      frsterr:ERRPTR;
      lasterr:ERRPTR;
      END;
   STDEMSG = PROCEDURE(STRING,BOOLEAN,CARDINAL);
(*  The STDEMSG procedure type is used to transalate an errnmbr into a
   message that will be displayed for the user.  Each program or module
   that uses RedoErrs should define a STDEMSG procedure.  *)
PROCEDURE FlgAsErr(fld,err:CARDINAL;majerr:BOOLEAN;VAR errs:ERRCNTRL);
(* This routine is used in conjunction with the deScreen routines to
   associate an error code with a specific deScreen field.  The error codes
   are defined in the procedure named STDEMSG and majerr defines whether or
   not the error is to be considered a Major error (i.e., must be corrected
   before further processing can be done).  The value parameters will be
   used to construct an errrcrd which will be appended to the chain of such
   records pointed to by frsterr and lasterr.  Note that the first time
   this routine is called, frsterr should be set = nil which will cause the
   other variables to be initialized before use.  If a calling program does
   not wish to use the standard error messages, it need only include a new
   StdEMsg procedure and not access the library.  *)
PROCEDURE ShowErrs(VAR thisscrn:ADDRESS;VAR errs:ERRCNTRL;blink:BYTE);
(* The color for all of the fields defined in ERRS will be set to blink. *)
PROCEDURE RedoErrs(VAR thisscrn:ADDRESS;showblst:FLPTR;
                   thisbox:CARDINAL;flds:FLPTR;VAR errs:ERRCNTRL;
                   VAR chgd:BOOLEAN;hlclr,blink:BYTE;hortab:CHAR;
                   VAR eascii:BOOLEAN;VAR kbchar:CHAR;stdemsg:STDEMSG);
(* This routine provides a standardized mechanicism for correcting errors
   on a descreen.  thisscrn must have been loaded using LoadScrn and
   thisbox refers to the box in which the errors occur.  If flds[1] = 0
   then all of the fields in the box may be accessed using ReadScrn.
   Otherwise, only the fields specified will be accessable using readflds.
   The list of errors and the associated fields must have been constructed
   from errs.frsterr using FlgAsErr.  When this routine is first entered,
   all errors fields in flds or in the associated box will be changed to
   the color specified by blink.  On return, errs.frsterr will be set to
   nil and the associated variables cleared.  This routine gives the user
   the option of accessing all fields in the box or list, or of only
   accessing those fields with errors.  If the latter is choosen, the error
```

Fig. 14-17 continued

reporting routine, STDEMSG, will be called to provide a description of
the error for display on the standard message lines. On return, kbchar
and eascii will indicate the character that ended the read. Standard
returns are:
```
     FK1 = Entry complete
     FK4 = Data contains only minor errors, accept as is
     FK9 = Start over
     FK10 = Abort
*)
PROCEDURE ClrErrs(VAR thisscrn:ADDRESS;VAR errs:ERRCNTRL;blink:BYTE);
(* This procedure will clear all of the deScreen errors defined in errs
   from the screen specified and turn off the color attribute given by
   blink.  *)
END EL1417.

IMPLEMENTATION MODULE EL1417;
  FROM SYSTEM IMPORT    ADDRESS,BYTE;
  FROM Storage IMPORT    ALLOCATE,DEALLOCATE;
  FROM EL0304 IMPORT    fk1,fk2,fk3,fk4,fk9;
  FROM EL0401 IMPORT    STRING,Literal;
  FROM EL0404 IMPORT    FixStr;
  FROM EL0501 IMPORT    CHARSET,MakeCSet,IncCSet,nullcset;
  FROM EL0505 IMPORT    FLPTR,MakFList,ClrFList;
  FROM EL0902 IMPORT    msgframe;
  FROM EL0905 IMPORT    Message;
  FROM EL1410 IMPORT    ChgColor;
  FROM EL1411 IMPORT    ShowBox;
  FROM EL1412 IMPORT    ReadScrn;
  FROM EL1413 IMPORT    ReadFlds;

PROCEDURE ClrErrs(VAR thisscrn:ADDRESS;VAR errs:ERRCNTRL;blink:BYTE);
CONST
  noblink = FALSE;
BEGIN
  WITH errs DO
    nmbrmaj:=0;
    nmbrmin:=0;
    WHILE (frsterr <> NIL) DO
      ChgColor(thisscrn,frsterr^.fldnmbr,blink,noblink);
      lasterr:=frsterr^.nexterr;
      DISPOSE(frsterr);
      frsterr:=lasterr;
      END;
    END;
  END ClrErrs;

PROCEDURE FlgAsErr(fld,err:CARDINAL;majerr:BOOLEAN;VAR errs:ERRCNTRL);
BEGIN
  WITH errs DO
    IF (frsterr = NIL)
      THEN
        NEW(frsterr);
        nmbrmaj:=0;
        nmbrmin:=0;
        lasterr:=frsterr;
      ELSE
        NEW(lasterr^.nexterr);
        lasterr:=lasterr^.nexterr;
          END;
        lasterr^.nexterr:=NIL;
        lasterr^.fldnmbr:=fld;
```

```
      lasterr^.errnmbr:=err;
      lasterr^.majerr:=majerr;
      IF (majerr)
        THEN nmbrmaj:=nmbrmaj+1
        ELSE nmbrmin:=nmbrmin+1;
        END;
      END;
    END FlgAsErr;

PROCEDURE ShowErrs(VAR thisscrn:ADDRESS;VAR errs:ERRCNTRL;blink:BYTE);
VAR
  thiserr:ERRPTR;
BEGIN
  thiserr:=errs.frsterr;
  WHILE (thiserr <> NIL) DO
    ChgColor(thisscrn,thiserr^.fldnmbr,blink,TRUE);
    thiserr:=thiserr^.nexterr;
    END;
  END ShowErrs;

PROCEDURE RedoErrs(VAR thisscrn:ADDRESS;showblst:FLPTR;
                   thisbox:CARDINAL;flds:FLPTR;VAR errs:ERRCNTRL;
                   VAR chgd:BOOLEAN;hlclr,blink:BYTE;hortab:CHAR;
                   VAR eascii:BOOLEAN;VAR kbchar:CHAR;StdEMsg:STDEMSG);
CONST
  oktochg = TRUE;
VAR
  lastbox,lastfld:CARDINAL;
  major:BOOLEAN;
  thiserr:ERRPTR;
  msg:STRING;
  errlist,boxlist:FLPTR;
BEGIN
  WITH errs DO
    MakFList(1,boxlist);
    boxlist^[1]:=thisbox;
    MakFList(1,errlist);
    ShowErrs(thisscrn,errs,blink);
    ShowBox(thisscrn,showblst);
    IF (nmbrmaj = 0)
      THEN Message(Literal(' Data contains minor errors'),
                   Literal(
        ' F2 = Modify All / F3 = Modify Errors / F4 = Save / F9 = Clear'),
                   msgframe,15,nullcset,easciis1,eascii,kbchar);
      ELSE Message(Literal(' Data contains major errors'),
             Literal(' F2 = Modify All / F3 = Modify Errors / F9 = Clear'),
                   msgframe,15,nullcset,easciis2,eascii,kbchar);
      END;
    thiserr:=frsterr;
    IF (kbchar = fk3)
      THEN
        REPEAT
          ChgColor(thisscrn,thiserr^.fldnmbr,blink,FALSE);
          StdEMsg(msg,thiserr^.majerr,thiserr^.errnmbr);
          errlist^[1]:=thiserr^.fldnmbr;
          Message(msg,
                  Literal(' F1 = Verify / F3 = Modify Next / F9 = Clear'),
                  msgframe,15,nullcset,nullcset,eascii,kbchar);
          ReadFlds(thisscrn,showblst,thisbox,errlist,0,lastfld,oktochg,
                   chgd,nullcset,easciis3,hlclr,hortab,eascii,kbchar);
          thiserr:=thiserr^.nexterr;
          UNTIL (thiserr = NIL) OR (kbchar <> fk3);
```

Fig. 14-17 continued

```
        IF (kbchar = fk3)
           THEN kbchar:=fk1;
           END;
     END;
   ShowBox(thisscrn,showblst);
   IF (kbchar = fk2)
     THEN
       Message(Literal(' Modify All'),
                 Literal(' F1 = Verify / F9 = Clear'),
                 msgframe,15,nullcset,nullcset,easciI,kbchar);
       IF (flds^[0] = 0)
         THEN ReadScrn(thisscrn,showblst,boxlist,0,lastbox,0,lastfld,
               oktochg,chgd,nullcset,easciis4,hlclr,hortab,easciI,kbchar);
         ELSE ReadFlds(thisscrn,showblst,thisbox,flds,0,lastfld,oktochg,
               chgd,nullcset,easciis4,hlclr,hortab,easciI,kbchar);
         END;
     END;
   END;
   ClrErrs(thisscrn,errs,blink);
   END RedoErrs;

VAR
   easciis1,easciis2,easciis3,easciis4:CHARSET;
BEGIN
   MakeCSet(FixStr(Literal(" fk2*fk3*fk4*fk9")),easciis1);
   MakeCSet(FixStr(Literal(" fk2*fk3*fk9")),easciis2);
   MakeCSet(FixStr(Literal(" fk1*fk3*fk9")),easciis3);
   MakeCSet(FixStr(Literal(" fk1*fk9")),easciis4);
END EL1417.
```

error records remaining in the list when *ReDoErrs* is completed. *ClrErrs* is available to the calling program.

StdEMsg. *ReDoErrs* calls a routine named *StdEMsg* to build error messages for the user. *StdEMsg* is intentionally in a separate module; it can be easily replaced. The basic routine shown in Fig. 14-18 defines just three messages (any program that uses *ChkDDate* must have those three messages), but any program that uses *ReDoErrs* should create its own *StdEMsq* routine. Note that the number associated with each message is the number the calling program should use when it calls *FlgAsErr*.

Dealing with Groups of Fields

Often, several fields in a deScreen must be treated together. It would be convenient to have a way of moving related fields to and from a deScreen at one time. A good example of that is the series of fields that constitute the birth date for each player on the Soccer Team Registration Form. It takes three fields to represent a date, and because many forms use dates, the deScreen routines include several routines for dealing with these three fields collectively.

PutDDate. The deScreen routine that moves a date to a SCREENMAP is called *PutDDate*. It is exported from EL1419, shown in Fig. 14-19. Note that *PutDDate* takes a date in the form *yymmdd* (six characters) and transfers it to the screen two characters at a time.

Fig. 14-18. Standard deScreen error messages.

```
DEFINITION MODULE EL1418;
   FROM EL0401 IMPORT    STRING;
   EXPORT QUALIFIED      StdEMsg;

PROCEDURE StdEMsg(msg:STRING;major:BOOLEAN;errnmbr:CARDINAL);
(* this procedure will return a msg describing the error associated with
   errnmbr.  The message will be prefixed by either 'Major error...' or
   'Minor error...' depending on the contents of major.  *)
END EL1418.

IMPLEMENTATION MODULE EL1418;
   FROM EL0401 IMPORT    STRING,Literal,CopyStr;
   FROM EL0402 IMPORT    Concat;

PROCEDURE StdEMsg(msg:STRING;major:BOOLEAN;errnmbr:CARDINAL);
BEGIN
   IF (major)
     THEN CopyStr(Literal('Major error...'),msg);
     ELSE CopyStr(Literal('Minor error...'),msg);
     END;
   CASE errnmbr OF
     1:Concat(Literal('Month is blank or invalid'),msg);
   : 2:Concat(Literal('Day is blank or invalid'),msg);
   : 3:Concat(Literal('Year is blank or invalid'),msg);
     ELSE
       Concat(Literal('Error'),msg);
     END;
   END StdEMsg;

END EL1418.
```

Fig. 14-19. Show a date on a deScreen.

```
DEFINITION MODULE EL1419;
   FROM SYSTEM IMPORT    ADDRESS;
   FROM EL0401 IMPORT    STRING;
   EXPORT QUALIFIED      PutDDate;

PROCEDURE PutDDate(yymmdd:STRING;yfld,mfld,dfld:CARDINAL;
                              VAR thisscrn:ADDRESS);
(* this procedure will move the contents of yymmdd into the descreen
   defined by thisscrn placing them in the appropriate fields.  Note that
   if dfld = 0, it will not be included in the operation, and only the yymm
   portion of the string will be accessed.  *)
END EL1419.

IMPLEMENTATION MODULE EL1419;
   FROM SYSTEM IMPORT    ADDRESS;
   FROM EL0401 IMPORT    STRING,SubStr;
   FROM EL1410 IMPORT    PutFld;

PROCEDURE PutDDate(yymmdd:STRING;yfld,mfld,dfld:CARDINAL;
                                 VAR thisscrn:ADDRESS);
BEGIN
   PutFld(yfld,SubStr(1,2,yymmdd),thisscrn);
   PutFld(mfld,SubStr(3,2,yymmdd),thisscrn);
   IF (dfld <> 0)
     THEN PutFld(dfld,SubStr(5,2,yymmdd),thisscrn);
     END;
   END PutDDate;

END EL1419.
```

GetDDate. To retrieve a date from a deScreen, use *GetDDate,* the routine shown in Fig. 14-20, exported from EL1420. It transfers two characters at a time into the six-character *yymmdd* parameter.

ChkDDate. It isn't enough to retrieve a date from a deScreen; you must also verify that the values make a valid date. The routine shown in Fig. 14-21, *ChkDDate,* will do both. Note that the routine calls *ChkDate* to actually validate the date. If *ChkDate* indicates that the data is invalid, *ChkDDate* uses one of the deScreen error handling routines to tell the user about it.

AN EXAMPLE

The Soccer Team Registration Form developed earlier in this chapter demonstrates how to use the deScreen techniques to define fairly sophisticated forms. For an example of using a deScreen form in an application, let's return to the Member List program begun in Chapter 11.

The SCD file

Figure 14-22 shows a SCD file listing for the deScreen used by the Membership List program. The screen that it generates allows the user to enter or change member data.

The screen in Fig. 14-22 has only two boxes; one that encloses only the "FAMILY

Fig. 14-20. Get a date from a deScreen.

```
DEFINITION MODULE EL1420;
  FROM SYSTEM IMPORT    ADDRESS;
  FROM EL0401 IMPORT    STRING;
  EXPORT QUALIFIED      GetDDate;

PROCEDURE GetDDate(yymmdd:STRING;yfld,mfld,dfld:CARDINAL;
                              VAR thisscrn:ADDRESS);
(* This procedure will access the appropriate fields in the descreen
   defined by thisscrn and assemble them in yymmdd.  Note that if dfld = 0,
   it will not be included in the operation, and only the yymm portion of
   the string will be accessed.  *)
END EL1420.

IMPLEMENTATION MODULE EL1420;
  FROM SYSTEM IMPORT    ADDRESS;
  FROM EL0401 IMPORT    STRING,SubStr;
  FROM EL0502 IMPORT    DATE;
  FROM EL1410 IMPORT    GetFld;

PROCEDURE GetDDate(yymmdd:STRING;yfld,mfld,dfld:CARDINAL;
                          VAR thisscrn:ADDRESS);
BEGIN
  GetFld(yfld,SubStr(1,2,yymmdd),thisscrn);
  GetFld(mfld,SubStr(3,2,yymmdd),thisscrn);
  IF (dfld <> 0)
    THEN GetFld(dfld,SubStr(5,2,yymmdd),thisscrn);
    END;
  END GetDDate;

END EL1420.
```

Fig. 14-21. Check a deScreen date.

```
DEFINITION MODULE EL1421;
  FROM SYSTEM IMPORT    ADDRESS;
  FROM EL0401 IMPORT    STRING;
  FROM EL1417 IMPORT    ERRCNTRL;
  EXPORT QUALIFIED      ChkDDate;

PROCEDURE ChkDDate(yymmdd:STRING;yfld,mfld,dfld:CARDINAL;
            VAR errs:ERRCNTRL;VAR thisscrn:ADDRESS);
(* This function will retrieve and check a date from a deScreen.  The
   values in the fields specified will be returned in the yymmdd string
   and, if an error is detected, the appropriate errors will be entered
   into the error list.  Note that if dfld = 0, only the yy and mm fields
   will be retrieved and checked.  Note that if all three fields are blank,
   yymmdd will return blank and no errors will be reported.  *)
END EL1421.


IMPLEMENTATION MODULE EL1421;
  FROM SYSTEM IMPORT    ADDRESS;
  FROM EL0401 IMPORT    STRING,StrChar,SetChar;
  FROM EL0403 IMPORT    Blank;
  FROM EL0502 IMPORT    DATE;
  FROM EL0708 IMPORT    ChkDate;
  FROM EL1417 IMPORT    ERRCNTRL,FlgAsErr;
  FROM EL1420 IMPORT    GetDDate;

PROCEDURE ChkDDate(yymmdd:STRING;yfld,mfld,dfld:CARDINAL;
            VAR errs:ERRCNTRL;VAR thisscrn:ADDRESS);
CONST
  major = TRUE;
VAR
  mok,dok,yok,blank:BOOLEAN;
  i:CARDINAL;
  date:DATE;
BEGIN
  GetDDate(yymmdd,yfld,mfld,dfld,thisscrn);
  IF (NOT Blank(yymmdd))
    THEN
      IF (dfld = 0)
        THEN
          SetChar(yymmdd,5,'0');
          SetChar(yymmdd,6,'1');
        END;
      FOR i:=1 TO 6 DO
        date[i]:=StrChar(yymmdd,i);
        END;
      IF (NOT ChkDate(date,yok,mok,dok))
        THEN
          IF (NOT mok)
            THEN FlgAsErr(mfld,1,major,errs);
            END;
          IF (dfld <> 0) AND (NOT dok)
            THEN FlgAsErr(dfld,2,major,errs);
            END;
          IF (NOT yok)
            THEN FlgAsErr(yfld,3,major,errs);
            END;
        END;
    END;
  END ChkDDate;

END EL1421.
```

Fig. 14-22. Mailing-list SCD file.

```
#
#
C,104,23,80,2;
B,1,1,1,2,80,1,1,2,80;
B,2,3,1,21,80,3,1,21,80
#                       1        2         3         4         5         6         7         8
#            12345678901234567890123456789012345678901234567890123456789012345678901234567890
T,1,1,80,7,  ╔═══════════════════════════════════════════════════════════════════════════╗
T,2,1,80,7,  ║FAMILY NAME: 1234567890123456789012345678901234567890012345                   ║
T,3,1,80,7,  ║   ADDRESS: 12345678901234567890123456789012345       PHONE (123) 123-1234    ║
T,4,1,80,7,  ║      CITY: 12345678901234567890  STATE: 123   ZIP: 123456789                 ║
T,5,1,80,7,  ╚═══════════════════════════════════════════════════════════════════════════╝
A,1,2,15,35,1, ,
A,2,3,15,35,1, ,
N,3,3,63,3,1, ,
A,4,3,68,3,1, ,
N,5,3,72,4,1, ,
A,6,4,15,20,1, ,
A,7,4,44,3,1, ,
A,8,4,55,9,1, ,
T,6,1,80,7,  ╔══════FIRST NAME═════════╤BIRTHDAY═╤PASS NUMBER═══════════NOTE══════════╗
R,16;
T,7,1,80,7,01║12345678901234567890123456789012345678901234567890│MM:DD:YY│12345678901234567890│
L,7,1,2,7,01;
A,9,7,4,30,1, ,
Z,25,7,35,2,1, ,
Z,41,7,38,2,1, ,
Z,57,7,41,2,1, ,
A,73,7,44,15,1, ,
A,89,7,60,20,1, ,
Q;
T,23,1,80,7,  ╚══════════════════════════╧═╧═╧════════════════════╧══════════════════╝
E;
```

NAME:" field, and a second that covers the rest of the screen. The area covered by both boxes fits on the display screen at the same time.

Accessing the IMG File

The IMG file is accessed by the procedures and functions defined in the module shown in Fig. 14-23. This module, EL1423, handles the "file maintenance" operations for the Membership List. It contains routines to add, change, delete, or list (on the screen) records obtained through the file access routines in EL1114.

The module has two internal routines: *ToScrn*, which moves data from the file to the screen; and *FromScrn*, which handles transfers from the screen to the file. The functions of the rest of the routines are obvious from their names.

Putting It All Together

In the last four chapters, I have discussed bits and pieces of the Member List program. The pieces have all been modules; to make it work, you need a program. The program, at least the source file that contains the keyword MODULE (without the IMPLEMENTATION), is shown in Fig. 14-23, and is called MAILLIST. After it initializes the appropriate variables and loads the MEMSCRN.IMG file into memory,

Fig. 14-23. The membership list deScreen access routines.

```
DEFINITION MODULE EL1423;
    FROM SYSTEM IMPORT    ADDRESS;
    FROM EL0401 IMPORT    STRING;
    FROM EL0503 IMPORT    LONGCARD;
    EXPORT QUALIFIED      ToScrn,FromScrn,GetName,AddName,
                          DltName,LstName,ChgName;

PROCEDURE ToScrn(VAR memscrn:ADDRESS;
                     name,address,city,state,zip,phone:STRING;
                     frstdtl:LONGCARD;
                     firstname,birthdate,pass,note:STRING):CHAR;
(* This routine will move data to the deScreen. *)
PROCEDURE FromScrn(VAR memscrn:ADDRESS;
                     name,address,city,state,zip,phone:STRING;
                 VAR frstdtl:LONGCARD;
                     firstname,birthdate,pass,note:STRING):CHAR;
(* This routine will move data from the deScreen to the file. *)
PROCEDURE GetName(VAR memscrn:ADDRESS;
                     name,address,city,state,zip,phone:STRING;
                 VAR frstdtl:LONGCARD;
                     firstname,birthdate,pass,note:STRING):CHAR;
(* This routine determines to which member the user is referring. *)
PROCEDURE AddName(VAR memscrn:ADDRESS;
                     name,address,city,state,zip,phone:STRING;
                 VAR frstdtl:LONGCARD;
                     firstname,birthdate,pass,note:STRING):CHAR;
(* This routine will add a new name to the file. *)
PROCEDURE DltName(VAR memscrn:ADDRESS;
                     name,address,city,state,zip,phone:STRING):CHAR;
(* This routine will oversee the deletion of the named record. *)
PROCEDURE LstName(VAR memscrn:ADDRESS;
                     name,address,city,state,zip,phone:STRING;
                 VAR frstdtl:LONGCARD;
                     firstname,birthdate,pass,note:STRING):CHAR;
(* This routine will locate the next name in the file. *)
PROCEDURE ChgName(VAR memscrn:ADDRESS;
                     name,address,city,state,zip,phone:STRING;
                 VAR frstdtl:LONGCARD;
                     firstname,birthdate,pass,note:STRING):CHAR;
(* This routine will handle changing data on the member screen. *)
END EL1423.

(* Copyright (c) 1987 TAB BOOKS INC.
    Author: Don Etling
*)
IMPLEMENTATION MODULE EL1423;
  FROM SYSTEM IMPORT    ADDRESS;
  FROM EL0303 IMPORT    equal;
  FROM EL0304 IMPORT    fk1,fk2,fk3,fk4,fk5,fk6,fk7,fk8,fk9,fk10;
  FROM EL0401 IMPORT    STRING,Literal,StrChar,StrLen,SetLen,SubStr,SetChar,
                        nullstr,ClearStr,MakeStr,MoveStr;
  FROM EL0403 IMPORT    Blank;
  FROM EL0404 IMPORT    FixStr;
  FROM EL0405 IMPORT    FillStr;
  FROM EL0501 IMPORT    CHARSET,MakeCSet,nullcset;
  FROM EL0503 IMPORT    LONGCARD,lczero,ComLCard;
  FROM EL0505 IMPORT    MakFList,FLPTR;
  FROM EL0801 IMPORT    FindParm;
  FROM EL0902 IMPORT    stdhilite,msgframe;
  FROM EL0905 IMPORT    Message;
  FROM EL0906 IMPORT    Cancel;
```

Fig. 14-23 continued

```
  FROM EL1410 IMPORT    BlankFld,GetFld,PutFld;
  FROM EL1411 IMPORT    ShowBox;
  FROM EL1412 IMPORT    ReadScrn;
  FROM EL1419 IMPORT    PutDDate;
  FROM EL1420 IMPORT    GetDDate;
  FROM EL1114 IMPORT    GetKid,DelName,GetNName,PutKid,
                        WrtName,ClsName,ReadName;

CONST
(*
  These constants are used to access the fields in memscrn.
*)
  maxentry = 16;
  nfld  = 1;    afld = 2;    p1fld = 3;    p2fld = 4;
  p3fld = 5;    cfld = 6;    sfld  = 7;    zfld  = 8;
  fffld = 9;
  fmmfld = fffld + maxentry;    fddfld = fmmfld + maxentry;
  fyyfld = fddfld + maxentry;    fpfld = fyyfld + maxentry;
  fnfld  = fpfld + maxentry;
  maxflds = fnfld + maxentry - 1;
  oktochg = TRUE;
  wait = 15;
VAR
  nbox,dbox,bboxes:FLPTR;
  hortab:CHAR;
  fk2fk5fk6fk7fk9fk10,fk5fk6fk7fk9fk10,fk1fk5fk6fk7fk10,
    fk1fk5fk9,fk4fk5fk9,fk9only,
    fk8fk9,fk5fk9,fk4fk8fk9:CHARSET;

PROCEDURE ToScrn(VAR memscrn:ADDRESS;
                     name,address,city,state,zip,phone:STRING;
                      frstdtl:LONGCARD;
                       firstname,birthdate,pass,note:STRING):CHAR;
VAR
  i:CARDINAL;
  kbchar:CHAR;
  eascii:BOOLEAN;
BEGIN
  FOR i:=1 TO maxflds DO
    BlankFld(i,memscrn);
    END;
  PutFld(nfld,name,memscrn);
  PutFld(afld,address,memscrn);
  PutFld(cfld,city,memscrn);
  PutFld(sfld,state,memscrn);
  PutFld(zfld,zip,memscrn);
  PutFld(p1fld,SubStr(1,3,phone),memscrn);
  PutFld(p2fld,SubStr(4,3,phone),memscrn);
  PutFld(p3fld,SubStr(7,4,phone),memscrn);
  i:=0;
  WHILE (ComLCard(frstdtl,lczero) <> equal) DO
    GetKid(firstname,birthdate,pass,note,frstdtl);
    PutFld(fffld+i,firstname,memscrn);
    PutDDate(birthdate,fyyfld+i,fmmfld+i,fddfld+i,memscrn);
    PutFld(fpfld+i,pass,memscrn);
    PutFld(fnfld+i,note,memscrn);
    i:=i+1;
    END;
  ShowBox(memscrn,bboxes);
  Message(Literal('Continue'),Literal(
  'F2 = Mod / F5 = Next / F6 = Lbls / F7 = List / F9 = Clear / F10 = Stop'),
```

```
             msgframe,0,nullcset,fk2fk5fk6fk7fk9fk10,eascii,kbchar));
    RETURN kbchar;
    END ToScrn;

PROCEDURE FromScrn(VAR memscrn:ADDRESS;
                       name,address,city,state,zip,phone:STRING;
                   VAR frstdtl:LONGCARD;
                       firstname,birthdate,pass,note:STRING):CHAR;
VAR
  i:INTEGER;
  junk,eascii:BOOLEAN;
  nmbr:LONGCARD;
  kbchar:CHAR;
BEGIN
  junk:=DelName(name,address,city,state,zip,phone);
  GetFld(nfld,name,memscrn);
  GetFld(afld,address,memscrn);
  GetFld(cfld,city,memscrn);
  GetFld(sfld,state,memscrn);
  GetFld(zfld,zip,memscrn);
  GetFld(p1fld,SubStr(1,3,phone),memscrn);
  GetFld(p2fld,SubStr(4,3,phone),memscrn);
  GetFld(p3fld,SubStr(7,4,phone),memscrn);
  i:=0;frstdtl:=lczero;nmbr:=lczero;
  FOR i:=0 TO maxentry-1 DO
    GetFld(fffld+i,firstname,memscrn);
    IF (NOT Blank(firstname))
      THEN
        GetDDate(birthdate,fyyfld+i,fmmfld+i,fddfld+i,memscrn);
        GetFld(fpfld+i,pass,memscrn);
        GetFld(fnfld+i,note,memscrn);
        PutKid(firstname,birthdate,pass,note,nmbr);
        IF (ComLCard(frstdtl,lczero) = equal)
          THEN frstdtl:=nmbr;
          END;
      END;
    END;
  IF (NOT WrtName(name,address,city,state,zip,phone,frstdtl))
    THEN Cancel(Literal('FromScrn'),name,1,0);
    END;
  ClsName;
  Message(Literal('Name saved'),
    Literal('F5 = Next / F6 = Lbls / F7 = List / F9 = Clear / F10 = Stop'),
          msgframe,wait,nullcset,fk5fk6fk7fk9fk10,eascii,kbchar);
  RETURN kbchar;
  END FromScrn;


PROCEDURE GetName(VAR memscrn:ADDRESS;
                      name,address,city,state,zip,phone:STRING;
                  VAR frstdtl:LONGCARD;
                      firstname,birthdate,pass,note:STRING):CHAR;
VAR
  eascii,chgd:BOOLEAN;
  kbchar:CHAR;
  i,lastbox,lastfld:CARDINAL;
BEGIN
  FOR i:=1 TO maxflds DO
    BlankFld(i,memscrn);
    END;
  ShowBox(memscrn,bboxes);
  FillStr(name,' ');        FillStr(address,' ');      FillStr(city,' ');
  FillStr(state,' ');       FillStr(zip,' ');          FillStr(phone,' ');
```

Fig. 14-23 continued

```
    FillStr(firstname,' ');   FillStr(birthdate,' ');   FillStr(pass,' ');
    FillStr(note,' ');
    Message(Literal('Enter Family Name and Number or use F6 or F7'),
      Literal('F1 = Check / F5 = Next / F6 = Lbls / F7 = List / F10 = Stop'),
          msgframe,wait,nullcset,nullcset,eascii,kbchar);
    ReadScrn(memscrn,bboxes,nbox,0,lastbox,0,lastfld,
             oktochg,chgd,nullcset,fk1fk5fk6fk7fk10,
             stdhilite,hortab,eascii,kbchar);
    GetFld(nfld,name,memscrn);
    IF (kbchar = fk1)
      THEN
        IF (Blank(name))
          THEN kbchar:=fk5;
          ELSE IF (ReadName(name,address,city,state,zip,phone,frstdtl))
            THEN kbchar:=ToScrn(memscrn,name,address,city,state,zip,phone,
                           frstdtl,firstname,birthdate,pass,note);
            ELSE Message(Literal('Family not on file'),
                 Literal('F1 = Add Name / F5 = Show Next / F9 = Clear Screen'),
                    msgframe,wait,nullcset,fk1fk5fk9,eascii,kbchar);
            END;
          END;
      END;
    RETURN kbchar;
    END GetName;

PROCEDURE AddName(VAR memscrn:ADDRESS;
                      name,address,city,state,zip,phone:STRING;
                      VAR frstdtl:LONGCARD;
                         firstname,birthdate,pass,note:STRING):CHAR;
VAR
  chgd,eascii:BOOLEAN;
  kbchar:CHAR;
  lastfld,lastbox:CARDINAL;
BEGIN
  Message(Literal('Family not on file...enter data,'),
    Literal('F4 = Save / F5 = Show Next / F9 = Clear Screen'),
         msgframe,wait,nullcset,nullcset,eascii,kbchar);
  ReadScrn(memscrn,bboxes,dbox,0,lastbox,0,lastfld,
           oktochg,chgd,nullcset,fk4fk5fk9,stdhilite,hortab,eascii,kbchar);
  IF (kbchar = fk4)
    THEN kbchar:=FromScrn(memscrn,name,address,city,state,zip,phone,
                            frstdtl,firstname,birthdate,pass,note);
    END;
  RETURN kbchar;
  END AddName;

PROCEDURE DltName(VAR memscrn:ADDRESS;
                     name,address,city,state,zip,phone:STRING):CHAR;
VAR
  i:CARDINAL;
  junk,eascii:BOOLEAN;
  nmbr:LONGCARD;
  kbchar:CHAR;
BEGIN
  Message(Literal('Verify...Delete this family?'),
          Literal('F8 = Delete / F9 = Clear Screen'),
             msgframe,wait,nullcset,fk8fk9,eascii,kbchar);
  IF (kbchar = fk8)
    THEN
      GetFld(nfld,name,memscrn);
      GetFld(afld,address,memscrn);
```

```
        GetFld(cfld,city,memscrn);
        GetFld(sfld,state,memscrn);
        GetFld(zfld,zip,memscrn);
        GetFld(p1fld,SubStr(1,3,phone),memscrn);
        GetFld(p2fld,SubStr(4,3,phone),memscrn);
        GetFld(p3fld,SubStr(7,4,phone),memscrn);
        IF (NOT DelName(name,address,city,state,zip,phone))
          THEN Cancel(Literal('DltName'),name,1,0);
          END;
        Message(Literal('Family deleted'),
                Literal('F5 = Show Next / F9 = Clear Screen'),
                msgframe,wait,nullcset,fk5fk9,eascii,kbchar);
      END;
  RETURN kbchar;
  END DltName;


PROCEDURE LstName(VAR memscrn:ADDRESS;
                      name,address,city,state,zip,phone:STRING;
                  VAR frstdtl:LONGCARD;
                      firstname,birthdate,pass,note:STRING):CHAR;
VAR
  eascii:BOOLEAN;
  kbchar:CHAR;
BEGIN
  GetFld(nfld,name,memscrn);
  GetFld(afld,address,memscrn);
  GetFld(cfld,city,memscrn);
  GetFld(sfld,state,memscrn);
  GetFld(zfld,zip,memscrn);
  GetFld(p1fld,SubStr(1,3,phone),memscrn);
  GetFld(p2fld,SubStr(4,3,phone),memscrn);
  GetFld(p3fld,SubStr(7,4,phone),memscrn);
  IF (NOT GetNName(name,address,city,state,zip,phone,frstdtl))
    THEN Message(Literal('No more Families in file'),
                          Literal('F9 = Clear Screen'),
                     msgframe,wait,nullcset,fk9only,eascii,kbchar);
    ELSE kbchar:=ToScrn(memscrn,name,address,city,state,zip,phone,
                          frstdtl,firstname,birthdate,pass,note);
    END;
  RETURN kbchar;
  END LstName;


PROCEDURE ChgName(VAR memscrn:ADDRESS;
                      name,address,city,state,zip,phone:STRING;
                  VAR frstdtl:LONGCARD;
                      firstname,birthdate,pass,note:STRING):CHAR;
VAR
  eascii,chgd:BOOLEAN;
  kbchar:CHAR;
  lastfld,lastbox:CARDINAL;
BEGIN
  Message(Literal('Enter changes'),
          Literal('F4 = Save / F8 = Delete / F9 = Clear Screen'),
              msgframe,wait,nullcset,nullcset,eascii,kbchar);
  ReadScrn(memscrn,bboxes,dbox,0,lastbox,0,lastfld,oktochg,chgd,nullcset,
              fk4fk8fk9,stdhilite,hortab,eascii,kbchar);
  IF (kbchar = fk4)
    THEN kbchar:=FromScrn(memscrn,name,address,city,state,zip,phone,
                          frstdtl,firstname,birthdate,pass,note);
    END;
  RETURN kbchar;
  END ChgName;
```

Fig. 14-23 continued

```
BEGIN
  MakFList(1,nbox);nbox^[1]:=1;
  MakFList(1,dbox);dbox^[1]:=2;
  MakFList(2,bboxes);bboxes^[1]:=1;bboxes^[2]:=2;
  hortab:=CHR(186);
  MakeCSet(FixStr(Literal('fk2*fk5*fk6*fk7*fk9*fk10')),
                                      fk2fk5fk6fk7fk9fk10);
  MakeCSet(FixStr(Literal('fk5*fk6*fk8*fk9*fk10')),fk5fk6fk7fk9fk10);
  MakeCSet(FixStr(Literal('fk1*fk5*fk6*fk7*fk10')),fk1fk5fk6fk7fk10);
  MakeCSet(FixStr(Literal('fk1*fk5*fk9')),fk1fk5fk9);
  MakeCSet(FixStr(Literal('fk4*fk5*fk9')),fk4fk5fk9);
  MakeCSet(FixStr(Literal('fk9')),fk9only);
  MakeCSet(FixStr(Literal('fk5*fk9')),fk5fk9);
  MakeCSet(FixStr(Literal('fk8*fk9')),fk8fk9);
  MakeCSet(FixStr(Literal('fk4*fk8*fk9')),fk4fk8fk9);
END EL1423.
```

Fig. 14-24. The mailing-list program.

```
(*  MAILLIST, Member list maintainence
    Copyright (c) 1987 TAB BOOKS INC.
    Author: Don Etling

  This program requires a paramter list containing at least the
  following entries:

      MEMSCRN=<membership list deScreen image>
      FAMILY=<Family name NDX file>
      KIDS=<Kids name LNK file>
      PRINTER=<printer control file>

MODULE MAILLIST;
  FROM SYSTEM IMPORT    ADDRESS;
  FROM EL0304 IMPORT    fk1,fk2,fk5,fk6,fk7,fk8,fk9,fk10;
  FROM EL0401 IMPORT    STRING,Literal,nullstr,MakeStr;
  FROM EL0503 IMPORT    LONGCARD;
  FROM EL0801 IMPORT    GetParms;
  FROM EL0902 IMPORT    msgframe,PstnCur;
  FROM EL0906 IMPORT    Cancel;
  FROM EL1409 IMPORT    LoadScrn;
  FROM EL1114 IMPORT    ClsName;
  FROM EL1203 IMPORT    PrtLbls,PrtList;
  FROM EL1423 IMPORT    AddName,LstName,DltName,ChgName,GetName;

CONST
  TITLE1 = 'MAILLIST - Membership list maintenance program.';
  TITLE2 = 'Copyright (c) 1987 TAB BOOKS INC.';
  TITLE3 = 'Author: Don Etling';
VAR
  kbchar:CHAR;
  memscrn:ADDRESS;
  name,address,city,state,zip,phone:STRING;
  frstdtl:LONGCARD;
  firstname,birthdate,pass,note,datestr:STRING;
BEGIN
  GetParms;
  MakeStr(name     ,35,nullstr);
  MakeStr(address  ,35,nullstr);
  MakeStr(city     ,20,nullstr);
```

```
MakeStr(state     , 3,nullstr);
MakeStr(zip       , 9,nullstr);
MakeStr(phone     ,10,nullstr);
MakeStr(firstname,30,nullstr);
MakeStr(birthdate, 6,nullstr);
MakeStr(pass      ,15,nullstr);
MakeStr(note      ,20,nullstr);
MakeStr(datestr   , 8,nullstr);
LoadScrn(Literal('MEMSCRN'),memscrn);
kbchar:=fk9;
REPEAT
  CASE kbchar OF
    fk1:kbchar:=AddName(memscrn,name,address,city,state,zip,phone,
                        frstdtl,firstname,birthdate,pass,note);
  ! fk2:kbchar:=ChgName(memscrn,name,address,city,state,zip,phone,
                        frstdtl,firstname,birthdate,pass,note);
  ! fk5:kbchar:=LstName(memscrn,name,address,city,state,zip,phone,
                        frstdtl,firstname,birthdate,pass,note);
  ! fk6:kbchar:=PrtLbls(name,address,city,state,zip,phone,
                        frstdtl,firstname,birthdate,pass,note);
  ! fk7:kbchar:=PrtList(name,address,city,state,zip,phone,
                        frstdtl,firstname,birthdate,pass,note);
  ! fk8:kbchar:=DltName(memscrn,name,address,city,state,zip,phone);
  ! fk9:kbchar:=GetName(memscrn,name,address,city,state,zip,phone,
                        frstdtl,firstname,birthdate,pass,note);
  ELSE
    Cancel(Literal('MAILLIST'),nullstr,2,1);
    END;
  UNTIL (kbchar = fk10);
ClsName;
WITH msgframe DO
  PstnCur(11,1c,msgframe);
  END;
END MAILLIST.
```

the program establishes a REPEAT loop that, depending on the value of *kbchar,* calls all of the other routines in the program.

Running the Program

To execute the MAILLIST program, you must first link the various pieces together. All of the Modula-2 packages include a suitable linker. Once the program is linked, enter:

MAILLIST PARMFILE=MAILLIST.PRM

Note that the program uses a parameter file, named MAILLIST.PRM. The I/O routines will look for that file on the default disk device. The MAILLIST.PRM file contains the following:

FAMILY=FAMILY.MST
KIDS=KIDS.MST
PRINTER=IBM.PTR
MEMSCRN=MEMSCRN.IMG

Fig. 14-25. Mailing-list help file.

```
{$HELPMSG:1}
Enter family last name.
{$HELPMSG:2}
Enter family street address.
{$HELPMSG:3}
Enter the area code of the family's phone.
{$HELPMSG:4}
Enter the family phone number exchange.
{$HELPMSG:5}
Enter the family phone number.
{$HELPMSG:6}
Enter the city in which the family lives.
{$HELPMSG:7}
Enter the state in which the family lives. Use the standard two character
abbreviation (3 characters in Canada).
{$HELPMSG:8}
Enter the family's zip code. Include all nine digits if you have them.
{$HELPMSG:9-24}
Enter the first name of one of the family members. Note that you should
use one line for each member...do not duplicate entries.
{$HELPMSG:25-40}
Enter the month in which this family member was born.
{$HELPMSG:41}
Enter the day on which this family member was born.
{$HELPMSG:42-56,USE:41}
{$HELPMSG:57-72}
Enter the year in which this family member was born.
{$HELPMSG:73-88}
If this member plays soccer, enter the Player Pass number assigned to
this member. Note that the number entered should correspond to the
number on the Players offical FIFA pass.
{$HELPMSG:81-104}
If you have any comments about this family member, enter them in this
space.
```

The file does not contain a parameter for PRTSPOOL; it could be added easily, if you wish, but the purpose of this program is to produce listings, not disk files.

Providing Help

Although the fields in the deScreen used by the MAILLIST program are fairly simple, Fig 14-24 defines a HLP file that can be used to offer help to the user. Remember, this file has to be run through the NDXHELP program before it is accessible to the deScreen routines. Figure 14-25 shows the mailing-list help messages.

Appendix

Library Member List

```
(*----------------------------------------------------------EL0906.abtstuff-*)
VAR
  abortfrm:FRAME;
  breakon :BOOLEAN;
(* abortfrm is a variable, but it should be treated as a constant that
   defines the area of the crt in which cancel messages should be
   displayed.  breakon is used to signal the internal BrkHndlr routine as
   to whether or not it should permit the Ctrl-Break or Ctrl-C key
   combination to interrupt program execution.  *)
(*----------------------------------------------------------EL0503.AddLCard-*)
PROCEDURE AddLCard(lcrd1,lcrd2:LONGCARD; VAR lcrdrslt:LONGCARD);
(* This routine will perform the equation :  lcrdrslt := lcrd1 + lcrd2   *)
(*----------------------------------------------------------EL1412.AlignNum-*)
PROCEDURE AlignNum(mc,ml:CARDINAL;VAR image:SMAP;VAR fld:FLDDEF);
(* This routine will align the characters in a numeric field so that the
   decimal point is properly positioned.  *)
(*----------------------------------------------------------EL0803.AskParm -*)
PROCEDURE AskParm(msg,parmid,parmval:STRING;VAR frame:FRAME);
(* This routine will use frame to ask the user to supply a value for the
   program parameter associated with parmid.  parmid and parmval will be
   added to the list of program parameters and parmval will be returned to
   the calling program.  *)
(*----------------------------------------------------------EL0403.Blank   -*)
PROCEDURE Blank(source:STRING):BOOLEAN;
(* If all of the characters in source are equal to blank, this routine will
   return TRUE...at the first occurence of a non-blank, this routine will
   return FALSE.  *)
(*----------------------------------------------------------EL1410.BlankFld-*)
PROCEDURE BlankFld(fldnmbr:CARDINAL;VAR thisscrn:ADDRESS);
(* This routine will fill the deScreen field associated with fldnmbr in
   thisscrn with blanks (except that the ":" in a numeric field will be
```

```
     left in its proper position).  Note that the change is made in the
     control area, not on the display.  *)
(*------------------------------------------------------------EL0801.BldParms-*)
PROCEDURE BldParms(parmlist:STRING);
(* This routine will parse parmlist into individual parameters that will be
   added to the list of program parameters.  If the routine encounters a
   parameter in the form PARMFILE=<filename>, the routine will attempt to
   read additional parameters from that file.  Further, if it encounters a
   parameter stating ENVIRON=<seg>:<off>, the routine will use that address
   as a DOS environment area and build additional parameters from there. *)
(*------------------------------------------------------------EL0301.ByWord  -*)
PROCEDURE ByWord(hibyte,lobyte:BYTE):WORD;
(* This routine will combine the two bytes to produce a single word.  *)
(*------------------------------------------------------------EL0906.Cancel  -*)
PROCEDURE Cancel(proc,msg:STRING;
                 msgnmbr:CARDINAL;status:BYTE);
(* This routine will terminate the current process and return to the
   invoker.  Usually, this means returning to the operating system.  This
   routine is intended to be used to indicate that a fatal error has
   occured, and the current process cannot continue to operate.  proc is
   used to identify the location where the cancel occurs...it is usually
   the name of the procedure where the call occurs, but, it can be any
   string of up to 20 characters.  msg can be used to show additional
   information about the error.  msgnmbr defines which standard error
   message should be displayed.  status will be used to set the error code
   that is passed to DOS...it can be accessed by the DOS IF and ERRORLEVEL
   commands.  The format of the error message that will be displayed is as
   follows:

        <message> (Status = <STATUS>)
        PROGRAM CANCELED

   The standard messages are:

        1 = Impossible error in <PROC> [<MSG]>
        2 = User requested abort in <PROC> [<MSG>]
        3 = Missing parm value for <MSG> in <PROC>
        4 = I/O error for <MSG> in <PROC>
        x = Undefined error code in <PROC> [<MSG>]
*)
(*-----------------------------------------------------------EL1412.CanDBox -*)
PROCEDURE CanDBox(VAR boxes:BDTBL;VAR readblst:FLPTR;
                  VAR currb,newbox:CARDINAL;
                      xmttabok:BOOLEAN;VAR flds:FDTBL):BOOLEAN;
(* This routine checks to see if another box is below the current one. *)
(*-----------------------------------------------------------EL1412.CanDTab -*)
PROCEDURE CanDTab (xmttabok:BOOLEAN;VAR box:BOXDEF;VAR flds:FDTBL;
                   VAR curtab:CARDINAL;curclmn:CARDINAL):BOOLEAN;
(* This routine will check to be sure that the screen includes a field to
   which the cursor can tab down.  *)
(*-----------------------------------------------------------EL1412.CanECur -*)
PROCEDURE CanECur (xmttabok:BOOLEAN;VAR box:BOXDEF;VAR flds:FDTBL;
                   VAR curtab:CARDINAL):BOOLEAN;
(* This routine will check to be certain that the cursor can be moved to
   the first field in the current box.  *)
(*-----------------------------------------------------------EL1412.CanHCur -*)
PROCEDURE CanHCur (xmttabok:BOOLEAN;VAR box:BOXDEF;VAR flds:FDTBL;
                   VAR curtab:CARDINAL):BOOLEAN;
(* This routine will check to be certain that the cursor can be moved to
   the last field in the current box.  *)
(*-----------------------------------------------------------EL1412.CanLTab -*)
PROCEDURE CanLTab(xmttabok:BOOLEAN;VAR box:BOXDEF;VAR flds:FDTBL;
                  VAR curtab:CARDINAL):BOOLEAN;
```

```
(* This routine will check to be sure that the screen includes a field to
   which the cursor can tab left.  *)
(*----------------------------------------------------------EL1412.CanPChr -*)
PROCEDURE CanPChr(mc,ml:CARDINAL;VAR image:SMAP;VAR fld:FLDDEF;
                  VAR curline,curclmn:CARDINAL;pchar:CHAR):BOOLEAN;
(* This routine will make sure that a character can be put to the current
   position.  *)
(*----------------------------------------------------------EL1412.CanRTab -*)
PROCEDURE CanRTab(xmttabok:BOOLEAN;VAR box:BOXDEF;VAR flds:FDTBL;
                  VAR curtab:CARDINAL):BOOLEAN;
(* This routine will check to be sure that the screen includes a field to
   which the cursor can tab right.  *)
(*----------------------------------------------------------EL1412.CanUBox -*)
PROCEDURE CanUBox(VAR boxes:BDTBL;VAR readblst:FLPTR;
                  VAR currb,newbox:CARDINAL;
                      xmttabok:BOOLEAN;VAR flds:FDTBL):BOOLEAN;
(* This routine checks to see if another box is above the current one. *)
(*----------------------------------------------------------EL1412.CanUTab -*)
PROCEDURE CanUTab (xmttabok:BOOLEAN;VAR box:BOXDEF;VAR flds:FDTBL;
                  VAR curtab:CARDINAL;curclmn:CARDINAL):BOOLEAN;
(* This routine will check to be sure that the screen includes a field to
   which the cursor can tab up.  *)
(*----------------------------------------------------------EL0605.CarToStr-*)
PROCEDURE CarToStr(nmbr,width:CARDINAL;dest:STRING);
(* This routine will convert nmbr into a sequence of width characters,
   with the value right justified in the STRING.  The routine assumes that
   dest is already defined and can hold at least width characters *)
(*----------------------------------------------------------EL0304.chars   -*)
(* This module assigns meaningful names to the special control characters
   associated with the IBM PC keyboard.  Note that these characters include
   both the normal ASCII controls, and, the "Extended ASCII" characters
   defined by IBM.  *)
CONST
  bksp = 010C;    break = 003C;    cr   = 015C;    deof  = 032C;
  lf   = 012C;    pgdn  = 121C;    pgup = 111C;    altdec = 072C;
(* STANDARD FUNCTION KEYS *)
  fk1  = 073C;    fk2 = 074C;    fk3 = 075C;    fk4 = 076C;    fk5 = 077C;
  fk6  = 100C;    fk7 = 101C;    fk8 = 102C;    fk9 = 103C;    fk10 = 104C;
(* SHIFT - FUNCTION KEYS *)
  fk11 = 124C;    fk12 = 125C;    fk13 = 126C;    fk14 = 127C;    fk15 = 130C;
  fk16 = 131C;    fk17 = 132C;    fk18 = 133C;    fk19 = 134C;    fk20 = 135C;
(* CNTRL - FUNCTION KEYS *)
  fk21 = 136C;    fk22 = 137C;    fk23 = 140C;    fk24 = 141C;    fk25 = 142C;
  fk26 = 143C;    fk27 = 144C;    fk28 = 145C;    fk29 = 146C;    fk30 = 147C;
(* ALT - FUNCTION KEYS *)
  fk31 = 150C;    fk32 = 151C;    fk33 = 152C;    fk34 = 153C;    fk35 = 154C;
  fk36 = 155C;    fk37 = 156C;    fk38 = 157C;    fk39 = 160C;    fk40 = 161C;
  (* FIELD TAB CHARS *)
  tabr  = 011C; (*normal tab          *) tabl = 017C; (*shift tab          *)
  rtab  = 115C; (*shift - NUM PAD 6 *) ltab = 113C; (*shift - NUM PAD 4 *)
  utab  = 110C; (*shift - NUM PAD 8 *) dtab = 120C; (*shift - NUM PAD 2 *)
  home  = 107C; (*shift - NUM PAD 7 *) end  = 117C; (*shift - NUM PAD 1 *)
  boxu  = 111C; (*shift - NUM PAD 9 *) boxd = 121C; (*shift - NUM PAD 0 *)
  (* CURSOR MOVEMENT CONTROLS*)
  curl  = 163C; (*ctrl NUM PAD 4      *) curr  = 164C; (*ctrl NUM PAD 6      *)
  insr  = 122C; (*shift - NUM PAD 0 *) del  = 123C; (*shift - NUM PAD . *)
  (* OVERALL CONTROL CHARACTERS *)
  esc       = 033C; (* Esc key          *)   allditto  = 023C; (*alt - R   *)
  nextval   = 027C; (*alt - I           *)   dittokey  = 040C; (*alt - D   *)
  xmtcntrl  = 055C; (*alt - X (toggles tabbing into xmtonly fld) *)
  clearfld  = 056C; (*alt - C           *)   seqval    = 061C; (*alt - N   *)
  help      = 043C; (*alt - H           *)
(*----------------------------------------------------------EL0501.CHARSET -*)
```

```
CONST
  piecesize = 16; setsize = 256; pieces = 16; maxpiece = pieces - 1;
TYPE
  PIECERANGE = [0..maxpiece];
  CHARSET = ARRAY PIECERANGE OF BITSET;
VAR
  nullcset,numbers,capitals,lowcases : CHARSET;
(* Although these symbols are defined as variables, they should be treated
   as constants. *)
(*-----------------------------------------------------EL1015.ChDir   -*)
PROCEDURE ChDir(ddname:STRING):WORD;
(* This routine will attempt to change the current directory according to
   the path defined in ddname.  If the operation is successful, the
   function will return = 0.  Otherwise, the routine will return equal to
   the error condition returned from DOS. *)
(*-----------------------------------------------------EL1412.ChgBox  -*)
PROCEDURE ChgBox(mc,ml:CARDINAL;VAR image:SMAP;VAR showblst:FLPTR;
                 VAR boxes:BDTBL;VAR flds:FDTBL;VAR newbox,curtab:CARDINAL;
                 oldbox,lastfld:CARDINAL;hortab:CHAR):BOOLEAN;
(* This routine handles the change from one box to another. *)
(*-----------------------------------------------------EL1412.ChgCAtt -*)
PROCEDURE ChgCAtt (VAR box:BOXDEF;VAR fld:FLDDEF;setcolor:BYTE);
(* This routine will change the color of the field associated with fld. *)
(*-----------------------------------------------------EL1410.ChgColor-*)
PROCEDURE ChgColor(VAR thisscrn:ADDRESS;fldnmbr:CARDINAL;
                       color:BYTE;switch:BOOLEAN);
(* thisscrn refers to a deScreen loaded by LoadScrn.  The color attribute
   of the indicated field will be changed.  If, on entry, switch is true
   color will be OR'd with existing attribute.  If false, color will be
   XOR'd to #FF and then AND'd to the exisiting attibute.  (i.e., switch =
   true turns color on, = false turns it off).  Note that the change is
   made in the control area, not on the crt. *)
(*-----------------------------------------------------EL1017.ChkAttrb-*)
PROCEDURE ChkAttrb(ddname:STRING; VAR attrib:WORD):BOOLEAN;
(* This routine will return the attribute recorded for the file associated
   with ddname.  If function returns = FALSE, the file does not exist.
   Otherwise, attrib will contain the appropriate value. *)
(*-----------------------------------------------------EL0708.ChkDate -*)
PROCEDURE ChkDate(yymmdd:DATE;VAR yok,mok,dok:BOOLEAN):BOOLEAN;
(* This routine will check the contents of yymmdd to verify that it
   contains a valid date.  If any of the fields are in error, the routine
   will return false, and the appropriate BOOLEAN(s) will be set false. *)
(*-----------------------------------------------------EL1421.ChkDDate-*)
PROCEDURE ChkDDate(yymmdd:STRING;yfld,mfld,dfld:CARDINAL;
           VAR errs:ERRCNTRL;VAR thisscrn:ADDRESS);
(* This function will retrieve and check a date from a deScreen.  The
   values in the fields specified will be returned in the yymmdd string
   and, if an error is detected, the appropriate errors will be entered
   into the error list.  Note that if dfld = 0, only the yy and mm fields
   will be retreived and checked.  Note that if all three fields are blank,
   yymmdd will return blank and no errors will be reported. *)
(*-----------------------------------------------------EL1008.ChkDisk -*)
PROCEDURE ChkDisk(ddname:STRING; VAR secperc,remc,totc,bytepers:WORD);
(* This routine will return with values indicating the amount of free
   space remaining on the device associated with ddname.

        secperc  = Sectors per cluster.
        remc     = Remaining clusters.
        totc     = Total clusters on the device.
        bytepers = Byte per sector.

  If ddname does specify a valid device, the routine will call Cancel.  *)
```

```
(*-------------------------------------------------------EL1110.ChkLnkF -*)
PROCEDURE ChkLnkF(ddname:STRING;rcrdlen:CARDINAL;VAR opnmode:FMODE);
(* This routine will ensure the LNK file associated with ddname is opened
    and ready for access.  If the operation results in a new file being
    created, this routine will initialize its header record correctly.  On
    entry, opnmode should be set to the value indicating the proper
    operation...on return, it will always equal oldfile.  This routine
    should be the first LNK routine called for a given file, and, it should
    be recalled periodically to ensure that the file is still open.  *)
(*-------------------------------------------------------EL1102.ChkLoad -*)
PROCEDURE ChkLoad(ddname:STRING;VAR p:NODEPTR;rcrdlen:CARDINAL);
(* This routine will determine if the record associated with p has been
    loaded into memory...if not, the routine will load it.  *)
(*-------------------------------------------------------EL1102.ChkNdxF -*)
PROCEDURE ChkNdxF(ddname:STRING;rcrdlen:CARDINAL; VAR opnmode:FMODE);
(* This procedure ensures that the NDX file associated with ddname is
    opened and ready for access.  Note that if the operation results in a
    new file being created, its header record will be properly initialized.
    On entry opnmode should be set to the value required for the desired
    operation...it will always return = oldfile.  This routine should be the
    first NDX routine called for a specific file and, if the file is on
    diskette, the routine should be recalled periodically to ensure that the
    proper diskette is still mounted.  *)
(*-------------------------------------------------------EL0706.CHKTIMER-*)
PROCEDURE ChkTimer(VAR hours,minutes,seconds:CARDINAL;
                   VAR ticsleft,timechkd:LONGCARD):BOOLEAN;
(* This function returns with the number of hours, minutes, and seconds
    remaining in ticsleft after being set by the appropriate call to
    SetTimer.  Note that all the parameters are changed by the call.  When
    ticsleft reaches zero, ChkTimer will return equal to FALSE.  *)
(*-------------------------------------------------------EL1009.ChkVol  -*)
PROCEDURE ChkVol(ddname:STRING;askfirst:BOOLEAN);
(* This routine will make certain that the correct volume is mounted in the
    device associated with ddname.  If askfirst = TRUE, the user will be
    prompted to mount the volume before the first check is made.  Control
    does not return to the caller until the correct diskette is mounted.  *)
(*-------------------------------------------------------EL0401.ChrPtr  -*)
PROCEDURE ChrPtr(s:STRING;n:CARDINAL):CHRPTR;
(* This routine will return a pointer to the character in s at the n'th
    position.  If n is greater than the StrLen(s), the routine will set n to
    StrLen(s).  If n = 0, the routine will set n = 1.  *)
(*-------------------------------------------------------EL1411.ClearBox-*)
PROCEDURE ClearBox(VAR thisscrn:ADDRESS;showblst:FLPTR);
(* This routine will clear the area of the display occupied by the deScreen
    boxes associated with showblst.  thisscrn refers to a deScreen control
    area loaded by LoadScrn.  *)
(*-------------------------------------------------------EL0401.ClearStr-*)
PROCEDURE ClearStr(VAR s:STRING);
(* This routine will deallocate the area defined by the STRING parameter.
    Note that this routine should only be used on STRING variables defined
    by MakeStr or SubStr.  If this routine is called with s pointing to a
    constant or stack STRING, the call will be ignored.  In either case, s
    will return NIL.  *)
(*-------------------------------------------------------EL0505.ClrArea -*)
PROCEDURE ClrArea(VAR p:AREAPTR);
(* This routine clears the area to which p points.  *)
(*-------------------------------------------------------EL1417.ClrErrs -*)
PROCEDURE ClrErrs(VAR thisscrn:ADDRESS;VAR errs:ERRCNTRL;blink:BYTE);
(* This procedure will clear all of the deScreen errors defined in errs
    from the screen specified and turn off the color attribute given by
    blink.  *)
(*-------------------------------------------------------EL1412.ClrFld  -*)
```

```
PROCEDURE ClrFld(mc,ml:CARDINAL;VAR image:SMAP;
                  VAR box:BOXDEF;VAR fld:FLDDEF);
(* This routine will clear all the field identified by fld. *)
(*------------------------------------------------------EL0505.ClrFList-*)
PROCEDURE ClrFList(VAR p:FLPTR);
(* This routine clears the list from the heap to which p points.  *)
(*------------------------------------------------------EL0504.ClrFrame-*)
PROCEDURE ClrFrame(VAR frame:FRAMEPTR);
(* This routine will clear the frame from the heap.  If frame.dyn = TRUE,
   the associated SCREENMAP will also be cleared.  *)
(*------------------------------------------------------EL1202.ClrLTbl -*)
PROCEDURE ClrLTbl(VAR h:LTBLPTR);
(* This routine will clear a line table. *)
(*------------------------------------------------------EL1102.ClrNdx  -*)
PROCEDURE ClrNdx(VAR hook:NODEPTR);
(* This routine will dispose of the chain of nodes specified by hook and
   thereby clear the heap for reuse.  *)
(*------------------------------------------------------EL0801.ClrParms-*)
PROCEDURE ClrParms;
(* This routine will clear all existing program parameters.  *)
(*------------------------------------------------------EL1007.ClrRcrd -*)
PROCEDURE ClrRcrd(VAR rcrd:RCRD);
(* This procedure will clear the record defintion specifed by rcrd.  *)
(*------------------------------------------------------EL1007.ClrRFlds-*)
PROCEDURE ClrRFlds(VAR rfldlist:RFLDLIST);
(* This routine clears the field definition controls specified by
   rfldlist. *)
(*------------------------------------------------------EL0902.ClrScrn -*)
PROCEDURE ClrScrn(VAR frame:FRAME;color:BYTE);
(* This routine will fill the display adapter memory with color blanks
   with the frame specified.  *)
(*------------------------------------------------------EL0504.ClrSMap -*)
PROCEDURE ClrSMap(nl,nc:CARDINAL;VAR smap:SMAPPTR);
(* This routine will clear the SCREENMAP defined by smap from the heap.
   Note that the two cardinal parameters must correspond to the values used
   when the smap was created.  *)
(*------------------------------------------------------EL0307.ClrTHeap-*)
PROCEDURE ClrTHeap(adr:ADDRESS);
(* This routine will clear all variables allocated on the temporary heap
   that were referenced by a variable on the stack whose ADDRESS was after
   adr.  *)
(*------------------------------------------------------EL1002.ClsFile -*)
PROCEDURE ClsFile(ddname:STRING;how:DISP);
(* This routine will close the file associated with ddname and update its
   place in the directory accordingly.  If how = clsanddel, the file will
   be deleted from the directory, regardless of whether the file was ever
   opened.  Otherwise, a call to close a file that has not been opened is
   ignored.  If ddname = '*.*', ALL open files will be closed.  Note that
   it is good policy to close files after writing a series of records to
   ensure that the directory is properly updated.  If the file is left
   open, and the program is aborted or the user swaps diskettes, the
   directory could be corrupted.  *)
(*------------------------------------------------------EL1201.ClsPrint-*)
PROCEDURE ClsPrint(eject:BOOLEAN);
(* This procedure will close the device associated with PPORT.  If eject is
   true on entry, a form feed will be written before the file is closed. *)
(*------------------------------------------------------EL0902.COLORS  -*)
VAR
   stdhilite,blink,nrmclr,undrline:BYTE;
   crtads:SMAPPTR;
   wrkframe,msgframe:FRAME;
(* These variables define general screen related values for use in
```

accessing the CRT. crtads points to the display buffer for the current
display. wrkframe and msgframe divide the display buffer into two
areas. The larger area, wrkframe is used for most of the work done by a
program...msgframe points to the last two lines on the CRT, which is the
area normally used to display error and status messages to the user. *)
(*---EL0503.ComLCard-*)
PROCEDURE ComLCard(lcrd1,lcrd2:LONGCARD):MATCHVAL;
(* This routine will compare the two LONGCARD parameters and return an
    integer indicating their relative value.

            If lcrd1 < lcrd2,   then ComLCard = less
            If lcrd1 = lcrd2,   then ComLCard = equal
            If lcrd1 > lcrd2,   then ComLCard = greater
*)
(*---EL0305.CompAddr-*)
PROCEDURE CompAddr(a1,a2:ADDRESS):MATCHVAL;
(* This routine will compare the two ADDRESS variables and return a
   corresponding value.
        If a1 < a2 then CompAddr = less
        If a1 = a2 then CompAddr = equal
        If a1 > a2 then CompAddr = greater
*)
(*---EL0303.CompArea-*)
PROCEDURE CompArea(VAR area1:ARRAY OF BYTE; s1,l1:CARDINAL;
                   VAR area2:ARRAY OF BYTE; s2,l2:CARDINAL;
                   nbytes:CARDINAL):MATCHVAL;
(* This routine will compare the two arrays beginning at s1 and s2. The
   compare is done according to the value of each corresponding byte in the
   areas. The compare will continue for nbytes.

        If area1 < area2 then CompArea = less
        If area1 = area2 then CompArea = equal
        If area1 > area2 then CompArea = greater
*)
(*---EL0402.Concat -*)
PROCEDURE Concat(source,dest:STRING);
(* This routine will concatenate source onto the end of the characters
   currently defined in dest. The length of dest will be adjusted
   accordingly. *)
(*---EL0401.CopyStr -*)
PROCEDURE CopyStr(source,dest:STRING);
(* This routine will copy the contents of the first STRING to the second.
   If StrLen(source) is shorter than StrSize(dest), StrLen(dest) will be
   set to StrLen(source)..if StrLen(source) is larger than StrSize(dest),
   the move will be truncated. *)
(*---EL0504.CRTTYPES-*)
TYPE
  DISPLAYWORD = RECORD
    chrbyte   : CHAR;
    colbyte   : BYTE;
    END;
  DWPTR = POINTER TO DISPLAYWORD;
  SCREENMAP = ARRAY [0..16383] OF DISPLAYWORD;
  SMAPPTR = POINTER TO SCREENMAP;
  FRAME = RECORD
    fl : CARDINAL;   (* first line   *)
    fc : CARDINAL;   (* first column   *)
    ll : CARDINAL;   (* last line   *)
    lc : CARDINAL;   (* last column   *)
    cl : CARDINAL;   (* current line   *)
    cc : CARDINAL;   (* current column   *)
    nl : CARDINAL;   (* number of lines   *)

```
      nc : CARDINAL;          (*  number of columns   *)
      s  : SMAPPTR;           (*  address of SCREENMAP *)
      dyn: BOOLEAN;           (*  kind of SCREENMAP    *)
      END;
  FRAMEPTR = POINTER TO FRAME;
(*------------------------------------------------------EL0704.Delay  -*)
PROCEDURE Delay(number:CARDINAL);
(* This routine will delay for the number of milliseconds specified.  Note
   that the delay is adjusted for XT or AT speeds, but is still
   approximate.  *)
(*------------------------------------------------------EL0402.Delete  -*)
PROCEDURE Delete(dest:STRING;s,n:CARDINAL);
(* This routine will delete n characters from dest, beginning at s.  Any
   characters to the right will be moved left.  Note that the current
   length of dest is adjusted.  *)
(*------------------------------------------------------EL1112.DelLink -*)
PROCEDURE DelLink(ddname:STRING;rcrdlen:INTEGER;
                  lastlink:LONGCARD;VAR thislink:LONGCARD);
(* This routine will remove a record from the current chain in the LNK file
   associated with ddname.  If lastlink is not equal to zero on entry, the
   corresponding record will be accessed and the next link to which it
   points will be removed from the chain.  If lastlink is equal to zero on
   entry, the record identified by thislink will be removed.  In either
   case, thislink will return pointing to the next record in the chain, or
   will return equal to zero if the end of chain has been reached.  *)
(*------------------------------------------------------EL1406.DESCREEN-*)
CONST
   maxtabs = 8192;    maxboxes = 255;    numtype = 7;    alptype = 6;
   xmttype = 5;       contype = 4;       zerofill = 3;   changed = 2;


TYPE
(* These are the internal types required for the operation of the deScreen
   routines.  They are only used by the MakeScrn program and the DESCREEN
   modules...not by the calling programs.  *)
   FLDTYPES =[0..15];
   FLDTYPE = SET OF FLDTYPES;
   FLDDEF = RECORD
     fldtype :FLDTYPE;
     fldlen  :CARDINAL;
     fldprec :CARDINAL;   (*Number of digits right
                                        of decimal for num *)
     fldline :CARDINAL;   (*Map line on which field appears *)
     fldclmn :CARDINAL;   (*Map column *)
     END;
   FDTBL = ARRAY [1..6500] OF FLDDEF;     (*  MAX POSSIBLE FIELDS *)
   FDTPTR = POINTER TO FDTBL;
   BOXDEF = RECORD
     fmlib     : CARDINAL;   (* FIRST MAP LINE IN BOX             *)
     fmcib     : CARDINAL;   (* FIRST MAP COLUMN IN BOX           *)
     nmlib     : CARDINAL;   (* NUMBER OF MAP LINES IN BOX        *)
     nmcib     : CARDINAL;   (* NUMBER OF MAP COLUMNS IN BOX      *)
     fslib     : CARDINAL;   (* FIRST SCREEN LINE IN BOX          *)
     fscib     : CARDINAL;   (* FIRST SCREEN COLUMN IN BOX        *)
     nslib     : CARDINAL;   (* NUMBER OF SCREEN LINES IN BOX     *)
     nscib     : CARDINAL;   (* NUMBER OF SCREEN COLUMNS IN BOX   *)
     cfmlibos  : CARDINAL;   (* CURRENT FIRST MAP LINE
                                          IN BOX ON SCREEN *)
     cfmcibos  : CARDINAL;   (* CURRENT FIRST MAP COLUMN
                                          IN BOX ON SCREEN *)
         (*NOTE:  CURRENT MAP LINE = fmlibox - fmlib
                                + CURRENT SCREEN LINE     *)
     tabs: RECORD
```

```
        ptr       : POINTER TO ARRAY [1..8192] OF CARDINAL;
        maxtabs : CARDINAL;
        END;
    END;
  BDTBL = ARRAY [1..maxboxes] OF BOXDEF;      (*MAX POSSIBLE BOXES*)
  BDTPTR = POINTER TO BDTBL;
  SDPTR =   POINTER TO SCRNDEF;
  SMAP =   ARRAY [1..maxarea] OF DISPLAYWORD;(*MAX POSSIBLE SIZE *)
  SMPTR = POINTER TO SMAP;
  SCRNDEF = RECORD
    dd                : STRING;          (* filename *)
    sdlen             : CARDINAL;
    smml              : CARDINAL;
    smmc              : CARDINAL;
    maxfield          : CARDINAL;
    maxbox            : CARDINAL;
    sm                : SMPTR;
    ct                : FDTPTR;
    bx                : BDTPTR;
  (*  SCREENMAP;
    FDTBL;
    BDTBL;
    BOXTABMAPS;*)
    END;
VAR
  hlpframe       : FRAME;
  ecntrl,ncntrl : CHARSET;
(*------------------------------------------------------------EL0503.DivLCard-*)
PROCEDURE DivLCard(lcrd1,lcrd2:LONGCARD; VAR lcrdrslt,lcrdrem:LONGCARD);
(*  This routine will perform the equation :
                  lcrdrslt.loword := lcrd1 / lcrd2.loword
    The remainder is returned in lcrdrem.loword *)
(*------------------------------------------------------------EL1002.DoClose -*)
PROCEDURE DoClose(handle:WORD);
(* This routine will close the file associated with the indicated file
   handle.  If the close is un-successful, the routine will call Cancel. *)
(*------------------------------------------------------------EL1002.DoCreate-*)
PROCEDURE DoCreate(dsname:STRING;VAR handle:WORD):BYTE;
(* This routine will attempt to create a new entry in the directory
   associated with dsname.  If a similar file already exists, it will be
   truncated by this call.  If the call is successful, the file handle will
   be returned in handle.  The results of the call will be returned as the
   function value.  *)
(*------------------------------------------------------------EL1002.DoDel   -*)
PROCEDURE DoDel(dsname:STRING);
(* This routine will delete the file associated with dsname from the
   appropriate directory.  If the delete is unsuccessful, the routine will
   call Cancel.  *)
(*------------------------------------------------------------EL1412.DoDelete-*)
PROCEDURE DoDelete(mc,ml:CARDINAL;VAR image:SMAP;VAR box:BOXDEF;
                       VAR fld:FLDDEF; VAR curclmn:CARDINAL);
(*  This routine will delete a character at the current cursor position. *)
(*------------------------------------------------------------EL1002.DoGet   -*)
PROCEDURE DoGet(thisfid:FID;length:WORD;buf:ADDRESS):WORD;
(* This routine will attempt to transfer length bytes from the current
   position of the file associated with handle.  If an error occurs the
   routine will call Cancel and terminate.  Otherwise, the function value
   will return indicating the number of bytes actually transferred.  If on
   return, DoGet = 0, the end of file has been reached.  *)
(*------------------------------------------------------------EL1002.DoOpen  -*)
PROCEDURE DoOpen(dsname:STRING; VAR handle:WORD;access:BYTE):BYTE;
(* This routine will attempt to open the file associated with dsname.  The
```

results of the attempt will be returned as the function value. The file
will be opened using the DOS access specified by access, and, if the
open is successful, the file handle will be returned in handle. *)
(*---EL1002.DoPut   -*)
PROCEDURE DoPut(thisfid:FID;length:WORD;buf:ADDRESS);
(* This routine will attempt to transfer length bytes to the file
associated with handle at the current location of the file pointer. If
an error occurs, the routine will call Cancel and terminate the program.
Note that if length bytes cannot be written, the routine assumes that
the disk is full and cancels with the appropriate error. *)
(*---EL1002.DoSet   -*)
PROCEDURE DoSet(method:BYTE;handle,rlen:WORD; VAR rnmbr:LONGCARD);
(* This routine will set the file pointer for the specifed handle according
to method:
        method = 0, The file will be set to the location specified by
                    rlen * (rnmbr - 1).
        method = 1, The file will be set to its current location
                    plus rlen * (rnmbr - 1).
        method = 2, The file will be set to the end of file plus
                    rlen * (rnmbr - 1).
    If an error occurs, this routine will call Cancel. Otherwise, on
    return, rnmbr will point to the new record number. *)
(*---EL1002.DrvNmbr -*)
PROCEDURE DrvNmbr(dsname:STRING):CARDINAL;
(* This routine will convert the drive letter to a number. If the dsname
specified does not have a device, this routine will insert the current
default drive in the name. *)
(*---EL0904.DsplyStr-*)
PROCEDURE DsplyStr(color:BYTE;msg:STRING;sl,sc:CARDINAL;VAR frame:FRAME);
(* This routine will display the contents of msg on the CRT with the
attribute of color. The characters will be moved to the display buffer
beginning at location [sl,sc] and, on return, the appropriate values in
frame will be adjusted. frame.cl and frame.cc will define the last
position used. frame.ll and frame.lc indicate the maximum values that
can be accessed. If, in the course of moving characters, frame.cc
should exceed frame.lc, frame.cl will be set to frame.cl+1 and frame.cc
will be set to frame.fc. Should line exceed frame.ll, the contents of
the screen from [frame.fl,frame.fc] to [frame.ll,frame.lc] will be
scrolled up, and line will be unchanged. *)
(*---EL0504.DsplyWrd-*)
PROCEDURE DsplyWrd(l,c:CARDINAL;VAR frame:FRAME):DWPTR;
(* This routine will return the address of the DISPLAYWORD in the SCREENMAP
associated with frame that is at line l, column c. *)
(*---EL1202.EndRprt -*)
PROCEDURE EndRprt;
(* This procedure will end the production of the report begun by SetRprt.
It will close the printer, thereby causing whatever is the buffer to
print, and reset the appropriate controls. *)
(*---EL1412.EnterFld-*)
PROCEDURE EnterFld(mc,ml:CARDINAL;VAR image:SMAP;
                   VAR showblst:FLPTR; VAR boxes:BDTBL;VAR flds:FDTBL;
                   VAR curbox,curtab,curfld,curline,curclmn:CARDINAL;
                   hlclr:BYTE;hortab:CHAR;fromleft:BOOLEAN);
(* This routine handles the operations for moving into a field. *)
(*---EL0501.EqCSet -*)
PROCEDURE EqCSet(chset1,chset2:CHARSET):BOOLEAN;
(* This routine will compare chset1 and chset2. The function will return
TRUE if the sets are equal. *)
(*---EL1417.ERRCNTRL-*)
TYPE
(* These definitions must be copied into any routine that uses the deScreen
error routines. Note that a variable of type ERRCNTRL should be

allocated by the calling routine in such a way that it remains
unmolested while error checking is occuring. The field frsterr in that
variable should be initialized to nil by the calling before the first
call to FlgAsErr. *)
```
ERRPTR  = POINTER TO ERRRCRD;
ERRRCRD = RECORD
   nexterr      :ERRPTR;
   fldnmbr      :CARDINAL;
   errnmbr      :CARDINAL;
   majerr       :BOOLEAN;
   END;
ERRCNTRL = RECORD
   nmbrmaj:CARDINAL;
   nmbrmin:CARDINAL;
   frsterr:ERRPTR;
   lasterr:ERRPTR;
   END;
 STDEMSG = PROCEDURE(STRING,BOOLEAN,CARDINAL);
```
(* The STDEMSG procedure type is used to transalate an errnmbr into a
    message that will be displayed for the user. Each program or module
    that uses RedoErrs should define a STDEMSG procedure. *)
(*---EL0501.ExcCSet -*)
PROCEDURE ExcCSet(ch:CHAR; VAR chset:CHARSET);
(* This routine will remove the character ch from the Character Set
   defined by chset. *)
(*---EL1011.FDateToW-*)
PROCEDURE FDateToW(VAR w:WORD;fdate:DATE);
(* This routine will convert the value of fdate, a string in the form
   yymmdd, into a single word in the format used by DOS to store the date a
   file was last modified. *)
(*---EL1017.FileAtt -*)
PROCEDURE FileAtt(opcode:BYTE;dsname:STRING; VAR attrib:WORD):BYTE;
(* This routine will attempt to return the attribute for the file
   associated with dsname. If an error occurs, the function will return
   set to the appropriate error code. Otherwise the function will return =
   0, and if opcode = 0 attrib will be set to the attribute byte for the
   file, or if opcode = 1, the file attribute will be set to attrib. *)
(*---EL0302.FillByte-*)
PROCEDURE FillByte(value:BYTE;VAR t:ARRAY OF BYTE;ti,n:CARDINAL);
(* This routine will fill the memory area beginning with t[ti] with n
   bytes of value. *)
(*---EL0405.FillStr -*)
PROCEDURE FillStr(s:STRING;c:CHAR);
   (* This routine will fill s with the CHAR supplied. *)
(*---EL0902.FindCRT -*)
PROCEDURE FindCRT;
(* This routine will determine which display adapter is currently in use,
   and set the appropriate address in the variable crtads. Note that
   FindCRT should normally be called before any other routine that uses the
   CRT, but, crtads will default to the monochrome adapter. *)
(*---EL1002.FindDS -*)
PROCEDURE FindDS(ddname,dsname:STRING);
(* This routine will locate the dsname associated with ddname. If the
   corresponding name entry cannot be found in the program parameters,
   dsname will equal ddname on return. *)
(*---EL1018.FindFile-*)
PROCEDURE FindFile(ddname:STRING;kind:WORD; filename:STRING;
                       VAR attrib:WORD; VAR ftime:TIME;VAR fdate:DATE;
                       VAR filesize:LONGCARD):BOOLEAN;
(* This routine will search the path and volume associated with ddname for
   a file that matches the associated file name. The file name may include
   global file search characters. If StrLen(filename) = 0 on entry, the

routine will assume that this is the first call; otherwise, the routine
will return the next matching file. If, on entry, kine = 0, only normal
files will be found. Otherwise, all files whose attribute matches one
of the attribute bits set will be returned. When no more files can be
found, the function will return FALSE. *)
(*--EL1002.FindHndl-*)
PROCEDURE FindHndl(ddname:STRING; VAR lastfid,thisfid:FIDPTR):BOOLEAN;
(* This routine will search the list of file definitions to locate the
file handle associated with the specified ddname. If the file handle is
not defined, the function will return FALSE. *)
(*--EL1104.FindNdx -*)
PROCEDURE FindNdx(ddname:STRING;VAR rcrd:RCRD; VAR nmbr:LONGCARD;
                        keyloc,keylen:CARDINAL;
                    VAR hook:NODEPTR;top:BOOLEAN):BOOLEAN;
(* This routine will attempt to locate a record in the file associated with
ddname whose key matches the key portion of rcrd. If a matching record
exists, its contents will be returned in rcrd, nmbr will be set to the
appropriate record number, and the function will return true. If a
record cannot be found, nmbr will return = 0 and the function will be
false. *)
(*--EL0801.FindParm-*)
PROCEDURE FindParm(parmid,parmval:STRING):BOOLEAN;
(* If a program parameter matching parmid can be found, this routine will
return TRUE and parmval will be set accordingly; otherwise the routine
will return FALSE and StrLLen(parmval) will equal zero. *)
(*--EL1002.FixName -*)
PROCEDURE FixName(dsname,volname:STRING);
(* This routine will fix up the dsname and separate out the volname, if one
is specified. If dsname includes the '!' character, each occurrence
will be replaced with the value of the DIRNAME parameter defined for the
main program. The routine expects dsname to be in the form of an ASCIIZ
string. *)
(*--EL0805.FixParm -*)
PROCEDURE FixParm(parmval:STRING);
(* This routine will replace all occurences of [<id>] in parmval with the
value associated with program parameter defined by <id>. For example:

        DEVICE=C
        CLNTNMBR=1231
        SUBDIR=CLNT[CLNTNMBR]
        ACCOUNTS=[DEVICE]:\[SUBDIR]\ACCOUNTS.MST

This sequence will be translated into:

        ACCOUNTS=C:\CLNT1231\ACCOUNTS.MST
*)
(*--EL0404.FixStr -*)
PROCEDURE FixStr(s:STRING):STRING;
(* This procedure rebuilds the contents of s, and returns, as its function
value, the rebuilt STRING. Normally, s contains special constructs and
is the result of a call to Literal, as in:

        CopyStr(FixStr(Literal("'An example'*cr*lf")),string);

Note that the constant is enclosed in double-quotes, with imbedded
single quotes, and the * operator. The * indicates that FixStr should
concatentate the cr and lf characters onto the end of the 'An example'
literal. Any characters within single quotes are copied into the
resulting string exactly as written. Other characters may be specified
by using their corresponding constant name (from EL0304); by specifying
CHR(x), where x defines the appropriate value; or, as #hh, where the #
indicates a hexi-decimal value defined by hh. For example:

```
        CopyStr(FixStr(Literal("CHR(0)*CHR(16)*#20*#20")),string);
*)
(*--------------------------------------------------------EL0701.flags   -*)
CONST
  carryflg = 0;  parflg  = 2;  auxcflg = 4;  zeroflg = 6;
  signflg  = 7;  trapflg = 8;  intflg  = 9;  dirflg  = 10;  ovrflg = 11;
(*--------------------------------------------------------EL1416.FldChgd -*)
PROCEDURE FldChgd(fldnmbr:CARDINAL;VAR thisscrn:ADDRESS):BOOLEAN;
(* This routine will return true if the flag maintained for the field in
   the specified scrn indicates that a change has been made to contents of
   the field since the last time that the flag was reset.  If no change has
   been made, the function will return false.  In either case, the field
   flag will be reset before control returns.  Note that when a screen is
   loaded, all flags are set to "No change".  *)
(*--------------------------------------------------------EL1415.FldLngth-*)
PROCEDURE FldLngth(fld:CARDINAL;VAR scrn:ADDRESS):CARDINAL;
(* This function will return the number of bytes in the deScreen field
   specified.  *)
(*--------------------------------------------------------EL0505.FLDS    -*)
CONST
  maxflds = 32766;
  maxarea = 32766;
TYPE
  FLDLIST = ARRAY [0..maxflds] OF CARDINAL;
  FLPTR = POINTER TO FLDLIST;
  AREA = ARRAY [0..maxarea] OF WORD;
  AREAPTR = POINTER TO AREA;
(*--------------------------------------------------------EL1417.FlgAsErr-*)
PROCEDURE FlgAsErr(fld,err:CARDINAL;majerr:BOOLEAN;VAR errs:ERRCNTRL);
(* This routine is used in conjunction with the deScreen routines to
   associate an error code with a specific deScreen field.  The error codes
   are defined in the procedure named STDEMSG and majerr defines whether or
   not the error is to be considered a Major error (i.e., must be corrected
   before further processing can be done).  The value parameters will be
   used to construct an errrcrd which will be appended to the chain of such
   records pointed to by frsterr and lasterr.  Note that the first time
   this routine is called, frsterr should be set = nil which will cause the
   other variables to be initialized before use.  If a calling program does
   not wish to use the standard error messages, it need only include a new
   StdEMsg procedure and not access the library.  *)
(*--------------------------------------------------------EL0901.FlushKB -*)
PROCEDURE FlushKB;
(* This routine will flush any pending characters from the keyboard
   buffer.  This can be used to prevent "type ahead" operations.  *)
(*--------------------------------------------------------EL1103.FlushNdx-*)
PROCEDURE FlushNdx(ddname:STRING;VAR p:NODEPTR);
(* This routine will ensure that the entire tree from a given node downward
   is written to the NDX file.  *)
(*--------------------------------------------------------EL1106.FreeNdx -*)
PROCEDURE FreeNdx(ddname:STRING;VAR rcrd:RCRD; keyloc,keylen:CARDINAL;
                   VAR hook:NODEPTR; top,updtdir:BOOLEAN);
(* This routine will attempt to delete the NDX record whose key matches the
   key portion of rcrd from the file associated with ddname.  If a record
   with a matching key exists, the record will be removed from the normal
   tree within the file, the record's contents will be set to binary
   zeroes, and the record's number will be added to the chain of free
   records in the file.  If a record with a matching key does not exist,
   the results of this routine are undefined.  If a record is removed, and
   updtdir = TRUE on entry, the file will be closed before returning so
   that the directory will be properly updated.  *)
(*--------------------------------------------------------EL1409.FreeScrn-*)
PROCEDURE FreeScrn(VAR thisscrn:ADDRESS);
```

(* This routine will clear the deScreen definition associated with thisscrn
   and release the space it occupies. *)
(*--EL1011.FTimeToW-*)
PROCEDURE FTimeToW(VAR w:WORD;ftime:TIME);
(* This routine will convert the value of ftime, a string in the form
   hhmmss, into a single word in the format used by DOS to store the time a
   file was last modified. *)
(*--EL0907.GetCursr-*)
PROCEDURE GetCursr(VAR line,column:CARDINAL);
(* This routine will return the current cursor position on the display
   currently in effect. Note that line will be between 1 and 25...column
   will be between 1 and 80. *)
(*--EL0707.GetDate -*)
PROCEDURE GetDate(VAR date:DATE);
(* This routine will return the current setting of the system date, in
   YYMMDD format. *)
(*--EL1420.GetDDate-*)
PROCEDURE GetDDate(yymmdd:STRING;yfld,mfld,dfld:CARDINAL;
                              VAR thisscrn:ADDRESS);
(* This procedure will access the appropriate fields in the descreen
   defined by thisscrn and assemble them in yymmdd. Note that if dfld = 0,
   it will not be included in the operation, and only the yymm portion of
   the string will be accessed. *)
(*--EL1016.GetDir -*)
PROCEDURE GetDir(ddname,dir:STRING):WORD;
(* This routine will attempt to locate the current path defined for the
   device associated with ddname. If no error occurs, dir will return the
   path. The function value will indicate the success or failure of the
   operation. *)
(*--EL1010.GetFcdt -*)
PROCEDURE GetFcdt(ddname:STRING; VAR fdate:DATE;VAR ftime:TIME):BOOLEAN;
(* If the file associated with ddname does not exist, the function will
   return FALSE...otherwise the function will return TRUE and fdate and
   ftime will be set to the date and time that the file was last modified.
   fdate is in the form yymmdd. ftime is in the form hhmmss. *)
(*--EL1410.GetFld -*)
PROCEDURE GetFld(fldnmbr:CARDINAL;fldvalue:STRING;VAR thisscrn:ADDRESS);
(* A deScreen procedure that returns the current value of the specified
   field from the identified screen definition. *)
(*--EL0901.GetKBChr-*)
PROCEDURE GetKBChr(VAR eascii:BOOLEAN;VAR kbchar:CHAR):BOOLEAN;
(* This routine will inspect the keyboard buffer and return FALSE if no
   character is pending. If a character is available, the routine will
   return TRUE and kbchar will contain the character. If the character is
   a standard ASCII character, eascii will return FALSE. If the character
   is Extended ASCII (such as one of the function keys or cursor control
   keys), eascii will return true. *)
(*--EL1003.GetLine -*)
PROCEDURE GetLine(ddname,line:STRING; getcrlf:LINECNTRL):BOOLEAN;
(* This routine will begin reading a character at a time from the current
   position of the file associated with ddname. Characters will be
   inserted in LINE until a carriage return/line feed sequence is
   encountered, or, until line is full. If getcrlf = rtrnend, the cr/lf
   sequence will be included in line. On return, StrLen(line) will be set
   accordingly. If GetLine returns FALSE, the file is at EOF. *)
(*--EL1110.GetLink -*)
PROCEDURE GetLink(ddname:STRING;VAR rcrd:RCRD;
                              thislink:LONGCARD;VAR nextlink:LONGCARD);
(* This routine will attempt to read the record pointed to by thislink from
   the LNK file associated with ddname. On return, nextlink will point to
   the next record in the same chain, or will be set to zero if thislink is
   the chain end. *)

```
(*-----------------------------------------------------EL1102.GetNdx  -*)
PROCEDURE GetNdx(ddname:STRING;nmbr:LONGCARD; VAR left,right:LONGCARD;
                     VAR bal:INTEGER;VAR thisrcrd:RCRD);
(* This routine will read the NDX record identified by nmbr from the file
   associated with ddname.  *)
(*-----------------------------------------------------EL0801.GetNParm-*)
PROCEDURE GetNParm(parmid,parmval:STRING):BOOLEAN;
(* If, on entry, StrLLen(parmid) = 0, this routine will return the parmid
   and parmval for the first parameter in the program parameter
   list...otherwise, the routine will return the next parameter in the
   list.  If no more program parameters are defined, the routine will
   return false and the length of both parmid and parmval will equal 0.  *)
(*-----------------------------------------------------EL0801.GetParms-*)
PROCEDURE GetParms;
(* This routine will gather all of the program parameters passed from the
   operating system.  This includes both parameters on the command line and
   those in the DOS environment when the program is loaded.  *)
(*-----------------------------------------------------EL1005.GetRcrd -*)
PROCEDURE GetRcrd(ddname:STRING;loccntrl:LOCCNTRL;
                  lastnmbr:LONGCARD;VAR nmbr:LONGCARD;
                  lentoget:WORD;VAR lengot:WORD; rcrd:ADDRESS):BOOLEAN;
(* This routine will attempt to read lentoget bytes from the file
   associated with ddname.  If, on entry, locate = setpostn, the file will
   be set to the byte indicated by:

        lentoget * (lastnmbr - 1)

   before the read is attempted.  Otherwise the file will be left at the
   position it was last set to.  If, in either case, the file is set to end
   of file, the function will return FALSE.  On return, lengot will
   indicate the number of bytes actually transferred.  *)
(*-----------------------------------------------------EL0307.GetTHeap-*)
PROCEDURE GetTHeap(VAR adr:ADDRESS;nbytes:CARDINAL);
(* This routine will allocate a variable on the temporary heap that is
   nbytes long and referenced by adr.  Note that any other temporary heap
   variables whose referenced ADDRESS is after adr will be cleared before
   the new area is allocated.  *)
(*-----------------------------------------------------EL0707.GetTime -*)
PROCEDURE GetTime(VAR time:TIME);
(* This routine will return the current setting of the system time, in
   HHMMDD format.  *)
(*-----------------------------------------------------EL0702.GetVectr-*)
PROCEDURE GetVectr(number:WORD):ADDRESS;
(* This routine will return the ADDRESS to which the interupt vector
   associated with number points.  *)
(*-----------------------------------------------------EL0707.GetWkDay-*)
PROCEDURE GetWkDay(wkday:STRING);
(* This routine will return a STRING containing the complete name of the
   day of week indicated by the current setting of the system clock.  *)
(*-----------------------------------------------------EL1302.Help    -*)
PROCEDURE Help(helpname,inxname:STRING;msgno:CARDINAL;VAR hlpframe:FRAME);
(* This routine will provide an on-screen help message corresponding to the
   contents of msgno.  The file identified by helpname contains the actual
   messages...the file associated with inxname is used as an index to those
   messages.  These files must be prepared by the NDXHELP program.  The
   messages appear on the screen in the area in hlpframe.  If the message
   requires more than that number of lines, this routine will permit the
   user to scroll them up and down, using the cursor control keys.  When
   the user presses the help key, this routine will clear that area and
   return to the calling procedure.  *)
(*-----------------------------------------------------EL0301.HiByte  -*)
PROCEDURE HiByte(twobytes:WORD):BYTE;
```

```
(* This routine will return the most significant byte of twobytes.  *)
(*------------------------------------------------------EL0501.IncCSet -*)
PROCEDURE IncCSet(ch:CHAR; VAR chset:CHARSET);
(* This routine will include the character ch in the Character Set defined
   by chset.  *)
(*------------------------------------------------------EL1412.IncFld  -*)
PROCEDURE IncFld(fld:STRING);
(* This routine will add '1' to the contents of the numeric field defined
   by fld.  *)
(*------------------------------------------------------EL0501.InCSet  -*)
PROCEDURE InCSet(ch:CHAR; chset:CHARSET):BOOLEAN;
(* This routine will determine if the character ch is in the set defined
   by chset, returning TRUE if it does.  *)
(*------------------------------------------------------EL0901.InitKB  -*)
PROCEDURE InitKB(caplock,numlock:BOOLEAN);
(* This routine will set the keyboard control states according to the
   values given.  *)
(*------------------------------------------------------EL0908.InputKB -*)
PROCEDURE InputKB(color:BYTE; msg,msgin:STRING;
                        VAR cl:CARDINAL;  VAR frame:FRAME);
(* This routine will display the contents of msg on the CRT and then read a
   string of characters from the keyboard up to but not including a
   carriage return.  When the carriage return is encountered, control
   returns to the calling routine, after a Line Feed is issued.  Normal
   backspace editing applies.  The characters entered by the user will be
   displayed in the color indicated.  All of the characters input must fit
   on the line at which input begins.  This routine is used in conjunction
   with TypeMsg.  Both routines restrict the cursor to within the limits
   defined by frame.  *)
(*------------------------------------------------------EL0402.Insert  -*)
PROCEDURE Insert(source,dest:STRING;d:CARDINAL);
(* This routine will insert source into dest, beginning at d.  Note that
   the current length of dest will be adjusted.  *)
(*------------------------------------------------------EL0701.Interupt-*)
PROCEDURE Interupt(    number:BYTE;
                VAR axreg,bxreg,cxreg,dxreg,dsreg,
                           esreg,direg,sireg,flags:WORD);
(*   This routine will issue a software interupt to the interupt vector
   associated with number.  The remaining variables correspond to the
   machine registers.  Usuage of these variables depends on the interupt
   issued.  *)
(*------------------------------------------------------EL0606.IntToStr-*)
PROCEDURE IntToStr(nmbr:INTEGER;width:CARDINAL;dest:STRING);
(* This routine will convert nmbr into a sequence of width characters,
   with the value right justified in dest.  If the number is less than
   zero, a '-' will be included in dest.  *)
(*------------------------------------------------------EL1002.IOCONSTS-*)
CONST
(* These constants define bit patterns for testing the attribute bits
   associated with a file.  *)
  nowrite = 0001H;   hidden = 0002H;   sysfile = 0004H;   volume = 0008H;
  subdir  = 0010H;   archive = 0020H;
(*------------------------------------------------------EL1002.IOTYPES -*)
TYPE
(* Non-Standard IO types. *)
  FMODE     = (newfile,oldfile,makenew,makeold,append);
  OPENKIND  = (insist,tryonce);
  DISP      = (clsonly,clsanddel);
  LINECNTRL = (endline,noendline,rtrnend,nortrnend);
  LOCCNTRL  = (setpostn,usepostn,seteof);
(* These type definitions are used by the IO control routines defined
   within the ETLING library.
```

FMODE refers to the status a file must have when it is first opened by a program.

newfile ...   The file must not exist on the volume. A new file
              with the indicated name will be created.
oldfile ...   The file must exist on the volume.
makenew ...   If a file with the indicated name already exists on
              the volume, it will be deleted and a new file created.
makeold ...   If a file with the indicated name already exists on the
              volume, it will be used, otherwise a new file will be
              created.
append ...   Just like MAKEOLD, except that if the file exists, its file
              pointer will be set to the end of the file before any new
              data is written.

OPENKIND defines how error conditions should be treated when opening a file.

insist ...   Do not return to caller until file can be opened
              successfully.
tryonce ...   Return to caller after one attempt to open file, regardless
              of error conditions.

DISP defines how a file should be handled after it is closed.

clsonly ...   Simply close the file.
clsanddel .   Close the file, then delete it from the directory.

LINCNTRL is used to control whether or not the Carriage Return / Line
Feed sequence is included in the read or write operation on a DOS text
file.

endline ... Write CR/LF after end of line.
noendline .   Do not write the CR/LF after end of line.
rtrnend ... Include the CR/LF in the line read from a file.
nortrnend .   Do not include the CR/LF in a read.

LOCCNTRL specifies how the file pointer is to be set before accessing a
file randomly.

setpostn ..   Set the file pointer to the position indicated.
usepostn ..   Use the current file pointer position.
seteof   ... Set the file pointer to the byte right after the end of file.
*)
  FIDPTR = POINTER TO FID;
  FID = RECORD
    nxtfid : FIDPTR;
    handle : WORD;
    ddname : STRING;
    END;
VAR
  frstfid : FIDPTR;
  vols   : ARRAY [0..25] OF STRING;
(*--EL1412.IsBlank -*)
PROCEDURE IsBlank(mc,ml:CARDINAL;VAR image:SMAP;VAR fld:FLDDEF):BOOLEAN;
(* This routine will check the contents of the field specified by fld and
   return TRUE if it is all blank. *)
(*--EL1108.LastNdx -*)
PROCEDURE LastNdx(ddname:STRING;VAR rcrd:RCRD;
                  VAR nmbr:LONGCARD;keyloc,keylen:CARDINAL;
                  VAR hook:NODEPTR;top,continue:BOOLEAN):BOOLEAN;
(* This routine will locate a record in the NDX file associated with ddname

whose key is equal to or less than the key in rcrd. If continue = TRUE
on entry, only a record with a lesser key will be returned. If a record
exists, the function will return true and nmbr will contain the number
of the record. If no more records exist, the function will return false
and nmbr = 0. *)

```
(*-------------------------------------------------EL1412.LeaveFld-*)
PROCEDURE LeaveFld(mc,ml:CARDINAL;VAR image:SMAP;VAR boxes:BDTBL;
                   VAR flds:FDTBL;curbox,curfld:CARDINAL);
(* This routine handles the operations required to leave a field. *)
(*-------------------------------------------------EL0401.Literal -*)
TYPE
  LITERAL  = PROCEDURE(ARRAY OF CHAR):STRING;
VAR
  Literal  : LITERAL;
(* The procedure variable, Literal, provides a way for a client module to
   use an array of chars as a STRING. The parameter may be a string
   constant or a normal ARRAY OF CHAR. Note that this routine creates a
   temporary STRING, referenced by an entry on the stack. The Literal
   procedure should only be used to create a calling parameter...the
   temporary STRING may be overwritten by any other stack reference.  *)
(*-------------------------------------------------EL1110.LNKTYPES-*)
TYPE
  LNKFCTRL = RECORD
    ddname    : STRING;
    rcrdnmbr  : LONGCARD;
    rcrd      : RCRD;
    rfldarea  : RFLDLIST;
    END;
(*-------------------------------------------------EL1409.LoadScrn-*)
PROCEDURE LoadScrn(scrnfile:STRING; VAR thisscrn:ADDRESS);
(* This is the first routine in the deScreen series. It is used to load a
   deScreen ".img" file and establish the required control variables in
   core. If the <dsname> associated with scrnfile can be opened and read
   successfully thisscrn will return pointing to the defined control area.
   (If the file cannot be loaded successfully, the routine will call
   Cancel). The variable thisscrn should be allocated by the caller in
   such a way that it is un-molested during screen access. The first call
   to any deScreen routine should be to LoadScrn which will allocate and
   initialize core for this area...subsequent calls use this variable to
   inform the screen handling routines which definition is being used.
   Therefore, a single program may use multiple screens with a different
   thisscrn for each.  *)
(*-------------------------------------------------EL0301.LoByte  -*)
PROCEDURE LoByte(twobytes:WORD):BYTE;
(* This routine will return the least significant byte of twobytes.  *)
(*-------------------------------------------------EL0503.LongCard-*)
PROCEDURE LongCard(loword,hiword:CARDINAL; VAR lcrd:LONGCARD);
(* This routine will create a double word CARDINAL on the heap, and return
   a pointer to it.  *)
(*-------------------------------------------------EL0602.MakCard -*)
PROCEDURE MakCard(source:STRING; s:CARDINAL; VAR stop:CARDINAL):CARDINAL;
(* This routine will convert the sequence of numeric characters in source
   (beginning at s) into a CARDINAL, which is returned as the function
   value. Conversion will stop when a non-numeric character is
   encountered, or the end of the STRING is reached. On exit, stop will be
   set to the last character processed, or, to the length of source +1.  *)
(*-------------------------------------------------EL0505.MakeArea-*)
PROCEDURE MakeArea(l:CARDINAL;VAR a:AREAPTR);
(* This routine will create an area on the heap capable of holding l words.
   Note that the first word contains a count of the number of additional
   words allocated. The routine assumes that the contents of a are of no
   consequence on entry.  *)
```

```
(*--------------------------------------------------------EL0501.MakeCSet-*)
PROCEDURE MakeCSet(chars:STRING;VAR chset:CHARSET);
(* This routine will create a CHARSET from the string defined by chars.
   Each character in chars will be included in chset.  *)
(*--------------------------------------------------------EL1111.MakeLink-*)
PROCEDURE MakeLink(ddname:STRING;oldlink:LONGCARD;
                      rcrd:RCRD;VAR newlink:LONGCARD);
(* This routine will add a new record to the LNK file associated with
   ddname.  On entry, if oldline = 0, a new chain will be started,
   otherwise, rcrd will be chained from the record specified by oldlink.
   newlink will return with the record number of the new record. Note that
   rcrd does not include space for the LNK pointers.  The LNK routines
   maintain the chain in an area that is separate from the rcrd area.  *)
(*--------------------------------------------------------EL1202.MakeLTbl-*)
PROCEDURE MakeLTbl(nlines,length:CARDINAL):LTBLPTR;
(* This procedure will build a Line Table, for use with the report handling
   routines in this module.  The table will have nlines lines, each of
   length characters.  *)
(*--------------------------------------------------------EL1102.MakeNode-*)
PROCEDURE MakeNode(VAR thisnode:NODEPTR;length:CARDINAL);
(* This routine will create a new NODEPTR record.  *)
(*--------------------------------------------------------EL1007.MakeRcrd-*)
PROCEDURE MakeRcrd(rcrdlen:CARDINAL;VAR rcrd:RCRD);
(* This procedure will create a record definition in memory capable of
   containing up to rcrdlen bytes.  *)
(*--------------------------------------------------------EL0504.MakeSMap-*)
PROCEDURE MakeSMap(nl,nc:CARDINAL;VAR s:SMAPPTR);
(* This routine will create a SCREENMAP on the heap, capable of containing
   the number of DISPLAYWORDs defined by the parameters.  Note that s is
   assumed to be undefined on entry.  *)
(*--------------------------------------------------------EL0401.MakeStr -*)
PROCEDURE MakeStr(VAR s:STRING;l:CARDINAL;init:STRING);
(* This routine will create a new STRING.  The CARDINAL, l, defines the
   total number of characters that the new STRING can contain...if it is
   zero, the length of the init parameter will determine the new STRING's
   maximum length.  The init parameter defines the new STRING's current
   length and initial contents.  Note that it is not logical to specify l =
   0 and init = nullstr.  On entry, the current value of s is assumed to be
   unknown.  *)
(*--------------------------------------------------------EL0505.MakFList-*)
PROCEDURE MakFList(l:CARDINAL;VAR f:FLPTR);
(* This routine will create a list on the heap capable of holding l
   cardinal values.  Note that the first word contains a count of the
   number of additional cardinals allocated.  The routines assumes that the
   contents of f are of no consequence on entry.  *)
(*--------------------------------------------------------EL0504.MakFrame-*)
PROCEDURE MakFrame(fl,fc,ll,lc,cl,cc,nl,nc:CARDINAL;
                      a:ADDRESS;VAR f:FRAMEPTR);
(* This routine will create a new Frame on the heap.  If a = NIL, the
   routine will also create an associated SCREENMAP, otherwise, f^.s will
   be set equal to a.  Note that f is assumed to be undefined on entry.  *)
(*--------------------------------------------------------EL0604.MakInt :-*)
PROCEDURE MakInt(source:STRING; s:CARDINAL;
                   VAR stop:CARDINAL):INTEGER;
(* This routine will convert the sequence of numeric characters in source
   (beginning at s) into an INTEGER, which is returned as the function
   value.  Conversion will stop when a non-numeric character is
   encountered, or the end of the STRING is reached.  On exit, stop will be
   set to the last character processed, or, to the length of source + 1. *)
(*--------------------------------------------------------EL0603.MakLCard-*)
PROCEDURE MakLCard(source:STRING; s:CARDINAL;
                     VAR stop:CARDINAL;VAR l:LONGCARD);
```

```
(* This routine will convert the sequence of numeric characters in source
   (beginning at s) into a LONGCARD, which is returned in l.  Conversion
   will stop when a non-numeric character is encountered, or the end of the
   STRING is reached.  On exit, stop will be set to the last character
   processed, or, set to the length of source + 1.  *)
(*-------------------------------------------------------EL0601.MakReal -*)
PROCEDURE MakReal(source:STRING; s:CARDINAL; VAR stop:CARDINAL):REAL;
(* This routine will convert the sequence of numeric characters in source
   (beginning at s) into a REAL, which is returned as the function value.
   Conversion will stop when a non-numeric character is encountered, or the
   end of the STRING is reached.  On exit, stop will be set to the last
   character processed, or, will equal the length of source + 1.  *)
(*-------------------------------------------------------EL1007.MakRFlds-*)
PROCEDURE MakRFlds(nmbrflds:CARDINAL;VAR rfldlist:RFLDLIST);
(* This routine will create field definition controls in memory capable of
   defining nmbrflds fields.  *)
(*-------------------------------------------------------EL1105.MarkNdx -*)
PROCEDURE MarkNdx(ddname:STRING;VAR rcrd:RCRD;
                  VAR nmbr:LONGCARD;keyloc,keylen:CARDINAL;
                  VAR hook:NODEPTR;top,updtdir:BOOLEAN);
(* This routine will add a record to the NDX file associated with ddname.
   If a matching record already exists, the results of this routine are
   undefined...be sure to call FindNdx first to see if a record exists.  If
   a new record is created, nmbr will return with the appropriate record
   number.  If, on entry, updtdir = TRUE, the file will be closed so that
   the directory will be properly updated.  *)
(*-------------------------------------------------------EL0403.MatchStr-*)
PROCEDURE MatchStr(string1,string2:STRING;s1,s2,l:CARDINAL):MATCHVAL;
(* This routine will compare l characters in the STRINGs, beginning at s
   and s2.  The compare is done according to the arrangement of characters
   in the normal ASCII collating sequence.  The results of the compare are
   returned as follows:

       If string1 < string2 then MatchStr = less
       If string1 = string2 then MatchStr = equal
       If string1 > string2 then MatchStr = greater

   If, on entry, l = 0, the length of the longer STRING will control the
   length.  If one string is longer than the other (but contain equal
   characters) the routine will return indicating that the shorter string
   comes before the longer in the collating sequence.  *)
(*-------------------------------------------------------EL0303.MATCHVAL-*)
CONST
  less = -1;   equal = 0;   greater = 1;
TYPE
  MATCHVAL = [less..greater];
(*-------------------------------------------------------EL1414.MaxFlds -*)
PROCEDURE MaxFlds(VAR scrn:ADDRESS):CARDINAL;
(* This function will return the total number of fields defined for the
   deScreen definiton specified.  Note that the count includes constant
   fields as well as variable fields.  *)
(*-------------------------------------------------------EL0305.MEMLOCTN-*)
TYPE
  MEMLOCTN = (inheap,instack,incode);
(* This TYPE is used to indicate where a given address falls within the
   currently executing program.  *)
(*-------------------------------------------------------EL0905.Message -*)
PROCEDURE Message(msg1,msg2:STRING; VAR msgframe:FRAME;
                  wait:CARDINAL; normals,easciis:CHARSET;
                  VAR eascii:BOOLEAN;VAR kbchar:CHAR);
(* This routine is a standardized error or instruction message handler.  It
   uses two lines on the display to show a message to the user and then,
```

either returns immediately (if both normals and easciis are equal to the
null set) or waits for the user to enter one of the keys corresponding
to a member of one of the sets. The character that terminates the
routine will return in kbchar. eascii will indicate whether or not the
character is an extended ASCII character. If the user enters a
character that is not in either set, an appropriate error message is
displayed and the standard error sound is made. Both messages are
displayed within msgframe. If StrLen(msg1) > O, it is displayed at
msgframe[fl,fc]. msg2 is displayed on msgframe[ll,lc]. Existing
contents of those lines are lost; the screen is not scrolled. If, on
entry, wait > O, the routine will use ChkTimer to allow the user
approximately wait seconds to respond...if the user doesn't respond
within that time, the routine will call Sound to attract attention. *)
(*--EL1013.MkDir   -*)
PROCEDURE MkDir(ddname:STRING):WORD;
(* This routine will attempt to create a directory according to the path
   defined in ddname. If the operation is successful, the function will
   return = O. Otherwise, the routine will return equal to the error
   returned from DOS. *)
(*--EL1002.MountVol-*)
PROCEDURE MountVol(volname:STRING;askfirst:BOOLEAN);
(* This routine will ensure that the correct disk or diskette is mounted in
   the device associated with volname. If, on entry, askfirst = TRUE, the
   user will be instructed to mount the correct volume...otherwise, the
   routine will check the device immediately. Control will not return to
   the caller until the device is mounted. *)
(*--EL0302.MovByteL-*)
PROCEDURE MovByteL(VAR f,t:ARRAY OF BYTE;fi,ti,n:CARDINAL);
(* This routine will move n bytes from the byte address specified by f[fi]
   to the byte address specified by t[ti]. Transfer starts with the
   leftmost (i.e., lowest) memory location of both areas. Note that there
   is no error checking done in conjunction with this routine. *)
(*--EL0302.MovByteR-*)
PROCEDURE MovByteR(VAR f,t:ARRAY OF BYTE;fi,ti,n:CARDINAL);
(* This routine will move n bytes from the byte address specified by f[fi]
   to the byte address specified by t[ti]. Transfer starts with the
   rightmost (i.e., highest) memory location of both areas. Note that
   there is no error checking done in conjunction with this routine. *)
(*--EL1412.MoveCur -*)
PROCEDURE MoveCur(VAR box:BOXDEF;VAR curline,curclmn:CARDINAL;
                        increment:INTEGER);
(* This routine moves the cursor to the new location. *)
(*--EL0401.MoveStr -*)
PROCEDURE MoveStr(source,dest:STRING;d:CARDINAL);
(* This routine will move all characters from source into dest, begining
   at d. If StrLen(dest) is not large enough to contain all of source, the
   move will be truncated. If StrLen(source) < StrLen(dest) − d then dest
   will be filled with blanks. Note that StrLen(dest) is not adjusted. *)
(*--EL0504.MovFrame-*)
PROCEDURE MovFrame(VAR f,t:FRAME);
(* This routine will move the contents of the screenmap refered to by f to
   the corresponsing area in t. The move is done line by line, beginning
   at f.cl and t.cl and will extend for only as many lines and columns as
   will fit in t. *)
(*--EL1007.MovFRcrd-*)
PROCEDURE MovFRcrd(VAR rcrd:RCRD;VAR rfldlist:RFLDLIST;
                        dest:ADDRESS;length,fldnmbr:CARDINAL);
(* This routine will move data from the rcrd^.area to the ADDRESS defined
   by dest. The location of the data in the rcrd^.area is controlled by
   rfldlist^.loc[fldnmbr]. The number of bytes moved is length (If length
   = O, length will be set to rfldlist^.len[fldnmbr]). If length is less
   than rfldlist^.len[fldnmbr], excess bytes in the record will be ignored.

If length is greater than rfldlist^.len[fldnmbr], the extra bytes in dest will be set to blank. The variable associated with dest must be large enough to contain the data. *)

(*--EL1007.MovTRcrd-*)
```
PROCEDURE MovTRcrd(VAR rcrd:RCRD;VAR rfldlist:RFLDLIST;
                        source:ADDRESS;length,fldnmbr:CARDINAL);
```
(* This routine will move data from the ADDRESS defined by source into rcrd^.area[rfldlist^.loc^[fldnmbr]]. The number of bytes moved is controlled by rfldlist^.len[fldnmbr]. If length is less than rfldlist^.len[fldnmbr] then the remaining bytes in the rcrd^.area field will be set to blanks. *)

(*--EL0503.MulLCard-*)
```
PROCEDURE MulLCard(lcrd1,lcrd2:LONGCARD; VAR lcrdrslt:LONGCARD);
```
(* This routine will perform the equation :

$$lcrdrslt := lcrd1.locard * lcrd2.locard$$

*)

(*--EL1102.NDXTYPES-*)
```
TYPE
  NODEPTR = RECORD
    ptr       : POINTER TO NODE;
    nmbr      : LONGCARD;
    END;
  NODE = RECORD
    left      : NODEPTR;
    right     : NODEPTR;
    balance   : INTEGER;
    rcrd      : RCRD;
    END;
  NDXFCTRL = RECORD
    ddname    : STRING;
    rcrdnmbr  : LONGCARD;
    rcrd      : RCRD;
    rfldarea  : RFLDLIST;
    hook      : NODEPTR;
    END;
CONST
  ndxclen = 10;
```
(*--EL1107.NextNdx -*)
```
PROCEDURE NextNdx(ddname:STRING;VAR rcrd:RCRD;
                  VAR nmbr:LONGCARD;keyloc,keylen:CARDINAL;
                  VAR hook:NODEPTR; top,continue:BOOLEAN):BOOLEAN;
```
(* This routine will locate a record in the NDX file associated with ddname whose key is equal to or greater than the key in rcrd. If continue is TRUE on entry, only a record with a greater key will be returned. If a record exists, the function will return true and nmbr will contain the number of the record. If no more records exist, the function will return false and nmbr = 0. *)

(*--EL0401.nullstr -*)
```
VAR
  nullstr : STRING;
```
(* The variable nullstr represents an empty string...zero length and no characters. *)

(*--EL0305.OnHeap -*)
```
PROCEDURE MemLoctn(a:ADDRESS):MEMLOCTN;
```
(* This routine will return a value specifing where the a ADDRESS is located. *)

(*--EL1002.OpnFile -*)
```
PROCEDURE OpnFile(ddname:STRING;VAR opnmode:FMODE;
                        VAR ioerr:BYTE;how:OPENKIND);
```
(* This routine will open the file associated with ddname. If a program parameter whose parmid matches ddname exists, the corresponding parmval will be used as the file's dsname; otherwise, ddname will be used for dsname. opnmode indicates what status the file must have to be

opened...it will return either newfile or oldfile to indicate if the
file was created. If the file is already open, the call is simply
ignored. If how = tryonce, only one attempt will be made to open the
file and ioerr will return with a DOS error code indicating the success
or failure of the attempt. Otherwise, the routine will not return to
the caller until the file can be opened. Note that the general format
for a file definition established via program parameters is:

        <ddname>=<dsname>[,<volumename>]

    If <volumename> is given, the device associated with <dsname> will be
    checked to verify that there is a file named <volumename> present on the
    device, BEFORE <dsname> is opened or closed. *)
(*--EL1201.OpnPrint-*)
PROCEDURE OpnPrint(asktoset,eject:BOOLEAN);
(* This procedure will open the file associated with the ddname PRINTER,
    and read that file to define the controls for the printer. If a program
    parameter for that ddname is not given, printed output will be directed
    to LPT1 with a default set of controls. If asktoset = true, this
    procedure will look for a parm named PRTSPOOL...if it exists, the user
    will be given the option of directing printed output there. Otherwise
    the user will be asked to align the paper before returning. If eject =
    TRUE, a form feed will be sent to the file. *)
(*--EL0703.PortIn -*)
PROCEDURE PortIn(number:WORD):WORD;
(* This routine inputs a single WORD (or BYTE, depending on the port
    accessed) from the I/O port specified by number. Note that it is the
    responsibility of the caller to determine whether the entire word is
    meaningful. *)
(*--EL0703.PortOut -*)
PROCEDURE PortOut(number,value:WORD);
(* This routine will send value to the I/O port idenitified by number.
    Note that it is the responsibility of the caller to determine whether
    both bytes of value have meaning. *)
(*--EL0403.Positn -*)
PROCEDURE Positn(pattern,source:STRING; s:CARDINAL):CARDINAL;
(* This routine will begin at s and search for an occurence of pattern in
    source. If a match is found, the index of the first character will be
    returned as the function value. If no match is found, or if s is
    greater than the length of source, the function will return 0. *)
(*--EL1201.Print   -*)
PROCEDURE Print(msg:STRING);
(* This routine will output the contents of msg to the device associated
    with PPORT. The actual assignment for that device is normally found in
    the file associated with the ddname PRINTER, and that file also contains
    the appropriate values for the printer control mnemonics. Any and all
    printer control to be done in the course of printing this message should
    be imbedded in the string in the form of mnemonics enclosed within two
    occurences of the ESC character...CHR(27). These mnemonics will be
    translated into an appropriate character string based on the translation
    table. For example, if msg includes:
                    ESC+'FF'+ESC
    and the printer involved is an IBM PC Graphics Printer, a CHR(12) will
    be written to the printer. The mnemonics are defined in PRTCONSTS. *)
(*--EL1201.PRTCONST-*)
VAR
(*
    Constants for defining printer mnemonics
*)
    pbl, (* ESC+'BL'+ESC   Ring Bell   *)
    pcb, (* ESC+'CB'+ESC   Begin compressed   *)
    pce, (* ESC+'CE'+ESC   End compressed   *)

```
  pcl, (* ESC+'CL'+ESC    Clear Printer Buffer      *)
  pcp, (* ESC+'CP'+ESC    Clear printer to default *)
  pcr, (* ESC+'CR'+ESC    Carriage Return          *)
  pff, (* ESC+'FF'+ESC    Form Feed                *)
  pdb, (* ESC+'DB'+ESC    Begin Double Strike      *)
  pde, (* ESC+'DE'+ESC    End Double Strike        *)
  peb, (* ESC+'EB'+ESC    Begin Emphasized         *)
  pee, (* ESC+'EE'+ESC    End Emphasized           *)
  pel, (* ESC+'EL'+ESC    End Line (usually CR*LF) *)
  plf, (* ESC+'LF'+ESC    Line feed                *)
  pub, (* ESC+'UB'+ESC    Begin Underline          *)
  pue, (* ESC+'UE'+ESC    End Underline            *)
  pwb, (* ESC+'WB'+ESC    Begin Double width       *)
  pwe, (* ESC+'WE'+ESC    End Double width         *)
  pfl: (* ESC+'FL66'+ESC Set form length  (66 may be replaced with
                          any two digits specifing the number of
                          lines per page  *)
      STRING;
(*-------------------------------------------------------EL1202.PRTLINES-*)
CONST
  maxlines = 256;
TYPE
  LTBLPTR = POINTER TO LINETBL;
  LINETBL = RECORD
    nmbr : CARDINAL;
    line : ARRAY [1..maxlines] OF STRING;
    END;
(*-------------------------------------------------------EL1202.PrtRprt -*)
PROCEDURE PrtRprt(prtline:STRING;VAR newpage:BOOLEAN; skiplines:CARDINAL;
                  hdgs:LTBLPTR;VAR pagenmbr,linenmbr:CARDINAL);
(* This procedure will print prtline on a report that has been previously
   defined by a call to SetRprt.  If newpage = true, a form feed will be
   issued and the lines pointed to by hdgs will be printed, before prtline.
   pagenmbr and linenmbr always reflect the current position of the print
   head after printing takes place.  SetRprt will set pagenmbr to
   zero...the first call to PrtRprt after that will cause the actual start
   of the first page.  skiplines indicates the number of lines to skip
   before printing prtline.  If, on entry, skiplines = 0, prtline will be
   printed on the current line of the current page.  The routine always
   issues a pel (the end-of-line printer mnemonic) after prtline...that
   control need not be imbedded in prtline.  Note that newpage will always
   return false.  *)
(*-------------------------------------------------------EL0902.PstnCur -*)
PROCEDURE PstnCur(line,column:CARDINAL;VAR frame:FRAME);
(* This routine will position the CRT cursor to the location specified, and
   frame.cl and frame.cc will be updated accordingly.  Note than no range
   checking is done, but, to avoid unpredictable results:

          1 <= line <= 25       1 <= column <= 80
*)
(*-------------------------------------------------------EL1412.PutChar -*)
PROCEDURE PutChar(mc,ml:CARDINAL;VAR image:SMAP;
                  VAR boxes:BDTBL;VAR flds:FDTBL;
                    VAR curbox,curfld,curline,curclmn:CARDINAL;
                      pchar:CHAR;VAR insrtchr:BOOLEAN):BOOLEAN;
(* This routine will move pchar to the current cursor position and adjust
   the field accordingly.  *)
(*-------------------------------------------------------EL0902.-PutCRT -*)
PROCEDURE PutCRT(color:BYTE;character:CHAR;VAR frame:FRAME);
(* This routine will output character to the CRT, positioned within the
   frame specified.  If the character is a backspace and frame.cc is
   greater than frame.fc, the cursor is moved to [cl,cc-1]; regardless, a
```

blank is moved to the new position. If character is a line feed,
frame.cl is set to frame.cl + 1. If character is a carriage return,
column is set to frame.cl. Any other value for character is moved to
the display buffer at [cl,cc], given the attribute specified by color,
and column is set to column + 1. *)

```
(*----------------------------------------------------------EL1419.PutDDate-*)
PROCEDURE PutDDate(yymmdd:STRING;yfld,mfld,dfld:CARDINAL;
                        VAR thisscrn:ADDRESS);
(* this procedure will move the contents of yymmdd into the descreen
   defined by thisscrn placing them in the appropriate fields. Note that
   if dfld = 0, it will not be included in the operation, and only the yymm
   portion of the string will be accessed.  *)
(*----------------------------------------------------------EL1410.PutFld  -*)
PROCEDURE PutFld(fldnmbr:CARDINAL;fldvalue:STRING;VAR thisscrn:ADDRESS);
(* A deScreen procedure that moves fldvalue into the identified screen
   definition.  *)
(*----------------------------------------------------------EL1004.PutLine -*)
PROCEDURE PutLine(ddname,line:STRING;putcrlf:LINECNTRL);
(* The contents of line will be written to the file associated with ddname.
   If putcrlf = endline, a carriage return / line feed sequence will be
   written after the end of the line.  *)
(*----------------------------------------------------------EL1110.PutLink -*)
PROCEDURE PutLink(ddname:STRING;thisnmbr,nextline:LONGCARD;rcrd:RCRD);
(* This routine will write a record to the LNK file associated with ddname.
   Note that this routine does not link records together and it should only
   be called by an application routine to replace the data portion of an
   existing LNK record.  *)
(*----------------------------------------------------------EL1102.PutNdx  -*)
PROCEDURE PutNdx(ddname:STRING; nmbr,left,right:LONGCARD;bal:INTEGER;
                    thisrcrd:RCRD);
(* This procedure will write the NDX record identified by nmbr to the file
   associated with ddname.  *)
(*----------------------------------------------------------EL1006.PutRcrd -*)
PROCEDURE PutRcrd(ddname:STRING;locate:LOCCNTRL; lastnmbr:LONGCARD;
                    VAR nmbr:LONGCARD; len:WORD;rcrd:ADDRESS);
(* If, on entry, locate = setpostn, the file will be set to the byte
   indicated by:

        lentoget * (lastnmbr - 1)

   before the write is attempted. Otherwise the file will be left at the
   position it was last set to. len bytes from rcrd will be transferred to
   the file. On return, nmbr will be updated accordingly.  *)
(*----------------------------------------------------------EL1103.R1ll    -*)
PROCEDURE R1ll(VAR p,p1:NODEPTR);
(*  Rotate tree once left to left. *)
(*----------------------------------------------------------EL1103.R1rr    -*)
PROCEDURE R1rr(VAR p,p1:NODEPTR);
(*  Rotate tree once right to right. *)
(*----------------------------------------------------------EL1103.R2lr    -*)
PROCEDURE R2lr(VAR p,p1,p2:NODEPTR);
(*  Rotate tree twice left to right *)
(*----------------------------------------------------------EL1103.R2rl    -*)
PROCEDURE R2rl(VAR p,p1,p2:NODEPTR);
(*  Rotate tree twice right to left. *)
(*----------------------------------------------------------EL1007.RCRDAREA-*)
CONST
  maxrlen = 32767;   maxrflds = 16383;
TYPE
  RCRDAREA = RECORD
    rcrdlen : CARDINAL;
    area    : ARRAY [1..maxrlen] OF BYTE;
```

```
        END;
    RCRD = POINTER TO RCRDAREA;
    RFLDAREA = RECORD
        nmbrflds : CARDINAL;
        loc      : ARRAY [1..maxrflds] OF CARDINAL;
        len      : ARRAY [1..maxrflds] OF CARDINAL;
        END;
    RFLDLIST = POINTER TO RFLDAREA;
```
(*--EL1413.ReadFlds-*)
```
PROCEDURE ReadFlds(VAR thisscrn:ADDRESS;showblst:FLPTR;
                       boxnumber:CARDINAL;flds:FLPTR;
                       frstfld:CARDINAL;VAR lastfld:CARDINAL;
                       oktochg:BOOLEAN;VAR chgd:BOOLEAN;
                   VAR normals,easciis:CHARSET;hlclr:BYTE;hortab:CHAR;
                   VAR eascii:BOOLEAN;VAR kbchar:CHAR);
```
(* This routine gives the calling program access to a subset of the fields
   defined for a single box in the deScreen defined by thisscrn. The
   routine operates by creating a new box with the definition defined for
   boxnumber, but with the list of fields defined by flds, and then calling
   the readscrn function. Refer to the explanation of ReadScrn for further
   details. *)
(*--EL0903.ReadKB -*)
```
PROCEDURE ReadKB(msg:STRING; normals,easciis:CHARSET;VAR eascii:BOOLEAN;
                 VAR kbChar:CHAR;VAR frame:FRAME;color:BYTE):BOOLEAN;
```
(* This routine will attempt to read from the keyboard. If no character is
   pending, control returns immediately to the caller, and the function
   will equal FALSE. If at least one character is read, reading continues
   until one of the characters in either normals or easciis is read, and
   then, control returns with the function equal to TRUE. msg is
   displayed, character by character as it is read, in the color specified.
   frame.cl and frame.cc are set accordingly. If an attempt is made to
   enter more characters than msg can contain, Sound will be called to warn
   the user. The character that ends the read is returned as kbchar with
   eascii set accordingly; the terminating character is NOT displayed, and
   the terminating character is NOT included in msg. The routine assumes
   that all of msg can fit within the frame defined. *)
(*--EL0802.ReadParm-*)
```
PROCEDURE ReadParm(ddname:STRING);
```
(* This routine will read program parameters from the file associated with
   ddname. *)
(*--EL1412.ReadScrn-*)
```
PROCEDURE ReadScrn(VAR thisscrn:ADDRESS;VAR showblst,readblst:FLPTR;
                       frstbox:CARDINAL;VAR lastbox:CARDINAL;
                       frstfld:CARDINAL;VAR lastfld:CARDINAL;
                       oktochg:BOOLEAN;VAR chgd:BOOLEAN;
                   VAR normals,easciis:CHARSET;hlclr:BYTE;hortab:CHAR;
                   VAR eascii:BOOLEAN;VAR kbchar:CHAR);
```
(* This routine gives the calling program access to a deScreen for
   controlling data entry. The appropriate screen must have been loaded
   (using LoadScrn) and is referred to by ThisScrn. ShowBLst defines the
   list of box numbers that are to appear on the screen during this
   access...these boxes will all scroll as appropriate. readblst defines
   the list of boxes into which data may be entered. Note the the two
   lists do not have to be the same, but every element in readblst should
   also be in showblst. frstbox defines the readblst box where reading is
   to be begin...(note: readblst[?] = frstbox). If frstbox = 0 on entry,
   reading will begin at readblst[1]. On exit, lastbox will be set to the
   box being accessed when the user decided that input was complete.
   frstfld defines the field number where reading is to begin. If frstfld
   = 0 on entry, reading will begin at the first field in frstbox. If
   frstfld <> 0 on entry, then frstbox must also not be zero, and reading
   will begin at the field specified. (If frstfld is not in frstbox, the

procedure will cancel). Calling this routine with frstbox and/or
frstfld not equal to zero allows a calling program to continue reading
where it left off, as opposed to starting over at the beginning of a
list. If oktochg is false on entry, this routine will not permit the
user to enter data into the screen...instead, the cursor control
characters can be used to view data. If oktochg is true on entry, and
any data is entered or changed, chgd will return true. hlclr defines
the color that is to be used to highlight the field currently being
read...this is usually stdhilite. hortab defines the character that is
to be used to mark a horizontal tab position of sideways scrolling...its
use depends on the screen being accessed. normals and easciis define
sets of characters that the routine is to use as a termination signal.
When a character from one of those sets is encountered, the routine will
return to the caller with kbchar equal to the character that terminated
the read, and, eascii set accordingly. *)
(*--EL1417.RedoErrs-*)
PROCEDURE RedoErrs(VAR thisscrn:ADDRESS;showblst:FLPTR;
                   thisbox:CARDINAL;flds:FLPTR;VAR errs:ERRCNTRL;
                   VAR chgd:BOOLEAN;hlclr,blink:BYTE;hortab:CHAR;
                   VAR eascii:BOOLEAN;VAR kbchar:CHAR;stdemsg:STDEMSG);
(* This routine provides a standardized mechanicism for correcting errors
   on a descreen. thisscrn must have been loaded using LoadScrn and
   thisbox refers to the box in which the errors occur. If flds[1] = 0
   then all of the fields in the box may be accessed using ReadScrn.
   Otherwise, only the fields specified will be accessable using readflds.
   The list of errors and the associated fields must have been constructed
   from errs.frsterr using FlgAsErr. When this routine is first entered,
   all errors fields in flds or in the associated box will be changed to
   the color specified by blink. On return, errs.frsterr will be set to
   nil and the associated variables cleared. This routine gives the user
   the option of accessing all fields in the box or list, or of only
   accessing those fields with errors. If the latter is choosen, the error
   reporting routine, STDEMSG, will be called to provide a description of
   the error for display on the standard message lines. On return, kbchar
   and eascii will indicate the character that ended the read. Standard
   returns are:
       FK1 = Entry complete
       FK4 = Data contains only minor errors, accept as is
       FK9 = Start over
       FK10 = Abort
*)
(*--EL1020.Remount -*)
PROCEDURE Remount;
(* This procedure is usually called at the end of a main program. It will
   search for a program parameter with <parmid> = REMOUNT. If the
   parameter is found, this routine will use its <parmval> to determine
   which diskettes should be mounted when the program ends. The format for
   <parmval> is:

       REMOUNT=<device>:,<volname> <device>:,<volname>[...]

   Note that, if neccessary, Remount can specify a volume for each of
   several devices. Each entry is delimited with a semicolon. *)
(*--EL1019.Rename -*)
PROCEDURE Rename(ddname,newname:STRING):BOOLEAN;
(* This routine will rename the file associated with ddname to the new name
   specified. The files need not be in the same directory, but must be on
   the same volume. Only the file associated with ddname may state the
   volumne name. If the file does not exist, the function will return
   FALSE. *)
(*--EL1113.ReplLink-*)
PROCEDURE ReplLink(ddname:STRING;rcrd:RCRD;thisline:LONGCARD);

```
(* This routine will replace the data in the LNK file record associated
   with ddname and identified by thislink.  No change is made to the
   associated chain.  *)
(*-----------------------------------------------------EL1104.ReplNdx -*)
PROCEDURE ReplNdx(ddname:STRING;VAR rcrd:RCRD;
               VAR nmbr:LONGCARD;keyloc,keylen:CARDINAL;
               VAR hook:NODEPTR;top:BOOLEAN; updtdir:BOOLEAN);
(* If a record with a matching key can be found in the NDX file associated
   with ddname, it will be replaced by rcrd, and its record number will be
   returned in nmbr.  If no match can be found, nmbr will return = 0, and
   no change will be made to the file.  If the record is replaced, and
   updtdir = TRUE, the file will be closed so that the directory will be
   properly updated.  *)
(*-----------------------------------------------------EL1014.RmDir   -*)
PROCEDURE RmDir(ddname:STRING):WORD;
(* This routine will attempt to delete the directory according to the path
   defined in ddname.  If the operation is successful, the function will
   return = 0.  Otherwise, the routine will return equal to the error code
   returned from DOS.  *)
(*-----------------------------------------------------EL1001.RptIOErr-*)
PROCEDURE RptIOErr(ioerr:BYTE;dsname,procname:STRING; comeback:BOOLEAN);
(* This routine will translate ioerr to an appropriate message and will
   call Message to display it within msgframe.  If comeback is not TRUE,
   or, if the user responds with a Ctrl-Break, this routine will call
   Cancel, reporting procname as the source of the abort.  The format of
   the message is:

        Msg #<nn>...<error message>...(<DSNAME>)...
        F1 = Continue
*)
(*-----------------------------------------------------EL1103.Sb1     -*)
PROCEDURE Sb1(VAR bal:INTEGER;VAR x,y:NODEPTR;VAR lower:BOOLEAN);
(*  This routine will set the appropriate balance for x and y. *)
(*-----------------------------------------------------EL1103.Sb2     -*)
PROCEDURE Sb2(VAR p2,p1,p:NODEPTR);
(*  This routine will set the appropriate balance for p1 and p.  *)
(*-----------------------------------------------------EL1412.ScrlScrn *)
PROCEDURE ScrlScrn (mc,ml:CARDINAL;VAR image:SMAP;
                 VAR showblst:FLPTR;VAR boxes:BDTBL;
                 VAR curbox,curfld:CARDINAL;VAR flds:FDTBL;
                 hortab:CHAR):BOOLEAN;
(* This routine scrolls the display. *)
(*-----------------------------------------------------EL0902.ScrollUp-*)
PROCEDURE ScrollUp(VAR frame:FRAME;color:BYTE);
(* This routine will scroll all of the lines on the display from frame.fl
   to frame.ll up one position, and the new line will be filled with color.
   On exit, frame.cl:=frame.ll.  *)
(*-----------------------------------------------------EL1017.SetAttrb-*)
PROCEDURE SetAttrb(ddname:STRING; attrib:WORD):BOOLEAN;
(* This routine will set the attribute recorded for the file associated
   with ddname.  If function returns = FALSE, the file does not exist.
   Otherwise, attrib will become the new file attribute recorded for the
   file.  *)
(*-----------------------------------------------------EL0401.SetChar -*)
PROCEDURE SetChar(s:STRING;n:CARDINAL;c:CHAR);
(* This routine will set the character in s at the n'th position to c.  If
   n is greater than the StrLen(s), the routine will set n to StrLen(s).
   If n = 0, the routine will set n = 1.  *)
(*-----------------------------------------------------EL1412.SetCur  -*)
PROCEDURE SetCur(mc,ml:CARDINAL;VAR image:SMAP;VAR fld:FLDDEF;
                           fromleft:BOOLEAN):CARDINAL;
(* This routine determines the cursor position. *)
```

```
(*---------------------------------------------------------EL0707.SetDate -*)
PROCEDURE SetDate(date:DATE):BOOLEAN;
(* This routine will set the system date to the corresponding value in
   date.  date is in YYMMDD format.  If the contents of date do not
   constitute a valid date, the routine will return FALSE.  *)
(*---------------------------------------------------------EL1002.SetDTA  -*)
PROCEDURE SetDTA(newdta:ADDRESS;VAR olddta:ADDRESS);
(* This routine will set the current DTA (disk transfer area) to the
   ADDRESS specified by newdta.  The DTA in effect when the routine is
   called will be returned in olddta.  *)
(*---------------------------------------------------------EL1011.SetFcdt -*)
PROCEDURE SetFcdt(ddname:STRING; fdate:DATE;ftime:TIME):BOOLEAN;
(* If the file associated with ddname does not exist, the function will
   return FALSE, otherwise the function will return TRUE, and the date and
   time stamp for the file will be set to the values indicated.  On entry,
   fdate has the form yymmdd;  ftime has the form hhmmdd.  *)
(*---------------------------------------------------------EL1012.SetFLoc -*)
PROCEDURE SetFLoc(ddname:STRING;method:LOCCNTRL;
                      rlen:WORD;VAR rnmbr:LONGCARD):BOOLEAN;
(* If the file associated with ddname does not exist, this function will
   return FALSE.  Otherwise, the function will return TRUE and the file
   pointer will be set according to the value in method.  If method =
   setpostn, the file pointer will be set to rlen * (rnmbr - 1).  If method
   = usepostn, the file pointer will be set to rlen * (rnmbr - 1) bytes
   past the current file position.  If method = seteof, the file pointer
   will be set to the end of file, and rnmbr will return with the number of
   rlen records the file contains.  *)
(*---------------------------------------------------------EL0401.SetLen  -*)
PROCEDURE SetLen(s:STRING;l:CARDINAL);
(* This routine will set the current length of the STRING parameter to the
   value specified by l.  If l > StrSize(s), the routine will set l =
   StrSize(s).  *)
(*---------------------------------------------------------EL0801.SetParm -*)
PROCEDURE SetParm(parmid,parmval:STRING);
(* If a parameter already exists for parmid, and StrLen(parmval) = 0 this
   routine will delete the associated parameter from the list of parameters
   for the program.  If parmid does not exist, it will be added to the
   program list.  If parmid does exist and StrLen(parmval) <> 0, the
   parameter will be set to the new value.  *)
(*---------------------------------------------------------EL0906.SetPStat-*)
PROCEDURE SetPStat(status:BYTE);
(* This routine will terminate the current process and set the process
   return code to status.  *)
(*---------------------------------------------------------EL1202.SetRprt -*)
PROCEDURE SetRprt(pcs:STRING;pagelength:CARDINAL;
                      asktoset,npage,dpage,tpage:BOOLEAN);
(* This procedure will define the control variables for a new report.  The
   character size used will be controlled by pcs...it should be set to the
   appropriate memnonic from PRTCONST.  The total number of lines that will
   be printed on a page (including headings) is controlled by pagelength.
   If asktoset = true, the user will be asked to position the paper to the
   top of a new page before printing begins.  If npage, dpage, and/or tpage
   are true, the first three lines of the headings printed on each page
   will include the page number, date, and time.  *)
(*---------------------------------------------------------EL0707.SETTIME -*)
PROCEDURE SetTime(time:TIME):BOOLEAN;
(* This routine will set the system time to the corresponding value in
   time.  time is in HHMMDD format.  If the contents of time do not
   constitue a valid time, the routine will return FALSE.  *)
(*---------------------------------------------------------EL0706.SetTimer-*)
PROCEDURE SetTimer(relative:BOOLEAN;
                      hours,minutes,seconds:CARDINAL;
```

```
                    VAR ticsleft,timechkd:LONGCARD);
(* If relative = TRUE on entry, then hours, minutes and seconds define a
   time to be added to the current system time to define a target;
   otherwise, the values given are the target time.  In either case,
   ticsleft will return with the number of clock tics required to reach the
   target time, and, timechkd will indicate the value of the DOS BIOS timer
   location when ticsleft was defined.  Subsequent calls to ChkTimer will
   decrement the value of ticsleft.  *)
(*------------------------------------------------------EL0702.SetVectr-*)
PROCEDURE SetVectr(number:WORD;server:ADDRESS);
(* This routine will set the interupt vector associated with number to the
   address defined by server.  *)
(*------------------------------------------------------EL1412.ShftLFld-*)
PROCEDURE ShftLFld(mc,ml:CARDINAL;VAR image:SMAP;
                         fldline,frstcol,lastcol:CARDINAL);
(* This routine will shift the contents of a field to the left. *)
(*------------------------------------------------------EL1412.ShftRFld-*)
PROCEDURE ShftRFld(mc,ml:CARDINAL;VAR image:SMAP;
                         fldline,frstcol,lastcol:CARDINAL);
(* This routine will shift the contents of a field to the right. *)
(*------------------------------------------------------EL1411.ShowBox -*)
PROCEDURE ShowBox(VAR thisscrn:ADDRESS;showblst:FLPTR);
(* This routine will move the appropriate contents of the deScreen boxes
   identified by showblst onto the display.  thisscrn refers to a descreen
   control area loaded by LoadScrn.  *)
(*------------------------------------------------------EL1417.ShowErrs-*)
PROCEDURE ShowErrs(VAR thisscrn:ADDRESS;VAR errs:ERRCNTRL;blink:BYTE);
(* The color for all of the fields defined in ERRS will be set to blink. *)
(*------------------------------------------------------EL1412.ShowFld -*)
PROCEDURE ShowFld(mc,ml:CARDINAL;VAR image:SMAP;
                         VAR box:BOXDEF;VAR fld:FLDDEF);
(* This routine moves a field from the image to the screen. *)
(*------------------------------------------------------EL1411.ShowScrn-*)
PROCEDURE ShowScrn (VAR image:SMAP;
        ml,              (*MAX LINES IN DEF               *)
        mc,              (*MAX COLUMNS IN DEF             *)
        fdl,             (*FIRST DEF LINE TO MOVE         *)
        fdc,             (*FIRST DEF COLUMN TO MOVE       *)
        fcl,             (*FIRST CRT LINE TO FILL         *)
        fcc,             (*FIRST CRT COLUMN TO FILL       *)
        ncltf,           (*NUMBER OF CRT LINES TO FILL   *)
        tnc:CARDINAL);   (*NUMBER OF CRT COLLUMN TO FILL*)
(* This routine is used to transfer a screen image from the definition to
   the crt screen.  It is used only internally by the deScreen routines and
   is not directly available to other procedures.  *)
(*------------------------------------------------------EL1301.ShwFrame-*)
PROCEDURE ShwFrame(VAR f,t:FRAME;VAR normals,easciis:CHARSET;
                   VAR eascii:BOOLEAN;VAR kbchar:CHAR);
(* This routine will display the contents of f on the crt within the area
   specified by t.  If the f contains more lines or columns than t, this
   routine will permit the user to scroll using the cursor control keys.
   When the user presses one of the keys specified, control will return to
   the calling program.  *)
(*------------------------------------------------------EL0705.Sound   -*)
PROCEDURE Sound(freq,duration:CARDINAL);
(* This routine uses the CPU timer to sound the PC's speaker.  freq is in
   cycles per second and duration is in milliseconds.  *)
(*------------------------------------------------------EL0705.sounds  -*)
CONST
  errfreq = 1046;  errdur  = 200;  qfreq  = 880;  qdur  = 100;
(*------------------------------------------------------EL1418.StdEMsg -*)
PROCEDURE StdEMsg(msg:STRING;major:BOOLEAN;errnmbr:CARDINAL);
```

(* this procedure will return a msg describing the error associated with
   errnmbr. The message will be prefixed by either 'Major error...' or
   'Minor error...' depending on the contents of major. *)
(*---EL0401.StrChar -*)
PROCEDURE StrChar(s:STRING;n:CARDINAL):CHAR;
(* This routine will return the character in s at the n'th position. If n
   is greater than the StrLen(s), the routine will set n = StrLen(s). If n
   = 0, the routine will set n = 1. *)
(*---EL0401.STRING   -*)
TYPE
  STRING;
(* A STRING variable is similar to an ARRAY OF CHARACTERS, except that the
   variable may be defined dynamically. Each STRING variable has two
   additional associated values, accessible by StrLen and StrSize. StrLen
   returns the number of characters in the STRING currently in use.
   StrSize returns the maximum number of characters the STRING may contain.
   The STRING routines include a Literal procedure that permits an array of
   char to be used anywhere a STRING is permitted. *)
(*---EL0401.StrLen -*)
PROCEDURE StrLen(s:STRING):CARDINAL;
(* This routine will return the current length of the STRING parameter. *)
(*---EL0401.StrSize -*)
PROCEDURE StrSize(s:STRING):CARDINAL;
(* This routine will return the maximum length of the STRING parameter. *)
(*---EL0305.strtheap-*)
VAR
  strtheap:ADDRESS;
(* This ADDRESS marks the first word of the heap area of the main process.
   Any variable between this ADDRESS and the current ADDRESS of the stack
   (i.e., SS:SP) must have been allocated by a call to NEW and is therefore
   a dynamic variable. *)
(*---EL0503.SubLCard-*)
PROCEDURE SubLCard(lcrd1,lcrd2:LONGCARD; VAR lcrdrslt:LONGCARD);
(* This routine will perform the equation : lcrdrslt := lcrd1 - lcrd2 *)
(*---EL0401.SubStr -*)
PROCEDURE SubStr(n,l:CARDINAL;s:STRING):STRING;
(* This routine creates a new STRING, containing the l characters from s,
   beginning at StrChar(s,n). Note that this routine creates a temporary
   STRING, similiar to the Literal routine. *)
(*---EL0705.ToneInit-*)
PROCEDURE ToneInit;
(* This routine will initialize the PC speaker system to produce a square
   wave using binary control values. *)
(*---EL0705.ToneOff -*)
PROCEDURE ToneOff;
(* This routine turns of the speaker timer. *)
(*---EL0705.ToneOn -*)
PROCEDURE ToneOn;
(* This routine will turn on the timer and the speaker according to the
   criteria established by ToneSet. *)
(*---EL0705.ToneSet -*)
PROCEDURE ToneSet(n:CARDINAL);
(* This routine selects the frequency of the square wave tone that will be
   output to the speaker system. n determines the frequency f according to
   the formula: f = 1,193,182 / n   *)
(*---EL0908.TypeStr -*)
PROCEDURE TypeStr(color:BYTE;homecur:BOOLEAN;
                  msg:STRING; VAR frame:FRAME);
(* This routine will display the contents of msg on the current display in
   the color indicated. If, on entry, homecur is TRUE, the cursor will be
   moved to the home position in the Frame, before the display. Otherwise,
   the cursor will be left in its current position. This routine works in

```
    conjunction with InputKB.  Both routines are restricted to the limits
    specified by frame.  *)
(*-----------------------------------------------------------EL1001.vols   ' -*)
VAR
  vols : ARRAY [0..25] OF STRING;
(* This array defines the volume lables the library routines think are
   associated with the corresponding device.  *)
(*-----------------------------------------------------------EL0804.WrtParm -*)
PROCEDURE WrtParm(ddname:STRING);
(* This routine will write all currently defined program parameters to the
   file associated with ddname.  Note that if any parmval includes a space,
   that entire parmval will be enclosed in double quote characters.  The
   double-quote character cannot be included in a parmval.  *)
(*-----------------------------------------------------------EL1010.WToFDate-*)
PROCEDURE WToFDate(w:CARDINAL;VAR fdate:DATE);
(* This routine will convert the value of w, a word in the format used by
   DOS to store the date a file was last modified, into a string in the
   form yymmdd.  *)
(*-----------------------------------------------------------EL1010.WToFTime-*)
PROCEDURE WToFTime(w:CARDINAL;VAR ftime:TIME);
(* This routine will convert the value of w, a word in the format used by
   DOS to store the time a file was last modified, into a string in the
   form hhmmss.  *)
```

Bibliography

Etling, Don.
Putting Pascal to Work
Blue Ridge Summit, Pennsylvania: TAB BOOKS Inc., 1986.

Joyce, Edward J.
Modula-2: A Seafarer's Manual and Shipyard Guide.
Reading, Massachusetts: Addison-Wesly, 1985.

Kaplan, Ian and Miller, Mike.
Modula-2 Programming.
Hasbrouck Heights, New Jersey: Hayden Book Company, 1986.

Meyers, Glenford J.
Reliable Software Through Composite Design.
New York: Petrocelli/Charter, 1975.

Norton, Peter.
Inside the IBM PC.
Bowie, Maryland: Robert J. Brady Company, 1983.

Rector, Russell and Alexy, George.
The 8086 Book.
Berkeley, California: OSBORNE/MCGraw-Hill, 1980.

Wiener, Richard and Ford, Gary A.
Modula-2: A Software Development Approach.
New York: John Wiley & Sons, 1985.

Niklaus Wirth.
Programming in Modula-2.
New York Berlin Heidelberg Tokyo: Springer-Verlag, 1985.

Niklaus Wirth.
Algorithms + Data Structures = Programs.
Englewood Cliffs, New Jersey: Prentice-Hall Inc., 1976.

Yourdon, Edward and Constantine, Larry L.
Structured Design.
Englewood Cliffs, New Jersey: Prentice-Hall Inc., 1979.

Index

Modula-2 Programmer's Resource Book

If you are intrigued with the possibilities of the data entry system and support programs included in Chapter 14 of *Modula-2 Programmer's Resource Book* (TAB Book No. 2741), you should definitely consider having the ready-to-run set of two disks containing the software applications. This software is guaranteed free of manufacturer's defects. (If you have any problems, return the disks within 30 days, and we'll send you a new one.) Not only will you save the time and effort of typing the programs, the disks eliminate the possibility of errors that can prevent the programs from functioning. Interested?

Available on two disks for the IBM PC and compatibles with DOS 2.0 or later at $29.95 for each set of disks plus $1.50 shipping and handling.